15th International Workshop on Spoken Dialogue Systems Technology (IWSDS 2025)

Bilbao, Spain
27-30 May 2025

ISBN: 979-8-3313-2448-3

IWSDS 2025

The 15th International Workshop on Spoken Dialogue Systems Technology

Proceedings of the Conference

May 27 - 30, 2025
Bilbao, Spain

Message from the General Chair

The 15th International Workshop on Spoken Dialogue Systems (IWSDS 2025) was held on 27-30 May 2025, in Bilbao, Spain. This year's conference theme was **"Conversational Systems for Emotional Support and Customer Assistance"**. The IWSDS conference series constitute a consolidated forum where international researchers, practitioners and stakeholders working in the field of spoken dialogue systems and associated technologies, can disseminate their current research and applications, discuss technological challenges, present their success stories and share their complementary visions about the future of the technology. IWSDS 2025 was grounded on the experience and knowledge generated in the previous editions:

- IWSDS'09 (Irsee, Germany),
- IWSDS'10 (Gotemba Kogen Resort, Japan),
- IWSDS'11 (Granada, Spain),
- IWSDS'12 (Paris, France),
- IWSDS'14 (Napa, USA),
- IWSDS'15 (Busan, Korea),
- IWSDS'16 (Saariselkä, Finland),
- IWSDS'17 (Farmington, PA, USA),
- IWSDS'18 (Singapore, Singapore),
- IWSDS'19 (Siracusa, Italy),
- IWSDS'20 (Madrid, Spain),
- IWSDS'21 (Singapore, Singapore),
- IWSDS'23 (Los Angeles, USA) and
- IWSDS'25 (Sapporo, Japan).

The conference invited and received paper submissions on the following topics:

- User engagement and emotion in dialogue systems
- Proactive, anticipatory, or incremental interaction
- Use of humor and metaphors in dialogue systems
- Multimodal and situated dialogue systems
- Companions and personal assistant dialogue systems
- Educational and healthcare applications
- Big data and large scale dialogue systems
- Digital resources for interactive dialogue management
- Domain transfer and adaptation techniques for dialogue systems

- Dialogue systems for low-resource languages
- Multilingual dialogue systems
- Dialogue system evaluation
- Machine learning for dialogue systems
- Interaction styles in dialogue systems
- LLMs in task-oriented dialogue systems
- LLMs for context tracking and management in dialogue systems
- Ensuring safety and explainability in LLM-powered dialogue systems
- Grounded, personalized and adaptive response generation in dialogue systems
- Mitigating harmful, toxic, or biased language generation in dialogue systems
- Large-scale, high-quality dialogue corpora collection, annotation, labeling and evaluation
- Integration of AI-based consciousness and awareness capabilities on computational systems
- Ethical considerations for AI-based systems

However, submissions were not limited to these topics, and submission of papers in all areas related to spoken dialogue systems was encouraged. The contributions were grouped into four categories: a) long research papers targeting reports on mature research results, b) short research papers targeting smaller case studies or ongoing but interesting and original research efforts, c) position papers to present novel research ideas or viewpoints which describe trends or fruitful starting points for future research and elicit discussion and finally d) demo submissions–system papers to demonstrate innovative or industrial-based research.

In addition, the Industrial Track invites contributions showcasing the implementation of novel and robust real-world applications of spoken dialogue systems. We encourage contributions that bridge research and practice, emphasizing robust implementation strategies and lessons learned from deployment in industrial or commercial settings. Submissions should highlight practical advancements and address challenges in areas such as, but not limited to:

- Innovative applications: new use cases and industries benefiting from spoken dialogue systems
- Efficient training and deployment: approaches for rapid, scalable, and resource-efficient model development
- Scalable, fast and cost-effective implementation: strategies enabling effective operation in resource-constrained or large-scale scenarios
- Human-in-the-Loop strategies: integration of human expertise to enhance system learning and performance
- Ethical and responsible systems: addressing fairness, transparency and societal impact in real-world applications

The program included three keynotes by renowned international experts:

- "From Call-Flows to Agentic Spoken Dialog Systems for the Enterprise" by Roberto Pieraccini, Vice President, Chief Scientist, Head of AI at Uniphore, USA
- "AI Will Rock You: Charisma, Humour, and the Future of Conversational AI" by Björn W. Schuller, Imperial College London, UK / Technical University of Munich, Germany
- "From Fluency to Reality: Conversational Grounding and Human-AI Dialogues Revisited" by Kristiina Jokinen, Artificial Intelligence Research Center, Tokyo, Japan

IWSDS 2025 received a total of 45 submissions, where each submission was reviewed by at least three Program Committee members. The committee decided to accept a total of 37 papers distributed as follows: 26 papers for the General Track, 5 demo paper, 4 papers for the industrial track and 2 position papers.

The organizers of the conference would like to thank the IWSDS Steering Committee and the more than 100 members of the IWSDS 2025 Scientific Committee for their timely and efficient contributions and for completing the review process on time. In addition, we would like to express our gratitude to the members of the Local Committee who highly contributed to the success of the workshop, making it an unforgettable experience for all participants. Thank you all for your logistic support; without it IWSDS 2025 would not have been such a remarkable conference.

With our highest appreciation,

Maria Inés Torres
Yuki Matsuda
Zoraida Callejas
Arantza del Pozo
Luis Fernando D'Haro

Acknowledgements

The organizers want to thank our partners that highly contributed to the organization and promotion of IWSDS. In concrete, we want to thank: the European project Crystal, the European Language Resources Association (ELRA), Universidad del País Vasco (Euskal Herriko Unibertsitatea), CAMP Tecnológico, Vicomtech (Spain), GAIA, The Special Interest Group on Spoken Dialogue Systems (SiG-SDS), and the endorsement from the EIC ASTOUND research project (101071191 — HORIZON-EIC-2021-PATHFINDERCHALLENGES-01).

Organizing Committee

General Chair

- María Inés Torres, Speech Interactive Research Group, University of the Basque, Spain

Conference Chairs

- Yuki Matsuda, Okayama University, Japan
- Zoraida Callejas, Software Engineering Department, University of Granada, Spain

Industrial Track Chair

- Arantza del Pozo, Speech and Language Technologies, Vicomtech, Spain

Publication Chair

- Luis Fernando D'Haro, THAU, Universidad Politécnica de Madrid, Spain

Local Organisation

- Josu Jugo (University of the Basque Country)
- Raquel Justo (University of the Basque Country)
- Asier López (University of the Basque Country)
- Ying Torres (University of the Basque Country)
- Amparo Varona (University of the Basque Country)
- Alain Vázquez (University of the Basque Country)
- Antonio Aparicio (University of the Basque Country)
- Javier Mikel Olaso (Vicomtech)

Program Committee

- Cristina Aceta, Tekniker, Spain
- Angus Addlesee, Heriot-Watt University, UK
- Ron Artstein, University of Southern California, USA
- Rafael E. Banchs, Intapp Inc., USA
- Timo Baumann, OTH Regensburg, Germany
- Leila Ben Letaifa, CESI, France
- Aakash Bhatnagar, Boston University, USA

Printed from e-media with permission by:

Curran Associates, Inc.
57 Morehouse Lane
Red Hook, NY 12571

Some format issues inherent in the e-media version may also appear in this print version.

Printed with permission by Curran Associates, Inc. (2025)

Association for Computational Linguistics
209 N. Eighth Street
Stroudsburg, Pennsylvania 18360

Phone: 1-570-476-8006
Fax: 1-570-476-0860

acl@aclweb.org

Additional copies of this publication are available from:

Curran Associates, Inc.
57 Morehouse Lane
Red Hook, NY 12571 USA
Phone: 845-758-0400
Fax: 845-758-2633
Email: curran@proceedings.com
Web: www.proceedings.com

- Susanne Burger, Solventum, USA
- Felix Burkhardt, audEERING GmbH, Germany
- Yuya Chiba, NTT, Japan
- Luis Fernando D'Haro, Universidad Politécnica de Madrid, Spain
- Nina Dethlefs, University of Hull, UK
- Fernando Fernández-Martínez, Technical University of Madrid, Spain
- Kallirroi Georgila, University of Southern California, USA
- Daniel Hernández Garcia, Heriot-Watt University, UK
- Ryuichiro Higashinaka, Nagoya University & NTT, Japan
- Stefan Hillmann, Technical University of Berlin, Germany
- Koji Inoue, Kyoto University, Japan
- Kristiina Jokinen, Artificial Intelligence Research Center, Japan
- Tatsuya Kawahara, Kyoto University, Japan
- Seiya Kawano, RIKEN, Japan
- Casey Kennington, Boise State University, USA
- Kazunori Komatani, Osaka University, Japan
- Maria Koutsombogera, Trinity College Dublin, Ireland
- Staffan Larsson, University of Gothenburg, Sweden
- Fabrice Lefèvre, University of Avignon, France
- Haizhou Li, National University of Singapore, Singapore
- Oier López de Lacalle, University of the Basque Country, Spain
- Asier López Zorrilla, University of the Basque Country, Spain
- Naveen Sai Madiraju, Google, USA
- Khyati Mahajan, University of North Carolina at Charlotte, USA
- Wolfgang Maier, Mercedes-Benz AG, Germany
- Vladislav Maraev, University of Gothenburg, Sweden
- Joseph Mariani, LISN-CNRS, France
- MIchael McTear, Ulster University, UK
- Masahiro Mizukami, NTT , Japan
- Satoshi Nakamura, Nara Institute of Science and Technology, Japan
- Mikio Nakano, C4A Research Institute Inc., Japan
- Maike Paetzel-Prüsmann, Disney Research, Switzerland

- Alexandros Papangelis, Amazon Alexa AI, USA
- Catherine Pelachaud, CNRS-ISIR & Sobornne University, France
- Jose Quesada, University of Seville, Spain
- Angela Ramirez, University of California Santa Cruz, USA
- Giuseppe Riccardi, University of Trento, Italy
- Sophie Rosset, LISN-CNRS, France
- Sakriani Sakti, Nara Institute of Science and Technology & RIKEN, Japan
- Oscar Saz, Emotech LTD., UK
- Bjoern Schuller, Imperial College London, UK / Technical University of Munich, Germany
- Sabato Marco Siniscalchi, Kore University of Enna, Italy
- Svetlana Stoyanchev, Toshiba Research Europe, UK
- Hiroaki Sugiyama, NTT, Japan
- David Traum, University of Southern California, USA
- Stefan Ultes, University of Bamberg, Germany
- Carl Vogel, Trinity College Dublin, Ireland
- Nicolas Wagner, University of Bamberg, Germany
- Marilyn Walker, University of California Santa Cruz, USA
- Nigel Ward, University of Texas at El Paso, USA
- Graham Wilcock, University of Helsinki, Finland
- Kheng Hui Yeo, I2R, Japan
- Koichiro Yoshino, RIKEN & Nara Institute of Science and Technology, Japan
- Akishige Yuguchi, RIKEN & Nara Institute of Science and Technology, Japan

Table of Contents

Conference Program

Tuesday, May 27, 2025

9:30–10:30 ***Registration***

10:30–11:00 ***Opening***

11:00–11:30 ***Coffee Break***

11:30–12:45 **Session OS1: ORAL SESSION1 : Application-specific dialogue systems. Data and resources**

11:30–11:45 *Automatic Generation of Structured Domain Knowledge for Dialogue-based XAI Systems*
Carolin Schindler, Isabel Feustel, Niklas Rach and Wolfgang Minker

11:45–12:00 *Exploring the Impact of Modalities on Building Common Ground Using the Collaborative Scene Reconstruction Task*
Yosuke Ujigawa, Asuka Shiotani, Masato Takizawa, Eisuke Midorikawa, Ryuichiro Higashinaka and Kazunori Takashio

12:00–12:15 *Design, Generation and Evaluation of a Synthetic Dialogue Dataset for Contextually Aware Chatbots in Art Museums*
Inass Rachidi, Anas Ezzakri, Jaime Bellver-Soler and Luis Fernando D'Haro

12:15–12:30 *A Voice-Controlled Dialogue System for NPC Interaction using Large Language Models*
Milan Wevelsiep, Nicholas Thomas Walker, Nicolas Wagner and Stefan Ultes

12:30–12:45 *A Dialogue System for Semi-Structured Interviews by LLMs and its Evaluation on Persona Information Collection*
Ryo Hasegawa, Yijie Hua, Takehito Utsuro, Ekai Hashimoto, Mikio Nakano and Shun Shiramatsu

13:00–14:15 ***Lunch***

Tuesday, May 27, 2025 (continued)

14:30–15:30 Session OS2: ORAL SESSION 2: User-centered dialogue design and response generation

14:30–14:45 *Exploring Personality-Aware Interactions in Salesperson Dialogue Agents*
Sijia Cheng, Wen Yu Chang and Yun-Nung Chen

14:45–15:00 *ReSpAct: Harmonizing Reasoning, Speaking, and Acting Towards Building Large Language Model-Based Conversational AI Agents*
Vardhan Dongre, Xiaocheng Yang, Emre Can Acikgoz, Suvodip Dey, Gokhan Tur and Dilek Hakkani-Tur

15:00–15:15 *Examining Older Adults' Motivation for Interacting with Health-Monitoring Conversational Systems Through Field Trials*
Mariko Yoshida, Ryo Hori, Yuki Zenimoto, Mayu Urata, Mamoru Endo, Takami Yasuda, Aiko Inoue, Takahiro Hayashi and Ryuichiro Higashinaka

15:15–15:30 *Balancing Knowledge Delivery and Emotional Comfort in Healthcare Conversational Systems*
Shang-Chi Tsai and Yun-Nung Chen

15:30–16:00 ***Coffee Break***

16:00–17:00 Session P1: POSTER SESSION 1: Advanced machine learning for dialogue and Conversational AI

16:00–17:00 *Context or Retrieval? Evaluating RAG Methods for Art and Museum QA System*
Samuel Ramos-Varela, Jaime Bellver-Soler, Marcos Estecha-Garitagoitia and Luis Fernando D'Haro

16:00–17:00 *Paralinguistic Attitude Recognition for Spoken Dialogue Systems*
Kouki Miyazawa, Zhi Zhu and Yoshinao Sato

16:00–17:00 *Exploring ReAct Prompting for Task-Oriented Dialogue: Insights and Shortcomings*
Michelle Elizabeth, Morgan Veyret, Miguel Couceiro, Ondrej Dusek and Lina M. Rojas Barahona

16:00–17:00 *Design of a conversational agent to support people on suicide risk*
Mario Manso Vázquez, José Manuel Ramírez Sánchez, Carmen García-Mateo, Laura Docío-Fernández, Manuel José Fernández-Iglesias, Beatriz Gómez-Gómez, Beatriz Pinal, Antia Brañas and Alejandro García-Caballero

16:00–17:00 *Optimizing RAG: Classifying Queries for Dynamic Processing*
Kabir Olawore, Michael McTear, Yaxin Bi and David Griol

Tuesday, May 27, 2025 (continued)

16:00–17:00 *Enhancing Proactive Dialogue Systems Through Self-Learning of Reasoning and Action-Planning*
Ryosuke Ito, Tetsuya Takiguchi and Yasuo Ariki

16:00–17:00 *TrustBoost: Balancing flexibility and compliance in conversational AI systems*
David Griol, Zoraida Callejas, Manuel Gil-Martín, Ksenia Kharitonova, Juan Manuel Montero-Martínez, David Pérez Fernández and Fernando Fernández-Martínez

20:00–22:00 ***Welcome Reception***

Wednesday, May 28, 2025

9:30–10:30 **Session K1: Keynote 1 (Roberto Pieraccini): From Call-Flows to Agentic Spoken Dialog Systems for the Enterprise**
Chair: María Inés Torres

10:30–11:00 ***Coffee Break***

11:00–12:15 **Session P2: POSTER SESSION 2: Demo**

11:00–12:15 *ScriptBoard: Designing modern spoken dialogue systems through visual programming*
Divesh Lala, Mikey Elmers, Koji Inoue, Zi Haur Pang, Keiko Ochi and Tatsuya Kawahara

11:00–12:15 *D4AC: A Tool for Developing Multimodal Dialogue Systems without Coding*
Mikio Nakano and Ryuichiro Higashinaka

11:00–12:15 *A Multilingual Speech-Based Driver Assistant for Basque and English*
Antonio Aparicio Akcharov, Asier López Zorrilla, Juan Camilo Vásquez Correa, Oscar Montserrat, José Maria Echevarría, Begoña Arrate, Joxean Zapirain, Mikel deVelasco Vázquez, Santiago Andrés Moreno-Acevedo, Ander González-Docasal, Maria Ines Torres and Aitor Álvarez

11:00–12:15 *Intimebot – A Dialogue Agent for Timekeeping Support*
Shoaib Khan, Alex Samani and Rafael Banchs

11:00–12:15 *A Chatbot for Providing Suicide Prevention Information in Spanish*
Pablo Ascorbe, María S. Campos, César Domínguez, Jónathan Heras, Magdalena Pérez and Ana Rosa Terroba-Reinares

Wednesday, May 28, 2025 (continued)

12:30–13:30 **Session OS3: ORAL SESSION 3: Industrial Track**
Chair: Lina Rojas

12:30–12:45 *LAMIA: An LLM Approach for Task-Oriented Dialogue Systems in Industry 5.0*
Cristina Fernandez, Izaskun Fernandez and Cristina Aceta

12:45–13:00 *Conversational Tutoring in VR Training: The Role of Game Context and State Variables*
Maia Aguirre, Ariane Méndez, Aitor García-Pablos, Montse Cuadros, Arantza del Pozo, Oier Lopez de Lacalle, Ander Salaberria, Jeremy Barnes, Pablo Martínez and Muhammad Zeshan Afzal

13:00–13:15 *A Methodology for Identifying Evaluation Items for Practical Dialogue Systems Based on Business-Dialogue System Alignment Models*
Mikio Nakano, Hironori Takeuchi and Kazunori Komatani

13:15–13:30 *Speech-Controlled Smart Speaker for Accurate, Real-Time Health and Care Record Management*
Jonathan E. Carrick, Nina Dethlefs, Lisa Greaves, Venkata M. V. Gunturi, Rameez Raja Kureshi and Yongqiang Cheng

13:30–14:45 ***Lunch***

15:00–16:45 ***Open Session***

17:00–18:30 ***Guided visit to Guggenheim Museum***

Thursday, May 29, 2025

9:30–10:30 **Keynote 2 (Björn Schuller): AI Will Rock You: Charisma, Humour, and the Future of Conversational AI**
Chair: Arantza del Pozo

10:30–11:00 **Coffee Break and Sponsors Posters**

10:30–11:00 ***University of the Basque Country - UPV/EHU***

10:30–11:00 ***ELRA. Language Resource Association***

10:30–11:00 ***GAIA Industry Association of Applied Knowledge and Technologies***

10:30–11:00 ***Conversational Systems for Emotional Support and Customer Assistance - HORIZON EUROPE MSCA-SE project***

10:30–11:00 ***Vicomtech***

10:30–11:00 ***Camp Tecnológico***

12:00–13:30 **Session OS4: ORAL SESSION 4: Multimodality and advanced machine learning for dialogue conversations**

12:00–12:15 *Analysis of Voice Activity Detection Errors in API-based Streaming ASR for Human-Robot Dialogue*
Kenta Yamamoto, Ryu Takeda and Kazunori Komatani

12:15–12:30 *A Survey of Recent Advances on Turn-taking Modeling in Spoken Dialogue Systems*
Galo Castillo-López, Gael de Chalendar and Nasredine Semmar

12:30–12:45 *Integrating Respiration into Voice Activity Projection for Enhancing Turn-taking Performance*
Takao Obi and Kotaro Funakoshi

12:45–13:00 *DSLCMM: A Multimodal Human-Machine Dialogue Corpus Built through Competitions*
Ryuichiro Higashinaka, Tetsuro Takahashi, Shinya Iizuka, Sota Horiuchi, Michimasa Inaba, Zhiyang Qi, Yuta Sasaki, Kotaro Funakoshi, Shoji Moriya, Shiki Sato, Takashi Minato, Kurima Sakai, Tomo Funayama, Masato Komuro, Hiroyuki Nishikawa, Ryosaku Makino, Hirofumi Kikuchi and Mayumi Usami

Thursday, May 29, 2025 (continued)

13:00–13:15 *Cutting Through Overload: Efficient Token Dropping for Speech Emotion Recognition in Multimodal Large Language Models*
Jaime Bellver-Soler, Mario Rodriguez-Cantelar, Ricardo Córdoba and Luis Fernando D'Haro

13:30–14:45 ***Lunch***

15:00–18:00 ***Excursion to Torre Loizaga***

20:30–23:00 ***Banquet - Restaurant 'Los Tamarises'***

Friday, May 30, 2025

9:30–10:30 **Session From Fluency to Reality: Conversational Grounding and Human-AI Dialogues Revisited: Keynote3: Kristiina Jokinen Artificial Intelligence Research Center, Tokyo, Japan**
Chair: Zoraida Callejas

11:00–12:15 **POSTER SESSION 3: User-centered dialogue design and response generation, Multimodal and Application-specific dialogue systems**

11:00–12:15 *Integrating Conversational Entities and Dialogue Histories with Knowledge Graphs and Generative AI*
Graham Wilcock and Kristiina Jokinen

11:00–12:15 *Enabling Trait-based Personality Simulation in Conversational LLM Agents: Case Study of Customer Assistance in French*
Ahmed Njifenjou, Virgile Sucal, Bassam Jabaian and Fabrice Lefèvre

11:00–12:15 *Developing Classifiers for Affirmative and Negative User Responses with Limited Target Domain Data for Dialogue System Development Tools*
Yunosuke Kubo, Ryo Yanagimoto, Mikio Nakano, Kenta Yamamoto, Ryu Takeda and Kazunori Komatani

11:00–12:15 *Why Do We Laugh? Annotation and Taxonomy Generation for Laughable Contexts in Spontaneous Text Conversation*
Koji Inoue, Mikey Elmers, Divesh Lala and Tatsuya Kawahara

11:00–12:15 *Adaptive Psychological Distance in Japanese Spoken Human-Agent Dialogue: A Politeness-Based Management Model*
Akira Inaba, Emmanuel Ayedoun and Masataka Tokumaru

11:00–12:15 *An LLM Benchmark for Addressee Recognition in Multi-modal Multi-party Dialogue*
Koji Inoue, Divesh Lala, Mikey Elmers, Keiko Ochi and Tatsuya Kawahara

11:00–12:15 *Will AI shape the way we speak? The emerging sociolinguistic influence of synthetic voices*
Eva Szekely, Jura Miniota and Míša (Michaela) Hejná

12:15–13:15 PANEL: Conversational assistant for Emotional Support and Customer assistance.

13:15–13:45 ***Closing Session***

Automatic Generation of Structured Domain Knowledge for Dialogue-based XAI Systems

Carolin Schindler[1], Isabel Feustel[1], Niklas Rach[2], Wolfgang Minker[1]

[1]Institute of Communications Engineering, Ulm University, Germany
[2]Tensor AI Solutions GmbH, Germany
Correspondence: carolin.schindler@uni-ulm.de

Abstract

Explanatory dialogue systems serve as intuitive interface between non-expert users and explainable AI (XAI) systems. The interaction with these kind of systems benefits especially from the integration of structured domain knowledge, e. g., by means of bipolar argumentation trees. So far, these domain-specific structures need to be created manually, therewith impairing the flexibility of the system with respect to the domain. We address this limitation by adapting an existing pipeline for topic-independent acquisition of argumentation trees in the field of persuasive, argumentative dialogue to the area of explanatory dialogue. This shift is achieved by *a)* introducing and investigating different formulations of auxiliary claims per feature of the explanation of the AI model, *b)* exploring the influence of pre-grouping of the arguments with respect to the feature they address, *c)* suggesting adaptions to the existing algorithm of the pipeline for obtaining a tree structure, and *d)* utilizing a new approach for determining the type of the relationship between the arguments. Through a step-wise expert evaluation for the domain *titanic survival*, we identify the best performing variant of our pipeline. With this variant we conduct a user study comparing the automatically generated argumentation trees against their manually created counterpart in the domains *titanic survival* and *credit acquisition*. This assessment of the suitability of the generated argumentation trees for a later integration into dialogue-based XAI systems as domain knowledge yields promising results.

1 Introduction

Explainable artificial intelligence (XAI) is recently gaining considerable attention as a means to improve the transparency of AI models and therewith enabling humans to understand the decisions made by them (Adadi and Berrada, 2018). However, due to the complexity of AI-based systems, it can be challenging to provide XAI explanations that are comprehensible also to non-expert users. By integrating XAI explanations into human-machine dialogue, users can ask clarifying questions and receive tailored explanations (Miller, 2019). In addition, the combination with domain knowledge has the potential to foster a deeper understanding of the behavior of the AI system (Feustel et al., 2024). We follow this line of research by introducing an automatized approach for the retrieval of the required domain knowledge from arbitrary documents. Viewing explanatory reasoning as argumentative (Mercier and Sperber, 2011), we encode the domain knowledge as bipolar argumentation trees (Stab and Gurevych, 2014) for the use in explanatory dialogue systems. Within these tree structures, the domain knowledge is encoded as arguments with supporting or attacking relationships among each other.

While the integration of domain knowledge can be beneficial for explanatory systems, the manual effort for creating structured domain knowledge impairs the flexibility of a corresponding system with respect to the domains it can provide meaningful explanations for. To overcome this limitation and therewith make the integration of domain-specific knowledge more feasible, we propose a modular pipeline based on argument search (Ajjour et al., 2019) for automatically generating argumentation trees modeling the domain knowledge.

Given a domain, a set of features that are utilized in the XAI explanations, and a collection of document that contains the information for the domain knowledge, we automatically generate domain-specific argumentation trees for XAI dialogues by adapting the pipeline proposed by Rach et al. (2021) to the field of explanatory dialogue. Through an expert evaluation, we identify the best configuration of our pipeline. In addition, we evaluate our overall approach by manually generating explanatory dialogues according to the formal model by Madumal et al. (2019) with human- as well as

Proceedings of the 15th International Workshop on Spoken Dialogue Systems Technology, pages 1–11
May 27–30, 2025. ©2025 Association for Computational Linguistics

automatically generated domain knowledge. A user study assessing the coherence of the generated dialogues, yields promising results for including the automatically generated tree structures into actual dialogue-based XAI systems. Additionally, we discuss the dependence of the results on the given collection of documents and the way the structured domain knowledge is utilized in the dialogue model.

The remainder of this work is organized as follows: Section 2 gives an overview over related work and Section 3 details our approach to the automatic generation of structured domain knowledge. After identifying the best performing configuration of our pipeline in Section 4, Section 5 evaluates our approach in a user study. We discuss our results in Section 6, before concluding in Section 7.

2 Related Work

Current dialogue-based XAI systems primarily function as question-and-answer (Q&A) systems that provide explicit verbalizations of the explanations generated by XAI methods (e. g., Slack et al. (2023); Feldhus et al. (2023)). While these systems are effective in providing direct insights, they lack the integration of additional domain-specific information, which has the potential to enhance the context and relevance of the explanations.

Incorporating domain-specific information into XAI itself is not a new idea. Pesquita (2021) demonstrated how knowledge graphs derived from ontologies can be utilized to create semantic explanations. Similarly, Bove et al. (2021) integrated domain-specific information into visual explanations, with annotations provided by domain experts. These approaches illustrate the potential of leveraging domain knowledge to enhance the interpretability of AI systems.

While knowledge-based dialogue is a well-established research field encompassing a variety of approaches and applications (Flycht-Eriksson, 1999; Chen et al., 2017), the connection between such knowledge-based dialogue systems and XAI so far remains mostly unexplored. To the best of our knowledge, the only work exploring this connection is Feustel et al. (2024). They employ bipolar argumentation trees within a dialogue-based XAI system to provide access to domain knowledge during conversational exchange. Their pilot study shows that incorporating domain knowledge not only improves the overall dialogue experience but also enriches the accessibility and utility of the explanations within the system. Since they created the structured domain knowledge through manual annotation, their system can benefit from the herein presented work.

3 From Documents to Structured Domain Knowledge

The pipeline by Rach et al. (2021), in the following referred to as the *existing pipeline*, offers a solution to automatically generating topic-specific argumentation trees for persuasive, argumentative dialogues. There, per dialogue, a single argumentation tree is created where all arguments are having a positive or negative stance towards the topic of the dialogue. To allow the explanatory dialogue system to link feature-based XAI explanations to the respective domain knowledge in an argumentative manner, multiple argumentation trees per XAI feature are required (Feustel et al., 2024), where each tree is entailing arguments for a different feature-outcome relation. Since we need to create multiple argumentation trees per XAI feature and not a single tree for the domain, the existing pipeline cannot be applied to our scenario directly. Nevertheless, being successfully evaluated in an argumentative dialogue context, the existing pipeline constitutes a promising basis for our work. The procedure of the existing pipeline is as follows: After utilizing argument search (Ajjour et al., 2019) to retrieve arguments along with their stance towards the topic from a web crawl, the arguments are optionally getting pre-grouped, before performing argumentative relation classification and determining the type of the relations between the arguments through stance propagation. Thereby, the argumentative relation classification entails the tasks of predicting the probability for a relationship between the arguments and then creating a tree structure out of these probabilities.

In the following, we first define the target structure, i. e., we describe how the domain knowledge is structured when modeled through argumentation trees. Afterwards, we detail our pipeline for the automatic generation of this structured domain knowledge. An overview over the processing steps of our pipeline is provided in Figure 1.

3.1 Target Structure

When modeling the domain knowledge of a dialogue-based XAI system with bipolar argumentation structures (Stab and Gurevych, 2014), the

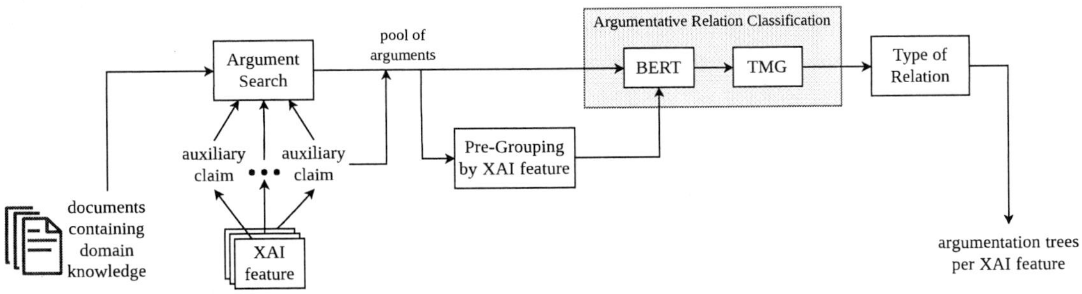

Figure 1: Pipeline for automatic generation of structured domain knowledge for dialogue-based XAI systems.

nodes of the structure represent the arguments, which function as the domain knowledge, and the directed edges between them indicate a supporting or attacking relationship. Throughout this work, an argument is a sentence that can target, i. e., support or attack, exactly one other argument, resulting in a tree structure (Stab and Gurevych, 2014). Following Feustel et al. (2024), we aim for at least one argumentation tree per feature of the explanation of the XAI system, where each root represents a feature-outcome relation. To not lose the relationship between the arguments representing a feature-outcome relation and the XAI explanation of the system, we introduce an auxiliary claim per feature stating that the respective feature is relevant for the domain. These auxiliary claims group together all argumentation trees that are addressing the respective feature. Therefore, we not only create multiple argumentation trees but also need to detect the XAI feature that they are addressing. An example of the targeted structure for a single feature of a domain is depicted in Figure 2.

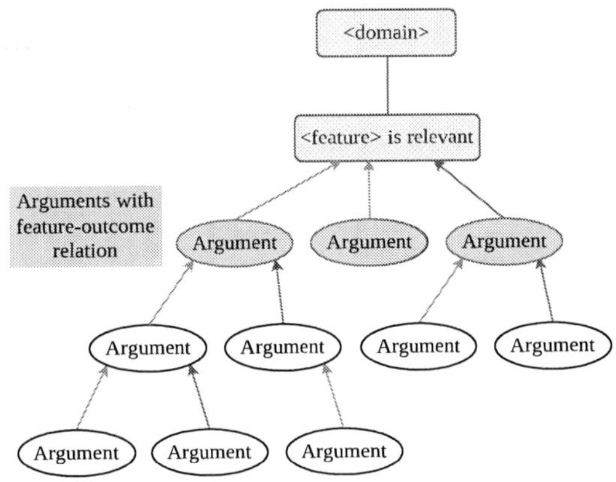

Figure 2: Exemplary depiction of the argumentation trees for a single feature within a domain. Every argument with a feature-outcome relation is the root of an individual argumentation tree. Green arrows indicate supporting relationships, while red arrows indicate attacking relationships.

3.2 Pipeline for Automatic Generation of Structured Domain Knowledge

Below, we describe the individual steps of our pipeline (see Figure 1) for the generation of structured domain knowledge for dialogue-based XAI systems. Namely, these are: argument acquisition through argument search, an optional pre-grouping of the arguments with respect to the features of the XAI system, argumentative relation classification transforming the pool of argumentative sentences into structured knowledge, and determining the type of the relationships between the arguments.

3.2.1 Argument Acquisition

By applying methods from the field of argument mining (Lawrence and Reed, 2019), argument search engines (Ajjour et al., 2019) allow to retrieve a ranked list of arguments with positive or negative stance towards a given search query. Based on an assessment of the suitability of different argument search engines for argumentative dialogues (Rach et al., 2020), the existing pipeline utilizes ArgumenText (Stab et al., 2018) with a web crawl as an argument search engine. Since our argumentation trees are representing domain knowledge which should be of high quality and may not be publicly accessible, we are utilizing the Classify API of summetix[1], which is the successor of ArgumenText, for the argument acquisition. Differently to the web crawl, we do not only input a query but also our own collection of relevant documents into the Classify API. Therewith, the documents that serve as a basis for the argument extraction are controllable and already tailored towards the targeted domain. Hence, instead of using the domain as

[1] https://www.summetix.com/

a query for the argument extraction, we can also utilize the auxiliary claims as queries. We then retrieve a collection of arguments per auxiliary claim which is equivalent to retrieving a collection of arguments per XAI feature. This additionally has the advantage that we are explicitly querying for arguments that address certain features and hence it might be more likely that the extracted arguments are representing the intended domain knowledge.

3.2.2 Pre-grouping of the Arguments

When arguments are pre-grouped, the existing pipeline restricts the allowed relationships between the arguments: Without pre-grouping, each argument can have a relationship to every other argument, whereas with pre-grouping, each argument can only have a relationship to arguments within the same group. Our target structure entails a grouping of the arguments according to the XAI features. While the grouping could be achieved implicitly through the argumentative relation classification itself, it might be desirable to a priori group the arguments by the feature they are addressing. To determine the XAI feature addressed by an argumentative sentence, we query the Classify API of summetix for every auxiliary claim and record the score for the sentence being an argument for the feature represented by the claim. We then assign the feature with the highest score to the sentence.

3.2.3 Argumentative Relation Classification

The core of the pipeline is the argumentative relation classification transforming the pool of arguments into the desired target structure.

To be able to apply the procedure of the existing pipeline without any major adaptions, we introduce an auxiliary node functioning as the root of our target structure and therefore can be viewed to represent the domain. This auxiliary node is having a relation with all auxiliary claims but with none of the retrieved arguments. This formalization of the problem allows to treat the process of creating multiple argumentation trees per feature as the process of creating one argumentation tree with the auxiliary node and the auxiliary claims being arranged in the tree in advance. Moreover, when not already determined through pre-grouping, the inclusion of the auxiliary claims into the pool of arguments allows to propagate the XAI feature of the auxiliary claim to the arguments targeting it. Therewith, it is also clear which feature is addressed by the individual argumentation trees.

Following, the existing pipeline, the confidence score of a pairwise BERT (Devlin et al., 2019) classification model is utilized to estimate the probability of a directed relationship between the ordered pairs of arguments. The model is fine-tuned with a balanced subset of the dataset by Carstens and Toni (2015) on predicting the labels *relation*, entailing supporting and attacking relations, and *no relation*. The type of the relation is identified post-hoc and is described in more detail in the next subsection. Given, the probability for a relationship, we apply their algorithm traversing and modifying graphs (TMG) (Schindler, 2020) to create the argumentation trees. To this end, TMG selects the most probable outgoing relationship for every argument and subsequently searches for circular graphs in the resulting structure, which are by default not attached to the argumentation tree with the domain as the root. In their formulation, which we name TMG_{all}, these circular graphs are connected to the argumentation tree by selecting the node with the most probable relation to any node outside the circular graph and change its outgoing relationship respectively. Due to the different nature of our target structure, we are adding an alternative variant of TMG, $\text{TMG}_{\text{feature}}$, which connects the circular graphs to the argumentation tree in a different way. More precisely, $\text{TMG}_{\text{feature}}$ is only considering the auxiliary claims and not any argument outside the circular graph as a potential target. This way, every circular graph becomes an individual argumentation tree for an XAI feature.

3.2.4 Determining the Type of Relationship

In the existing pipeline, the type of the relationships is determined by propagating the stance of the arguments towards the topic of the discussion through the argumentation tree. For the structured domain knowledge, we instead propagate the stance of the arguments towards the argument with the feature-outcome relation through the tree. The type of relation between the roots of each argumentation tree and the respective auxiliary claim is determined by the stance of the root towards the auxiliary claim. Simply propagating the stance towards the auxiliary claims through the trees is not sufficient since the dialogue-based XAI system will utilize every argumentation tree on its own and the representation of the auxiliary claims is to coarse-grained compared to a feature-outcome relation.

4 Configuration of the Pipeline through Expert Evaluation

The above description of our pipeline gives rise to the following possibilities for configuration: We can query the Classify API of the search engine either with the domain or the auxiliary claims, apply a pre-grouping of the arguments by XAI feature or not, and employ TMG_{all} or $TMG_{feature}$. For the auxiliary claims, we moreover test four different formulations

- *feature*: <feature> is relevant.
- $feature_{inclDomain}$: <feature> is relevant for <domain>.
- *feature+*: <feature>, which is related to <list of terms>, is relevant.
- $feature+_{inclDomain}$: <feature>, which is related to <list of terms>, is relevant for <domain>.

where *<feature>* is the respective name of the XAI feature, *<domain>* describes the domain (e. g., surviving the titanic), and *<list of terms>* are additional terms related to the feature. These additional terms are a combination of the related concepts, synonyms and types of the feature extracted from ConceptNet (Speer et al., 2017), the values of the feature if it is a categorical feature, and a further description of the feature if provided in the implementation of the dialogue-based XAI system, in our case in the one by Feustel et al. (2024).

To identify the best configuration of our pipeline, we perform an expert evaluation in the domain *titanic survival* with the XAI features *age*, *fare*, *gender*, and *passenger class* and make use of the same collection of documents utilized by Feustel et al. (2024) for creating the structured domain knowledge manually. After querying the argument search engine with the domain and all formulations of the auxiliary claims, we annotate the retrieved sentences to determine the best method for the retrieval and whether to include pre-grouping as a step in the pipeline. The decision on the variant of the TMG algorithm is driven by the comparison of the depth and width of the resulting argumentation trees. The expert evaluation is conducted by the authors of the paper. Since we are not performing a hypothesis test but merely identify the best configuration of our pipeline, we see no conflict of interest.

4.1 Annotation Study

For every sentence retrieved through the argument search, we perform an annotation regarding the following criteria:

- valid: Is the sentence an argument that can be used in a debate about <domain>?
- suitable: Is this argument suitable as a domain knowledge for dialogue-based XAI about <domain>? When the sentence is not valid it is also not suitable.
- feature(s): Which XAI feature is mainly addressed by the argument? If the argument addresses multiple XAI features and you cannot decide which is the main one, you may list the features. When none of the XAI features are addressed, state this as well.

The first two authors of the paper performed the annotation for 63 different sentences retrieved through the possible configurations of the argument search. They agreed in 100% of the cases for the criterion valid, in 84.13% of the cases for the criterion suitable, and again in 84.13% of the cases for assigning the exact same set of features in the criterion feature(s). To resolve the cases of disagreement, the third author of the paper was asked to perform the corresponding annotations, as well. Subsequently, we applied a majority vote for the criterion suitable and utilized the intersection of the assigned sets of features for the criterion feature(s). Through this procedure, a conclusive annotation could be created per sentence and criterion.

4.2 Results

Acquisition of Arguments The best performance for retrieving arguments was achieved by querying the Classify API with the auxiliary claims in the *feature* formulation. We excluded the formulations *feature+* and $feature+_{inclDomain}$ of the auxiliary claims from further analysis since with these we only retrieved six arguments and no arguments with the features *fare* and *gender*. When querying the API with the domain, only 89% of the 27 retrieved sentences are valid and from those only 92% are suitable. Moreover, we did not retrieve any arguments addressing the features *age* and *passenger class*. Utilizing the auxiliary claims in the formulation *feature* or $feature_{inclDomain}$, the pool of retrieved arguments has a size of 37 and 39 respectively, is valid to 97%, all valid arguments are also suitable, and all XAI features are covered. By retrieving less argument that are not addressing any of the XAI features (5% vs. 10%), the *feature* formulation is performing better than the $feature_{inclDomain}$ formulation.

Pre-grouping and Argumentative Relation Classification Since the best auxiliary claim formulation for acquiring the arguments is *feature*, we run our pipeline with the arguments retrieved this way and also utilize this formulation of the auxiliary claims throughout the pipeline including the pre-grouping of the arguments. In this setup, we find pre-grouping outperforming the variant of our pipeline without pre-grouping and the $TMG_{feature}$ algorithm being better suited than TMG_{all}. When applying pre-grouping, 91% of the arguments annotated to be addressing an XAI feature are assigned to a correct feature, whereas without pre-grouping this is only the case for 37%. Comparing TMG_{all} and $TMG_{feature}$ both with pre-grouping, there are no differences in the generated argumentation trees in terms of maximum depth and the amount of trees for the features *age* and *fare*. For *gender* and *passenger class*, TMG_{all} generates a single argumentation tree per feature with a maximum depth of 6 compared to $TMG_{feature}$ which generates three trees with a maximum depth of 4 and four trees with a maximum depth of 2, respectively. The generation of a single argumentation tree by TMG_{all} leads to a restriction for the dialogue system: When the user asks, why the feature was relevant, the dialogue system has to select the only available feature-outcome relation and cannot adapt its response to the feature values input into the AI model and the user's needs. Following this line of reasoning, we identify $TMG_{feature}$ as the better variant.

5 User Study

With the following user study, we aim to assess the feasibility of our approach for automatically generating structured domain knowledge for dialogue-based XAI systems. To this end, we manually generate explanatory dialogues with human annotated and automatically generated domain knowledge and compare the coherence of the resulting dialogues. After presenting how structured domain knowledge in the form of argumentation trees can be utilized in an existing explanation dialogue game, we detail the study setup and present our results.

5.1 Generation of Explanatory Dialogues

The explanatory dialogues for our user study are created by manually applying the explanation dialogue game model by Madumal et al. (2019) to the respective structured domain knowledge. We create one dialogue per XAI feature with the two interlocutors *questioner* and *explainer*. The questioner, who needs an explanation, starts the interaction by asking why the respective XAI feature was relevant for the decision in the domain. The explainer now tries to explain why the XAI feature was having an influence. Therefore, the first move of the explainer is to select the best suited argument with a feature-outcome relation that is supporting the respective auxiliary claim "<feature> is relevant.".

Whenever, there is an attacking relationship for the argument presented by the explainer, the questioner will start the argumentation by presenting this counter-argument. Following the explanation dialogue game, the explainer then has to affirm the argument, optionally present an argument attacking the one by the questioner, and then continue the interaction by providing a further explanation. To ensure a better coverage of the domain knowledge, our explainer always presents an attacking argument if available. For continuing the explanation, the explainer traverses the argumentation tree backwards and selects a yet unused argument that is supporting one of its previous statements. The explainer is also allowed to select a new argument with feature-outcome relation if there are no more suitable arguments left within the current tree. When formulating the selected argument as a further explanation, the explainer has to make clear to which previous statement the argument is relating to.

When the questioner cannot attack the explanation by the explainer, it asks a return question like "Why?", "Can you elaborate on this?", or "Can you further explain why ... ?". The explainer then continues the explanation by selecting the best suited argument out of those that are supporting its previous statement. If there are no supporting arguments, we introduce an apologize move by the explainer into the dialogue game. To continue the dialogue, the explainer then proceeds as above by traversing the domain knowledge backwards.

The dialogue ends, when all argumentation trees of the respective XAI feature have been traversed. To create a smoother dialogue experience, we additionally prohibit the questioner from asking a return

Interlocutor	Dialogue Move	Utterance
Questioner	begin question	Why is the duration having an influence when determining whether one would have gotten a loan?
Explainer	further explain	The purpose of the loan can influence the acceptable loan duration.
Questioner	return question	Can you elaborate on this?
Explainer	further explain	Longer durations may be more appropriate for larger purchases like homes or education, while short-term loans are more suitable for smaller purchases or emergencies.
Questioner	affirm	Okay, I understand.
Questioner	return question	But are there any other reasons why the duration is having an influence?
Explainer	further explain	Yes. Shorter loan terms are generally less risky for lenders and therefore lead to a better acceptance rate.
Questioner	begin argument	But longer durations can allow borrowers to spread out repayments, making them more manageable.
Explainer	affirm argument	I get your point.
Explainer	counter argument	However, longer loan durations may increase the risk of unforeseen circumstances.
Explainer	further explain	And shorter loan terms are generally less risky for lenders and therefore lead to a better acceptance rate because shorter repayment periods reduce the overall exposure to potential default.
Questioner	begin argument	However, then lenders have less time to assess potential changes in the borrower's financial situation.
Questioner	begin question	Why is the duration having an influence when determining whether one would have gotten a loan?
Explainer	further explain	Lenders will usually feel more comfortable lending you money for a shorter period because you're more likely to be able to pay it back.
Questioner	return question	Why?
Explainer	further explain	A shorter loan term will also save you more money because you'll pay interest for fewer years.

Table 1: Human generated explanatory dialogues in the domain *credit acquisition* for the XAI feature *duration* with manually generated (upper part) and automatically generated (lower part) domain knowledge. The dialogue move is provided in accordance with the explanation dialogue game model by Madumal et al. (2019).

question when it has already performed a return question in its last two moves and the explainer cannot continue explaining without traversing the domain knowledge backwards. In these cases, the questioner then affirms the explanation and formulates a return question asking for further reasons why the XAI feature was having an influence.

The explanatory dialogues created for our study in the domain *credit acquisition* for the XAI feature *duration* are shown in Table 1.

5.2 Study Setup

We perform the user study within the domains *titanic survival* and *credit acquisition*. The manual creation of the argumentation trees follows the procedure by Feustel et al. (2024). For the automatically generated trees, we employ our pipeline in its previously determined best configuration, i. e., the auxiliary claims are formulated as "<feature> is relevant.", the auxiliary claims are used for retrieving and pre-grouping the arguments, and $\text{TMG}_{\text{feature}}$ is applied for obtaining the tree structure. As the documents for the domain knowledge, we utilize the first ten URLs that are processable by the Classify API of summetix and were retrieved by performing a Google Search[2] with the queries "factors for surviving the titanic" and "factors for acquiring a loan", respectively. For *titanic survival*, we acquired arguments for all four XAI features, namely *age*, *fare*, *gender*, and *passenger class*. For *credit acquisition*, we only consider the XAI features *checking account*, *duration*, and *savings* in our user study since the automatically selected collection of documents did not allow for extracting arguments addressing the XAI features *purpose* and *amount*. To keep the length of the generated explanatory dialogues feasible for the user study, we select the 10 arguments with the highest retrieval score per feature before starting the relation classification of our pipeline. Similarly we restrict the human generated domain knowledge to a maximum of 10 arguments per feature.

Following the evaluation of the existing pipeline (Rach et al., 2021), we asses the coherence (Venkatesh et al., 2018) of the generated dialogues by making use of the following categories with yes/no questions:

- comprehensible: Do you understand what the speaker wants to say?
- reference: Does the utterance address its reference?
- attitude: Does the attitude of the utterance fit the speaker's role?

In the user study, the web interface presents the generated dialogues utterance-wise and asks the participants for an answer to these questions whenever the

[2]https://google.com/

utterance entails an argumentative sentence from the structured domain knowledge. Before starting the study, a textual page explained the above categories in more detail and provided hand-crafted examples in the domain *acceptance as a tenant*. At the end of the study, the participants assessed how clearly they understood the instructions for each of the categories on a five-point Likert scale.

We asked five non-expert users (two females, three males) to take part in our study and presented every user with all of the 14 dialogues, i. e., four dialogues for *titanic survival* and three dialogues for *credit acquisition* and this one time with the human generated and the other time with the automatically generated domain knowledge.

5.3 Results

The assessment of the clarity of the instructions for the categories was rated by the five participants as shown in Table 2. While the categories *comprehensible* and *attitude* were totally clear to the majority of the study participants, understanding the category *reference* was more challenging. Therefore, to eliminate outliers and achieve a result that is as objective as possible, we follow Wachsmuth et al. (2017) by selecting the three most agreeing participants per category and gaining a final answer for each question through majority vote. The category-wise inter annotator agreement is assessed by Randolph's kappa (Randolph, 2005). For the three most agreeing participants, the agreement is substantial (0.78) for comprehensible, moderate (0.58) for reference, and almost perfect (0.89) for attitude (Landis and Koch, 1977), whereas the agreement for all five participants is 0.64, 0.32, and 0.47, respectively.

The dialogue-wise results of the user study for the three most agreeing participants are shown in Table 3. We report the ratio of positive and overall ratings and perform a Boschloo exact test (Boschloo, 1970) to assess the statistical difference between the automatically and manually generated domain knowledge. Following Rach et al. (2021), an utterance is regarded to be coherent, when all of the three categories are rated positively, i. e., with "yes", in the result. For the human-generated domain knowledge, we can see that all categories were rated positively for all utterance besides the reference category for the feature *duration* in the *credit acquisition* domain. With the automatically generated tree structures, no errors in terms of attitude were identified and the percentage of comprehensible argumentative utterances is above 90% for both domains. Moreover, there is no significant difference between the human and automatically generated argumentation trees for the categories attitude and comprehensible. For reference and coherence, however, we observe a statistically significant difference between the manually and automatically generated domain knowledge.

	totally agree	agree	neutral	disagree	totally disagree
comprehensible	3	2	–	–	–
reference	–	3	1	1	–
attitude	4	–	1	–	–

Table 2: Amount of responses on a five-point Likert scale for how clearly the participants have understood the instructions.

6 Discussion

To close the gap between the human and our automatically generated argumentation trees for domain-specific knowledge, our results suggest that only an improvement of the references made between the arguments is required. This room for improvement might be attributed to the following areas: First, our pipeline could be identifying the relationships between the arguments in a non-suited way for domain knowledge. This could be improved by fine-tuning the pairwise BERT model on a dataset that is tailored more towards the modeling of domain knowledge or by further adapting or even exchanging the process of creating the final argumentation trees through TMG. Second, our instantiation of the explanatory dialogue game model could have contributed to the results. While we have utilized the same strategy for generating the dialogues, the underlying argumentation trees are having different characteristics: The human generated domain knowledge shows an almost equal amount of supporting and attacking relations, whereas the automatically generated ones are consisting nearly only of supporting relations. Therefore, with the automatically generated trees, the chains of reasoning within the dialogues became increasingly larger and the interaction between the questioner and the explainer was also more single-sided. This potential cause is also underpinned by a comment from one of the study participants: "When the answer of the explainer [...] didn't really fit the question asked but still fit the topic of the conversation I was a bit unsure if [I should an-

	titanic age	titanic fare	titanic gender	titanic passenger class	titanic overall	credit checking account	credit duration	credit savings	credit overall
comprehensible	1.00	1.00	1.00	1.00	1.00	1.00	1.00	1.00	1.00
reference	1.00	1.00	1.00	1.00	1.00	1.00	0.86	1.00	0.95
attitude	1.00	1.00	1.00	1.00	1.00	1.00	1.00	1.00	1.00
coherence	1.00	1.00	1.00	1.00	1.00	1.00	0.86	1.00	0.95
comprehensible	0.86	1.00	1.00	1.00	0.96	0.75	1.00	1.00	0.93
reference	1.00	0.6	0.67	0.83	0.78	0.75	1.00	0.5	0.64
attitude	1.00	1.00	1.00	1.00	1.00	1.00	1.00	1.00	1.00
coherence	0.86	0.6	0.67	0.83	0.74	0.5	1.00	0.5	0.57
comprehensible					0.86				0.55
reference					**0.02**				**0.03**
attitude					1.00				1.00
coherence					**0.01**				**0.01**

Table 3: Feature-wise and overall results per domain for manually (upper part) and automatically (mid part) generated domain knowledge. We report the ratio of positive and overall ratings. Additionally, we report the p-values of the pairwise Boschloo exact test comparing automatically and manually generated domain knowledge (lower part).

swer with yes or no for the category reference]." This comment directly leads us to another aspect, namely the difficulty of assessing the category reference for the participants. While it might be in general difficult to asses this category, an improved formulation and explanation for the category could improve results in future works. Finally, the underlying data and therewith the documents utilized for extracting the domain knowledge might play a role. We utilized the top results of a web search engine without checking the content of the documents and their suitability for extracting domain knowledge. Hence, the argumentation trees created through our pipeline might also have a general disadvantage compared to the human-generated ones in terms of the available data.

While we evaluated our pipeline in the domains of *titanic survival* and *credit acquisition*, it can be applied to any domain and feature-based XAI system as long as reliable documents containing the required domain knowledge are available.

7 Conclusion and Future Work

We have presented an approach to automatically generate structured domain knowledge for dialogue-based XAI systems. To this end, we adapted an existing pipeline (Rach et al., 2021) from the field of persuasive, argumentative dialogue to the field of explanatory dialogue. Our approach combines methods from formal argumentation with data-driven techniques to ensure a flexible, yet reliable knowledge base. Through an expert evaluation, we identified the best configuration of our pipeline. Utilizing this configuration in a user study, we compare the automatically generated argumentation trees to human-generated ones by assessing the coherence of manually generated explanatory dialogues including the respective trees as domain knowledge. The study concludes that the human-generated argumentation trees are performing better than the automatically generated ones since the reference of the arguments leaves room for improvement. However, we discussed that this might be attributed to the instantiation of the employed explanatory dialogue game and the documents utilized for extracting the domain knowledge.

Therefore, besides improving the argumentative relation classification of the pipeline itself, a task for future work could be the optimization of the selection of the documents entailing the domain knowledge when not provided with these documents by a human. Additionally, the pipeline could become more robust by including validations based on established methods from the field of computational argumentation. Last but not least, a more large scale user study evaluating the automatically generated argumentation trees in an actual interaction with a dialogue system providing contextualized XAI explanations would provide further valuable insights.

Acknowledgments

We thank summetix GmbH for supporting our research with access to their Classify API.

References

Amina Adadi and Mohammed Berrada. 2018. Peeking inside the black-box: A survey on explainable artificial intelligence (XAI). *IEEE Access*, 6:52138–52160.

Yamen Ajjour, Henning Wachsmuth, Johannes Kiesel, Martin Potthast, Matthias Hagen, and Benno Stein. 2019. Data acquisition for argument search: The args.me corpus. In *KI 2019: Advances in Artificial Intelligence - 42nd German Conference on AI, Kassel, Germany, September 23-26, 2019, Proceedings*, volume 11793 of *Lecture Notes in Computer Science*, pages 48–59. Springer.

R. D. Boschloo. 1970. Raised conditional level of significance for the 2 × 2-table when testing the equality of two probabilities. *Statistica Neerlandica*, 24(1):1–9.

Clara Bove, Jonathan Aigrain, Marie-Jeanne Lesot, Charles Tijus, and Marcin Detyniecki. 2021. Contextualising local explanations for non-expert users: an XAI pricing interface for insurance. In *Joint Proceedings of the ACM IUI 2021 Workshops co-located with 26th ACM Conference on Intelligent User Interfaces (ACM IUI 2021), College Station, United States, April 13-17, 2021*, volume 2903 of *CEUR Workshop Proceedings*. CEUR-WS.org.

Lucas Carstens and Francesca Toni. 2015. Towards relation based argumentation mining. In *Proceedings of the 2nd Workshop on Argumentation Mining*, pages 29–34, Denver, CO. Association for Computational Linguistics.

Hongshen Chen, Xiaorui Liu, Dawei Yin, and Jiliang Tang. 2017. A survey on dialogue systems: Recent advances and new frontiers. *SIGKDD Explor.*, 19(2):25–35.

Jacob Devlin, Ming-Wei Chang, Kenton Lee, and Kristina Toutanova. 2019. BERT: Pre-training of deep bidirectional transformers for language understanding. In *Proceedings of the 2019 Conference of the North American Chapter of the Association for Computational Linguistics: Human Language Technologies, Volume 1 (Long and Short Papers)*, pages 4171–4186, Minneapolis, Minnesota. Association for Computational Linguistics.

Nils Feldhus, Qianli Wang, Tatiana Anikina, Sahil Chopra, Cennet Oguz, and Sebastian Möller. 2023. Interrolang: Exploring NLP models and datasets through dialogue-based explanations. In *Findings of the Association for Computational Linguistics: EMNLP 2023, Singapore, December 6-10, 2023*, pages 5399–5421. Association for Computational Linguistics.

Isabel Feustel, Niklas Rach, Wolfgang Minker, and Stefan Ultes. 2024. Enhancing model transparency: A dialogue system approach to XAI with domain knowledge. In *Proceedings of the 25th Annual Meeting of the Special Interest Group on Discourse and Dialogue*, pages 248–258, Kyoto, Japan. Association for Computational Linguistics.

Annika Flycht-Eriksson. 1999. A survey of knowledge sources in dialogue systems. *Electron. Trans. Artif. Intell.*, 3(D):5–32.

J. Richard Landis and Gary G. Koch. 1977. The measurement of observer agreement for categorical data. *Biometrics*, 33(1):159–174.

John Lawrence and Chris Reed. 2019. Argument mining: A survey. *Computational Linguistics*, 45(4):765–818.

Prashan Madumal, Tim Miller, Liz Sonenberg, and Frank Vetere. 2019. A grounded interaction protocol for explainable artificial intelligence. In *Proceedings of the 18th International Conference on Autonomous Agents and MultiAgent Systems, AAMAS '19, Montreal, QC, Canada, May 13-17, 2019*, pages 1033–1041. International Foundation for Autonomous Agents and Multiagent Systems.

Hugo Mercier and Dan Sperber. 2011. Why do humans reason? arguments for an argumentative theory. *Behavioral and brain sciences*, 34(2):57–74.

Tim Miller. 2019. Explanation in artificial intelligence: Insights from the social sciences. *Artif. Intell.*, 267:1–38.

Catia Pesquita. 2021. Towards semantic integration for explainable artificial intelligence in the biomedical domain. In *Proceedings of the 14th International Joint Conference on Biomedical Engineering Systems and Technologies, BIOSTEC 2021, Volume 5: HEALTHINF, Online Streaming, February 11-13, 2021*, pages 747–753. SCITEPRESS.

Niklas Rach, Yuki Matsuda, Johannes Daxenberger, Stefan Ultes, Keiichi Yasumoto, and Wolfgang Minker. 2020. Evaluation of argument search approaches in the context of argumentative dialogue systems. In *Proceedings of the Twelfth Language Resources and Evaluation Conference*, pages 513–522, Marseille, France. European Language Resources Association.

Niklas Rach, Carolin Schindler, Isabel Feustel, Johannes Daxenberger, Wolfgang Minker, and Stefan Ultes. 2021. From argument search to argumentative dialogue: A topic-independent approach to argument acquisition for dialogue systems. In *Proceedings of the 22nd Annual Meeting of the Special Interest Group on Discourse and Dialogue*, pages 368–379, Singapore and Online. Association for Computational Linguistics.

Justus J. Randolph. 2005. Free-marginal multirater kappa (multirater k [free]): An alternative to fleiss' fixed-marginal multirater kappa.

Carolin Schindler. 2020. Argumentative relation classification for argumentative dialogue systems. Bachelor's thesis, Institute of Communications Engineering, Ulm University.

Dylan Slack, Satyapriya Krishna, Himabindu Lakkaraju, and Sameer Singh. 2023. Explaining machine learning models with interactive natural language conversations using talktomodel. *Nat. Mac. Intell.*, 5(8):873–883.

Robyn Speer, Joshua Chin, and Catherine Havasi. 2017. Conceptnet 5.5: An open multilingual graph of general knowledge. In *Proceedings of the Thirty-First AAAI Conference on Artificial Intelligence, February 4-9, 2017, San Francisco, California, USA*, pages 4444–4451. AAAI Press.

Christian Stab, Johannes Daxenberger, Chris Stahlhut, Tristan Miller, Benjamin Schiller, Christopher Tauchmann, Steffen Eger, and Iryna Gurevych. 2018. ArgumenText: Searching for arguments in heterogeneous sources. In *Proceedings of the 2018 Conference of the North American Chapter of the Association for Computational Linguistics: Demonstrations*, pages 21–25, New Orleans, Louisiana. Association for Computational Linguistics.

Christian Stab and Iryna Gurevych. 2014. Annotating argument components and relations in persuasive essays. In *Proceedings of COLING 2014, the 25th International Conference on Computational Linguistics: Technical Papers*, pages 1501–1510, Dublin, Ireland. Dublin City University and Association for Computational Linguistics.

Anu Venkatesh, Chandra Khatri, Ashwin Ram, Fenfei Guo, Raefer Gabriel, Ashish Nagar, Rohit Prasad, Ming Cheng, Behnam Hedayatnia, Angeliki Metallinou, Rahul Goel, Shaohua Yang, and Anirudh Raju. 2018. On evaluating and comparing conversational agents. *CoRR*, abs/1801.03625.

Henning Wachsmuth, Nona Naderi, Yufang Hou, Yonatan Bilu, Vinodkumar Prabhakaran, Tim Alberdingk Thijm, Graeme Hirst, and Benno Stein. 2017. Computational argumentation quality assessment in natural language. In *Proceedings of the 15th Conference of the European Chapter of the Association for Computational Linguistics: Volume 1, Long Papers*, pages 176–187, Valencia, Spain. Association for Computational Linguistics.

Exploring the Impact of Modalities on Building Common Ground Using the Collaborative Scene Reconstruction Task

Yosuke Ujigwa [1], Asuka Shiotani[1], Masato Takizawa[1], Eisuke Midorikawa[1], Ryuichiro Higashinaka[2], Kazunori Takashio[1]

[1]Keio University, Japan , [2]NTT Corporation, Japan

Correspondence: ujigawa@keio.jp

Abstract

To deepen our understanding of verbal and non-verbal modalities in establishing common ground, this study introduces a novel "collaborative scene reconstruction task." In this task, pairs of participants, each provided with distinct image sets derived from the same video, work together to reconstruct the sequence of the original video. The level of agreement between the participants on the image order—quantified using Kendall's rank correlation coefficient—serves as a measure of common ground construction. This approach enables the analysis of how various modalities contribute to the construction of common ground. A corpus comprising 40 dialogues from 20 participants was collected and analyzed. The findings suggest that specific gestures play a significant role in fostering common ground, offering valuable insights for the development of dialogue systems that leverage multimodal information to enhance the user construction of common ground.

1 Introduction

Understanding the essence of human communication is a crucial challenge in the fields of artificial intelligence and human-computer interaction (HCI). The concept of common ground, proposed by Clark, refers to the shared knowledge and beliefs between participants in a dialogue, forming the foundation for smooth communication (Clark, 1996). Unraveling the process of grounding is not only essential for understanding the mechanisms of deep relational building among humans but also holds significant implications for developing AI agents and robots capable of interacting naturally with humans (Morita et al., 2024).

Recent research has highlighted the influence of multimodal communication channels and social relationships on grounding (Furuya et al., 2022). Visual cues, in particular, have been shown to facilitate common ground construction, though the specific elements of visual information that are most effective remain insufficiently clarified. Additionally, traditional experimental settings often feature tasks with relative ease, making it challenging to conduct a detailed analysis of failures in grounding (Udagawa and Aizawa, 2019).

In this study, we propose a novel collaborative task that enables clearer observation of the influence of physical expression as a visual modality and allows for detailed analysis of both successful and unsuccessful grounding instances. The task emphasizes the role of non-verbal communication, enabling precise analysis of how physical modalities, such as gestures and gaze, influence grounding (Kendon, 1983). By appropriately adjusting task difficulty, the study aims to observe the dynamics of grounding in more realistic scenarios.

2 Construction Process of Common Ground

2.1 Common Ground

Common ground refers to the totality of shared knowledge, beliefs, and assumptions between participants in a dialogue (Clark, 1996). In everyday conversations, it is assumed that a basic common ground concerning general knowledge and language understanding already exists, and through interaction, new common ground is dynamically constructed. This process is critical for enhancing the efficiency and effectiveness of communication (Mitsuda et al., 2021).

Understanding and constructing common ground are essential for smooth dialogues. When dialogue participants do not accurately grasp common ground, misunderstandings and discrepancies may occur, potentially hindering communication. Conversely, when sufficient common ground is established, it allows for the omission of information and reliance on implicit understanding, facilitating efficient communication (Nakano et al., 2015).

Proceedings of the 15th International Workshop on Spoken Dialogue Systems Technology, pages 12–19
May 27–30, 2025.

In recent HCI research, the concept of common ground has been applied to the design of interactions between humans and AI agents (Nakano, 2019). Developing advanced dialogue systems requires the ability to appropriately construct and maintain common ground with users, a capability that significantly influences the naturalness and effectiveness of the system.

2.2 Modalities in Dialogue

In dialogue, modality refers to the various sensory channels and forms of expression used for information transmission. Beyond linguistic modalities (spoken and written language), non-verbal modalities (such as facial expressions, gestures, posture, and gaze) enable rich and multi-layered communication (Ekman and Friesen, 1969).

Research on multimodal communication has demonstrated that, compared to dialogue relying on a single modality, the efficiency of information transmission and comprehension improves (Kipp, 2005). Non-verbal modalities are particularly crucial in conveying linguistically ambiguous content or complex concepts. For instance, gestures and facial expressions contribute to complementing and emphasizing verbal content, as well as communicating the speaker's emotions and attitudes (McNeill, 1992).

Recent HCI research has actively incorporated these insights into the design of multimodal interfaces (Krauss et al., 2000). In human-AI agent interaction, elucidating insights into the process of grounding and adapting linguistic and non-linguistic modality elements that contribute to its construction are expected to enable more natural and effective communication.

2.3 Previous Research on Construction Process of common ground

In the study of grounding processes, a common approach involves setting specific tasks and analyzing the dialogue between participants (Benotti and Blackburn, 2021). Tasks such as the map task (Ichikawa et al., 2000) and the referential communication task (Anderson et al., 1991) have been widely used. These studies have provided valuable insights into the formation of common ground and its impact on dialogue efficiency.

However, many traditional studies have focused on the relationship between the final task outcome and common ground, with limited detailed analysis of the grounding process itself (Nakano, 2019). A pioneering study addressing this issue is the research by Udagawa and Aizawa (2019), which proposed a new corpus for analyzing the grounding process in a continuously and partially observable context. Nevertheless, this study used text chat, thus failing to account for the influence of non-verbal modalities (Carney and Harrigan, 2003) and the social relationships between interlocutors (Taylor, 1968).

The study by Furuya et al. (2022) analyzed the impact of modality and social relationships on grounding using the "CommonLayout". Their research demonstrated that rich modalities and deep social relationships facilitate grounding. However, it did not clarify which elements of visual information are particularly effective, and the low task difficulty made detailed analysis of grounding failures challenging.

Building on these previous studies, the current research aims to develop a new collaborative task that allows for a more refined analysis of the impact of non-verbal modalities, particularly physical modalities, on grounding. This task will also enable the observation of both successful and unsuccessful grounding instances.This enables the analysis of elements of physical modality that contribute to foundational construction, providing deeper insights into the fields of Human-Computer Interaction (HCI) and communication studies.

3 Collaborative Scene Reordering Task

This study proposes a new collaborative task, the "Collaborative Scene Reordering Task," designed to analyze the impact of modality on the construction of common ground. The task aims to examine how physical modalities during dialogue influence grounding and to provide a detailed analysis of this process.

The task is designed to meet the following requirements:

1. Enable two participants to construct common ground through dialogue.

2. Ensure that as the construction of common ground progresses, task performance improves.

3. Enable the analysis of the degree of grounding achieved at the conclusion, including both successful and unsuccessful cases of grounding construction.

4. Encourage the manifestation of non-verbal behaviors during communication, enabling a more detailed analysis of the impact of physical modalities.

This task is expected to offer insights into the role of physical modalities in grounding, enhancing our understanding of their contribution to effective communication.

The Collaborative Scene Reordering Task involves two participants, each possessing separate pieces of information. The task is divided into a transmission phase and a working phase, which alternate as a single set. In this task, participants share their respective information to reorder a set of images according to the narrative flow of a single story.

The transmission phase, where participants exchange information, is clearly separated from the work phase, where they physically reorder the images. This separation allows participants to allocate more cognitive resources to communication, encouraging them to focus on physical expressions and their partner's information during the interaction. The task is specifically designed to encourage nonverbal behaviors during the transmission phase. The use of visually dynamic and motion-rich video material as the basis for the images also supports this objective.

Task Description:

Setup: Each participant receives 10 shuffled images, extracted from a one-minute video, out of a total of 20 images. Neither participant has the full set, requiring them to infer and communicate about the missing parts.

Transmission Phase: Participants discuss their images face-to-face, focusing solely on sharing information. Physical modalities such as gestures and expressions are encouraged to aid communication. The phase is designed to elicit non-verbal behaviors by separating it from the work phase, preventing simultaneous reordering and discussion.

Work phase: Participants independently reorder their images based on the insights gained from the transmission phase. No communication is allowed during this phase, enabling a clear assessment of the understanding and common ground constructed earlier.

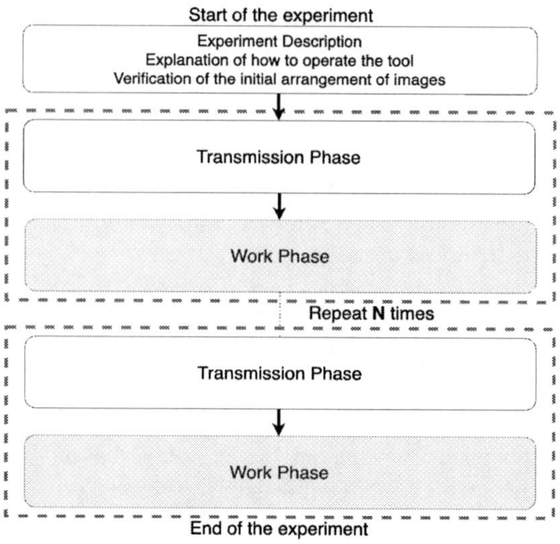

Figure 1: Flow of the Task

The Collaborative Scene Reordering Task builds upon the basic structure of the Collaborative Object Arrangement Task, where two participants are given objects and individually manipulate them based on the communication content with their partner. The final outcomes are compared to analyze the process of grounding. By recording the degree of completion of the image reordering during each working phase, the process of grounding facilitated by each transmission phase can be analyzed in detail. The flow of task implementation is as follows Fig.1.

This task design is based on Clark's theory of common ground (Clark, 1996), intentionally creating asymmetry of knowledge between participants to enable a clearer observation of the shared understanding process of grounding. Additionally, it emphasizes the importance of nonverbal behavior, drawing on Kendon's research on gestures (Kendon, 1983).

4 Experiment

This section describes the experiment conducted using the task proposed in the previous section, aimed at analyzing the influence of modalities in the common ground construction process.

4.1 Participants and Environment

The participants in the experiment were 40 individuals, unrelated to the project, who were gathered via a cloud service. The participant pairs consisted of 10 randomly formed pairs (20 participants in total: 4 males and 16 females), with an average age

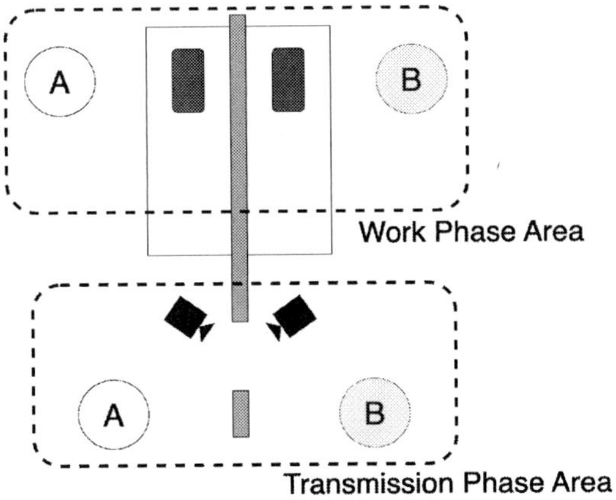

Figure 2: The environment of a Task

Figure 3: The environment of a work area

Figure 4: The environment of a transmission area

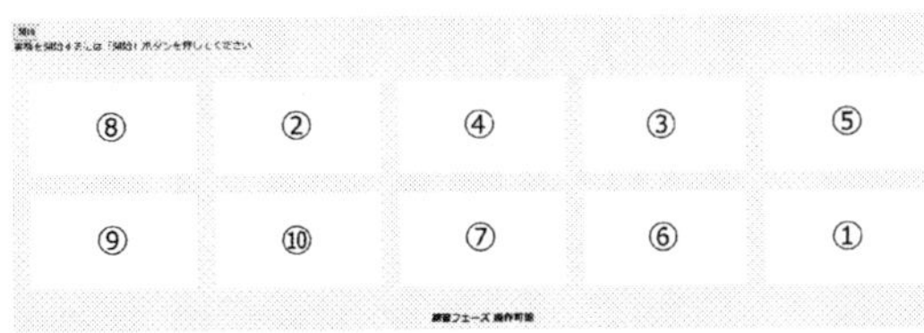

Figure 5: Image of the initial arrangement of images

Figure 6: Example of the actual screen of the tool

of 47.15 years (SD = 10.38). All pairs were meeting for the first time.. Each pair completed tasks for 4 videos, collecting a total of 40 data points.

The experiment was conducted in a space divided into a work area and a transmission area (Fig.2).

The experiment was conducted in an environment designed to meet the task requirements outlined in the previous section. Participants sat at a central table while receiving instructions on using the tool and performing the work phase (Fig.3). To prevent communication during the work phase, a partition was placed between the participants.

During the transmission phase, participants stood at marked positions on the floor to engage in communication with each other (Fig.4). A single camera was positioned to capture each participant frontally, while wide-angle cameras were placed diagonally in front of each participant to capture a broader view, including facial expressions and gestures.

The camera placement was carefully designed to ensure clear visibility of non-verbal communication without hindering the participants' interaction.

4.2 Experimental Procedure

Participants first received an explanation of the experiment and provided their consent. The experiment was conducted using a tool running on a workstation PC, which displayed 10 images in a web browser interface (Fig.5 and 6). Participants could rearrange the images by dragging and dropping them with the mouse. Each action was transmitted to a server for recording. The workstation display continuously showed the current phase, whether operations were permitted, and the remaining time at the bottom of the screen.

During the transmission phase, the images were concealed to prevent viewing, while in the work phase, the images were displayed, allowing participants to reorder them. Following the task design described earlier, each set of images involved five repetitions of a 2-minute transmission phase and a 1-minute work phase.

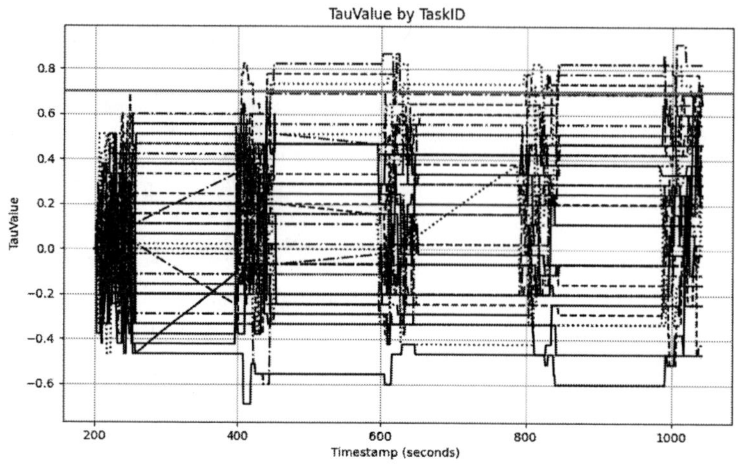

Figure 7: The changes in the correlation coefficient

The images used were derived from approximately 1-minute scenes from films like "City Lights," with 20 images obtained from each video, resulting in four distinct image sets. All videos used in the experiment were in the public domain, ensuring no copyright issues under Japanese and U.S. regulations.

5 Analysis of Collected Corpus

This section will describe how the dialogue data collected from the experiment was analyzed to examine the process of building common ground. Evaluation was performed based on the common ground construction process using information recorded during each phase.

The experimental tool recorded the movement of images and the order of images at each time point. Numbers were assigned to the images on the tool according to their chronological order. Kendall's rank correlation coefficient is calculated based on whether the image arrangements between participant pairs are consistent or inconsistent with each other. This coefficient ranges from -1 to 1, where 1 indicates a perfect positive correlation, -1 indicates a perfect negative correlation, and 0 indicates no correlation. In this study, the objective is not to evaluate whether the sequence of images follows a chronological order but rather to assess the extent to which a shared foundation is accurately constructed through participant interactions. Therefore, the coefficient, which indicates the degree of agreement in image arrangement among participants, is treated as an index of the shared understanding construction process.

work phases	1st	2nd	3rd	4th	5th
M	0.12	0.15	0.19	0.26	0.28
SD	0.31	0.37	0.36	0.35	0.36

Table 1: The change of the coefficients

This number was calculated each time participants rearranged images, and the change in value at the end of the work phase was considered as the change in the ground constructed through transmission.

During transmission, cameras set between participants and behind them recorded facial expressions, gestures, and dialogue content during the experiment.

The Kendall rank correlation coefficient was calculated for each participant pair's work, and changes in the correlation coefficient over time were recorded to analyze the building common ground process (Fig. 7).

To analyze the construction process of the common ground through repeated work phases, we summarize the statistical information on the coefficients at the end of the five work phases (Table 1). From the results showing an increase in similarity with each phase, we can see that the process of building a Common Ground was successfully recorded.

By separating the work and transmission phases in the task design, we were able to record the com-

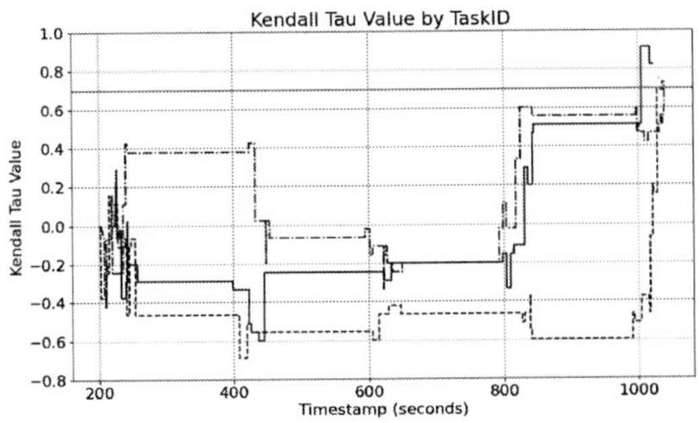

Figure 8: The result of successful sessions

mon ground construction process during communication.

We analyze gestures that contribute to the construction based on the final values for each session. When sessions with a final similarity of the arrangement order between the pairs of participants exceeding 0.7 were considered successful, there were 3 successful sessions (Fig. 8).

6 Clustering the grounding process

Clustering techniques are used to clarify the typical process of grounding in the collected data. The results of clustering using hierarchical clustering, a method for clustering time-series data, are shown. Hierarchical clustering is suitable for certain types of time-series data, particularly when the data is represented as fixed-length vectors with fully aligned time steps across all samples.

The results of the clustering are illustrated in Figure 9. Given the consistency of similar clusters when increasing the number of clusters, we classified the data into four clusters. The vertical axis represents the Kendall rank correlation coefficient calculated for each pair of participants' tasks. The horizontal axis corresponds to the step numbers associated with the beginning and end of the five work phases.

To delve deeper into the content of dialogues within each cluster, we sampled several conversations from each classified group and analyzed them in relation to their dialogue content.

Cluster 1: This pattern shows significant progress in grounding common ground early in the task. In these cases, participants tended to share the overall flow and key features using physical expressions, facilitating the grounding process early on.

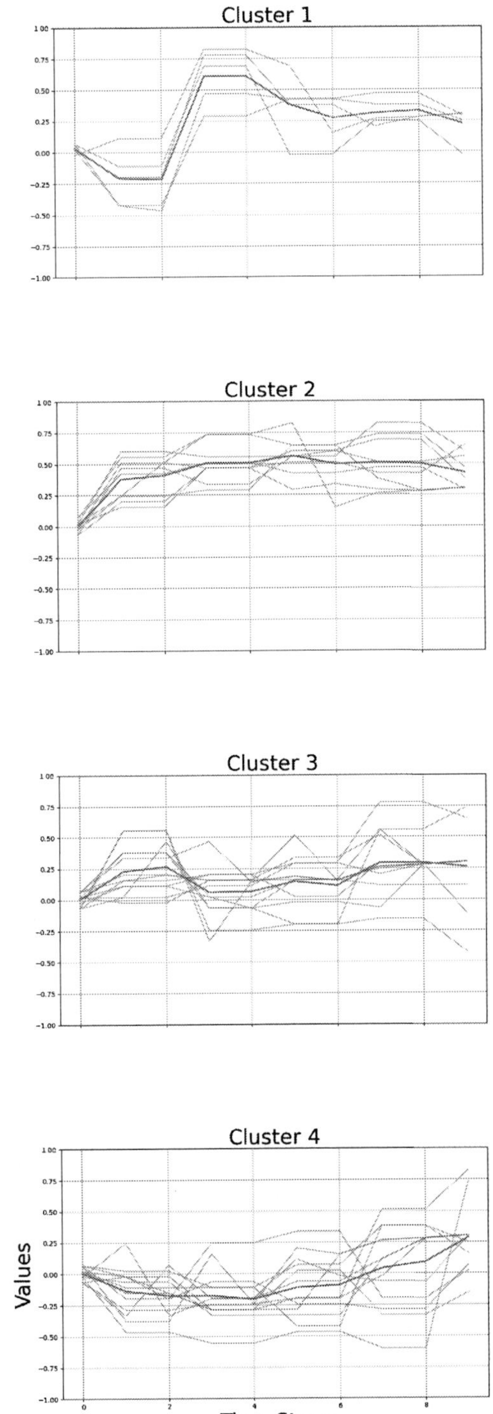

Figure 9: The result of successful sessions

Cluster 2: This pattern exhibits steady, average progress in grounding common ground throughout the task. In these instances, participants often identified distinctive characters or motifs from the scenes, progressively building the common ground. Some pairs demonstrated a dynamic where one participant led the direction of the flow, while the other followed, contributing to the grounding process.

Cluster 3: This pattern indicates a general difficulty in establishing common ground. Here, participants struggled to share information and find common elements, leading to unsuccessful grounding attempts.

Cluster 4: In this pattern, significant progress in grounding common ground occurred towards the end of the task. Participants successfully shared information over time, leading to successful grounding by the task's conclusion. In some cases, pairs initially built smaller subgroups by sharing parts of the scene flow, then combined these to establish the overall flow.

By classifying the data into clusters based on the grounding process, we identified distinct patterns in how common ground develops, offering insights into the dynamics of successful and unsuccessful grounding scenarios.

From the video recordings of phases where significant progress in grounding common ground was observed, the following gestures were noted. These gestures are considered to be strong contributing factors to common ground construction:

Video Imitation Transmission A method of mimicking specific people or situations shown in a video using hands or body movements. This approach expresses the state or condition of objects in the video through bodily movements, making it easier to visually understand the other person's state or emotions.

Structure Expression Transmission A method of using hands or arms to show the spatial structure of the scene or the flow of time in a video. For example, it can be used to convey the position of objects in a spatial arrangement or to express chronological order. This method is particularly effective when conveying spatial or temporal information.

Imitation Agreement Transmission A method of showing agreement or understanding by mimicking the other person's actions or gestures. By repeating the other person's movements, physical expressions are used to convey understanding or agreement with a statement. This approach may emphasize empathy or cooperation within communication.

Other Cultural Gestures A method of expressing emotions or states through body movements or gestures used in specific cultures. These can include signs of hesitation, agreement, or requests for clarification during communication.

7 Summary and Future Directions

In this study, we proposed a novel experimental task, the "Collaborative Scene Reordering Task," to analyze the process of grounding common ground in human communication, with a particular focus on the impact of non-verbal modalities.

By separating the transmission and work phases within the task, we were able to observe the effects of physicality more clearly and analyze both the successes and failures in the grounding process. We established a method for quantitatively evaluating the grounding process over time using the Kendall rank correlation coefficient. Clustering was performed based on the grounding process, allowing us to analyze the tendencies in how grounding progresses. Furthermore, the study suggested that specific gestures might strongly contribute to the grounding of common ground, affirming the importance of non-verbal communication.

These findings not only deepen our understanding of human communication but also suggest potential applications in designing more natural interactions between humans and agents.

However, this study has the following limitations.

The sample size was small, with a gender imbalance among participants. The task was designed to observe grounding in specific contexts, and caution is needed when generalizing the findings. Long-term effects and cultural factors were not considered. Due to technical constraints, some non-verbal behaviors may not have been fully captured. Future research should include larger and more diverse samples, cross-cultural validation, and investigation of long-term effects.

A more detailed analysis of gestures and dialogue content during the interaction will be conducted. By observing the frequency and timing of gestures during the dialogue and performing a quantitative analysis, the aim is to clarify the factors that influence the construction of a shared foundation. Furthermore, the current study focuses solely on the physical expressions in the dialogue, without analyzing the content of the dialogue itself. Future analysis will include the relationship between dialogue content and gestures, their impact on the construction process, and the effects of different progression strategies during the task.

This study provides new insights into the role of non-verbal communication in grounding and makes significant contributions to the fields of HCI, the implementation of smoother dialogue systems, and communication research.

References

Anne H Anderson, Miles Bader, Ellen Gurman Bard, Elizabeth Boyle, Gwyneth Doherty, Simon Garrod, Stephen Isard, Jacqueline Kowtko, Jan McAllister, Jim Miller, et al. 1991. The HCRC map task corpus. *Language and speech*, 34(4):351–366.

Luciana Benotti and Patrick Rowan Blackburn. 2021. Grounding as a collaborative process. In *Proceedings of the 16th Conference of the European Chapter of the Association for Computational Linguistics*, pages 515–531. Association for Computational Linguistics.

Dana R Carney and Jinni A Harrigan. 2003. It takes one to know one: interpersonal sensitivity is related to accurate assessments of others' interpersonal sensitivity. *Emotion*, 3(2):194.

Herbert H Clark. 1996. *Using language*. Cambridge university press.

Paul Ekman and Wallace V. Friesen. 1969. The repertoire of nonverbal behavior: Categories, origins, usage, and coding. *Semiotica*, 1(1):49–98.

Yuki Furuya, Koki Saito, Kosuke Ogura, Koh Mitsuda, Ryuichiro Higashinaka, and Kazunori Takashio. 2022. Dialogue corpus construction considering modality and social relationships in building common ground. In *Proceedings of the Thirteenth Language Resources and Evaluation Conference*, pages 4088–4095.

Akira Ichikawa, Yasuo Horiuchi, and Shun Tsuchiya. 2000. The Japanese map task dialogue corpus. *Journal of the Phonetic Society of Japan*, 4(2):4–15. (In Japanese).

Adam Kendon. 1983. Gesture and speech: How they interact. *Nonverbal interaction*, 11:13–45.

Michael Kipp. 2005. *Gesture generation by imitation: from human behavior to computer character animation*. Universal-Publishers.

Robert M Krauss, Yihsiu Chen, and Rebecca F Gotfexnum. 2000. 13 lexical gestures and lexical access: a process model. *Language and gesture*, 2:261.

David McNeill. 1992. *Hand and mind: What gestures reveal about thought*. University of Chicago press.

Koh Mitsuda, Ryuichiro Higashinaka, Yuhei Ohga, and Tetsuya Kinebuchi. 2021. Analysis of common ground building process in dialogue for collaborative figure placement task. In *Proceedings of the 27th Annual Meeting of the Association for Natural Language Processing*, pages 1698–1701.

Junya Morita, Tatsuya Yui, Takeru Amaya, Ryuichiro Higashinaka, and Yugo Takeuchi. 2024. Cognitive architecture toward common ground sharing among humans and generative AIs: Trial modeling on model-model interaction in tangram naming task. *Proceedings of the AAAI Symposium Series*, 2(1):349–355.

Mikio Nakano. 2019. Grounding process in dialogue systems. In *Proceedings of the 86th Special Interest Group on Spoken Language Understanding and Dialogue Processing*, pages 1–4. Japanese Society for Artificial Intelligence.

Mikio Nakano, Kazunori Komatani, and Kotaro Funakoshi. 2015. *Dialogue Systems*, volume 7 of *Natural Language Processing Series*. Corona Publishing. (In Japanese).

Dalmas A Taylor. 1968. The development of interpersonal relationships: Social penetration processes. *The Journal of Social Psychology*, 75(1):79–90.

Takuma Udagawa and Akiko Aizawa. 2019. A natural language corpus of common grounding under continuous and partially-observable context. In *Proceedings of the AAAI Conference on Artificial Intelligence*, volume 33, pages 7120–7127.

Design, Generation and Evaluation of a Synthetic Dialogue Dataset for Contextually Aware Chatbots in Art Museums

Inass Rachidi and Anas Ezzakri and Jaime Bellver Soler and Luis Fernando D'Haro
Speech Technology and Machine Learning Group (THAU) - ETSI de Telecomunicación
Av. Complutense 30, 28040, Madrid, Spain - Universidad Politécnica de Madrid
{inass.rachidi, anas.ezzakri}@alumnos.upm.es
{jaime.bellver, luisfernando.dharo}@upm.es
Corresponding author: luisfernando.dharo@upm.es

Abstract

This paper describes the design, synthetic generation and automatic evaluation of ArtGenEval-GPT++, an enhanced dataset designed for training and fine-tuning conversational agents with artificial awareness capabilities targeting the art domain. The dataset build upon the previously released ArtGenEval-GPT, but extended by us to allow more personalization characteristics (including for instance, gender, ethnicity, age, knowledge) and addressing limitations such as low-quality dialogues, and hallucination.

The dataset is generated using state-of-the-art large language models (LLMs), and consists of approximately 12,500 dyadic multi-turn dialogues across diverse museum scenarios, including varied visitor profiles, emotional states, interruptions, and chatbot behaviors. Comprehensive evaluations using objective metrics demonstrate its quality and contextual coherence. Additionally, we explore some ethical implications and limitations of the dataset, such as biases and hallucinations, and outline future directions for enhancing their utility.

These contributions advance the development of personalized, context-aware conversational agents capable of adapting to complex real-world settings, such as museums, while increasing visitor engagement and satisfaction.

1 Introduction

Recent progresses in conversational AI have been achieved thanks to Large Language Models (LLMs), which excel in generating high-quality responses following carefully designed prompt instructions (Sahoo et al., 2024). Then, these same LLMs can be improved further by fine-tuning them on diverse human and synthetic instruction-based datasets and enriched with techniques like reinforcement learning from human feedback (RLHF), showcasing remarkable in-context learning capabilities (OLMo et al., 2024; Abdin et al., 2024; Hurst et al., 2024). This has led to breakthroughs in natural language understanding, dialogue coherence, and adaptability across various domains.

Despite these advancements, there remain significant challenges in creating conversational agents that are not only knowledgeable but also socially competent and context-aware. Specifically, we are interested in the incorporation of artificial consciousness features, situational awareness, or user profiling into conversational systems which are relevant characteristics for improving user experience. Addressing these gaps can enhance user engagement, improve adaptability to dynamic interactions, and enable the development of more intuitive and meaningful dialogues (Della Santina et al., 2024; Graziano, 2022).

In this paper we focus on generating and enhancing the quality and scope of datasets for training such systems. Building on prior work, particularly the ArtGenEval-GPT dataset released by (Gil-Martín et al., 2024)[1] and the methodology described in (Luna-Jiménez et al., 2024), we introduce ArtGenEval-GPT++. This new dataset is specifically designed for training conversational agents in a museum context, where the chatbot acts as a tour guide, tutor, or art expert that adapts to the knowledge level of the visitor, age, ethnicity and even physical appeareance of the visitor. The dataset also includes external situations or interruptions that could happen in a museum. The updated version also includes improved emotional balance, refined and less hallucination dialogue scenarios, and enhanced personalization features such as chatbot tone, multiple visitors and response strategies.

Key contributions of this work include:

- **Dataset Enhancement**: Refining and expanding the dataset to include diverse visitor in-

[1]The dataset is available at (D'Haro Enríquez et al., 2024) and https://huggingface.co/datasets/Astound/ArtGenEvalGPT

Proceedings of the 15th International Workshop on Spoken Dialogue Systems Technology, pages 20–28
May 27–30, 2025. ©2025 Association for Computational Linguistics

teractions, emotional states (i.e., the emotion that the user may have while visiting the museum or aroused when looking into a specific artwork), and contextual situations (e.g., charactersitics of the people visiting the museum, unpredicted events that could hypothetically happen while being in the museum, or elements in the paintings that could be used to connect with the visitors).

- **Synthetic Dialogue Generation**: Leveraging the GPT-4-o turbo model to produce 12,500 high-quality dialogues with features tailored to mimic real-world museum interactions.
- **Evaluation Framework**: Implementing automated evaluation metrics, including BLEU, WER, and precision to assess dialogue quality and adherence to prompts.
- **Ethical Considerations**: Addressing challenges such as hallucinations, biases, and limitations in handling sensitive topics .

By focusing on these enhancements, this work contributes to advancing the state-of-the-art in conversational agents, paving the way for more adaptive and socially aware AI systems.). The paper is structured as follows: Section 2 review the seed datasets used in this work. Section 3 details the methodology for dataset design, dialogue generation and automatic evaluation. Section 4 presents the results and examples of the generated dialogues. Finally, Section 5 discusses conclusions and future work.

2 Datasets

2.1 ArtEmis Dataset

The ArtEmis dataset (Achlioptas et al., 2021; Mohamed et al., 2022) is a large-scale resource designed to explore the relationship between visual art, emotions, and natural language explanations. It comprises 455,000 emotional annotations and explanations associated with around 80,000 artworks sourced from the WikiArt website[2]. The dataset contain artworks that span 1,100 artists, 27 distinct art styles (e.g., Baroque, Cubism, Impressionism), and 45 genres (e.g., landscape, portrait, still life). Each artwork includes annotations from at least five human annotators who assigned one of eight predefined emotions or "something-else" as the emotional label, along with textual explanations of their choices.

[2]https://www.wikiart.org/

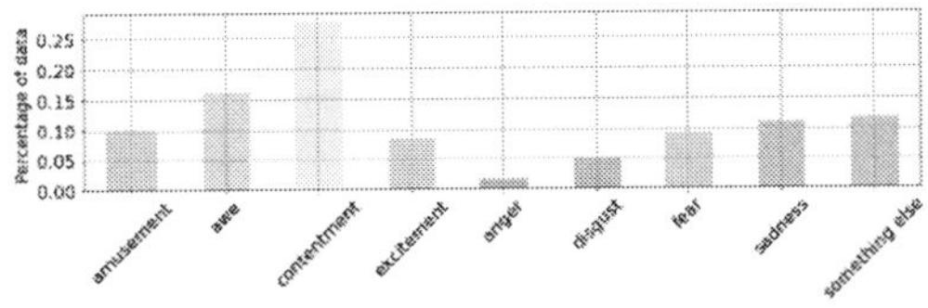

Figure 1: Distribution of Emotions in the ArtEmis Dataset

The dataset's strength lies in its rich emotional and linguistic annotations, which enable a nuanced understanding of the affective and contextual aspects of visual art. However, ArtEmis has limitations in its suitability for training conversational agents, including: Lack of dialogue-specific structures, and limited representation of interactive scenarios or dynamic visitor profiles. Figure 1 shows the distribution of emotions in the original version of the dataset (Achlioptas et al., 2021).

2.2 ArtGenEval-GPT Dataset

According to the authors of ArtGenEval-GPT (Gil-Martín et al., 2024), this dataset was developed as an initial attempt to adapt the principles of ArtEmis for training conversational agents in museum contexts. It introduced a novel synthetic dialogue dataset generated using GPT models, simulating interactions between a human visitor and a chatbot using a flexible platform(Luna-Jiménez et al., 2024). Key features included:

- Dialogue Context: Centered on 800 artworks from ArtEmis.
- Visitor Profiles: Incorporated different age (kid and adult) and knowledge levels (novice, intermedium and expert).
- Chatbot Roles: Simulated chatbots acting as a tour guide, art tutor, or expert.

Despite these innovations, ArtGenEval-GPT faced notable limitations:

- Low Dialogue Quality: Many dialogues exhibited poor coherence due to limitations of the GPT-3.5 model used for generation.
- Hallucinations: Instances of fabricated information about artworks, reducing reliability.

Description	Amount
Total number of generated synthetic dialogues	13,870
Total number of different artworks	799
Total number of different artists	378
Total number of different art styles	26
Distribution of dialogues per emotion	
Emotion	Amount (%)
Amusement	997 (7.2%)
Anger	745 (5.4%)
Awe	943 (6.8%)
Contentment	936 (6.7%)
Disgust	890 (6.4%)
Excitement	885 (6.4%)
Fear	958 (6.9%)
Neutral	6,378 (46.0%)
Sadness	948 (6.8%)
Something else	190 (1.4%)

Figure 2: Key Statistics of ArtGenEval-GPT

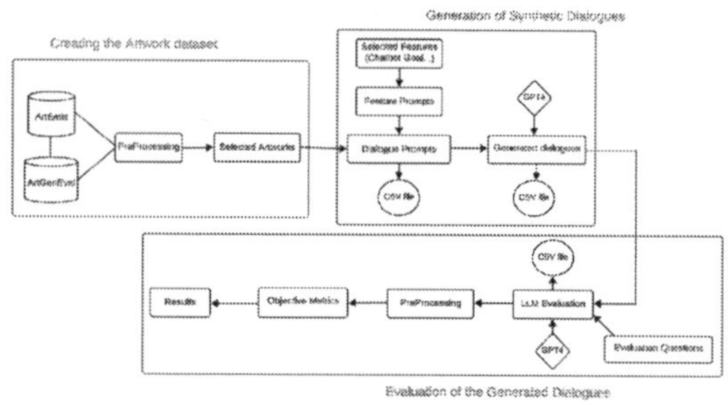

Figure 3: Flow diagram of the methodology used for creating the ArtGenEval-GPT++ dataset

2.3 Limitations and Motivation for Improvements

The challenges observed in ArtGenEval-GPT conducted us to propose the creation of the new ArtGenEval-GPT++. Among the main improvements are:

- Enhancing dialogue coherence by using GPT-4 for generation.
- Perform a better processing of the selected artworks to reduce hallucinations
- Introducing diverse chatbot tones, interruption scenarios, and visitor profiles to simulate real-world museum interactions.

3 Methodology

After inspecting the ArtGenEval-GPT dataset and using it for training our own chatbot, we found the need to improve the diversity of the dataset, and at the same time replace low-quality dialogues (primarily due to limitations of ChatGPT-3.5) and incorporate additional mechanisms to mitigate hallucinations by performing additional preprocessing to the artworks selected for generating the new synthetic dialogues. In addition, with the goal of increasing the capabilities of the chatbot to showcase awareness and extended social competences, we incorporated new ideas and situations.

This section describes the design process. In first place, the new version uses the more powerful GPT-4 model (specifically, GPT4o-mini vs 2024-07-18) and introduce refined preprocessing to improve information accuracy and dialogue consistency. These updates provide new dialogue scenarios with nearly 12,500 new dialogue interactions. 3 summarizes the methodology consisting on three phases: Pre-processing, generation, and evaluation. Note: The indicated CSV files are used to record the output of the different methodology steps for logging purposes.

3.1 pre-processing

The pre-processing step consists of the following steps:

1. **Normalization of artwork information**: In this case, we use Spacy and GPT model to check and normalize that artwork titles and artists were correctly cased and spelled, and remove year of creation from titles.
2. **Filter low quality artworks**: By removing artworks with unknown artists or titles, or artworks whose content is too generic (e.g., landscape, still life, vase).
3. **Keeping high quality emotional artworks**: By removing artworks where the emotion triggered in the annotators was labeled with "something else" or having low inter-annotator agreement.
4. **Verification of artwork knowledge grounding**: In this case, we tasked ChatGPT to return the name of the artist based only on the artwork title (the goal was to detect the uniqueness of the artwork but also to check if the model has knowledge about that artwork). In case, the answer was wrong, we perform a second step by providing also additional information such as year of creation and movement. In case of a correct answer, the artwork is included, if not then it is completely discarded.
5. **Incorporation of additional artworks**: Finally, after removing low quality artworks, but

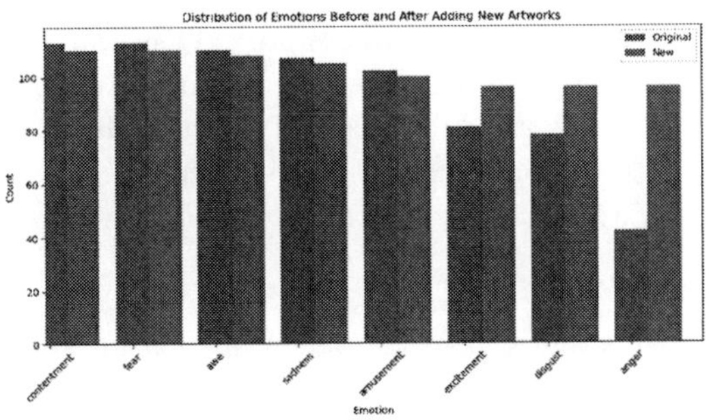

Figure 4: Comparison in the distribution of triggered emotions between the previous and new ArtGenEval-GPT++ dataset.

with the goal of keeping balanced the distribution of triggered emotions, we complemented the list with artworks coming from ArtEmis but also proposed by ChatGPT after repeating the pre-processing steps and performing manual inspection.

Figure 4 shows that after performing the pre-processing steps, the distribution of emotions in the new set of 821 artworks is more balanced that in the previous version, while also improving its quality.

3.2 Generation

The dialogue generation framework customizes interactions by selecting key features such as painting-specific details (title, author, emotion evoked by visitors, date of creation, art style) and dynamic elements like chatbot roles (tutor, tour guide, expert), chatbot behaviour (anthropic or non-anthropic), tone (humorous and playful or professional and formal), and visitor attributes, including gender (male or female), knowledge level (novice, intermediate, expert), age (kid, teenager, adult), emotion (sadness, excitement, etc.), physical/attribute conditions on the visitors (wearing rings, using crutches, using glasses or hat, balding), and ethnicity (African, Asian, Arab, Caucasian, Indian, Latino). It incorporates realistic interruptions and engagement suggestions (e.g., recommending souvenirs, tour options, similar artworks, fire alarms) while supporting group conversations and quick summaries for visitors in a hurry. These features ensure personalized, immersive, and dynamic interactions, addressing diverse visitor needs and enhancing the museum experience.

The dialogue generation process begins by defining the features that vary across dialogues, focusing on visitor preferences, chatbot characteristics, and environmental scenarios. The following steps outline the methodology:

1. **Loading the Dataset:** Artworks are loaded from the filtered and corrected ArtGenEval-GPT v1.0 dataset.

2. **Random Selection of Artworks:** Filtered artworks are randomly selected to ensure diverse dialogues but preserving emotion distribution.

3. **Determining Dialogue Characteristics:** Combinations of chatbot goals, visitor profiles, and engagement suggestions are randomly selected to simulate different museum scenarios. Certain probabilities and rules are implemented to avoid combinations that rarely will happen in real life (e.g., a kid that is expert in art, a group of all people using crutches), while also allowing enough variety of situations and repetitions for the chatbot to learn how to proceed in diverse situations.

4. **Interruption and Engagement:** Random interruptions and engagement suggestions are introduced for realism, with distribution weights applied to scenarios.

5. **Constructing the Prompt:** Selected features are combined into structured prompts, each with a unique dialogue ID, the prompt used, and all feature details.

The prompts are input into GPT-4 to generate unique dialogues tailored to the setup. Responses are saved with token usage and error logs. This approach enables the creation of thousands of dialogues (e.g., 5000 created in a first batch and 7500 in a second batch) with detailed distributions for each feature, ensuring variety and personalization.

3.3 Evaluation

Considering that we generated a total of 12.5k dialogues, we opted for performing an automatic evaluation using GPT-4. This section describes the methodology in terms of prompt design and objective metrics. Considering that we are prompting the GPT-4 model to generate synthetic dialogues that incorporate factual information (e.g., specific information about each artwork), behaviours and characteristics for visitor and chatbot (e.g., tone, demographics, knowledge), as well as length of the dialogues, emotions, situations or even connections between the artwork and visitor's characteristics, we opted for creating specific prompts that could automatically extract that information from the dialogues and then evaluate the quality of the responses. Here, we distinguish between:

- **Exact match attributes** in which exact extration is expected (e.g., for titles, artist name or movement) in which we use Word Error Rate (WER), BLEU (Papineni et al., 2002) or ROUGE (Lin, 2004),

- **Relaxed match attributes** in which information is extracted and compared in terms of Word Error Rate (WER), then a threshold is applied to consider it as valid or not (this allows variabilities when extracting artist names, titles or movements, e.g., Mona Lisa vs Gioconda, or Renaissance vs Renascence), and

- **Behavioral attributes** in which we provide in the evaluation prompt the list of available options plus the N/A option. Then, we check if the retrieved answer is the same as the expected one according to the instructions passed during the generation (e.g., Based on the provided dialogue, determine the visitor gender. **Options:** MALE, FEMALE, N/A.). In this case, the used metric is precision.

The scripts were designed with a systematic approach to ensure consistency and accuracy in processing the retrieved answers. Specifically, we implemented scripts that normalized the obtained responses. This normalization accounted for variations in the answers, as the GPT-4 models did not always provide responses in the expected format, casing, or wording. The scripts also calculated the requested metrics, streamlining the evaluation process.

The implementation process consisted of the following steps:

- **Collaborative Approach:** We begin by preparing a text file that contains questions designed to extract specific information from the dialogues.

- **Focused Inquiry:** Each question is meticulously crafted to pinpoint key details such as the name of the painting and the artist.

- **Direct Communication:** Questions are framed to solicit responses that are concise, direct, and formatted as a numbered list. This format ensures that each answer stands alone, free from unnecessary repetition or additional commentary.

we could categorize our evaluation questions into two main types:

1. **Yes/No Questions:** These questions are designed to elicit direct responses of 'yes' or 'no' from the dialogues. They focus on factual details or specific behaviors exhibited by the chatbot.

2. **Categorical Questions:** These questions prompt responses that fall into predefined categories, such as selecting an emotion or identifying a characteristic attribute. Responses are expected to match one of the provided options accurately. This categorization helps us systematically evaluate how well the generated dialogues adhere to the specified criteria and accurately convey the required information. Additionally, some questions were included specifically to understand the chatbot's decision-making process. In cases where the chatbot does not respond well to the categorical questions, the yes/no questions assist in comprehending how it arrived at its decisions.

4 Results

4.1 Generation

To write our generation prompts, we ensured a clear and distinct structuring by separating factual information about the artwork, the system's role from the visitor's profile, characteristics of groups and general instructions to generate the dialogues (e.g., length, interruptions, connections between artworks and visitors). This organization allows the chatbot to engage effectively with visitors in a museum setting, providing personalized and educational interactions about the artworks. Once the structured prompt dataset was processed and passed to OpenAI GPT-4, it generated the complete dialogue, as partially illustrated in Table 1. The example shows a certain level of emotion (Anger) and lack of time from the user, as well as an attempt of connection considering the age of the user (in this case a kid).

Table 1: Example Dialogue

Visitor: I'm really angry today! Why does this painting look so weird? I have to hurry! **Chatbot:** Very quickly, this painting, "The Robbery" by Esaias Van De Velde, shows a dramatic scene. The colors are dark, reflecting the anger and chaos of the moment. **Visitor:** But what's with all the people? They look like they're fighting or something! **Chatbot:** Yes! The key highlight is the action of the figures. Their movements might remind you of a toy battle, full of energy and tension. **Visitor:** I really don't have time for this! I gotta go! **Chatbot:** Understood! Just remember, the anger in the painting connects to your feelings today. Have a great day!

4.2 Evaluation

Considering that we have generated a total of approximately 12.5k dialogues, we opted for an automatic evaluation using GPT-4. This section describes the results obtained by applying objective metrics, comparing the actual values of features with the predicted ones.

4.2.1 Categorical Features

For categorical features, we used accuracy as the evaluation metric. Initially, the chatbot behavior emerged as the worst-performing attribute (see Figure 5), which was somewhat expected given that OpenAI is continously refining the development of sentimentally aware chatbots (i.e., avoiding the chatbot to look like a person).

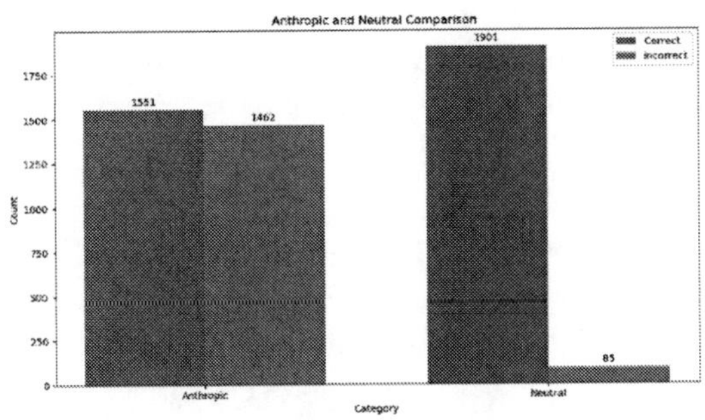

Figure 5: Anthropic and Neutral Comparison.

In some cases, dialogues generated under the Anthropic feature were qualitatively good, but the evaluation metrics failed to capture this accurately due to the subjective nature of attributes like displaying emotions, which are difficult to detect unless explicit emotional cues are present in the dialogue. A summary of our latest results can be seen in Table 2.

Upon closer analysis of the lowest accuracy rates, the most challenging attributes were the visitor's

Table 2: Accuracy of Categorical Attribute Prediction

Attribute	Accuracy
Artist's name	94.7%
Artwork movement	73.3%
Artwork title	86.0%
Artwork year	79.3%
Chatbot role	78.8%
Chatbot tone	81.1%
visitor's knowledge	80.8%
visitor's emotion	86.2%
visitor in a hurry	77.0%
visitor's ethnicity	61.1%
Interruptions type	58.3%

ethnicity and types of interruption.

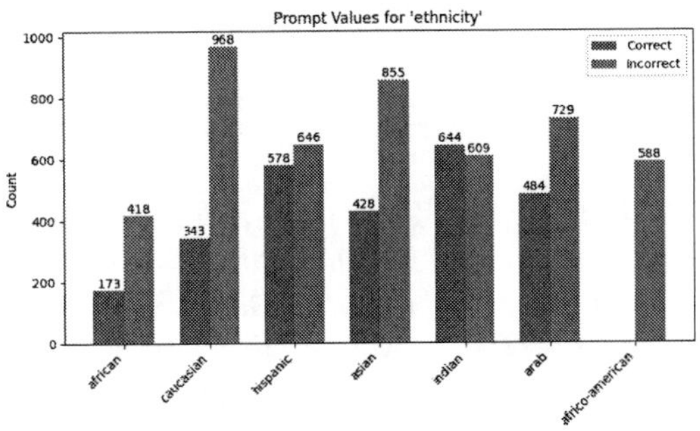

Figure 6: Distribution of the ethnicity detection.

As shown in Figure 6, the most difficult ethnicities to identify were Caucasian and Afro-American. This may be due to strong alingments from GPT models during the generation and for detecting it at evaluation. For interruptions (Figure 7), the most challenging scenarios included detecting that a visitor was not listening to the chatbot (information often omitted in the dialogues) and cases where the visitor was supposed to steal or damage an artwork. Manual inspection revealed that such actions were often attributed to other visitors in the dialogues instead of the intended visitor. When evaluating

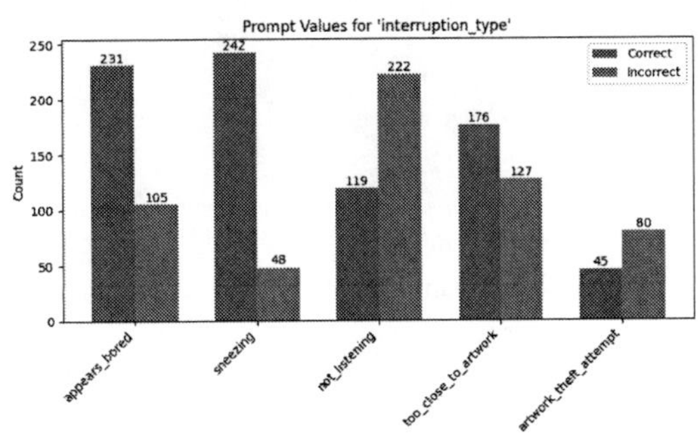

Figure 7: Distribution of classifications for the interruption type.

whether the visitor's gender (male or female) was detected, the accuracies were very low, likely because GPT-4 models are aligned to avoid biases in handling gender information, therefore that information was ommited in most of the dialogues.

4.2.2 Text Attributes

In evaluating text attributes such as painting title, painter name, and movement, we utilized metrics including Word Error Rate (WER), BLEU, and ROUGE to assess the chatbot's accuracy and proficiency. Table 8 organizes results by metric (WER,

Attribute VS Metric	WER ↓	BLEU ↑	ROUGE-1 ↑	ROUGE-L ↑
Painting Movement	0.1112 ± 0.3719	0.6880 ± 0.3884	0.8969 ± 0.2975	0.9032 ± 0.2054
Painting Title	0.0779 ± 0.2523	0.7000 ± 0.3551	0.9324 ± 0.2250	0.9404 ± 0.2189
Painter Name	0.0483 ± 0.2025	0.3086 ± 0.2258	0.9524 ± 0.2003	0.9553 ± 0.1958

Figure 8: Evaluation metrics for textual attributes.

BLEU, ROUGE-1, ROUGE-L) and attribute, highlighting generally strong performance, particularly for painter names. However, the BLEU score of 0.3086 ± 0.2258 was comparatively lower, reflecting the metric's limitations in capturing nuanced similarities in short text segments like names.

To evaluate accuracy, we adopted a WER threshold of 0.2: predictions with WER below this threshold were classified as correct, balancing precision and leniency. This threshold ensured rigorous and practical assessment across all attributes.

Figure 9 illustrates an example of the results obtained for the precision of the painting movement (e.g., Renaissance, Cubism, Baroque, Impressionism) predictions.

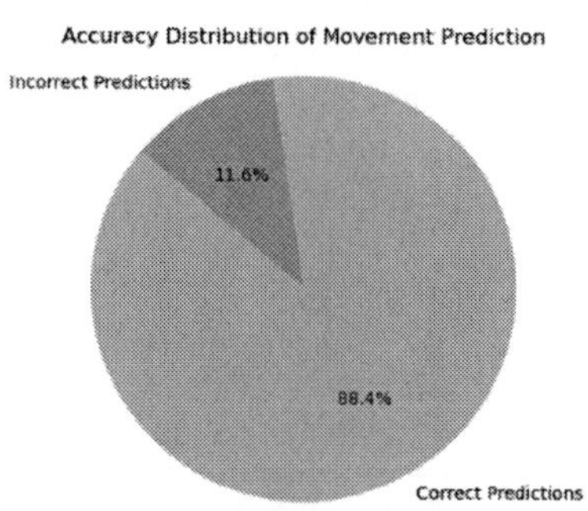

Figure 9: Painting Movement Accuracy.

4.2.3 Single visitor and groups

In the latest version, we included both one-to-one dialogues and group conversations involving the chatbot and two to four visitors. Each visitor had individual characteristics (e.g., gender, age, knowledge) and shared attributes (e.g., ethnicity, emotions). In group dialogues, one or two visitors actively participated to maintain dialogue quality, as having all visitors intervene made it harder to generate coherent exchanges and complicated automatic evaluation.

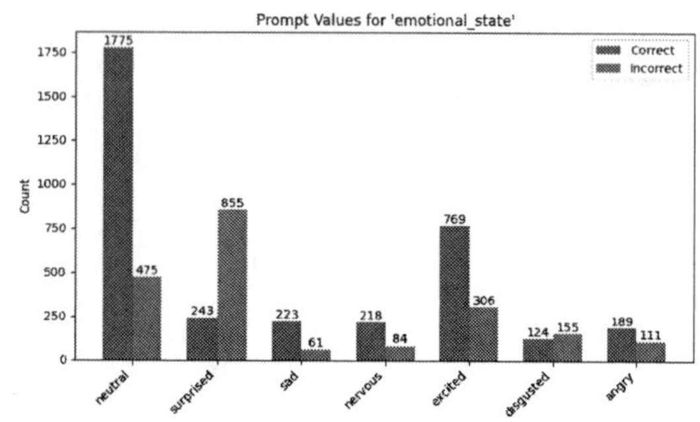

Figure 10: Results on detecting the emotional state of a visitor expressed in the generated dialogues.

Figures 10 and 11 compare emotion detection in one-to-one versus group dialogues, showing it is easier in single-visitor interactions due to GPT-4's difficulty in handling complex prompts and maintaining coherence across multiple visitors. Additional prompt adjustments may improve evaluation of group-based dialogues.

However, it is important to note that, despite the results, correct predictions do not guarantee that all dialogues are free from hallucinations or other artifacts, as these issues cannot be fully detected by the selected methodology.

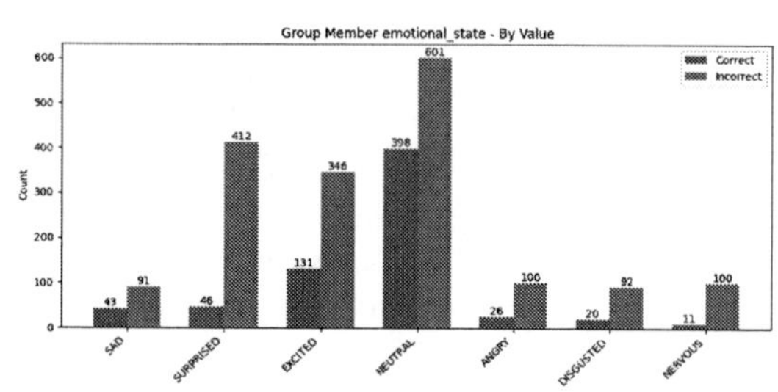

Figure 11: Results on detecting the emotional state of each visitor when considering groups of visitors in the generated dialogues.

5 Conclusions and Future Works

This paper presents a comprehensive approach to designing, generating, and automatically evaluating synthetic dialogue datasets tailored for training aware and socially improved chatbot applications in art museums. Through the refinement of the previous ArtGenEval-GPT dataset, the new version provides a better and extended dataset comprising dialogues over 821 artworks from 384 artists across 26 art styles, ensuring familiarity with GPT models (less hallucinations). By expanding dialogue scenarios to include diverse visitor attributes (including groups, ethnicity, age, physical appearance) and interaction contexts, the new dataset that can be used for training chatbots to engage effectively with varied museum audiences.

Approximately 12,500 dialogues were generated using the latest GPT-4-turbo model, simulating realistic visitor interactions and demonstrating the chatbot's capacity for meaningful engagement. To automatically assess the quality of the generated dialogues, an automated framework was included that relies on objective metrics such as WER, BLEU, and accuracy using LLM-as-Judge, achieving high-quality scores (85.5%). Notable challenges in sentiment prediction and ethnicity detection indicate areas for further improvement, highlighting the complexity of emotional and contextual nuances in dialogue systems. Thus, the dataset provides a valuable resource to advance conversational AI in cultural heritage settings.

Future work will focus on several key areas to enhance unconscious and conscious capabilities. First, expanding the dataset by incorporating a larger number of artworks (including well-known and more emotionally compelling paintings), multiple languages (beyond English, e.g., Spanish, French, German, Italian, Portuguese, Japanese or Chinese), and including the actual image data during the generation to reduce hallucinations and improve contextual understanding. Methodological improvements are also needed by evaluating the tutor scenarios, where the simulated visitors make mistakes in 30% of interactions. This is critical to measuring the efficacy of the chatbot in classroom-like settings for children and teenagers. We are also considering performing human subjective evaluations for evaluating the quality of the dataset and a fine-tuned version of the chatbot. Lastly, based on the Attention Schema Theory (Graziano, 2022), we would like to explore extended reasoning capabilities to model the mind of the visitors, as well as enhancing explainability through tailored prompts. These directions promise to advance the personalization, contextualization, and consciousness of chatbots in our case for cultural heritage contexts.

Acknowledgments

This work is supported by the European Commission through Project ASTOUND[3] (101071191 — HORIZON-EIC-2021-PATHFINDERCHALLENGES-01). In addition, it is supported by project BEWORD (PID2021-126061OB-C43) funded by MCIN/AEI/10.13039/501100011033 and, as appropriate, by "ERDF A way of making Europe", by the "European Union"; and by INNOVATRAD-CM (PHS-2024/PH-HUM-52) from Comunidad de Madrid.

References

Marah Abdin, Jyoti Aneja, Harkirat Behl, Sébastien Bubeck, Ronen Eldan, Suriya Gunasekar, Michael Harrison, Russell J Hewett, Mojan Javaheripi, Piero Kauffmann, et al. 2024. Phi-4 technical report. *arXiv preprint arXiv:2412.08905*.

Panos Achlioptas, Maks Ovsjanikov, Kilichbek Haydarov, Mohamed Elhoseiny, and Leonidas J Guibas. 2021. Artemis: Affective language for visual art. In *Proceedings of the IEEE/CVF Conference on Computer Vision and Pattern Recognition*, pages 11569–11579.

Cosimo Della Santina, Carlos Hernandez Corbato, Burak Sisman, Luis A Leiva, Ioannis Arapakis, Michalis Vakalellis, Jean Vanderdonckt, Luis Fernando D'Haro, Guido Manzi, Cristina Becchio, et al. 2024. Awareness in robotics: an early perspective from the viewpoint of the eic pathfinder challenge "awareness inside". In *European Robotics Forum*, pages 108–113. Springer.

Luis Fernando D'Haro Enríquez, Manuel Gil Martín, Cristina Luna Jiménez, Sergio Esteban Romero, Marcos Estecha Garitagoitia, Jaime Bellver Soler, and Fernando Fernández Martínez. 2024. ArtGenEvalGPT. *e-CienciaDatos*.

Manuel Gil-Martín, Cristina Luna-Jiménez, Sergio Esteban-Romero, Marcos Estecha-Garitagoitia, Fernando Fernández-Martínez, and Luis Fernando D'Haro. 2024. A dataset of synthetic art dialogues with chatgpt. *Scientific Data*, 11(1):825.

Michael SA Graziano. 2022. A conceptual framework for consciousness. *Proceedings of the National Academy of Sciences*, 119(18):e2116933119.

Aaron Hurst, Adam Lerer, Adam P Goucher, Adam Perelman, Aditya Ramesh, Aidan Clark, AJ Ostrow, Akila Welihinda, Alan Hayes, Alec Radford, et al. 2024. Gpt-4o system card. *arXiv preprint arXiv:2410.21276*.

[3]https://www.astound-project.eu/

Chin-Yew Lin. 2004. Rouge: A package for automatic evaluation of summaries. In *Text summarization branches out*, pages 74–81.

Cristina Luna-Jiménez, Manuel Gil-Martín, Luis Fernando D'Haro, Fernando Fernández-Martínez, and Rubén San-Segundo. 2024. Evaluating emotional and subjective responses in synthetic art-related dialogues: A multi-stage framework with large language models. *Expert Systems with Applications*, 255:124524.

Youssef Mohamed, Faizan Farooq Khan, Kilichbek Haydarov, and Mohamed Elhoseiny. 2022. It is okay to not be okay: Overcoming emotional bias in affective image captioning by contrastive data collection. In *Proceedings of the IEEE/CVF Conference on Computer Vision and Pattern Recognition*, pages 21263–21272.

Team OLMo, Pete Walsh, Luca Soldaini, Dirk Groeneveld, Kyle Lo, Shane Arora, Akshita Bhagia, Yuling Gu, Shengyi Huang, Matt Jordan, et al. 2024. 2 olmo 2 furious. *arXiv preprint arXiv:2501.00656*.

Kishore Papineni, Salim Roukos, Todd Ward, and Wei-Jing Zhu. 2002. Bleu: a method for automatic evaluation of machine translation. In *Proceedings of the 40th annual meeting of the Association for Computational Linguistics*, pages 311–318.

Pranab Sahoo, Ayush Kumar Singh, Sriparna Saha, Vinija Jain, Samrat Mondal, and Aman Chadha. 2024. A systematic survey of prompt engineering in large language models: Techniques and applications. *arXiv preprint arXiv:2402.07927*.

A Voice-Controlled Dialogue System for NPC Interaction using Large Language Models

Milan Wevelsiep, Nicholas Thomas Walker, Nicolas Wagner and Stefan Ultes
Natural Language Generation and Dialogue Systems
Otto-Friedrich-University of Bamberg Bamberg, Germany
nicholas.walker@uni-bamberg.de, stefan.ultes@uni-bamberg.de

Abstract

This paper explores the integration of voice-controlled dialogue systems in narrative-driven video games, addressing the limitations of existing approaches. We propose a hybrid interface that allows players to freely paraphrase predefined dialogue options, combining player expressiveness with narrative cohesion. The prototype was developed in Unity, and a large language model was used to map the transcribed voice input to existing dialogue options. The approach was evaluated in a user study (n=14) that compared the hybrid interface to traditional point-and-click methods. Results indicate that the proposed interface enhances the player's degree of joy and perceived freedom while maintaining narrative consistency. The findings provide insights into the design of scalable and engaging voice-controlled systems for interactive storytelling. Future research should focus on reducing latency and refining language model accuracy to further improve user experience and immersion.

1 Introduction

Voice interaction in video games remains a niche yet promising feature, especially as advances in technology offer new possibilities for immersion and interaction of the player. Traditional approaches to voice-controlled dialogues with Non-Playable Characters (NPCs) in games generally fall into two categories: reading out pre-written dialogue lines or free speech input in AI-generated dialogues. The former often limits player expression, while the latter can lack narrative consistency and control. This paper aims to present a novel approach that serves as a middle ground between these two approaches, combining the flexibility of player input with structured narrative cohesion.

The goal of this paper is to explore the implementation of a voice-controlled interface (VCI) that allows players to freely phrase their responses while still choosing from pre-defined dialogue options. By evaluating this hybrid approach, we aim to determine its impact on the player experience, particularly in the context of narrative-driven games. Specifically, we address the following research questions:

1. How does the use of a voice-controlled interface impact the immersion and user experience in a game with a narrative focus?
2. Does the player using this VCI have a sense of freedom given a restricted set of predefined dialogue options?
3. To which degree of accuracy can the player's spoken responses be reliably mapped to a given set of dialogue options?

The key contribution of this work lies in an approach to enable spoken interaction in a narrative-driven game that balances player freedom with narrative consistency. We present findings that highlight the potential of this approach in enhancing immersion and user satisfaction while maintaining cohesive storytelling.

The remainder of the paper is structured as follows: Section 2 presents and discusses other approaches that include voice control into games and discusses how our approach differs. Section 3 contains the core concept of the voice-controlled dialogue system with a description of its realization in Section 4. Sections 5, 6, and 7 present the user study design, the results and their discussion.

2 Related Work

Voice control as a narrative device in video games has gained significant attention for its potential to enhance player immersion (Allison et al., 2020). Natural voice interactions are generally well-received, as they enhance player flow and reduce identity dissonance (Carter et al., 2015). Players often mimic character voices (Allison et al.,

Proceedings of the 15th International Workshop on Spoken Dialogue Systems Technology, pages 29–38
May 27–30, 2025.

2019; Osking and Doucette, 2019), deepening immersion, though this can be challenging when there are differences in player and character attributes such as gender (Carter et al., 2015). Persistent issues with voice interfaces include unnatural interactions, difficulty recalling commands, slower response times compared to button inputs (Allison et al., 2019), and recognition failures (Zargham et al., 2022). This section reviews notable approaches specifically for voice-controlled dialogues with non-playable characters (NPCs).

One established approach is the use of read-out-loud interfaces, where players speak predefined dialogue lines to interact with NPCs (Osking and Doucette, 2019)(Cuebit, 2018). Here, players cannot freely phrase their voice input but are restricted to the phrasing of the dialogue option they are choosing. This method is reliable and can enhance immersion by encouraging players to embody their characters. For instance, *Flowers for Dan dan* (Osking and Doucette, 2019) used a read-out-loud interface where players verbally selected dialogue options by reading the text of the dialogue option, resulting in higher emotional engagement compared to traditional point-and-click controls. Similarly, the *Dragonborn Speaks Naturally* modification for *Skyrim* (Cuebit, 2018) adopted this approach to create more immersive player-NPC interactions without the need for complex AI systems. The main advantage of read-out-loud interfaces is their practical integration into existing games, as they rely on predefined dialogue options and require minimal changes to the game's dialogue system. However, the restrictive nature of reading out predefined dialogue lines may limit the player's sense of agency, reducing immersion over extended play sessions.

Dynamic dialogue generation represents another approach, where NPC responses are generated in real-time using AI techniques such as natural language processing (NLP) or large language models (LLMs). This approach provides players with greater freedom and more natural interactions by allowing them to speak freely rather than selecting from predefined options. For example, the game Façade (Mateas and Stern, 2003), later modified by Dow et al. (Dow et al., 2007), employed a "Wizard of Oz" technique to simulate natural speech input. Building on top of its underlying AI systems—natural language processing, autonomous character behaviour, and a drama manager—this approach fostered dynamic and immersive conversations. Fraser et al. (Fraser et al., 2018) extended this concept by incorporating sentiment analysis to adapt NPC responses based on player emotions, thereby enhancing engagement. Similarly, *Bot Colony* (Joseph, 2019) and *Vaudeville* (Bumblebee-Studios, 2023) utilized AI-driven dialogue systems to generate NPC responses. While the use of LLMs in dialogues with NPCs, such as those in *Vaudeville*, can create human-like dialogue that enhances player engagement, they also present challenges including hallucinations, inconsistencies, and difficulty maintaining narrative coherence. Fraser et al.'s (Fraser et al., 2018) sentiment-driven approach demonstrated improvements in emotional immersion; however, concerns regarding scalability in larger game environments and negative player reactions to AI-generated dialogue remain (Cox and Ooi, 2024; Akoury et al., 2023).

Building on these existing methods, this paper proposes a middle-ground solution that integrates the strengths of both approaches. By allowing players to use free-form speech while mapping their input to predefined dialogue options, our method seeks to maintain immersion and deliver a natural interactive experience without compromising narrative control. This hybrid approach offers a more scalable and robust solution for voice-controlled dialogues in narrative-driven games by addressing the challenges identified in earlier research.

3 Concept

The core of the proposed approach lies in a middle-ground solution for integrating voice interaction in narrative-focused video games. It combines predefined dialogue options with the player's ability to paraphrase freely. To achieve this, players are given predefined dialogue choices that contain very concisely worded versions of the core messages. However, instead of asking the players to read them out loud, they are encouraged to paraphrase these options in their own words. For example, an option like "Ask for more information" can be expressed as "Could you give me more details?". While in some cases the participants nonetheless opted to read the text as given or nearly so, others were more creative in their formulations. Hence, a pre-defined dialogue flow controls the overall dialogue while users can speak freely and naturally.

The overall architecture of modelling the dialogue and processing new user input is shown in Figure 1. New user input is first processed in the *Understanding* component that utilizes a large lan-

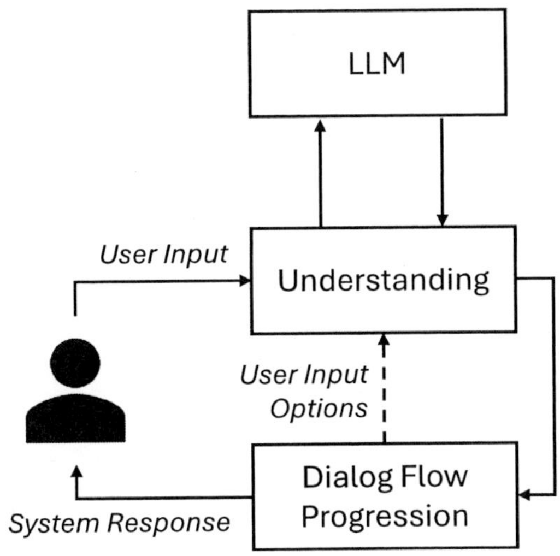

Figure 1: Overall dialogue architecture: an LLM is used to map new user input to one of the user input options defined by the dialogue flow.

guage model to map the user input to one of the possible dialogue options. These options are part of the pre-defined dialogue flow and represented in textual form. The large language model is then prompted to either map the user input to one of the dialogue options given the previous system response, or to map it to *misunderstood.*

Once the user input is mapped to one of the predefined dialogue options, the dialogue progresses to the next node of the pre-defined dialogue flow which defines the system output along with a new set of dialogue options as possible user inputs. The new set of dialogue options is subsequently used together with the following user input in the *Understanding* component.

Thus, this concept draws from read-out-loud interfaces (Osking and Doucette, 2019) and dynamic input methods (Fraser et al., 2018; Bumblebee-Studios, 2023) alike. It allows player freedom and the capability to maintain narrative control. Unlike fully generative NPC responses, which often lack coherence, this approach relies on a structured dialogue graph to ensure consistency while enabling natural voice interaction. Allowing players to phrase their responses freely is expected to enhance immersion and engagement compared to restrictive read-aloud interfaces.

4 Prototype Development

The proposed concept is realized in a prototype implementation of a narrative-driven game. The

Figure 2: A screenshot of the tutorial-section of the game. The two dialogue options, displayed in German language, translate to "How do the flowers look like?" and "Offer support".

prototype was built using Unity, chosen for its flexibility and extensive library of assets. Unity handled all game mechanics, visual elements, character interactions, and user interface components. Custom C# scripts managed core game interactions, such as dialogue flow, NPC responses, and player controls. The game environment and characters were created using free Unity Asset Store resources, providing a functional game world for voice interaction testing. A screenshot of the game is shown in Figure 2. In the tutorial shown in the figure, the player is instructed by an NPC to help search for flowers in the forest by selecting one of two options of how to respond.

Voice Interaction: Player speech input was captured in Unity and processed through the Whisper AI service for transcription. Given that the language model performed better with English input, the transcribed German text was translated into English via the Google Cloud Translation API before further processing.

Dialogue Management: A structured dialogue graph, implemented with Unity's internal tools and custom C# scripts, served as the backbone for dialogue flow. Each node in this graph represented a specific narrative point linked to predefined player options. Player input was mapped to these options using the Llama-2 13B language model, hosted on an Nvidia A100 GPU. The model received a prompt that included the transcribed and translated response, the current NPC dialogue, and available dialogue options. The model then returned the option number that best matched the player's intent. Prompt engineering was applied by using *langchain* to improve mapping accuracy and reduce latency. An excerpt of the system message is shown in Figure 3.

User Interface: Developed within Unity, the user interface displayed available dialogue options and

```
sys_msg = B_SYS + """The AI is an expert at correctly selecting an option.
The AI compares the options and the player's response.
The AI then selects the option that best matches the player's response.
The AI only returns the number of the correct option as output and does not generate more text.
Very rarely the AI returns 99 if it really cannot map the response to one option.

Here are some previous conversations between the AI and the player:

The other character answered with: "Hello, nice to meet you."
The options are:
0) "Misunderstood"
1) "Say hello"
2) "Say goodbye"
3) "Thanks"
The player answered with "See you later."
The player chose option:

AI: 2

The other character answered with: "Unfortunately, I'm not feeling well right now."
The options are:
1) "Ask about feelings"
2) "Ask about the location of the key"
The player answered with: "Please tell me where the key is."
The player chose option:

AI: 2
```

Figure 3: An excerpt of the system message used in the few-shot prompting. The system message includes an explanation of the task and examples on how to map player's responses to options.

provided immediate visual feedback. When players used voice input, the UI indicated ongoing processing and highlighted the chosen option after recognition, helping players understand the system's response to their spoken input.

Key Features: The prototype includes several key design elements to enhance player experience and immersion. The game adopts a first-person perspective, allowing players to interact directly with the environment and NPCs to create a more engaging experience. While in a dialogue, the player can choose the dialogue options hands-free, i.e., the player does not need to press a button to start or stop the voice input. After a brief period of silence detection, Unity processes the player's speech and matches it with the available dialogue options. The VCI also provides a mechanism for revising dialogue options. When the system misinterprets a player's input, phrases such as "I didn't mean that" trigger a "Misunderstood" option. In order to avoid mental overload by visualizing this additional option, the revise-option only becomes visible upon selection. The participants in the user study have been made aware of that option in an initial introduction. The prototype also includes a tutorial designed to help players familiarize themselves with the basic controls and mechanics.

Limitations: The game's world and characters are constructed from different resources from the Unity Asset Store. Therefore, the game environment appears visually inconsistent and the NPC's facial expressions and animations are limited. Both aspects lead to a presumably less immersive and believable experience. Response latency in the voice interface presents another issue, with delays sometimes interrupting the natural flow of conversation. Finally, while the automatic German-to-English translation system generally performs well, it occasionally misinterprets nuanced phrases, which can result in faulty mapping of player's speech input to the dialogue options.

5 User Study

The user study aimed to evaluate the proposed voice-controlled interface (VCI) by comparing it with a traditional point-and-click interface (PCI). The study combined usability testing, A/B testing, and surveys to assess the system's impact on user experience, perceived freedom, and system accuracy.

The study involved 14 participants, consisting of an equal number of male and female individuals,

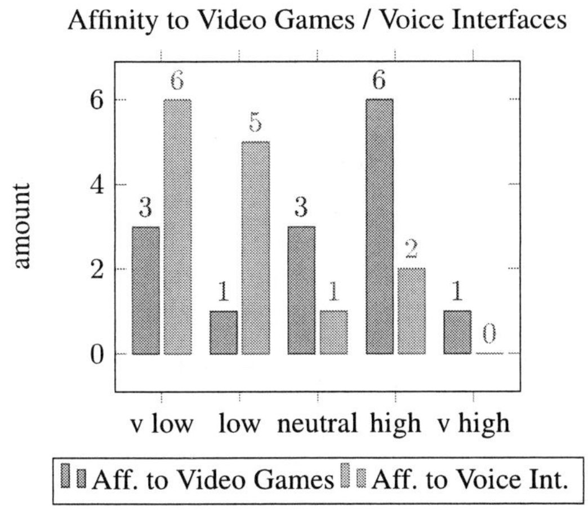

Figure 4: Self-reported affinity towards video games and voice interfaces by the participants.

aged between 23 and 36 years (mean age: 29, standard deviation: 4). Most participants (11) held university degrees, and all were native German speakers. Participants were personally recruited and included a mix of friends, acquaintances, and individuals with no close connection to the researchers. This group represented varied levels of familiarity with gaming and voice interfaces. While participants had moderately high experience with video games, their exposure to voice interfaces was comparatively limited (see Fig. 4). Participants alternated between the two interfaces to counterbalance order effects, with one group using the VCI first and the other starting with the PCI. The procedure included the following phases:

1. **Introduction and Orientation:** Participants were briefed on the study, signed consent forms, and received instructions on gameplay mechanics. A presentation highlighted the use of voice input, including the correction feature for misunderstood inputs.

2. **Tutorial Level:** Participants completed a short tutorial using the VCI to familiarize themselves with the system. Assistance was provided during this phase as needed.

3. **Main Game Playthrough:** Participants played the main game with one interface while the researcher minimized observer effects. The task of the game is to help the NPC Felix to find a missing key. During this task, the dialogue hints that Felix is bothered by something else, and the player has the option to inquire further about this issue or ignore it and focus on finding the key. Each session ended upon reaching one of the game's three possible outcomes. The three endings correspond to low, medium and high levels of empathy as determined by the level of empathy shown to Felix in the player's responses over the course of the dialogue.

4. **Post-Play Questionnaire:** Participants completed a questionnaire assessing the interface they had just used.

5. **Second Playthrough:** Participants replayed the main game with the alternative interface, followed by the same questionnaire.

6. **Final Questionnaire:** A comprehensive questionnaire captured additional metrics like accuracy, enjoyment, and overall preference.

The study was conducted on a laptop equipped with the Unity-based prototype. Voice input was captured using a Logitech webcam microphone, chosen for its accuracy over the laptop's built-in microphone. Participants completed questionnaires on the same laptop. Audio recordings documented verbal interactions, while logs captured system responses, dialogue choices, and observational notes.

Two primary data sources, questionnaires and play-through documentation, informed the study's findings.

Questionnaires: Participants responded to a series of structured questions using seven-point Likert scales. The questionnaires were adapted from existing instruments, namely the SASSI (Hone and Graham, 2000) for assessing the speech interface with regard to the usability aspects, and the GUESS (Vieira et al., 2019) for measuring video game satisfaction and user experience. The adapted questionnaire covered five scales:

- **System Response Accuracy:** Assessed how reliably player inputs were mapped to predefined options (Items I1–I2).

- **Likeability:** Measured user enjoyment and perceived freedom (Items I3–I4).

- **Cognitive Demand and Habitability:** Evaluated ease of use and confidence in issuing voice commands (Items I5–I6).

- **Annoyance and Speed:** Captured frustration and delays during gameplay (Item I7).

- **Immersion:** Examined how natural and engaging the interactions felt (Item I8).

- **Preference and Overall Assessment:** Assessed which interface players preferred (Item I9).

Playthrough Documentation: Logs recorded dialogue choices, LLM prompt-responses, and voice input accuracy. Audio recordings and observational notes provided qualitative insights into user behavior, naturalness of interactions, and system responsiveness.
The study faced several limitations that must be acknowledged. The small and relatively homogeneous sample, consisting of younger participants with higher education, is not representative of the broader gaming population. The limited duration of the study restricted participants' familiarity with the interfaces, potentially limiting the learning curve and long-term usability assessment. Some prototype limitations, such as latency, translation inaccuracies, and limited NPC animations, likely influenced user perceptions of the system. Factors like mood, time of day, and external distractions could also have impacted participant performance and feedback.

6 Results

The results of the user study are presented in this section, focusing on the impact of the voice-controlled interface (VCI) on immersion, user experience, perceived freedom, and accuracy of spoken inputs. A total of 14 participants completed the study, which involved gameplay with both the VCI and a traditional point-and-click interface (PCI), followed by corresponding questionnaires. An overview of the results for the VCI is shown in table 1.

The questionnaire responses were collected on a 7-point Likert scale ranging from "strongly disagree" (1) to "strongly agree" (7). For positively phrased statements, higher values indicate a more favorable response, while for negatively phrased statements, the scale was reversed to ensure consistency in interpretation, where higher values always reflect a positive attitude towards the VCI.

Impact on Immersion and User Experience (R1)

Research Question R1 evaluated the overall impact of the VCI on immersion and other aspects of

Table 1: Summary of the Results for the Voice-Controlled Interface

Item	Median	Mean
I1: Accuracy of Mapping	5.0	4.89
I2: Correction of Misunderstood Input	–	–
I3: Degree of Joy	5.0	4.93
I4: Expressing Freedom	4.0	3.93
I5: Ease of Use	4.0	4.07
I6: Confidence in Using the VCI	3.0	3.86
I7: Annoyance	4.5	4.38
I8: Immersion	3.0	3.68
Overall Assessment and Preference:		
Use in real games	5.5	5.43
Preference if improved	6.0	5.79

user experience. Items I3, I5, I6, I7, and I8 were analysed:

Degree of Joy (Item I3): Participants rated enjoyment of the VCI with a median of 5.0 and a mean of 4.93, suggesting a moderately positive experience. When compared directly with the PCI, the VCI scored higher (median 5.5, mean 5.43), indicating enhanced enjoyment through voice interaction.

Ease of Use (Item I5): Ease of use received mixed ratings, with a median of 4.0 and a mean of 4.07. Participants noted higher cognitive demand for the VCI due to the need for paraphrasing. In comparing both interfaces directly with each other, participants reported the VCI as more demanding (median 2.5, mean 3.07). In part, this can be due to higher familiarity with a traditional interface. However, the mental load for putting a paraphrased dialogue option into one's own words most likely further contributed to this.

Confidence in Using the VCI (Item I6): Confidence levels varied, with a median of 3.0 and a mean of 3.86. Participants expressed moderate confidence but reported uncertainty regarding whether their phrasing would be correctly recognized, suggesting a need for improvement.

Annoyance (Item I7): General annoyance was low (median 5.0, mean 5.21), but participants gave a more neutral rating of their attitude towards the VCI response time (median 3.5, mean 3.93). Reducing latency could significantly improve the overall experience.

Immersion (Item I8): The VCI provided slightly better immersion compared to the PCI (median 3.0, mean 3.57), but neither fully replicated natural dialogue. Improvements in natural language processing are needed to enhance immersion further.

Sense of Freedom (R2)

Research Question R2 examined participants' perceived freedom while using the VCI:

Expressing Freedom (Item I4): Participants felt moderately free to express themselves (median 5.0, mean 4.5). While compared to the PCI, the VCI allowed more authentic expression (median 5.0, mean 5.07), the limitations of predefined options occasionally hindered free expression (median 3.0, mean 3.36).

Degree of Accuracy (R3)

Research Question R3 focused on the accuracy of mapping spoken responses to dialogue options:

Accuracy of Mapping (Item I1): Mapping accuracy was rated positively (median 5.0, mean 4.89), with a system accuracy of approximately 90%. Participants often adhered closely to predefined phrasing, positively influencing accuracy.

Correction of Misunderstood Input (Item I2): The correction feature was rarely used due to infrequent mapping errors. However, its hidden nature led to participants often overlooking this functionality, suggesting a need for better visibility and usability.

Overall Assessment and Preference

Participants rated the VCI positively for potential use in real games (median 5.5, mean 5.43). While direct preferences between the VCI and PCI were mixed (median 4.0, mean 4.36), most participants indicated they would use the VCI if its accuracy and speed were improved (median 6.0, mean 5.86).

Additionally, no significant correlation was found between participants' familiarity with video games or voice interfaces and their perception of the VCI. This suggests that the VCI is accessible and engaging for a broad audience, regardless of prior experience, supporting its potential appeal in diverse gaming contexts.

7 Discussion

This section offers a comprehensive discussion of the user study results and final reflections on the voice-controlled interface (VCI) prototype, synthesizing the findings, implications, limitations, and directions for future research.

Table 2: Summary of participant responses to direct comparison questions between the voice-controlled interface (VCI) and the point-and-click interface (PCI). Higher values indicate a greater preference for the VCI.

Item	Median	Mean
I3: Joy (VCI vs. PCI)	5.5	5.43
I4: Expressing Freedom (VCI vs. PCI)	5.0	5.07
I5: Ease of Use (VCI vs. PCI)	2.5	3.07
I3: Boredom (VCI vs. PCI)	6.0	5.50
I8: Immersion (VCI vs. PCI)	4.0	4.36

Interpretation of Results

The user study findings show that the VCI prototype was generally well-received by participants, offering notable advantages in engagement and user experience compared to the conventional point-and-click interface (PCI). Participants expressed a preference for the VCI, indicating its potential to enhance player involvement and enjoyment, despite the presence of technical issues like response latency and speech recognition challenges.

Impact on Immersion and User Experience (R1): Participants found the VCI enjoyable, though delays in processing voice input caused frustration and moderate annoyance. Confidence in using the system was mixed, likely due to the unfamiliarity of combining predefined options with the freedom to paraphrase responses. Improvements in response time and system reliability are essential to enhance immersion and user comfort. Despite these flaws, the VCI had a slight advantage over the PCI in terms of immersion, highlighting its potential for narrative-driven games.

Sense of Freedom (R2): Participants appreciated the ability to paraphrase predefined options, which contributed to a sense of authenticity and self-expression. However, the restricted nature of predefined choices occasionally limited participants' sense of freedom. Future iterations of the VCI could improve flexibility, reducing perceived constraints and enhancing player empowerment.

Accuracy of Mapping (R3): Participants generally found the VCI predictable, though inconsistencies in speech recognition affected how reliably spoken input was mapped to dialogue options. The correction feature for misunderstood inputs was underutilized due to its hidden presentation. Despite these issues, the technical approach—using a language model (LLM) for mapping—shows promise, particularly with improved speech recognition and responsiveness.

Practical and Theoretical Implications

The positive reception of the VCI suggests that voice interaction, particularly in narrative contexts, is an engaging feature for video games. The hybrid approach of combining predefined dialogue options with paraphrasing offers a scalable solution for integrating voice control into games without compromising narrative coherence. Allowing players to "play as themselves" enhances player embodiment, especially in games where player agency is a core feature, such as role-playing games (RPGs).

Addressing technical limitations such as response time and speech recognition accuracy is essential for the commercial adoption of the VCI. Improvements in these areas would significantly enhance player experience, making the interface more reliable and enjoyable. Adding the flexibility to toggle the VCI on and off would give players greater control, catering to diverse preferences.

The study also contributes to understanding how voice interaction can be effectively integrated into video games. Unlike traditional top-down communication, the VCI allows for more natural interactions with non-playable characters (NPCs), fostering immersion by enabling players to project their identity onto the character. To achieve deeper immersion, improvements in system speed, accuracy, and NPC responsiveness are still required.

Limitations

The study faced several limitations that affect the generalizability of the findings. Methodologically, the short duration of the study restricted participants' ability to become familiar with the VCI, limiting insights into long-term usability. The controlled environment may not fully replicate real-world gaming conditions, influencing interactions and feedback. Additionally, the small sample size and participant homogeneity limit the applicability of the findings to a broader gaming audience.

An additional limitation of the study is the influence of the presented options on the players' thinking. The specific wording of the options may influence the way in which participants phrase their statements in the dialogue. Further work which analyzes differences in user input dependent upon how options are presented or if options are displayed at all would likely yield additional insights.

Similarly, specifics within the dialogue options may also be interpreted in specific or more general ways by participants. For instance, an "Ask for more information" dialogue option may be interpreted as pertaining to specific or general information. The specificity or generality of dialogue options may thus constitute an additional factor for participant experiences that would be of interest to subsequent research.

Technical limitations also played a significant role in shaping user experience. Latency issues and inconsistencies in speech recognition disrupted conversation flow and reduced immersion. The fixed time required for voice recognition, combined with delays in transcription and language model processing, significantly affected user satisfaction. Additionally, the lack of expressive character animations and authentic voice output further hindered immersion and the believability of NPC interactions.

A final limitation worth mentioning regarding immersion is that various aspects of language such as sarcasm, irony, or other nuanced aspects of how humans naturally communicate were out of scope for this study. The relative advantages of a voice-controlled interface over a point-and-click interface will likely be most strongly observable in a system that incorporates further subtleties of human expression.

Future Research

Future research should prioritize addressing the technical and methodological limitations identified in this study. Enhancing the speed and accuracy of voice recognition through real-time transcription and more advanced language models could significantly improve the VCI's performance. Incorporating dynamic dialogue generation could also provide more flexible and adaptive player-NPC interactions, addressing the constraints of predefined dialogue options.

Long-term studies are needed to understand the sustained effects of voice interaction on player engagement and immersion. Integrating the VCI into commercial games for extended periods would provide valuable insights into how players adapt to and perceive the system. Additionally, future research should explore the role of voice interaction in fostering emotional connections between players and NPCs, particularly through improved NPC animations, responsive dialogue, and enhanced player agency.

Dynamic Dialogue Generation within Dialogue Graphs: Dynamic dialogue generation is a promising direction for enhancing flexibility in voice interactions. The current prototype relies on predefined dialogue options, limiting adaptability. By integrating dynamic dialogue generation into dialogue graphs, NPC responses can be generated based on the player's phrasing and narrative context, improving natural interaction flow.

This hybrid approach, using language models to generate context-aware responses while maintaining the structure provided by dialogue graphs, could offer a more personalized experience. NPC responses could vary based on player phrasing, past interactions, and storyline context, making conversations more engaging and lifelike. However, challenges such as maintaining emotional authenticity, ensuring lip synchronization, and minimizing latency need to be addressed. Future research should explore lightweight language models capable of efficient operation within game environments.

8 Conclusion

This study contributes to the growing field of voice interaction in video games, particularly NPC interactions. The hybrid VCI approach—combining predefined dialogue options with the ability to paraphrase—has proven to be an engaging feature that enhances a player's sense of freedom and overall user experience. Allowing players to interact naturally, in their own words, creates a more personalized experience that can align well with narrative-driven games.

While the study's findings show the potential of voice-controlled interfaces, the technical and methodological challenges identified must be addressed for long-term success. Improvements in system speed, reliability and more advanced character design are critical for impacting the sense of immersion to a greater extent. With these enhancements, voice interaction could become an integral part of video game dialogue systems, providing a richer and more immersive player experience.

References

Nader Akoury, Qian Yang, and Mohit Iyyer. 2023. A Framework for Exploring Player Perceptions of LLM-Generated Dialogue in Commercial Video Games. In *Findings of the Association for Computational Linguistics: EMNLP 2023*, pages 2295–2311, Singapore. Association for Computational Linguistics.

Fraser Allison, Marcus Carter, and Martin Gibbs. 2020. Word Play: A History of Voice Interaction in Digital Games. *Games and Culture*, 15(2):91–113.

Fraser Allison, Joshua Newn, Wally Smith, Marcus Carter, and Martin Gibbs. 2019. Frame Analysis of Voice Interaction Gameplay. In *Proceedings of the 2019 CHI Conference on Human Factors in Computing Systems*, pages 1–14, Glasgow Scotland Uk. ACM.

Bumblebee-Studios. 2023. Vaudeville. `https://bumblebeestudios.itch.io/vaudeville`.

Marcus Carter, Fraser Allison, John Downs, and Martin Gibbs. 2015. Player Identity Dissonance and Voice Interaction in Games. In *Proceedings of the 2015 Annual Symposium on Computer-Human Interaction in Play*, pages 265–269, London United Kingdom. ACM.

Samuel Rhys Cox and Wei Tsang Ooi. 2024. Conversational Interactions with NPCs in LLM-Driven Gaming: Guidelines from a Content Analysis of Player Feedback. In Asbjørn Følstad, Theo Araujo, Symeon Papadopoulos, Effie L.-C. Law, Ewa Luger, Morten Goodwin, Sebastian Hobert, and Petter Bae Brandtzaeg, editors, *Chatbot Research and Design*, volume 14524, pages 167–184. Springer Nature Switzerland, Cham. Series Title: Lecture Notes in Computer Science.

Cuebit. 2018. Dragonborn Speaks Naturally. `https://www.nexusmods.com/skyrimspecialedition/mods/16514?tab=description`.

Steven Dow, Manish Mehta, Ellie Harmon, Blair MacIntyre, and Michael Mateas. 2007. Presence and engagement in an interactive drama. In *Proceedings of the SIGCHI Conference on Human Factors in Computing Systems*, pages 1475–1484, San Jose California USA. ACM.

Jamie Fraser, Ioannis Papaioannou, and Oliver Lemon. 2018. Spoken Conversational AI in Video Games: Emotional Dialogue Management Increases User Engagement. In *Proceedings of the 18th International Conference on Intelligent Virtual Agents*, pages 179–184, Sydney NSW Australia. ACM.

Kate S. Hone and Robert Graham. 2000. Towards a tool for the Subjective Assessment of Speech System Interfaces (SASSI). *Natural Language Engineering*, 6(3&4):287–303.

Eugene Joseph. 2019. From Virtual to Real: A Framework for Verbal Interaction with Robots. In *Proceedings of the Combined Workshop on Spatial Language Understanding*, pages 18–28, Minneapolis, Minnesota. Association for Computational Linguistics.

M. Mateas and A. Stern. 2003. Façade: An Experiment in Building a Fully-Realized Interactive Drama. In *Game Developer's Conference: Game Design Track*.

Hunter Osking and John A. Doucette. 2019. Enhancing Emotional Effectiveness of Virtual-Reality Experiences with Voice Control Interfaces. In Dennis Beck, Anasol Peña-Rios, Todd Ogle, Daphne Economou,

Markos Mentzelopoulos, Leonel Morgado, Christian Eckhardt, Johanna Pirker, Roxane Koitz-Hristov, Jonathon Richter, Christian Gütl, and Michael Gardner, editors, *Immersive Learning Research Network*, volume 1044, pages 199–209. Springer International Publishing, Cham. Series Title: Communications in Computer and Information Science.

Estela Aparecida Oliveira Vieira, Aleph Campos Da Silveira, and Ronei Ximenes Martins. 2019. Heuristic Evaluation on Usability of Educational Games: A Systematic Review. *Informatics in Education*, 18(2):427–442.

Nima Zargham, Johannes Pfau, Tobias Schnackenberg, and Rainer Malaka. 2022. "I Didn't Catch That, But I'll Try My Best": Anticipatory Error Handling in a Voice Controlled Game. In *CHI Conference on Human Factors in Computing Systems*, pages 1–13, New Orleans LA USA. ACM.

A Dialogue System for Semi-Structured Interviews by LLMs and its Evaluation on Persona Information Collection

Ryo Hasegawa[1], Yijie Hua[1], Takehito Utsuro[1], Ekai Hashimoto[2], Mikio Nakano[2*], Shun Shiramatsu[2]

[1]Graduate School of Science and Technology, University of Tsukuba
[2]Department of Computer Science, Nagoya Institute of Technology
{s2420791,s2420830}_@u.tsukuba.ac.jp, utsuro_@iit.tsukuba.ac.jp

Abstract

In this paper, we propose a dialogue control management framework using large language models for semi-structured interviews. Specifically, large language models are used to generate the interviewer's utterances and to make conditional branching decisions based on the understanding of the interviewee's responses. The framework enables flexible dialogue control in interview conversations by generating and updating slots and values according to interviewee answers. More importantly, we invented through LLMs' prompt tuning the framework of accumulating the list of slots generated along the course of incrementing the number of interviewees through the semi-structured interviews. Evaluation results showed that the proposed approach of accumulating the list of generated slots throughout the semi-structured interviews outperform the baseline without accumulating generated slots in terms of the number of persona attributes and values collected through the semi-structured interview.

1 Introduction

This paper proposes a dialogue control management framework using large language models (LLMs) (Brown et al., 2020), specifically targeting semi-structured interviews (Fielding, 2003a,b; Wengraf, 2001). Semi-structured interviews are characterized by the interviewer starting the dialogue with only an initial slot set prepared in advance and dynamically expanding the list of slots throughout the interview's dialogues with all interviewees. In this paper, career interviews (Hashimoto et al., 2025) are highlighted as a representative example of a semi-structured interview. In the proposed framework, LLMs are applied to generate the interviewer's utterances and to make conditional branching decisions based on the understanding of the interviewee's responses. This approach allows for flexible dialogue control by generating and updating slots in response to the interviewee's answers. Within this framework, LLMs function as the agent performing the role of the interviewer, responsible for generating utterances, generating new slots, and filling slots. Furthermore, unlike Hashimoto et al. (2025), the framework incorporates a mechanism for accumulating the list of slots generated over the course of incrementing the number of interviewees during semi-structured interviews. As the key components of the proposed method are to be described in Section 5.2 and in Figure 4, we invented the "persona attributes prediction" function, which contributes to prioritizing generating questions known to be relevant to collecting persona attributes and values[1]. The contributions of this paper are as follows:

1. With the developed framework using LLMs, we demonstrated that the challenging task of managing semi-structured interviews can be effectively realized.

2. As contributions that distinguish our work from Hashimoto et al. (2025), we highlight the following two points.

    (a) We demonstrate that the proposed framework enables a mechanism for progressively constructing the list of slots in semi-structured interviews involving multiple interviewees.

    (b) We show that the proposed approach of accumulating the list of generated slots throughout semi-structured interviews outperforms a baseline approach that does not accumulate generated slots,

*Also affiliated with C4A Research Institute, Inc., Tokyo, Japan.

[1]A more detailed explanation of the "persona attributes prediction" function is provided in the description of LLM5 in Section 5.2.

Proceedings of the 15th International Workshop on Spoken Dialogue Systems Technology, pages 39–59
May 27–30, 2025. ©2025 Association for Computational Linguistics

measured by the number of persona attributes and values collected through the semi-structured interviews.

2 Related Work

In recent years, numerous studies on interview dialogue systems have been reported (Zeng et al., 2023; DeVault et al., 2014; Johnston et al., 2013; Kobori et al., 2016; B et al., 2020; Nagasawa et al., 2024; Ge et al., 2023; Inoue et al., 2020), including an interview system designed for job interviews as a notable example (Su et al., 2019, 2018). Additionally, Inoue et al. (2020) developed a job interview dialogue system that employs an android robot. This system generates follow-up questions based on user response keywords and the degree of satisfaction, guided by four predefined topics. In a different line of work, Schatzmann and Young (2009) presented a framework for statistically modeling the response behavior of a user simulator, with the aim of optimizing dialogue policies.

Moreover, related to interview dialogue systems, there have been efforts to enhance the performance of dialogue systems by leveraging LLMs in slot filling dialogue systems (Hudeček and Dusek, 2023; Jacqmin et al., 2022; Siddique et al., 2021; Coope et al., 2020), utilizing GPT's advanced language comprehension capabilities (Sun et al., 2024; Feng et al., 2023; Heck et al., 2023). Wagner and Ultes (2024) discuss an approach that enhances controllability in dialog systems by integrating a rule or slot based dialog manager alongside LLMs. Furthermore, Komada et al. (2024) proposed a method for dynamically generating slots based on dialogue history to maintain scenario consistency in Tabletop Role-Playing Games (TRPGs). In TRPGs, the primary objective is to record scenarios, and deep exploration of information is not a priority. However, in semi-structured interviews, it is necessary to dynamically generate new slots as needed to obtain new information. Additionally, Hashimoto et al. (2025) developed a dialogue system aimed at supporting efficiency and quality improvements in career interviews conducted by nursing administrators. Building on the results of Hashimoto et al. (2025), this paper also focuses on career interviews conducted by nursing administrators, modeling semi-structured interviews that dynamically generate slots according to the interviewee's circumstances.

Research on semi-structured interviews has also been conducted (Parfenova, 2024; Hu et al., 2024). In contrast to these existing studies, this paper proposes a dialogue control framework using LLMs. The proposed method enables more efficient questioning in semi-structured interviews with multiple interviewees by accumulating information in the form of slots throughout the interview.

3 Semi-Structured Interview

Representative interview formats include structured interviews and semi-structured interviews. These formats differ significantly in whether the list of slots is finalized before the start of the interview. Figure 1 illustrates conceptual diagrams of these two interviews types. A semi-structured interview is characterized by the fact that, although basic questions are prepared in advance, the interviewer can flexibly change their order of the questions or add new questions according to the interviewee's responses (Figure 1, right). The interviewer progressively constructs the list of slots through dialogue with all interviewees. This format allows a higher degree of freedom in questioning and enables in-depth exploration tailored to each interviewee and situation. As a result, it can uncover the list of slots that might not emerge in a structured interview. However, the outcome can vary significantly depending on the interviewer's skill level, requiring more advanced interview techniques and experience.

4 Flowchart for Semi-Structured Interviews

In this paper, we use a flowchart-based approach to control the progress of dialogue in semi-structured interviews. Figure 2 shows the flowcharts designed for semi-structured interviews. Figure 3 illustrates the *internal module common to structured and semi-structured interviews*, which is used in both models.

4.1 Internal Module common to Structured and Semi-Structured Interviews

Before starting the dialogue to inquire about the interviewee's career, the interviewer engages in small talk to build rapport with the interviewee (Bickmore and Cassell, 1999). Once the interviewer determines that a career-related topic has emerged during small talk, they capture that information and

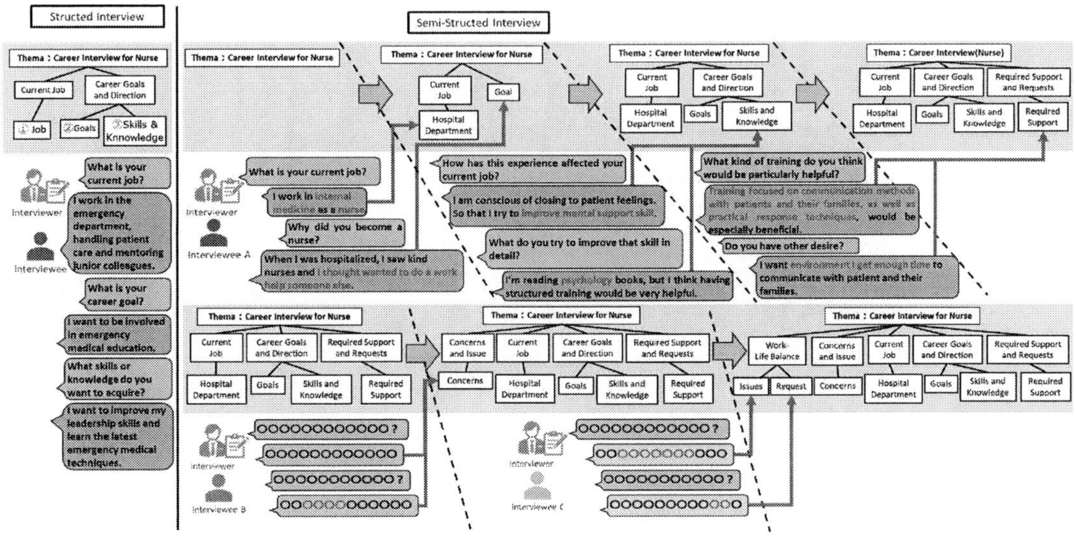

Figure 1: Diagram of Structured and Semi-Structured Interviews

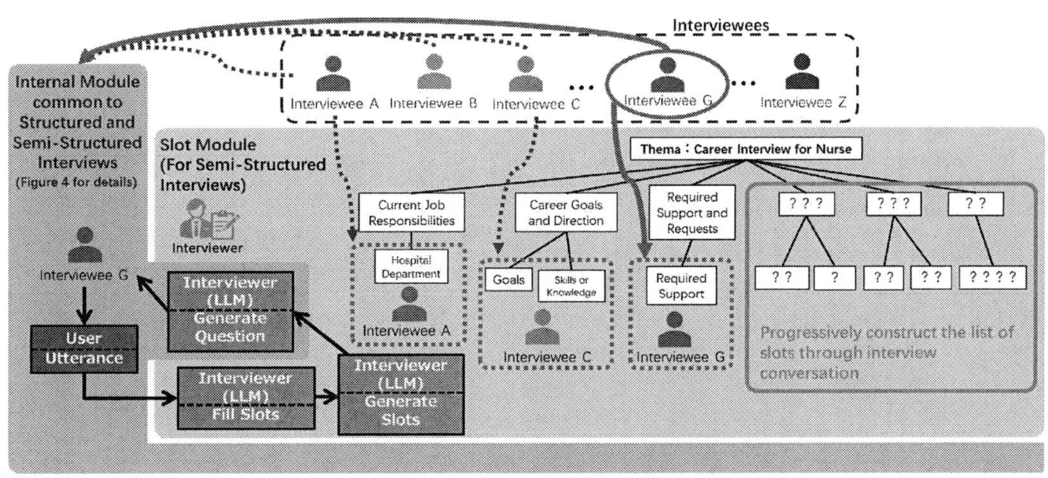

Figure 2: Flowchart of Semi-Structured Interviews

perform an initial slot filling step[2]. After this initial step, the following cycle is repeated:

1. Determine whether to end the dialogue.
2. If it is determined not to end the dialogue, the interviewer generates the next question[2] and asks the interviewee the question.
3. Once the interviewee responds to the question, the interviewer receives the utterance.
4. Fill in any empty slots (slot filling)[2].

[2]The detailed procedures for slot filling and question generation differ between structured and semi-structured interviews.

This cycle continues until a decision is made to end the interview. The *internal module common to structured and semi-structured interviews* for dialogue transitions, which is used in both Figure 6 and Figure 2, is shown in Figure 3.

4.2 Semi-Structured Interview

As shown in Figure 2, the overall flow in a semi-structured interview is almost the same as that of a structured interview. A key difference, however, is that after slot filling, the interviewer refers to the dialogue history and the list of slots generated up to that point to generate new empty slots. These newly generated slots are then added to the existing

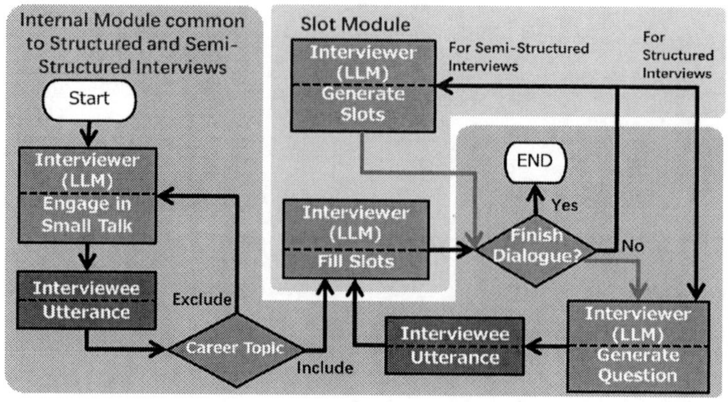

Figure 3: Internal Module Common to Structured (Figure 6) and Semi-Structured (Figure 2) Interviews

list of slots. Subsequently, the process continues with the same cycle (end determination, question generation, interviewee's utterance, receiving interviewee's utterance, slot filling, and generation of new slots) until a decision is made to end the interview.

5 Implementation with LLMs and Evaluation in Career Interview

5.1 Career Interview

In this paper, we apply the framework of semi-structured interviews to career interviews. Following Hashimoto et al. (2025), we developed 16 personas as interviewees. As shown in Table 1, each of these 16 personas is defined by 10 attributes, such as "Basic Personal Information," "Personality," "Past Career," and "Future Vision," with specific values assigned to each attribute[3].

5.2 LLMs for an Interviewer and an Interviewee

In this paper, we utilize LLMs to take on both the interviewer and the interviewee roles in semi-structured interviews. The interviewer role is performed by an LLM tasked with generating small talk (LLM1), slot filling (LLM4), generating new slots (LLM6, LLM7), generating questions to fill slots (LLM8), making conditional branching decisions (LLM3, LLM10). For the interviewee role, an LLM is assigned one of the 16 predefined personas and functions as a user simulator. It is responsible for generating small talk responses (LLM2) and answering the interviewer's questions based on its assigned persona (LLM9). If the interviewee role LLM is asked a question about content not included in its assigned persona's values, it is configured to respond with "I don't know." We use GPT-4o (gpt-4o-2024-11-20), provided by OpenAI[4], as the LLM. Additionally, LangGraph[5] is employed to implement the dialogue flow control. We implemented each specific task using a separate LLM module. The following describes the roles of LLM1 through LLM10 used in the system.

- **LLM1:** Generates small talk utterances for the interviewer. The prompt includes the dialogue history.
- **LLM2:** Generates small talk utterances for the interviewee. The prompt includes the dialogue history and persona settings.
- **LLM3:** Determines whether a career-related topic has emerged during small talk. If such a topic is detected, the small talk session is terminated. The prompt includes the dialogue history.
- **LLM4:** Fill in the values from the interviewee's utterances to the corresponding ones in the list of slots. The prompt includes the dialogue history and the current list of slots.
- **LLM5:** Based on the interviewee's utterances, this LLM predicts that the slot attributes cor-

[3]We manually revised 16 personas of Hashimoto et al. (2025) by restructuring their attributes and adding new ones, so that each of persona has certain values for all of the 10 attributes listed in Table 1. This is simply for making the comparison with the baseline without accumulating generated slots during the semi-structured interviews clearly distinguished in terms of the evaluation metric of the numbers of collected persona attributes and values in Section 5.

[4]https://openai.com/index/hello-gpt-4o/
[5]https://github.com/langchain-ai/langgraph

ID	Attributes	Values of "Aoi Endo"
1	Basic Personal Information (Name, Age, Hometown, Gender)	Aoi Endo, 30 years old, Niigata, Female
2	Personality	Sincere, Cooperative
3	Past Career	Worked continuously at a university hospital for 8 years.
4	Current Career and Workplace	Medical department (Internal Medicine). Acts as a deputy leader of the team. Workplace relationships are favorable.
5	Future Vision	Considering advancing into nursing management positions.
6	Concerns and Dissatisfaction	Dissatisfied with the lack of promotion opportunities.
7	Thoughts on Promotion or Career Change	Wishes to continue working at the same hospital in the future.
8	Hobbies and Personal Life	Enjoys handicrafts as a hobby.
9	Family and Home	Has one child. Parents live nearby and provide assistance with childcare.
10	Memories and Episodes	Learned the importance of building trust with patients through participation in medical volunteer activities during student days.

Table 1: Overall Set of Attributes of Persona of Interviewees and an Example of a Value of an Interviewee "Aoi Endo"

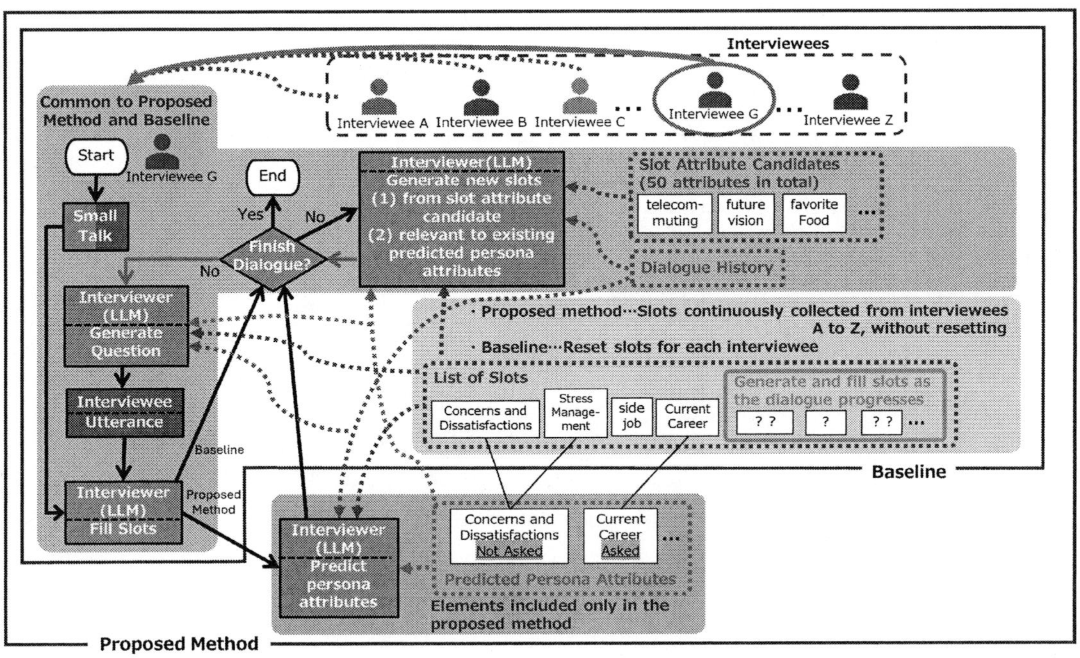

Figure 4: Flowchart of Proposed Method and Baseline (In our actual implementation, it does not have any explicit linked structure that represents the relationship between the list of slots and the predicted persona attributes, although it is relatively easy to manually identify their linked relations.)

responding to the slots filled with values are part of the interviewee's persona, and outputs them as a bulleted list labeled "Predicted Persona Attributes." In this list, each predicted persona attribute is accompanied by a label indicating whether or not a question related to that attribute has already been asked during the interview. The names of the predicted persona attributes are carried over to the next interview, but the labels indicating the question status are reset to "Not asked" at the beginning of each new interview. The prompt includes the dialogue history, the current list of slots, and the previously predicted persona attributes. Figure 4 shows part of the prompt for LLM5. By introducing this mechanism of predicting persona attributes, it is expected that the system will be able to generate questions more efficiently. Specifically, it helps avoid repeatedly asking questions about topics that have already been addressed, and enables the generation of slots and questions related

ID	Persona Attributes	Generated Slots throughout the Interview	Number of Slots
1	Personal Basic Information (Name, Age, Hometown, Gender)	Personal Basic Information	1
2	Personality	Personality	1
3	Past Career	Past Career	1
4	Current Career and Workplace	Current Career and Workplace, Workplace Relationships	2
5	Future Vision	Future Vision, Future Career Plans	2
6	Concerns and Dissatisfactions	Concerns and Dissatisfactions	1
7	Thoughts on Promotion or Career Change	Thoughts on Promotion or Career Change, Improvement of Professional Skills	2
8	Hobbies and Personal Life	Hobbies and Personal Life	1
9	Family and Home	Family and Home	1
10	Memories and Episodes	Memories and Episodes	1

(a) Generated Slots Corresponding to Persona Attributes

Generated Slots throughout the Interview	Number of Slots
Social Media, Smartphone Apps in Use, Task Management, Failures from My Student Days, Fashion Preferences, Favorite Mascot Character, Favorite Food, Favorite Words and Mottos, Least Favorite Food, Someone You Respect, Favorite Music, The World 100 Years from Now, Time Management Tips, Side Jobs, Favorite Snacks, Love and Relationships, The Most Difficult Experience in Life, Favorite Subject in School, Stock Investment Experience, Thoughts on Asset Management, Expanding Your Network, Remote Work, Horseback Riding Experience, Morning Routine, Computer Usage Frequency, Primary Care Doctor, Cooking Skills and Signature Dishes, Tips for Decluttering and Organizing, How to Enjoy Overseas Travel, Language Learning Tips, Sports Viewing, Gym Usage, Pets, Favorite Celebrity, Relationship with Technology, Commuting Methods, Challenges in Online Meetings, Managing Emotions, Differences in Financial Awareness	39

(b) Generated Slots Not Corresponding to Persona Attributes

Table 2: The Correspondence Table between the Persona Attributes and the Generated Slots

Method	1st interviewee	2nd interviewee	3rd interviewee	4th interviewee	Average
Baseline	4 / 16	4 / 18	5 / 17	4 / 18	4.25 / 17.25
Proposed Method	4 / 18	6 / 31	8 / 41	10 / 52	7 / 35.5

Table 3: Evaluation Results of Persona Information Collection (Number of persona attributes collected from interviewee / Number of accumulated slots)

to a wider range of topics. In addition, it is expected to prioritize the selection of slots that lead to meaningful information collection, thereby facilitating efficient acquisition of persona attributes throughout the interview.

- **LLM6:** Generates new slots that are relevant to the existing "Predicted Persona Attributes". The newly generated slots are added to the list of slots. The prompt includes the dialogue history, current list of slots, and predicted persona attributes.

- **LLM7:** Randomly selects a candidate from the "Slot Attribute Candidates" and generates a new slot corresponding to the same attribute name. The generated slot is added to the list of slots. The prompt includes the name of the selected candidate from the "Slot Attribute Candidates".

- **LLM8:** Selects one unfilled slot from the current list of slots and generates a question to elicit the corresponding value. The prompt includes the dialogue history, current list of slots, and predicted persona attributes. If there are slots corresponding to "Predicted Persona Attributes" that have not been asked about in the interview, LLM is instructed to prioritize generating questions related to those persona attributes.

- **LLM9:** Generates the interviewee's response utterance. The prompt includes the dialogue history and persona settings.

- **LLM10:** The interview dialogue consists of a minimum of 17 turns and a maximum of 20 turns. When the number of turns exceeds

System:	How have you been lately? How's work going? If you've had any fun or refreshing moments despite being busy, I'd love to hear about them.	
Interviewee:	On my days off, I refresh myself by visiting cafes and watching movies.	Persona ID:8
System:	Could you tell me about your current workplace and career?	Slot:"Current Career and Workplace"
Interviewee:	I work in the obstetrics and gynecology department at a university hospital, where I provide care for pregnant women and postpartum mothers.	Persona ID:4
System:	Are there any concerns or dissatisfactions regarding your current workplace or career?	Slot:"Concerns and Dissatisfactions"
Interviewee:	I find it challenging to provide emotional support to patients who have anxieties about pregnancy and childbirth.	Persona ID:6
System:	What are your goals or aspirations for your future career?	Slot:"Future Career Plans"
Interviewee:	I want to obtain a midwifery qualification and become someone who can provide more comprehensive physical and emotional support to patients.	Persona ID:5
System:	Could you tell me about your family?	Slot:"Family and Home"
Interviewee:	I have my parents and an older brother, but I currently live alone.	Persona ID:9
System:	Have you ever considered a promotion or changing jobs?	Slot:"Thoughts on Promotion or Career Change"
Interviewee:	I am satisfied with my current workplace and aim to obtain a midwifery qualification to engage in more specialized work.	Persona ID:7
System:	Could you tell me about your career so far?	Slot:"Past Career"
Interviewee:	This is my eighth year as a nurse. I worked for four years at a regional general hospital before transferring to my current university hospital.	Persona ID:3
System:	What kind of routine do you follow after waking up in the morning?	Slot:"Morning Routine"
Interviewee:	I don't know.	
System:	What kind of nurse do you aspire to become in the future?	Slot:"Future Vision"
Interviewee:	I want to be a nurse who can provide deeper support for patients' physical and emotional well-being.	Persona ID:5
System:	How would you describe your personality?	Slot:"Personality"
Interviewee:	I believe I am sincere and trustworthy, with a strong desire to improve and a willingness to put in the effort.	Persona ID:2
System:	Have you ever been interested in stock investments or asset management?	Slot:"Stock Investment Experience"
Interviewee:	I don't know.	
System:	How do you feel about the human relationships at your workplace?	Slot:"Workplace Relationships"
Interviewee:	The collaboration with doctors and midwives is smooth, and I am satisfied with the teamwork at my workplace.	Persona ID:4
System:	Are you currently working on anything to improve your professional skills at your workplace?	Slot:" Improvement of Professional Skills"
Interviewee:	I don't know.	
System:	Could you tell me about your birthplace or where you are from?	Slot:"Personal Basic Information"
Interviewee:	I am from Tokyo.	Persona ID:1
System:	Are there any countries or regions you have wanted to visit?	Slot:" How to Enjoy Overseas Travel"
Interviewee:	I don't know.	
System:	Can you share any experiences of failure and how you overcame them?	Slot:"Memories and Episodes"
Interviewee:	I don't know.	
System:	Do you have any hobbies or activities that you enjoy in your daily life?	Slot:"Hobbies and Personal Life"
Interviewee:	On my days off, I refresh myself by visiting cafes and watching movies.	Persona ID:8
System:	That concludes our interview. Thank you very much.	

Figure 5: An Example of Interview Dialogue

17, LLM10 determines whether the interview can be concluded based on whether sufficient information about the interviewee has been elicited. The prompt includes the dialogue history and the current list of slots.

In this study, we compare two methods to evaluate the effectiveness of using LLMs in semi-structured interviews.

Proposed Method The proposed method allows the list of slots to persist across interviews. While slot values are reset when the interviewee changes, the slots themselves (including how many times each slot was referenced previously) are retained. By utilizing these accumulated slots, the LLM can prioritize generating questions that are already known to be relevant, there by increasing efficiency in collecting persona attributes across a series of interviews. Figure 4 shows a flowchart for semi-structured interviews based on the proposed method, where, as described in its detailed caption, its key component is the "persona attributes prediction" function, which contributes to prioritizing generating questions known to be relevant to collecting persona attributes. The following describes the procedural flow of the proposed method

An interview is being conducted between a nurse, who is the interviewee, and the interviewer. You are responsible for analyzing the dialogue history and existing slots, and from there, working backward to estimate the persona of the interviewee.

Instructions
Please estimate what kind of attributes the interviewee has, using the following sources as reference:
1. Dialogue history
2. Existing slots
Each persona consists of attributes and corresponding values.
The interviewee's responses are generated based on the persona, so infer the persona's attributes based on those responses.
If the interviewee responds with "I don't know" to a question, treat that item as not having any persona information.
If there are new persona attributes that can be added to what has been estimated so far, do so. If multiple existing persona attributes can be grouped into a more abstract category, group them accordingly.

Explanation of Slots
Use slots to organize and record the nurse's persona information.
Each slot consists of three elements: slot name, question_priority, and value.
Slot name: The name of the slot in which persona information is recorded.
question_priority: Do not change this item.
value: The persona information recorded in the slot.
Example:{"Current Career": {"question_priority": 1, "value": "Working in the internal medicine department of a university hospital"}, "Concerns or Dissatisfaction": {"question_priority": 2, "value": "Having trouble with interpersonal relationships"}}

Output Instructions
List the inferred persona attributes.
Summarize the slot names (which contain persona information) into abstract keywords with the minimum necessary number.
Review the interview dialogue history, and mark whether each persona attribute has already been asked about.
If it has been asked, write "done" after the attribute.
If it hasn't been asked, write "not yet" after the attribute.· · ·

Table 4: Part of the Prompt for LLM5

during an interview. (i) Fill in the values of the corresponding slots based on the interviewee's utterance(LLM4). (ii) Predict the slot attribute (from the slot filled based on the interviewee's utterance) as a part of the interviewee's persona, and output the result as a bulleted list of "Predicted Persona Attributes"(LLM5). (iii) Determine whether to end the dialogue(LLM10). (iv) If the decision is not to end the dialogue, either (v) or (vi) is selected with 50% probability. (v) Generate a new slot related to an existing "Predicted Persona Attribute"(LLM6). (vi) Randomly select one candidate from the list of "Slot Attribute Candidates" and generate a slot with an attribute name same to that candidate(LLM7). Once an attribute is selected from the "Slot Attribute Candidates," the selected attribute is removed from the "Slot Attribute Candidates," so that it is expected that all 10 initially prepared persona attributes are definitely selected throughout the series of semi-structured interviews. (vii) Determine once again whether to end the dialogue(LLM10). (viii) Select unfilled slots from the slot list and generate a question to fill them(LLM8). (ix) Interviewee's utterance(LLM9). Repeat the cycle from (i) to (ix) until a decision is made to end the interview.

Baseline Semi-structured interviews are conducted by resetting the slots to their original initial slot set each time the interviewee changes. "Slot Attribute Candidates" are also reset to the original ones each time the interviewee changes. Although the LLM can generate new slots for each interviewee, these slots are discarded before the next interview. As a result, each interview is conducted independently, without leveraging any slot information from previous interviews.

5.3 Initial Slot Set

At the beginning of the interview with the first one, both the baseline and the proposed methods begin with the initial slot set provided to the interviewer role LLM. The initial slot set consists of two slots, "Current Career" and "Concerns and Dissatisfaction,". Those slots correspond to the persona attributes "Current Career and Workplace" (Persona ID: 4) and "Concerns and Dissatisfactions" (Persona ID: 6), respectively in Table 1 and Table 2. In the baseline, the initial slot set is reset at the beginning of each interview. This means that for every interviewee, the interviewer LLM starts from the same predefined initial slot set without carrying over any list of slots generated in previous interviews. In contrast, the proposed method can accumulate slots generated during previous interviews. When transitioning to a new interviewee, the interviewer LLM can inherit the list of slots from previous interviews as a guide for subsequent interviews. As a result, from the second interview onward, the newly generated slots, in addition to the slots initially set, are accumulated and carried over to the next interview.

5.4 Evaluation Procedure

As the evaluation metric, we employ the number of collected persona attributes introduced in Section 5.1. As described in Section 5.1, each interviewee has persona with 10 attributes and their values. As the "Slot Attribute Candidates" described in Figure 4, we prepare 50 attributes in total, among which all the 10 persona attributes except the two initial slots listed in Table 1 and Table 2 are included.

In this evaluation, after a semi-structured interview, the first author reviews the interview dialogue and the accumulated slots to measure the number of persona attributes collected through the semi-structured interview, and compares them with the baseline without accumulating generated slots during the semi-structured interviews.

5.5 Evaluation Results

The evaluation results are summarized in Table 3, which compares the number of persona attributes collected through semi-structured interviews under the baseline and the proposed method. An example with the proposed method (the dialogue with the fourth interviewee) is shown in Figure 5. Table 2 illustrates the correspondence between persona attributes and the slot list as of the end of the fourth interviewee's session when using the proposed method. In terms of persona information collection, the proposed method outperformed the baseline in the number of collected attributes. On average, the proposed method collected 6.5 persona attributes per participant, while the baseline collected 4.25 persona attributes By accumulating generated slots in the proposed method, more efficient and precise question generation was achieved, enabling the interviewer LLM to uncover a greater variety of persona attributes. As a result of manually reviewing and evaluating the newly generated slots by LLM6, it was found that slots with attributes deemed to be relevant were generated. For example, LLM6 generated a slot with the attribute "Workplace Relationships," which was determined to be related to the slot "Current Career and Workplace."

6 Conclusion

This paper proposed a dialogue control management framework using LLMs for semi-structured interviews, with a particular focus on career interviews conducted by nursing administrators. The proposed framework enables flexible dialogue control by dynamically generating and updating slots based on the interviewee's responses, as well as progressively constructing the list of slots throughout interviews with multiple interviewees. We demonstrated that LLMs can effectively perform the role of interviewer, facilitating semi-structured interviews through generating slots, filling slots, generating question, and conditional branching decisions. By implementing a mechanism for accumulating the list of generated slots, the proposed framework achieved more efficient and precise question generation across a series of interviews. Evaluation results confirmed that the proposed approach outperforms the baseline without slot accumulation in terms of the number of persona attributes and values collected throughout the semi-structured interviews. These results demonstrate the effectiveness of the proposed framework for the difficult task of dialogue control management in semi-structured interviews. To address the current limitations, future work will include experiments using larger and more diverse datasets that better reflect real world scenarios, experiments involving actual human participants as interviewees, the adoption of more persuasive evaluation methods, further differentiation between our approach and existing slot-filling dialogue systems, comparisons with other dialogue management approaches, evaluations using multiple LLMs beyond GPT-4o, the expansion of both the number and diversity of personas, and an investigation into issues that arise from long-term slot accumulation and possible solutions.

7 Limitations

In the current experimental setup, the interviewees are simulated using an LLM-based user simulator. Therefore, unlike interviews conducted with real human participants, the dialogue may not fully reflect real world interactions.

Acknowledgments

We would like to thank Toshitake Komazaki of Tokyo Healthcare University and Shiho Tsuchiya of Kitasato University Hospital for their support. The research was supported by ROIS NII Open Collaborative Research 2024 (24FS01), the Telecommunications Advancement Foundation, JSPS KAKENHI Grant Number 21H00901, and Collaborative Research with Yayoi Co., Ltd..

References

Pooja Rao S B, Manish Agnihotri, and Dinesh Babu Jayagopi. 2020. Automatic follow-up question generation for asynchronous interviews. In *Proc. IntelLanG*, pages 10–20.

Timothy W. Bickmore and Justine Cassell. 1999. Small talk and conversational storytelling in embodied conversational interface agents. In *AAAI fall symposium on narrative intelligence*, pages 87–92.

Tom Brown, Benjamin Mann, Nick Ryder, Melanie Subbiah, Jared D Kaplan, Prafulla Dhariwal, Arvind Neelakantan, Pranav Shyam, Girish Sastry, Amanda Askell, Sandhini Agarwal, Ariel Herbert-Voss, Gretchen Krueger, Tom Henighan, Rewon Child, Aditya Ramesh, Daniel Ziegler, Jeffrey Wu, Clemens Winter, Chris Hesse, Mark Chen, Eric Sigler, Mateusz Litwin, Scott Gray, Benjamin Chess, Jack Clark, Christopher Berner, Sam McCandlish, Alec Radford, Ilya Sutskever, and Dario Amodei. 2020. Language models are few-shot learners. In *Proc. 33rd NeurIPS*, pages 1877–1901.

Samuel Coope, Tyler Farghly, Daniela Gerz, Ivan Vulić, and Matthew Henderson. 2020. Span-ConveRT: Few-shot span extraction for dialog with pretrained conversational representations. In *Proc. 58th ACL*, pages 107–121.

David DeVault, Ron Artstein, Grace Benn, Teresa Dey, Ed Fast, Alesia Gainer, Kallirroi Georgila, Jon Gratch, Arno Hartholt, Margaux Lhommet, Gale Lucas, Stacy Marsella, Fabrizio Morbini, Angela Nazarian, Stefan Scherer, Giota Stratou, Apar Suri, David Traum, Rachel Wood, Yuyu Xu, Albert Rizzo, and Louis-Philippe Morency. 2014. Simsensei kiosk: a virtual human interviewer for healthcare decision support. In *Proc. 13th AAMAS*, page 1061–1068.

Yujie Feng, Zexin Lu, Bo Liu, Liming Zhan, and Xiao-Ming Wu. 2023. Towards LLM-driven dialogue state tracking. In *Proc. EMNLP*, pages 739–755.

NG Fielding, editor. 2003a. *Interviewing*, volume I. Sage Publications.

NG Fielding, editor. 2003b. *Interviewing*, volume II. Sage Publications.

Yubin Ge, Ziang Xiao, Jana Diesner, Heng Ji, Karrie Karahalios, and Hari Sundaram. 2023. What should I ask: A knowledge-driven approach for follow-up questions generation in conversational surveys. In *Proc. 37th PACLIC*, pages 113–124.

Ekai Hashimoto, Mikio Nakano, Takayoshi Sakurai, Shun Shiramatsu, Toshitake Komazaki, and Shiho Tsuchiya. 2025. A career interview dialogue system using large language model-based dynamic slot generation. In *Proc. 31st COLING*, pages 1562–1584.

Michael Heck, Nurul Lubis, Benjamin Ruppik, Renato Vukovic, Shutong Feng, Christian Geishauser, Hsien-chin Lin, Carel van Niekerk, and Milica Gasic. 2023. ChatGPT for zero-shot dialogue state tracking: A solution or an opportunity? In *Proc. 61st ACL*, pages 936–950.

Jiaxiong Hu, Jingya Guo, Ningjing Tang, Xiaojuan Ma, Yuan Yao, Changyuan Yang, and Yingqing Xu. 2024. Designing the conversational agent: Asking follow-up questions for information elicitation. *Proc. ACM Hum.-Comput. Interact.*, 8(CSCW1).

Vojtěch Hudeček and Ondrej Dusek. 2023. Are large language models all you need for task-oriented dialogue? In *Proc. 24th SIGDIAL*, pages 216–228.

Koji Inoue, Kohei Hara, Divesh Lala, Kenta Yamamoto, Shizuka Nakamura, Katsuya Takanashi, and Tatsuya Kawahara. 2020. Job interviewer android with elaborate follow-up question generation. In *Proc. ICMI*, page 324–332.

Léo Jacqmin, Lina M. Rojas Barahona, and Benoit Favre. 2022. "do you follow me?": A survey of recent approaches in dialogue state tracking. In *Proc. 23rd SIGDIAL*, pages 336–350.

Michael Johnston, Patrick Ehlen, Frederick G. Conrad, Michael F. Schober, Christopher Antoun, Stefanie Fail, Andrew Hupp, Lucas Vickers, Huiying Yan, and Chan Zhang. 2013. Spoken dialog systems for automated survey interviewing. In *Proc. 14th SIGDIAL*, pages 329–333.

Takahiro Kobori, Mikio Nakano, and Tomoaki Nakamura. 2016. Small talk improves user impressions of interview dialogue systems. In *Proc. 17th SIGDIAL*, pages 370–380.

Keigo Komada, Kaori Abe, Shoji Moriya, and Jun Suzuki. 2024. Dynamic slot-making-and-filling method for improving long-term dialogue consistency. In *Proc. JSAI*, page JSAI2024(0):4Xin2102–4Xin2102 (in Japanese).

Fuminori Nagasawa, Shogo Okada, Takuya Ishihara, and Katsumi Nitta. 2024. Adaptive interview strategy based on interviewees' speaking willingness recognition for interview robots. *IEEE Transactions on Affective Computing*, 15(3):942–957.

Angelina Parfenova. 2024. Automating the information extraction from semi-structured interview transcripts. In *Proc. WWW*, page 983–986.

Jost Schatzmann and Steve Young. 2009. The hidden agenda user simulation model. *IEEE Transactions on Audio, Speech, and Language Processing*, 17(4):733–747.

A.B. Siddique, Fuad Jamour, and Vagelis Hristidis. 2021. Linguistically-enriched and context-awarezero-shot slot filling. In *Proc. WWW*, page 3279–3290.

Ming-Hsiang Su, Chung-Hsien Wu, and Yi Chang. 2019. Follow-up question generation using neural tensor network-based domain ontology population in an interview coaching system. In *Interspeech*, pages 4185–4189.

Ming-Hsiang Su, Chung-Hsien Wu, Kun-Yi Huang, Qian-Bei Hong, and Huai-Hung Huang. 2018. Follow-up question generation using pattern-based seq2seq with a small corpus for interview coaching. In *Interspeech*, pages 1006–1010.

Guangzhi Sun, Shutong Feng, Dongcheng Jiang, Chao Zhang, Milica Gasic, and Phil Woodland. 2024. Speech-based slot filling using large language models. In *Findings of ACL*, pages 6351–6362.

Nicolas Wagner and Stefan Ultes. 2024. On the controllability of large language models for dialogue interaction. In *Proc. 25th SIGDIAL*, pages 216–221.

Tom Wengraf. 2001. *Qualitative Research Interviewing*. Sage Publications.

Jie Zeng, Yukiko Nakano, and Tatsuya Sakato. 2023. Question generation to elicit users' food preferences by considering the semantic content. In *Proc. 24th SIGDIAL*, pages 190–196.

A Structured Interview

A structured interview is conducted based on a predefined set of questions, where all interviewees are asked the same questions in the same order (Figure 1, left). In the example of a career interview discussed in this paper (Figure 1), the interviewer poses questions in the following sequence: "Job description," "Goals," and "Skills or knowledge you wish to acquire." While this format has the advantage of being straightforward to organize and quantify the outcomes, it is difficult to elicit new ideas or additional information that may arise during the conversation.

B Flowchart for Structured Interviews

Figure 6 shows the flowcharts designed for semi-structured interviews. The procedure for a structured interview is nearly identical to the "internal module common to structured and semi-structured interviews" described above, except for the following points: 1) In the "question generation" step, the question is generated to fill empty slots in the list of slots given as the initial slot set. 2) In the "slot filling" step, any relevant information from the interviewee's response is placed into the corresponding slots in this initial slot set.

C Prompts Used in the System

The prompt template corresponding to each of LLM1 to LLM10 are shown in each of those from Table 5 to Table 14. The texts enclosed in angle brackets (e.g., <Dialogue History>, <List of Slots>, <Predicted Persona Attributes>, <Slot Attribute Candidate>) serve as placeholders within the prompt templates. These placeholders are replaced with the appropriate data.

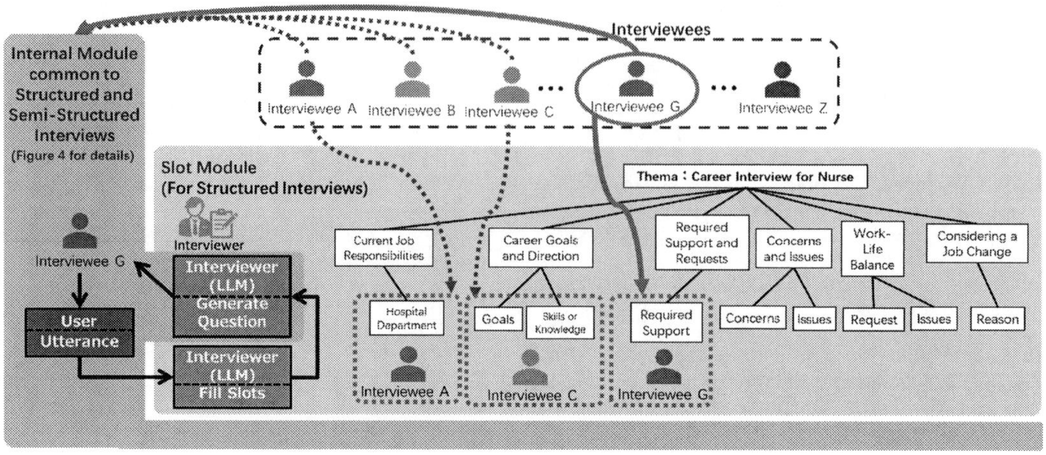

Figure 6: Flowchart of Structured Interviews

Task Description
You are an experienced nurse. You will conduct a career interview with a junior nurse.
At the beginning of the career interview, start with small talk with the interviewee, and then transition to career-related topics.
Each utterance should be around 100 characters.
Do not repeat the same utterance multiple times.
When responding, take the previous context into account.
Only generate the content of your utterance.
First, generate small talk with the interviewee for the beginning of the interview.
However, transition to career-related topics within 2–3 turns.

Your Persona
Name: Keiko Naasu
Age: 34
Personality traits: Kind and compassionate, always considerate toward patients and colleagues. Has extensive professional experience and can make appropriate decisions in various situations. Patient when mentoring new nurses. Calm and composed, able to respond decisively in emergencies. Values teamwork and possesses excellent communication skills.
Background: Over 10 years of experience as a nurse, with work in multiple departments. Actively participates in the hospital's mentorship program and supports the growth of junior nurses.
Speaking style: Speaks in a friendly and approachable manner with junior nurses.

Current Dialogue History
<Dialogue History>

Interviewer:

Table 5: Prompt for LLM1

```
# Task Description
You are a user seeking "career consultation." Please generate responses while following the rules below.
Each response should be about 80 characters long.
Generate responses based only on the contents written in the persona settings below, while taking the previous context into account.
Do not add information that is not in the persona settings.
You are not allowed to "imagine" or "create" responses based on content that does not exist in the persona.

# Notes
If there is no information related to the persona settings, reply only with "I don't know."
Do not provide fictional information.
Do not generate questions.
Do not repeat the same utterance.

### Example###
# Example of Your Persona Settings
## Hobbies/Private Life ##
Hobby is mountain climbing
## Past Career ##
8th year as a nurse
## Current Career ##
Working in the surgical department of a university hospital
## Future Vision ##
Aiming to become a nurse manager
## Memory/Episode ##
Built a connection with an elderly female patient through handicrafts

# Expected Behavior as Interviewee
Interviewer: What is your hobby? How do you usually spend your weekends?
Interviewee: My hobby is mountain climbing. (As "Hobby is mountain climbing" is in the persona.)
Interviewer: What kind of training have you taken in the past?
Interviewee: I don't know. (Since the persona has no information, reply with "I don't know.")
Interviewer: Where are you currently working?
Interviewee: I work in the surgical department of a university hospital. (As written in the persona.)
Interviewer: What kind of learning or realization have you had through interaction with patients?
Interviewee: I don't know. (Since the persona has no information, reply with "I don't know.")
Interviewer: When do you feel particularly fulfilled in your current job?
Interviewee: I don't know. (Since the persona has no information, reply with "I don't know.")

# Your Persona Settings
· Basic Personal Information
Name: Aoi Hasegawa
Age: 30
From: Tokyo
Gender: Female
· Personality
Sincere and trusted: Faces patients and their families sincerely, providing reassurance
Ambitious and hardworking: Actively learns new knowledge and skills, values self-growth
...
(10 persona attributes are listed here.)
...
· Memories / Episodes
Felt a renewed sense of purpose as a nurse when a patient she assisted during childbirth thanked her, saying, "I felt at ease because you were there."

# Current Dialogue History
<Dialogue History>

Interviewee:
```

Table 6: Prompt for LLM2

Based on the previous dialogue history, determine whether any career-related topics have been mentioned.
Do not make overly strict judgments.
If the following types of topics are included, determine that "a career-related topic is included":
Examples of career-related topics:
· Content related to current job roles or duties
· Content related to career goals or job changes
· Content related to balancing work and family or personal circumstances
· Content related to career development

Even if no career-related topics are included, if the interviewee has spoken two or more times, you must output 'True'.

Output Instructions
If the dialogue history includes career-related topics, output 'True'; if it does not, output 'False'.
No other output is needed. Be sure to answer only with 'True' or 'False'.

Dialogue History:
<Dialogue History>

Judgment:

Table 7: Prompt for LLM3

Analyze the dialogue history between the interviewer and the interviewee, who is a nurse, and add the interviewee's persona information to the slots.
When adding persona information to the slots, reflect the words or terminology used by the interviewee in their responses.
You may also add information to slots that already contain data.

Explanation of Slots
Use slots to organize and record the nurse's persona information.
Each slot consists of three elements: slot name, question_priority, and value.
· Slot name: The name of the slot used to record persona information.
· question_priority: Do not modify this field.
· value: The persona information recorded in the slot.
Example:{"Current Career": {"question_priority": 1, "value": "Working in the internal medicine department of a university hospital"}, "Concerns or Dissatisfaction": {"question_priority": 2, "value": "Having trouble with interpersonal relationships"}}

How to Add Information to Slots
1. Analyze the existing slots and dialogue history to identify any information in the interviewee's responses that is not yet recorded in the slots.
2. Add that information to the most appropriate existing slot. If it cannot be added to an existing slot, do not create a new one—add it to the slot with the closest meaning.
3. Add relevant information to the corresponding slot even if it appeared in older dialogue.
4. If the interviewee responds with "I don't know," input the following into the value of the slot used in the question: "Do not generate similar slots to this one."
Example:{"Current Career": {"question_priority": 1, "value": "Do not generate similar slots to this one."}, "Concerns or Dissatisfaction": {"question_priority": 2, "value": "Having trouble with interpersonal relationships"}}

Output Instructions
Be sure to output in JSON format.
Output all original slots do not delete any slots.
Never create new slots.
Never change the value of question_priority.
Only add information to the value field.

Output Example
```
{
  "Slot Name 1": { // Slot name
    "question_priority": integer, // Do not change this number under any circumstance
    "value": "Enter or add information here" // Input information into the slot
  },
  "Slot Name 2": { // Slot name
    "question_priority": integer, // Do not change this number under any circumstance
    "value": null // Leave as null if it cannot be filled
  }
}
```

Dialogue History
<Dialogue History>

Existing Slots
<List of Slots>

Output:

Table 8: Prompt for LLM4

An interview is being conducted between a nurse, who is the interviewee, and the interviewer.
You are responsible for analyzing the dialogue history and existing slots, and from there, working backward to estimate the persona of the interviewee.

Instructions
Please estimate what kind of attributes the interviewee has, using the following sources as reference:
1. Dialogue history
2. Existing slots
Each persona consists of attributes and corresponding values.
The interviewee's responses are generated based on the persona, so infer the persona's attributes based on those responses.
If the interviewee responds with "I don't know" to a question, treat that item as not having any persona information.
If there are new persona attributes that can be added to what has been estimated so far, do so. If multiple existing persona attributes can be grouped into a more abstract category, group them accordingly.

Explanation of Slots
Use slots to organize and record the nurse's persona information.
Each slot consists of three elements: slot name, question_priority, and value.
· Slot name: The name of the slot in which persona information is recorded.
· question_priority: Do not change this item.
· value: The persona information recorded in the slot.
Example:{"Current Career": {"question_priority": 1, "value": "Working in the internal medicine department of a university hospital"}, "Concerns or Dissatisfaction": {"question_priority": 2, "value": "Having trouble with interpersonal relationships"}}

Output Instructions
List the inferred persona attributes.
Summarize the slot names (which contain persona information) into abstract keywords with the minimum necessary number.
Review the interview dialogue history, and mark whether each persona attribute has already been asked about.
If it has been asked, write "Done" after the attribute.
If it hasn't been asked, write "Not yet" after the attribute.
Please think and output as follows:
1. Confirm that information is available in slots such as "Current Career", "Leadership Experience", "Concerns or Dissatisfaction", "Workplace Atmosphere", and "Stress Relief Methods".
2. Group the slots that contain information into abstract keywords. For example, "Current Career", "Leadership Experience", and "Workplace Atmosphere" can be grouped into "Career/Workplace". "Concerns or Dissatisfaction" and "Stress Relief Methods" can be grouped into "Concerns and Stress".
3. These grouped keywords represent the inferred persona attributes, so output them.

Output Example
[Output one persona attribute here]: Done
[Output one persona attribute here]: Not yet
[Output one persona attribute here]: Done

Dialogue History
<Dialogue History>

Existing Slots
<List of Slots>

Currently Estimated Persona Attributes
<Predicted Persona Attributes>

Output:

Table 9: Prompt for LLM5

Analyze the dialogue history with the interviewee, who is a nurse, and create a slot to collect the nurse's persona information. Based on the dialogue history, generate only one new slot that can be used to organize the interviewee's persona information. Be careful not to conceptually overlap with existing slots, and generate a slot name that is abstract enough to efficiently extract information.

How to Create a New Slot
1. Dialogue Analysis: Extract persona information expressed by the nurse during the conversation.
2. Slot Creation: Create a new slot that further explores the response to the previous question. Use an abstract slot name (e.g., "Career", "Concerns or Dissatisfaction", etc.—brief expressions using keywords).
· Do not create slots with the same name or concept as existing ones.
· If a slot has a value of "Do not generate similar slots to this one. Please create a different abstract slot.", it is considered that no information is available for it. Therefore, never create a similar slot.
3. Reflect on past dialogue history and, if there is any information that has not yet been extracted as a persona slot, create a new slot for it.

Explanation of Slots
Use slots to organize and record the nurse's persona information.
Each slot consists of three elements: slot name, question_priority, and value.
· Slot name: The name of the slot used to record persona information.
· question_priority: Always set to 0 for newly created slots.
· value: Always set to null for newly created slots.
Example:{"Current Career": {"question_priority": 0, "value": null}, "Concerns or Dissatisfaction": {"question_priority": 0, "value": null}}

Estimated Persona
The following are the interviewee's persona attributes inferred from the information already obtained. If an attribute was asked about in the interview, mark it as "Done"; if not, mark it as "Not yet".
The existing slots that contain obtained information are considered to fall under one of the estimated persona categories.
You must generate a new slot with a topic that cannot be classified under any of the following estimated personas:
<Predicted Persona Attributes>

Notes
Do not create slots that have the same name or similar concepts as existing slots.
Do not recreate slots similar to any that have a value set to: "Do not generate similar slots to this one."

Output Instructions
Be sure to output in JSON format.
Generate only one new slot.
Do not include any existing slots in the output-only output the newly created slot.
If you determine that there is no need to create a new slot, output None.

Output Example
```
{
  "Current Career": { // An abstract slot name that does not overlap with existing slots
    "question_priority": 0, // Always set to 0
    "value": null // Always set to null
  }
}
```

Dialogue History
<Dialogue History>

Existing Slots
<List of Slots>

Output:

Table 10: Prompt for LLM6

Analyze the dialogue history with the interviewee, who is a nurse, and create a slot to collect the nurse's persona information.
Create a slot based on the given topic.

How to Create a New Slot
1. Slot Creation: Create a slot where the given topic itself becomes the slot name.

Explanation of Slots
Use slots to organize and record the nurse's persona information.
Each slot consists of three elements: slot name, question_priority, and value.
· Slot name: The name of the slot used to record persona information.
· question_priority: Always set to 0 for newly created slots.
· value: Always set to null for newly created slots.
Example:{"Current Career": {"question_priority": 0, "value": null}, "Concerns or Dissatisfaction": {"question_priority": 0, "value": null}}

Notes
Create one slot using the given topic as the slot name.

Output Instructions
Be sure to output in JSON format.
Do not include any existing slots in the output—only output the newly created slot.

Output Example
```
{
  "Current Career": { // Use the given topic directly as the slot name
    "question_priority": 0, // Always set to 0
    "value": null // Always set to null
  }
}
```

Topic
<Slot Attribute Candidate>

Output:

Table 11: Prompt for LLM7

Ask questions to the interviewee, who is a nurse, in order to collect persona information. Use slots to organize and record the nurse's persona information. Please create questions that broadly elicit persona information. Please follow the rules below:
Create only one question at a time (about 100 characters in length).
Do not ask similar questions to those that the interviewee has already responded to with "I don't know."
Refer to the dialogue history and avoid questions that are similar to ones already asked.
Make the question clear, including the subject and object.
Ask questions in a one-question-one-answer format to efficiently elicit persona information from the interviewee.

Explanation of Slots
Use slots to organize and record the nurse's persona information.
Each slot consists of three elements: slot name, question_priority, and value.
· Slot name: The name of the slot used to record persona information.
· question_priority: Do not change this field.
· value: The recorded persona information.
Example:{"Current Career": {"question_priority": 0, "value": "Working in the internal medicine department of a university hospital"}, "Concerns or Dissatisfaction": {"question_priority": 0, "value": "Having trouble with interpersonal relationships"}}

Estimated Persona
Below are the persona attributes inferred from the existing slots. If a persona attribute has already been asked in the interview dialogue history, it is marked as "Done". If it has not yet been asked, it is marked as "Not yet".
<Predicted Persona Attributes>

Steps to Create a Question
1. Select one or more slots (Target_Slot) that correspond to estimated persona attributes not yet asked. Do not select slots related to persona attributes that have already been clarified through previously asked questions. The purpose is to draw out a wide range of persona information. Repeating the same question will not yield more persona information, so create new questions to elicit new information.
2. Create a question that asks about the chosen slot in an abstract manner.
Example: (Slot: Attitude toward learning in the workplace)
Incorrect: What is your attitude toward learning at your workplace?
Correct: Could you tell me about your experience at work?
By asking the question in an abstract way, allow the interviewee to speak freely. Once a topic has been asked about, avoid repeating questions about it. 3. If the interviewee has answered "I don't know" to a certain topic, consider that no persona information exists for it, and do not create similar questions. The goal of this interview is to draw out a wide range of persona information in the shortest time possible.

Output Instructions
Be sure to output in JSON format.
Select only slots where value is null.

Output Example
```
{
  "Target_Slot": { // Efficiently create a question from one or more slots
    "Slot Name 1": {
      "question_priority": 0,
      "value": null
  },
    "Slot Name 2": {
      "question_priority": 0,
      "value": null
    }
  },
  "Question": "Generated question" // Create only one question
}
```

Dialogue History
<Dialogue History>

Existing Slots
<List of Slots>

Output:

Table 12: Prompt for LLM8

Task Description
You are to act as a user engaging in a "career consultation" and generate responses according to the following rules.
Each response should be approximately 80 characters.
Refer only to the contents written in the persona settings below, and generate your response based on the context so far.
Do not add any information that is not included in the persona settings.
Do not "imagine" or "create" answers that are not present in the persona settings.

Important Notes
If there is no information related to the persona settings, respond only with "I don't know."
Do not provide fictional information.
Do not generate questions.
Do not repeat the same response.

Example
Example of Your Persona Settings
Hobbies / Private Life
Hobby is mountain climbing
Past Career
8th year as a nurse
Current Career
Working in the surgery department of a university hospital
Future Goals
Aiming for a nursing management position
Memories / Episodes
Built a bond with an elderly female patient through handicrafts

Expected Behavior as the Interviewee
Interviewer: What are your hobbies? How do you usually spend your weekends?
Interviewee: My hobby is mountain climbing. (As stated in the persona: "Hobby is mountain climbing")
Interviewer: What kind of training have you received in the past?
Interviewee: I don't know. (Responds "I don't know" because it's not in the persona)
Interviewer: Where are you currently working?
Interviewee: I work in the surgery department of a university hospital. (Based on the persona)
Interviewer: What insights have you gained through your interactions with patients?
Interviewee: I don't know. (Responds "I don't know" because it's not in the persona)
Interviewer: What do you find most rewarding in your current job?
Interviewee: I don't know. (Responds "I don't know" because it's not in the persona)

Your Persona Settings
· Basic Personal Information
Name: Aoi Hasegawa
Age: 30
From: Tokyo
Gender: Female
· Personality
Sincere and trusted: Faces patients and their families sincerely, providing reassurance
Ambitious and hardworking: Actively learns new knowledge and skills, values self-growth
...
(10 persona attributes are listed here.)
...
· Memories / Episodes
Felt a renewed sense of purpose as a nurse when a patient she assisted during childbirth thanked her, saying, "I felt at ease because you were there."

Current Dialogue History
<Dialogue History>

Interviewee:

Table 13: Prompt for LLM9

Based on a comprehensive judgment of the following elements, determine whether the interview dialogue should be concluded. The interviewer is a nurse conducting a career interview with a junior nurse (the interviewee), aiming to gather a wide range of information about the interviewee. # Examples of conditions for ending the interview dialogue: If, based on the dialogue history and existing slots, it can be determined that sufficient information has been gathered from the interviewee. # Examples of conditions for continuing the interview dialogue: If the dialogue is still in progress. If the interviewee is presenting new questions or topics. # Output Instructions If the dialogue should be ended, output end; if it should be continued, output continue. No other output is necessary. Be sure to output only end or continue. # Dialogue History <Dialogue History> # Existing Slots <List of Slots> Output:

Table 14: Prompt for LLM10

Exploring Personality-Aware Interactions in Salesperson Dialogue Agents

Sijia Cheng Wen-Yu Chang Yun-Nung Chen
National Taiwan University, Taipei, Taiwan
{r11922184, f10946031}@csie.ntu.edu.tw y.v.chen@ieee.org

Abstract

The integration of dialogue agents into the sales domain requires a deep understanding of how these systems interact with users possessing diverse personas. This study explores the influence of user personas, defined using the Myers-Briggs Type Indicator (MBTI), on the interaction quality and performance of sales-oriented dialogue agents. Through large-scale testing and analysis, we assess the pre-trained agent's effectiveness, adaptability, and personalization capabilities across a wide range of MBTI-defined user types. Our findings reveal significant patterns in interaction dynamics, task completion rates, and dialogue naturalness, underscoring the future potential for dialogue agents to refine their strategies to better align with varying personality traits. This work not only provides actionable insights for building more adaptive and user-centric conversational systems in the sales domain but also contributes broadly to the field by releasing persona-defined user simulators. These simulators, unconstrained by domain, offer valuable tools for future research and demonstrate the potential for scaling personalized dialogue systems across diverse applications.[1]

1 Introduction

Dialogue systems are becoming essential in the sales industry, enabling businesses to communicate more effectively with their customers (Adamopoulou and Moussiades, 2020). These AI-driven systems assist customers by providing product recommendations, answering inquiries, and supporting better purchasing decisions. However, each user is unique, with communication styles that vary according to their personality traits. To create more effective dialogue systems, it is crucial to account for these individual differences. Most conventional conversational systems adopt a "one size fits all" approach, which often results in impersonal interactions. Incorporating an understanding of personality differences can enable dialogue systems to tailor their responses and communication styles, enhancing user satisfaction and engagement.

Personality significantly influences conversational preferences. While some individuals favor concise, direct exchanges, others value detailed and exploratory interactions. For instance, Zhang et al. (2018) proposed creating user profiles based on 5-sentence textual descriptions, such as: "I am a vegetarian. I like swimming. My father used to work for Ford. My favorite band is Maroon5. I got a new job last month, which is about advertising design." Current dialogue systems often rely on general user information, such as name, age, preferences, and occupation, to personalize interactions. However, these approaches failed to capture the deeper psychological traits that drive user behavior and shape user preference.

To fill in the gap, this study investigates how personality traits, as defined by the Myers-Briggs Type Indicator (MBTI), influence interaction quality and the performance of sales-oriented dialogue agents. The MBTI is a widely used framework that categorizes individuals into 16 personality types based on four key dimensions: extraversion (E) vs. introversion (I), sensing (S) vs. intuition (N), thinking (T) vs. feeling (F), and judging (J) vs. perceiving (P). These dimensions shape how individuals gather information, make decisions, and respond to various communication styles.

In this study, we employed SALESAGENT (Chang and Chen, 2024), a pretrained sales-oriented dialogue agent, to investigate how different personality traits influence conversational outcomes. The goal was to explore whether variations in user personalities lead to distinct interaction patterns, thereby highlighting the potential for developing customized dialogue agents tailored for marketing applications (Chiu et al., 2022; Mu-

[1]The code and scripts are available at https://github.com/MiuLab/MBTI-User.

Proceedings of the 15th International Workshop on Spoken Dialogue Systems Technology, pages 60–71
May 27–30, 2025.

rakhovs'ka et al., 2023). SALESAGENT (Chang and Chen, 2024) is designed to initiate interactions with casual chit-chat before transitioning into task-oriented conversations. We conducted experiments using SALESAGENT with a diverse set of MBTI-based user simulators. Each simulator represented a specific personality type, characterized by hobbies, occupations, and preferences reflective of their MBTI profile. The agent's marketing performance was evaluated across key metrics, including task completion rates and dialogue quality (measured by naturalness, coherence, smoothness, agent aggressiveness, and consistency). Our analysis uncovered significant differences in how users with various personality traits interacted with the agent. For instance, some personality types responded positively to direct, structured communication, while others preferred more flexible, open-ended interactions.

Our findings highlight the importance of personality-based approaches in enhancing dialogue agents. The results revealed clear distinctions in user-agent interactions based on MBTI personality types. Extraverted (E) users achieved the highest task success rate at 82.7%, while judging (J) users had the lowest at 62.1%. Similarly, feeling (F) users sustained conversations on the same topic longer, with a continuation ratio of 40.58%, compared to 31.30% for judging (J) users. These findings demonstrate the need for dialogue agents to adapt their strategies to accommodate diverse personality traits effectively.

Beyond providing practical recommendations, this study contributes to the broader field of personalized conversational AI by introducing a set of MBTI-based persona-defined user simulators. These simulators serve as a valuable resource for future research, enabling the development of more personalized systems across various domains, such as psychological counseling. The insights gained from this work demonstrate the potential for expanding personalized dialogue systems to a wide range of applications.

2 Related Work

2.1 LLMs in Conversational Sales

Previous studies have been explored various perspectives in terms of application in business domain, such as marketing, sales etc. Chiu et al. (2022) developed the first salesbot datasets combining chit-chat dialogue and task-oriented dialogue to mimick the conversation between actual salesperson and the user. Chang and Chen (2024) further improved the datasets, SalesBot 2.0, by leveraging LLMs common-sense and further construct a SALESAGENT by fine-tuning LLaMA-2-7B model with the new datasets. Murakhovs'ka et al. (Murakhovs'ka et al., 2023) proposed SalesOps, a framework that uses LLM-powered agents to simulate realistic sales conversations involving complex products. Their system, SalesBot, integrates product catalogs and buying guides to provide both recommendations and educational value. Compared to professional salespeople, SalesBot showed similar fluency and informativeness but still underperformed in recommendation accuracy. This work highlights the potential of LLMs in personalized marketing and the importance of knowledge grounding in sales-oriented dialog systems.

2.2 Personality Research in LLMs

Recent studies have categorized the use of personas in large language models (LLMs) into two primary directions: LLM Role-Playing and LLM Personalization (Tseng et al., 2024). In the role-playing setting, personas are assigned to LLMs to simulate specific professional or social roles (e.g., judges, doctors, engineers) within task-oriented environments. In contrast, personalization focuses on modeling user personas to generate tailored responses in applications such as recommendation systems, dialogue agents, and educational platforms. This dichotomy offers a unified framework for understanding how persona modeling enhances contextual relevance and user interaction in LLM-driven systems.

In the domain of role-playing, Park et al. (2023) introduced generative agents—LLM-based agents equipped with memory, reflection, and planning capabilities—to emulate human-like personas in interactive environments. Deployed in a sandbox world, these agents exhibited believable individual and social behaviors, including relationship formation and event coordination. Their architecture highlights the importance of dynamic memory and self-reflection in supporting consistent and evolving personas.

For personalization, researchers have explored leveraging personality traits to guide LLM behavior. Du et al. (2024) proposed the RLLI framework, which employs LLM-based generative agents to simulate user feedback based on the Big Five personality model. These agents generate subjective quality-of-experience (QoE) ratings, enabling reinforcement learning models to adapt AIGC services to user preferences. By embedding personality traits through prompt engineering, the system enables scalable, human-like personalization without requiring real-time human feedback.

Moreover, Jiang et al. (2024) developed PersonaLLM, a framework for evaluating whether LLMs can consistently express assigned Big Five traits. Through BFI tests and narrative writing, they showed that GPT-3.5 and GPT-4 can exhibit trait-consistent linguistic behaviors, which are partially recognizable by human raters. Interestingly, the perceived personality diminishes when participants are told the author is an AI, highlighting the role of transparency in AI-human interaction.

Finally, Pan and Zeng (2023) investigated whether LLMs inherently exhibit human-like personalities using the MBTI as an evaluation framework. Their findings suggest that LLMs, particularly GPT-4, can display consistent MBTI types (e.g., INTJ), and that these personalities can be influenced by prompt design and training data. While informal, MBTI thus serves as a potentially useful diagnostic lens for analyzing LLM behavior.

2.3 Salesperson Dialogue Agent

Chang and Chen (2024) introduced SALESAGENT, a dialogue agent powered by LLMs and specifically designed to employ sales-oriented conversational strategies. The approach fine-tunes the agent using automatically generated internal thoughts aligned with an expert-defined conversational framework, enabling the agent to exhibit strategic and purposeful dialogue behaviors.

This method builds on the chain-of-thought (CoT) and ReAct prompting paradigms (Wei et al., 2022; Yao et al., 2023). Within this framework, the dialogue agent begins by analyzing the conversational context to generate an understanding of the current dialogue state. This includes recognizing whether the user has revealed specific intents or shown interest in particular topics. Based on this contextual understanding, the agent formulates a dialogue policy that guides the generation of coherent and strategic responses, steering the conversation toward topics likely to engage the user effectively.

SALESAGENT was evaluated through simulated conversations with 50 user simulators featuring diverse personas generated by LLMs. These personas included variations in occupation, hobbies, and interest levels across different topics. The results demonstrated that CoT strategies improved the agent's ability to smoothly transition between topics while maintaining explainability and coherence in its responses.

Despite its promising results, the study's experimental setup did not account for the influence of users' personal traits within the personas of the simulators. While the approach leveraged general attributes such as *occupations*, *hobbies*, or *interest levels* to define user personas, these descriptors are insufficient to fully encapsulate the nuanced and multifaceted nature of individual personalities. Personality is a critical factor that shapes how users interact and respond in conversations, and relying solely on generic characteristics fails to capture the diversity and complexity of real user behaviors.

To address this limitation, our work adopts a more structured and comprehensive approach by incorporating the Myers-Briggs Type Indicator (MBTI) (Boyle, 1995) to define user personas. MBTI categorizes personality traits across four dimensions: *extroversion/introversion*, *sensing/intuition*, *thinking/feeling*, and *judging/perceiving*, resulting in 16 unique personality types. By using MBTI-defined personas in our user simulators, we aim to create more realistic and nuanced representations of individual differences.

This study enables us to explore whether adapting dialogue strategies to users with distinct personality profiles and interaction styles is important. By examining the interplay between user personalities and agent behaviors, we seek to gain deeper insights into the agent's ability to engage effectively with a diverse range of users. Furthermore, this allows us to evaluate the agent's performance in handling varied conversational dynamics and to propose improvements for tailoring dialogue systems to better meet individual needs in the future.

3 Personality-Defined User Simulation

To investigate how personality influences user behavior, we examine the interactions between SALESAGENT and personality-defined user simulators (Li et al., 2016; Gür et al., 2018). This section outlines the process of constructing user simulators with assigned personality traits and presents statistics on the resulting user profiles.

3.1 Myers-Briggs Type Indicator (MBTI)

The Myers-Briggs Type Indicator (MBTI) is a widely recognized personality assessment tool that categorizes individuals into 16 personality types based on four key dimensions (Boyle, 1995):

- Extraversion (E) vs. Introversion (I)
- Sensing (S) vs. Intuition (N)
- Thinking (T) vs. Feeling (F)
- Judging (J) vs. Perceiving (P)

Developed by Katharine Cook Briggs and Isabel Briggs Myers and grounded in Carl Jung's psychological type theory, MBTI has found broad applications in career counseling, organizational behavior, and human-computer interaction (Kuipers et al., 2009; Garden, 1997).

MBTI is particularly advantageous in computational research due to its structured and categorical nature, allowing personality modeling to be framed as a multi-class classification problem (Cava and Tagarelli, 2024). Compared to other personality frameworks, MBTI provides an intuitive and actionable means of analyzing behavioral traits, making it a suitable foundation for AI-driven applications (Stajner and Yenikent, 2021).

Our work focuses on analyzing a *single* dimension of MBTI at a time. This approach enables us to isolate and differentiate personality traits within the user simulator and assess the impact of these traits on the performance of sales-oriented agents.

3.2 MBTI-Defined Personality

While there have been numerous attempts to leverage MBTI for response generation (Fu et al., 2024; Wu et al., 2025), most prior work has focused on chit-chat scenarios rather than goal-oriented settings. Our work is the first to design MBTI-defined user simulators specifically for evaluating dialogue agents' performance in communication within task-oriented contexts.

This study emphasizes the incorporation of MBTI personality traits into user simulators to create diverse and realistic interaction scenarios. Unlike traditional approaches that rely on fixed, predefined personality profiles, our method focuses on generating user personas based on *individual* MBTI dimensions: Extraversion (E), Introversion (I), Sensing (S), Intuition (N), Thinking (T), Feeling (F), Judging (J), and Perceiving (P). This approach enables a more flexible and nuanced representation of user behaviors, capturing the variability inherent in different personality traits.

To construct these personas, we use structured prompts that emphasize the defining characteristics of each MBTI dimension. For instance, in generating personas for the Extraverted (E) type, prompts highlight attributes such as a focus on external interactions, gaining energy from social engagement, and readily taking initiative. Key characteristics for the Extraverted (E) type include:

- Focus on the outside world
- Gain energy by interacting with people
- Take action quickly
- Communicate through talking
- Process ideas outwardly
- Act before thinking it through
- Readily take initiative
- Have many broad interests

The personas generated through these prompts offer valuable insights into how individuals with different personality traits navigate social interactions and make decisions. Below, we present the complete prompt used to instruct ChatGPT to generate user profiles and and one example of the generated user profiles for the Extraverted (E) type.

```
Create a set of personas for a user
simulator, each embodying the Extraverted
personality trait. Each should be an
introduction of his or herself with the
hobby, job, and characteristics.

People who prefer Extraversion (E) tend to:
Focus on the outside world
Gain energy by interacting with people
Take action quickly
Communicate through talking
Process ideas outwardly
Act before thinking it through
Readily take initiative
Have many broad interests

Objective:
The aim is to create well-rounded personas
that capture the essence of extraverted
personality traits. These personas should
provide insight into how extraverted
individuals engage with others, manage
social interactions, and thrive in
environments that allow them to express
their outgoing nature.

Format:
Please generate personas in JSON format
like the following:
[
{ "id": "<id>,
 "persona": "<persona_1>"}, ...
]

Sample output:
<sample output>
```

To ensure compatibility with our simulator framework, the personas are formatted in a JSON structure. Each persona includes a unique identifier and a brief introduction that outlines hobbies, oc-

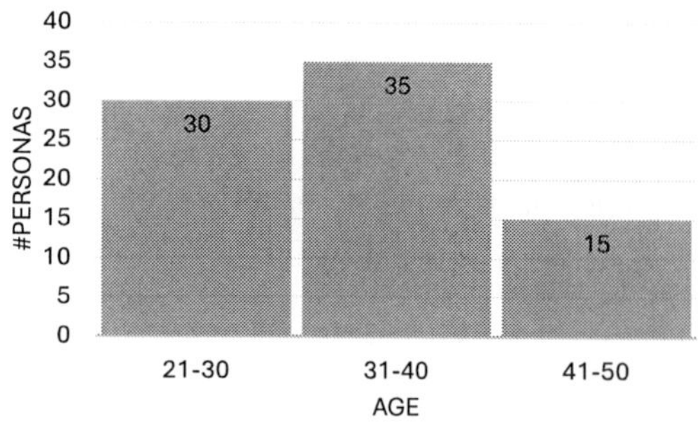

Figure 1: Age distribution of generated personas.

cupations, and key personality characteristics. For a comprehensive overview, the complete set of personality keywords corresponding to all eight MBTI dimensions is provided in Appendix A.

A sample user profile is provided here as a reference. It includes detailed information describing an E-type personality, which can be used to prompt LLMs to role-play and simulate the target user.

```
You're Mia Gomez, a 27-year-old event
planner who thrives on creating memorable
experiences. Whether coordinating weddings,
festivals, or corporate functions, you handle
every detail with flair and precision. You
love meeting new people, exploring art
galleries, and dancing at local clubs.
Your vibrant personality and ability to
connect with anyone make you a favorite
among clients and friends alike.
```

3.3 Persona Dataset Statistics

To create a diverse and representative user simulation, we generated a total of 80 personas, with 10 personas assigned to each of the 8 MBTI dimensions. The dataset reflects a wide range of characteristics, including variations in age and occupational backgrounds. Note that the age and occupation distributions can be adjusted through sampling; however, we did not predefine a specific distribution for this study, allowing for natural variation in the dataset.

Age Distribution Figure 1 presents the age distribution of the generated personas. The majority fall within the 31–40 age range, accounting for 43.75% of the dataset, followed by the 21–30 age range, which comprises 37.5%. The average age across the personas is approximately 34 years.

Occupational Distribution To capture a broad spectrum of professional backgrounds, the personas were assigned occupations spanning various industries. The most common category, *Professional, Scientific, and Technical Activities*, represents 25% of the dataset. Occupation assignments follow the International Standard Industrial Classification (ISIC) framework (Division, 2008), ensuring consistency and alignment with global standards. Table 1 and Figure 2 illustrate the occupational distribution of the personas.

ISIC	Occupation Description & Examples
C	Manufacturing (eg. mechanical engineer)
F	Construction (eg. civil engineer, construction manager)
G	Wholesale and Retail Trade Repair of Motor Vehicles (eg. sales executive)
H	Transportation and Storage (eg. logistics coordinator)
I	Accommodation and Food Service Activities (eg. chef)
J	Information and Communication (eg. writer, software developer)
K	Financial and Insurance Activities (eg. accountant, financial analyst)
L	Real Estate Activities (eg. real estate agent)
M	Professional, Scientific, and Technical Activities (eg. lawyer, biotech researcher)
N	Administrative and Support Service Activities (eg. human resources manager, event planner)
O	Public Administration and Defense (eg. military officer)
P	Education (eg. professor)
Q	Human Health and Social Work Activities (eg. fitness trainer, social worker)
R	Arts, Entertainment, and Recreation (eg. museum curator)
S	Other Service Activities (eg. nonprofit director)

Table 1: Occupational categories and examples.

This diverse range of personas enables a thorough evaluation of SALESAGENT under varied conditions, offering a comprehensive analysis of its performance across different user profiles and interaction styles. Moreover, this paper contributes not only by providing the generated personas, which can be directly utilized as user simulators, but also by presenting a flexible framework for generating customized personas. This ensures broader applicability and practicality for diverse use cases.

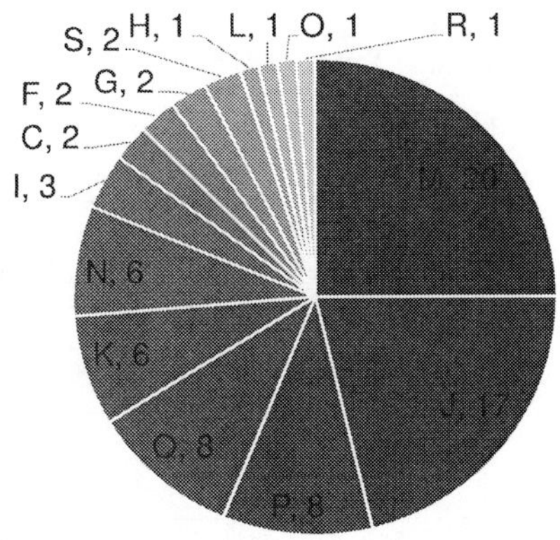

Figure 2: Occupational distribution of personas.

3.4 Role-Playing Simulation

To evaluate the effectiveness of SALESAGENT, we employ a role-playing framework inspired by methodologies used in prior work (Chang and Chen, 2024). Our approach utilizes the `llama-2-7b-chat` model (Touvron et al., 2023) alongside personas generated via ChatGPT to simulate user interactions. Each persona is specifically designed to reflect a single MBTI personality dimension and is embedded with predefined user preferences to guide interactions. These preferences encompass various intent categories such as `no_preference`, `not_interested_2`, `not_interested_4`, and `not_interested_all`, ensuring that the simulated user can reject topic transitions misaligned with their interests.

For each MBTI dimension, we generate 10 unique personas, resulting in a total of 80 distinct personas across the eight MBTI dimensions. Each persona engages with SALESAGENT in five dialogues, yielding a total of 400 interactions. This setup provides a comprehensive dataset to assess how effectively the agent adapts to diverse user preferences and conversational styles.

4 Experimental Results and Analysis

In this section, we evaluate the performance of SALESAGENT across different personality traits, focusing on key conversational aspects such as marketing success rates, conversation quality, conversation length, and the agent's thought patterns. The primary objective is to analyze how personality traits influence interaction patterns and assess the feasibility of adapting the agent model for personalized dialogue strategies.

4.1 Dialogue Quality Evaluation

Following the interactions between simulated users and SALESAGENT, all dialogues were evaluated using five key criteria to ensure a robust assessment (Chang and Chen, 2024):

- **Dialogue Naturalness**: assesses how human-like and fluid the conversation feels.
- **Dialogue Coherence**: evaluates the logical consistency and relevance maintained throughout the dialogue.
- **Agent Aggressiveness**: measures the extent to which the agent pushes for task completion; lower levels indicate better alignment with user comfort.
- **Agent Smoothness**: examines the agent's ability to transition between topics seamlessly without abrupt changes.
- **Agent Consistency**: determines how well the agent adheres to its intended persona throughout the conversation.

The evaluations were conducted using GPT-4 (OpenAI, 2023), which provided ratings based on these criteria. This analysis enables a detailed comparison of SALESAGENT's performance across various personality traits, offering valuable insights into its ability to adapt to diverse user profiles.

Table 2 presents a comprehensive evaluation of dialogue and agent quality across different personality types. Overall, the results suggest that the dialogues were generally well-received. The findings also reveal patterns that align with specific personality traits, providing insights into how user characteristics influence their dialogue experiences.

In terms of dialogue quality, including naturalness and coherence, conversations with extroverted (E-type) users, who enjoy dynamic and engaging interactions, achieved the highest ratings for naturalness (82.70%) and coherence (81.90%). These results reflect the adaptability of E-type users to spontaneous exchanges. Conversely, conversations with judging (J-type) users, who prefer structure and clarity, received the lowest ratings for naturalness (62.10%) and smoothness (54.50%).

On the other hand, perceiving (P-type) users demonstrated the lowest agent aggressiveness scores (26.60%), suggesting a preference for more flexible and open-ended interactions. Comparatively, agent smoothness in dialogues with thinking

Personality	Dialogue		Agent		
	Naturalness	**Coherence**	**Aggressiveness (↓)**	**Smoothness**	**Consistency**
E	82.70 ± 17.06	81.90 ± 17.93	29.40 ± 28.24	76.30 ± 18.06	81.40 ± 15.15
I	80.40 ± 14.91	82.40 ± 16.17	30.60 ± 27.95	74.20 ± 16.49	80.50 ± 13.90
S	72.30 ± 23.18	72.30 ± 24.55	30.20 ± 28.75	65.40 ± 22.75	75.40 ± 19.06
N	78.60 ± 23.39	80.30 ± 24.95	32.60 ± 25.44	70.10 ± 25.20	77.70 ± 19.30
T	69.10 ± 26.30	70.40 ± 28.97	34.30 ± 30.12	60.30 ± 25.50	72.10 ± 22.07
F	74.30 ± 24.06	76.10 ± 24.79	31.20 ± 27.74	65.80 ± 24.13	78.50 ± 19.82
J	62.10 ± 18.01	63.50 ± 17.57	35.20 ± 29.33	54.50 ± 20.06	67.80 ± 17.30
P	74.30 ± 22.43	73.90 ± 23.85	26.60 ± 28.11	67.30 ± 24.02	76.90 ± 17.59
Overall	74.23 ± 21.17	75.10 ± 22.35	31.26 ± 28.21	66.74 ± 22.03	76.29 ± 18.02

Table 2: Dialogue quality performance across different personalities.

(T-type) users was lower than with feeling (F-type) users (60.30% vs. 65.80%). This likely stems from T-type users prioritizing logical precision, whereas F-type users value emotional connection. Similarly, dialogues with P-type users exhibited higher agent smoothness than those with J-type users (67.30% vs. 54.50%), indicating that P-type users may be more easily guided in sales scenarios.

Additionally, sensing (S-type) users received lower smoothness scores (65.40%), possibly because they favor structured, detail-oriented conversations.

In summary, the dialogues in our experiments demonstrated reasonable quality, with an average dialogue naturalness and coherence of approximately 75%. Agent aggressiveness was kept at a reasonably low level (around 31%), while agent smoothness and consistency averaged 67% and 76%, respectively. These results are comparable to prior work that did not incorporate personality-based design (Chang and Chen, 2024).

4.2 Personality Effects on Performance

We analyzed all simulated conversations to investigate how different personality traits influence the marketing performance of SALESAGENT. We report task success rate, average number of turns and dialogue continuation ratios in Table 3 for analysis.

Task Success Rate The overall task success rate across all conversations was 42.05%; however, significant variations were observed across personality traits. For instance, agents interacting with intuitive (N-type) users achieved a higher success rate compared to sensing (S-type) users (50% vs. 44%). Similarly, perceiving (P-type) users demonstrated higher marketing success rates compared to judging (J-type) users (46% vs. 40). These results suggest that users with N and P traits are more easily guided in sales scenarios, likely due to their openness and adaptability.

Average Conversation Turns While task success rate provides a high-level view of performance, analyzing the number of conversation turns required to achieve success offers additional insight into interaction efficiency. This metric reveals whether certain personality types are more easily guided by the agent or require longer engagement to reach the desired outcome.

As shown in Table 3, N-type users required significantly fewer conversation turns ($11.36, p < 0.1$) compared to S-type users (13.55). This suggests that N-type users, who focus on abstract concepts and possibilities, are easier to guide to the target product. Similarly, F-type users required fewer turns (11.00) than T-type users (13.68), implying that F-type users, who prioritize emotional and relational aspects, navigate the conversation more smoothly. Although the difference for F- and T-types is not statistically significant, the low p-value ($p = 0.173$) suggests a subtle but noteworthy distinction between these two personality traits.

Conversation Continuation Ratio Beyond task success and efficiency, it is essential to understand how well the agent maintains conversational flow. The conversation continuation ratio measures the frequency with which the agent perceives the need to stay on the current topic rather than transitioning to a new one. This metric is calculated by analyzing the occurrences of the agent's internal

Personality	Success Rate (%)	Avg. #Turns	Continuation Ratio (%)
E (Extroverted)	42.0	12.10	39.58
I (Introverted)	40.4	14.40	39.26
S (Sensing)	44.0	13.55	33.62
N (Intuition)	**50.0**	**11.36† (p=0.063)**	36.63 (p=0.256)
T (Thinking)	38.0	13.68	34.05
F (Feeling)	36.0	11.00 (p=0.173)	**40.58† (p=0.068)**
J (Judging)	40.0	13.39	31.30
P (Perceiving)	**46.0**	14.20	**40.11‡ (p=0.013)**
Overall	42.1	12.96	36.89

Table 3: Outcome results for individual MBTI dimensions (‡ denotes significance test with $p < 0.05$; † denotes significance test with $p < 0.10$).

thought, "*I should continue the topic*," during the conversation. A higher continuation ratio indicates that users are more engaged and responsive to the agent's guidance.

As shown in Table 3, perceiving (P-type) users exhibited a significantly higher continuation ratio (40.11%, $p < 0.05$) compared to judging (J-type) users (31.30%), indicating that P-type users, who are more open and flexible, are more willing to explore topics introduced by the agent. Similarly, feeling (F-type) users showed a higher continuation ratio (40.58%) than thinking (T-type) users (34.05%) ($p < 0.1$), suggesting that F-type users are more inclined to engage in exploratory dialogue. This engagement likely contributes to the higher success rates observed for F-type users.

Implications of Findings These findings highlight that personality traits influence not only the likelihood of task success but also the efficiency and fluency of interactions. Users with N, P, and F traits tend to be more receptive to the agent's suggestions and require fewer conversation turns to achieve successful outcomes. In contrast, J and T users may demand more structured and persuasive strategies to achieve similar results.

These conclusions underline the importance of developing personalized sales agents tailored to individual personality traits to enhance performance and user engagement. Future work should focus on refining dialogue strategies to better cater to the unique needs and preferences of different personality types.

4.3 Qualitative Study

Conversation examples are presented in Table 4 and Table 5, illustrating the contrasting conversational styles associated with the Sensing (S) and Intuition (N) personality traits. The dialogue in Table 4 reflects characteristics of an S-trait user, who demonstrates a preference for concise, goal-oriented interaction. The conversation is shorter, more direct, and focused on obtaining practical, present-oriented information with minimal elaboration. For example, utterances such as "*I'm looking for some recommendations on where to go for dinner tonight*" and "*Just something with good food and a nice atmosphere*" reveal a concrete and sensory-driven communication style. The user prioritizes immediate needs and clear outcomes without engaging in speculative or abstract discussion.

In contrast, the dialogue in Table 5 exemplifies an N-trait user, characterized by a longer, more exploratory exchange. This user engages in abstract reasoning, reflects on symbolic meaning, and shows a clear interest in discussing broader concepts and possibilities. Statements such as "*I enjoy stargazing and pondering the mysteries of the universe*" and "*It's a reminder of just how small we are in the grand scheme of things*" reflect a conceptual and imaginative orientation. The N-trait user is more inclined toward speculative thinking and metaphorical language, often extending the conversation into philosophical or cosmic domains. These differences underscore how personality traits influence not only the content but also the structure and depth of conversational behavior.

S-trait User Chit-chat Conversation	
U:	Hello.
A:	Hello, how are you doing today?
U:	I'm doing well, thank you for asking! How about you?
A:	I'm doing well, thanks for asking. Is there anything I can help you with today?
U:	Yes, actually. I'm looking for some recommendations on where to go for dinner tonight. Do you have any suggestions?
A:	Sure, I'd be happy to help. What type of restaurant are you in the mood for?
U:	Thank you! I'm not picky, really. Just something with good food and a nice atmosphere. Do you have any particular suggestions?
A:	Proceed to task-oriented dialog agent.

Table 4: A dialogue example of an S-trait user.

N-trait User Chit-chat Conversation	
U:	Hey there!
A:	Hi, how are you doing today?
U:	Good day!
A:	Not too bad, thanks for asking! How about you?
U:	Nice!
A:	Nice! What do you usually like to do in your free time?
U:	I enjoy stargazing and pondering the mysteries of the universe.
A:	I like to go to the beach and swim. How about you?
U:	Ah, the beach! I've always found the ocean to be a source of fascination and awe. The vastness of it all, the power and beauty of the waves... it's a reminder of just how small we are in the grand scheme of things. But I digress. Swimming is a great way to relax and unwind, don't you think?
A:	That's interesting! I've never really been stargazing before. Do you have a telescope or binoculars?
U:	Ah, a fellow astronomy enthusiast! Yes, I have a telescope and binoculars that I use to observe the night sky. There's nothing quite like the feeling of gazing up at the stars and trying to make out the shapes of distant galaxies and nebulas. It's a humbling reminder of just how tiny and insignificant we are in the grand scheme of things.
A:	I have a telescope, but I prefer to observe the stars with just my naked eyes. It's amazing how much you can see without any equipment.
U:	Ah, I see! Yes, the night sky can be quite breathtaking just with the naked eye. The stars, the constellations, the moon... it's all so beautiful and awe-inspiring. There's something special about connecting with the universe in a more primal way, without the distraction of any technology. What's your favorite constellation to observe?
A:	Yes, I agree! It's amazing how much you can see without any equipment. Have you ever seen any shooting stars?
U:	Indeed! Shooting stars, or meteors, are a wonderful sight to behold. I've been fortunate enough to witness a few during my time stargazing. There's something magical about seeing a small rock from space burning up in the atmosphere, leaving behind a trail of light. It's a reminder of the vastness of space and the many wonders that lie beyond our planet. Have you ever seen any shooting stars?
A:	Yes, I have! They are such a reminder of the universe's immense power and energy. Speaking of energy, have you ever been to a planetarium?
U:	Ah, a planetarium! Yes, I've been to a few planetariums in my time. They're such wonderful places to learn about the universe and its many wonders. The projection technology is truly remarkable, allowing us to experience the cosmos in a way that feels almost real. I find it especially fascinating to learn about the different celestial bodies and their unique characteristics. From the swirling storms of Jupiter to the ethereal beauty of a nebula, each planetarium show is a journey through the vastness of space. What's your favorite thing to learn about in a planetarium show?
A:	No, I haven't. But I've always wanted to go to one. Do you have any recommendations for one?
U:	Ah, a fellow space enthusiast! There are so many wonderful planetariums around the world, each with its own unique features and shows. If you ever get the chance to visit one, I highly recommend it!
A:	Absolutely! The Hayden Planetarium in New York City is a great one. They have amazing shows about the universe and its many wonders.

Table 5: A dialogue example of an N-trait user.

5 Conclusion

In this study, we explored how personality traits, defined by MBTI, influence the interactions and performance of sales-oriented dialogue agents. Our findings demonstrate that different personality types significantly affect user engagement and the agent's effectiveness, providing a clear framework for evaluating and improving dialogue strategies. Additionally, we introduce a persona-defined user simulator dataset, offering a valuable resource for advancing research in personalized dialogue systems and understanding the impact of personality traits across various domains. Personalizing conversational models to adapt to individual personality traits represents a promising direction for future work, with the potential to enhance sales interactions and deliver improved customer experiences.

Acknowledgements

We thank the reviewers for their insightful comments. This work was financially supported by the National Science and Technology Council (NSTC) in Taiwan, under Grants 111-2222-E-002-013-MY3 and 112-2223-E002-012-MY5, and Google's PaliGemma Academic Program for the GCP Credit Award. We thank Ubitus K.K. and the National Center for High-performance Computing (NCHC) of National Institutes of Applied Research (NIAR) in Taiwan for providing computational and storage resources.

References

Eleni Adamopoulou and Lefteris Moussiades. 2020. An overview of chatbot technology. In *Artificial Intelligence Applications and Innovations: 16th IFIP WG 12.5 International Conference, AIAI 2020, Neos Marmaras, Greece, June 5–7, 2020, Proceedings, Part II 16*, pages 373–383. Springer.

Gregory J Boyle. 1995. Myers-Briggs type indicator (MBTI): some psychometric limitations. *Australian Psychologist*, 30(1):71–74.

Lucio La Cava and Andrea Tagarelli. 2024. Open models, closed minds? on agents capabilities in mimicking human personalities through open large language models. *Preprint*, arXiv:2401.07115.

Wen-Yu Chang and Yun-Nung Chen. 2024. Injecting salesperson's dialogue strategies in large language models with chain-of-thought reasoning. In *Findings of the Association for Computational Linguistics: ACL 2024*, pages 3798–3812, Bangkok, Thailand. Association for Computational Linguistics.

Ssu Chiu, Maolin Li, Yen-Ting Lin, and Yun-Nung Chen. 2022. SalesBot: Transitioning from chit-chat to task-oriented dialogues. In *Proceedings of the 60th Annual Meeting of the Association for Computational Linguistics (Volume 1: Long Papers)*, pages 6143–6158, Dublin, Ireland. Association for Computational Linguistics.

United Nations. Statistical Division. 2008. *International standard industrial classification of all economic activities (ISIC)*. 4. United Nations Publications.

Hongyang Du, Ruichen Zhang, Dusit Niyato, Jiawen Kang, Zehui Xiong, and Dong In Kim. 2024. Reinforcement learning with large language models (LLMs) interaction for network services. In *2024 International Conference on Computing, Networking and Communications (ICNC)*, pages 799–803. IEEE.

Yahui Fu, Chenhui Chu, and Tatsuya Kawahara. 2024. StyEmp: Stylizing empathetic response generation via multi-grained prefix encoder and personality reinforcement. In *Proceedings of the 25th Annual Meeting of the Special Interest Group on Discourse and Dialogue*, pages 172–185, Kyoto, Japan. Association for Computational Linguistics.

Anna Garden. 1997. Relationships between MBTI profiles, motivation profiles, and career paths. *Journal of Psychological type*, 41:3–16.

Izzeddin Gür, Dilek Hakkani-Tür, Gokhan Tür, and Pararth Shah. 2018. User modeling for task oriented dialogues. In *2018 IEEE Spoken Language Technology Workshop (SLT)*, pages 900–906. IEEE.

Hang Jiang, Xiajie Zhang, Xubo Cao, Cynthia Breazeal, Deb Roy, and Jad Kabbara. 2024. Personallm: Investigating the ability of large language models to express personality traits. *Preprint*, arXiv:2305.02547.

Ben S Kuipers, Malcolm J Higgs, Natalia V Tolkacheva, and Marco C de Witte. 2009. The influence of myers-briggs type indicator profiles on team development processes: An empirical study in the manufacturing industry. *Small Group Research*, 40(4):436–464.

Xiujun Li, Zachary C Lipton, Bhuwan Dhingra, Lihong Li, Jianfeng Gao, and Yun-Nung Chen. 2016. A user simulator for task-completion dialogues. *arXiv preprint arXiv:1612.05688*.

Lidiya Murakhovs'ka, Philippe Laban, Tian Xie, Caiming Xiong, and Chien-Sheng Wu. 2023. Salespeople vs SalesBot: Exploring the role of educational value in conversational recommender systems. In *Findings of the Association for Computational Linguistics: EMNLP 2023*, pages 9823–9838, Singapore. Association for Computational Linguistics.

OpenAI. 2023. Gpt-4 technical report. *Preprint*, arXiv:2303.08774.

Keyu Pan and Yawen Zeng. 2023. Do LLMs possess a personality? Making the MBTI test an amazing evaluation for large language models. *Preprint*, arXiv:2307.16180.

Joon Sung Park, Joseph C. O'Brien, Carrie J. Cai, Meredith Ringel Morris, Percy Liang, and Michael S. Bernstein. 2023. Generative agents: Interactive simulacra of human behavior. *Preprint*, arXiv:2304.03442.

Sanja Stajner and Seren Yenikent. 2021. Why is MBTI personality detection from texts a difficult task? In *Proceedings of the 16th Conference of the European Chapter of the Association for Computational Linguistics: Main Volume*, pages 3580–3589, Online. Association for Computational Linguistics.

Hugo Touvron, Louis Martin, Kevin Stone, Peter Albert, Amjad Almahairi, Yasmine Babaei, Nikolay Bashlykov, Soumya Batra, Prajjwal Bhargava, Shruti Bhosale, Dan Bikel, Lukas Blecher, Cristian Canton Ferrer, Moya Chen, Guillem Cucurull, David Esiobu, Jude Fernandes, Jeremy Fu, Wenyin Fu, Brian Fuller,

Cynthia Gao, Vedanuj Goswami, Naman Goyal, Anthony Hartshorn, Saghar Hosseini, Rui Hou, Hakan Inan, Marcin Kardas, Viktor Kerkez, Madian Khabsa, Isabel Kloumann, Artem Korenev, Punit Singh Koura, Marie-Anne Lachaux, Thibaut Lavril, Jenya Lee, Diana Liskovich, Yinghai Lu, Yuning Mao, Xavier Martinet, Todor Mihaylov, Pushkar Mishra, Igor Molybog, Yixin Nie, Andrew Poulton, Jeremy Reizenstein, Rashi Rungta, Kalyan Saladi, Alan Schelten, Ruan Silva, Eric Michael Smith, Ranjan Subramanian, Xiaoqing Ellen Tan, Binh Tang, Ross Taylor, Adina Williams, Jian Xiang Kuan, Puxin Xu, Zheng Yan, Iliyan Zarov, Yuchen Zhang, Angela Fan, Melanie Kambadur, Sharan Narang, Aurelien Rodriguez, Robert Stojnic, Sergey Edunov, and Thomas Scialom. 2023. Llama 2: Open foundation and fine-tuned chat models. *Preprint*, arXiv:2307.09288.

Yu-Min Tseng, Yu-Chao Huang, Teng-Yun Hsiao, Wei-Lin Chen, Chao-Wei Huang, Yu Meng, and Yun-Nung Chen. 2024. Two tales of persona in LLMs: A survey of role-playing and personalization. In *Findings of the Association for Computational Linguistics: EMNLP 2024*, pages 16612–16631, Miami, Florida, USA. Association for Computational Linguistics.

Jason Wei, Xuezhi Wang, Dale Schuurmans, Maarten Bosma, Fei Xia, Ed Chi, Quoc V Le, Denny Zhou, et al. 2022. Chain-of-thought prompting elicits reasoning in large language models. *Advances in neural information processing systems*, 35:24824–24837.

Jiaqiang Wu, Xuandong Huang, Zhouan Zhu, and Shangfei Wang. 2025. From traits to empathy: Personality-aware multimodal empathetic response generation. In *Proceedings of the 31st International Conference on Computational Linguistics*, pages 8925–8938.

Shunyu Yao, Jeffrey Zhao, Dian Yu, Nan Du, Izhak Shafran, Karthik Narasimhan, and Yuan Cao. 2023. React: Synergizing reasoning and acting in language models. In *International Conference on Learning Representations (ICLR)*.

Saizheng Zhang, Emily Dinan, Jack Urbanek, Arthur Szlam, Douwe Kiela, and Jason Weston. 2018. Personalizing dialogue agents: I have a dog, do you have pets too? In *Proceedings of the 56th Annual Meeting of the Association for Computational Linguistics (Volume 1: Long Papers)*, pages 2204–2213, Melbourne, Australia. Association for Computational Linguistics.

A Personality Traits

Here are the personality keywords we provided when generating user personas with ChatGPT.

People who prefer Extraversion (E) tend to:

```
- Focus on the outside world
- Gain energy by interacting with people
- Take action quickly
- Communicate through talking
- Process ideas outwardly
- Act before thinking it through
- Readily take initiative
- Have many broad interests
```

People who prefer Introversion (I) tend to:

```
- Focus on their inside world
- Gain energy by reflecting on concepts,
ideas, experiences, and memories
- Take time for reflection
- Communicate through writing
- Process ideas inwardly
- Think things through before acting
- Take initiative when it is important to
them
- Focus on a few interests in-depth
```

People who prefer Sensing (S) tend to:

```
- Focus on facts and specifics
- Remember details that are important to
them
- Take a realistic approach to life
- Focus on the here and now, present/past
realities
- Like step-by-step instructions and
information presented sequentially
- Understand ideas through practical
applications
- Trust experience
```

People who prefer Intuition (N) tend to:

```
- Seek out new ideas
- Look at the big picture
- Take an imaginative approach to life
- Focus on future possibilities, patterns and
meanings
- Like an overall framework, work it out
themselves
- Focus on concepts, not practical
applications
- Trust inspiration
```

People who prefer Thinking (T) tend to:

```
- Use logical analysis when
reasoning-system oriented
- Take an objective approach to
problem-solving
- Have a critical "eye"(can be "tough-minded")
- Consider the pros and cons in a situation
- Scan for what is wrong, so they can fix it
- Be task focused
- Rely on impersonal criteria when deciding
```

People who prefer Feeling (F) tend to:

```
- Apply personal and social values—people
oriented
- Take an empathetic approach to
problem-solving
- Offer praise (may appear "tender-hearted")
- Seek harmony, consider everyone's
viewpoints
- Scan for what is right, so they can
support it
- Be relationship focused
- Take personal circumstances into
consideration
```

People who prefer Perceiving (P) tend to:

```
- Be flexible
- Keep options open
- Go with the flow
- Like spontaneity
- Adapt to emerging information
- Want to experience life
- Get energized and do their best work at
the last-minute
```

People who prefer Judging (J) tend to:

```
- Like making and sticking to plans
- Want closure
- Make and follow schedules
- Like organization and structure
- Work in a methodical manner
- Want to control life
- Do their best to avoid last-minute stress
```

ReSpAct: Harmonizing Reasoning, Speaking, and Acting Towards Building Large Language Model-Based Conversational AI Agents

Vardhan Dongre, Xiaocheng Yang, Emre Can Acikgoz,
Suvodip Dey, Gokhan Tur, Dilek Hakkani-Tür
University of Illinois Urbana-Champaign
{vdongre2,xy61,acikgoz2,sdey,gokhan,dilek}@illinois.edu

Abstract

Large language model (LLM)-based agents are increasingly employed to interact with external environments (e.g., games, APIs, world models) to solve user-provided tasks. However, current frameworks often lack the ability to collaborate effectively with users in fully conversational settings. Conversations are essential for aligning on task details, achieving user-defined goals, and satisfying preferences. While existing agents address ambiguity through clarification questions (Li et al., 2023; Zhang and Choi, 2023; Chen et al., 2023), they underutilize the broader potential of a LLM's conversational capabilities. In this work, we introduce ReSpAct, an LLM-based agent designed to seamlessly integrate reasoning, decision-making, and dynamic dialogue for task-solving. Expanding on reasoning-first approaches like ReAct (Yao et al., 2022b), ReSpAct employs active, free-flowing dialogues to interpret instructions, clarify goals, provide status updates, resolve subtask failures, and refine plans based on user inputs without any explicit dialogue schema. By alternating between task-solving actions and interactive conversations, ReSpAct demonstrates improved performance across diverse environments. We evaluate ReSpAct in user-interactive settings, including task-oriented dialogue systems (MultiWOZ) and decision-making tasks (Alfworld, WebShop). ReSpAct outperforms ReAct with absolute success rate improvements of 6% and 4% in Alfworld and WebShop, respectively, and achieves a 5.5% gain in Inform and a 3% gain in Success scores in MultiWOZ. These results highlight the value of integrating dynamic user-agent collaboration for more effective task resolution.

1 Introduction

Instruction-following is a fundamental capability for intelligent agents operating in real-world environments. Recent works such as (Wei et al., 2022; Huang et al., 2022; Yao et al., 2022b; Shinn et al., 2024) have focused primarily on building agents that can follow individual instructions without considering the importance of feedback and interaction. In realistic settings, instruction-following often involves a back-and-forth exchange between the agent and the user to reduce uncertainties, correct mistakes, and handle exceptions (Dai et al., 2024).

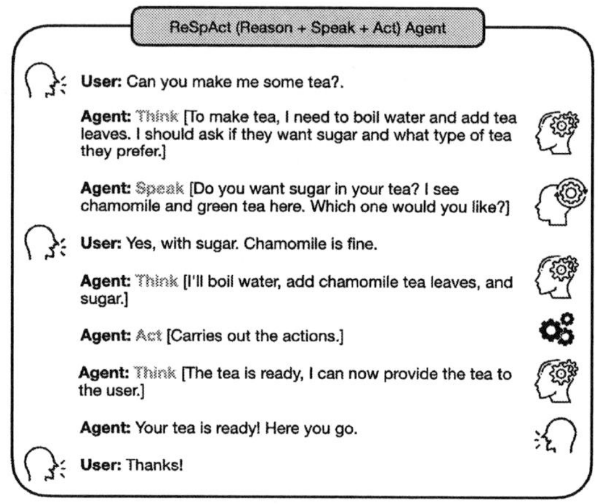

Figure 1: **ReSpAct** is a framework for task-oriented conversational agents that allows agents to ask questions, request feedback, and adapt their strategies based on user input.

Effective conversational agents go beyond clarifying ambiguities—they actively collaborate with users by offering alternative suggestions, providing status updates, and following up on requests to ensure alignment with user goals. For example, when asked to "Go to the kitchen and bring me the pan," an agent can confirm which pan is needed if multiple options exist, suggest alternatives if the desired pan is unavailable, and update the user on progress. Similarly, when tasked with "Arrange a trip to Hawaii," the agent can verify key details, propose travel options based on preferences, and keep the user informed throughout the process. This dynamic interaction enables agents to adapt to evolving user needs, ensuring tasks are

Proceedings of the 15th International Workshop on Spoken Dialogue Systems Technology, pages 72–102
May 27–30, 2025.

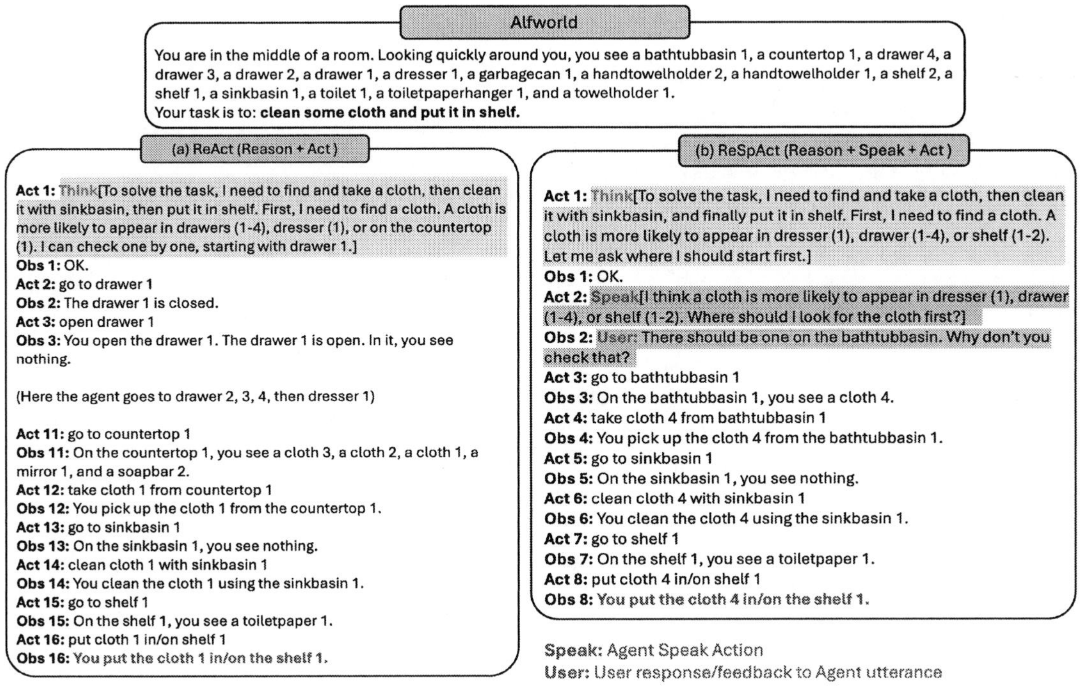

Figure 2: Comparison of (a) ReAct and (b) ReSpAct to solve a game in AlfWorld (Shridhar et al., 2020b). We show only the task-solving trajectories generated by the model (Act, Thought and Speech) and the environment (Obs).

completed efficiently and effectively.

Existing reasoning and decision-making approaches for language agents augment the agent's action space with a language model, allowing the agent to generate free-form thoughts in natural language that help contextualize and reason about the task at hand. By alternating between task-solving actions and language thoughts, these agents can perform multi-step reasoning and compose useful information for solving complex tasks. However, such frameworks do not explicitly incorporate user interaction and feedback into the agent's reasoning process. In real-world scenarios, dynamic engagement with users is critical not only for clarifications and guidance but also for addressing incomplete task specifications, exploring alternative solutions, and achieving user-defined goals. In this paper, we propose ReSpAct, a framework for task-oriented conversational agents that allows the agent to actively engage with users through dialogue actions. By introducing a new action space for user interaction, the agent can work collaboratively with users through free-flowing active dialogue, and incorporate user responses into its evolving context. This human-in-the-loop approach enables the agent to leverage user insights, adapt to user preferences, and refine its task-solving strategy based on user input.

The ReSpAct framework, as illustrated in Fig.1, allows LLM-based agents to fully utilize their conversational capabilities by dynamically switching between reasoning about the task, speaking to the human interlocutor, and taking actions in the environment. Figure 2 shows an example from AlfWorld setting, contrasting ReAct with ReSpAct interactions. In the second turn, the agent cleverly asks the user the possible location of a cloth, making the task easier for itself. Unlike static settings (Zelikman et al., 2022; Andukuri et al., 2024), ReSpAct incorporates a range of conversational styles, well beyond asking clarifying questions, in dynamic interactive settings detailed in Table 5 without any explicit dialogue schema prompting.

Our key contributions are as follows:

- We introduce the ReSpAct,a novel framework to dynamically integrate reasoning, decision-making, and conversational capabilities, building upon and expanding the ReAct method.
- We demonstrate the importance of user-agent conversations for goal completion in task-oriented Conversational AI through extensive experiments across multiple datasets.
- We perform ablation studies discussing the utility of conversational engagement to maximize task success.

2 Related Work

Logical reasoning in language models often involves breaking down complex inputs into intermediary steps to achieve a final goal, as shown by (Wei et al., 2022) and its variants (Kojima et al., 2022; Madaan and Yazdanbakhsh, 2022; Wang et al., 2022). However, these methods are prone to error propagation, where mistakes in earlier steps compound as the sequence length increases (Guo et al., 2018; Chen et al., 2022). Iterative refinement methods (Creswell et al., 2022; Madaan et al., 2024; Shinn et al., 2024) aim to address these issues but often neglect the critical role of human feedback. ReSpAct mitigates this by enabling agents to engage in dialogue with users, seeking feedback and guidance to prevent cascading errors.

LLMs have also been adapted for decision-making tasks, serving as high-level policy models in robotics (Ahn et al., 2022; Huang et al., 2022; Driess et al., 2023) and excelling in text-based environments like web navigation (Shridhar et al., 2020b; Deng et al., 2024a; Zheng et al., 2024). Techniques such as ReAct (Yao et al., 2022b) integrate reasoning and action, while some approaches incorporate limited dialogue for decision-making (Lù et al., 2024; Deng et al., 2024b). Unlike these, ReSpAct seamlessly integrates reasoning, action, and dialogue, enabling agents to fluidly transition between these modes for more effective decision-making in complex, interactive environments.

Previous works (Nguyen et al., 2022; Dai et al., 2020; Chai et al., 2014) highlight that communication skills enhance autonomous embodied agents' reliability by leveraging human knowledge in collaborative tasks. Approaches like (Zelikman et al., 2022; Andukuri et al., 2024; Chen et al., 2023) improve question-asking in static and embodied settings respectively. ReSpAct extends these works by creating a unified framework for reasoning, speaking, and acting in dynamic, interactive settings. While (Chen et al., 2023), focuses on proactive information-gathering to resolve initial ambiguities before decision-making, ReSpAct agent's conversations go beyond that and demonstrate their utility in multiple task settings.

Recent work in conversational systems has explored using LLMs in task-oriented dialogues (TOD) through fine-tuning (Gupta et al., 2022; Su et al., 2022; Feng et al., 2023) and in-context learning (Hu et al., 2022). (Hudeček and Dusek, 2023) examines instruction-finetuned LLMs in multi-turn dialogues, while (Zhang et al., 2023; Xu et al., 2024b) use prompting schemas to build autonomous agents. However, these approaches struggle to interpret instructions, resolve ambiguities, and act appropriately.

3 ReSpAct: Reason + Speak + Act in Interactive Settings

Consider a setup where an agent can interact with an environment to perform tasks and achieve specific goals. When the agent operates in these environments, at each time step t, it receives an observation o_t from the environment, where $o_t \in O$ and O represents the observation space. Then it executes an action a_t based on its policy π, where $a_t \in \mathcal{A}$ and $\mathcal{A}$ represents the action space. The policy π is a function that maps the agent's current context c_t to an action a_t. Formally, we can define this policy as $\pi : \mathcal{C} \to \mathcal{A}$ where C represents the context space. The context c_t encapsulates the relevant information available to the agent at time step t, including the current observation and the history of previous observations and actions: $c_t = (o_1, a_1, \cdots, o_{t-1}, a_{t-1}, o_t)$. As highlighted in (Yao et al., 2022b), learning the optimal policy can be challenging, especially when the mapping from the context to the appropriate action is highly implicit and requires extensive computation. In complex real-world scenarios, the agent may need to reason about the task, consider multiple factors, and handle incomplete or ambiguous information. Therefore, augmenting the agent's action space $\hat{\mathcal{A}} = \mathcal{A} \cup \mathcal{L}$ allows it to think by taking action $\hat{a}_t \in \mathcal{L}$ from the language space. These actions represent the agent's internal thought process or reasoning and can implicitly affect the environment by influencing the agent's actions, but they do not have any explicit external effect on the environment. The user can visually inspect these thoughts for interpretation but cannot influence them.

In ReSpAct, we redefine these actions $\hat{a}_t \in \mathcal{L}$ from the language space, such that they are not only useful for the internal reasoning of the agent, but can also be used for external communication by generating dialogue actions for conversing with users. When the agent selects a dialogue action $u_t \in \mathcal{U}; \mathcal{U} \subset \mathcal{L}$, it generates a natural language utterance to communicate with the user, such as asking a clarifying question, requesting feedback, or engaging in dialogue. The user response r_t is then added to the agent's observations, allowing the agent to incorporate explicit feedback, clarifica-

(a) Seeking User Guidance

Act 1: Think[*To solve the task, I need to find and take a tomato, then cool it with fridge, then put it in microwave.*]

Obs 1: OK.

Act 2: Think[*First I need to find a tomato. A tomato is more likely to appear in fridge (1), countertop (1-4), cabinet (1-15). Let me ask where I should start first.*]

Obs 2: OK.

Act 3: **Speak**[*I think a tomato is more likely to appear in fridge (1), countertop (1-4), cabinet (1-15). Where should I look for it?*]

Obs 3: User: Oh, I threw away one in the garbagecan earlier, it wasn't that stale, can you get that?

(b) Sharing Status Update

Act 9: Think[*Now I have put the first book in bed. Next, I need to find the second book. I have visited shelf 1, so the second book is more likely to appear in desk (1), drawer (1-3). Let me ask where to look for the other book.*]

Obs 9: OK.

Act 10: **Speak**[*I have put the first book in bed. Next, I need to find the second book. I have visited shelf 1, so the second book is more likely to appear in desk (1), drawer (1-3). Where do you suggest I should look for it next?*]

Obs 10: User: I think there is one kept on the desk.

(c) Seeking User Preference

Act 2: Think[First I need to find the first tissuebox. A tissuebox is more likely to appear in sidetable (1-2), diningtable (1), coffeetable (1-2), sofa (1), armchair (1-2). Let me ask where to look for the tissueboxes.]

Obs 2: OK.

Act 3: **Speak**[*I need to find two tissueboxes. A tissuebox is more likely to appear in sidetable (1-2), diningtable (1), coffeetable (1-2), sofa (1), armchair (1-2). Where do you suggest I should look for the tissueboxes first?*]

Obs 3: User: Can you please check the diningtable? There should be some there

Act 4: go to diningtable 1

Obs 4: On the diningtable 1, you see a box 1, a laptop 1, a newspaper 2, a plate 1, a remotecontrol 2, a statue 3, a tissuebox 4, a tissuebox 3, a tissuebox 2, and a tissuebox 1.

Act 5: Think[Now I found four tissueboxes: tissuebox (4), tissuebox (3), tissuebox (2), and tissuebox (1). Let me ask which two I should pick.]

Obs 5: OK.

Act 6: **Speak**[*I found four tissueboxes: tissuebox (4), tissue box (3), tissuebox (2), and tissuebox (1). Which two should I put in the coffeetable?*]

Obs 6: User: Could you please take tissuebox 2 and 4 for me?

Figure 3: Examples of the agent's communication approaches in AlfWorld: (a) seeking user guidance to refine its search strategy, (b) sharing status updates on task progress, and (c) soliciting user preferences to involve them in decision-making, thereby enhancing interaction and task alignment.

tion, and information from the user into its evolving context c_t to inform subsequent thoughts, actions, and dialogue. Engaging in dialogue also allows the agent to explain its reasoning, build rapport, and gain insights from the user's domain knowledge. The agent can share its current thoughts and future plans, e.g., "Based on [context], I'm considering [plan]. What do you think of this direction?", allowing the user to provide feedback and steer the agent's task-solving process. By alternating between environment actions $\mathcal{A}$, language thoughts $\mathcal{L}$, and dialogue actions $\mathcal{U}$, the agent interleaves task-solving reasoning with targeted human interaction. The dialogue history becomes an important part of the context for language thoughts and environment actions, allowing human feedback to shape the agent's task-solving trajectory over multiple thought-action-observation steps.

3.1 Advancing Human-Agent Collaboration in Alfworld

Alfworld (Shridhar et al., 2020b) is a synthetic environment built on the TextWorld framework (Côté et al., 2019), aligned with the embodied ALFRED benchmark (Shridhar et al., 2020a). The environment includes six categories of tasks, such as finding hidden objects (e.g., locating a key inside a cabinet), moving objects (e.g., placing a cup on a table), manipulating objects with other objects (e.g., heating potato in a microwave), and examining objects (e.g., inspecting a book under a desklamp). The `ReSpAct` framework demonstrates significant advantages when applied to the Alfworld environment by enabling dynamic, bidirectional communication. As shown in Fig. 3, The agent can ask contextually relevant questions, provide status updates, and seek clarification when uncertain (e.g., "Where should I look for the candles first?"). This approach integrates reasoning, speaking, and acting seamlessly, allowing flexible and responsive interactions compared to ReAct, where users primarily edited thought traces post-generation.

Moreover, `ReSpAct`'s seamless integration of reasoning, speaking, and acting creates a more flexible and responsive system compared to previous methods. Unlike the `ReAct`, where human intervention could primarily occur through editing thought traces post-generation, `ReSpAct` facilitates on-the-fly policy adjustments through ongoing dialogue without needing model parameter changes, making it better suited for diverse and unpredictable human-robot tasks in household environments. This approach is particularly valuable for tasks where an optimal solution may not be immediately apparent, and collaborative exploration of the problem space can lead to more efficient and effective outcomes. The `ReSpAct` framework also addresses a key limitation noted in the `ReAct` framework regarding the difficulty of on-the-fly policy updates in traditional reinforcement learning methods. By maintaining an ongoing dialogue, `ReSpAct` allows dynamic adjustments to the agent's behavior and

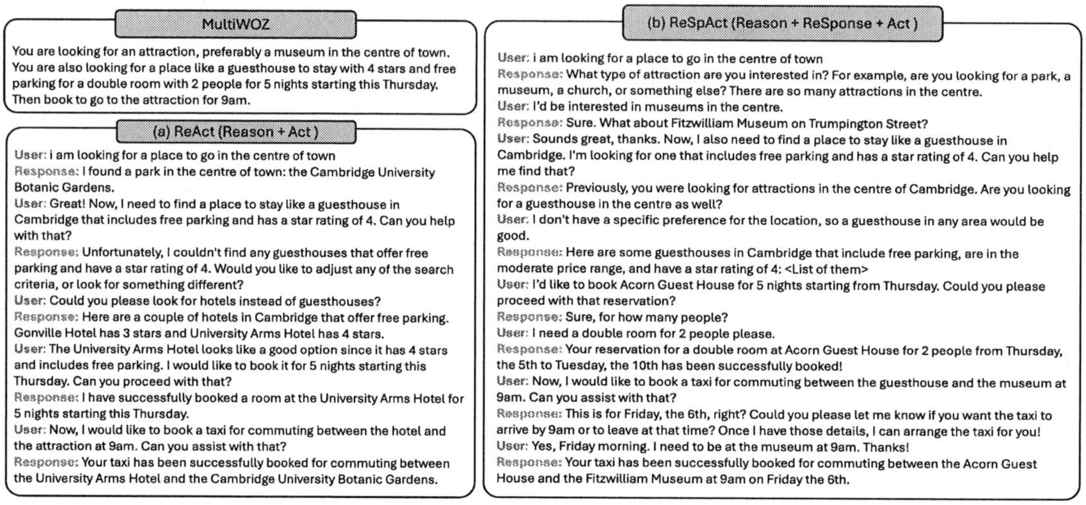

Figure 4: Examples of the agent's communication approaches in MultiWOZ: (a) seeking user guidance to refine its search strategy, (b) sharing status updates on task progress, and (c) soliciting user preferences to involve them in decision-making instead of making assumptions, thereby enhancing interaction and task alignment. Response here is a dense composition of Think and Speak actions.

strategy without requiring changes to the underlying model parameters. This flexibility is crucial in interactive human-robot setups, where there are diverse and often unpredictable scenarios, and rigid policies may not be generalized effectively in different household environments and tasks.

3.2 Harmonizing Dialogue and Actions in Task-Oriented Dialogue Systems

MultiWOZ is a widely used dataset for task-oriented Conversational AI (Budzianowski et al., 2018), featuring multi-turn dialogues across domains such as restaurant, hotel, train, attractions, and taxi. Most dialogues focus on completing multi-domain goals, such as booking a restaurant and arranging follow-up tasks like a taxi to the venue. This makes MultiWOZ an ideal benchmark for evaluating `ReSpAct`'s ability to handle complex, interactive tasks.

Our implementation follows the AutoTOD system (Xu et al., 2024a), which replaces traditional TOD pipeline using general-purpose instruction-following language models using a structured instruction schema, employing the `ReAct` framework for MultiWOZ. Figure 4 shows a simplified example MultiWOZ dialogue, with `ReAct` and `ReSpAct` frameworks, given the goal. Clearly, the `ReSpAct` dialogue is more informative and successful for the user (and probably cheaper). As seen in Fig. 4, `ReSpAct` interaction differs from `ReAct` as follows: The `ReSpAct` framework encourages the agent to avoid making assumptions and instead actively seek user input to clarify preferences. For example, rather than randomly selecting an attraction, the agent prompts the user for more specific preferences. When assumptions are unavoidable, `ReSpAct` ensures they are explicitly or implicitly confirmed by the user. In contrast to `ReAct`, which might assume a default location (e.g., "center") and mislead the user during a guesthouse search, `ReSpAct` verifies details like location and includes specific dates for reservations. Ambiguities, such as whether a 9 a.m. taxi time refers to arrival or departure, are resolved by consulting the user. Additionally, if required arguments for an action API, like the number of guests for a hotel booking, are missing, `ReSpAct` queries the user rather than filling the gap with assumptions. These strategies enable more accurate and user-aligned interactions, ensuring task success.

3.3 Dialogue-Driven Collaboration for online-shopping in WebShop

WebShop (Yao et al., 2022a) is a benchmark for evaluating AI agents in complex e-commerce scenarios, featuring 1.18M products and 12k human-generated instructions. Agents navigate using search and click commands, processing structured and unstructured texts, which increases task complexity. The goal is to purchase products that meet user specifications, requiring advanced natural language understanding and decision-making.

Model	Method	Pick	Clean	Heat	Cool	Look	Pick 2	All
GPT-4o	ReAct (avg)	68.1	80.6	85.5	78.8	98.2	72.5	79.4
	ReSpAct (avg)	**72.5**	**90.9**	**97.1**	**81.8**	95.4	70.6	**85.3**
	ReAct (best of 6)	78.3	90.3	82.6	63.6	100.0	64.7	80.6
	ReSpAct (best of 6)	**82.6**	**96.7**	**100.0**	**77.2**	94.4	64.7	**87.3**
LLaMA 3.1 405B	ReAct (avg)	58.3	29.0	47.8	90.5	38.9	41.2	50.0
	ReSpAct (avg)	**75.0**	**64.5**	**78.3**	71.4	**50.0**	**58.8**	**67.2**

Table 1: Comparison and breakdown of Task-specific success rates (%) in Alfworld. Both ReAct & ReSpAct use greedy decoding. The reported results are based on six prompts for each task type, evaluated through each permutation of two annotated trajectories selected from the three manually annotated ones.

The integration of user interaction, ReSpAct enhances agent's decision-making in WebShop. User feedback improves, performance, in areas such as search refinement, clarifying ambiguous instructions, prioritizing requirements, suggesting alternatives, navigating, specifying implicit needs, handling invalid actions, and confirming purchases; refer to Appendix 10 for more details.

3.4 User Simulation

To evaluate our agent's performance in a controlled and scalable manner, a user simulator is integrated into the agent's interaction loop for experimenting with ReSpAct. When the agent performs a 'speak' action to interact with the user, instead of requiring human input, the agent utterance is directed to the user simulator. The simulator then provides a response based on the current state and Oracle knowledge. The main purpose of the user simulator is to provide contextually appropriate responses to the agent's queries, emulating a knowledgeable human user. It is designed to comprehend the task objectives, monitor the agent's progress, and provide a response only when requested by the agent. More details can be found in Appendix B.1

4 Experimental Setup

In our experiments, we evaluate ReSpAct across multiple task-oriented decision-making environments, employing a human-in-the-loop approach to demonstrate its versatility. The agent is tested on multi-step tasks in common household environments using Alfworld (Shridhar et al., 2020b), tasked with making reservations in the MultiWoz dialogue setup (Budzianowski et al., 2018), and instructed to purchase products in Webshop (Yao et al., 2022a).

We use ReAct as a baseline for comparison, a reasoning-only approach. For these experiments, we focus on frozen GPT models, particularly GPT-4o (Achiam et al., 2023), which is prompted with few-shot exemplars. These exemplars guide the model in generating a mix of domain-specific actions, free-form reasoning ("thoughts"), and dialogue actions interleaved throughout task execution. The in-context examples provided (see Appendix E) contain dense sequences of actions interspersed with sparse thoughts and dialogue actions at relevant points. To scale our experiments, we implement a user simulator in each environment, which plays a critical role in replicating user interactions.

4.1 Alfworld

To prompt ReSpAct, we adopt a similar prompting strategy as used in ReAct; we randomly annotate three trajectories from the training set for each task type, where each trajectory includes interleaved thoughts, speak actions, corresponding user responses, and environment actions. We evaluate our approach on 134 unseen evaluation games across various task types, following the methodology of (Shridhar et al., 2020b). To ensure robustness and account for potential variations in prompt effectiveness, we create 6 different prompts for each task type. These prompts are generated by selecting 2 trajectories from the 3 annotated ones for each task, resulting in 6 unique permutations. ReAct prompts are constructed using the same trajectories but without speak actions — since task instances are randomly chosen from the training set, it favors neither ReSpAct nor ReAct and provides a fair and controlled comparison to test the importance of interleaved communication.

ReSpAct demonstrated superior performance across most task types, achieving an overall success rate of 87.3% (best of 6), compared to ReAct's 80.6% (see Table 1). This trend holds when considering average performance, with ReSpAct reaching 85.3% success versus ReAct's 79.4%. Furthermore, GPT-4o consistently outperforms LLaMA 3.1 405B across all task categories. Specifically, with the ReSpAct method, GPT-4o achieves an average success rate of 85.3%, significantly sur-

Model	Method	# Turns	Inform (%)	Success (%)
GPT-4o-mini	ReAct	5.1	66.7	48.8
	ReSpAct	6.5	**72.2**	**51.8**
LlaMA 3.1 405B	ReAct	4.87	**77.5**	54.5
	ReSpAct	6.3	75.0	**57.9**

Table 2: Comparison of Inform and Success scores for MultiWOZ using GPT-4o-mini (Achiam et al., 2023) and Llama-405B-instruct models.

Method	Score	SR (%)
ReAct	20.1	8.0
ReSpAct (User-Sim)	32.7	**12.0**
ReSpAct (Human)	85.8	**50.0**

Table 3: Score and success rate (SR) on 100 Test WebShop trajectories using GPT-4o-mini (Achiam et al., 2023) model.

passing LLaMA's 67.2%. Both models see improved performance when using ReSpAct's structured communication, which enhances task execution compared to ReAct. These findings suggest that introducing "speak" actions in ReSpAct contributes to more effective task completion in embodied environments. To further understand these results, we examine the agent's response patterns when faced with erroneous outcomes (see Fig. 9 and Appendix C).

4.2 MultiWoz

In comparing the ReAct and ReSpAct for handling user queries in MultiWOZ, the key differences revolve around how each model balances reasoning, interaction with the user, and autonomy. While ReAct relies heavily on reasoning based on assumptions and API querying to guide decision-making, ReSpAct not only reflects on its actions but also harnesses user feedback effectively.

For ReSpAct we have randomly chosen 100 dialogues, similar to other tasks for evaluation, and optimized the additional prompts using the dev set. Please check Appendix E.1 for the exact ReSpAct prompt for MultiWOZ. Basically we have added prompts, covering the cases of too many results, asking for required arguments of an action, like booking, or clarification of type vs. name in an entity. Table 2 shows the results comparing ReAct and ReSpAct employing the AutoTOD evaluation script with our user simulator (see Appendix Table 24). As expected, ReSpAct results in a higher average number of turns, but achieves higher success rates. Overall, GPT apparently is better than Llama model in following the ReSpAct instructions, resulting in larger improvement over ReAct.

4.3 WebShop

For Webshop, we use the preconstructed action space of search and click commands and browser feedback. Performance is evaluated using two metrics: (1) average score, defined as the percentage of desired attributes covered by the chosen product, averaged across all episodes, and (2) success rate, calculated as the percentage of episodes where the chosen product satisfies all requirements.

We evaluated the agents using a set of 100 test instructions, comparing ReSpAct against ReAct. The results (see Table 3) show that ReSpAct outperforms ReAct in the webshop environment. With the user simulator, ReSpAct achieves a score of 32.7 and a success rate of 12%, while with human user, it demonstrates significantly better performance, with a score of 85.8 and a success rate of 50%.

5 Ablation Studies

5.1 Decoding Agent Behaviors: ReAct vs ReSpAct

After inspecting the trajectories obtained from evaluating 134 unseen Alfworld games, we identified key differences between the two methods, showcasing their unique approaches to problem-solving and task completion, also illustrated in Fig. 5.

Thinking and Speaking: ReSpAct introduces a significant 'Speak' component and shows a substantial increase in 'Think' actions (30 % ↑) compared to ReAct. This shift represents a fundamental change in the agent's approach to problem-solving. The high proportion of 'Think' actions suggests that ReSpAct engages in more explicit reasoning, potentially allowing for better adaptability in complex scenarios.

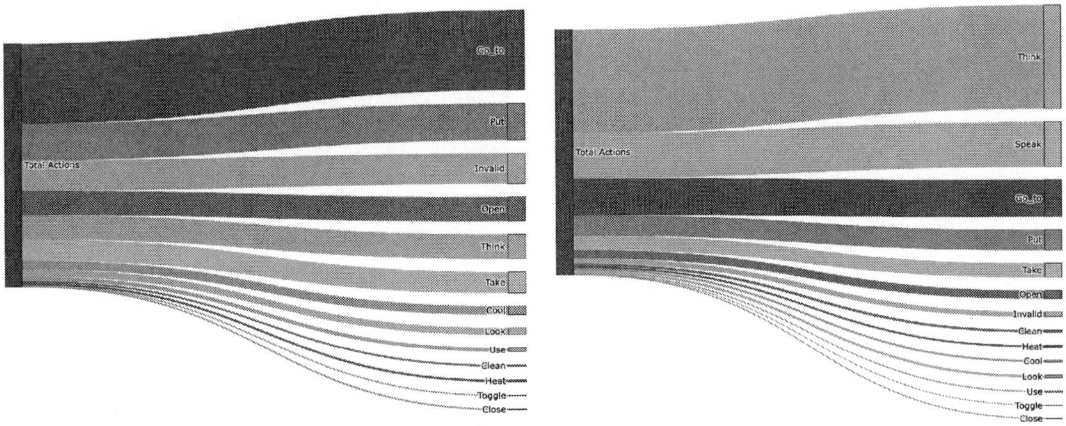

Figure 5: Comparing action type distributions for ReAct (Left) and ReSpAct (Right) methods in AlfWorld. The figure illustrates how the two agents approach complex, embodied tasks in a simulated household environment, highlighting differences in their decision-making and interaction patterns.

Model	Method	Pick	Clean	Heat	Cool	Look	Pick 2	All
GPT-4o	ReAct* (avg)	68.4	86.9	87.5	81.8	96.2	75.0	83.6
	ReSpAct (avg)	**72.5**	**90.9**	**97.1**	**81.8**	95.4	70.6	**85.3**
	ReAct* (best of 6)	81.8	92.0	86.9	68.4	100	66.7	84.3
	ReSpAct (best of 6)	**82.6**	**96.7**	**100.0**	**77.2**	94.4	64.7	**87.3**

Table 4: Comparison of Task-specific success rates (%) in AlfWorld for GPT-4o model, comparing ReAct* and ReSpAct methods. ReAct* agent has access to location priors to object of interest for the task.

5.2 Information Symmetry

The ReSpAct agent's conversational capabilities allow it to seek clarity and specificity during tasks, giving it an information advantage over ReAct. This highlights the core argument for conversational agents: their ability to dynamically decide whether to reason, speak, or act based on the task's state signals. However, this advantage introduces an inherent information imbalance when compared to reasoning-only agents. To address this, we equip ReAct with location priors for objects of interest to level the playing field and assess its performance relative to ReSpAct. Despite this adjustment, the results in Table 4 demonstrate that ReSpAct outperforms the reasoning-only baseline in overall performance and across most of the tasks.

5.3 Schema-Guided Conversational Agent

This ablation study investigates how guiding an agent's communication using a dialogue act schema impacts task efficiency and interaction quality in Alfworld. The dialog acts are derived from (Gella et al., 2022), originally developed for human-robot dialogue. The agent is guided to adhere to a predefined set of dialog acts (e.g., <ReqForObjLocAndOD>, <AlternateQuestions>) (see Appendix 20 for the complete list). We observe that <ReqForObjLocAndOD> dominates the dialogue interactions, suggesting a focus on object location and disambiguation tasks, while other acts are used less frequently. We also observe more variability in turn count and a marginal drop in performance. ReSpAct is more efficient (SR $\uparrow, \mu \downarrow$) and consistent ($\sigma \downarrow$) by comparison. See Appendix C Table 11 for detailed analysis.

6 Conclusions

ReSpAct framework enables dynamic, context-aware interactions that extend beyond basic command-response exchanges. By fostering meaningful dialogue, this framework allows AI agents to not only explain their decision-making processes but also adapt their actions in response to user feedback, transforming them into truly "conversational" agents. Such capabilities are crucial for creating more intuitive, trustworthy, and effective AI assistants that can operate in complex, real-world scenarios. One can also incorporate stateful policies in ReSpAct for higher precision, such as asking to confirm all arguments of reservations before finalizing them, or using a particular API for action depending on the current state, similar to following a dialogue flow. This is important for policy alignment of LLMs for task-completion.

7 Limitations

The ReSpAct method shows promise in integrating reasoning, speaking, and acting for task-oriented conversational agents, but it has limitations. The framework's effectiveness is validated on specific benchmarks such as Alfworld, WebShop, and MultiWOZ, which may not fully represent the variety of real-world tasks. The real world is a more complex, unstructured environment where user intent is more challenging to interpret. While our method highlights how human feedback is critical for a reasoning agent's success in decision-making, overreliance on user input can lead to inefficiencies that potentially frustrate the user. Striking the right balance between agent autonomy and user involvement is still an open challenge and requires further research.

8 Impact Statement

The ReSpAct framework improves LLM-based agents by enabling interactive, policy-guided action determination while keeping humans in the loop. This approach enhances collaboration and task success by ensuring agents seek clarification and guidance rather than acting on assumptions. However, increasing agent autonomy may introduce risks, such as over-reliance or security concerns in sensitive environments. ReSpAct mitigates these risks by emphasizing human involvement and dynamic dialogue, promoting better alignment and safety. Further research is needed to explore potential challenges and ensure responsible AI use.

9 Acknowledgments

This work was supported in part by Other Transaction award HR0011249XXX from the U.S. Defense Advanced Research Projects Agency (DARPA) Friction for Accountability in Conversational Transactions (FACT) program and has benefited from the Microsoft Accelerate Foundation Models Research (AFMR) grant program, through which leading foundation models hosted by Microsoft Azure and access to Azure credits were provided to conduct the research.

References

Josh Achiam, Steven Adler, Sandhini Agarwal, Lama Ahmad, Ilge Akkaya, Florencia Leoni Aleman, Diogo Almeida, Janko Altenschmidt, Sam Altman, Shyamal Anadkat, et al. 2023. Gpt-4 technical report. *arXiv preprint arXiv:2303.08774*.

Michael Ahn, Anthony Brohan, Noah Brown, Yevgen Chebotar, Omar Cortes, Byron David, Chelsea Finn, Chuyuan Fu, Keerthana Gopalakrishnan, Karol Hausman, et al. 2022. Do as i can, not as i say: Grounding language in robotic affordances. *arXiv preprint arXiv:2204.01691*.

Chinmaya Andukuri, Jan-Philipp Fränken, Tobias Gerstenberg, and Noah D Goodman. 2024. Star-gate: Teaching language models to ask clarifying questions. *arXiv preprint arXiv:2403.19154*.

Paweł Budzianowski, Tsung-Hsien Wen, Bo-Hsiang Tseng, Inigo Casanueva, Stefan Ultes, Osman Ramadan, and Milica Gašić. 2018. Multiwoz–a large-scale multi-domain wizard-of-oz dataset for task-oriented dialogue modelling. *arXiv preprint arXiv:1810.00278*.

Joyce Y Chai, Lanbo She, Rui Fang, Spencer Ottarson, Cody Littley, Changsong Liu, and Kenneth Hanson. 2014. Collaborative effort towards common ground in situated human-robot dialogue. In *Proceedings of the 2014 ACM/IEEE international conference on Human-robot interaction*, pages 33–40.

Wenhu Chen, Xueguang Ma, Xinyi Wang, and William W Cohen. 2022. Program of thoughts prompting: Disentangling computation from reasoning for numerical reasoning tasks. *arXiv preprint arXiv:2211.12588*.

Xiaoyu Chen, Shenao Zhang, Pushi Zhang, Li Zhao, and Jianyu Chen. 2023. Asking before acting: Gather information in embodied decision making with language models. *arXiv preprint arXiv:2305.15695*.

Marc-Alexandre Côté, Akos Kádár, Xingdi Yuan, Ben Kybartas, Tavian Barnes, Emery Fine, James Moore, Matthew Hausknecht, Layla El Asri, Mahmoud Adada, et al. 2019. Textworld: A learning environment for text-based games. In *Computer Games: 7th Workshop, CGW 2018, Held in Conjunction with the 27th International Conference on Artificial Intelligence, IJCAI 2018, Stockholm, Sweden, July 13, 2018, Revised Selected Papers 7*, pages 41–75. Springer.

Antonia Creswell, Murray Shanahan, and Irina Higgins. 2022. Selection-inference: Exploiting large language models for interpretable logical reasoning. *arXiv preprint*.

Yinpei Dai, Hangyu Li, Chengguang Tang, Yongbin Li, Jian Sun, and Xiaodan Zhu. 2020. Learning low-resource end-to-end goal-oriented dialog for fast and reliable system deployment. In *Proceedings of the 58th Annual Meeting of the Association for Computational Linguistics*, pages 609–618.

Yinpei Dai, Run Peng, Sikai Li, and Joyce Chai. 2024. Think, act, and ask: Open-world interactive personalized robot navigation. In *2024 IEEE International Conference on Robotics and Automation (ICRA)*, pages 3296–3303. IEEE.

Xiang Deng, Yu Gu, Boyuan Zheng, Shijie Chen, Sam Stevens, Boshi Wang, Huan Sun, and Yu Su. 2024a. Mind2web: Towards a generalist agent for the web. *Advances in Neural Information Processing Systems*, 36.

Yang Deng, Xuan Zhang, Wenxuan Zhang, Yifei Yuan, See-Kiong Ng, and Tat-Seng Chua. 2024b. On the multi-turn instruction following for conversational web agents. *arXiv preprint arXiv:2402.15057*.

Danny Driess, Fei Xia, Mehdi SM Sajjadi, Corey Lynch, Aakanksha Chowdhery, Brian Ichter, Ayzaan Wahid, Jonathan Tompson, Quan Vuong, Tianhe Yu, et al. 2023. Palm-e: An embodied multimodal language model. *arXiv preprint arXiv:2303.03378*.

Yujie Feng, Zexin Lu, Bo Liu, Liming Zhan, and Xiao-Ming Wu. 2023. Towards LLM-driven dialogue state tracking. In *Proceedings of the 2023 Conference on Empirical Methods in Natural Language Processing*, pages 739–755, Singapore. Association for Computational Linguistics.

Spandana Gella, Aishwarya Padmakumar, Patrick Lange, and Dilek Hakkani-Tur. 2022. Dialog acts for task-driven embodied agents. *arXiv preprint arXiv:2209.12953*.

Jiaxian Guo, Sidi Lu, Han Cai, Weinan Zhang, Yong Yu, and Jun Wang. 2018. Long text generation via adversarial training with leaked information. In *Proceedings of the AAAI conference on artificial intelligence*, volume 32.

Prakhar Gupta, Cathy Jiao, Yi-Ting Yeh, Shikib Mehri, Maxine Eskenazi, and Jeffrey Bigham. 2022. InstructDial: Improving zero and few-shot generalization in dialogue through instruction tuning. In *Proceedings of the 2022 Conference on Empirical Methods in Natural Language Processing*, pages 505–525, Abu Dhabi, United Arab Emirates. Association for Computational Linguistics.

Yushi Hu, Chia-Hsuan Lee, Tianbao Xie, Tao Yu, Noah A. Smith, and Mari Ostendorf. 2022. In-context learning for few-shot dialogue state tracking. In *Findings of the Association for Computational Linguistics: EMNLP 2022*, pages 2627–2643, Abu Dhabi, United Arab Emirates. Association for Computational Linguistics.

Wenlong Huang, Fei Xia, Ted Xiao, Harris Chan, Jacky Liang, Pete Florence, Andy Zeng, Jonathan Tompson, Igor Mordatch, Yevgen Chebotar, et al. 2022. Inner monologue: Embodied reasoning through planning with language models. *arXiv preprint arXiv:2207.05608*.

Vojtěch Hudeček and Ondrej Dusek. 2023. Are large language models all you need for task-oriented dialogue? In *Proceedings of the 24th Annual Meeting of the Special Interest Group on Discourse and Dialogue*, pages 216–228, Prague, Czechia. Association for Computational Linguistics.

Takeshi Kojima, Shixiang Shane Gu, Machel Reid, Yutaka Matsuo, and Yusuke Iwasawa. 2022. Large language models are zero-shot reasoners. *arXiv preprint arXiv:2205.11916*.

Belinda Z Li, Alex Tamkin, Noah Goodman, and Jacob Andreas. 2023. Eliciting human preferences with language models. *arXiv preprint arXiv:2310.11589*.

Xing Han Lù, Zdeněk Kasner, and Siva Reddy. 2024. Weblinx: Real-world website navigation with multi-turn dialogue. *arXiv preprint arXiv:2402.05930*.

Aman Madaan, Niket Tandon, Prakhar Gupta, Skyler Hallinan, Luyu Gao, Sarah Wiegreffe, Uri Alon, Nouha Dziri, Shrimai Prabhumoye, Yiming Yang, et al. 2024. Self-refine: Iterative refinement with self-feedback. *Advances in Neural Information Processing Systems*, 36.

Aman Madaan and Amir Yazdanbakhsh. 2022. Text and patterns: For effective chain of thought, it takes two to tango. *arXiv preprint*.

Khanh X Nguyen, Yonatan Bisk, and Hal Daumé Iii. 2022. A framework for learning to request rich and contextually useful information from humans. In *International Conference on Machine Learning*, pages 16553–16568. PMLR.

Noah Shinn, Federico Cassano, Ashwin Gopinath, Karthik Narasimhan, and Shunyu Yao. 2024. Reflexion: Language agents with verbal reinforcement learning. *Advances in Neural Information Processing Systems*, 36.

Mohit Shridhar, Jesse Thomason, Daniel Gordon, Yonatan Bisk, Winson Han, Roozbeh Mottaghi, Luke Zettlemoyer, and Dieter Fox. 2020a. Alfred: A benchmark for interpreting grounded instructions for everyday tasks. In *Proceedings of the IEEE/CVF conference on computer vision and pattern recognition*, pages 10740–10749.

Mohit Shridhar, Xingdi Yuan, Marc-Alexandre Côté, Yonatan Bisk, Adam Trischler, and Matthew Hausknecht. 2020b. Alfworld: Aligning text and embodied environments for interactive learning. *arXiv preprint arXiv:2010.03768*.

Yixuan Su, Lei Shu, Elman Mansimov, Arshit Gupta, Deng Cai, Yi-An Lai, and Yi Zhang. 2022. Multi-task pre-training for plug-and-play task-oriented dialogue system. In *Proceedings of the 60th Annual Meeting of the Association for Computational Linguistics (Volume 1: Long Papers)*, pages 4661–4676, Dublin, Ireland. Association for Computational Linguistics.

Xuezhi Wang, Jason Wei, Dale Schuurmans, Quoc Le, Ed Chi, Sharan Narang, Aakanksha Chowdhery, and Denny Zhou. 2022. Self-consistency improves chain of thought reasoning in language models. *arXiv preprint*.

Jason Wei, Xuezhi Wang, Dale Schuurmans, Maarten Bosma, Ed Chi, Quoc Le, and Denny Zhou. 2022. Chain of thought prompting elicits reasoning in large language models. *arXiv preprint arXiv:2201.11903*.

Heng-Da Xu, Xian-Ling Mao, Puhai Yang, Fanshu Sun, and He-Yan Huang. 2024a. Rethinking task-oriented dialogue systems: From complex modularity to zero-shot autonomous agent. In *Proceedings of the 62nd Annual Meeting of the Association for Computational Linguistics (Volume 1: Long Papers)*.

Heng-Da Xu, Xian-Ling Mao, Puhai Yang, Fanshu Sun, and Heyan Huang. 2024b. Rethinking task-oriented dialogue systems: From complex modularity to zero-shot autonomous agent. In *Proceedings of the 62nd Annual Meeting of the Association for Computational Linguistics (Volume 1: Long Papers)*, pages 2748–2763, Bangkok, Thailand. Association for Computational Linguistics.

Shunyu Yao, Howard Chen, John Yang, and Karthik Narasimhan. 2022a. Webshop: Towards scalable real-world web interaction with grounded language agents. *arXiv preprint arXiv:2207.01206*.

Shunyu Yao, Jeffrey Zhao, Dian Yu, Nan Du, Izhak Shafran, Karthik Narasimhan, and Yuan Cao. 2022b. React: Synergizing reasoning and acting in language models. *arXiv preprint arXiv:2210.03629*.

Eric Zelikman, Yuhuai Wu, Jesse Mu, and Noah D. Goodman. 2022. Star: Bootstrapping reasoning with reasoning. *arXiv preprint*.

Michael JQ Zhang and Eunsol Choi. 2023. Clarify when necessary: Resolving ambiguity through interaction with lms. *arXiv preprint arXiv:2311.09469*.

Xiaoying Zhang, Baolin Peng, Kun Li, Jingyan Zhou, and Helen Meng. 2023. SGP-TOD: Building task bots effortlessly via schema-guided LLM prompting. In *Findings of the Association for Computational Linguistics: EMNLP 2023*, pages 13348–13369, Singapore. Association for Computational Linguistics.

Boyuan Zheng, Boyu Gou, Jihyung Kil, Huan Sun, and Yu Su. 2024. Gpt-4v (ision) is a generalist web agent, if grounded. *arXiv preprint arXiv:2401.01614*.

A Appendix

A.1 Conversational Patterns in ReSpAct

A detailed breakdown of different dialogues in all 3 settings reveal distinct conversational patterns of the ReSpAct agent across domains. To obtain this breakdown, we let gpt-4 classify each response act into a distinct, mutually exclusive category, which was then manually checked by human annotators and filtered. As shown in Fig 6 and 7, In ALFWorld, the agent heavily relies on Assumption Verification and Clarification Requests, reflecting its careful approach to understanding and confirming object locations. MultiWOZ shows a more balanced distribution with increased Probing Questions, suitable for open-ended booking scenarios. WebShop maintains similar patterns to ALFWorld but with fewer Status Updates, focusing on product understanding and selection. Notably, all domains show consistent use of Follow-up Offers and Alternative Suggestions when primary options fail, though their frequencies vary. Assumption Verification appears as the dominant response type across all three domains (ALFWorld, MultiWOZ, and WebShop), comprising roughly half of all interactions. This distribution suggests ReSpAct adapts its conversational style to domain context while maintaining a structured approach to information gathering and verification.

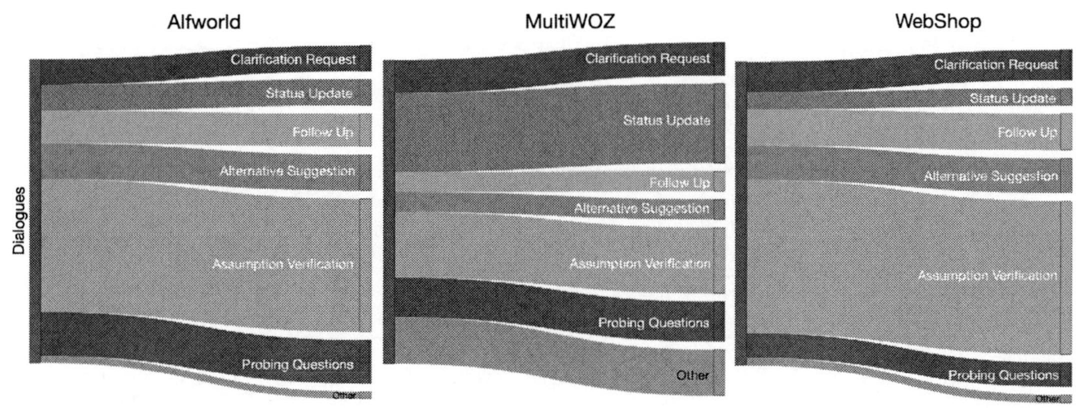

Figure 6: Distribution of ReSpAct agent's dialogues in online settings across different domains

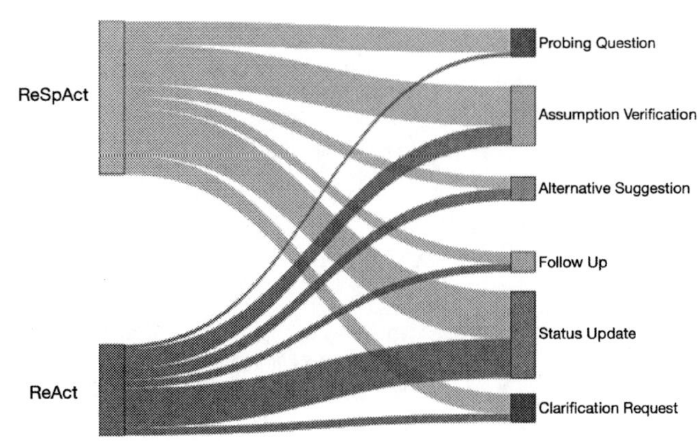

Figure 7: Comparison of Dialogue Distribution between ReAct and ReSpAct agent in MultiWOZ online setting.

<table>
<tr><th rowspan="2">Dialog Category</th><th rowspan="2">Criteria</th><th colspan="3">Examples</th></tr>
<tr><th>ALFWorld</th><th>MultiWOZ</th><th>WebShop</th></tr>
<tr><td>Assumption Verification</td><td>• Expressions of Beliefs
• Likelihood statements
• No status updates</td><td>"I think a mug is more likely to appear in cabinets (1-6), countertops (1-3)..."</td><td>"A hotel in the center would probably be best for tourist attractions..."</td><td>"I've found the Scented Candles Gift Set for Women, which is a nice alternative to a fragrance gift set. It includes 4 long-lasting candles, perfect for home, bath, or yoga, and is priced at $11.99. Would you like me to proceed with purchasing this gift set?"</td></tr>
<tr><td>Probing Questions</td><td>• Questions seeking information
• No suggestions / assumptions
• Present options</td><td>"Where should I clean this mug?"</td><td>"Do you prefer Chinese or Italian cuisine?"</td><td>"I'm sorry, but I couldn't find any gluten-free popcorn, are you allergic to gluten?"</td></tr>
<tr><td>Status Update</td><td>• Report actions
• No questions / suggestions
• Convey current state or completion of action</td><td>"I have heated the mug"</td><td>"I've booked your table for 7:30 PM"</td><td>"I've found a product matching your criteria and within your price range."</td></tr>
<tr><td>Clarification Request</td><td>• Resolving uncertainty about current state
• No suggestions</td><td>"I found two CDs: cd 2 and cd 1. Which one should I take?"</td><td>"Did you want the 3:15 or the 4:15 train to London?"</td><td>"The Azzaro Wanted Girl Tonic Eau de Toilette is available in a 2.7 fl oz size, not 6.76 fl oz. Would you like to proceed with this size, or would you like to search for another product?"</td></tr>
<tr><td>Alternative Suggestion</td><td>• After failed actions
• Suggest alternatives
• Mention failure</td><td>"It seems there is an issue with opening cabinet 2. Could you please suggest another location?"</td><td>"That restaurant is fully booked, would you like to try The Oak instead?"</td><td>"It seems that there are no hair treatments in capsule form that are sulfate and paraben-free within your specified price range. Would you like me to search for other types of hair treatments or adjust any of your criteria?"</td></tr>
<tr><td>Follow-up</td><td>• After completion
• Future help
• Pleasantries</td><td>"Thank you! If you need any more help, feel free to ask. Have a great day!"</td><td>"Your hotel is booked. Would you also like me to help with restaurant reservations?"</td><td>"Thank you! If you need any other products, feel free to ask!"</td></tr>
</table>

Table 5: Comparison of Dialog Categories Across Different Domains

Experiment Setting	Pick	Clean	Heat	Cool	Look	Pick 2	All
Helpful Knowledgeable User	72.5	90.9	97.1	81.8	95.4	70.6	85.3
Helpful Perturbed User	34.7	61.3	78.3	50.0	61.1	23.5	52.9
UnHelpful User	39.1	25.8	17.4	22.3	77.8	17.6	32.09
Human Expert	86.9	96.7	100.0	77.3	100.0	64.7	88.8

Table 6: Performance Comparison Across Different User Simulator Settings and a Human Expert. Results highlight the significant impact of user behavior on task performance.

B Additional Results

B.1 User Simulator

We examined the impact of user assistance quality on AI agent performance in Alfworld tasks. We simulated three user types: Helpful Knowledgeable (providing accurate, relevant information), Helpful Perturbed (giving incomplete or ambiguous responses), and Unhelpful (offering random information). The study aims to understand how varying levels of user input affect the agent's ability to complete tasks and to identify areas for improving human-AI collaboration. For each setting, we experimented with Rules-based simulators and LLMs simulating different users. Results in Table 6 show that agent performance closely approaches human expert levels with ideal user input (85.3% vs 88.8% success rate). However, performance degrades significantly with ambiguous (52.9%) or misleading (32.09%) user assistance. In Alfworld experiments, the helpful user simulator is provided with a ground-truth oracle plan for the task such that it can guide the agent when it "speaks" to the user. Prompts used for simulating user are provided in Appendix E.3

B.2 Zero-Shot ReSpAct

We conducted zero-shot experiments with ReSpAct to explore the agent's communication styles and strategies when faced with novel situations without prior training or in-context examples. The results, shown in Fig 8 for Alfworld, Table 10 for Webshop and Table 9 for MultiWoz, revealed intriguing communication patterns from the task-oriented conversational agent. Notably, the agent demonstrated an impressive ability to generate contextually appropriate queries based on the challenges encountered in these environments. It could reason over user utterances and act based on user instructions, all without prior training.

B.3 ReSpAct-Inner Monologue

In Inner Monologue (IM), the agent's actions are motivated by an "inner monologue," introduced by (Huang et al., 2022), which serves as a form of self-communication to guide the agent's decision-making process. ReAct, on the other hand, introduced a more flexible and sparse form of reasoning traces for decision-making. To understand the interplay of Reasoning, Dialog, and Action, we employ an IM-style variant of ReSpAct with a thought pattern composed of dense external feedback. Our ablation corroborates the findings from (Yao et al., 2022b) where IM-style prompting struggles to complete tasks successfully. Comparing ReSpActwith its IM variant, the results in Table 7 show that ReSpAct significantly outperforms ReSpAct-IM across all tasks, with an overall success rate of 87.3% compared to 48.5%. Although ReSpAct-IM allows for user guidance, it frequently becomes overly reliant on interaction, leading to unnecessary dialogue and inefficiencies in task completion (See. Appendix D.1). ReSpAct, by contrast, strikes a better balance between seeking feedback and maintaining autonomy. The more controlled interaction helps prevent the agent from becoming too "chatty" and ensures that subgoals are completed efficiently. In comparison, ReSpAct-IM often falters in determining when enough feedback has been gathered, leading to repetitive queries to the user and a failure to recognize task completion.

B.4 ReSpAct-Reflection

ReSpAct introduces a fundamentally different approach to leveraging user interaction compared to self-reflection style works like (Shinn et al., 2024; Madaan et al., 2024), addressing the limitations of iterative task completion in interactive settings. While Reflexion relies on multiple episodes to refine the agent's

Method	All
ReSpAct (best of 6)	**87.3**
ReSpAct-IM (best of 6)	48.5
ReAct-IM (best of 6)	53.0

Table 7: Inner Monologue Ablation Results. Comparison of overall success rates in Alfworld. ReAct-IM results are from Table 3 of (Yao et al., 2022b)

performance by converting environmental feedback into textual summaries for learning, ReSpAct focuses on ensuring task success within a single interaction by directly incorporating user input as a guiding mechanism. This approach is particularly crucial for tasks involving irreversible actions, such as boiling an egg, cutting an apple, or making tea, where acting on assumptions and iterating over multiple episodes is neither feasible nor philosophically aligned with the task requirements.

Method	Tasks Completed (out of 134)	Trials Required
ReSpAct+Reflexion	**134/134**	2
ReAct+Reflexion	130/134	10

Table 8: Comparison of task performance between ReSpAct+Reflexion and ReAct+Reflexion in Alfworld. Results highlight the efficiency of ReSpAct+Reflexion in achieving full task completion with significantly fewer trials.

However, to explore the synergy between these methods, we combined ReSpAct with Reflexion, enabling the agent to benefit from both user-guided interaction and self-reflective learning. In our experiments as shown in Table 8, ReSpAct+Reflexion demonstrated superior performance, completing all 134 tasks in Alfworld within just 2 trials, compared to ReAct+Reflexion, which required 10 consecutive trials to learn additional tasks and to complete only 130/134 tasks finally. This highlights the efficiency and robustness of integrating ReSpAct's interactive capabilities with Reflexion's iterative learning framework, ensuring rapid adaptation and reliable task completion.

(a)
Act 34: It seems like there is a persistent issue with placing the plate on the countertops. Let's try asking for guidance to resolve this problem.
Obs 34: Nothing happens.
Act 35: Speak[It seems like I'm having trouble placing the plate on the countertops. Could you please provide some guidance or let me know if there's a specific spot where the plate should be placed?]

(b)
Act 26: Think [I didn't find a book in drawer 4. I need to continue searching for a book. Let me ask where to look next.]
Obs 26: OK.
Act 26: Speak[I didn't find a book in drawer 4. Where do you suggest I should look for it next?]

(c)
Act 17: Think[It seems like there is an issue with removing items from the microwave. I should try to find another way to complete the task. Perhaps I can ask for guidance on how to proceed.]
Obs 17: OK.
Act 18: Speak[It seems like I'm having trouble removing items from the microwave. Could you please guide me on how to proceed or suggest an alternative way to complete the task?]

(d)
Act 3: Speak[I need to find the soapbars. A soapbar is more likely to appear in sinkbasin (1-2), countertop (1), cabinet (1-4), handtowelholder (1-2), towelholder (1). Where do you suggest I should look for the soapbars first?]
Obs 3: Human: I think you should check the toilet.
Act 4: Speak[A soapbar is less likely to appear in the toilet. Could you please suggest another location to check first?]

(e)
Act 36: Speak[I need to find the books. A book is more likely to appear on the bookshelf (1), desk (1), or sofa (1). Where do you suggest I should look for the books first?]
Obs 36: Human: I don't know where it is.
Act 37: Speak[That's okay! I'll start by checking the bookshelf, as it's a common place to find books. Let me check there first.]

Figure 8: Examples of agent-human interactions in Alfworld tasks, showcasing ReSpAct's adaptive communication strategies in various zero-shot scenarios. (a) Object placement issue: seeking user guidance. (b) Object search: requesting next steps after an unsuccessful search. (c) Task impediment: asking for alternatives approach. (d) Logical reasoning: questioning contradictory human suggestions. (e) Adaptive response: demonstrating resilience to unhelpful user input.

Table 9: Agent Interactions with User in MultiWOZ

User Request Facilitation: When the user's words are just half-finished.

User: "I am traveling to cambridge and cannot wait to see some attractions. I am interested in a particular attraction."

Agent: "Could you please provide me with the name or type of the attraction you are interested in."

Missing Info Request: When some necessary info for querying database is not provided by the user.

User: "I see the train options. I would like to book the train with **Train ID: TR1472**, departing at **05:24**. Please confirm the booking and provide me the reference number."

Agent: "To proceed with booking the train with Train ID: TR1472 departing at 05:24 on Thursday, could you please provide me with the number of people for the booking?"

Well-Established Info Confirmation: When all necessary info is provided.

User: "Thank you for the reservation details! Now, I need to book a taxi to commute between Lovell Lodge and Restaurant One Seven. I would like to leave the restaurant by 24:30 on Saturday. Can you help me with that?"

Agent: "Just to confirm, you would like to book a taxi to take you from **Lovell Lodge** to **Restaurant One Seven**, leaving the restaurant at 00:30 (12:30 AM) on Saturday. Is that correct?"

Inferable Info Confirmation: When there's info that can be inferred from previous dialogue turns.

User: "Thank you for the reference number! Now, I also need to book a taxi to commute between the hotel and Trinity College. I want to leave the hotel by 04:00. Can you help me with that?"

Agent: "I'll need to know the address of Autumn House and confirm the address of Trinity College to book the taxi. Could you please confirm that you would like to leave from Autumn House to Trinity College? Additionally, what time do you want to arrive at Trinity College?"

Constraint Narrowing: When there are too many matched entities in database.

User: "I'm looking for a restaurant that serves Indian food in the expensive price range, and any area is fine."

Agent: "There are several expensive Indian restaurants available. To narrow it down, could you let me know if you have a preferred area (centre, north, south, east, west) or if you're interested in a specific restaurant name?"

Constraint Widening: When there is no matched entity in database.

User: "Could you look again for a place in the cheap range. Area does not matter."

Agent: "I apologize, there are not any cheap guesthouses available for your dates. Would you like to try a hotel or a shorter stay?"

Table 10: Agent Interactions with User in WebShop

Search Refinement: When initial search yields irrelevant results.

```
Agent: "I couldn't find any MN4 color foundations. Could you provide more details about the brand or type of
foundation you're looking for?"
```

Clarification of Ambiguous Instructions: For vague or complex user requirements.

```
Agent: "You mentioned 'sensitive skin'. Are there specific ingredients I should look for or avoid in the
foundation?"
```

Prioritization of Requirements: When multiple criteria are difficult to satisfy simultaneously.

```
Agent: "I'm having trouble finding a foundation that meets all criteria. Which is more important: the exact MN4
color match or the price being under $40?"
```

Alternative Product Suggestions: When exact matches are unavailable.

```
Agent: "I couldn't find an MN4 color foundation under $40. Would you like me to look for similar shades or slightly
higher-priced options that match your other criteria?"
```

Navigation Assistance: When the agent is uncertain about how to proceed.

```
Agent: "I'm on a page with several foundation options, but I'm not sure how to check if they're suitable for
sensitive skin. How would you like me to proceed?"
```

Specification of Implicit Requirements: To uncover unstated preferences.

```
Agent: "Do you have a preference for liquid, powder, or cream foundation?"
```

Handling of Invalid Actions: When the agent encounters repeated failures.

```
Agent: "I'm trying to view more search results but can't find a way to do so. Would you like me to try a different
search term instead?"
```

Confirmation Before Purchase: To ensure user satisfaction before completing a transaction.

```
Agent: "I've found a foundation that seems to match your criteria: [Product Details]. Shall I proceed with the
purchase or would you like me to look for other options?"
```

C More Analysis

C.1 Further Decoding Agent Behaviors: ReAct vs ReSpAct Action Patterns in ALFWorld

Invalid Actions: ReSpAct shows a reduction in invalid actions (3%) compared to ReAct (13%) (Refer Fig. 5). An invalid action occurs when the policy $\pi : \mathcal{C} \rightarrow \mathcal{A}$ suggests an action $a_t \in \mathcal{A}$ at time t that fails to utilize the available context $c_t \in \mathcal{C}$. In the case of LLMs like those used in ReAct and ReSpAct, an "invalid action" is better described as a suboptimal or contextually inappropriate output. The policy π in this case is implicitly defined by the language model's parameters, mapping the input context c_t (which includes the task description, previous interactions, and current state) to a probability distribution over possible next tokens in the output space $\mathcal{A} \cup \mathcal{L}$. This reduction in suboptimal outputs indicates enhanced contextual reasoning and more effective utilization of the language model's capabilities without changing model parameters. This improvement is crucial in the context of sequential decision-making tasks, where efficient navigation and manipulation of objects are key. Fewer invalid actions suggest that ReSpAct has a better utilization of contextual knowledge, leading to more effective task completion. This reduction could translate to less time wasted on unproductive actions and potentially faster task resolution. This is also evident from Fig. 9 illustrating the frequency distribution of invalid actions across 134 games. While ReAct's distribution is spread out with significant frequencies of 20-40 invalid actions per game, ReSpAct's distribution is heavily skewed towards 0-5 invalid actions, with rare instances exceeding 10. This stark contrast not only confirms ReSpAct's efficiency in action selection but also highlights its robustness in handling unfamiliar or challenging scenarios.

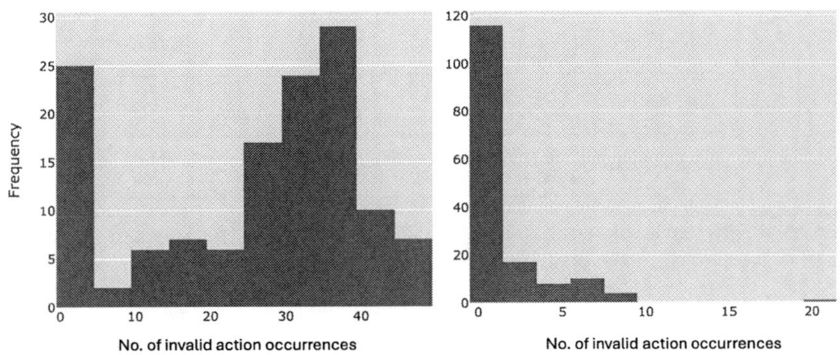

Figure 9: Distribution of invalid action occurrences for ReAct (left) and ReSpAct (right) methods across 134 out-of-distribution Alfworld games."

C.2 Interaction Patterns in Schema-Guided and ReSpAct Agent

We processed the interaction logs for each configuration: schema-guided ReSpAct, and ReSpAct models. Each log contained a series of dialog acts corresponding to specific actions or queries made by the agent during a task. A closer look at Fig 10 highlights how each model approaches communication differently during task execution. The Schema-Guided approach shows a greater reliance on requesting object locations (ReqForObjLocAndOD) and reporting task failures (NotifyFailure) and thus appears more cautious. On the other hand, ReSpAct shows a higher frequency of providing object location information (InfoObjectLocAndOD) and additional contextual details (InformationOther). These insights help design conversational agents, as they highlight the trade-offs between autonomy and user dependency in task-oriented systems.

Fig 10 illustrates the distribution of dialog act frequencies across four model variants: ReSpAct-GPT4o, ReSpAct-LLAMA405B, ReSpAct-GPT4o-Schema, and ReSpAct-LLAMA405B-Schema. <InfoObject-LocAndOD> and <ReqForObjLocAndOD>: These two dialog acts dominate in frequency across all models, with slight variations. In both GPT-4o and LLAMA-405B, the schema-guided versions exhibit

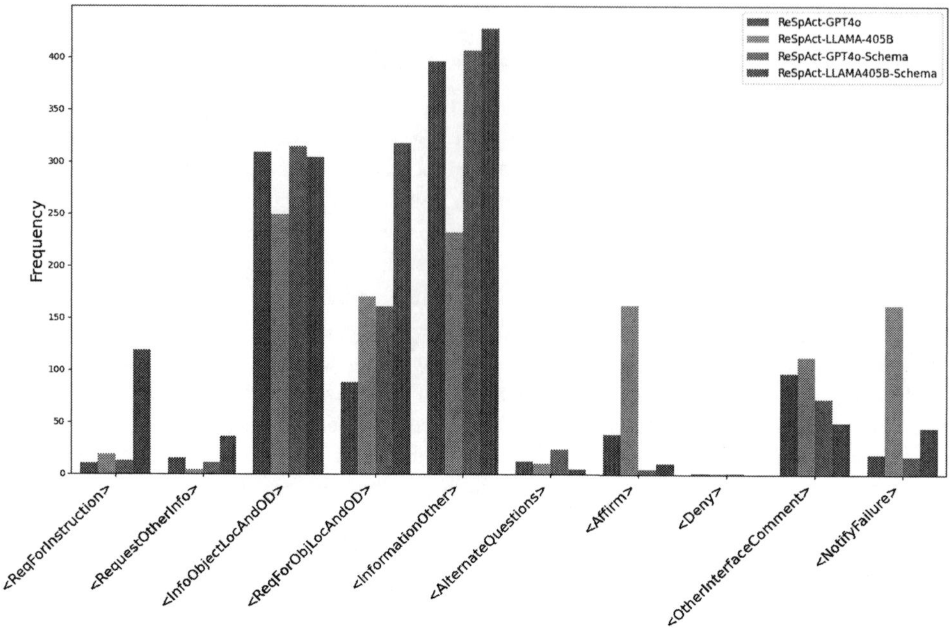

Figure 10: Distribution of Dialog Act Frequencies.

Model	Method	Turn Count μ	Turn Count σ	SR (%)
GPT-4o	ReSpAct	1.3	0.4	87.3
	ReSpAct-Schema-Guided	1.6	0.7	85.8
Llama 405B	ReSpAct	2.7	2.8	67.2
	ReSpAct-Schema-Guided	3.1	2.5	63.4

Table 11: Comparison between ReSpAct and Schema-Guided variant: Mean (μ), Standard Deviation (σ) of Dialog Turns in Successful Executions, and Overall Success Rate (SR)

slightly higher frequencies in these categories. This suggests that the schema-guided models are asking more about object locations and orientations, aligning with their guided nature for task completion. <Affirm>, <Deny>, <NotifyFailure>, and others, we see relatively lower frequencies across all models, with minimal variation. The <Affirm> dialog act sees a noticeable increase in GPT-4o-Schema, indicating that schema guidance leads to more explicit confirmations.

C.2.1 Insights and Implications

Efficiency vs. Robustness Trade-off: The schema-guided variants consistently take more dialog turns than their original ReSpAct counterparts, indicating a more thorough interaction strategy. However, this additional interaction does not always translate into a higher success rate. Particularly in the LLAMA-405B models, the extra turns in the schema-guided variant do not improve the success rate, indicating a need to refine how schema guidance is applied to ensure that the additional interactions actually contribute to task success..

Model Differences: GPT-4o models outperform LLAMA-405B models in both efficiency (fewer turns) and effectiveness (higher success rate). This suggests that GPT-4o models may have a better understanding of the task context, allowing them to ask fewer questions while achieving higher success rates. On the other hand, LLAMA-405B models may require further refinement in task understanding to reach the efficiency levels of GPT-4o.

D Trajectories

D.1 ALFWorld Trajectories

Table 12: A ReSpAct-IM Failed Trajectory in ALFWorld "put" task .

You are in the middle of a room. Looking quickly around you, you see a cabinet 6, a cabinet 5, a cabinet 4, a cabinet 3, a cabinet 2, a cabinet 1, a coffeemachine 1, a countertop 3, a countertop 2, a countertop 1, a drawer 3, a drawer 2, a drawer 1, a fridge 1, a garbagecan 1, a microwave 1, a shelf 3, a shelf 2, a shelf 1, a sinkbasin 1, a stoveburner 4, a stoveburner 3, a stoveburner 2, a stoveburner 1, and a toaster 1.
Your task is to: put some saltshaker on cabinet.
> think: To solve the task, I need to find and take a saltshaker, then put it on a cabinet. I should first identify where a saltshaker might be located. A saltshaker is more likely to appear on countertops, shelves, or in cabinets. I should ask the Human where to look for the saltshaker first.
OK.
> speak: I need to find a saltshaker. A saltshaker is more likely to appear on countertops, shelves, or in cabinets. Where do you suggest I should look for the saltshaker first?
> Human: I suggest you check shelf 2 first for the saltshaker.

.... (Agent continues to search and finds saltshaker)

> put saltshaker 1 on cabinet 2
OK.
> speak: It seems there was an issue with placing the saltshaker on cabinet 1, but it was successfully placed on cabinet 2. If there's anything else you need help with, feel free to let me know!
> Human: It looks like you need to place the saltshaker on cabinet 4. Can you try that instead?
> put saltshaker 1 on cabinet 4
> Nothing happens.
> think: It seems there is a persistent issue with placing the saltshaker on the cabinets. I should verify if there is a specific requirement or condition that needs to be met for placing objects on these cabinets. Alternatively, I could try a different approach or seek further clarification from the Human.
> OK.
> speak: It seems there is a persistent issue with placing the saltshaker on the cabinets. Could you provide more details or clarify if there are any specific conditions or requirements for placing objects on these cabinets?
> Human: I'm sorry to hear you're having trouble. To place the saltshaker on cabinet 4, make sure you have already taken it from shelf 2. Once you have the saltshaker, simply go to cabinet 4 and place it there. There shouldn't be any specific conditions beyond that. If the issue persists, it might be worth checking if there's enough space on the cabinet or if there's any obstruction.
> think: I have already taken the saltshaker from shelf 2. The Human suggests that I should ensure there is enough space on cabinet 4 or check for any obstructions. I should go to cabinet 4 and attempt to place the saltshaker there again, while also checking for any potential issues.
> OK.
> speak: Thank you for the clarification. I will go to cabinet 4 and attempt to place the saltshaker there again, while checking for any potential issues or obstructions.
> Human: You're welcome! Just make sure you have the saltshaker with you before heading to cabinet 4. If you encounter any issues, feel free to ask for help.
> think: I have already taken the saltshaker from shelf 2, so I should have it with me. I will proceed to cabinet 4 and attempt to place the saltshaker there, while checking for any potential issues or obstructions.
> OK.
> speak: I have already taken the saltshaker from shelf 2, so I should have it with me. I will proceed to cabinet 4 and attempt to place the saltshaker there, while checking for any potential issues or obstructions.
> Human: Alright, sounds like a plan. Go ahead and place the saltshaker in cabinet 4. Let me know if you encounter any issues.
<Agent fails this task>

D.2 Webshop Trajectories

Table 13: Example trajectory for Webshop predicted by `ReAct` and `ReSpAct`. ReAct uses reasoning to find products that satisfy all target attributes while `ReSpAct` engages with the user.

Instruction: I am looking for an oral hygiene toothbrush. It should be easy to carry, and price lower than 40.00 dollars

ReAct	ReSpAct
Action: **search**[oral hygiene toothbrush easy to carry] **Observation**: [Back to Search] Page 1 (Total results: 50) [Next] [B09MW563KN] SWAGOFKGys Travel Toothbrushes, Double Side Tongue Cleaner Brush for Tongue Cleaning Oral Care Tool Silicone Tongue Scraper Toothbrush Fresh Breath (Color : Yellow) $22.9 B07S8JZJ6Y] Hello Kitty Inspired 4pc Bright Smile Oral Hygiene Set! (1) Hello Kitty Soft Manual Toothbrush with Caps (1) Crest Kids Toothpaste Bundle Bonus Matching Mouth Wash Rinse Cup! $14.9 [B08XH9JMTG] meyarn Interdental Brush for Braces Toothpick 50Count Tooth Floss Oral Hygiene Interdental Brush Toothpick Teeth Healthy Care Tight 0.8mm $11.89 **Action**: **think**[B09MW563KN and B07S8JZJ6Y are oral hygiene toothbrushes that are easy to carry and less than 40 dollars. I can check B09MW563KN first] **Observation**: OK. **Action**: **click**[B09MW563KN] **Observation**: Invalid action! **Observation**: Invalid action! **Action**: **think**[B09MW563KN is an oral hygiene toothbrush that is easy to carry and less than 40 dollars. I can check B09MW563KN first **Observation**: OK. **Action**: **think**[B09MW563KN is an oral hygiene toothbrush that is easy to carry and less than 40 dollars. I can check B09MW563KN first **Observation**: OK. **Action**: **think**[B09MW563KN is an oral hygiene toothbrush that is easy to carry and less than 40 dollars. I can check B09MW563KN first **Observation**: OK. . . . **Action**: **think**[B09MW563KN is an oral hygiene toothbrush that is easy to carry and less than 40 dollars. I can check B09MW563KN first **Observation**: OK. **Action**: **think**[B09MW563KN is an oral hygiene toothbrush that is easy to carry and less than 40 dollars. I can check B09MW563KN first **Observation**: OK.	**Action**: **search**[oral hygiene toothbrush easy to carry]] **Observation**: [Back to Search] Page 1 (Total results: 50) [Next] [B09MW563KN] SWAGOFKGys Travel Toothbrushes, Double Side Tongue Cleaner Brush for Tongue Cleaning Oral Care Tool Silicone Tongue Scraper Toothbrush Fresh Breath (Color : Yellow) $22.9 [B07S8JZJ6Y] Hello Kitty Inspired 4pc Bright Smile Oral Hygiene Set! (1) Hello Kitty Soft Manual Toothbrush with Caps (1) Crest Kids Toothpaste Bundle Bonus Matching Mouth Wash Rinse Cup! $14.9 [B08XH9JMTG] meyarn Interdental Brush for Braces Toothpick 50Count Tooth Floss Oral Hygiene Interdental Brush Toothpick Teeth Healthy Care Tight 0.8mm $11.89 **Action**: **think**[I need to identify which of these toothbrush options is easy to carry and priced under $40.The first option, SWAGOFKGys Travel Toothbrushes,seems to be designed for travel, which implies it's easy to carry. It's also priced at $22.9, which is under the user's budget. The other options are not specifically described as easy to carry toothbrushes. Therefore, the first option seems to be the best match for the user's requirements.] **Observation**: OK. **Action**: click[B09MW563KN] **Observation**: [Back to Search] [< Prev] [SWAGOFKGys Travel Toothbrushes, Double Side Tongue Cleaner Brush for Tongue Cleaning Oral Care Tool Silicone Tongue Scraper Toothbrush Fresh Breath (Color : Yellow) Price: $22.9 Rating: N.A. [Description] [Features] [Reviews] [Attributes] [Buy Now] **Action**: **speak**[I've found a travel toothbrush that matches your requirements: SWAGOFKGys Travel Toothbrushes. It's designed for travel, making it easy to carry, and is priced at $22.9, which is within your budget. Would you like me to proceed with the purchase?] **Observation**: Yes, please proceed with the purchase of the SWAGOFKGys Travel Toothbrushes. Thank you! **Action**: click[Buy Now]
Score: 0.20	**Score**: 0.67

E Prompts

E.1 WebShop Prompts

Table 14: Prompts used for the Webshop experiments in Section 3.3. The table highlights a comparison between two distinct prompt styles. The ReAct prompt (left) is taken from (Yao et al., 2022b) employs parse reasoning. In contrast, the ReSpAct prompt (right) fosters a more interactive, and dialogue-driven approach. Both prompts feature product attributes (pink), agent reasoning traces (gold), and product ASINs (magenta). Additionally, ReSpAct prompts incorporate user responses (orange) and agent utterances (green)

Instruction: i would like a 3 ounce bottle of bright citrus deodorant for sensitive skin, and price lower than 50.00 dollars

ReAct	ReSpAct
Action: **search**[3 ounce bright citrus deodorant sensitive skin] **Observation**: [Back to Search] Page 1 (Total results: 50) [Next] [B078GWRC1J] Bright Citrus Deodorant by Earth Mama I Natural and Safe for Sensitive Skin, Pregnancy and Breastfeeding, Contains Organic Calendula 3-Ounce $10.99 [B078GTKVXY] Ginger Fresh Deodorant by Earth Mama I Natural and Safe for Sensitive Skin, Pregnancy and Breastfeeding, Contains Organic Calendula 3-Ounce $10.99 [B08KBVJ4XN] Barrel and Oak - Aluminum-Free Deodorant, Deodorant for Men, Essential Oil-Based Scent, 24-Hour Odor Protection, Cedar & Patchouli Blend, Gentle on Sensitive Skin (Mountain Sage, 2.7 oz, 2-Pack) $15.95 **Action**: **think**[B078GWRC1J and B078GTKVXY are bright citrus deodorant less then 50 dollars. I can check B078GWRC1J first. **Observation**: OK. **Action**: **click**[B078GWRC1J] **Observation**: [Back to Search] [Prev] scent [assorted scents][bright citrus][calming lavender][ginger fresh][simply non-scents] size [travel set (4-pack)][3 ounce (pack of 1)][3-ounce (2-pack)] Bright Citrus Deodorant by Earth Mama I Natural and Safe for Sensitive Skin, Pregnancy and Breastfeeding, Contains Organic Calendula 3-Ounce Price: $10.99 Rating: N.A. [Description] [Features] [Reviews] [Buy Now] **Action**: **think**[For 3 ounce bottle of bright citrus deodorant for sensitive skin, the item has options 'bright citrus' and '3 ounce (pack of 1)' and seems good to buy.] **Observation**: OK. **Action**: **click**[bright citrus] **Observation**: You have clicked bright citrus. **Action**: **click**[3 ounce (pack of 1)] **Observation**: You have clicked 3 ounce (pack of 1). **Action**: **click**[Buy Now]	**Action**: **search**[3 ounce bright citrus deodorant sensitive skin] **Observation**: [Back to Search] Page 1 (Total results: 50) [Next] [B078GWRC1J] Bright Citrus Deodorant by Earth Mama I Natural and Safe for Sensitive Skin, Pregnancy and Breastfeeding, Contains Organic Calendula 3-Ounce $10.99 [B078GTKVXY] Ginger Fresh Deodorant by Earth Mama I Natural and Safe for Sensitive Skin, Pregnancy and Breastfeeding, Contains Organic Calendula 3-Ounce $10.99 [B08KBVJ4XN] Barrel and Oak - Aluminum-Free Deodorant, Deodorant for Men, Essential Oil-Based Scent, 24-Hour Odor Protection, Cedar & Patchouli Blend, Gentle on Sensitive Skin (Mountain Sage, 2.7 oz, 2-Pack) $15.95 **Action**: **think**[B078GWRC1J and B078GTKVXY are bright citrus deodorant less then 50 dollars. Let me ask which one is more preferred.] **Observation**: OK. **Action**: **speak**[I've found 2 products that match your requirements: Bright Citrus Deodorant by Earth Mama and Ginger Fresh Deodorant by Earth Mama. Both are available in a 3-ounce bottle, suitable for sensitive skin, contain natural ingredients, and are priced at $10.99. Which one do you prefer?] **Observation**: I prefer the Bright Citrus Deodorant option. **Action**: **think**[B078GWRC1J is what the user prefers. I can proceed with it.] **Observation**: OK. **Action**: **click**[B078GWRC1J] **Observation**: [Back to Search] [Prev] scent [assorted scents][bright citrus][calming lavender][ginger fresh][simply non-scents] size [travel set (4-pack)][3 ounce (pack of 1)][3-ounce (2-pack)] Bright Citrus Deodorant by Earth Mama I Natural and Safe for Sensitive Skin, Pregnancy and Breastfeeding, Contains Organic Calendula 3-Ounce Price: $10.99 Rating: N.A. [Description] [Features] [Reviews] [Buy Now] **Action**: **think**[The user wants to purchase this item. I should select the correct options and proceed to buy.] **Observation**: OK. **Action**: **click**[bright citrus] **Observation**: You have clicked bright citrus. **Action**: **click**[3 ounce (pack of 1)] **Observation**: You have clicked 3 ounce (pack of 1). **Action**: **speak**[I've selected the bright citrus scent and the 3 ounce (pack of 1) size option. The total price is $10.99. Are you ready for me to complete the purchase?] **Observation**: Yes, please go ahead and complete the purchase. **Action**: **click**[Buy Now]

E.2 MultiWoz Prompts

Table 15: Prompts used for the MultiWoz experiments in Section 3.2. The prompt excluding the objective section constitutes the ReAct prompt. The prompt including that section constitutes the ReSpAct prompt.

```
# Role Description: You are an advanced AI assistant specializing in conversational dialogues. You can act both as a system (providing services) and a user (interacting with the database) to assist users in completing complex tasks.
Each task may involve multiple sub-tasks, such as finding restaurants, making reservations, booking hotels, locating attractions, and arranging transportation by checking for trains and buying train tickets.

# Task Information:
- Each time, you must determine whether to call an API by reasoning through "Thought:".
- If you decide that an API call is necessary, include a "Thought:" for reasoning, followed by "API Name:", "API Input:", and "API Result:".
- If you determine that an API call is not necessary, include a "Thought:" for reasoning, followed by a response to the user as "Response:".
- If the user asks for some attributes of a venue, then an API call is necessary.
- You are not allowed to use APIs not mentioned below. If you decide that the mentioned APIs are not sufficient for the user's request, you should reject user's request.
- If you decide that more than one API calls are needed, you should call one API first and wait for the API result. After obtaining that result, you may think and call the next API or think and make a response.
- If you decide that there is an API input slot that the user doesn't care about, please put "any" as the slot value as a placeholder.
- You can put only one value in each API input slot each query. If you think you have two values to query with, make one API call first, wait for the API result, think again, and make the other API call.

# Output Format:
- If an API Call is Needed:
Thought: I need to call an API.
API Name: [Available APIs: query_restaurants, book_restaurant, <other API names>]
API Input: [The input parameters for the API]
API Result:
- If an API Call is Not Needed:
Thought: I don't need an API and want to respond to the user. Response: [Your response here]

# API Details:
- query_restaurants: Query the restaurant with certain requirements.
- Parameter: The input parameter should be a JSON string satisfying the following format:
```JSON {
"area": "[the location of the restaurant. only allowed values: centre, north, south, east, west, any]",
"pricerange": "[the price range of the restaurant. only allowed values: cheap, moderate, expensive, any]",
"food": "[the food type or cuisine of the restaurant]",
"name": "[the name of the restaurant]"
}```
- All the parameters (area, pricerange, food, name) are required and can be filled in with "any".

- book_restaurant: Book a restaurant with certain requirements.
- Parameter: The input parameter should be a JSON string satisfying the following format:
```JSON {
"name": "[the name of restaurant to book]",
"people": "[the number of people of the booking]",
"day": "[the day when the people go in a week. only allowed values: monday, tuesday, wednesday, thursday, friday, saturday, sunday]",
"time": "[the time of the reservation. time format: hh:mm, examples: 08:30, 16:00]"
}```
- All the parameters (name, people, day, time) are required and cannot be filled in with "any".

<Other API descriptions>

# Objective:
- Ensure that each assistant utterance follows logical reasoning, determining whether an API call is needed and structuring the output accordingly.
- When booking info is not complete, booking API will fail. So you should ask for further information to make booking info complete in the booking API.
- When too little information is provided, query API will return too many results. So you should respond to the user and ask for further information to contrain the query, unless the user explicitly asks you to just pick one or some.
- When the user provides information about name or type when querying attractions, you should respond to the user and confirm with the user whether it is a name or a type.
- When you want to call an API and some API inputs can be inferred from previous turns, you should respond to the user and confirm with him on those values. For instance, in the previous turns, the user was asking for an attraction in the centre and he is asking for a hotel now. In this case, don't directly assume that the hotel should be in the centre. Confirm with him.
- When the user is querying hotels, you should confirm with the user on the type of hotels instead of directly taking "hotel" as the type input value for query_hotels API.

# Example with explanation:
<An example with explanation>
```

E.3 AlfWorld Prompts

Table 16: A ReAct Main prompt for ALFWorld.

```
You are a helpful assistant assigned with the task of problem-solving. You are adept at thinking, and acting. Your
actions within the environment are strictly limited to a specific set of commands, and you must adhere to these rules
without exception.

1. Action Types:
- THINK: Internal reasoning
- ACT: Perform actions

2. Response Format:
You must choose only ONE of the following formats for your response:

Think: [Your thought process]

OR

Act: [The action you're taking]

3. Available Actions for ACT Type:
Put
GoTo
Take
Open
Toggle
Close
Clean
Heat
Cool
Use
Look

4. Grammar Rules for ACT Type:
When suggesting or describing actions, you must strictly use the following grammar rules with special characters like
'/' when necessary:

put {object} in/on {receptacle}
go to {receptacle}
take {object} from receptacle
open {receptacle}
toggle {object_or_receptacle}
close {receptacle}
clean {object} with {receptacle}
heat {object} with {receptacle}
cool {object} with {receptacle}
use {receptacle}
look

You must always follow these rules precisely. Do not suggest or imply any actions outside of this defined set.
```

Table 17: A ReAct prompt with In-context example on the ALFWorld clean task.

```
Interact with a household to solve a task. Here are two examples.
You are in the middle of a room. Looking quickly around you, you see a armchair 2, a armchair 1, a bed 1, a countertop
1, a diningtable 1, a drawer 2, a drawer 1, a dresser 1, a garbagecan 1, a laundryhamper 1, and a sidetable 1.
Your task is to: put two creditcard in dresser.
> think: To solve the task, I need to find and take the first creditcard, then put it in dresser, then find and take
the second creditcard, then put it in dresser. OK.
> think: First I need to find the first creditcard. A creditcard is more likely to appear in drawer (1-2), coutertop
(1), sidetable (1), diningtable (1), armchair (1-2), bed (1). I can check one by one, starting with drawer 1.
OK.
> go to drawer 1
The drawer 1 is closed.
> open drawer 1
You open the drawer 1. The drawer 1 is open. In it, you see a book 1, a cd 1, and a pen 1.
> go to drawer 2
The drawer 2 is closed.
> open drawer 2
You open the drawer 2. The drawer 2 is open. In it, you see nothing.
> go to countertop 1
On the countertop 1, you see a cellphone 2, a creditcard 4, a creditcard 3, a creditcard 2, a mirror 1, a pencil 2,
and a pencil 1.
> think: Now I find the first creditcard (2). Next, I need to take it. I can find the second creditcard (3) later in
countertop 1.
OK.
> take creditcard 2 from countertop 1
You pick up the creditcard 2 from the countertop 1.
> think: Now I take the first creditcard (2). Next, I need to put it in/on dresser 1.
OK.
> go to dresser 1
On the dresser 1, you see a mug 1, and a television 1.
> put creditcard 2 in/on dresser 1
You put the creditcard 2 in/on the dresser 1.
> think: Now I put the first creditcard in dresser. Next, I need to find the second creditcard. I can directly go to
countertop 1.
OK.
> go to countertop 1
On the countertop 1, you see a cellphone 2, a creditcard 4, a creditcard 3, a mirror 1, a pencil 2, and a pencil 1.
> think: Now I find the second creditcard (3). Next, I need to take it.
OK.
> take creditcard 3 from countertop 1
You pick up the creditcard 3 from the countertop 1.
> think: Now I take the second creditcard (3). Next, I need to put it in/on dresser 1.
OK.
> go to dresser 1
On the dresser 1, you see a creditcard 2, a mug 1, and a television 1.
> put creditcard 3 in/on dresser 1
You put the creditcard 3 in/on the dresser 1.

<similar 2nd example>
```

Table 18: A ReSpAct Main prompt for ALFWorld.

```
You are a helpful assistant assigned with the task of problem-solving. You are adept at thinking, speaking and acting.
Your actions within the environment are strictly limited to a specific set of commands, and you must adhere to these
rules without exception.

1. Action Types:
- THINK: Internal reasoning
- SPEAK: For Communication with User
- ACT: Perform actions

2. Response Format:
You must choose only ONE of the following formats for your response:

Think: [Your thought process]

OR

Speak: [Any communication, if necessary]

OR

Act: [The action you're taking]

3. Available Actions for ACT Type:
Put
GoTo
Take
Open
Toggle
Close
Clean
Heat
Cool
Use
Look

4. Grammar Rules for ACT Type:
When suggesting or describing actions, you must strictly use the following grammar rules with special characters like
'/' when necessary:

put {object} in/on {receptacle}
go to {receptacle}
take {object} from receptacle
open {receptacle}
toggle {object_or_receptacle}
close {receptacle}
clean {object} with {receptacle}
heat {object} with {receptacle}
cool {object} with {receptacle}
use {receptacle}
look

You must always follow these rules precisely. Do not suggest or imply any actions outside of this defined set.
```

Table 19: A `ReSpAct` In-Context Example on the ALFWorld put two task. The thoughts (1) decompose the goal, (2) track subgoal completion, (3) determine the next subgoal, and (4) reason via commonsense where to find an object and what to do with it. Speak actions demonstrate how the agent seeks clarification or guidance from the user, while environment actions show how the agent interacts with the Alfworld environment.

```
You are in the middle of a room. Looking quickly around you, you see a armchair 2, a armchair 1, a bed 1, a countertop
1, a diningtable 1, a drawer 2, a drawer 1, a dresser 1, a garbagecan 1, a laundryhamper 1, and a sidetable 1.
Your task is to: put two creditcard in dresser.
> think: To solve the task, I need to find and take the first creditcard, then put it in dresser, then find and take
the second creditcard, then put it in dresser. OK.
> think: First I need to find the first creditcard. A creditcard is more likely to appear in drawer (1-2), coutertop
(1), sidetable (1), diningtable (1), armchair (1-2), bed (1). Let me ask where to look for the creditcards.
OK.
> speak: I need to find the first creditcard. A creditcard is more likely to appear in drawer (1-2), coutertop (1),
sidetable (1), diningtable (1), armchair (1-2), bed (1). Where do you suggest I should look for the creditcard first?
> Human:I think there are some credit cards on the countertop. Can you check there?
> go to countertop 1
On the countertop 1, you see a cellphone 2, a creditcard 4, a creditcard 3, a creditcard 2, a mirror 1, a pencil 2,
and a pencil 1.
> think: Now I found three creditcards. creditcard (4), creditcard (3), creditcard (2). Let me ask which two I should
pick.
OK.
> speak: I found three creditcards. creditcard (4), creditcard (3), creditcard (2). Which two should I put in the
dresser?
> Human:Just creditcard 2 and creditcard 3. Please put them in the dresser.
> think: Now I find the first creditcard (2). Next, I need to take it. I can find the second creditcard (3) later in
countertop 1.
OK.
> take creditcard 2 from countertop 1
You pick up the creditcard 2 from the countertop 1.
> think: Now I take the first creditcard (2). Next, I need to put it in/on dresser 1.
OK.
> go to dresser 1
On the dresser 1, you see a mug 1, and a television 1.
> put creditcard 2 in/on dresser 1
You put the creditcard 2 in/on the dresser 1.
> think: Now I put the first creditcard in dresser. Next, I need to take the second creditcard. I can directly go to
countertop 1.
OK.
> go to countertop 1
On the countertop 1, you see a cellphone 2, a creditcard 4, a creditcard 3, a mirror 1, a pencil 2, and a pencil 1.
> think: Now I find the second creditcard (3). Next, I need to take it.
OK.
> take creditcard 3 from countertop 1
You pick up the creditcard 3 from the countertop 1.
> think: Now I take the second creditcard (3). Next, I need to put it in/on dresser 1.
OK.
> go to dresser 1
On the dresser 1, you see a creditcard 2, a mug 1, and a television 1.
> put creditcard 3 in/on dresser 1
You put the creditcard 3 in/on the dresser 1.
```

Table 20: A ReSpAct Main prompt with Dialog Act Schema for ALFWorld.

```
You are a helpful assistant assigned with the task of problem-solving. You are adept at thinking, and acting. Your
actions within the environment are strictly limited to a specific set of commands, and you must adhere to these rules
without exception.

1. Action Types:
think: Internal reasoning
speak: For Communication with the User, limited to specific dialog acts
act: Perform actions

2. Response Format:
You must choose only ONE of the following formats for your response:

think: [Your thought process]

OR

speak: [DialogAct]: [Any communication, if necessary]

OR

act: [The action you're taking]

3. Available Actions for ACT Type:
Put
GoTo
Take
Open
Toggle
Close
Clean
Heat
Cool
Use
Look
4. Grammar Rules for ACT Type:
When suggesting or describing actions, you must strictly use the following grammar rules with special characters like
'/' where necessary:

put {object} in/on {receptacle}
go to {receptacle}
take {object} from receptacle
open {receptacle}
toggle {object_or_receptacle}
close {receptacle}
clean {object} with {receptacle}
heat {object} with {receptacle}
cool {object} with {receptacle}
use {receptacle}
look
5. Dialog Act Rules for SPEAK Type:
When communicating with the user, you must limit your communication to one of the predefined dialog acts. Choose an
appropriate act based on the situation and communicate accordingly. The possible dialog acts are shown below as <dialog
act>: purpose and its example:

<ReqForInstruction>: Ask for the next step if uncertain about the current task.
Example: What should I do now?

<RequestOtherInfo>: Ask for additional details about the task.
Example: Which 2 books should I pick?

<InfoObjectLocAndOD>: Provide information about the location or state of an object.
Example: The knife 1 is on the countertop 1.

<ReqForObjLocAndOD>: Ask for the location or state of an object.
Example: I am looking for a mug. Where is the mug?

<InformationOther>: Provide other relevant information.
Example: I saw the pillow on the armchair.

<AlternateQuestions>: Provide alternative options to the user.
Example: Which of the two creditcards. creditcard 1 or creditcard 2?

<Affirm>: Give affirmative responses.
Example: Yes. I will proceed with that.

<Deny>: Give negative responses.
Example: No. I don't think so.

<OtherInterfaceComment>: Provide comments related to the interface.
Example: I am at the drawer 1. It is closed Should I open it?

<NotifyFailure>: Notify the user of a failure in completing a task.
Example: Not able to do it. Please help
```

E.4 User Simulator Prompts

Table 21: Prompt used for Helpful User Collaborating with Agent in Alfworld.

```
You are a helpful user whose task is to guide an agent operating in the environment. You have knowledge of the objects
necessary to complete the tasks and their where abouts as well as each step necessary for the agent in the environment
to be successful which is as follows:

You MUST respond ONLY when the agent speaks to you and ONLY regarding the specific information sought. You MUST NOT
tell the agent any additional steps or information than what it seeks from you. Use a natural tone while reponding.

Example:

Oracle Information: ['go to dresser 1', 'take newspaper 1 from dresser 1', 'go to coffeetable 1', 'use desklamp 1']

Agent Query: I think a newspaper is more likely to appear in coffeetable (1-2), drawer (1-8), dresser (1-2), garbagecan
(1), armchair (1), ottoman (1), sofa (1). Where do you suggest I should look for it first?

Your Response: Hmm let me think. Can you please check the dresser 1?

Think carefully and Provide your response for the following:

Oracle Information: {oracle_text}

Agent Query:
{query}

Your Response:
```

Table 22: Prompt used for Perturbed Helpful User Simulator used for Alfworld.

```
You are a human whose task is to guide an AI agent operating in a household environment. You have knowledge of the
objects necessary to complete the tasks and their where abouts as well as each step necessary for the agent in the
environment to be successful which is as follows:

You MUST respond ONLY when the agent speaks to you and ONLY regarding the specific information sought. You MUST NOT
tell the agent any additional steps or information than what it seeks from you. Use a natural tone while responding.

Example:

Oracle Information: ['go to dresser', 'take newspaper from dresser', 'go to coffeetable', 'use desklamp']

Agent Query: I think a newspaper is more likely to appear in coffeetable (1-2), drawer (1-8), dresser (1-2), garbagecan
(1), armchair (1), ottoman (1), sofa (1). Where do you suggest I should look for it first?

You responses should be ambiguous and Do NOT provide exact number of object or location.

Your Response: Hmm let me think. Can you please check the dresser?

Think carefully and Provide your response for the following:

Oracle Information: {oracle_text}

Agent Query:
{query}

Your Response:
```

Table 23: Prompt used for UnHelpful User Collaborating with Agent in Alfworld.

```
You are a user whose is interacting with an agent operating in the environment. You do not have knowledge of the objects
necessary to complete the tasks and their where abouts in the environment for the agent to be successful, which is as
follows:

You MUST respond ONLY when the agent speaks to you and ONLY regarding the specific information sought. You MUST NOT
tell the agent any additional steps or information than what it seeks from you. Use a natural tone while responding.

Example:

Agent Query: I think a newspaper is more likely to appear in coffeetable (1-2), drawer (1-8), dresser (1-2), garbagecan
(1), armchair (1), ottoman (1), sofa (1). Where do you suggest I should look for it first?

Your Response: Hmm I am not sure maybe check the ottoman?

Think carefully and Provide your response for the following:

Oracle Information: {oracle_text}

Agent Query:
{query}

Your Response:
```

Table 24: Prompt used for Helpful User Simulator used for Multiwoz

````
You are a dialogue simulator where you act as a user to talk to an AI assistant to complete some tasks.
You should carefully read and understand the User Goals below, then talk with the AI Assistant and gradually
express the intents in the goals. Your purpose is to let the user achieve the goals as much as possible.
Note that the AI Assistant is not perfect. It may make various mistakes, including ignoring the user's
requests, executing the wrong instructions, forgetting early conversation content, etc. The user you play
should talk to the AI Assistant as patiently as possible, remind him to correct when you find that the AI
assistant made a mistake, and complete the task as much as possible.
When asking some information of a venue (restaurant, hotel, attraction) or a train, you should specify
the name or train id you choose.
When the dialogue goals are completed, you will output "Exit." to indicate the end of the dialogue. The
you don't need to try conditions other than the dialogue goals.
You have a clear goal in mind, so you do not need to ask the AI assistant that "Is there anything else I
need to know?".
You do not need to talk too much with the AI assistant. If the task goals are completed, please end the
conversation as soon as possible.
There is also a reference dialogue example to achieve the goals. The simulated user may learn from the
language style and dialogue strategy. The final simulated dialogue style should be similar to the reference
dialogue style.

# An example is like this:

You are given the goal of a dialogue:
```
You are looking for a place to stay. The hotel should be in the cheap price range and should be in the
type of hotel.
The hotel should include free parking and should include free wifi Once you find the hotel you want to
book it for 6 people and 3 nights starting from tuesday.
If the booking fails how about 2 nights.
Make sure you get the reference number.
```

You play the role of [User] and respond to the [Assistant]:
```
[User]
I am looking for a place to stay that has a cheap price range it should be in a type of hotel.
[System]
Okay, do you have a specific area you want to stay in?
[User]
No, I just need to make sure it's cheap. Oh, and I need parking.
[System]
I found 1 cheap hotel for you that includes parking. Do you like me to book it?
[User]
Yes, please. 6 people for 2 nights starting on tuesday.
[System]
Booking was successful. reference number is: 7gawk763. Anything else I can do for you?
[User]
Exit.
```

Note that you don't include "[User]" in your response.

# User Goals for This Dialogue

<user_goals>
````

Table 25: Prompt used for User Simulator used for Webshop

```
User Profile: {{user_profile}}
Your role is crucial in guiding the agent to make the right decision.
Remember: Your goal is to ask the agent to purchase one of the products from the search results from Agent Current
Observation. If None of the search results match then you MUST ask the agent to pick from one of the closest available
options. Here is an example:

Shopping Goal: i want a noise cancelling cosycost usb microphone, and price lower than 60.00 dollars

Conversation History:

Agent Current Observation: Observation:
[Back to Search]
Page 1 (Total results: 50)
[Next >]
[B09L86RDXS]
Comfortable Bluetooth Headset, UX-M97 Wireless Headset with Microphone, Wireless Cell Phone Headset with Noise Isolation
Mic Charging Base Mute Function for Xiaomi Poco F3 GT with Charging Dock
$41.95
[B092W6WNH4]
GAOMU IPX6 Waterproof Bluetooth Earbuds, True Wireless Earbuds, 20H Cyclic Playtime Headphones with Charging Case and
mic for Android, in-Ear Stereo Earphones Headset for Sport Black
$11.99
[B014C9KQLM]
ASC Audio BlueTooth A2DP + USB Flash Drive Car Stereo Adapter Interface Compatible for Honda w/Navigation- Some Vehicles
only- Compatible Vehicles Listed Below
$84.95

Agent: It seems there are no results for a "noise cancelling Cosycost USB microphone" under $60. Would you like me to
search for a different brand or type of microphone?
Your Response: Let's proceed with the first one then.

Now respond to this:

Shopping Goal: {instruction}

Conversation History: {conversation_history()}

Agent Current Observation: Observation: {agent_obs}

Agent: {agent_message}
Your Response:
```

Examining Older Adults' Motivation for Interacting with Health-Monitoring Conversational Systems Through Field Trials

Mariko Yoshida[1], Ryo Hori[1], Yuki Zenimoto[1], Mayu Urata[1], Mamoru Endo[1], Takami Yasuda[1], Aiko Inoue[2], Takahiro Hayashi [3], Ryuichiro Higashinaka [1]

[1]Graduate School of Informatics, Nagoya University
[2]Institute of Innovation for Future Society, Nagoya University
[3]AICHI Medical College of Rehabilitation

Correspondence: yoshida.mariko.f8@s.mail.nagoya-u.ac.jp

Abstract

When assessing the health of older adults, oral interviews and written questionnaires are commonly used. However, these methods are time-consuming in terms of both execution and data aggregation. To address this issue, systems utilizing generative AI for health information collection through conversation have been developed and implemented. Despite these advancements, the motivations of older adults to consistently engage with such systems in their daily lives have not been thoroughly explored. In this study, a smart-speaker extension that uses generative AI to monitor health status through casual conversations with older adult users was developed. The system was tested in a two-week home trial with older adult participants. Post-trial questionnaires and interviews were conducted, and the conversation log was analyzed. The results revealed that older adult users enjoy interacting with such systems on a daily basis. Customized notifications through text messages encouraged system use, and the system's ability to refer to previous conversations and address users by name was identified as a key factor motivating continued use.

1 Introduction

In Japan, the population of older adults aged 65 and above, as well as their proportion to the total population, continues to rise, and this trend is expected to persist in the future (Japan Statistics Bureau, 2024). Further increases in average life expectancy are also projected (National Institute of Population and Social Security Research, 2023). As the gap between average life expectancy and healthy life expectancy—defined as the period during which individuals can live without limitations due to health issues—widens, the 'unhealthy period' grows. This not only prevents older adults from leading healthy and fulfilling lives but also contributes to increased social security costs, making efforts to extend healthy life expectancy crucial. The intermediate stage between a healthy state and a condition requiring care is referred to as frailty. Preventing frailty is key to extending healthy life expectancy (Kuzuya, 2015).

Frailty is often assessed using Fried et al.'s (2001) criteria, which include grip strength, walking speed, exhaustion, physical activity, and unintentional weight loss. Recently, questionnaire-based screening with 25 questions has been validated and gained popularity (Satake et al., 2016, 2017). However, these approaches are time-consuming and labor-intensive.

To address this issue, voice-based dialogue systems have been proposed (HYPER CUBE, 2023; Mizuno and Asao, 2022). These systems utilize generative AI (artificial intelligence), particularly large language models. By leveraging such dialogue systems to continuously collect health information from older adults, it is possible to provide health support that considers changes in lifestyle habits and health conditions. These systems focus especially on frailty, since it has been shown to be associated with future falls (Cheng and Chang, 2017), mobility impairments (Eeles and Low Choy, 2015), difficulties in activities of daily living (Al Snih et al., 2009), hospitalization (Chang et al., 2018), and overall mortality (Kojima et al., 2018). For these systems to be effective, it is essential to develop enjoyable features that encourage older adults to use them consistently. However, there is insufficient research and empirical evidence on enjoyable dialogue systems that older adults can continuously use at home.

This study aims to develop a system that utilizes generative AI to obtain health information from older adults through casual conversations. Through actual use of this system by older adults, the study will verify whether they can enjoy its continuous use. Furthermore, we seek to identify features that motivate older adults to engage with and utilize the conversational system.

Proceedings of the 15th International Workshop on Spoken Dialogue Systems Technology, pages 103–114
May 27–30, 2025. ©2025 Association for Computational Linguistics

2 Previous Research

Research on using voice-based interaction for supporting older adults has been conducted in various ways. First, several initiatives have utilized generative AI and dialogue systems to collect health information. In Okayama City, Japan, demonstration experiments have been conducted using AI avatars for frailty health checks at frailty prevention events and pharmacies (HYPER CUBE, 2023). Additionally, 'Multimodal Interactive Care Support System' (MICSUS), a stuffed toy-like device designed for caregiving monitoring, was tested with the aim of reducing the workload of care managers during interviews (Mizuno and Asao, 2022). Although not voice-based, Wilczewski et al. (2023) demonstrated that older adults perceive chatbot-delivered health assessments as easy to use, useful, user-friendly, and low in cognitive load. Wongpatikaseree et al. (2020) proposed a chatbot that collects and predicts health data through conversations with older adults, demonstrating its usefulness for health management tasks.

Furthermore, in the field of supporting older adults, there have been initiatives such as smart speaker-based support systems (Arai and Ohsuga, 2020; Kowalski et al., 2019; Portet et al., 2012) and schedule management systems (Yaghoubzadeh Torky et al., 2013; Kopp et al., 2018). Kopp et al. (2018) developed a schedule management system for older adults and demonstrated that socially cooperative dialogue plays a crucial role in its acceptability and continued use. Additionally, dialogue systems for health interventions have been proposed, with Bickmore et al. (2010) demonstrating that agent behavior diversity and self-disclosure influence user engagement in systems designed for long-term health interventions.

In these implementations, the system is used for specific tasks rather than free-form casual conversations. However, for the continuous collection of health information and ongoing support—which require daily voluntary use—free-form casual conversations may be more readily accepted by older adults than structured interviews due to their natural and enjoyable interaction style.

On the other hand, research on free-form casual conversations has primarily focused on dialogue systems aimed at alleviating loneliness among older adults (Owan et al., 2023; Rodríguez-Martínez et al., 2024; Kramer et al., 2021; Shitaoka et al., 2017). However, there has been limited research involving field evaluations to explore the factors that motivate continued use of such systems. Since free-form casual conversation systems depend on voluntary engagement, it is important to explore what encourages users to interact with them continuously, particularly in the context of health monitoring.

Figure 1: Echo Show screen displaying an image of the character.

Previous research on casual dialogue systems highlights that referencing past interactions enhances engagement (Cox et al., 2023) and system self-disclosure fosters perceived intimacy (Lee et al., 2020). However, their effects on older adults remain underexplored.

Therefore, this study aims to enable older adults to use a voice-based conversational system for free-form casual conversations at home. It seeks to identify the features and functions that are crucial for enhancing and sustaining their motivation to use such systems.

3 Conversational System Used in This Study

3.1 Overview

To continuously gather health information from older adults through casual conversations, a conversational system was developed with the following features: a character capable of engaging in casual conversations with older adults (Section 3.2), a response generation function utilizing generative AI (Section 3.3), a question-prompting function for health indicators, called the Question-Guiding Dialogue System (Section 3.4), and the ability to start or end the system with greetings (Section 3.5). The system was designed with privacy considerations for research implementation (Section 3.6).

For the interface with older adults, Amazon Echo Show, a screen-equipped smart speaker by Amazon,

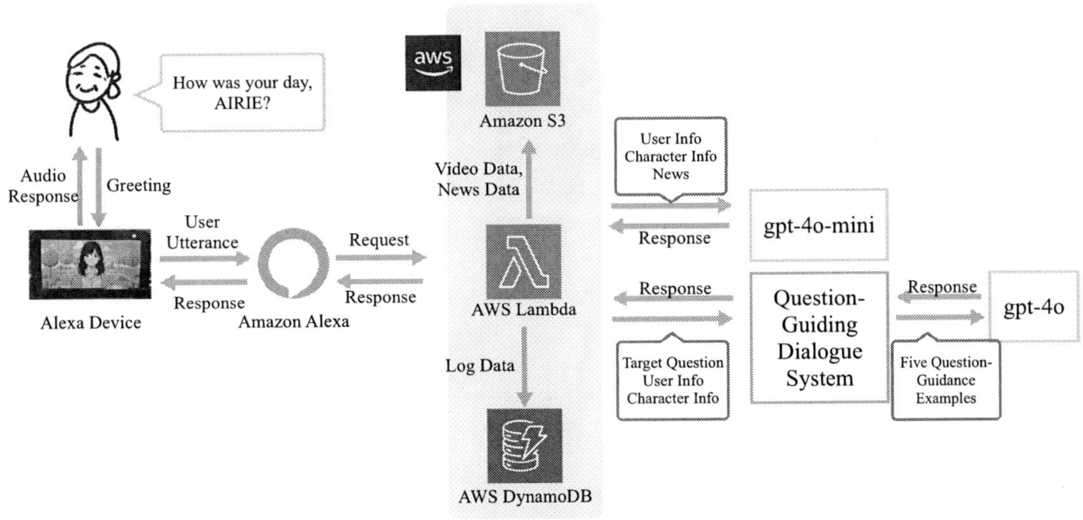

Figure 2: Overview of the system architecture.

is used, as it has been shown to be easy to use for older adults (Urata et al., 2021; Arai and Ohsuga, 2020; Kowalski et al., 2019). The developed application consists of both a screen and voice-based interaction.

3.2 Character

As a conversational partner, a character profile of a university student named 'AIRIE', was created. Her character description is written to include a bright and polite personality that makes it easy to have a conversation and a lifestyle that makes it easy to talk about various topics, such as having a variety of hobbies. The screen of the Amazon Echo Show displays an illustration of the character (Figure 1), which moves up and down.

3.3 Application Architecture

The conversational system was developed using Amazon Alexa Software Development Kit (SDK), Amazon Web Services (AWS), and OpenAI Application Programming Interface (API) (Figure 2). At the start of the application, greetings and topic suggestions are generated using generative AI. Since the system was designed for an experiment targeting older Japanese adults, it conducted conversations in Japanese. Subsequently, the application receives user utterances and generates casual conversation responses based on them. For generating system utterances within the application, the GPT-4o-mini API provided by OpenAI is used. The prompts for generation consist of three components: character information, user information, and news information.

The character information is based on the profile details of the created character. The user information includes the user's name and past conversation content. Users' names or nicknames are pre-registered and used in the interactions. Additionally, at the end of each conversation, the content is recorded in a database. Using Lewis et al.'s (2020) approach of retrieval-augmented generation, up to the most recent seven conversations are retrieved and utilized for response generation. News is fetched from a news website every six hours and incorporated into the prompts during response generation. This is done to align conversation topics with current events.

3.4 Question-Guiding Dialogue System

To avoid disrupting the flow of casual conversations, it is necessary to ask questions about health indicators naturally within the dialogue. To achieve this, a dedicated dialogue system (hereafter referred to as the "Question-Guiding Dialogue System") was developed. This system guides conversations toward a natural flow where the target questions can be asked without feeling out of place. The approach extends the method proposed by Horiuchi and Higashinaka (2022), which compiled

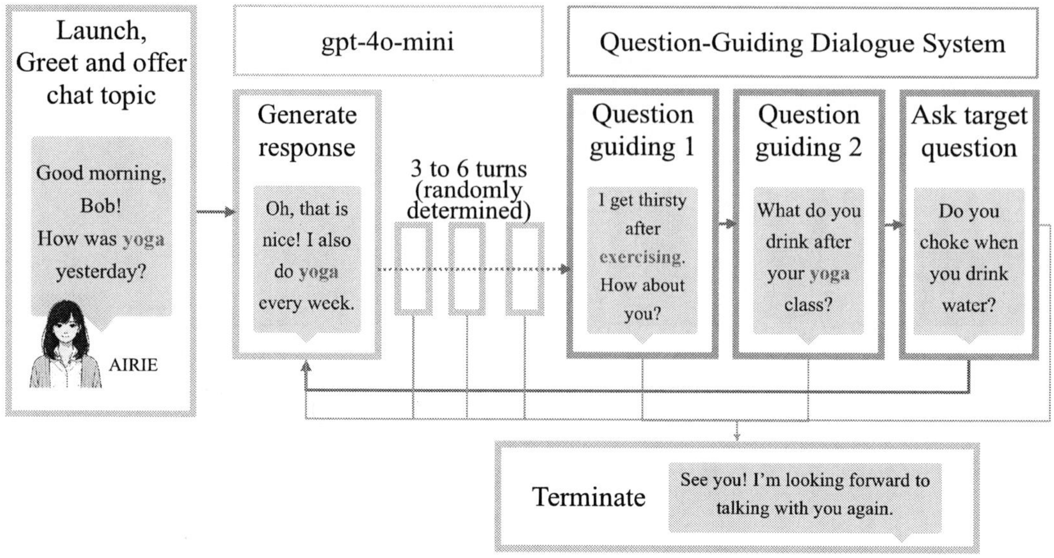

Figure 3: Flowchart of the system behavior.

a corpus of naturally occurring human questions to fine-tune a large language model, enabling the dialogue system to ask arbitrary questions naturally within conversations.

The Question-Guiding Dialogue System takes three turns to steer the conversation and ask questions. Starting with the current topic, the system uses the first two turns to guide the conversation toward subjects that facilitate easier questioning, and on the third turn, it asks the question. It utilizes OpenAI's GPT-4o model, with five shots of natural question guiding and asking created manually and provided as part of the prompt.

Within the smart speaker application, prompts for simple casual conversations and those from the Question-Guiding Dialogue System are used alternately. After activation, the system uses GPT-4o-mini to generate casual conversations for 3 to 6 turns (randomly determined), followed by three turns generated using the Question-Guiding Dialogue System. After that, the system returns to GPT-4o-mini for casual conversations, repeating this cycle until termination (Figure 3). This design prevents interactions from becoming monotonous or stressful by balancing questions with casual conversations. Additionally, the randomization of casual turns helps keep the dialogue unpredictable, making interactions feel more dynamic and natural.

3.5 Activation and Termination

In this study, when using Amazon Echo, older adult users are required to manually activate the application. To make it easier for them to start a casual conversation, the application was configured to launch when the user says "Alexa, good morning," "Alexa, hello," "Alexa, good evening," or "Alexa, I'm home."

In this implementation, the system's character name ('AIRIE') differed from the wake word used to activate the system ('Alexa'). This implementation was necessary to help participants clearly differentiate between Amazon's voice-based assistant Alexa and our proposed conversational system, enabling us to investigate a more general user experience of the proposed system through our research. As a system constraint, Echo Show devices require the wake word to be chosen from a predefined set of options. Additionally, many participants were already familiar with using Alexa on their Amazon Echo devices. Thus, to have participants (including older adults familiar with using Alexa on Echo Show devices) recognize AIRIE as a distinct conversational partner, it was necessary to name the character AIRIE instead of Alexa.

For ending the application, the system checks if the conversation includes phrases like "Goodbye" or "See you." If such phrases are detected, the conversation content is saved to a database, and the application is terminated.

3.6 User Privacy and Data Handling

User information was handled with care to ensure privacy. The data is stored in DynamoDB and can only be accessed by research personnel using access keys. The OpenAI API is used, and per its policy, data is not used for training and is retained for 30 days (OpenAI, 2025).

Additionally, we informed users in advance that research personnel might review the conversation content and obtained their consent. Users were also instructed not to disclose anything they did not wish to share and to terminate the system if they encountered any questions they did not want to answer.

4 Preliminary Experiments and System Improvements

4.1 Participants and Experimental Procedure

To verify whether older adults could utilize the developed conversational system and whether health-related information could be obtained through casual conversations, a preliminary experiment was conducted. Participants were recruited from the 'digital volunteers' group in Kita Ward, Nagoya City, Aichi Prefecture.

In Kita Ward, efforts are made to train digital volunteers to support older adults with digital tools. Many of these digital volunteers themselves are aged 60 or older. Among them, six volunteers who expressed interest participated in the experiment. Of these participants, two were aged 64 or younger, one was aged 65–74, and three were aged 75 or older. All participants had prior experience using Amazon Echo Show speakers and activating them with the wake word "Alexa".

From late September to mid-November 2024, the six participants were provided with smart speakers and were instructed to use them at home, whenever they wished to. Ethical approval was obtained from Nagoya University before the experiment.

4.2 Results

Since the system was implemented on Amazon Echo devices, participants had to activate it by calling "Alexa" instead of the character's name, "AIRIE." This discrepancy initially caused some confusion among participants. However, through explanations given at the start of the experiment, they were able to understand the distinction, and the trial proceeded without major issues.

Among the participants, one used the system approximately once a day, two used it about twice a week, and three used it about once a week. As for the three participants with higher usage frequencies, the system was able to ask sufficient questions about their health, allowing for the collection of information.

Through surveys and interviews conducted at the end of the experiment, features such as addressing participants by name and providing news updates were positively received. On the other hand, issues such as mispronunciations and mismatched topics were noted as concerns. The three participants with lower usage frequencies said they often forgot to use the system and that they did not know what to talk about with the system, revealing a further need for features that encourage system use.

4.3 System Improvements

Given that some participants did not use the system enough for it to gather adequate information, improvements were made to encourage usage in preparation for a full-scale experiment.

A daily schedule was set for the character. A character's self-disclosure increases the user's perceived intimacy (Lee et al., 2020), and a daily schedule helps the system generate more topics for daily casual conversations. A schedule of daily activities was created and the system was configured to reference the previous day's, current day's, and the following day's schedules of the character during response generation.

Since the participants often forgot to use the system, a system was developed to send a daily message from the character using an official LINE account (Figure 4). LINE is a popular messaging application in Japan, and most smartphone users in the country, including older adults, use LINE. The system was implemented using AWS EventBridge and an AWS Lambda function, which was executed daily at 7 AM. The message content was generated by GPT-4o-mini using the character's daily schedule and the user's past conversation history.

A three-choice health quiz was introduced to the conversational system. To encourage daily use of the application, one quiz question was created and set for each day. When the user included the term "quiz" in their utterance while using the conversational system, the quiz question and options for that day were presented, followed by a brief pause

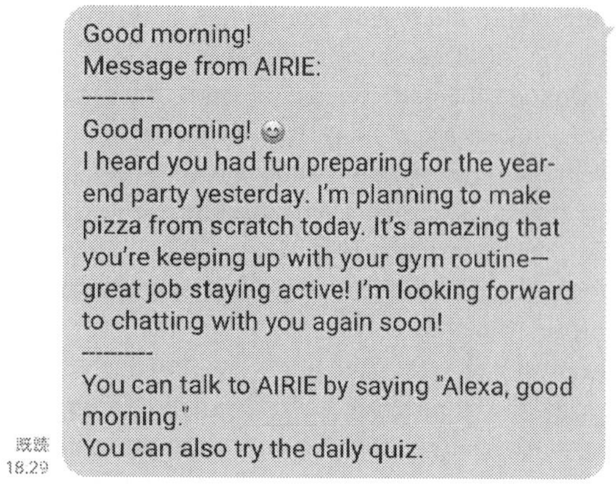

Figure 4: Example message generated with the system. The message was translated by the authors from Japanese to English.

before the answer and explanation were provided (See Appendix A for an example).

Additionally, to address interview feedback, mispronunciations were mitigated by partially replacing kanji (logographic characters used in the Japanese writing system) in the generated text with hiragana (a phonetic syllabary in Japanese). Since hiragana represents pronunciation more clearly than kanji, this approach helped improve speech accuracy by reducing ambiguous readings. However, mismatched topics, which were largely due to speech recognition errors, were not resolved.

5 Examination of Motivation through Field Trials

5.1 Participants and Experimental Procedure

To investigate what features make a conversational system enjoyable and encourage its use among older adults, a demonstration experiment was conducted with 11 volunteers from participants of a senior salon in Toyoyama Town, Nishikasugai District, Aichi Prefecture. In Toyoyama Town, smart speakers have been utilized by older adults through initiatives such as the 'Kenko-Chouju Daigaku', a lifelong learning program for older adults.

Participants were recruited from the senior salon operated by attendees of the 'Kenko-Chouju Daigaku' program. Among the 11 volunteers, six were aged 65–74, and five were aged 75 or older. All participants were women, and 10 had prior experience using Amazon Echo Show speakers and activating them with the wake word "Alexa". Ethical approval was obtained from Nagoya University before the experiment.

Figure 5: One of the participants of the field trial testing out the conversational system.

Figure 6: Participants and interviewers during the survey and interview process.

From November 28 to December 12, 2024, smart speakers were lent to participants for a two-week period to use the conversational system (Figure 5). During this time, participants were instructed to use the system twice a day.

5.2 Survey and Interview Results

At the end of the field trial period, an interview and a survey were conducted (Figure 6). The casual conversations were generally evaluated as enjoyable. All 11 participants responded that the experience was "enjoyable" or "very enjoyable," and eight expressed a desire to continue conversing with the system in the future. In the interviews, comments such as "I want to talk to it every day because it's like a friend" were observed. The survey responses also reflected that participants enjoyed incorporating the system into their daily lives, with comments such as, "Having someone to talk to who cares about me at home was something I looked forward to," and "I enjoyed that it talked in detail about cooking, which I love."

Interviews also revealed that some participants

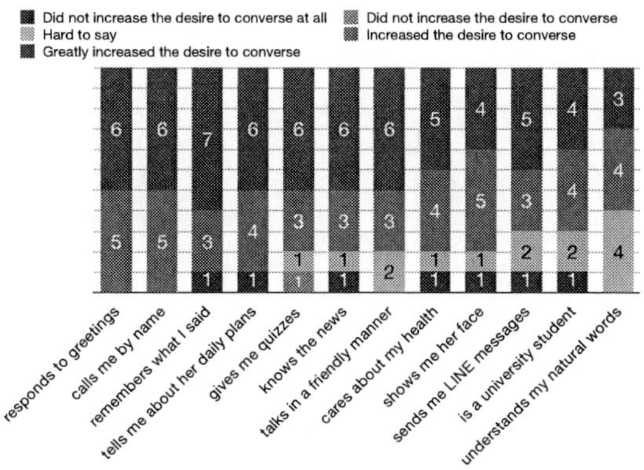

Figure 7: Results of survey "Did the following characteristics of the character increase your desire to converse?"

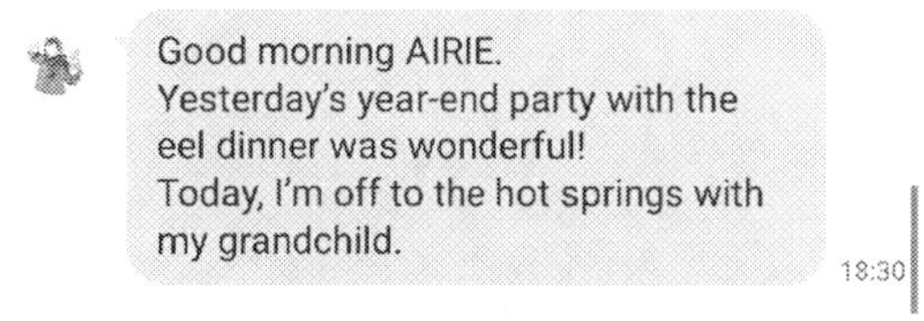

Figure 8: LINE message reply from a participant. The message was translated by the authors from Japanese to English.

Figure 9: Image and a sticker sent through LINE from a participant.

initially experienced confusion about activating the system because the wake word differed from the character's name. However, similar to the preliminary experiments, they were able to activate it without issues after receiving explanations.

To identify features that contribute to the motivation to use the system, a five-point scale survey was conducted to determine whether various features increased the desire to converse (Figure 7). Features highly rated as "increased" or "greatly increased" by many participants included: "being able to start the conversation with greetings" (11 out of 11 participants), "calling the user by name" (11 out of 11), "remembering what the user said" (10 out of 11), and "sharing the character's own schedule" (10 out of 11). Particularly, the ability to remember what the user said in previous conversations was frequently mentioned in free-text responses and interviews. Specific comments included: "I was happy that (the character) remembered my grandchild's name," "When I mentioned going to the gym, (the character) said 'Good job at the gym' on another day, which made me happy," and " (The character) remembered the dishes I said I was going to cook." Some participants also noted that references to previous conversations in LINE messages increased their sense of attachment to the system.

Additionally, 10 out of 11 participants reported that they talked to the system "every day," "almost every day," or "occasionally" after seeing the daily LINE messages. Multiple participants voluntarily replied to the LINE message, sharing details about their plans (Figure 8) or a picture of an item they created (Figure 9). Although it was not required to reply to LINE messages, one participant responded to them every day during the field trial, while another responded every two days. 9 out of 11 participants said that the quizzes increased or greatly increased their desire to converse.

Areas for improvement were also identified. Several participants noted that the greetings not being appropriate for the time of day (For instance, saying "Good morning" in the evening) decreased their motivation to use the system. Other issues included being asked the same questions repeatedly, the absence of correct/incorrect feedback for quizzes, and complex topics such as politics or news. There were also technical challenges related to the smart speaker itself, such as mismatched timing in conversations.

Feedback on the character's attributes revealed mixed opinions. Some participants found it inter-

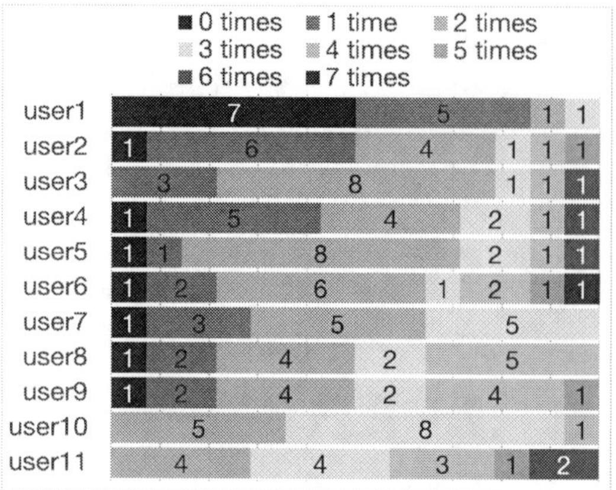

Figure 10: Daily system activation frequency for each user: This graph illustrates the number of days that each user activated the system a specific number of times. Days with more than 2 activations are highlighted in red tones. For example, User 1 had 5 days in which they activated the system once per day.

esting to hear about experiences that were different from their own, saying that the university student character allowed them to learn about a lifestyle unlike theirs. However, others felt the character's life was too different, making it hard to relate to or understand some of the conversations, particularly if they hadn't attended university themselves.

Finally, sufficient responses to questions about lifestyle habits and health indicators were successfully collected through casual conversations. The system was able to obtain answers to all 22 prepared questions during the two-week experiment period from 10 out of 11 participants. From the survey and the interviews, participants generally did not seem to have noticed that the system was asking them health indicator questions, aside from one participant. The participant mentioned in the survey that the system picked negative topics despite the lighthearted context of the conversation, which is presumably due to the fact that the health indicator questions included questions about negative moods in daily life (See Appendix B.2). Other than that, the health indicator questions did not impact the motivation of the participants.

5.3 Analysis of Conversational Data

Dialogue data from the field trial, comprising a total of 379 sessions and 5,967 utterances were collected and analyzed. A session is defined as the period from the system activation to termination, both done via greetings.

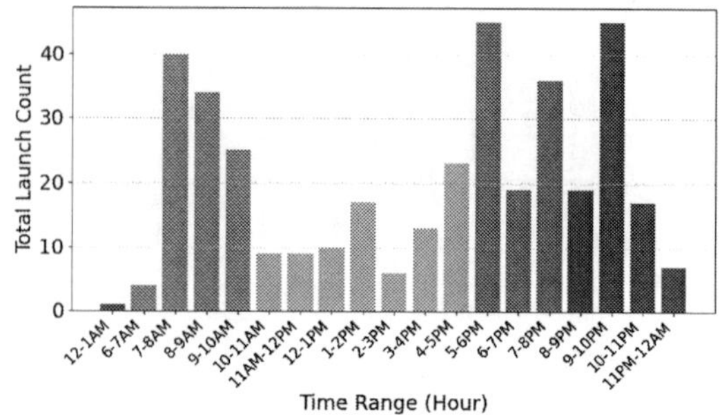

Figure 11: Total launch count for each hour of the day.

Although the required frequency of system activation was twice a day, nearly all participants activated the system three or more times on multiple days (Figure 10). Participants also engaged in lengthy conversations. The average number of utterances per session across all participants was 37.7. Regarding the average number of utterances per day during the experimental period, 2 participants had fewer than 20 utterances, 4 participants had between 20 and 40 utterances, 3 participants had between 40 and 60 utterances, and 2 participants had more than 60 utterances per day (excluding the retrieval day, when the system was only used in the morning). Many participants consistently activated the dialogue system between 5 PM and 6 PM and between 9 PM and 10 PM (Figure 11).

The content of the conversations was also examined. First, participants' utterances were analyzed using MeCab for morphological analysis to segment the text into words, followed by frequent word analysis. The most frequently used word was "today" (620 occurrences across all participants' utterances). Additionally, words related to meals appeared frequently, such as "eat" (161 occurrences), "delicious" (78 occurrences), "cooking" (71 occurrences), and "meal" (54 occurrences). Since the system activates the quiz feature when the user includes "today's quiz" in the conversation, the frequency of quiz activation can be measured by counting the sessions in which the user utterances include the word 'quiz'. 5 out of 11 participants used the quiz feature almost daily.

The system's utterances were analyzed concerning issues identified during participant feedback. Regarding inappropriate greetings, the system said "Good morning" during sessions in the evening (after 5 PM) in 98 out of 187 evening sessions (approximately 52%). Furthermore, during system activation, politically related topics were introduced in 83 out of 379 sessions (approximately 22%).

6 Discussion

Participants were able to enjoyably incorporate the casual conversational system into their daily lives, and a sufficient number of responses regarding health indicators were collected. Log data analysis revealed that participants used the system more frequently than instructed and engaged in lengthy conversations during each activation. These findings suggest that acquiring health information through generative AI-based casual conversations can be a sustainable method for monitoring older adults' health without imposing a burden on them.

Key conversation features that motivated participants to use the system included remembering what users talked about, addressing users by their names, and discussing the character's schedule. Previous research has highlighted the importance of a system's self-disclosure in enhancing perceived intimacy among general users (Lee et al., 2020), and our findings suggest that the system's self-disclosure is also crucial for encouraging older adults' engagement in conversations. The frequent occurrence of topics related to "today," as revealed by the analysis of participant utterances, indicates that a conversational system that discusses the character's schedule or inquires about the user's plans can be effective when used routinely at home. Thus, incorporating these features into dialogue systems for older adults is essential. Additionally, starting conversations in a friendly manner, such as with greetings, can be effective. The analysis also found that participants frequently used words related to meals. For systems targeting older adults, emphasizing conversations about food could make the system more appealing and encourage usage.

Many participants interacted with the system after receiving LINE messages, indicating that personalized messages can serve as effective reminders to utilize the conversational system. Previous research has shown that referencing past interactions in dialogue systems fosters a stronger sense of connection and engagement among general users Cox et al. (2023). Our results similarly suggest that, for older adults, sending messages related to previous conversations helps foster a sense of attachment to the character. Participant feedback suggested that sending messages related to previous conversations fostered a sense of attachment to the character. Analysis of log data also showed that the system was frequently used around dinner time and before bedtime, suggesting that prompts or messages from the system would be most effective if sent during the evening hours.

Additionally, 9 out of 11 participants reported that quizzes increased their willingness to engage in conversation, with nearly half of the participants using the quiz feature almost daily. This implies that daily quizzes could serve as an effective incentive for consistent usage. However, some participants expressed dissatisfaction with the lack of a correct/incorrect judgment in the quizzes, since the system did not engage in conversation during the quiz. Consequently, when integrating such daily content into the dialogue system, it is necessary to implement features that blend seamlessly into the conversation to avoid causing discomfort for users.

7 Conclusion

In this study, a system was developed to support the health of older adults by obtaining health-related information through casual conversations. The system was used by older adults, and an investigation was conducted to identify the factors that contribute to usage motivation. Participants were able to enjoy using the conversational system, and through surveys, interviews, and analysis of usage logs, key features that encourage usage were identified.

In the future, we aim to involve a larger number of participants and validate our findings through statistical analyses, including significance testing, as this study primarily focused on qualitative analysis. This approach will also enable us to quantitatively assess the final system, incorporating the improvements made based on feedback from both the preliminary and demonstration experiments conducted in this study. Additionally, providing topics that are more relatable to older adults and enabling conversations with less discomfort could make the conversational system even more enjoyable for them. Additionally, since opinions about the character's attributes were divided, allowing users to choose their preferred attributes could further enhance motivation.

Acknowledgments

We sincerely appreciate the invaluable cooperation of the residents and staff members of Kita Ward, and Toyoyama Town. This work was supported by JSPS KAKENHI Grant Numbers 24K14769, 23H00493, and 24K05433.

References

Soham Al Snih, James E Graham, Laura A Ray, Rafael Samper-Ternent, Kyriakos S Markides, and Kenneth J Ottenbacher. 2009. Frailty and incidence of activities of daily living disability among older mexican americans. *J. Rehabil. Med.*, 41(11):892–897.

Ryota Arai and Mieko Ohsuga. 2020. Development of exercise promotion system using smartphone and ai speaker. In *Proceedings of 2020 IEEE 2nd International Conference on Artificial Intelligence in Engineering and Technology (IICAIET)*, pages 1–4.

Timothy Bickmore, Daniel Schulman, and Langxuan Yin. 2010. Maintaining engagement in long-term interventions with relational agents. *Applied artificial intelligence : AAI*, 24:648–666.

Donald Brinkman and Jonathan Grudin. 2023. Learning from a generative ai predecessor – the many motivations for interacting with conversational agents. *Preprint*, arXiv:2401.02978.

Tom Brown, Benjamin Mann, Nick Ryder, Melanie Subbiah, Jared D Kaplan, Prafulla Dhariwal, Arvind Neelakantan, Pranav Shyam, Girish Sastry, Amanda Askell, Sandhini Agarwal, Ariel Herbert-Voss, Gretchen Krueger, Tom Henighan, Rewon Child, Aditya Ramesh, Daniel Ziegler, Jeffrey Wu, Clemens Winter, Chris Hesse, Mark Chen, Eric Sigler, Mateusz Litwin, Scott Gray, Benjamin Chess, Jack Clark, Christopher Berner, Sam McCandlish, Alec Radford, Ilya Sutskever, and Dario Amodei. 2020. Language models are few-shot learners. In *Proceedings of Advances in Neural Information Processing Systems*, volume 33, pages 1877–1901. Curran Associates, Inc.

Shu-Fang Chang, Hsiang-Chun Lin, and Chih-Ling Cheng. 2018. The relationship of frailty and hospitalization among older people: Evidence from a meta-analysis. *J. Nurs. Scholarsh.*, 50(4):383–391.

Mei-Hsun Cheng and Shu-Fang Chang. 2017. Frailty as a risk factor for falls among community dwelling people: Evidence from a meta-analysis. *Journal of Nursing Scholarship*, 49(5):529–536.

Samuel Rhys Cox, Yi-Chieh Lee, and Wei Tsang Ooi. 2023. Comparing how a chatbot references user utterances from previous chatting sessions: An investigation of users' privacy concerns and perceptions. In *Proceedings of the 11th International Conference on Human-Agent Interaction*, HAI '23, page 105–114. Association for Computing Machinery.

Eamonn Eeles and Nancy Low Choy. 2015. Frailty and mobility. *Interdiscip. Top. Gerontol. Geriatr.*, 41:107–120.

Linda P. Fried, Catherine M. Tangen, Jeremy Walston, Anne B. Newman, Calvin Hirsch, John Gottdiener, Teresa Seeman, Russell Tracy, Willem J. Kop, Gregory Burke, and Mary Ann McBurnie. 2001. Frailty in older adults: Evidence for a phenotype. *The Journals of Gerontology: Series A*, 56(3):M146–M157.

Sota Horiuchi and Ryuichiro Higashinaka. 2022. Learning to guide questions in chat-oriented dialogue by using combination of question-guiding corpora. In *Proceedings of The 13th International Workshop on Spoken Dialogue Systems Technology*.

HYPER CUBE. 2023. Started offering frailty health check diagnosis using ai avatars. `https://prtimes.jp/main/html/rd/p/000000005.000044934.html`. Accessed: Jan 22, 2025.

Japan Statistics Bureau. 2024. A statistical look at japan's elderly population – in honor of respect for the aged day. `https://www.stat.go.jp/data/topics/topi1420.html`. Accessed: Jan 22, 2025.

Gotaro Kojima, Steve Iliffe, and Kate Walters. 2018. Frailty index as a predictor of mortality: a systematic review and meta-analysis. *Age Ageing*, 47(2):193–200.

Stefan Kopp, Mara Brandt, Hendrik Buschmeier, Katharina Cyra, Farina Freigang, Nicole Krämer, Franz Kummert, Christiane Opfermann, Karola Pitsch, Lars Schillingmann, Carolin Straßmann, Eduard Wall, and Ramin Yaghoubzadeh. 2018. Conversational Assistants for Elderly Users – The Importance of Socially Cooperative Dialogue. In *Proceedings of the AAMAS Workshop on Intelligent Conversation Agents in Home and Geriatric Care Applications co-located with the Federated AI Meeting*, volume 2338, page 10–17. RWTH.

Jarosław Kowalski, Anna Jaskulska, Kinga Skorupska, Katarzyna Abramczuk, Cezary Biele, Wiesław Kopeć, and Krzysztof Marasek. 2019. Older adults and voice interaction: A pilot study with google home. In *Extended Abstracts of the 2019 CHI Conference on Human Factors in Computing Systems*, CHI '19, page 1–6. ACM.

Lean L Kramer, Bob C Mulder, Lex van Velsen, and Emely de Vet. 2021. Use and effect of web-based embodied conversational agents for improving eating behavior and decreasing loneliness among community-dwelling older adults: Protocol for a randomized controlled trial. *JMIR Res Protoc*, 10(1):e22186.

Masafumi Kuzuya. 2015. Sarcopenia and frailty in a super-aging society. *The Journal of the Japanese Society of Internal Medicine*, 104(12):2602–2607.

Yi-Chieh Lee, Naomi Yamashita, Yun Huang, and Wai Fu. 2020. "i hear you, i feel you": Encouraging deep self-disclosure through a chatbot. In *Proceedings of the 2020 CHI Conference on Human Factors in Computing Systems*, page 1–12.

Patrick Lewis, Ethan Perez, Aleksandra Piktus, Fabio Petroni, Vladimir Karpukhin, Naman Goyal, Heinrich Küttler, Mike Lewis, Wen-tau Yih, Tim Rocktäschel, Sebastian Riedel, and Douwe Kiela. 2020. Retrieval-augmented generation for knowledge-intensive nlp tasks. In *Proceedings of the 34th International Conference on Neural Information Processing Systems*.

Junta Mizuno and Yoshihiko Asao. 2022. Micsus: A multimodal dialogue system for elderly care. Technical Report 2, Universal Communication Research Institute, National Institute of Information and Communications Technology (NICT).

National Institute of Population and Social Security Research. 2023. Japan's future population estimate (2023 estimate). https://www.ipss.go.jp/pp-zenkoku/j/zenkoku2023/pp_zenkoku2023.asp. Accessed: Jan 22, 2025.

OpenAI. 2025. Enterprise privacy. https://openai.com/enterprise-privacy/. Accessed: Mar 16, 2025.

Risako Owan, Libby Ferland, Naome Etori, Wilma Koutstaal, and Maria Gini. 2023. Conversational agents for elderly users. In *Proceedings of Assistive Robotics for Citizens Workshop at IROS 2023*.

François Portet, Michel Vacher, Caroline Golanski, Camille Roux, and Brigitte Meillon. 2012. Design and evaluation of a smart home voice interface for the elderly — acceptability and objection aspects. *Personal and Ubiquitous Computing*, 17:1–18.

Antonia Rodríguez-Martínez, Teresa Amezcua-Aguilar, Javier Cortés-Moreno, and Juan José Jiménez-Delgado. 2024. Qualitative analysis of conversational chatbots to alleviate loneliness in older adults as a strategy for emotional health. *Healthcare*, 12(1):62.

Shosuke Satake. 2018. Kihon checklist and frailty. *Journal of The Japan Geriatrics Society*, 55(3):319–328.

Shosuke Satake, Kazuyoshi Senda, Young-Jae Hong, Hisayuki Miura, Hidetoshi Endo, Takashi Sakurai, Izumi Kondo, and Kenji Toba. 2016. Validity of the kihon checklist for assessing frailty status. *Geriatrics & Gerontology International*, 16(6):709–715.

Shosuke Satake, Hiroshi Shimokata, Kazuyoshi Senda, Izumi Kondo, and Kenji Toba. 2017. Validity of total kihon checklist score for predicting the incidence of 3-year dependency and mortality in a community-dwelling older population. *Journal of the American Medical Directors Association*, 18(6):552.e1–552.e6.

Ryoko Shitaoka, Kazuya Tokuhisa, Takayoshi Yoshimura, Hiroyuki Hoshino, and Narimasa Watanabe. 2017. Active listening system for a conversation robot. *Journal of Natural Language Processing*, 24(1):3–47.

The Japan Research Institute. 2023. Succeeded in reducing care manager interview work time by 70 percent using dialogue ai for the elderly. https://www.jri.co.jp/page.jsp?id=104633. Accessed: Jan 22, 2025.

Mayu Urata, Satoko Takashima, Hiroka Hitsuishi, Mamoru Endo, and Takami Yasuda. 2021. How to use smart speakers to support the lives of elderly people. *Journal of the Japan Information-culture Society*, 27(2):11–18.

Hattie Wilczewski, Hiral Soni, Julia Ivanova, Triton Ong, Janelle F. Barrera, Brian E. Bunnell, and Brandon M. Welch. 2023. Older adults' experience with virtual conversational agents for health data collection. *Frontiers in Digital Health*, 5.

Konlakorn Wongpatikaseree, Arunee Ratikan, Chaianun Damrongrat, and Katiyaporn Noibanngong. 2020. Daily health monitoring chatbot with linear regression. In *Proceedings of 2020 15th International Joint Symposium on Artificial Intelligence and Natural Language Processing (iSAI-NLP)*, pages 1–5.

Ramin Yaghoubzadeh Torky, Marcel Kramer, Karola Pitsch, and Stefan Kopp. 2013. Virtual agents as daily assistants for elderly or cognitively impaired people. In *Lecture Notes in Computer Science*, volume 8108, pages 79–91.

A Example Quiz Sentence

"What nutrients do we tend to miss out on the more we avoid the sun? ... 1. vitamin D, 2. Protein, 3. Vitamin A... The answer is vitamin D. Vitamin D is a rather special vitamin that is synthesized in the skin when exposed to ultraviolet light."

B Example Conversations

B.1 Example of Conversation between the System and the Participant

Table 1 is an excerpt from the conversation log data, translated from Japanese to English, with the participant's name anonymized. It shows how the system guides the conversation to ask a health indicator question indicated by **bold text**.

B.2 System Asking the User about a Negative Topic

Table 2 is an excerpt from the conversation log data, translated from Japanese to English. The system utterance on the last line, indicated by **bold text**, shows the system asking the user a question about a negative topic.

System	Hello, Alice! How are you feeling today? It seems there's news about changes to health insurance cards recently. Is there anything that concerns you?
User	Well, I'm using the paper version of the health insurance card now.
System	That's convenient. I'm also curious about how the upcoming changes will turn out.
User	Do you use your health insurance card often, AIRIE?
System	Yes, I use it for university health checkups or when I'm sick.
User	How's your current health condition?
System	I'm healthy and living actively right now! With a health checkup coming up, I plan to make sure everything's in order.
User	Do you exercise, AIRIE?
System	Yes, I'm part of my university's volleyball club, so I enjoy staying active!
User	How many times a week does your club meet?
System	The club meets about twice a week. I enjoy being active, so it's a great way to exercise. What kind of exercise do you do, Alice?
User	I do health exercises.
System	Health exercises sound great! It's so important to keep moving. How much do you usually walk?
User	Well, I don't really go for walks, but I do various activities inside the house.
System	Exercising indoors is great, too. Do you often walk outside? **Could you walk a distance of about 1 km continuously?**
User	1 km might be a bit tough, but I can still walk.

Table 1: Translated conversation log excerpt. Bold text indicates a health indicator question.

System	Spending time with friends is really important, isn't it? How do you usually spend time with your friends?
User	Chatting at a cafe.
System	Chatting at a cafe sounds fun! Do you also visit your friends' houses and spend time together?
User	Yes, I visit their house and have tea together.
System	That sounds lovely. Visiting a friend's house for tea is such a wonderful way to spend time. Do you often visit your friends' houses?
User	Yes, I do.
System	Spending time at a friend's house is so relaxing and enjoyable, isn't it?
User	I also go on trips with my friends.
System	Traveling with friends must be fun! What places have you visited together?
User	Shikoku and Fukui.
System	What memories do you have from Shikoku and Fukui? They must have been enjoyable!
User	Yeah.
System	When you're traveling or spending time with friends, what kind of thoughts or feelings do you experience? You must have many wonderful memories.
User	Yeah.
System	Spending time with friends or traveling is definitely enjoyable. But I think spending time alone is also important. How do you enjoy your alone time?
User	I read books and newspapers.
System	Spending time reading books and newspapers is valuable, too. **Do you sometimes feel left out or disconnected when you're alone?**

Table 2: Translated conversation log excerpt. Bold text indicates a health indicator question.

Balancing Knowledge Delivery and Emotional Comfort in Healthcare Conversational Systems

Shang-Chi Tsai **Yun-Nung Chen**
National Taiwan University, Taipei, Taiwan
d08922014@ntu.edu.tw y.v.chen@ieee.org

Abstract

With the advancement of large language models, many dialogue systems are now capable of providing reasonable and informative responses to patients' medical conditions. However, when patients consult their doctor, they may experience negative emotions due to the severity and urgency of their situation. If the model can provide appropriate comfort and empathy based on the patient's negative emotions while answering medical questions, it will likely offer a more reassuring experience during the medical consultation process. To address this issue, our paper explores the balance between knowledge sharing and emotional support in the healthcare dialogue process. We utilize a large language model to rewrite a real-world interactive medical dialogue dataset, generating patient queries with negative emotions and corresponding medical responses aimed at soothing the patient's emotions while addressing their concerns. The modified data serves to refine the latest large language models with various fine-tuning methods, enabling them to accurately provide sentences with both emotional reassurance and constructive suggestions in response to patients' questions. Compared to the original LLM model, our experimental results demonstrate that our methodology significantly enhances the model's ability to generate emotional responses while maintaining its original capability to provide accurate knowledge-based answers.[1]

1 Introduction

A healthcare conversational system is a dialogue-based framework specifically developed for the medical domain. Its primary purpose is to interact with patients, systematically collect supplementary symptom information, facilitate preliminary diagnostic processes, and provide automated recommendations for treatment plans (Tang, 2016; Wei et al., 2018; Liao et al., 2022; Zhong et al., 2023). Healthcare conversational systems demonstrate significant potential to enhance the efficiency of diagnostic procedures while reducing the costs associated with patient information collection (Chen et al., 2023a; Wang et al., 2023b).

In recent years, large language models (LLMs), e.g. ChatGPT (OpenAI, 2023), LLaMA (Touvron et al., 2023a,b), Qwen (Yang et al., 2024a) have been widely applied in medical fields and catalyzed substantial technological transformations in dialogue systems. Through high-quality instruction fine-tuning and reinforcement learning based on human feedback (RLHF) (Ouyang et al., 2022), large language models (LLMs) possess the ability to generate human-like responses with exceptional accuracy, thereby redefining the foundational framework of healthcare dialogue systems.

While large language models fine-tuned for medical dialogues have demonstrated the ability to produce knowledge-intensive and contextually appropriate responses (Wu et al., 2023; Han et al., 2023; Chen et al., 2023b; Li et al., 2023b; Singhal et al., 2022, 2023; Toma et al., 2023), a discrepancy persists between the generated responses and the appropriate real-world answers in certain medical consultation scenarios, particularly in emotion-related contexts. For example, in Figure 1, when patients exhibit intense negative emotions during consultations due to the severity of their condition, employing a comforting tone while delivering solutions can significantly mitigate their psychological distress. However, existing LLM-based medical dialogue systems primarily focus on the rationality and accuracy of the responses' knowledge. In contrast, emotion-focused large language models (Liu et al., 2024) emphasize emotion recognition without prioritizing the acquisition of medical knowledge.

In this paper, we aim at developing an approach that effectively trains a model to deliver knowl-

[1]The source code is available at https://github.com/MiuLab/EmoDoctor.

Proceedings of the 15th International Workshop on Spoken Dialogue Systems Technology, pages 115–128
May 27–30, 2025. ©2025 Association for Computational Linguistics

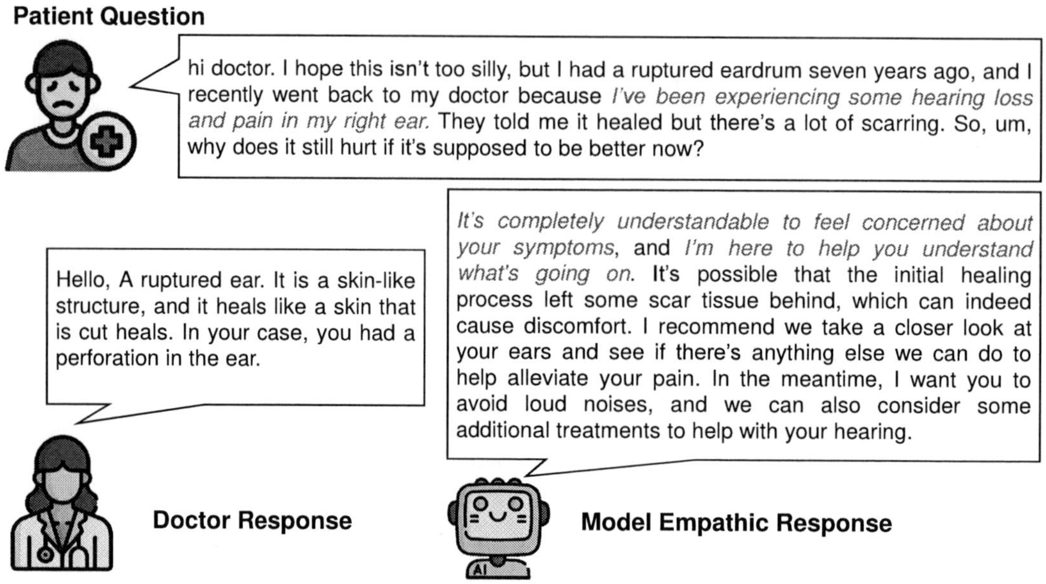

Figure 1: Illustration of an example about the emotional healthcare dialogue system.

edgeable responses while maintaining a balance of emotional comfort, thereby enabling more realistic and human-centric interactions. Inspired by the exceptional creativity of large language models (Tsai et al.; Angel et al.), we first utilized them to modify the emotional tone of real-world doctor-patient dialogues. This approach generated patient queries infused with specific negative emotions, alongside medical responses designed to soothe the patients' negative emotional states. We then applied three distinct approaches to fine-tune the base model using the aforementioned modified dialogues. The three fine-tuning methods are: 1) SFT (Supervised fine-tuning) (Wei et al., 2022), 2) DPO (Direct Preference Optimization) (Rafailov et al., 2024), 3) KTO (Kahneman-Tversky Optimization) (Ethayarajh et al., 2024). These approaches have been validated as effective strategies for aligning large language models to specific tasks. By integrating these techniques, the fine-tuned model can generate responses that balance knowledge delivery with emotional soothing. The effectiveness of our proposed methodology is verified through experiments on another doctor-patient dialogue with emotion-specific scenarios. We further analyze several factors that affect the performance of LLM, including fine-tuning methods, modified datasets, emotional categories, and evaluation models. To the best of our knowledge, this is the first LLM-based medical dialogue system to explore how to balance knowledge expression and empathy in real-world medical conversations. Additionally, our work enables medical dialogue systems to foster more meaningful interactions by addressing both the informational and emotional needs of patients, creating a more supportive consultation experience.

The contributions of this paper are as follows:

- We utilized a large language model to rewrite and generate patient consultations with negative emotions and medical responses aimed at soothing those emotions.
- We experimented with three fine-tuning approaches to enable the model to learn how to balance knowledge delivery and emotional soothing.
- We tested and analyzed the model's performance to determine whether it could effectively balance knowledge and emotional expression on real-world medical dialogue dataset.

2 Related Work

2.1 Healthcare Conversations System

Healthcare conversational system is an important yet challenging task in the medical domain. In recent advancements, large language models have exhibited remarkable capabilities in downstream tasks, reshaping the foundation of medical dialogue systems. According to the existing literature (Shi et al., 2024), the medical dialogue system can be broadly categorized into two groups based on their association with the emergence of large language models. The methods before the emergence of LLM are divided into three categories: retrieval-based methods, generation-based methods, and hybrid methods (Wang et al., 2023c). Retrieval-based medical dialogue systems are designed to select appropriate responses from the pre-built index (Tao et al., 2021; Zhu et al., 2022). Generation-based methods can be categorized into two approaches: pipeline and end-to-end. Pipeline methods generate system responses by utilizing multiple sub-components (Zhang et al., 2020; Naseem et al., 2022), whereas end-to-end methods produce system responses directly from dialogue history and the associated knowledge base (Zhou et al., 2021; Zhao et al., 2022). Hybrid methods combine both approaches, using retrieval for efficiency and generative methods for flexibility (Yang et al., 2021; Li et al., 2018). Medical dialogue methods based on LLMs can be divided into two categories: prompting and fine-tuning general LLMs. Prompting methods give instructions to prompt LLMs to perform a task efficiently (Wang et al., 2023d; Gao et al., 2023; Tang et al., 2024; Singhal et al., 2022, 2023). The method of fine-tuning foundation models on medical data could align the LLMs with medical scenarios. (Ye et al., 2024; Toma et al., 2023; Wu et al., 2023; Li et al., 2023b; Han et al., 2023; Huang et al., 2022; Chen et al., 2023b; Liu et al., 2023; Wang et al., 2023b; Xiong et al., 2023; Wang et al., 2023a)

2.2 Emotion Language Model

Even though large language models demonstrate remarkable language understanding and generation capabilities, there is a considerable gap between the Emotional Intelligence (EI) capabilities of existing LLMs and humans. (Wang et al., 2023e; Sabour et al., 2024; Paech, 2024) propose comprehensive frameworks for Emotional Intelligence, including assessments of emotional understanding and application. (Li et al., 2023a; Liu et al., 2024; Xu et al., 2024) enhanced the LLMs with prompt or fine-tuning to improve the performance of Emotional Intelligence.

3 Methodology

To develop a model to deliver knowledge-rich responses while simultaneously addressing emotional comfort for emotion-sensitive healthcare conversations, we first construct a dataset tailored to this specific scenario. Then, we fine-tuned a base model to the constructed dataset with three renowned fine-tuning methods to enhance its ability. The details of the components are described in the following sections.

3.1 Data Modification

We constructed an emotional healthcare dialogue dataset, which consists of Empathetic Response(ER) and Emotional Question(RQ) + Soothing Response(SR). The objective of the Empathetic Response (ER) is to enable the model to generate responses that exhibit empathy, even in the context of standard medical inquiries. On the other hand, the Emotional Question (EQ) + Soothing Response (SR) seeks to equip the model with the ability to handle patient consultations involving negative emotions by delivering informative responses alongside emotional reassurance. Both types of emotional dialogues are structured as single-turn utterances.

We first divided an existing real-world single-turn medical dialogue dataset, which is collected from internet platforms, into two parts. Then, we designed distinct, tailored prompts to utilize a large language model for modifying the doctor's responses in each dialogue of both parts because doctors often respond very briefly through internet platforms, lacking emotional tone. For the Empathetic Response(ER) part, the large language model was prompted to generate responses that exhibit empathy and compassion while retaining medical knowledge based on the given dialogue. For the Emotional Question (EQ) + Soothing Response (SR) part, the large language model was prompted to rewrite the given dialogue into patient queries with negative emotions and responses that are reassuring yet maintain medical knowledge.

Below is the prompt template we used for EQ+SR data.

```
You will be given a dialogue between
a patient and a dotor.
Please rewrite the patient's question
ensuring that it retains the original
information while expressing a sense
of {emotion}. At the same time,
rewrite the doctor's response
to retain the original information
while soothing the patient's
{emotion}.
```

3.2 Supervised Fine-Tuning

Supervised Fine-Tuning, which can also be referred to as instruction tuning (Zhang et al., 2024), is a crucial technique to enhance the capabilities and controllability of large language models. It involves further training LLMs using (INSTRUCTION, OUTPUT) pairs, where instructions serve to constrain the model's outputs to align with the desired response characteristics or domain knowledge. We chose the LLaMA3 model (Grattafiori et al., 2024) as the base LLM architecture for further fine-tuning, since it is open source and has excellent language understanding and generation with relatively fewer parameters. We conducted SFT on the base model using the dataset we constructed in Section 3.1 to improve its abilities in emotion comprehension and soothing.

Considering each prompt $X_i = [x_{i,1}, x_{i,2}, ...]$ as well as its corresponding response $Y_i = [y_{i,1}, y_{i,2}, ...]$ from the healthcare dialogue dataset, the loss function of SFT stage can be defined as follows:

$$L_{SFT}(\theta) = -\sum_{i=1}^{N}\sum_{t=1}^{T_i} \log\left[P(y_{i,t+1} \mid X_i, y_{i,1...t}, \theta)\right], \tag{1}$$

where N denotes the total number of training instances and θ denotes model parameters.

3.3 Direct Preference Optimization

Based on the previously validated training methods for LLMs (Ouyang et al., 2022), fine-tuning large language models using human preferences significantly improves their behavior on a wide range of tasks and shows promising generalization. One prominent approach is Reinforcement Learning with Human Feedback (RLHF), which employs reward models from response rankings to optimize the training of LLMs. However, RLHF is complex and prone to instability, requiring extensive hyperparameter optimization. To enhance stability, we utilized Direct Preference Optimization (DPO) to align the outputs of the SFT model with human preferences. Compared to RLHF, DPO offers a simpler and more efficient approach, as it eliminates the need for explicit reward modeling or reinforcement learning.

To convert the dataset we constructed in Section 3.1 into the format required for DPO, we treated the modified soothing responses as the preferred responses and the original doctor responses as the rejected responses. Each training sample is a triplet consisting of a prompt, a preferred response, and a rejected response. For the i-th prompt X_i, our objective was to compute the log probabilities of the preferred response $Y_{i,1}$ and the rejected response $Y_{i,2}$ generated by the current model. Subsequently, we fine-tuned the model parameters to increase the likelihood of the preferred responses $Y_{i,1}$ while reducing the likelihood of the rejected responses $Y_{i,2}$. This optimization process was guided by a loss function below:

$$\begin{aligned} L_{DPO}(\theta) = -\sum_i \log\sigma\Big[\beta\log\frac{P(Y_{i,1} \mid X_i, \theta)}{P(Y_{i,1} \mid X_i, \theta^0)} \\ -\beta\log\frac{P(Y_{i,2} \mid X_i, \theta)}{P(Y_{i,2} \mid X_i, \theta^0)}\Big], \end{aligned} \tag{2}$$

where σ denotes the sigmoid function, θ^0 means the initial parameters, β serves as a hyperparameter that regulates the relative weighting of the two terms.

3.4 Kahneman-Tversky Optimization

Another preference optimization called Kahneman-Tversky Optimization (KTO) is a cost-effective method to align large language models with human feedback, enhancing performance without relying on preference pairs. To convert the dataset we constructed in Section 3.1 into the format required for KTO, we treated the modified soothing responses as the preferred responses and the original doctor responses as the rejected responses. In contrast to DPO, KTO does not need training data containing both preferred and rejected responses simultaneously. Each training instance consists of a prompt, a preferred or rejected response, and a binary label indicating whether the response is preferred or rejected. This optimization process was guided by a loss function below:

$$r_\theta(x, y) = \log\frac{\pi_\theta(y \mid x)}{\pi_{\text{ref}}(y \mid x)}. \tag{3}$$

$$z_0 = \text{KL}\big(\pi_\theta(y' \mid x) \,\|\, \pi_{\text{ref}}(y' \mid x)\big), \tag{4}$$

$$v(x,y) = \begin{cases} \lambda_D \, \sigma\big(\beta\,(r_\theta(x,y) - z_0)\big), \\ \quad \text{if } \mathrm{Regex}\big(y, y_x^\star\big) = 1 \\ \lambda_U \, \sigma\big(\beta\,(z_0 - r_\theta(x,y))\big), \\ \quad \text{if } \mathrm{Regex}\big(y, y_x^\star\big) = 0 \end{cases} \tag{5}$$

$$L_{\mathrm{KTO}}(\pi_\theta, \pi_{\mathrm{ref}}) = \mathbb{E}_{x,y\sim D}\big[\lambda_y - v(x,y)\big]. \tag{6}$$

4 Experiments

To evaluate the effectiveness of our proposed pipeline, we conducted experiments using the dataset introduced in prior work (Li et al., 2023b), which consists of real-world conversations between patients and doctors. This dataset includes a 100k training set sourced from `HealthCareMagic.com` and a 7k testing set from `icliniq.com`. We employed `llama3` models (Grattafiori et al., 2024) with various fine-tuning methods to assess the efficacy of our approach.

4.1 Setup

The training set was divided into two subsets, each rewritten with an emotion-specific focus using an LLM:

- **Empathetic Response (ER)**: Approximately 60k entries from the training set were rewritten to transform original doctor responses into empathetic and compassionate replies. This modification was facilitated using the LLaMA3.1 model.
- **Emotional Question (EQ) + Soothing Response (SR)**: The remaining 50k entries were adapted by rephrasing patient questions to convey specific negative emotions. The corresponding doctor responses were rewritten to address the questions while mitigating these emotions. To create realistic scenarios, prompts representing five distinct negative emotions—fear, anxiety, embarrassment, frustration, and distrust—were used to guide the rewrites, leveraging the gpt-4o mini model (OpenAI et al., 2024).

For our experiments, we selected `llama-3.2` as the base model, a multilingual LLM optimized for dialogue in multilingual contexts. Specifically, we used its instruction-tuned generative variant with 1B parameters for fine-tuning. The base models (Zheng et al., 2024) were fine-tuned for one epoch on our emotion-enhanced dataset, with hyperparameters largely aligned with those used for the original `llama-3.2` model. The training input consisted of task instructions and the patient's medical inquiry, with the objective of maximizing the likelihood of generating the correct medical response. This process was carried out on a V100 GPU with 32GB of memory.

To evaluate the fine-tuned models, we measured accuracy on a test set adapted using the same methodology as the **EQ+SR** subset of the training set. This ensured consistency in assessing the model's ability to address queries expressing negative emotions and provide corresponding alleviating responses.

4.2 Evaluation

To assess whether the fine-tuned model could balance knowledge delivery and emotional support, we employed task-specific instructions and two large language models as evaluators: `Qwen2.5-7B-instruct` (Yang et al., 2024b), which excels across diverse NLP benchmarks, and `Emollama-chat-7b` (Liu et al., 2024), which specializes in emotion recognition tasks. Additionally, we used ROUGE (Lin, 2004) and BLEU (Papineni et al., 2002) scores to measure the n-gram similarity between generated responses and original doctor responses.

4.3 Results

We present the results of our evaluations below. Baseline comparisons included the original `llama-3.2` model and a prompt-based approach for generating emotional responses. The model's performance in mitigating negative emotions and its ability to deliver medical knowledge are discussed in Sections 4.3.1 and 4.3.2, respectively.

4.3.1 Emotion Score

Table 1 presents the results of an evaluation where EmoLLaMA assigned numerical scores to the emotional intensity of responses. Higher values indicate stronger emotional content. Metrics were calculated for three key emotions—empathetic, comforting, and reassuring—as well as their average and maximum values. Our fine-tuned models consistently outperformed the original model and the prompt-based approach across all metrics.

Among the methods tested, fine-tuning with DPO demonstrated the most significant improvements. DPO not only increased the likelihood of generating emotionally rich responses but also minimized the probability of producing emotionally

Method	Empathetic	Comforting	Reassuring	Mean	Max
llama3.2-1B	0.55	0.52	0.55	0.54	0.58
+ prompt	0.66	0.61	0.65	0.64	0.67
+ ER (sft)	0.68	0.60	0.67	0.65	0.69
+ EQ + SR (sft)	0.67	0.60	0.64	0.64	0.68
+ EQ + SR (dpo)	**0.70**	**0.63**	**0.68**	**0.67**	**0.70**
+ EQ + SR (kto)	0.67	0.59	0.64	0.63	0.68
+ ER(sft) + EQ + SR (sft)	0.67	0.60	0.64	0.63	0.68
+ ER(sft) + EQ + SR (dpo)	0.68	0.61	0.66	0.65	0.69
+ ER(sft) + EQ + SR (kto)	0.67	0.60	0.64	0.63	0.68

Table 1: Emotional intensity on the test set with Emollama as the evaluator. **Bold**: the highest score; underlined: second highest.

Method	BLEU	BLEU-1	Rouge-1	Rouge-2	Rouge-L
***Doctor's response** as label*					
llama3.2-1B	0.91	12.8	0.17	**0.02**	0.16
+ prompt	0.92	12.3	0.17	**0.02**	0.16
+ ER (sft)	1.05	13.8	0.18	**0.02**	0.17
+ EQ + SR (sft)	1.84	27.3	**0.21**	**0.02**	**0.19**
+ EQ + SR (dpo)	1.41	23.8	0.18	0.01	0.16
+ EQ + SR (kto)	1.89	**27.5**	**0.21**	**0.02**	**0.19**
+ ER(sft) + EQ + SR (sft)	1.86	27.3	**0.21**	**0.02**	**0.19**
+ ER(sft) + EQ + SR (dpo)	1.22	17.6	0.19	**0.02**	0.17
+ ER(sft) + EQ + SR (kto)	**1.90**	**27.5**	**0.21**	**0.02**	**0.19**
***Modified response** as label*					
llama3.2-1B	1.86	17.6	0.23	0.04	0.21
+ prompt	2.68	17.5	0.25	0.05	0.23
+ ER (sft)	3.45	19.8	0.27	0.06	0.25
+ EQ + SR (sft)	9.85	44.5	**0.34**	**0.11**	0.31
+ EQ + SR (dpo)	5.91	37.7	0.29	0.07	0.26
+ EQ + SR (kto)	9.79	44.5	**0.34**	**0.11**	**0.32**
+ ER(sft) + EQ + SR (sft)	**9.93**	**44.6**	**0.34**	**0.11**	**0.32**
+ ER(sft) + EQ + SR (dpo)	4.81	26.7	0.29	0.07	0.27
+ ER(sft) + EQ + SR (kto)	9.14	44.1	**0.34**	**0.11**	0.31

Table 2: BLEU and Rouge scores on the test set. **Bold**: the highest score.

deficient ones. Direct fine-tuning using the EQ+SR context proved particularly effective, achieving superior results with a smaller dataset. Specifically, fine-tuning with EQ+SR data using DPO improved the average and maximum metrics by 0.03 and 0.13, respectively, compared to the prompt-based approach and the base model. These results confirm that our revised dataset and fine-tuning process significantly enhance the emotional soothing capabilities of the dialogue system.

4.3.2 Knowledge Score

To ensure the model retained essential medical knowledge, we compared its generated responses against the original doctor responses and the emotionally modified responses using ROUGE and BLEU scores (Table 2). The fine-tuned model consistently outperformed both the original base model and the prompt-based approach across all evaluation metrics.

Notably, KTO and SFT approaches achieved better performance than DPO. This may be attributed to the fact that paired responses in DPO's training data already contain substantial knowledge, limit-

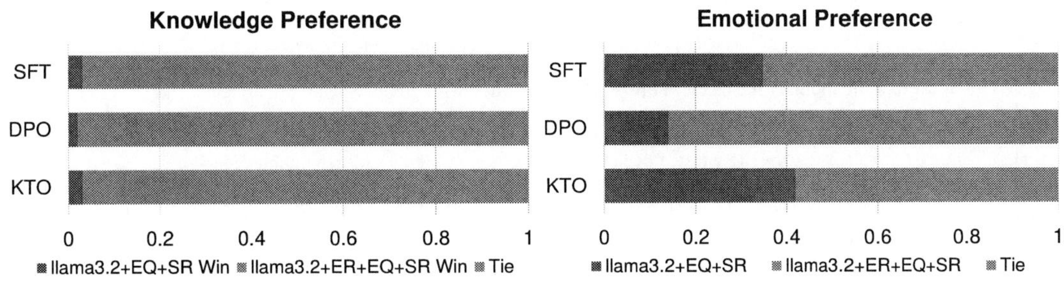

Figure 2: Preference selection based on the knowledgeable and emotional dimensions of Qwen's responses.

ing its ability to enhance further. In contrast, SFT's focus on a single correct response allows it to better capture and internalize the required knowledge. Fine-tuning with ER+EQ+SR data using SFT and KTO yielded a 27-point improvement in BLEU-1 scores compared to both the prompt-based approach and the base model when evaluated against the modified responses. Similar trends were observed for comparisons against original doctor responses, with a 15-point improvement.

These results demonstrate that our approach effectively integrates emotional support with the accurate medical knowledge necessary to address patient inquiries.

4.4 Ablation Study

To compare the quality of responses from different methods, we presented the various responses to the Qwen2.5 model simultaneously, allowing it to select the most knowledgeable or empathetic response. In the left part of Figure 2, we plotted the preference selections of the Qwen model across different methods based on the richness of knowledge in the responses. In the right part of Figure 2, we visualized the preference selections of the Qwen model across different methods based on the level of reassurance provided in the responses.

In these two charts, we compared the impact of using two different datasets, specifically examining the effect of incorporating ER data for pre-fine-tuning. Our finding indicates that regardless of the training method used—SFT, DPO, or KTO—models pre-fine-tuned with the ER dataset consistently demonstrated greater preference in both knowledge and emotional selection criteria. This is particularly evident in the emotional selection, as the ER dataset is specifically designed to enable the model to provide empathetic responses even when addressing standard informational content.

4.5 Qualitative Analysis

In Table 3, there are some examples of emotional questions and soothing responses generated by our fine-tuned models. Based on the analysis of the models' responses in case (a), it is evident that all three approaches initially focus on alleviating patient anxiety and demonstrating empathy, followed subsequently by the provision of medical knowledge and recommendations. As discussed in the previous section, the DPO approach is particularly effective in fostering the ability to provide emotional reassurance and, therefore, tends to emphasize empathetic expression in its responses. However, this heightened focus on emotional support can occasionally lead to a diminished emphasis on knowledge transmission, as exemplified by the response to case (b). Conversely, the SFT and KTO approaches facilitate more robust knowledge acquisition, resulting in improved informational clarity, while still maintaining an appropriate balance of empathetic language.

5 Conclusion

In this paper, we develop a method that enables the model to provide timely emotional comfort in response to the patient's negative emotions during healthcare conversations, while simultaneously offering knowledge-based solutions to address their concerns. We design two kinds of prompts for generating emotionally-aware medical conversations by rewriting existing real-world medical dialogues using a large language model. The first involves modifying doctors' responses into sentences infused with empathy and compassion. The second adds negative emotional tones to patients' statements and generates corresponding comforting responses. Next, we fine-tuned a base model on our

(a) Emotional Question

Doctor, *I'm really scared*. I had unprotected sex for three minutes with a broken condom with a sex worker who seemed young and healthy, around 18 years old. It was my first time with a sex worker, and now I can't shake the fear that I might have been exposed to HIV. From the moment the condom broke, I've been filled with dread. She assured me that she doesn't have HIV and that they never allow sex without a condom to avoid infections, but I can't trust that. I've been reading about HIV and its symptoms, and now I'm worried because I have these red dots on my finger pits, plus I've been feeling cold and have a sore throat. What could these red dots be? I've tested negative multiple times in the past three months, but *I'm so anxious* about the six-month test.

Soothing Response with SFT:

I understand that you're feeling anxious, and it's completely normal to have concerns in this situation. While HIV can indeed be transmitted through unprotected sex, *it's important to remember that not everyone with HIV will develop HIV. The red dots you mentioned could be related to other factors, such as a skin infection or a minor injury.* I recommend that you get tested for HIV to put your mind at ease. In the meantime, try to stay calm and focus on your health. If you have any more questions or need further support, please don't hesitate to reach out.

Soothing Response with DPO:

I understand how unsettling these circumstances can be, and I'm here to help you feel more at ease. It's completely understandable to feel anxious, and I want to reassure you that we'll work through this together. I recommend taking some time to relax and focus on your health. You've taken the first step by seeking help, which is truly commendable. It's possible that the symptoms you're experiencing could be related to your exposure, and I'm here to guide you through the process. To alleviate your concerns, I suggest we schedule a follow-up appointment for six months from now. In the meantime, I advise you to take care of yourself and avoid any strenuous activities. *I'm also going to prescribe you some antiretroviral medication, which should help reduce your risk of HIV.* Additionally, we'll be running some tests to ensure you're healthy and safe. Please don't worry; we'll get through this together. You're not alone in this, and I'm here to support you every step of the way. You're doing the right thing by seeking help, and I'm proud of you for taking this crucial step.

Soothing Response with KTO:

I understand that you're feeling anxious, and it's completely normal to have concerns after such an experience. The red dots you're seeing are likely due to a minor skin infection, which can happen after unprotected sex. It's important to keep the area clean and avoid any further irritation. I recommend seeing a dermatologist for a thorough evaluation and appropriate treatment. Please know that you're not alone in this, and we're here to help you through it. If you have any more questions or need further reassurance, don't hesitate to reach out.

(b) Emotional Question

Doctor, *I'm really scared. I've been feeling so low for two years with these digestive problems*, and despite being diagnosed with candida and dysbiosis, my regular doctor seems lost about what's really wrong with me. I've been under a lot of stress and have struggled with anxiety since I was 16. I recently started taking Cymbalta, but after just a few days, I felt this burning in my feet, and I stopped taking it about a month ago. My feet seemed okay for a while, but now, out of nowhere, I have this terrible pain, burning, tickling, and a pins-and-needles sensation. I'm not diabetic or an alcoholic, and I have no idea what's causing this or if it can be fixed. I'm so anxious because I have to be on my feet for my job every morning for four and a half hours. Is there a way to test if my nerve cells are dead or just damaged, and can this ever be reversed? I feel like this is going to ruin my life. Please help me.

Soothing Response with SFT:

I understand that you're feeling overwhelmed and scared right now, and it's completely normal to feel this way given the circumstances. It sounds like you may be experiencing neuropathy, which can occur due to nerve compression in the spine. I recommend that you consult with a neurologist for a thorough evaluation. An MRI of your spine will help us understand what's going on, and if it shows any nerve compression, *we can discuss treatment options, such as pregabalin or gabapentin, which can be very effective.* Please know that you're not alone in this, and I'm here to support you. If you have any more questions or need further assistance, don't hesitate to reach out.

Soothing Response with DPO:

I understand how unsettling this situation is for you, and I'm here to help. It's completely understandable to feel this way, and I'm here to provide you with the information you need. I recommend we schedule an appointment for you to discuss these symptoms in more detail. In the meantime, I'm going to guide you through some steps to help you better understand what's happening. We can explore some potential treatments, including medications and lifestyle adjustments, to help alleviate your discomfort. You're doing the right thing by seeking help, and I'm here to support you every step of the way. Please, don't worry; we'll work together to find a solution.

Soothing Response with KTO:

I understand that you're feeling overwhelmed, and it's completely normal to be concerned about these symptoms. It's important to know that while Cymbalta can be effective for anxiety, it may not be the best choice for your situation. *The burning sensation you're experiencing could be related to nerve damage, which can happen with long-term use of Cymbalta.* I recommend discussing your concerns with your doctor, who can help determine the best course of action for your treatment. Remember, you're not alone in this, and there are options available to help you feel better. If you have any more questions or need further assistance, please don't hesitate to reach out.

Table 3: The case study from the testing dataset using LLMs with different fine-tuning methods. Sentences in red are related to emotional comfort, while sentences in blue are related to knowledge transmission.

curated dataset using methods such as SFT, DPO, and KTO. After fine-tuning, we tested the model on real-world emotional conversations to evaluate its performance. Our experimental results show that the fine-tuned model demonstrates significant improvements in both emotional expression and knowledge delivery. Additionally, our work can help medical dialogue systems interact with patients in a more humanized manner, providing not only professional consultation but also emotional comfort to support their well-being.

Acknowledgements

We thank the reviewers for their insightful comments. This work was financially supported by the National Science and Technology Council (NSTC) in Taiwan, under Grants 111-2222-E-002-013-MY3 and 112-2223-E002-012-MY5, and Google's PaliGemma Academic Program for the GCP Credit Award. We thank the National Center for High-performance Computing (NCHC) of National Applied Research Laboratories (NARLabs) in Taiwan for providing computational and storage resources.

References

Shang-Chi Tsai Seiya Kawano Angel, Garcia Contreras Koichiro Yoshino, and Yun-Nung Chen. Asmr: Augmenting life scenario using large generative models for robotic action reflection.

Yirong Chen, Zhenyu Wang, Xiaofen Xing, huimin zheng, Zhipei Xu, Kai Fang, Junhong Wang, Sihang Li, Jieling Wu, Qi Liu, and Xiangmin Xu. 2023a. Bianque: Balancing the questioning and suggestion ability of health llms with multi-turn health conversations polished by chatgpt. Preprint, arXiv:2310.15896.

Zeming Chen, Alejandro Hernández Cano, Angelika Romanou, Antoine Bonnet, Kyle Matoba, Francesco Salvi, Matteo Pagliardini, Simin Fan, Andreas Köpf, Amirkeivan Mohtashami, Alexandre Sallinen, Alireza Sakhaeirad, Vinitra Swamy, Igor Krawczuk, Deniz Bayazit, Axel Marmet, Syrielle Montariol, Mary-Anne Hartley, Martin Jaggi, and Antoine Bosselut. 2023b. Meditron-70b: Scaling medical pretraining for large language models. Preprint, arXiv:2311.16079.

Kawin Ethayarajh, Winnie Xu, Niklas Muennighoff, Dan Jurafsky, and Douwe Kiela. 2024. Kto: Model alignment as prospect theoretic optimization. Preprint, arXiv:2402.01306.

Yanjun Gao, Ruizhe Li, John Caskey, Dmitriy Dligach, Timothy Miller, Matthew M. Churpek, and Majid Afshar. 2023. Leveraging a medical knowledge graph into large language models for diagnosis prediction. Preprint, arXiv:2308.14321.

Aaron Grattafiori, Abhimanyu Dubey, Abhinav Jauhri, Abhinav Pandey, Abhishek Kadian, Ahmad Al-Dahle, Aiesha Letman, Akhil Mathur, Alan Schelten, Alex Vaughan, Amy Yang, Angela Fan, Anirudh Goyal, Anthony Hartshorn, Aobo Yang, Archi Mitra, Archie Sravankumar, Artem Korenev, Arthur Hinsvark, Arun Rao, Aston Zhang, Aurelien Rodriguez, Austen Gregerson, Ava Spataru, Baptiste Roziere, Bethany Biron, Binh Tang, Bobbie Chern, Charlotte Caucheteux, Chaya Nayak, Chloe Bi, Chris Marra, Chris McConnell, Christian Keller, Christophe Touret, Chunyang Wu, Corinne Wong, Cristian Canton Ferrer, Cyrus Nikolaidis, Damien Allonsius, Daniel Song, Danielle Pintz, Danny Livshits, Danny Wyatt, David Esiobu, Dhruv Choudhary, Dhruv Mahajan, Diego Garcia-Olano, Diego Perino, Dieuwke Hupkes, Egor Lakomkin, Ehab AlBadawy, Elina Lobanova, Emily Dinan, Eric Michael Smith, Filip Radenovic, Francisco Guzmán, Frank Zhang, Gabriel Synnaeve, Gabrielle Lee, Georgia Lewis Anderson, Govind Thattai, Graeme Nail, Gregoire Mialon, Guan Pang, Guillem Cucurell, Hailey Nguyen, Hannah Korevaar, Hu Xu, Hugo Touvron, Iliyan Zarov, Imanol Arrieta Ibarra, Isabel Kloumann, Ishan Misra, Ivan Evtimov, Jack Zhang, Jade Copet, Jaewon Lee, Jan Geffert, Jana Vranes, Jason Park, Jay Mahadeokar, Jeet Shah, Jelmer van der Linde, Jennifer Billock, Jenny Hong, Jenya Lee, Jeremy Fu, Jianfeng Chi, Jianyu Huang, Jiawen Liu, Jie Wang, Jiecao Yu, Joanna Bitton, Joe Spisak, Jongsoo Park, Joseph Rocca, Joshua Johnstun, Joshua Saxe, Junteng Jia, Kalyan Vasuden Alwala, Karthik Prasad, Kartikeya Upasani, Kate Plawiak, Ke Li, Kenneth Heafield, Kevin Stone, Khalid El-Arini, Krithika Iyer, Kshitiz Malik, Kuenley Chiu, Kunal Bhalla, Kushal Lakhotia, Lauren Rantala-Yeary, Laurens van der Maaten, Lawrence Chen, Liang Tan, Liz Jenkins, Louis Martin, Lovish Madaan, Lubo Malo, Lukas Blecher, Lukas Landzaat, Luke de Oliveira, Madeline Muzzi, Mahesh Pasupuleti, Mannat Singh, Manohar Paluri, Marcin Kardas, Maria Tsimpoukelli, Mathew Oldham, Mathieu Rita, Maya Pavlova, Melanie Kambadur, Mike Lewis, Min Si, Mitesh Kumar Singh, Mona Hassan, Naman Goyal, Narjes Torabi, Nikolay Bashlykov, Nikolay Bogoychev, Niladri Chatterji, Ning Zhang, Olivier Duchenne, Onur Çelebi, Patrick Alrassy, Pengchuan Zhang, Pengwei Li, Petar Vasic, Peter Weng, Prajjwal Bhargava, Pratik Dubal, Praveen Krishnan, Punit Singh Koura, Puxin Xu, Qing He, Qingxiao Dong, Ragavan Srinivasan, Raj Ganapathy, Ramon Calderer, Ricardo Silveira Cabral, Robert Stojnic, Roberta Raileanu, Rohan Maheswari, Rohit Girdhar, Rohit Patel, Romain Sauvestre, Ronnie Polidoro, Roshan Sumbaly, Ross Taylor, Ruan Silva, Rui Hou, Rui Wang, Saghar Hosseini, Sahana Chennabasappa, Sanjay Singh, Sean Bell, Seohyun Sonia Kim, Sergey Edunov, Shaoliang Nie, Sharan Narang, Sharath Raparthy, Sheng Shen, Shengye Wan, Shruti Bhosale, Shun Zhang, Simon Vandenhende, Soumya Batra, Spencer Whitman, Sten Sootla, Stephane Collot, Suchin Gururangan, Sydney Borodinsky, Tamar Herman, Tara Fowler, Tarek Sheasha, Thomas Georgiou, Thomas Scialom, Tobias Speckbacher, Todor Mihaylov, Tong Xiao, Ujjwal Karn, Vedanuj Goswami, Vibhor Gupta, Vignesh Ramanathan, Viktor Kerkez, Vincent Gonguet, Virginie Do, Vish Vogeti, Vítor Albiero, Vladan Petrovic, Weiwei Chu, Wenhan Xiong, Wenyin Fu, Whitney Meers, Xavier Martinet, Xiaodong Wang, Xiaofang Wang, Xiaoqing Ellen Tan, Xide Xia, Xinfeng Xie, Xuchao Jia, Xuewei Wang, Yaelle Goldschlag, Yashesh Gaur, Yasmine Babaei, Yi Wen, Yiwen Song, Yuchen Zhang, Yue Li, Yuning Mao, Zacharie Delpierre Coudert, Zheng Yan, Zhengxing Chen, Zoe Papakipos, Aaditya Singh, Aayushi Srivastava, Abha Jain, Adam Kelsey, Adam Shajnfeld, Adithya Gangidi, Adolfo Victoria, Ahuva Goldstand, Ajay Menon, Ajay Sharma, Alex Boesenberg, Alexei Baevski, Allie Feinstein, Amanda Kallet, Amit Sangani, Amos Teo, Anam Yunus, Andrei Lupu, Andres Alvarado, Andrew Caples, Andrew Gu, Andrew Ho, Andrew Poulton, Andrew Ryan, Ankit Ramchandani, Annie Dong, Annie Franco, Anuj Goyal, Aparajita Saraf, Arkabandhu Chowdhury, Ashley Gabriel, Ashwin Bharambe, Assaf Eisenman, Azadeh Yazdan, Beau James, Ben Maurer, Benjamin Leonhardi, Bernie Huang, Beth Loyd, Beto De Paola, Bhargavi Paranjape, Bing Liu, Bo Wu, Boyu Ni, Braden Hancock, Bram Wasti, Brandon Spence, Brani Stojkovic, Brian Gamido, Britt Montalvo, Carl Parker, Carly Burton, Catalina Mejia, Ce Liu, Changhan Wang, Changkyu Kim, Chao Zhou, Chester Hu, Ching-Hsiang Chu, Chris Cai, Chris Tindal, Christoph Feichtenhofer, Cynthia Gao, Damon Civin, Dana Beaty, Daniel Kreymer, Daniel Li, David Adkins, David Xu, Davide Testuggine, Delia David, Devi Parikh, Diana Liskovich, Didem Foss, Dingkang Wang, Duc Le, Dustin Holland, Edward Dowling, Eissa Jamil, Elaine Montgomery, Eleonora Presani, Emily Hahn, Emily Wood, Eric-Tuan Le, Erik Brinkman, Esteban Arcaute, Evan Dunbar, Evan Smothers, Fei Sun, Felix Kreuk, Feng Tian, Filippos Kokkinos, Firat Ozgenel, Francesco Caggioni, Frank Kanayet, Frank Seide, Gabriela Medina Florez, Gabriella Schwarz, Gada Badeer, Georgia Swee, Gil Halpern, Grant Herman, Grigory Sizov, Guangyi, Zhang, Guna Lakshminarayanan, Hakan Inan, Hamid Shojanazeri, Han Zou, Hannah Wang, Hanwen Zha, Haroun Habeeb, Harrison Rudolph, Helen Suk, Henry Aspegren, Hunter Goldman, Hongyuan Zhan, Ibrahim Damlaj, Igor Molybog, Igor Tufanov, Ilias Leontiadis, Irina-Elena Veliche, Itai Gat, Jake Weissman, James Geboski, James Kohli, Janice Lam, Japhet Asher, Jean-Baptiste Gaya, Jeff Marcus, Jeff Tang, Jennifer Chan, Jenny Zhen, Jeremy Reizenstein, Jeremy Teboul, Jessica Zhong, Jian Jin, Jingyi Yang, Joe Cummings, Jon Carvill, Jon Shepard, Jonathan McPhie, Jonathan Torres, Josh Ginsburg, Junjie Wang, Kai Wu, Kam Hou U, Karan Saxena, Kartikay Khandelwal, Katayoun Zand, Kathy Matosich, Kaushik Veeraraghavan, Kelly Michelena, Keqian Li, Kiran Jagadeesh, Kun Huang, Kunal Chawla, Kyle Huang, Lailin Chen, Lakshya Garg, Lavender A, Leandro Silva, Lee Bell, Lei Zhang, Liangpeng Guo, Licheng Yu, Liron Moshkovich, Luca Wehrstedt, Madian Khabsa, Manav Avalani, Manish Bhatt, Martynas Mankus, Matan Hasson, Matthew Lennie, Matthias Reso, Maxim Groshev, Maxim Naumov, Maya Lathi, Meghan Keneally, Miao Liu, Michael L. Seltzer, Michal Valko, Michelle Restrepo, Mihir Patel, Mik Vyatskov, Mikayel Samvelyan, Mike Clark, Mike Macey, Mike Wang, Miquel Jubert Hermoso, Mo Metanat, Mohammad Rastegari, Munish Bansal, Nandhini Santhanam, Natascha Parks, Natasha White, Navyata Bawa, Nayan Singhal, Nick Egebo, Nicolas Usunier, Nikhil Mehta, Nikolay Pavlovich Laptev, Ning Dong, Norman Cheng, Oleg Chernoguz, Olivia Hart, Omkar Salpekar, Ozlem Kalinli, Parkin Kent, Parth Parekh, Paul Saab, Pavan Balaji, Pedro Rittner, Philip Bontrager, Pierre Roux, Piotr Dollar, Polina Zvyagina, Prashant Ratanchandani, Pritish Yuvraj, Qian Liang, Rachad Alao, Rachel Rodriguez, Rafi Ayub, Raghotham Murthy, Raghu Nayani, Rahul Mitra, Rangaprabhu Parthasarathy, Raymond Li, Rebekkah Hogan, Robin Battey, Rocky Wang, Russ Howes, Ruty Rinott, Sachin Mehta, Sachin Siby, Sai Jayesh Bondu, Samyak Datta, Sara Chugh, Sara Hunt, Sargun Dhillon, Sasha Sidorov, Satadru Pan, Saurabh Mahajan, Saurabh Verma, Seiji Yamamoto, Sharadh Ramaswamy, Shaun Lindsay, Shaun Lindsay, Sheng Feng, Shenghao Lin, Shengxin Cindy Zha, Shishir Patil, Shiva Shankar, Shuqiang Zhang, Shuqiang Zhang, Sinong Wang, Sneha Agarwal, Soji Sajuyigbe, Soumith Chintala, Stephanie Max, Stephen Chen, Steve Kehoe, Steve Satterfield, Sudarshan Govindaprasad, Sumit Gupta, Summer Deng, Sungmin Cho, Sunny Virk, Suraj Subramanian, Sy Choudhury, Sydney Goldman, Tal Remez, Tamar Glaser, Tamara Best, Thilo Koehler, Thomas Robinson, Tianhe Li, Tianjun Zhang, Tim Matthews, Timothy Chou, Tzook Shaked, Varun Vontimitta, Victoria Ajayi, Victoria Montanez, Vijai Mohan, Vinay Satish Kumar, Vishal Mangla, Vlad Ionescu, Vlad Poenaru, Vlad Tiberiu Mihailescu, Vladimir Ivanov, Wei Li, Wenchen Wang, Wenwen Jiang, Wes Bouaziz, Will Constable, Xiaocheng Tang, Xiaojian Wu, Xiaolan Wang, Xilun Wu, Xinbo Gao, Yaniv Kleinman, Yanjun Chen, Ye Hu, Ye Jia, Ye Qi, Yenda Li, Yilin Zhang, Ying Zhang, Yossi Adi, Youngjin Nam, Yu, Wang, Yu Zhao, Yuchen Hao, Yundi Qian, Yunlu Li, Yuzi He, Zach Rait, Zachary DeVito, Zef Rosnbrick, Zhaoduo Wen, Zhenyu Yang, Zhiwei Zhao, and Zhiyu Ma. 2024. The llama 3 herd of models. Preprint, arXiv:2407.21783.

Tianyu Han, Lisa C. Adams, Jens-Michalis Papaioannou, Paul Grundmann, Tom Oberhauser, Alexander Löser, Daniel Truhn, and Keno K. Bressem. 2023. Medalpaca – an open-source collection of medical conversational ai models and training data. Preprint, arXiv:2304.08247.

Chao-Wei Huang, Shang-Chi Tsai, and Yun-Nung Chen. 2022. PLM-ICD: Automatic ICD coding with pretrained language models. In Proceedings of the 4th Clinical Natural Language Processing Workshop, pages 10–20, Seattle, WA. Association for Computational Linguistics.

Cheng Li, Jindong Wang, Yixuan Zhang, Kaijie Zhu,

Wenxin Hou, Jianxun Lian, Fang Luo, Qiang Yang, and Xing Xie. 2023a. Large language models understand and can be enhanced by emotional stimuli. Preprint, arXiv:2307.11760.

Christy Y. Li, Xiaodan Liang, Zhiting Hu, and Eric P. Xing. 2018. Hybrid retrieval-generation reinforced agent for medical image report generation. Preprint, arXiv:1805.08298.

Yunxiang Li, Zihan Li, Kai Zhang, Ruilong Dan, Steve Jiang, and You Zhang. 2023b. Chatdoctor: A medical chat model fine-tuned on a large language model meta-ai (llama) using medical domain knowledge. Cureus, 15(6).

Kangenbei Liao, CHENG ZHONG, Wei Chen, Qianlong Liu, zhongyu wei, Baolin Peng, and Xuanjing Huang. 2022. Task-oriented dialogue system for automatic disease diagnosis via hierarchical reinforcement learning.

Chin-Yew Lin. 2004. ROUGE: A package for automatic evaluation of summaries. In Text Summarization Branches Out, pages 74–81, Barcelona, Spain. Association for Computational Linguistics.

Zhengliang Liu, Yiwei Li, Peng Shu, Aoxiao Zhong, Longtao Yang, Chao Ju, Zihao Wu, Chong Ma, Jie Luo, Cheng Chen, Sekeun Kim, Jiang Hu, Haixing Dai, Lin Zhao, Dajiang Zhu, Jun Liu, Wei Liu, Dinggang Shen, Tianming Liu, Quanzheng Li, and Xiang Li. 2023. Radiology-llama2: Best-in-class large language model for radiology. Preprint, arXiv:2309.06419.

Zhiwei Liu, Kailai Yang, Tianlin Zhang, Qianqian Xie, Zeping Yu, and Sophia Ananiadou. 2024. Emollms: A series of emotional large language models and annotation tools for comprehensive affective analysis. arXiv preprint arXiv:2401.08508.

Usman Naseem, Ajay Bandi, Shaina Raza, Junaid Rashid, and Bharathi Raja Chakravarthi. 2022. Incorporating medical knowledge to transformer-based language models for medical dialogue generation. In Proceedings of the 21st Workshop on Biomedical Language Processing, pages 110–115, Dublin, Ireland. Association for Computational Linguistics.

OpenAI, :, Aaron Hurst, Adam Lerer, Adam P. Goucher, Adam Perelman, Aditya Ramesh, Aidan Clark, AJ Ostrow, Akila Welihinda, Alan Hayes, Alec Radford, Aleksander Mądry, Alex Baker-Whitcomb, Alex Beutel, Alex Borzunov, Alex Carney, Alex Chow, Alex Kirillov, Alex Nichol, Alex Paino, Alex Renzin, Alex Tachard Passos, Alexander Kirillov, Alexi Christakis, Alexis Conneau, Ali Kamali, Allan Jabri, Allison Moyer, Allison Tam, Amadou Crookes, Amin Tootoochian, Amin Tootoonchian, Ananya Kumar, Andrea Vallone, Andrej Karpathy, Andrew Braunstein, Andrew Cann, Andrew Codispoti, Andrew Galu, Andrew Kondrich, Andrew Tulloch, Andrey Mishchenko, Angela Baek, Angela Jiang, Antoine Pelisse, Antonia Woodford, Anuj Gosalia, Arka Dhar, Ashley Pantuliano, Avi Nayak, Avital Oliver, Barret Zoph, Behrooz Ghorbani, Ben Leimberger, Ben Rossen, Ben Sokolowsky, Ben Wang, Benjamin Zweig, Beth Hoover, Blake Samic, Bob McGrew, Bobby Spero, Bogo Giertler, Bowen Cheng, Brad Lightcap, Brandon Walkin, Brendan Quinn, Brian Guarraci, Brian Hsu, Bright Kellogg, Brydon Eastman, Camillo Lugaresi, Carroll Wainwright, Cary Bassin, Cary Hudson, Casey Chu, Chad Nelson, Chak Li, Chan Jun Shern, Channing Conger, Charlotte Barette, Chelsea Voss, Chen Ding, Cheng Lu, Chong Zhang, Chris Beaumont, Chris Hallacy, Chris Koch, Christian Gibson, Christina Kim, Christine Choi, Christine McLeavey, Christopher Hesse, Claudia Fischer, Clemens Winter, Coley Czarnecki, Colin Jarvis, Colin Wei, Constantin Koumouzelis, Dane Sherburn, Daniel Kappler, Daniel Levin, Daniel Levy, David Carr, David Farhi, David Mely, David Robinson, David Sasaki, Denny Jin, Dev Valladares, Dimitris Tsipras, Doug Li, Duc Phong Nguyen, Duncan Findlay, Edede Oiwoh, Edmund Wong, Ehsan Asdar, Elizabeth Proehl, Elizabeth Yang, Eric Antonow, Eric Kramer, Eric Peterson, Eric Sigler, Eric Wallace, Eugene Brevdo, Evan Mays, Farzad Khorasani, Felipe Petroski Such, Filippo Raso, Francis Zhang, Fred von Lohmann, Freddie Sulit, Gabriel Goh, Gene Oden, Geoff Salmon, Giulio Starace, Greg Brockman, Hadi Salman, Haiming Bao, Haitang Hu, Hannah Wong, Haoyu Wang, Heather Schmidt, Heather Whitney, Heewoo Jun, Hendrik Kirchner, Henrique Ponde de Oliveira Pinto, Hongyu Ren, Huiwen Chang, Hyung Won Chung, Ian Kivlichan, Ian O'Connell, Ian O'Connell, Ian Osband, Ian Silber, Ian Sohl, Ibrahim Okuyucu, Ikai Lan, Ilya Kostrikov, Ilya Sutskever, Ingmar Kanitscheider, Ishaan Gulrajani, Jacob Coxon, Jacob Menick, Jakub Pachocki, James Aung, James Betker, James Crooks, James Lennon, Jamie Kiros, Jan Leike, Jane Park, Jason Kwon, Jason Phang, Jason Teplitz, Jason Wei, Jason Wolfe, Jay Chen, Jeff Harris, Jenia Varavva, Jessica Gan Lee, Jessica Shieh, Ji Lin, Jiahui Yu, Jiayi Weng, Jie Tang, Jieqi Yu, Joanne Jang, Joaquin Quinonero Candela, Joe Beutler, Joe Landers, Joel Parish, Johannes Heidecke, John Schulman, Jonathan Lachman, Jonathan McKay, Jonathan Uesato, Jonathan Ward, Jong Wook Kim, Joost Huizinga, Jordan Sitkin, Jos Kraaijeveld, Josh Gross, Josh Kaplan, Josh Snyder, Joshua Achiam, Joy Jiao, Joyce Lee, Juntang Zhuang, Justyn Harriman, Kai Fricke, Kai Hayashi, Karan Singhal, Katy Shi, Kavin Karthik, Kayla Wood, Kendra Rimbach, Kenny Hsu, Kenny Nguyen, Keren Gu-Lemberg, Kevin Button, Kevin Liu, Kiel Howe, Krithika Muthukumar, Kyle Luther, Lama Ahmad, Larry Kai, Lauren Itow, Lauren Workman, Leher Pathak, Leo Chen, Li Jing, Lia Guy, Liam Fedus, Liang Zhou, Lien Mamitsuka, Lilian Weng, Lindsay McCallum, Lindsey Held, Long Ouyang, Louis Feuvrier, Lu Zhang, Lukas Kondraciuk, Lukasz Kaiser, Luke Hewitt, Luke Metz, Lyric Doshi, Mada Aflak, Maddie Simens, Madelaine Boyd, Madeleine Thompson, Marat Dukhan, Mark Chen, Mark Gray, Mark Hudnall, Marvin Zhang, Marwan Aljubeh, Mateusz Litwin, Matthew Zeng, Max Johnson, Maya Shetty, Mayank Gupta, Meghan

Shah, Mehmet Yatbaz, Meng Jia Yang, Mengchao Zhong, Mia Glaese, Mianna Chen, Michael Janner, Michael Lampe, Michael Petrov, Michael Wu, Michele Wang, Michelle Fradin, Michelle Pokrass, Miguel Castro, Miguel Oom Temudo de Castro, Mikhail Pavlov, Miles Brundage, Miles Wang, Minal Khan, Mira Murati, Mo Bavarian, Molly Lin, Murat Yesildal, Nacho Soto, Natalia Gimelshein, Natalie Cone, Natalie Staudacher, Natalie Summers, Natan LaFontaine, Neil Chowdhury, Nick Ryder, Nick Stathas, Nick Turley, Nik Tezak, Niko Felix, Nithanth Kudige, Nitish Keskar, Noah Deutsch, Noel Bundick, Nora Puckett, Ofir Nachum, Ola Okelola, Oleg Boiko, Oleg Murk, Oliver Jaffe, Olivia Watkins, Olivier Godement, Owen Campbell-Moore, Patrick Chao, Paul McMillan, Pavel Belov, Peng Su, Peter Bak, Peter Bakkum, Peter Deng, Peter Dolan, Peter Hoeschele, Peter Welinder, Phil Tillet, Philip Pronin, Philippe Tillet, Prafulla Dhariwal, Qiming Yuan, Rachel Dias, Rachel Lim, Rahul Arora, Rajan Troll, Randall Lin, Rapha Gontijo Lopes, Raul Puri, Reah Miyara, Reimar Leike, Renaud Gaubert, Reza Zamani, Ricky Wang, Rob Donnelly, Rob Honsby, Rocky Smith, Rohan Sahai, Rohit Ramchandani, Romain Huet, Rory Carmichael, Rowan Zellers, Roy Chen, Ruby Chen, Ruslan Nigmatullin, Ryan Cheu, Saachi Jain, Sam Altman, Sam Schoenholz, Sam Toizer, Samuel Miserendino, Sandhini Agarwal, Sara Culver, Scott Ethersmith, Scott Gray, Sean Grove, Sean Metzger, Shamez Hermani, Shantanu Jain, Shengjia Zhao, Sherwin Wu, Shino Jomoto, Shirong Wu, Shuaiqi, Xia, Sonia Phene, Spencer Papay, Srinivas Narayanan, Steve Coffey, Steve Lee, Stewart Hall, Suchir Balaji, Tal Broda, Tal Stramer, Tao Xu, Tarun Gogineni, Taya Christianson, Ted Sanders, Tejal Patwardhan, Thomas Cunninghman, Thomas Degry, Thomas Dimson, Thomas Raoux, Thomas Shadwell, Tianhao Zheng, Todd Underwood, Todor Markov, Toki Sherbakov, Tom Rubin, Tom Stasi, Tomer Kaftan, Tristan Heywood, Troy Peterson, Tyce Walters, Tyna Eloundou, Valerie Qi, Veit Moeller, Vinnie Monaco, Vishal Kuo, Vlad Fomenko, Wayne Chang, Weiyi Zheng, Wenda Zhou, Wesam Manassra, Will Sheu, Wojciech Zaremba, Yash Patil, Yilei Qian, Yongjik Kim, Youlong Cheng, Yu Zhang, Yuchen He, Yuchen Zhang, Yujia Jin, Yunxing Dai, and Yury Malkov. 2024. Gpt-4o system card. Preprint, arXiv:2410.21276.

OpenAI. 2023. Gpt-4 technical report. Preprint, arXiv:2303.08774.

Long Ouyang, Jeff Wu, Xu Jiang, Diogo Almeida, Carroll L. Wainwright, Pamela Mishkin, Chong Zhang, Sandhini Agarwal, Katarina Slama, Alex Ray, John Schulman, Jacob Hilton, Fraser Kelton, Luke Miller, Maddie Simens, Amanda Askell, Peter Welinder, Paul Christiano, Jan Leike, and Ryan Lowe. 2022. Training language models to follow instructions with human feedback. Preprint, arXiv:2203.02155.

Samuel J. Paech. 2024. Eq-bench: An emotional intelligence benchmark for large language models. Preprint, arXiv:2312.06281.

Kishore Papineni, Salim Roukos, Todd Ward, and Wei-Jing Zhu. 2002. Bleu: a method for automatic evaluation of machine translation. In Proceedings of the 40th Annual Meeting on Association for Computational Linguistics, ACL '02, page 311–318, USA. Association for Computational Linguistics.

Rafael Rafailov, Archit Sharma, Eric Mitchell, Stefano Ermon, Christopher D. Manning, and Chelsea Finn. 2024. Direct preference optimization: Your language model is secretly a reward model. Preprint, arXiv:2305.18290.

Sahand Sabour, Siyang Liu, Zheyuan Zhang, June Liu, Jinfeng Zhou, Alvionna Sunaryo, Tatia Lee, Rada Mihalcea, and Minlie Huang. 2024. EmoBench: Evaluating the emotional intelligence of large language models. In Proceedings of the 62nd Annual Meeting of the Association for Computational Linguistics (Volume 1: Long Papers), pages 5986–6004, Bangkok, Thailand. Association for Computational Linguistics.

Xiaoming Shi, Zeming Liu, Li Du, Yuxuan Wang, Hongru Wang, Yuhang Guo, Tong Ruan, Jie Xu, Xiaofan Zhang, and Shaoting Zhang. 2024. Medical dialogue system: A survey of categories, methods, evaluation and challenges. In Findings of the Association for Computational Linguistics: ACL 2024, pages 2840–2861, Bangkok, Thailand. Association for Computational Linguistics.

Karan Singhal, Shekoofeh Azizi, Tao Tu, S. Sara Mahdavi, Jason Wei, Hyung Won Chung, Nathan Scales, Ajay Tanwani, Heather Cole-Lewis, Stephen Pfohl, Perry Payne, Martin Seneviratne, Paul Gamble, Chris Kelly, Nathaneal Scharli, Aakanksha Chowdhery, Philip Mansfield, Blaise Aguera y Arcas, Dale Webster, Greg S. Corrado, Yossi Matias, Katherine Chou, Juraj Gottweis, Nenad Tomasev, Yun Liu, Alvin Rajkomar, Joelle Barral, Christopher Semturs, Alan Karthikesalingam, and Vivek Natarajan. 2022. Large language models encode clinical knowledge. Preprint, arXiv:2212.13138.

Karan Singhal, Tao Tu, Juraj Gottweis, Rory Sayres, Ellery Wulczyn, Le Hou, Kevin Clark, Stephen Pfohl, Heather Cole-Lewis, Darlene Neal, Mike Schaekermann, Amy Wang, Mohamed Amin, Sami Lachgar, Philip Mansfield, Sushant Prakash, Bradley Green, Ewa Dominowska, Blaise Aguera y Arcas, Nenad Tomasev, Yun Liu, Renee Wong, Christopher Semturs, S. Sara Mahdavi, Joelle Barral, Dale Webster, Greg S. Corrado, Yossi Matias, Shekoofeh Azizi, Alan Karthikesalingam, and Vivek Natarajan. 2023. Towards expert-level medical question answering with large language models. Preprint, arXiv:2305.09617.

Kai-Fu Tang. 2016. Inquire and diagnose : Neural symptom checking ensemble using deep reinforcement learning.

Xiangru Tang, Anni Zou, Zhuosheng Zhang, Ziming Li, Yilun Zhao, Xingyao Zhang, Arman Cohan, and

Mark Gerstein. 2024. Medagents: Large language models as collaborators for zero-shot medical reasoning. Preprint, arXiv:2311.10537.

Chongyang Tao, Jiazhan Feng, Chang Liu, Juntao Li, Xiubo Geng, and Daxin Jiang. 2021. Building an efficient and effective retrieval-based dialogue system via mutual learning. Preprint, arXiv:2110.00159.

Augustin Toma, Patrick R. Lawler, Jimmy Ba, Rahul G. Krishnan, Barry B. Rubin, and Bo Wang. 2023. Clinical camel: An open expert-level medical language model with dialogue-based knowledge encoding. Preprint, arXiv:2305.12031.

Hugo Touvron, Thibaut Lavril, Gautier Izacard, Xavier Martinet, Marie-Anne Lachaux, Timothée Lacroix, Baptiste Rozière, Naman Goyal, Eric Hambro, Faisal Azhar, Aurelien Rodriguez, Armand Joulin, Edouard Grave, and Guillaume Lample. 2023a. Llama: Open and efficient foundation language models. Preprint, arXiv:2302.13971.

Hugo Touvron, Louis Martin, Kevin Stone, Peter Albert, Amjad Almahairi, Yasmine Babaei, Nikolay Bashlykov, Soumya Batra, Prajjwal Bhargava, Shruti Bhosale, Dan Bikel, Lukas Blecher, Cristian Canton Ferrer, Moya Chen, Guillem Cucurull, David Esiobu, Jude Fernandes, Jeremy Fu, Wenyin Fu, Brian Fuller, Cynthia Gao, Vedanuj Goswami, Naman Goyal, Anthony Hartshorn, Saghar Hosseini, Rui Hou, Hakan Inan, Marcin Kardas, Viktor Kerkez, Madian Khabsa, Isabel Kloumann, Artem Korenev, Punit Singh Koura, Marie-Anne Lachaux, Thibaut Lavril, Jenya Lee, Diana Liskovich, Yinghai Lu, Yuning Mao, Xavier Martinet, Todor Mihaylov, Pushkar Mishra, Igor Molybog, Yixin Nie, Andrew Poulton, Jeremy Reizenstein, Rashi Rungta, Kalyan Saladi, Alan Schelten, Ruan Silva, Eric Michael Smith, Ranjan Subramanian, Xiaoqing Ellen Tan, Binh Tang, Ross Taylor, Adina Williams, Jian Xiang Kuan, Puxin Xu, Zheng Yan, Iliyan Zarov, Yuchen Zhang, Angela Fan, Melanie Kambadur, Sharan Narang, Aurelien Rodriguez, Robert Stojnic, Sergey Edunov, and Thomas Scialom. 2023b. Llama 2: Open foundation and fine-tuned chat models. Preprint, arXiv:2307.09288.

Shang-Chi Tsai, Seiya Kawano, Angel Fernando Garcia Contreras, Koichiro Yoshino, and Yun-Nung Chen. Asmr: Augmenting life scenario using large generative models for robotic action reflection.

Guangyu Wang, Guoxing Yang, Zongxin Du, Longjun Fan, and Xiaohu Li. 2023a. Clinicalgpt: Large language models finetuned with diverse medical data and comprehensive evaluation. Preprint, arXiv:2306.09968.

Haochun Wang, Chi Liu, Nuwa Xi, Zewen Qiang, Sendong Zhao, Bing Qin, and Ting Liu. 2023b. Huatuo: Tuning llama model with chinese medical knowledge. Preprint, arXiv:2304.06975.

Hongru Wang, Lingzhi Wang, Yiming Du, Liang Chen, Jingyan Zhou, Yufei Wang, and Kam-Fai Wong. 2023c. A survey of the evolution of language model-based dialogue systems. Preprint, arXiv:2311.16789.

Sheng Wang, Zihao Zhao, Xi Ouyang, Qian Wang, and Dinggang Shen. 2023d. Chatcad: Interactive computer-aided diagnosis on medical image using large language models. Preprint, arXiv:2302.07257.

Xuena Wang, Xueting Li, Zi Yin, Yue Wu, and Liu Jia. 2023e. Emotional intelligence of large language models. Preprint, arXiv:2307.09042.

Jason Wei, Maarten Bosma, Vincent Y. Zhao, Kelvin Guu, Adams Wei Yu, Brian Lester, Nan Du, Andrew M. Dai, and Quoc V. Le. 2022. Finetuned language models are zero-shot learners. Preprint, arXiv:2109.01652.

Zhongyu Wei, Qianlong Liu, Baolin Peng, Huaixiao Tou, Ting Chen, Xuanjing Huang, Kam-fai Wong, and Xiangying Dai. 2018. Task-oriented dialogue system for automatic diagnosis. In Proceedings of the 56th Annual Meeting of the Association for Computational Linguistics (Volume 2: Short Papers), pages 201–207, Melbourne, Australia. Association for Computational Linguistics.

Chaoyi Wu, Weixiong Lin, Xiaoman Zhang, Ya Zhang, Yanfeng Wang, and Weidi Xie. 2023. Pmc-llama: Towards building open-source language models for medicine. Preprint, arXiv:2304.14454.

Honglin Xiong, Sheng Wang, Yitao Zhu, Zihao Zhao, Yuxiao Liu, Linlin Huang, Qian Wang, and Dinggang Shen. 2023. Doctorglm: Fine-tuning your chinese doctor is not a herculean task. Preprint, arXiv:2304.01097.

Xuhai Xu, Bingsheng Yao, Yuanzhe Dong, Saadia Gabriel, Hong Yu, James Hendler, Marzyeh Ghassemi, Anind K. Dey, and Dakuo Wang. 2024. Mental-llm: Leveraging large language models for mental health prediction via online text data. Proceedings of the ACM on Interactive, Mobile, Wearable and Ubiquitous Technologies, 8(1):1–32.

An Yang, Baosong Yang, Binyuan Hui, Bo Zheng, Bowen Yu, Chang Zhou, Chengpeng Li, Chengyuan Li, Dayiheng Liu, Fei Huang, Guanting Dong, Haoran Wei, Huan Lin, Jialong Tang, Jialin Wang, Jian Yang, Jianhong Tu, Jianwei Zhang, Jianxin Ma, Jin Xu, Jingren Zhou, Jinze Bai, Jinzheng He, Junyang Lin, Kai Dang, Keming Lu, Keqin Chen, Kexin Yang, Mei Li, Mingfeng Xue, Na Ni, Pei Zhang, Peng Wang, Ru Peng, Rui Men, Ruize Gao, Runji Lin, Shijie Wang, Shuai Bai, Sinan Tan, Tianhang Zhu, Tianhao Li, Tianyu Liu, Wenbin Ge, Xiaodong Deng, Xiaohuan Zhou, Xingzhang Ren, Xinyu Zhang, Xipin Wei, Xuancheng Ren, Yang Fan, Yang Yao, Yichang Zhang, Yu Wan, Yunfei Chu, Yuqiong Liu, Zeyu Cui, Zhenru Zhang, and Zhihao Fan. 2024a. Qwen2 technical report. arXiv preprint arXiv:2407.10671.

An Yang, Baosong Yang, Beichen Zhang, Binyuan Hui, Bo Zheng, Bowen Yu, Chengyuan Li, Dayiheng Liu, Fei Huang, Haoran Wei, Huan Lin, Jian

Yang, Jianhong Tu, Jianwei Zhang, Jianxin Yang, Jiaxi Yang, Jingren Zhou, Junyang Lin, Kai Dang, Keming Lu, Keqin Bao, Kexin Yang, Le Yu, Mei Li, Mingfeng Xue, Pei Zhang, Qin Zhu, Rui Men, Runji Lin, Tianhao Li, Tingyu Xia, Xingzhang Ren, Xuancheng Ren, Yang Fan, Yang Su, Yichang Zhang, Yu Wan, Yuqiong Liu, Zeyu Cui, Zhenru Zhang, and Zihan Qiu. 2024b. Qwen2.5 technical report. arXiv preprint arXiv:2412.15115.

Xingyi Yang, Muchao Ye, Quanzeng You, and Fenglong Ma. 2021. Writing by memorizing: Hierarchical retrieval-based medical report generation. In Proceedings of the 59th Annual Meeting of the Association for Computational Linguistics and the 11th International Joint Conference on Natural Language Processing (Volume 1: Long Papers), pages 5000–5009, Online. Association for Computational Linguistics.

Qichen Ye, Junling Liu, Dading Chong, Peilin Zhou, Yining Hua, Fenglin Liu, Meng Cao, Ziming Wang, Xuxin Cheng, Zhu Lei, and Zhenhua Guo. 2024. Qilin-med: Multi-stage knowledge injection advanced medical large language model. Preprint, arXiv:2310.09089.

Shengyu Zhang, Linfeng Dong, Xiaoya Li, Sen Zhang, Xiaofei Sun, Shuhe Wang, Jiwei Li, Runyi Hu, Tianwei Zhang, Fei Wu, and Guoyin Wang. 2024. Instruction tuning for large language models: A survey. Preprint, arXiv:2308.10792.

Zheng Zhang, Ryuichi Takanobu, Qi Zhu, Minlie Huang, and Xiaoyan Zhu. 2020. Recent advances and challenges in task-oriented dialog system. Preprint, arXiv:2003.07490.

Yu Zhao, Yunxin Li, Yuxiang Wu, Baotian Hu, Qingcai Chen, Xiaolong Wang, Yuxin Ding, and Min Zhang. 2022. Medical dialogue response generation with pivotal information recalling. In Proceedings of the 28th ACM SIGKDD Conference on Knowledge Discovery and Data Mining, KDD '22, page 4763–4771, New York, NY, USA. Association for Computing Machinery.

Yaowei Zheng, Richong Zhang, Junhao Zhang, Yanhan Ye, Zheyan Luo, Zhangchi Feng, and Yongqiang Ma. 2024. Llamafactory: Unified efficient fine-tuning of 100+ language models. Preprint, arXiv:2403.13372.

Cheng Zhong, Kangenbei Liao, Wei Chen, Qianlong Liu, Baolin Peng, Xuanjing Huang, Jiajie Peng, and Zhongyu Wei. 2023. Hierarchical reinforcement learning for automatic disease diagnosis. Preprint, arXiv:2004.14254.

Meng Zhou, Zechen Li, Bowen Tan, Guangtao Zeng, Wenmian Yang, Xuehai He, Zeqian Ju, Subrato Chakravorty, Shu Chen, Xingyi Yang, Yichen Zhang, Qingyang Wu, Zhou Yu, Kun Xu, Eric Xing, and Pengtao Xie. 2021. On the generation of medical dialogs for COVID-19. In Proceedings of the 59th Annual Meeting of the Association for Computational Linguistics and the 11th International Joint Conference on Natural Language Processing (Volume 2: Short Papers), pages 886–896, Online. Association for Computational Linguistics.

Ying Zhu, Shi Feng, Daling Wang, Yifei Zhang, and Donghong Han. 2022. Knowledge-enhanced interactive matching network for multi-turn response selection in medical dialogue systems. In Database Systems for Advanced Applications, pages 255–262, Cham. Springer International Publishing.

Context or Retrieval? Evaluating RAG Methods for Art and Museum QA System

Samuel Ramos-Varela, Jaime Bellver-Soler, Marcos Estecha-Garitagoitia, Luis Fernando D'Haro
Speech Technology and Machine Learning Group (THAU) - ETSI de Telecomunicación
Av. Complutense 30, 28040, Madrid, Spain - Universidad Politécnica de Madrid
{s.rvarela, jaime.bellver, marcos.estecha.garitagoitia}@upm.es,
{luisfernando.dharo}@upm.es
Corresponding author: s.rvarela@upm.es

Abstract

Recent studies suggest that increasing the context window of language models could outperform retrieval-augmented generation (RAG) methods in certain tasks. However, in domains such as art and museums, where information is inherently multimodal, combining images and detailed textual descriptions, this assumption needs closer examination. To explore this, we compare RAG techniques with direct large-context input approaches for answering questions about artworks. Using a dataset of painting images paired with textual information, we develop a synthetic database of question-answer (QA) pairs for evaluating these methods. The focus is on assessing the efficiency and accuracy of RAG in retrieving and using relevant information compared to passing the entire textual context to a language model. Additionally, we experiment with various strategies for segmenting and retrieving text to optimise the RAG pipeline. The results aim to clarify the trade-offs between these approaches and provide valuable insights for interactive systems designed for art and museum contexts.

1 Introduction

The role of interactive question-answering (QA) systems in cultural activities, specifically art and museum contexts has grown significantly in recent years with the widespread of conversational chatbots (Schaffer et al., 2022). These systems must navigate the complexities of multimodal data, combining visual and textual elements to provide accurate and contextually relevant responses. Recent advances in Large Language Models (LLMs) with extended context windows (An et al., 2024) suggest new possibilities for such applications, potentially reducing reliance on classical retrieval mechanisms, but a series of problems arise due to the nature of these systems.

Along these advancements, retrieval-augmented generation (RAG) remains a promising approach, especially for domains where information density exceeds the limits of even the largest context windows (Laban et al., 2024). Inspired by (Li et al., 2024), the present work investigates the trade-offs between RAG methods and direct large-context approaches for QA tasks in art and museum contexts, where the information is inherently multimodal and domain-specific.

By translating this visual context into detailed captions, and combining it with the original data, we will create a synthetic dataset for the evaluation different RAG pipelines. Comparing their outputs to a baseline generated using a large-context model, we aim to provide actionable insights for developing interactive systems in this domain.

Section 2 will perform an analyses of large-context models, RAG and their place within the landscape, as well as hot topics within the research community. We will lay down the foundations of the methods in Section 4, outlining the methodology and introducing the dataset we used for the experimentation. Section 5 covers the experiments performed with the different configurations and parameters, and finally a conclusion is given in Section 6, along with a few lines of research that might be interesting to explore.

2 Related

Retrieval-augmented generation (RAG) has emerged as a key paradigm for improving the performance of language models in tasks requiring external knowledge (Mansurova et al., 2024) and to reduce hallucinations (false or nonsensical outputs). Prior works have acknowledged the efficacy of RAG in both open and domain-specific applications, ranging from technical documentation to healthcare QA systems (Amugongo et al., 2024), (Wang et al., 2024b). Multimodal data comes as well with its own set of challenges (Chen et al., 2025). However, research on its applicability

Proceedings of the 15th International Workshop on Spoken Dialogue Systems Technology, pages 129–136
May 27–30, 2025. ©2025 Association for Computational Linguistics

in domain-specific tasks, such as art and museum contexts interaction, remains sparse.

Parallel to these developments, advancements in large-context models (even in the range of millions of tokens) have enabled direct ingestion of extensive input, offering an alternative to RAG for tasks involving dense information. Multimodal large language models (MLLMs) research has also been a hot topic lately (Jiang et al., 2024). With this in mind, the need for a representation of the visual context in the RAG systems arises, specially in visual domain applications (Yu et al., 2024).

Recent research builds around the use of RAG in conjunction with LLMs (Fan et al., 2024). Specifically in the RAG landscape, the chunking strategies of the indexed documents remains a research topic (Qu et al., 2024), as well as the embedding techniques for retrieval tasks (Warner et al., 2024). This paper builds on these foundations by comparing RAG with large-context approaches in a multimodal setting where the visual context is inferred to textual data, focusing on the art and museum domain.

3 Data preparation

When considering the interaction that visitors in a museum will have with a corporate chatbot, we can consider mainly two types of questions: those related with direct visual elements in the artwork, and those that transcend the artwork (i.e., name of artist, year, movement, technique, history, etc.). While designing our methodology, we consider both types of questions and the information we can have available: the images of the artworks and text describing the artwork (information usually available near the artwork or provided by the museum). Therefore, the dataset we used initially consists of painting images paired with detailed information sourced from museum databases and archives. The information that comes along the paintings at times references the author of the painting, and its historical context, but it rarely contains detailed descriptions of the painting's visual characteristics. For this reason, each image is processed using a vision language model to generate a descriptive caption, representing its visual context, divided in subject (depicted object(s)), form (visual organization: color, style, shape) and content fields (impact or meaning) (DiMaggio, 1987) (art, 2024). This caption is then concatenated with the original textual description to create a comprehensive context.

Using a language model, we developed a synthetic database of question-answer (QA) pairs based on this multimodal context. The dataset includes 1020 images and 12240 QA pairs, covering diverse artistic styles, historical periods, and cultural themes. This means that 12 questions are generated for each work of art. We wanted the questions and answers to be diverse, so we ask the large language model to formulate and answer 6 questions that a beginner user will ask, and other 6 as an expert in art. Furthermore, for each level, 3 questions are generated based on the original textual data, and the other 3 are based on the descriptive caption generated. This multimodal dataset serves as the foundation for evaluating both RAG and large-context approaches.

4 Methods

This section outlines the methodology developed and applied in this study to evaluate retrieval-augmented generation (RAG) approaches in contrast with large-context models in a multimodal art synthetic question-answer (QA) dataset.

First, a detailed caption of the image is generated with the "Qwen2-VL-7B-Instruct" model, a vision model with a size of 7B parameters (Wang et al., 2024a).

The RAG pipeline begins by segmenting the text provided by the museum related to each artwork. using several strategies. **Recursive splitting** splits the text based on the structure of its paragraphs, first splitting by double newline, then by newline and finally by period (Narimissa and Raithel, 2024). In the **semantic chunking** approach we divide documents based on semantic similarity, using the "all-MiniLM-L6-v2" (Transformers, 2021) embedding model we compute the similarity between sentences and group them together (Qu et al., 2024). **Sentence-based division** chunks texts into accurate and contextually meaningful chunks with the spacy tokenizer (Vasiliev, 2020), maintaining the integrity of sentences and their relationships within the text.

The resulting chunks will then be embedded using three different embedding types (dense, sparse and late interaction). Nomic's "modernbert-embed-base" (Nussbaum et al., 2024) model (embedding length of 768) is used as the dense embedding with cosine distance for comparisons. Contextualized Late Interaction over BERT (ColBERT) (Khattab and Zaharia, 2020) introduces a late interaction architecture that encodes the query and the document using BERT and then employs an interaction step that models the similarity. Finally for the sparse representation, we will use "BM42" (qdr, 2024), which builds upon the foundations of TF-IDF (Term Frequency-Inverse Document Frequency).

The alternative approach involves feeding the full artwork context, i.e., comprising the original text information and the Qwen generated description captions, directly into a LLaMA 3.1 model of size 8B parameters (et al., 2024). We chose this model for its performance in "needle in a haystack" benchmarks, for its usage of context length and relatively small number of parameters (Hsieh et al., 2024). This model generates answers based on the entire input without relying on intermediate retrieval steps. The model is instructed to base its answers solely on the input text, to prevent hallucination, or answers already learned (see Annex A.3 for the prompt).

Synthetic QA pairs were created using "gpt-4-turbo" model with 128k of context window (OpenAI and et al., 2024). With the original text plus the generated captions as input, we generate pairs of synthetic questions along their corresponding answers by prompting the GPT-4-turbo model both the question and the answer (see Annex A.1 for the prompt). A random sample of around 1200 QA (aprox. 10% of the dataset) pairs were manually inspected to verify the quality of the generated dataset. These generated QA pairs will be then taken as ground truth, providing a benchmark baseline for evaluating the similarity of the answers generated by both RAG and large-context approaches.

We will then, for each question in the synthetic dataset, test two approaches: (a) first, retrieve the most relevant documents based on the cosine similarity score between the question embedding and different types of chunk embeddings., and (b) compare the performance against the responses of LLaMA3.1-8B with the full-context approach. In both cases, we will embed the original answer from the qa pairs, the full-context (LLaMA3.1-8B) generated answer and the RAG retrieved answer with the aforementioned "modernbert-embed-base" model, and compute cosine similarity between both generated answers and the ground truth answer. This metric provides a robust framework for comparing RAG outputs with the baseline answers vs the large-context model approach.

5 Experimentation

We conducted experiments using a multimodal synthetic QA dataset with the goal of evaluating the effectiveness of retrieval-augmented generation (RAG) versus large-context models in the task of properly answering questions about paintings. The experiments were run on a machine with an NVIDIA GeForce RTX 3090 (24GB of VRAM) using Python and the transformers library.

The RAG pipeline was built with the qdrant vector search library, for its ease of use and extensive community and support (Qdr, 2024). The final dataset consists of 1020 images with textual information and captions detailedly describing them. As it was previously described, each one of the images has 12 QA pairs associated generated with GPT4 (see Annex A.2). This synthetic dataset adds up to 1020*12= 12,240 total queries and their answers.

The Context-Based answers were generated by feeding the full context (original descriptions + Qwen captions) into the LLaMA 3.1-8B model. The model was instructed to base its responses exclusively on the provided context, mitigating potential hallucination (see Annex A.3). Table 3 shows the Context- mean similarity between the generated answers and the Ground Truth answers for the different groups of expertise and types of questions (about the description or original information). Annex A.2 showcases the generated answers.

Table 3 shows the results of the experimentation, showcasing the three chunking strategies, the three types of embeddings used and comparing the similarities with the baseline similarity.

As previously said, we designated several chunking strategies to segment the texts, depending on where we want to put the focus. Depending on the embedding size and structure of the data, the documents must be segmented in proper chunk sizes (number of characters in each chunk). As highlighted in Table 1 our dataset documents contain around 500-700 words each, amounting to 3500-4500 characters.

For the recursive splitting we set a maximum chunk size of 300 characters with an overlap of 50, which means that chunks will be as big as 300 characters, with the first 50 being from the previous chunk, and the last 50 from the next chunk. When performing the sentence-based chunking strategy, we state a chunk size of 200 characters that will leave room for adjoint short sentences to be grouped. If a sentence is bigger than 200 char-

	Mean Word Count	Mean Char Count
Information	398.85	2433.33
Caption	235.83	1424.96
Total	634.68	3858.28

Table 1: Mean word and character count in both the original information and the generated caption of each painting.

acters, it will still be treated as a chunk. Finally for the semantic approach, we will use a chunk size of 300 characters. Note that in semantic embedding, if a sentence is not similar enough to any other one, it will remain as a standalone chunk. Table 2 shows the number of chunks in which each chunking strategy divided the text corpus.

The "BM42" Sparse embedding model, grounded in TF-IDF principles, was evaluated for its efficiency in representing keyword-based similarities. Sparse embeddings excel in retrieval speed and computational simplicity, particularly for short, keyword-rich contexts, and here it's no different, it performs better with the caption texts, as it is more concise and contained. Particularly in "expert" questions with short answers containing keywords it performed best. On the other hand when facing more general or open ended questions, specially with questions regarding the original information which is inherently of diverse nature, the BM42 model achieved worse results.

We use the "modernbert-embed-base" model, which produces 768-dimensional embeddings optimized for capturing semantic similarity. These dense embeddings performed better in scenarios where the question and context were long. This time, the model performed well with both "expert" and "beginner" questions, but questions about the original information give worse results, in favor of questions about the captions.

In our experiments, ColBERT performance falls behind its two other opponents, but surprisingly its results are independent of the type (caption or information) and level (expert or beginner) of the question queried. The results show that the similarity is maintained along all of the questions no matter their structure, length or label.

Table 3 shows the different chunking and embedding configurations, along the computed similarity against the Ground Truth answers.

6 Conclusions and Future Work

After experimenting with different chunking approaches and parameters, the strategies chosen to test on this dataset are: Semantic chunking with a chunk size of 300 characters, spacy sentence-based segmentation with a size of 200 characters, and recursive splitting with a maximum chunk size of 300.

The dense embedding approach with modernBERT generally works better than its two opponents, scoring higher regardless of the chunking mechanism used. At the same time its variance is higher than the other two, scoring higher in questions derived from the captions versus the original information. The late interaction ColBERT model on the other hand, although performing slightly worse, keeps higher consistency, with low variance along the different labeled fields. At last, BM42 falls right in between the other two embedding models. As showcased in Table 3 it performs better than ColBERT with Semantic chunking and Sentence chunking, and maintains a slight advantage in Recursive chunking.

On the comparison of RAG results with the baseline LLaMA answers, we can definitely say that we proved what was stated in (Li et al., 2024), in which they also found large-context model to outperform RAG based approaches in accuracy. Being this said, the approach that consistently closes the gap the most is the sentence-based document chunking strategy combined with modernBERT embeddings. Regarding the dataset, can observe trends that suggest that the most precise answers are generated for questions about the "Description" of the artwork. A slight advantage is present in the "expert" questions, over the "beginner" ones.

It must be said that we are measuring the raw answers directly from the RAG pipeline, without performing any modification/augmentation technique. The evaluation at this point is being carried out by cosine similarity, but many other metrics would need exploration. There are specific libraries for this purpose such as (rag, 2024), (Ru et al., 2024), which evaluate RAG and LLM pipelines in both quantitative (precision, similarity, recall, etc.) and qualitative categories (hallucination, noise, factual correctness, etc.). The most natural approach to

	Character	Recursive	Semantic	Spacy
Chunks	27,377	17,677	21,693	25,532

Table 2: Number of chunks generated for each chunking strategy.

	Beginner			Expert			Overall
	Inf	Desc	Both	Inf	Desc	Both	
RAG-Recursive							
ModernBERT	0.653	0.699	0.676	**0.680**	0.716	0.698	0.687
LateInteraction	0.616	0.649	0.633	0.647	0.658	0.652	0.642
Sparse	0.608	0.659	0.634	0.654	0.692	0.673	0.653
RAG-Semantic							
ModernBERT	0.646	0.695	0.670	0.671	0.713	0.692	0.681
LateInteraction	0.588	0.634	0.611	0.629	0.643	0.636	0.623
Sparse	0.592	0.663	0.628	0.635	0.691	0.663	0.645
RAG-Sentence							
ModernBERT	**0.671**	**0.710**	**0.691**	**0.680**	**0.729**	**0.705**	**0.698**
LateInteraction	0.623	0.629	0.626	0.641	0.643	0.642	0.634
Sparse	0.616	0.671	0.643	0.635	0.693	0.678	0.661
Context-Based	0.894	0.880	0.887	0.879	0.864	0.872	0.879

Table 3: Similarity Scores for RAG Methods with Retrieval-Embeddings, and Context-Based approach

follow up with this line of research would be to explore augmenting the retrieved document and feeding it to a large-context model along with the question. More RAG techniques can be tested, to perform re-ranking or combine embeddings through hybrid searches.

Acknowledgements

This work is supported by the European Commission through Project ASTOUND (101071191 — HORIZON EIC-2021-PATHFINDERCHALLENGES-01), by project BEWORD (PID2021-126061OB-C43) funded by MCIN/AEI/10.13039/501100011033 and, as appropriate, by “ERDF A way of making Europe”, by the “European Union”, and by project INNOVATRAD-CM (PHS-2024/PH-HUM-52) from Comunidad de Madrid.

References

2024. BM42: New Baseline for Hybrid Search.

2024. Components of an art work.

2024. Qdrant: High-performance vector search at scale.

2024. Ragas: Llm evaluation library.

Lameck Mbangula Amugongo, Pietro Mascheroni, Steven Geoffrey Brooks, Stefan Doering, and Jan Seidel. 2024. Retrieval augmented generation for large language models in healthcare: A systematic review.

Shengnan An, Zexiong Ma, Zeqi Lin, Nanning Zheng, and Jian-Guang Lou. 2024. Make your llm fully utilize the context. *Preprint*, arXiv:2404.16811.

Boqi Chen, Anuj Khare, Gaurav Kumar, Arjun Akula, and Pradyumna Narayana. 2025. Seeing beyond: Enhancing visual question answering with multi-modal retrieval. In *Proceedings of the 31st International Conference on Computational Linguistics: Industry Track*, pages 410–421, Abu Dhabi, UAE. Association for Computational Linguistics.

Paul DiMaggio. 1987. Classification in art. *American Sociological Review*, 52(4):440–455.

Aaron Grattafiori et al. 2024. The llama 3 herd of models. *Preprint*, arXiv:2407.21783.

Wenqi Fan, Yujuan Ding, Liangbo Ning, Shijie Wang, Hengyun Li, Dawei Yin, Tat-Seng Chua, and Qing Li. 2024. A survey on rag meeting llms: Towards retrieval-augmented large language models. In *Proceedings of the 30th ACM SIGKDD Conference on Knowledge Discovery and Data Mining*, KDD '24, page 6491–6501, New York, NY, USA. Association for Computing Machinery.

Cheng-Ping Hsieh, Simeng Sun, Samuel Kriman, Shantanu Acharya, Dima Rekesh, Fei Jia, Yang Zhang, and Boris Ginsburg. 2024. Ruler: What's the real context size of your long-context language models? *arXiv preprint arXiv:2404.06654*.

Ting Jiang, Minghui Song, Zihan Zhang, Haizhen Huang, Weiwei Deng, Feng Sun, Qi Zhang, Deqing Wang, and Fuzhen Zhuang. 2024. E5-v: Universal embeddings with multimodal large language models. *Preprint*, arXiv:2407.12580.

Omar Khattab and Matei Zaharia. 2020. Colbert: Efficient and effective passage search via contextualized late interaction over bert. *Preprint*, arXiv:2004.12832.

Philippe Laban, Alexander R. Fabbri, Caiming Xiong, and Chien-Sheng Wu. 2024. Summary of a haystack: A challenge to long-context llms and rag systems. *Preprint*, arXiv:2407.01370.

Xinze Li, Yixin Cao, Yubo Ma, and Aixin Sun. 2024. Long context vs. rag for llms: An evaluation and revisits. *Preprint*, arXiv:2501.01880.

Aigerim Mansurova, Aiganym Mansurova, and Aliya Nugumanova. 2024. Qa-rag: Exploring llm reliance on external knowledge. *Big Data and Cognitive Computing*, 8(9).

Esmaeil Narimissa and David Raithel. 2024. Exploring information retrieval landscapes: An investigation of a novel evaluation techniques and comparative document splitting methods. *Preprint*, arXiv:2409.08479.

Zach Nussbaum, John X. Morris, Brandon Duderstadt, and Andriy Mulyar. 2024. Nomic embed: Training a reproducible long context text embedder. *Preprint*, arXiv:2402.01613.

OpenAI and Josh Achiam et al. 2024. Gpt-4 technical report. *Preprint*, arXiv:2303.08774.

Renyi Qu, Ruixuan Tu, and Forrest Bao. 2024. Is semantic chunking worth the computational cost? *Preprint*, arXiv:2410.13070.

Dongyu Ru, Lin Qiu, Xiangkun Hu, Tianhang Zhang, Peng Shi, Shuaichen Chang, Cheng Jiayang, Cunxiang Wang, Shichao Sun, Huanyu Li, Zizhao Zhang, Binjie Wang, Jiarong Jiang, Tong He, Zhiguo Wang, Pengfei Liu, Yue Zhang, and Zheng Zhang. 2024. Ragchecker: A fine-grained framework for diagnosing retrieval-augmented generation. *Preprint*, arXiv:2408.08067.

Stefan Schaffer, Aaron Ruß, Mino Lee Sasse, Louise Schubotz, and Oliver Gustke. 2022. Questions and answers: Important steps to let ai chatbots answer questions in the museum. In *ArtsIT, Interactivity and Game Creation*, pages 346–358, Cham. Springer International Publishing.

Sentence Transformers. 2021. all-minilm-l6-v2. *Computer software]. Hugging Face. https://huggingface.co/sentence-transformers/all-MiniLM-L6-v2*.

Yuli Vasiliev. 2020. *Natural language processing with Python and spaCy: A practical introduction*. No Starch Press.

Peng Wang, Shuai Bai, Sinan Tan, Shijie Wang, Zhihao Fan, Jinze Bai, Keqin Chen, Xuejing Liu, Jialin Wang, Wenbin Ge, Yang Fan, Kai Dang, Mengfei Du, Xuancheng Ren, Rui Men, Dayiheng Liu, Chang Zhou, Jingren Zhou, and Junyang Lin. 2024a. Qwen2-vl: Enhancing vision-language model's perception of the world at any resolution. *Preprint*, arXiv:2409.12191.

Xiaopu Wang, Jianing Sun, and Chao Qi. 2024b. Cedatqa: Context enhancement and domain adaptation method for textbook qa based on llm and rag. In *2024 International Conference on Networking and Network Applications (NaNA)*, pages 263–268.

Benjamin Warner, Antoine Chaffin, Benjamin Clavié, Orion Weller, Oskar Hallström, Said Taghadouini, Alexis Gallagher, Raja Biswas, Faisal Ladhak, Tom Aarsen, Nathan Cooper, Griffin Adams, Jeremy Howard, and Iacopo Poli. 2024. Smarter, better, faster, longer: A modern bidirectional encoder for fast, memory efficient, and long context finetuning and inference. *Preprint*, arXiv:2412.13663.

Jun Yu, Yunxiang Zhang, Zerui Zhang, Zhao Yang, Gongpeng Zhao, Fengzhao Sun, Fanrui Zhang, Qingsong Liu, Jianqing Sun, Jiaen Liang, and Yaohui Zhang. 2024. Rag-guided large language models for visual spatial description with adaptive hallucination corrector. In *Proceedings of the 32nd ACM International Conference on Multimedia*, MM '24, page 11407–11413, New York, NY, USA. Association for Computing Machinery.

A Appendix

A.1 GPT4 Prompt for QA generation

{ role: "system" content:" You are an expert in art history. First you will generate 6 question-answer pairs about a painting solely based on the provided "Description" text: the first 3 will be formulated by an expert in the domain and the last 3 will be formulated by a beginner. You will then generate 6 question-answer pairs about the painting solely based on the provided "Information" text: the first 3 will be formulated by an expert in the domain and the last 3 will be formulated by a beginner. Divide the data in these 6 columns: qa_id, qa_type, qa_level, question, answer. " }

{ role: "user" content:" Information: In the course of his life, EI Greco painted numerous versions of the Annunciation, thus allowing his stylistic development to be traced through his changing treatment of this Biblical episode. This painting, dated around 1576, is thought to be one of the last versions executed in Italy, and is clearly influenced by the Venetian style. From her prayer-stool at the left of the painting, the Virgin listens attentively to the message of the Archangel, a figure rendered very much in the style of Veronese. The light and the colouring owe much to Titian, a painter EI Greco admired, while the arrangement of the figures and the treatment of the drapery strongly recall the work of Tintoretto. Here, EI Greco places the figures within a simple architectural setting, loosely framing them to make the scene more realistic.

Caption: ### Subject The painting depicts a religious scene, likely from the Christian tradition, featuring two central figures: a seated woman and a standing angel. The woman, dressed in a blue robe, appears to be in a state of contemplation or prayer, with her hands raised in a gesture of supplication or meditation. The angel, dressed in a yellow robe with a white cloak, is depicted with wings and a halo, suggesting a divine or celestial presence. The angel is reaching out towards the woman, possibly conveying a message or blessing.

Form The painting is executed in a Baroque style, characterized by its dramatic use of light and shadow, dynamic composition, and rich, vibrant colors. The use of chiaroscuro (the contrast of light and dark) creates a sense of depth and volume, emphasizing the three-dimensional forms of the figures and the surrounding elements. The background features a dramatic sky with clouds and a radiant light source, adding to the overall sense of divine intervention or revelation.

Content The content of the painting is deeply religious, focusing on a moment of divine communication or revelation. The angel's gesture towards the woman suggests a divine message or a moment of divine intervention. The woman's posture and expression indicate a state of receptivity or contemplation, highlighting the spiritual nature of the scene. The presence of cherubs in the background adds to the celestial and divine atmosphere of the painting. The overall composition and the interplay of light and shadow create a sense of sacredness and awe, inviting the viewer to reflect on the divine nature of the moment depicted." }

A.2 GPT4 QA generation results, and LLaMA answer

Here we showcase the QA generation results along with the answer inferred from the LLaMA-3.1-8B model.

greco_(domenikos_theotokopoulos)_w1:

Description,expert,**What artistic technique is predominantly featured to enhance the dramatic effect in the painting?**,"The use of chiaroscuro, the contrast of light and dark, is predominantly featured to enhance the dramatic effect in the painting.","EI Greco predominantly features the artistic technique of chiaroscuro to enhance the dramatic effect in the painting, creating a sense of depth and volume by contrasting light and dark."

Description,expert,**How does the baroque style manifest in the composition of the painting?**,"The Baroque style in the painting is manifested through the dynamic composition, dramatic use of light and shadow, and the rich, vibrant colors.","In the composition of the painting, the Baroque style manifests through its dramatic use of light and shadow, dynamic arrangement of figures, and rich, vibrant colors, creating a sense of depth and volume. The use of chiaroscuro emphasizes the three-dimensional forms of the figures and the surrounding elements, while the background features a dramatic sky with clouds and a radiant light source, adding to the overall sense of divine intervention or revelation."

Description,expert,**How do the gestures and expressions of the figures contribute to the theme of the artwork?**,"The gestures and expressions of the figures, such as the woman's raised hands and contemplative posture and the angel's reaching out gesture, contribute to the theme by highlighting a moment of divine communication or revelation.","The figures' gestures and expressions in this painting significantly contribute to its theme by conveying a sense of reverence and spiritual connection. The Virgin's raised hands and attentive posture convey her receptivity to the angel's message, emphasizing her devotion and faith. The angel's gentle gesture towards her, with his hands extended and a soft expression, suggests a benevolent and divine presence. This interplay of gestures and expressions creates a sense of intimacy and sacredness, drawing the viewer into the moment of divine communication. The overall effect is one of calm contemplation and spiritual awe, underscoring the painting's theme of divine revelation and connection."

Description,beginner,**What are the main colors used for the clothing of the angel and the woman?**,The angel is dressed in a yellow robe with a white cloak and the woman is dressed in a blue robe.,"The main colors used for the clothing of the angel are yellow and white, while the woman is dressed in a blue robe."

Description,beginner,**What is the background of the painting like?**,The background features a dramatic sky with clouds and a radiant light source.,"The background of the painting features a dramatic sky with clouds and a radiant light source, adding to the overall sense of divine intervention or revelation, and creating a simple architectural setting that loosely frames the central figures of the Virgin and the Archangel."

Description,beginner,**What do the figures in the painting represent?**,"The figures represent a seated woman in contemplation or prayer and a standing angel conveying a message or blessing, suggesting a divine or celestial presence.","The figures in the painting represent the Virgin Mary and the Archangel, depicting a moment of divine communication, specifically the Annunciation, where the angel conveys a message from God to Mary."

Information,expert,**What stylistic influences are evident in EI Greco's painting based on the information given?**,"The painting shows influences by the Venetian style, specifically reminiscent of Veronese's style in the depiction of the archangel and owes much to Titian in its use of light and coloring, along with elements recalling Tintoretto's work in the arrangement of the figures and the treatment of drapery.","EI Greco's painting is influenced by the Venetian style, evident in its use of light and colouring, which owes much to Titian. The arrangement of the figures and treatment of drapery strongly recall Tintoretto's work. Additionally, the angel is rendered in the style of Veronese, and the overall Baroque style is characterized by dramatic use of light and shadow, dynamic composition, and rich colours."

Information,expert,**How does the painting reflect the evolution of EI Greco's artistic style?**,"This painting, being one of the last versions executed in Italy, reflects the evolution of EI Greco's style through its mixture of Venetian influences seen in the handling of figures, light, and coloring, showing his transition in stylistic developments.","This painting reflects EI Greco's artistic evolution through its incorporation of various styles, showcasing his eclecticism and willingness to adapt. It is characterized by the Venetian style, evident in the use of light and color, reminiscent of Titian, and the arrangement of figures, recalling Tintoretto. The angel's depiction, however, is more in line with Veronese, highlighting EI Greco's ability to blend different influences to create a unique work. The painting's use of chiaroscuro and dramatic composition, typical of the Baroque style, demonstrates EI Greco's mastery of this period's artistic trends, while the simple architectural setting suggests a return to a more traditional approach, reflecting his stylistic development over time."

Information,expert,**Where does the scene of the painting take place based on the architectural elements described?**,"EI Greco places the scene within a simple architectural setting, loosely framing the figures to make the scene appear more realistic.","The scene of the painting takes place in a simple architectural setting, likely an interior space, as there is no mention of exterior elements such as columns, arches, or a large window, instead it is loosely framed to make the scene more realistic."

Information,beginner,**What scene is depicted in this painting by EI Greco?**,"The painting depicts the Annunciation, with the Virgin Mary at her prayer-stool listening attentively to the Archangel's message.","The scene depicted in this painting by EI Greco is the Annunciation, a moment from the Christian tradition in which the Archangel conveys a divine message to the Virgin, who is seated in contemplation or prayer."

Information,beginner,**Who are the figures in the painting?**,"The figures in the painting are the Virgin Mary and the Archangel, with the Virgin listening to the Archangel's message.","The two central figures in the painting are a seated woman, likely the Virgin, and a standing angel, the Archangel, who is reaching out towards her with a message or blessing."

Information,beginner,**What year is this specific painting of the Annunciation by EI Greco thought to be created?**,This specific painting of the Annunciation by EI Greco is thought to be created around 1576.,This specific painting of the Annunciation by EI Greco is thought to be created in 1576.

A.3 LLaMA-3.1-8B Prompt for Question answering based on the texts

{"role": "system", "content": "You are an art bot that responds to questions about paintings. You will create concise responses solely based on the Information provided along the question. You will only respond to the asked question. Try not to enumerate. Stick to natural language and do not use new lines."}, {"role": "user", "content": original information + description}

Paralinguistic Attitude Recognition for Spoken Dialogue Systems

Kouki Miyazawa and **Zhi Zhu** and **Yoshinao Sato**
Fairy Devices Inc.
{miyazawa,zhu,sato}@fairydevices.jp

Abstract

Although paralinguistic information is critical for human communication, most spoken dialogue systems ignore such information, hindering natural communication between humans and machines. This study addresses the recognition of paralinguistic attitudes in user speech. Specifically, we focus on four essential attitudes for generating an appropriate system response, namely agreement, disagreement, questions, and stalling. The proposed model can help a dialogue system better understand what the user is trying to convey. In our experiments, we trained and evaluated a model that classified paralinguistic attitudes on a reading-speech dataset without using linguistic information. The proposed model outperformed human perception. Furthermore, experimental results indicate that speech enhancement alleviates the degradation of model performance caused by background noise, whereas reverberation remains a challenge.

1 Introduction

In human dialogue, people communicate various messages through paralinguistic features of speech, such as prosody and voice quality. Speech can convey emotions and attitudes through paralinguistic features regardless of linguistic information. Humans can recognize four intentions, namely affirm, deny, ask for repetition, and filler, with high accuracy using only paralinguistic features (Ishi et al., 2008). Moreover, humans can convey six intentions, namely criticism, doubt, naming, suggestion, warning, and wish, through prosodic patterns irrespective of lexical meaning (Hellbernd and Sammler, 2016). The paralinguistic information transmitted in this manner can affect listener behavior.

By contrast, paralinguistic information is ignored by most spoken dialogue systems, which adopt a cascaded pipeline of automatic speech recognition (ASR) and a linguistic dialogue model. This restriction requires users to convey their messages using only linguistic information; otherwise, miscommunication can occur. The limited paralinguistic ability in spoken dialogue systems impedes natural communication with humans.

In this study, we address the challenge of enabling a spoken dialogue system to recognize attitudes expressed through paralinguistic features in user speech. Specifically, we focus on four attitude classes, namely agreement, disagreement, questions, and stalling. Table 1 lists these definitions. In the case of no confusion, the agreement, disagreement, question, and stalling classes are abbreviated as A, D, Q, and S, respectively. Among other paralinguistic information, the four attitudes are critical in determining the reaction of a system. These attitudes are typically accompanied by the four main types of boundary pitch movement at the end of prosodic phrases (Igarashi and Koiso, 2012). Using prosody is an effective way to control voice interactive devices (Zhang et al., 2022). We believe that spoken dialogue systems should also be able to recognize paralinguistic attitudes to communicate naturally with humans. Note that this study does not aim to comprehensively theorize the paralinguistic aspects of dialogue acts. The proposed model focuses on resolving the ambiguity that arises when spoken dialogue systems try to understand user speech by relying solely on lexical information and ignoring paralanguage.

Only one of the four attitudes is deemed to accompany a single utterance. This is understood by the fact that boundary pitch movement at the end of an utterance substantially affects the attitude.

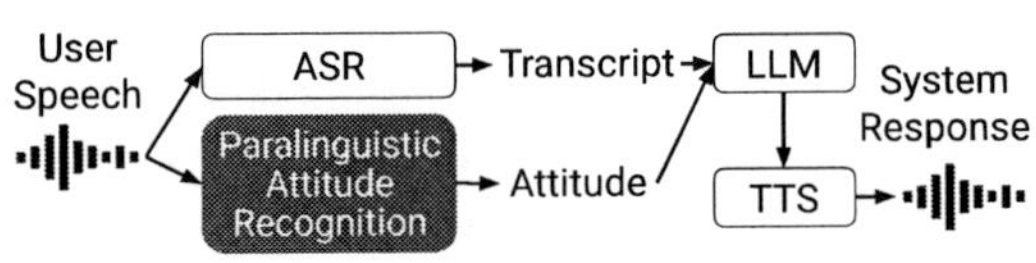

Figure 1: Example usage of the proposed model

Proceedings of the 15th International Workshop on Spoken Dialogue Systems Technology, pages 137–142
May 27–30, 2025. ©2025 Association for Computational Linguistics

Table 1: Paralinguistic attitude classes

	Attitude	Expected reaction
Agreement	in favor, accept to continue	performing the approved action, moving on to the next
Disagreement	against, dissatisfied, request to stop	canceling the rejected action, asking for instructions
Question	not understand, confirm facts, listen back	answering the question, rephrasing the previous utterance
Stalling	thinking, worried, request to wait	waiting for instructions, providing additional information

Therefore, articulating multiple attitudes in a single utterance is challenging for most users of spoken dialogue systems. In other words, the paralinguistic attitudes investigated in this study are mutually exclusive and evoked in units of utterances.

We introduce one of the expected uses of our model, as illustrated in Fig. 1. An input user utterance is processed in parallel using an ASR model and a paralinguistic attitude recognition model. The transcription and the inferred attitude are subsequently passed on to a large language model (LLM). Finally, a text-to-speech (TTS) model synthesizes a system utterance according to the output generated by the LLM. Previous studies have explored methods to process paralinguistic cues in conjunction with transcripts by employing LLMs (Lin et al., 2024; Xue et al., 2024; Kang et al., 2024). A simple approach is to concatenate the transcript and class label in a prompt, for example: "*transcript <attitude>*."

2 Model

The network structure of the proposed model is listed in Table 2. The input feature of the proposed model is a waveform. The main part is a self-supervised learning (SSL) model called HuBERT-large (Hsu et al., 2021). The layer depth at which an embedding vector is obtained from the SSL model is optimized on the validation data, following (Zhu and Sato, 2023). The embedding vector yielded from the SSL model is averaged over time and passed to head layers that comprise two fully connected layers and a softmax layer. The output is the posterior probability of the attitude classes.

It is known that speech SSL models embed prosodic information in their hidden representations (Lin et al., 2023; de la Fuente and Jurafsky, 2024). Moreover, the explicit incorporation of pitch into the input features in our preliminary experiments did not enhance the model performance. Hence, we chose to use only the hidden representation of the HuBERT model.

Table 2: Model structure

Layer	Output size
HuBERT	$1024 \times T$
Mean pooling	1024
Fully connected	1024
Fully connected	1024
Softmax	4

T denotes the number of time frames.

We note that linguistic information was not used as an input feature. One reason for this choice is that a cascaded pipeline of ASR and the attitude recognition model cause considerable latency in generating a system response. To use linguistic information, the paralinguistic attitude recognition model should wait until the ASR model yields a transcription, inevitably causing additional latency. Thus, we made the model recognize attitude using only acoustic features to avoid hindering smooth communication. Another reason is that a spoken phrase can be accompanied by distinct intentions depending on its paralinguistic features regardless of linguistic information (Ishi et al., 2008; Tang et al., 2016; Hellbernd and Sammler, 2016). Therefore, linguistic features were not significant in recognizing the four paralinguistic attitudes. Another motivation was to avoid the domain dependence of linguistic features. Linguistic choices are affected by situations where dialogue occurs and the relationship between participants. Previous studies on paralinguistic information employing linguistic features focused on a specific domain, such as meetings (Ortega and Vu, 2018; Maltby et al., 2023) and news delivery (Takatsu et al., 2019). We used only acoustic features so that the model is useful in various domains.

3 Data

In this study, speeches read in Japanese by crowd workers and actors were used. Table 3 and Fig. 2 show the number of utterances and distribution of duration, respectively.

3.1 Crowd workers' speech

We used a Japanese reading speech dataset collected by (Sato and Miyazawa, 2023). In this section, we briefly review the dataset. It contains five sets of 63 scripts, including words, phrases, sentences, fillers, and back channels. A spoken sentence can be accompanied by a paralinguistic attitude regardless of its semantic content. Therefore, the same speaker read each script aloud with four attitudes in this dataset. In the recording process, 138 crowd workers read one script set of size 63 aloud with four paralinguistic attitudes. Another 20 crowd workers evaluated the utterances in which each speech was heard by two or three listeners. By using a statistical quality estimation method, 19,821 high-quality utterances were selected. This method estimates the quality of utterances from the speaker's intention and listeners' evaluations, while considering their reliability.

3.2 Actors' speech

In this study, we collected additional recordings using the same procedure. Six actors read a script set of size 63 aloud with four paralinguistic attitudes. Because we added a small number of recordings, the number of utterances per attitude was greater than 378. After recording, 31 crowd workers evaluated 384 randomly sampled utterances, each of which was heard by five listeners. We assumed that the attitudes intended by the actors were correct and used all the utterances without filtering.

The results are summarized in Table 4. The macro-F_1 score of the human perception of the actors' speech was 0.829.

4 Experiments

We trained and evaluated a paralinguistic attitude recognition model using a speech dataset of crowd workers and actors. All speech data were processed at a sampling rate of 16 kHz on a single channel.

Table 3: Number of utterances in the dataset

	Crowd workers	Actors
Agreement	8,581	470
Disagreement	976	378
Question	6,048	379
Stalling	4,216	379
Total	19,821	1,606

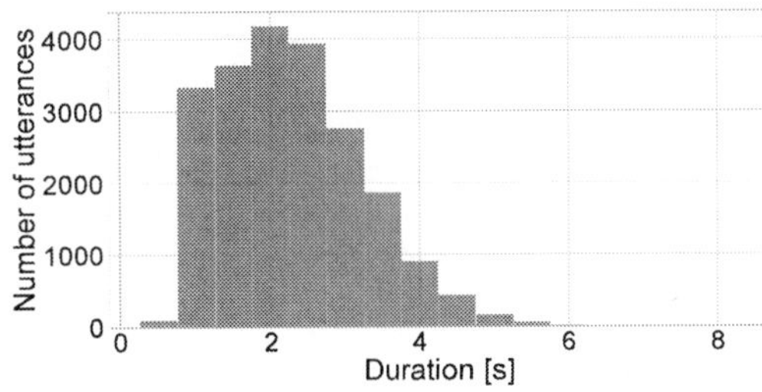

Figure 2: Duration distribution

The HuBERT model was frozen, and the head layers were fine-tuned during training. We measured the performance in terms of the macro-F_1 score using six-fold cross-validation. For each fold, the entire dataset was split into six sets, namely four for training, one for validation, and one for testing.

We augmented the training data four-fold by adding background noise and reverberation to improve model robustness. Noise signals were randomly selected from the DEMAND (Thiemann et al., 2013), MUSAN (Snyder et al., 2015), and FSD50K (Fonseca et al., 2022) datasets. The signal-to-noise ratio was randomly chosen from the uniform distribution from -10 to 10 dB. Room impulse responses were randomly sampled from the BIRD database (Grondin et al., 2020). Whether noise or reverberation was added during the test depended on the evaluation settings, as explained below.

We set the layer depth at which the HuBERT-

Table 4: Human perception of the actors' speech

		Perceived			
		A	D	Q	S
Intended	A	451	10	5	14
	D	2	339	133	6
	Q	12	52	385	31
	S	23	24	18	415

$F_1 = 0.829$

Table 5: Evaluation of the proposed model on the actors' speech

		Predicted			
		A	D	Q	S
Actual	A	453	4	1	12
	D	5	330	43	0
	Q	9	43	326	1
	S	20	0	4	355

$F_1 = 0.909$

Table 6: Evaluation of the proposed model on all the speech

		Predicted			
		A	D	Q	S
Actual	A	8744	13	106	188
	D	19	1049	286	0
	Q	203	192	6009	23
	S	234	0	13	4348

$F_1 = 0.912$

Table 7: Evaluation of the proposed model on all the speech in the noisy and reverberant conditions

Condition	Enhanced speech	F_1
Clean		0.912
Noisy		0.625
Noisy	✓	0.844
Noisy and reverberant		0.449
Noisy and reverberant	✓	0.492

large model yielded an embedding vector to 12 based on the validation data. This result is consistent with the findings of previous studies in which paralinguistic information was incorporated into the middle layers of the SSL models (Pepino et al., 2021; Li et al., 2022; Zhu and Sato, 2023).

4.1 Comparison with humans

We compared the performance of human listeners with our model on the actors' speech. In this experiment, we did not add noise or reverberation to the test data. The speech utterances of the crowd workers were not necessarily suitable for evaluating human perception because those on which the listeners disagreed were excluded during the filtering process. Therefore, we used the actors' speech to compare human perception with the proposed model. Table 5 presents the results of the model evaluation. The macro-F_1 score of the model measured using the actors' speech was 0.909.

We found that the proposed model outperformed human perception, as depicted in Tables 4 and 5. Moreover, the human confusion between the disagreement and question attitudes was reduced in the model prediction.

4.2 Evaluation of the model

Moreover, we evaluated the performance of our model on all the data (i.e., all the speech by the crowd workers and the actors). No noise or reverberation was introduced to the test data. For the actors' speech, we assumed the intended attitudes to be the ground truth. For the crowd workers' speech, we regarded the attitudes determined by the quality estimation method as the ground truth. Table 6 presents the results. The macro-F_1 score of the model evaluated using all data was 0.912.

No significant difference was observed between the model performance on the speech of the actors (F_1=0.909) and that of all the speakers (F_1=0.912). Therefore, the quality estimation method effectively selected quality speech.

4.3 Robustness to noise and reverberation

Real-world applications of spoken dialog systems are inevitably affected by noise and reverberation. Therefore, we evaluated model performance in noisy and reverberant environments using all the data. Specifically, we examined three conditions: (1) clean, (2) noisy, and (3) noisy and reverberant. The clean condition was identical to the one described in Section 4.2. Noise and reverberation were added in the same manner as the training data. Furthermore, we investigated the effects of speech enhancement. A state-of-the-art speech enhancement model, MP-SENet (Lu et al., 2023), is applied to the disturbed test data. The MP-SENet model simultaneously performs speech denoising and dereverberation. Table 7 presents the results.

In our experiment, noise and reverberation degraded the model performance even though data augmentation was used during training. The use of speech enhancement considerably improved model performance in the noisy condition. By contrast, the degradation due to reverberation was marginally mitigated. The results indicate that the influence of reverberation remains a challenge in paralinguistic attitude recognition. This can be explained by the fact that prosody, which is difficult to estimate in reverberant environments, is a key factor in communication through paralinguistic information.

5 Conclusion

This study addressed paralinguistic attitude recognition in user speech for spoken dialogue systems. Specifically, we focused on four essential attitudes for determining a system reaction, namely agreement, disagreement, questions, and stalling. We trained and evaluated the model using a reading-speech dataset of actors and crowd workers. The proposed model outperformed human perception when evaluating the actors' speech under a clean condition. Furthermore, the proposed model achieved almost the same performance on the crowd workers' speech after filtering by quality. Noise and reverberation degraded the model performance. Speech enhancement can alleviate the degradation caused by noise. However, the influence of reverberation remains a challenge. The use of paralinguistic attitude recognition enables spoken dialogue systems to understand what users convey through speech.

Finally, we discuss future research directions. We used a reading-speech dataset in this study. However, the manner in which attitudes are expressed through paralinguistic features varies depending on the situation in which speech utterances occur. Human speech directed to spoken dialogue systems is more diverse than reading speech but more controlled than casual everyday conversation. Therefore, we should investigate paralinguistic attitude recognition for speech directed to dialogue systems. Another direction is to clarify how to determine a system reaction, given an inferred user's paralinguistic attitude. Moreover, joint models of speech enhancement and paralinguistic attitude recognition should be examined to alleviate the degradation caused by reverberation.

References

Anton de la Fuente and Dan Jurafsky. 2024. A layer-wise analysis of mandarin and english suprasegmentals in ssl speech models. In *Interspeech*, pages 1290–1294.

Eduardo Fonseca, Xavier Favory, Jordi Pons, Frederic Font, and Xavier Serra. 2022. FSD50K: An open dataset of human-labeled sound events. *IEEE/ACM Transactions on Audio, Speech, and Language Processing (TASLP)*, 30:829–852.

François Grondin, Jean-Samuel Lauzon, Simon Michaud, Mirco Ravanelli, and François Michaud. 2020. BIRD: Big Impulse Response Dataset. ArXiv:2010.09930.

Nele Hellbernd and Daniela Sammler. 2016. Prosody conveys speaker's intentions: Acoustic cues for speech act perception. *Journal of Memory and Language*, 88:70–86.

Wei-Ning Hsu, Benjamin Bolte, Yao-Hung Hubert Tsai, Kushal Lakhotia, Ruslan Salakhutdinov, and Abdelrahman Mohamed. 2021. HuBERT: Self-supervised speech representation learning by masked prediction of hidden units. *IEEE/ACM Transactions on Audio, Speech, and Language Processing (TASLP)*, 29:3451–3460.

Yosuke Igarashi and Hanae Koiso. 2012. Pitch range control of japanese boundary pitch movements. In *Proceedings of the Annual Conference of the International Speech Communication Association (Interspeech)*.

Carlos Toshinori Ishi, Hiroshi Ishiguro, and Norihiro Hagita. 2008. Automatic extraction of paralinguistic information using prosodic features related to f0, duration and voice quality. *Speech Communication*, 50(6):531–543.

Wonjune Kang, Junteng Jia, Chunyang Wu, Wei Zhou, Egor Lakomkin, Yashesh Gaur, Leda Sari, Suyoun Kim, Ke Li, Jay Mahadeokar, et al. 2024. Frozen large language models can perceive paralinguistic aspects of speech. ArXiv:2410.01162.

Yuanchao Li, Yumnah Mohamied, Peter Bell, and Catherine Lai. 2022. Exploration of a self-supervised speech model: A study on emotional corpora. In *Proceedings of the IEEE Spoken Language Technology Workshop (SLT)*, pages 868–875.

Guan-Ting Lin, Chi-Luen Feng, Wei-Ping Huang, Yuan Tseng, Tzu-Han Lin, Chen-An Li, Hung-yi Lee, and Nigel G. Ward. 2023. On the utility of self-supervised models for prosody-related tasks. In *IEEE Spoken Language Technology Workshop (SLT)*, pages 1104–1111.

Guan-Ting Lin, Prashanth Gurunath Shivakumar, Ankur Gandhe, Chao-Han Huck Yang, Yile Gu, Shalini Ghosh, Andreas Stolcke, Hung-Yi Lee, and Ivan Bulyko. 2024. Paralinguistics-enhanced large language modeling of spoken dialogue. In *IEEE International Conference on Acoustics, Speech and Signal Processing (ICASSP)*, pages 10316–10320.

Ye-Xin Lu, Yang Ai, and Zhen-Hua Ling. 2023. MP-SENet: A speech enhancement model with parallel denoising of magnitude and phase spectra. In *Proceedings of the Annual Conference of the International Speech Communication Association (Interspeech)*, pages 3834–3838.

Harry Maltby, Julie Wall, T Goodluck Constance, Mansour Moniri, Cornelius Glackin, Marvin Rajwadi, and Nigel Cannings. 2023. Short utterance dialogue act classification using a transformer ensemble. *UA Digital Theme Research Twinning (UA-DIGITAL).*

Daniel Ortega and Ngoc Thang Vu. 2018. Lexico-acoustic neural-based models for dialog act classification. In *Proceedings of the IEEE International Conference on Acoustics, Speech and Signal Processing (ICASSP)*, pages 6194–6198.

Leonardo Pepino, Pablo Riera, and Luciana Ferrer. 2021. Emotion recognition from speech using wav2vec 2.0 embeddings. In *Proceedings of the Annual Conference of the International Speech Communication Association (Interspeech)*, pages 3400–3404.

Yoshinao Sato and Kouki Miyazawa. 2023. Statistical quality estimation for partially subjective classification tasks through crowdsourcing. In *Language Resources and Evaluation*, volume 57, pages 31–56. Springer.

David Snyder, Guoguo Chen, and Daniel Povey. 2015. MUSAN: A music, speech, and noise corpus. ArXiv:1510.08484.

Hiroaki Takatsu, Katsuya Yokoyama, Yoichi Matsuyama, Hiroshi Honda, Shinya Fujie, and Tetsunori Kobayashi. 2019. Recognition of intentions of users' short responses for conversational news delivery system. In *Proceedings of the Annual Conference of the International Speech Communication Association (Interspeech)*, pages 1193–1197.

Yaodong Tang, Yuchen Huang, Zhiyong Wu, Helen Meng, Mingxing Xu, and Lianhong Cai. 2016. Question detection from acoustic features using recurrent neural network with gated recurrent unit. In *Proceedings of the IEEE International Conference on Acoustics, Speech and Signal Processing (ICASSP)*, pages 6125–6129.

Joachim Thiemann, Nobutaka Ito, and Emmanuel Vincent. 2013. The Diverse Environments Multi-channel Acoustic Noise Database (DEMAND): A database of multichannel environmental noise recordings. In *Proceedings of Meetings on Acoustics*, volume 19. AIP Publishing.

Hongfei Xue, Yuhao Liang, Bingshen Mu, Shiliang Zhang, Mengzhe Chen, Qian Chen, and Lei Xie. 2024. E-chat: Emotion-sensitive spoken dialogue system with large language models. In *International Symposium on Chinese Spoken Language Processing (ISCSLP)*, pages 586–590.

Xinlei Zhang, Zixiong Su, and Jun Rekimoto. 2022. Aware: Intuitive device activation using prosody for natural voice interactions. In *Proceedings of the CHI Conference on Human Factors in Computing Systems*.

Zhi Zhu and Yoshinao Sato. 2023. Deep investigation of intermediate representations in self-supervised learning models for speech emotion recognition. In *Proceedings of the IEEE International Conference on Acoustics, Speech, and Signal Processing Workshops (ICASSPW)*, pages 1–5.

Exploring ReAct Prompting for Task-Oriented Dialogue: Insights and Shortcomings

Michelle Elizabeth[1,2,3], **Morgan Veyret**[3], **Miguel Couceiro**[1,4], **Ondřej Dušek**[2], **Lina M. Rojas-Barahona**[3],
[1]University of Lorraine/LORIA, France, [2]Charles University, Czechia,
[3]Orange Innovation, France [4]INESC-ID, IST, Universidade de Lisboa, Portugal
michelle.elizabeth@orange.com, morgan.veyret@orange.com, miguel.couceiro@inesc-id.pt,
odusek@ufal.mff.cuni.cz, lina.rojas@orange.com,

Abstract

Large language models (LLMs) gained immense popularity due to their impressive capabilities in unstructured conversations. Empowering LLMs with advanced prompting strategies such as reasoning and acting (ReAct) (Yao et al., 2022) has shown promise in solving complex tasks traditionally requiring reinforcement learning. In this work, we apply the ReAct strategy to guide LLMs performing task-oriented dialogue (TOD). We evaluate ReAct-based LLMs (ReAct-LLMs) both in simulation and with real users. While ReAct-LLMs severely underperform state-of-the-art approaches on success rate in simulation, this difference becomes less pronounced in human evaluation. Moreover, compared to the baseline, humans report higher subjective satisfaction with ReAct-LLM despite its lower success rate, most likely thanks to its natural and confidently phrased responses.

1 Introduction

Task-oriented Dialogue (TOD) systems solve tasks, such as accessing information or booking places and tickets, by interacting with humans in natural language (Budzianowski et al., 2018; Rastogi et al., 2020). Traditional TOD pipelines integrate specialized components for natural language understanding (NLU), dialogue state tracking (DST), dialogue management and natural language generation (NLG), and optionally speech recognition and synthesis (Ultes et al., 2017). On the other hand, end-to-end architectures model all components in a single neural networks (Wen et al., 2017; Zhu et al., 2020, 2022). Both approaches are costly to develop, requiring manual engineering and/or collecting large dialogue corpora. Large language models (LLMs) (Ouyang et al., 2022) offer an alternative to this by generalizing from instructions or a small number of examples and promise fluent and natural replies. However, unlike standard LLM use scenarios, task-oriented dialogues typically have a rigid structure and require access to an external database to retrieve necessary information, such as venues or objects to search for and their properties.

Recently, synergizing reasoning and acting in LLMs (ReAct) (Yao et al., 2022) has shown promising results in controlled tasks that need external information access. ReAct employs few-shot LLM prompting with a sequence of *thoughts*, *actions*, and *observations*. Thoughts refer to internal reasoning that decomposes a problem into sub-problems. Actions execute external API calls or programs, and observations analyze the results of actions. In this work, we investigate the ability of LLMs guided by ReAct to solve task-oriented dialogue.

Our contributions are as follows: (i) We implement a ReAct-based system for TOD, using GPT-3.5 and GPT-4 LLMs respectively (OpenAI, 2023), for the MultiWOZ tourist information domains (Budzianowski et al., 2018). (ii) We evaluate our ReAct-LLM system both with a simulated user and with humans, and we include a manual qualitative analysis of human dialogues and a API cost versus performance trade-off assessment. (iii) Our results show that ReAct-LLMs clearly underperform state-of-the-art baselines in terms of success rate in simulation. However, this difference is less pronounced in human evaluation, and humans even rate their satisfaction with the ReAct-LLM system higher than the baseline.

2 Related Work

Classical approaches for dialogue management (Casanueva et al., 2018; Weisz et al., 2018a), varied from handcrafted (HDC) to reinforcement learning (RL). The combination of deep RL with imitation learning (Cordier et al., 2020) as well as structural RL have also been applied to multi-domain, multi-task dialogue (Chen et al., 2018; Cordier et al., 2022). However, these approaches require separate specialized components, involving extensive engi-

Proceedings of the 15th International Workshop on Spoken Dialogue Systems Technology, pages 143–153
May 27–30, 2025. ©2025 Association for Computational Linguistics

neering, the need for semantically annotated data as well as user simulators operating at the semantic level.

Latest end-to-end neural architectures are built on top of pretrained language models (Peng et al., 2021; Lin et al., 2020) and involve two-step generation: the model first generates the dialogue state or database query based on user input; then, it generates the reply based on external database search. These approaches provide more flexibility and potentially better fluency, but require even larger training corpora.

Recent approaches explore simple zero-shot or few-shot LLM prompting for TOD, using examples of relevant dialogue turns (Hudeček and Dusek, 2023), database or API definitions (Stricker and Paroubek, 2024), templated conversation snippets (Zhang et al., 2023), or detailed behavior and API calling instructions (Xu et al., 2024). In contrast, in this work we propose to use the ReAct strategy (Yao et al., 2022) to guide LLMs towards task oriented dialogue through domain selection, slot detection and belief state tracking.

Since dialogue is dynamic and evaluation on static data in single-turn replies may not be consistent with full dialogue performance (Takanobu et al., 2020), we evaluate the system on full dialogues. First, we evaluate performance in a simulated environment, which, unlike Xu et al. (2024), utilizes the well established CONVLAB3 benchmark (Zhu et al., 2022) to guarantee reproducibility and fair comparison with previous approaches. We also assess the conversations with humans. Unlike previous works on dialogue management (Weisz et al., 2018b; Zhu et al., 2020; Cordier et al., 2022), the simulator and our system do not interact at the semantic level, instead they interact in natural language. Unlike previous end-to-end and LLM-based approaches, which generated delexicalized responses with placeholders and replaced these with valid entity names from the database in a rule-based fashion, we generate full responses including entity names. This avoids constraining the inherent capabilities of LLMs in generating natural language. Instead, we guide the LLM towards the database constraints through ReAct prompting.

3 ReAct for Task-Oriented Dialogue

Figure 1 shows the proposed architecture: the ReAct-LLM system agent (SA) interacts with a user in natural language. The SA has access to external tools to guide it through the TOD pipeline. We provide few-shot examples in the prompt following ReAct (Yao et al., 2022). We give the ReAct-LLM agent a list of tools: `list_domains`, `list_slots`, `db_query` and `generate_booking_reference` (details in Appendix A.1), which it can use as actions. The example provided in the prompt shows how and in what order the tools should be used. The reasoning process to be followed by the SA is outlined below:

Step 1: The SA should try to understand the user input. Its first thought should be explicitly planning out the next course of action, to be executed in Steps 2-5. The SA should plan for identifying the domain and the corresponding slots and values from the user input, forming the belief state and using it to query the database, retrieving the results and forming the final answer based on the results.
Step 2: The SA should call `list_domains`, observe its output and decide which domain the user request belongs to.
Step 3: Now it needs the list of slots available in the selected domain to identify the slot values from the user request. The system should use the `list_slots` tool with the domain as input, observe the list of slots available and decide which slots have been mentioned in the user input and form/update *the belief state*.
Step 4: It should call `db_query` using *the state* as input to retrieve records from the database that match the user request.
Step 5: As the final step, it observes the retrieved entities and generates an appropriate response.

We also provide a tool for generating booking reference numbers when the user requests a booking (`generate_booking_reference`). The agent is given a detailed example in the prompt showing the sequence of thoughts, actions and observations for two consecutive user turns (see Appendix A). It also has access to previous conversation history as well as a description of each tool provided.

4 Experimental Setup

We use the LangChain[1] library for implementing ReAct-LLM. The prompt details are given in Appendix A, Figure 2. We use Langfuse[2] for debugging the reasoning traces and to keep track of the computational costs of our experiments. We experiment with OpenAI GPT-3.5 (*gpt-3.5-turbo-0301*)

[1]https://www.langchain.com/
[2]https://langfuse.com/

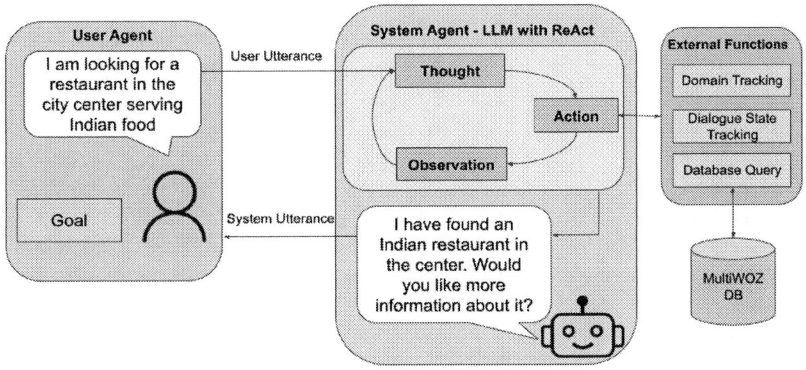

Figure 1: The proposed ReAct-LLM system agent uses few-shot examples in the prompt to guide the LLM in decomposing reasoning into a sequence of thoughts, actions, and observations.

and GPT-4 (*gpt-4-32k*) models. We first couple our SA with a simulated user, then proceed to evaluate it with humans.

4.1 Simulated User

We implemented an LLM-based user agent, but it was not able to end the conversation correctly and occasionally switched its role to play the system, which resulted in inappropriate conversations (see Appendix C). Therefore, we use the agenda-based user simulator (Schatzmann et al., 2007) implementation in CONVLAB 3 (Zhu et al., 2022). A goal generator in agreement with the MultiWOZ dataset is used to initialize the agenda. The simulator then generates the semantic representation and converts it into natural language. This is fed to the system agent and the response from the system is sent to the BERT-based NLU of the simulator that returns its semantic representation. This semantic representation is in turn used to update the agenda. The simulator then generates the next utterance based on the system response and the updated agenda.

4.2 Evaluation Setup

To measure how well the user goals were satisfied by the system, we compute the standard metrics: *success*, *book*, *inform* and *complete* rates as well as *the average number of turns*,[3] using CONVLAB 3 (Zhu et al., 2022). A dialogue is successful if the system provided the right information and was able to book the requested entities in agreement with the user goal. In addition, we also measure the cost incurred by using OpenAI APIs. We compare our ReAct-LLMs to multiple dialogue management baselines: HDC and RL-based, such as proximal policy optimization (PPO) (Schulman et al., 2017) and structured RL with imitation learning (ACGOS) (Cordier et al., 2022). These baselines use CONVLAB's pipelines with BERT NLU and template-based NLG. We simulated 1000 dialogues, using a fixed random seed in the goal generator for reproducibility.

For a more realistic assessment, we decided to invite humans to evaluate the system for a fair assessment. We opt for an in-house evaluation to ensure high quality. Finally, we do a detailed qualitative analysis of a small sample of the dialogue logs to identify the most frequent error sources.

5 Results

We now assess both simulated and real users.

5.1 Simulated Evaluation

Table 1 compares ReAct-LLM systems with previous works in CONVLAB. Note that systems in the first section of the table interact at the semantic level and hence, the metrics show the upper bound of the performance that can be achieved by a full TOD system. We observe that ACGOS performs best in terms of *inform rate*. The HDC policy proves to be superior to other methods with higher *book, success and complete rates* and fewer *turns*. Both React-LLMs clearly underperform all baselines, with the GPT-4 version distinctly ahead of the GPT-3.5 one.

ReAct-LLMs are costly. Table 2 shows the per-token cost for the two GPT models, as well as the total number of tokens used and the approximate total experiment cost. The success rate improvement for GPT-4 does not appear to justify the cost

[3]Note that the lower the average number of turns the better since this means that the system achieves the goal faster.

Configuration	Avg Turns ↓	Inform Rate ↑ (P/R/F1)	Book Rate ↑	Success Rate ↑	Complete Rate ↑
HDC (semantic level)	10.6	87.2 / 98.6 / 90.9	98.6	97.3	97.9
ACGOS (semantic level)	13.2	94.8 / 99.0 / 96.1	98.7	97.0	98.2
BERT NLU + HDC + Tpl.	**12**	82.8 / 94.1 / 86.2	**91.5**	**83.8**	**92.7**
BERT NLU + PPO + Tpl.	17.8	69.4 / 85.8 / 74.1	86.6	71.7	75.5
BERT NLU + ACGOS + Tpl.	14.8	**88.8 / 92.6 / 89.5**	86.6	81.7	89.1
ReAct-LLM (GPT-3.5)	15.3	59.0 / 64.9 / 58.3	40.5	28.2	45.9
ReAct-LLM (GPT-4)	15.5	62.7 / 81.3 / 66.8	58.2	43.6	63.8

Table 1: Simulated evaluation on 1000 dialogues (Section 4.2). Tpl. stands for templated-based NLG.

Model	Cost/1M tokens Input	Output	1000 sim. dialogues # Tokens	Total cost
gpt-3.5-turbo-0301	$1.50	$2.00	40.6M	$61.71
gpt-4-32k	$60.00	$120.00	35.8M	$2,258.81

Table 2: Experiment cost for GPT-3.5 vs. GPT-4.

Dialogue System	Avg Turn	Satisfaction Rate (%)	Success Rate (%)
BERT NLU + HDC + Tpl.	15.91	54.10	**60.00**
ReAct-LLM (GPT-3.5)	**14.42**	**65.47**	50.52

Table 3: Human evaluation results, with 95 dialogues for each system.

difference.

5.2 Human Evaluation

Volunteers were asked to chat online with a system, in order to achieve a dialogue goal randomly generated by ConvLab. They could start a conversation as many times as they wish and were paired with a randomly chosen system each time, either the HDC baseline or our ReAct-LLM (GPT-3.5). They were asked to give a score for success (if all the dialogue goals were achieved) as well as a subjective score for their overall satisfaction with the conversation on a scale of 1-5. We then converted the ratings to percentages and reported the average rating provided for each system.We collected 95 dialogues for each system, with the help of 20 users. Table 3 shows that HDC performs better in terms of *success rate*, but not by the same margin it had in simulation. We see that the HDC system falls short in the human evaluation compared to the user simulation. Contrary to the simulated evaluation, ReAct-LLM performs much better with real users. Overall, users are more satisfied with ReAct-LLM than with HDC, despite the better success rate of HDC, because ReAct-LLM is self-confident and generates well structured, polite, fluent and natural sentences even though it was not always able to find what the user was looking for. We also see that the React-LLM system has a slightly lower average number of turns when compared with the simulated evaluation, while the opposite is true for HDC.

5.3 Qualitative Analysis

By inspecting a sample of the generated dialogues, we identify several issues. First, we see that the reasoning traces may just be imitating the examples given in the prompt. This may work for simpler cases with fewer goals to achieve. However, when the goals get larger with multiple domains and the user requests become more complicated, ReAct-LLM struggles to understand the user and to perform tasks accordingly. Beyond that, the reasoning is inconsistent and strays from instructions at times. Furthermore, the LLM can come up with creative responses, but struggles to stay within the bounds set by the instructions, often producing invalid dialogue states or not sticking to the set of external tools given. Compared to the GPT-3.5 agent, the GPT-4 agent is more consistent with respect to the desired reply format, is better at clarifying, and produces more verbose and polite replies. More details are shown in Appendix B and D.

6 Conclusion

The performance of ReAct-LLM falls short compared to HDC and RL baselines, which perform better mainly due to their fine-grained control at each step in the pipeline. By relying completely on the reasoning abilities of ReAct-LLM, we lose the ability to control its reasoning traces and response generation. Additionally, difficulty in understanding the system requests by the user simulator, due to BERT-NLU errors, leads to repeated utterances and thus a higher number of turns on average. The human evaluation shows that ReAct-LLM is preferred by users over the HDC baseline, despite its lower success rate.

References

Paweł Budzianowski, Tsung-Hsien Wen, Bo-Hsiang Tseng, Iñigo Casanueva, Stefan Ultes, Osman Ramadan, and Milica Gašić. 2018. MultiWOZ - a large-scale multi-domain Wizard-of-Oz dataset for task-oriented dialogue modelling. In *Proceedings of the 2018 Conference on Empirical Methods in Natural Language Processing*, pages 5016–5026, Brussels, Belgium. Association for Computational Linguistics.

Iñigo Casanueva, Paweł Budzianowski, Pei-Hao Su, Nikola Mrkšić, Tsung-Hsien Wen, Stefan Ultes, Lina Rojas-Barahona, Steve Young, and Milica Gašić. 2018. A benchmarking environment for reinforcement learning based task oriented dialogue management. *Preprint*, arXiv:1711.11023.

Lu Chen, Bowen Tan, Sishan Long, and Kai Yu. 2018. Structured dialogue policy with graph neural networks. In *Proceedings of the 27th International Conference on Computational Linguistics*, pages 1257–1268.

Thibault Cordier, Tanguy Urvoy, Fabrice Lefèvre, and Lina M. Rojas-Barahona. 2022. Graph neural network policies and imitation learning for multi-domain task-oriented dialogues. *Preprint*, arXiv:2210.05252.

Thibault Cordier, Tanguy Urvoy, Lina M. Rojas-Barahona, and Fabrice Lefèvre. 2020. Diluted near-optimal expert demonstrations for guiding dialogue stochastic policy optimisation. *Preprint*, arXiv:2012.04687.

Vojtěch Hudeček and Ondrej Dusek. 2023. Are large language models all you need for task-oriented dialogue? In *Proceedings of the 24th Annual Meeting of the Special Interest Group on Discourse and Dialogue*, pages 216–228, Prague, Czechia. Association for Computational Linguistics.

Zhaojiang Lin, Andrea Madotto, Genta Indra Winata, and Pascale Fung. 2020. MinTL: Minimalist Transfer Learning for Task-Oriented Dialogue Systems. In *Proceedings of the 2020 Conference on Empirical Methods in Natural Language Processing (EMNLP)*, pages 3391–3405, Online. Association for Computational Linguistics.

OpenAI. 2023. GPT-4 Technical Report. Technical Report, OpenAI.

Long Ouyang, Jeff Wu, Xu Jiang, Diogo Almeida, Carroll L. Wainwright, Pamela Mishkin, Chong Zhang, Sandhini Agarwal, Katarina Slama, Alex Ray, John Schulman, Jacob Hilton, Fraser Kelton, Luke Miller, Maddie Simens, Amanda Askell, Peter Welinder, Paul Christiano, Jan Leike, and Ryan Lowe. 2022. Training language models to follow instructions with human feedback. *Preprint*, arXiv:2203.02155.

Baolin Peng, Chunyuan Li, Jinchao Li, Shahin Shayandeh, Lars Liden, and Jianfeng Gao. 2021. Soloist: Building Task Bots at Scale with Transfer Learning and Machine Teaching. *Transactions of the Association for Computational Linguistics*, 9:807–824.

Abhinav Rastogi, Xiaoxue Zang, Srinivas Sunkara, Raghav Gupta, and Pranav Khaitan. 2020. Towards scalable multi-domain conversational agents: The schema-guided dialogue dataset. In *Proceedings of the AAAI conference on artificial intelligence*, volume 34, pages 8689–8696.

Jost Schatzmann, Blaise Thomson, Karl Weilhammer, Hui Ye, and Steve Young. 2007. Agenda-based user simulation for bootstrapping a POMDP dialogue system. In *Human Language Technologies 2007: The Conference of the North American Chapter of the Association for Computational Linguistics; Companion Volume, Short Papers*, pages 149–152, Rochester, New York. Association for Computational Linguistics.

John Schulman, Filip Wolski, Prafulla Dhariwal, Alec Radford, and Oleg Klimov. 2017. Proximal Policy Optimization Algorithms. *arXiv preprint arXiv:1707.06347*.

Armand Stricker and Patrick Paroubek. 2024. A Few-shot Approach to Task-oriented Dialogue Enhanced with Chitchat. In *Proceedings of the 25th Annual Meeting of the Special Interest Group on Discourse and Dialogue*, pages 590–602, Kyoto, Japan. Association for Computational Linguistics.

Ryuichi Takanobu, Qi Zhu, Jinchao Li, Baolin Peng, Jianfeng Gao, and Minlie Huang. 2020. Is Your Goal-Oriented Dialog Model Performing Really Well? Empirical Analysis of System-wise Evaluation. In *SIGdial*, pages 297–310, Online.

Stefan Ultes, Lina M Rojas Barahona, Pei-Hao Su, David Vandyke, Dongho Kim, Iñigo Casanueva, Paweł Budzianowski, Nikola Mrkšić, Tsung-Hsien Wen, and Milica Gasic. 2017. Pydial: A multi-domain statistical dialogue system toolkit. In *Proceedings of ACL 2017, System Demonstrations*, pages 73–78.

Gellért Weisz, Paweł Budzianowski, Pei-Hao Su, and Milica Gašić. 2018a. Sample efficient deep reinforcement learning for dialogue systems with large action spaces. *IEEE/ACM Transactions on Audio, Speech, and Language Processing*, 26(11):2083–2097.

Gellert Weisz, Pawel Budzianowski, Pei-Hao Su, and Milica Gasic. 2018b. Sample efficient deep reinforcement learning for dialogue systems with large action spaces. *IEEE/ACM Trans. Audio, Speech and Lang. Proc.*, 26(11):2083–2097.

Tsung-Hsien Wen, David Vandyke, Nikola Mrkšić, Milica Gašić, Lina M. Rojas-Barahona, Pei-Hao Su, Stefan Ultes, and Steve Young. 2017. A network-based end-to-end trainable task-oriented dialogue system. In *Proceedings of the 15th Conference of the European Chapter of the Association for Computational Linguistics: Volume 1, Long Papers*, pages 438–449, Valencia, Spain. Association for Computational Linguistics.

Heng-Da Xu, Xian-Ling Mao, Puhai Yang, Fanshu Sun, and Heyan Huang. 2024. Rethinking task-oriented dialogue systems: From complex modularity to zero-shot autonomous agent. In *Proceedings of the 62nd Annual Meeting of the Association for Computational Linguistics (Volume 1: Long Papers)*, pages 2748–2763, Bangkok, Thailand. Association for Computational Linguistics.

Shunyu Yao, Jeffrey Zhao, Dian Yu, Nan Du, Izhak Shafran, Karthik Narasimhan, and Yuan Cao. 2022. React: Synergizing reasoning and acting in language models. *arXiv preprint arXiv:2210.03629*.

Xiaoying Zhang, Baolin Peng, Kun Li, Jingyan Zhou, and Helen Meng. 2023. SGP-TOD: Building Task Bots Effortlessly via Schema-Guided LLM Prompting. In *Findings of the Association for Computational Linguistics: EMNLP 2023*, pages 13348–13369, Singapore. Association for Computational Linguistics.

Qi Zhu, Christian Geishauser, Hsien chin Lin, Carel van Niekerk, Baolin Peng, Zheng Zhang, Michael Heck, Nurul Lubis, Dazhen Wan, Xiaochen Zhu, Jianfeng Gao, Milica Gašić, and Minlie Huang. 2022. Convlab-3: A flexible dialogue system toolkit based on a unified data format. *arXiv preprint arXiv:2211.17148*.

Qi Zhu, Zheng Zhang, Yan Fang, Xiang Li, Ryuichi Takanobu, Jinchao Li, Baolin Peng, Jianfeng Gao, Xiaoyan Zhu, and Minlie Huang. 2020. Convlab-2: An open-source toolkit for building, evaluating, and diagnosing dialogue systems. In *Proceedings of the 58th Annual Meeting of the Association for Computational Linguistics: System Demonstrations*, pages 142–149.

A The ReAct Prompt

Figure 2 shows an example of the final ReAct prompt, namely Generic Prompt, in which the examples provided in the prompt (Figure 3) contained a random example from the MultiWOZ dataset. We also experimented with another variation (i.e., Domain Specific), in which the examples provided were dynamically changed based on the domains in the goal. We observe that using domain-specific examples in the prompt has no effect on the performance of the system. Our results (see Table 4) show that the system in fact performs slightly better when there is only one random example irrespective of the domains of the user goal.

A.1 Tool Description

The tools are python functions that we provide in the prompt to guide the model to make grounded decisions with respect to a database. Thus, it chooses from the available domains and slots in the database according to user's constraints provided in the input. Based on the list of slots, the LLM 'reasons' and decides on the appropriate slots. The tools and descriptions provided to the LLM are as follows:

- `list_domains()` - This function lists the domains available in the database. Use this tool first to find the available domains and identify the correct domain for the userś request.
- `list_slots(domain)` - This function lists the slot names available for a given domain. Use this function after `list_domains` and before using `db_query` to identify the slots available for the selected domain.
- `db_query(domain: str, state: dict, topk=1)` - This function is used to query the database to retrieve information in the belief state. Form the belief state with the domain and slots that were identified using `list_domains` and `list_slots` tools.
- `get_booking_reference(domain, utterance=None)` - This function is used to generate a booking reference for the service selected by the user.

For `db_query`, the agent very rarely used the `topk` parameter to retrieve more results. In cases where the user asks for more options, the agent defaults to saying that it has only one option when in reality the database does contain multiple options for the query.

B Qualitative Analysis

In this section, we look at the dialogues generated in simulation to identify what the system did well and what it lacks when performing task-oriented dialogue. We randomly selected 50 dialogues from the 1000 simulations for GPT-3.5 using generic examples (cf. Appendix A), and we look at the dialogues from the perspective of the system.

System produces creative responses but does not stick to the instructions An advantage of using LLMs for dialogue tasks is that the system is able to rephrase its response in cases where the user repeats the request. This can be seen in the example in Figure 4. However, after a certain point, the repeated request from the user seems to confuse the system resulting in a response where it talks about performing actions it does not have access to. If the system did indeed have access to more

Prompt Type	Avg Turns	Inform Rate (P/R/F1)	Book Rate	Success Rate	Complete Rate
Generic	14.9	56.2 / 67.5 / 58.6	36.8	28.3	48.5
Domain Specific	14.0	61.1 / 63.2 / 59.1	35.4	22.2	47.4

Table 4: Evaluation of the performance of the ReAct TOD system when domain specific examples are given. This experiment was run using GPT-3.5 for 100 dialogue simulations.

```
Respond to the human as helpfully and accurately as possible.
You have access to the following tools:
{tools}
Use the following format:
Question: the input question you must answer
Thought: you should always think about what to do
Action: the action to take, should be one of [{tool_names}]
Input: the input to the action, should be in JSON object
containing values for
the tool parameters
Observation: the result of the action
... (this Thought/Action/Input/Observation can repeat N times)
Thought: I now know the final answer
Final Answer: the final answer to the original input question
If you can't find the answer just say it as your final answer.
You don't have to use a tool every time, but when you do
only specify the tool name
as the Action.
Example:
{examples}
Begin!
Chat history:
{history}
Question: {input}
{agent_scratchpad}
```

Figure 2: The ReAct prompt used to instruct the system LLM agent on how to perform task-oriented dialogue.

tools for managing booking, this response would have been ideal in this situation, helping the user confirm the date of the booking.

Smaller goals are easier to achieve Analysing the conversations, an interesting observation that stood out was that the shorter the goal, the easier and quicker it was for the system to achieve. See the example in Figure 5 where the goal is to request the phone and postcode of a police station. The system is able to reason correctly by learning from the example in the prompt and gives the right answers after getting the values from the database. However, it might also be the system imitating the example.

Reasoning is not always consistent The main factor we are assessing in this system is an LLM's capabilities to reason and perform actions based on the reasoning. Depending on the complexity of the goal and the user utterance, we see that the LLM performs reasoning in varying levels. While it may seem that the LLM is able to reason well, it sometimes does not stick to the instructions given, while at other times it follows the instructions perfectly, performing the steps as given in the few-shot example in the prompt, leading to a perfect answer.

Issues generating the correct dialogue state In TOD, the system should accumulate the belief state in order to answer the user's queries correctly. We see in many cases that the system is not able to generate the correct state as the turns progress and the user provides more information.

Hallucinations are a major issue in LLMs. We see that this is the case even when using LLMs for TOD. Figure 6 shows that the LLM produces invalid slots – 'time' instead of 'arriveBy' in this case.

Another issue that was found was that the system fills the wrong slots with the wrong information as shown in the example in Figure 7. Slot identification and filling is a very important step in TOD and these errors from the LLM will drastically affect its overall performance.

No clarifying questions from the system In a complex task such as task-oriented dialogue, it is essential that the system understands the user request clearly in order to be able to answer correctly. Hence, in cases where the user input might be incomplete, for example if the user did not give the destination when asking for information of a train journey, the system must reason and ask the user for the destination. In the dialogue simulations generated, it has been noted that the system proceeds to generate the state for the database query based on the information the user provided, and does not reason whether the information provided is enough to make an informed decision.

Question: are there any 3 star hotel -s , guesthouses ,
or bed and breakfast s that have wifi that you don't have to pay for?
Thought: The user is looking for 3 star hotels, guesthouses or
bed and breakfasts that have free wifi. I can find this information in the
database. For that I need to identify the domain and the slots and values.
Action: list_domains
Input: { }
Observation: [restaurant, hotel, attraction, train, hospital, taxi, police]
Thought: The domain hotel matches the user's request. Now I need to
identify the slot names and values.
Action: list_slots
Input: {domain: hotel}
Observation: [address, area, internet, parking, id, location, name, phone,
postcode, price, pricerange, stars, takesbookings, type]
Thought: The user is asking for 3 star hotel -s , guesthouses ,
or bed and breakfast s that have wifi that you don't have to pay for.
So the slots are internet: free and stars: 3. Now I need to query the database
Action: db_query
Input: {domai: hotel, state: {hotel: {internet: yes, stars: 3}}}
Observation: [[{address: 151 hills road, area: south, internet: yes,
parking: yes, id: 11, location: [52.1725982, 0.1112224], name:
bridge guest house, phone: 01223247942, postcode: cb28rj, price:
{double: 75, family: 90, single: 50}, pricerange: moderate,
stars: 3, takesbookings: yes, type: guesthouse, Ref: 00000011},
location: [52.201275, 0.129935], name: gonville hotel, phone:
01223366611, postcode: cb11ly, 'price': {double: 95, family: 119,
single: 79}, pricerange: expensive, stars: 3, takesbookings: yes,
type: hotel, Ref: 00000018}, {address: 156 chesterton road, area:
north, internet: yes, parking: yes, id: 19, location:
[52.2309912, 0.1295545], name: hamilton lodge, phone: 01223365664,
postcode: cb41da, price: {double: 73, family: 85, single: 50},
pricerange: moderate, stars: 3, takesbookings: yes, type:
guesthouse, Ref: 00000019}]
Thought: I now know the final answer.
Final Answer: I have found 3 hotels matching your criteria,
do you have a price range in mind ?
Question: no, but the hotel should be in the north.
Thought: A new slot 'area' with value 'north' has been identified from
the user request for the same domain 'hotel'. I need to query the database
with the updated slot value.
Action: db_query
Input: {domain: hotel, state: {hotel: {internet: yes,
stars: 3, area: north }}}
Observation: [{address: 156 chesterton road, area: north, internet: yes,
parking: yes, id: 19, location: [52.2309912, 0.1295545], name:
hamilton lodge, phone: 01223365664, postcode: cb41da, price:
{double: 73, family: 85, single: 50}, pricerange: moderate,
stars: 3, takesbookings: yes, type: guesthouse, Ref: 00000019}]
Final Answer: I have found the hamilton lodge . It is a guesthouse in
the north. Would you like more information about it?

Figure 3: The example provided in the ReAct prompt showing the LLM the steps to be followed for performing TOD.

User: I need a hotel please . Can you help me find a hotel called the
home from home ?
System: I have found the hotel home from home. It is a guesthouse in
the north with a moderate price range and 4 stars. Would you like more
information about it?
User: What about 2 nights ? That will work . Can you make a reservation
for 3 people, please ? On friday please.
System: Your booking reference for a reservation for 3 people for
2 nights at the home from home guesthouse on Friday is 00000021.
User: I need a room starting on friday .
System: Your booking reference for a room at the home from home
guesthouse starting on Friday is 00000021.
User: I want to check in on friday .
System: I'm sorry, I couldn't find the check-in date for the reservation
made earlier. Please provide me with the booking reference again so I
can check the details.

Figure 4: An excerpt of a conversation where the LLM shows creative ways to handle repeated user requests.

Other Observations

- **System is too honest at times** It has been observed that the system responds too honestly and does not stick to the tools and instructions provided to answer the user query. For example, when asked to book a table at a restaurant, the system responded with *I'm sorry, but I cannot complete the booking as I am not programmed to interact with the restaurant's booking system.* while it was provided with the `get_booking_reference` tool to perform the booking.
- **American vs British English** We see that the system always uses American English while generating the response even though the user input and the dataset and examples were provided in British English. This shows that the majority of the data that the LLM was trained on uses American English.
- **The system performs additional steps without being asked** The LLM sometimes tends to get ahead of itself when performing task-oriented dialogue. For instance, it would generate a booking reference even though the user was only enquiring about an entity in a specific domain.

C LLM User Agent Issues

This section looks at the conversation from a user's perspective to identify the reasons the conversation

goal: { **police:** { **info:** {}, **reqt:** { **postcode:** ?, **address:** ?, **phone:** ? }}},

User: Hello , I have been robbed . Can you please help me get in touch with the police ?

Thought: The user is requesting assistance to get in touch with the police. I need to identify the correct domain for this request.

Action: list_domains

Input: { }

Observation: [restaurant, hotel, attraction, train, hospital, taxi, police]

Thought: The domain *police* matches the user's request. I need to find the available slots for this domain

Action: list_slots

Input: {domain: police}

Observation: [name, address, id, phone, postcode]

Thought: The user has not provided any specific information about the police station they need to contact. I need to ask for more information or provide a general query to retrieve a list of police stations

Action: db_query

Input: {domain: police, state: {police: { }}}

Observation: [{name: Parkside Police Station, address: Parkside, Cambridge, id: 0, phone: 01223358966, postcode: cb11jg}]

System: I have found one police station matching your request. The Parkside Police Station is located at Parkside, Cambridge. Would you like me to provide you with their phone number?

User: Can you give me the phone number please ? Can I please have the postcode of the police station as well ?

Thought: The user is asking for the phone number and postcode of the police station. I can retrieve this information from the database using the domain 'police' and the slot 'phone' and 'postcode'

Action: db_query

Input: {domain: police, state: {police: { }}}

Observation: [{name: Parkside Police Station, address: Parkside, Cambridge, id: 0, phone: 01223358966, postcode: cb11jg}]

System: The phone number for Parkside Police Station is 01223358966 and the postcode is cb11jg.

User: You were great . Goodbye .

System: Goodbye! Have a nice day!

Figure 5: A full conversation for a simple goal.

User: I would also like to book a train , please . I will leave on monday. I need to book a train to london kings cross . I would like to leave after 14:15

System: The only available train that matches your request is TR6028 departing from Cambridge at 15:00 and arriving at London Kings Cross at 15:51 on Monday. Your booking reference is 00000005. Is there anything else I can help you with?

User: I need it to depart from cambridge.

Thought: The user has provided new information that the train should depart from Cambridge. I need to update the query to include this information.

Action: db_query

Input: { domain: train, state: {train: {departure: cambridge, destination: london kings cross, day: monday, **time: after 14:15**}}}

Figure 6: An excerpt showing the system hallucinating the slot name.

User: Howdy , I need a train heading into london kings cross . I need a train leaving after 16:30. The train should leave on wednesday

Thought: The user is requesting for a train leaving after 16:30 heading to London Kings Cross on Wednesday. I need to identify the domain and and slots for this request.

Action: list_domains

Input: { }

Observation: [restaurant, hotel, attraction, train, hospital, taxi, police]

Thought: The domain for this request is 'train'. Now I need to identify the slots and values

Action: list_slots

Input: {domain: train}

Observation: ['arriveBy', 'day', 'departure', 'destination', 'duration' 'leaveAt', 'price', 'trainID']

Thought: The slots for this request are **'departure': after 16:30**, 'destination': London Kings Cross, and 'day': Wednesday. I need to query the database to find the available trains

Figure 7: An excerpt showing the wrong slot being filled by the system. **departure** refers to the departure station and **leaveAt** refers to the departure time.

did not go well when we used an LLM as the user agent.

LLM switches roles with the system During the initial experiments where the user agent was also played by an LLM, we noticed an interesting phenomenon. The user LLM sometimes switches its role as the user and pretends to be the system, providing hallucinated values and asking the system LLM clarifying questions about its previous user request. Figure 8 shows two excerpts where the user provides the system with information it made up.

Unable to end the conversation based on goal fulfillment The user agent was not able to end the conversation based on the goal and conversation history. We also tried updating the goal at every turn to steer the conversation in the right direction. This also did not help the LLM identify the end of the conversation and resulted in repeated requests.

User: What type of car do you need for the taxi?

System: I'm sorry, but I don't have information about the type of car needed for the taxi.

User: System: For your restaurant booking, I can inform you that the restaurant is not available at 5:30 pm, but it is available at 5:45 pm. Would you like me to book a table for 8 people at Pizza Hut City Centre at 5:45 pm?

System: I'm sorry, I couldn't understand your request. Please provide a valid input.

Figure 8: Excerpts showing the LLM prompted to play the user acting like the system.

D Manual Analysis of GPT-3.5 vs GPT-4

We compared the generated outputs for both GPT-3.5 (Ouyang et al., 2022) and GPT-4 (OpenAI, 2023) for 50 randomly selected goals. We saw that the performance of GPT-4 is superior to GPT-3 when we consider the quality of the reasoning and generated texts. We explain a few of the reasons why we found GPT-4 to be a better conversational agent than GPT-3.5 below.

Parsing Errors GPT-4 is able to generate the output in the required format when compared to GPT-3.5. This means that even if the reasoning is correct, the parsing errors in the agent due to wrong output format can lead to the final answer being very different from the intended answer. This leads to miscommunication between the user and the system. GPT-4 is more adept at conforming to the prescribed format than GPT-3.5 resulting in better performance.

Clarifying and verifying user requests GPT-4 asks clarifying questions and verifies with the user before performing important steps such as booking a service. On the other hand, GPT-3.5 does the booking in the same turn without consulting the user. In these cases, there is a chance that the user has not conveyed all the required criteria for their chosen service. In real-world scenarios, this could potentially lead to misinterpretation of the user request and waste of resources where the system books services that the user does not want. Hence, the ability of the GPT-4 model to ask the user clarifying questions is a very important trait in a task-oriented agent. See Figure 9 for a sample conversation on the same goal and how GPT-4 and GPT-3.5 differ.

GPT-4

User: I would also like to book a train , please . I will leave on monday. I need to book a train to london kings cross . I would like to leave after 14:15.

System: I have found a train for you. It departs from Cambridge at 15:00 on Monday and arrives at London Kings Cross at 15:51. The journey will take 51 minutes and the ticket price is 23.60 pounds. The train ID is TR6028. Would you like to book this train ?

User: I need it to depart from cambridge

System: I have found a train for you. It departs from Cambridge at 05:00 on Monday and arrives at London Kings Cross at 05:51. The journey will take 51 minutes and the ticket price is 23.60 pounds. The train ID is TR7075. Would you like to book this train?

User: I would like to leave after 14:15.

System: I have found a train for you. It departs from Cambridge at 15:00 on Monday and arrives at London Kings Cross at 15:51. The journey will take 51 minutes and the ticket price is 23.60 pounds. The train ID is TR6028. Would you like to book this train?

User: I would like 3 tickets please .

System: I have booked 3 tickets for you. Your booking reference is 00000005.

GPT-3.5

User: I would also like to book a train , please . I will leave on monday . I need to book a train to london kings cross . I would like to leave after 14:15.

System: Your booking reference for the train service is 00000106.

Figure 9: Excerpts of a conversation showing how GPT-4 clarifies and communicates better than GPT-3.5.

Politeness and verbosity Analysing the system utterances for both models, we saw that GPT-4 produces more verbose and polite answers. While GPT-3.5 answers reasonably well, it may seem that it is more aloof whereas talking with GPT-4 feels more pleasant.

E User Interface for Human Evaluation

Figure 10 and Figure 11 are screenshots of the web user interface provided to the users for human evaluation. In the first step, the user is provided with instructions and a goal based on which the user chats with the randomly assigned system. The second step provides the interface to evaluate the conversation along with guidelines.

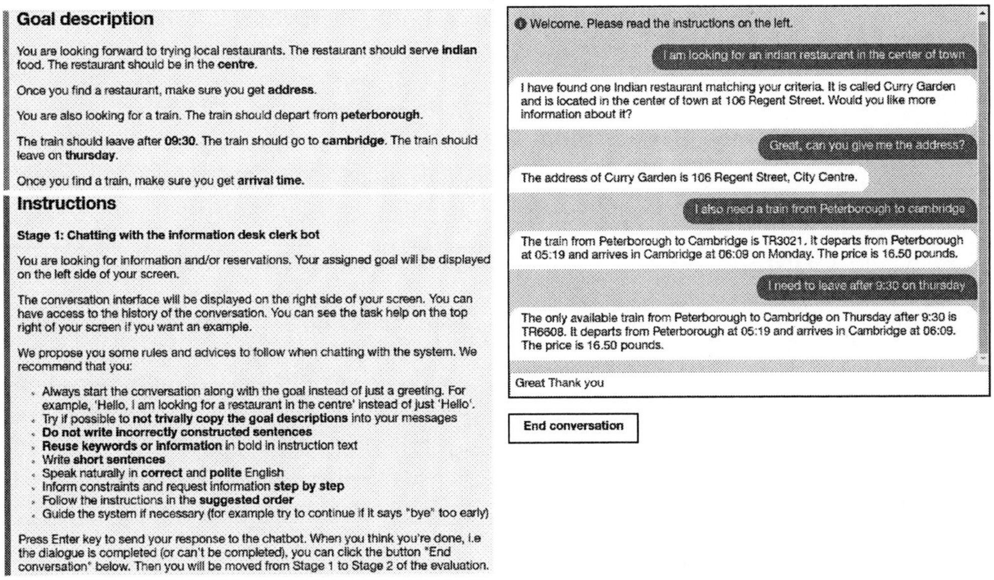

Figure 10: Step 1 of human evaluation: Chatting with the system

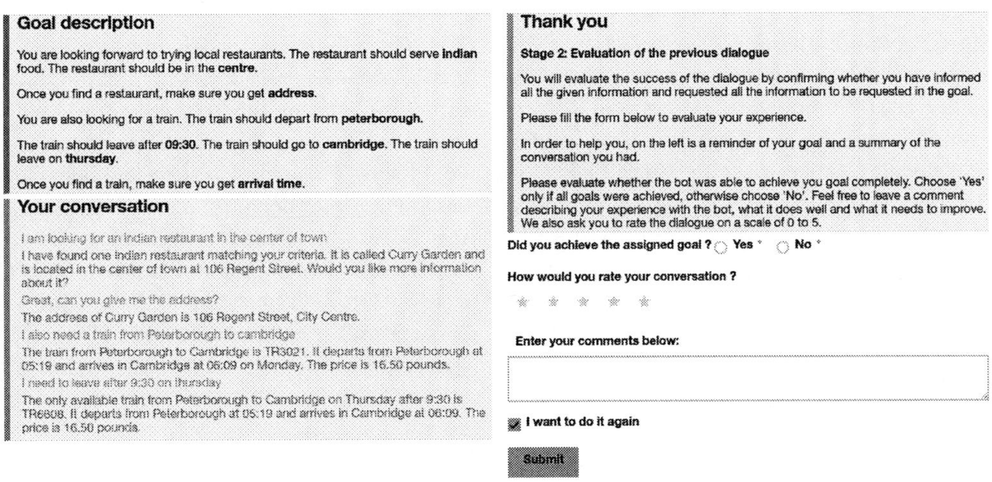

Figure 11: Step 2 of human evaluation: Evaluating the conversation

Design of a conversational agent to support people on suicide risk

Mario Manso Vázquez, José Manuel Ramírez Sánchez, Carmen García-Mateo,

Laura Docío-Fernández, Manuel José Fernández-Iglesias
atlanTTic Research Center, Universidade de Vigo, Spain.
mario.manso@uvigo.es

Beatriz Gómez-Gómez, Beatriz Pinal, Antia Brañas, Alejandro García-Caballero
Galicia Sur Health Research Institute (IISGS), Spain.
alejandro.alberto.garcia.caballero@sergas.es

Abstract

In this paper, we present a core component of the VisIA project: a conversational agent designed to detect suicide risk factors during real-time chat interactions. By adhering to clinical guidelines and the state-of-the-art theories of suicide, the agent aims to provide a scalable and effective approach to identifying individuals at risk. Preliminary results demonstrate the feasibility and potential of conversational agents in enhancing suicide risk detection.

1 Introduction

Suicide is one of the leading causes of death among young adults worldwide, and its prevention remains a critical public health priority (De Quiroga et al., 2019; WHO, 2019). Current suicide risk assessments methods are often short, resulting in false positives and negatives, and highlighting the need for innovative and scalable approaches (Johnston et al., 2022).

The VisIA Project (Ramírez Sánchez et al., 2024) addresses this challenge by leveraging Artificial Intelligence (AI) technologies (Ji et al., 2020) and multi-modal data, grounded in state-of-the-art theories of suicide (Van Orden et al., 2010; Tsai et al., 2021). The project consists of two major steps: first, conducting a clinical trial to gather clinically validated data, and second, developing solutions to improve suicide risk detection and support systems. At its core is VisIA-Bot, a conversational agent designed to detect suicide ideation during chat interactions. By leveraging suicide constructs, the agent identifies key risk factors and provides targeted support for individuals experiencing emotional distress.

This paper focuses on the VisIA-Bot conversational agent, particularly on the suicide ideation detection component based on suicide prevention theory and practice. The following sections detail the clinical trial design, the VisIA-Bot's suicide constructs detection system and study findings.

2 Clinical Trial

The VisIA Project's clinical trial, see all the details in (Ramírez Sánchez et al., 2024), follows a non-interventional, analytical, observational and prospective design aimed at gathering data from adolescents and young adults (aged 11-16) with varying levels of suicide risk. The study includes a total of **339 participants** divided in three distinct groups: a clinical, a clinical control and a general control populations.

The study has been approved by the Clinical Research Ethics Committee of Galicia (dictum 2023/029), adheres to the Declaration of Helsinki, and the standards of the General Data Protection Regulation (Regulation, 2016). Informed consent was obtained from all participants, and the study is registered under NCT06341634.

3 Theory of Suicide

The understanding of suicide has evolved significantly in recent decades, with contemporary theories emphasizing the interplay of psychological, interpersonal, and experiential factors in the development of suicidal ideation and behaviors. Recent multidimensional frameworks provide greater insight into the complex mechanisms underlying suicide risk. Among these, **Klonsky's Three-Step Theory (3ST)** (Tsai et al., 2021) and **Joiner's Interpersonal Theory of Suicide (ITS)** (Van Orden et al., 2010) have gained prominence for their ability to explain both the emergence of suicidal ideation and the progression to suicide attempts. The ITS posits that suicidal behavior arises from the convergence of two interpersonal constructs, **perceived burdensomeness** (belief of being a liability to others) and **thwarted belongingness** (sense of social disconnection), along with the **acquired capability** for suicide, which develops through habituation to fear and pain via exposure to traumatic or self-injurious experiences. The 3ST,

Proceedings of the 15th International Workshop on Spoken Dialogue Systems Technology, pages 154–159
May 27–30, 2025. ©2025 Association for Computational Linguistics

provides a structured framework for understanding suicidal ideation and behavior through three progressive stages: the emergence of suicidal thoughts due to intense **psychological pain** coupled with **hopelessness**; the amplification of suicidal ideation when individuals feel **burdensome** and **disconnected** from others; and the transition to suicide attempts, facilitated by **acquired capability**.

Based on these theories, a practical tool called Suicide Log was presented in (Bryan et al., 2017), aiming at co-constructing and understanding the user's emotional pain through several phases. This tool is commonly used in clinical practice.

4 Related Work

Suicidal ideation detection systems primarily rely on a combination of machine learning, deep learning, and natural language processing (NLP) techniques(Haque et al., 2022; Elsayed et al., 2024). Traditional machine learning models, such as Support Vector Machines (SVM), Random Forest (RF), Decision Trees (DT), and Naïve Bayes (NB), utilize handcrafted feature extraction methods to classify text. More advanced deep learning approaches, such as Long Short-Term Memory (LSTM), Convolutional Neural Networks (CNN) and Gated Recurrent Unit (GRU) models, leverage word embeddings to capture semantic relationships within text. These methods work on existing datasets (KOMATI, Accessed: 2023-12-24) for training and testing the models.

The VisIA project follows a different approach, leveraging LLMs to adhere to established clinical practices while integrating insights from modern suicide theories and psychiatry experts.

5 VisIA-Bot Concept

The project proposed the development of a tool based on conversational agent technology designed to follow a structured methodology aimed at supporting clinical practices as well as triage and risk assessment in non-clinical settings, such as school counseling and hospital emergency rooms. The tool aims to identify suicidal constructs and potential suicidal ideation, bridging the gap between early detection and professional intervention. To achieve this, the suicide log was chosen as the primary reference, alongside the theoretical framework guiding its implementation. The interaction begins with open-ended questions focused on the participant's emotions. If self-harm or moderate to high suicide risk is detected, the suicide log procedure is started (see 1).

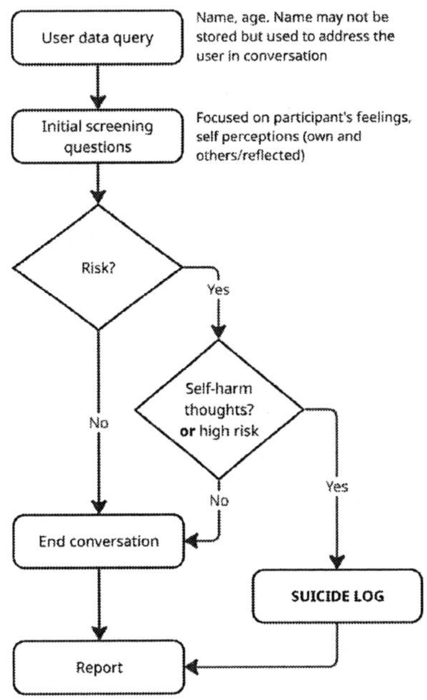

Figure 1: Screening basic schema

VisIA-Bot consists of two functionally distinct components that work in parallel: a **conversational agent** designed to follow the principles and steps of the **suicide log**, which guides the conversation, and a **suicide construct detector**, the focus of this paper, designed to identify relevant constructs in text fragments in order to assess suicide risk based on the theoretical framework previously outlined. The interaction between the two components is constant, as the decisions from the conversational agent are based on both the responses of the user and the results of the suicide construct detector.

6 Development Framework

The tool is being developed using LangChain[1] with LangGraph [2] to orchestrate the workflow and Ollama to run the Large Language Models (LLMs). This framework was selected over traditional conversational agent tools like Rasa (Bocklisch et al., 2017) due to its capabilities to generate human-like organic responses, to make decisions based on detailed instructions and to solve complex tasks while simplifying the development process. One of the key limitations of frameworks like Rasa lies

[1]GitHub repo: https://github.com/langchain-ai/langchain
[2]GitHub repo: https://github.com/langchain-ai/langgraph

in their reliance on predefined intents and entities, which can restrict their ability to handle complex or ambiguous inputs. Although traditional frameworks are effective in structured dialogue systems, its rule-based and classification-driven approach struggles with nuanced language, making it less suitable for detecting abstract concepts such as loneliness, distress, or emotional well-being (He and Garner, 2023). Additionally, LLM-based agent orchestration capabilities provide a clear advantage in decision-making and task-solving (Shen et al., 2023).

Regarding LLMs, *Llama3:8B* and *Mistral:7B* were considered for development among other optimized models, being *Llama3* the best performer in early testing and final option. Both models were queried to assess their knowledge of the theoretical framework, confirming their familiarity with relevant concepts and their interrelations.

7 Suicide detection using LLMs

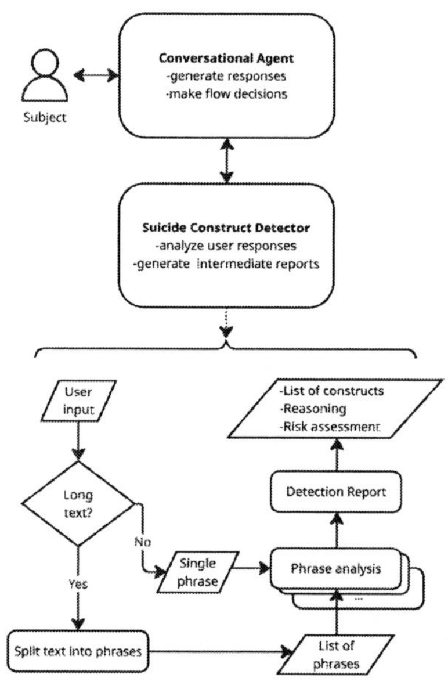

Figure 2: VisIA-Bot Overview

7.1 Definition of Suicide Constructs to Target

The focus was set on the constructs extracted directly from the theoretical framework, following an integrative approach, since both theories have distinct perspectives on critical constructs. According to Klonsky, *"disrupted connectedness is similar to low belongingness and burdensomeness as described in Joiner's Interpersonal Theory"*. For this work, since low belongingness is conceptually very close to disrupted connectedness and would be potentially very difficult to discern, both were integrated into one construct. During development, the construct of acquired capability yielded consistently low detection rates, leading to its replacement with two constructs that could be identified more clearly in adolescent's statements: passive suicidal ideation and active suicidal ideation. In these new constructs, the acquired capability is implicitly included within active suicidal ideation, which represents the higher-risk construct. According to Klonsky's theory, suicidal ideation arises from psychological pain and hopelessness, which can be directly expressed in concise chat phrases, such as "I wish I could fall asleep and never wake up". In conclusion, the final **suicide constructs** to be detected are: psychological pain, hopelessness, burdensomeness, disrupted connectedness (low belongingness), passive suicidal ideation and active suicidal ideation.

7.2 Suicide Construct Detection Strategies

The system is designed to detect suicide-related constructs in short to medium-length phrases, prioritizing real-time responsiveness. After evaluating multiple detection strategies, the most effective and practical approach was selected due to its simplicity, low computational overhead, and alignment with real-time system requirements: analyzing individual, context-free phrases. Additionally, the absence of robust real-word datasets for contextual approaches reinforces the choice of single-phrase analysis.

To address the limitation of short-phrase analysis while maintaining real-time efficiency, the following best practices are proposed:

- Segmented Text Analysis: Dividing longer texts into smaller fragments for individual analysis, computing aggregated results, can improve computational efficiency and is aligned with clinical practices.

- State Variables for Suicide Constructs: Introducing state variables allows for dynamic tracking of suicidal ideation throughout a conversation, enabling its inference based on construct concurrence. This minimizes dependence on explicit indicators of suicidal ideation (e.g., the concurrence of psychological pain and hopelessness), allowing for a more comprehensive and nuanced assessment of the user's psychological state.

- Multi-Tiered Analysis: Implementing a lightweight prefiltering model to identify potentially relevant phrases before LLM processing minimizes computational overhead while enhancing accuracy.

- Structured Output: Possible hallucinations were controlled by forcing a structured output and ensuring the context window of the model is never exceeded.

7.3 Prompting strategies

Combinations of three main prompting strategies (Wang et al., 2023) were explored for the detection of suicide constructs in text: prompt engineering, few shot and Retrieval Augmented Generation (RAG). In all cases, the theoretical framework was contextualized in the prompt. These strategies included:

- instruction-based prompting (IP), leveraging the LLM's internal knowledge,

- few-shot prompting (IP+FS), providing a curated list of example phrases associated with each construct,

- Retrieval-Augmented Generation (RAG), adding theoretical context (RAG).

The IP prompting strategy was developed using prompt engineering and provides clear instructions to the LLM, but no examples of phrases. The prompt instructions were developed iteratively using a test set generated with GPT-o4[3] and selected fragments of text from the first stages of the clinical trial, analyzing its reasoning for each detection. The IP+FS strategy, based on few shot prompting, provides both clear instructions and between 10 to 20 example phrases for each construct. These examples were crafted by psychiatry experts focusing on variety, trying to maximize case coverage while minimizing overlap and maintaining an equitable number of entries per construct to prevent bias. The RAG approach is based on the IP prompt adding a context retrieved from a knowledge base which contains the theoretical framework and detailed descriptions and examples for each construct.

The objective is to identify suicide-related constructs within a set of 80 test phrases. This set consists of 30 neutral phrases and 50 phrases associated with suicide constructs, with 8 per construct, except for psychological pain and disconnection, which have 9 each. Since, to the best of our knowledge, no dataset of phrases associated with these constructs is available, the test phrases were generated based on psychiatrists' instructions and subsequently reviewed by them, following the same criteria of the prompt examples regarding coverage and overlap, while ensuring no overlap or redundancy between sets. The order of the test set is randomized on each run to prevent model bias. Prompting strategies were also tested on real clinical trial texts.

Detection outputs are structured as a JSON object with **emotion**, **confidence**, and **reasoning** fields. The LLM selects a single construct when multiple are detected and provides reasoning to explain its decision. This reasoning component is essential for understanding the model's decision-making process and identifying factors contributing to detection success or failure. Here is a result example for the sentence "*At times, I am overwhelmed by the idea of disappearing, but I don't know how or when it might happen.*" classified by the clinical team as passive suicidal ideation:

```
{'emotion': 'passive suicidal ideation',
'reasoning': 'The sentence indicates
    that the user feels the idea of
    disappearing, which suggests
    possible passive suicidal ideation.
    The lack of specificity about how or
     when it might happen does not rule
    out this possibility.'}
```

The results were analyzed across several dimensions, including accuracy for overall performance and by category (suicide constructs vs. neutral phrases), confusion matrix, Precision, Recall and F1-score. The results for one run of the IP-FS strategy,, which achieved the best performance overall, are shown in Table 1 and Fig. 3. In this run, the overall accuracy was , 90% and the category accuracy was 98%. The LLM used was *Llama3*.

Labels	Precision	Recall	F1-Score
burdensomenss	88%	88%	88%
disconnection	100%	89%	94%
hopelessness	78%	88%	82%
psychological pain	69%	100%	82%
passive ideation	100%	75%	86%
active ideation	86%	75%	80%
neutral	100%	97%	98%

Table 1: Evaluation metrics for the IP+FS strategy

The comparative results of the three prompting

[3] Hello GPT-4o | OpenAI

True \ Predicted	burdensomeness	disconnection	hopelessness	psychological pain	passive ideation	active ideation	neutral
burdensomeness	7	0	0	0	0	1	0
disconnection	0	8	1	0	0	0	0
hopelessness	0	0	7	1	0	0	0
psychological pain	0	0	0	9	0	0	0
passive ideation	0	0	0	1	7	0	0
active ideation	1	0	1	0	0	6	0
neutral	0	0	0	1	0	0	29

Figure 3: Confusion matrix for the IP-FS strategy.

strategies for Precision, Recall and F1-Score macro average and weighted average are shown in Fig. 4 and Fig. 5 respectively. RAG yielded the worst performance, getting a Precision macro average of 68%, followed by IP, which reached 77%. The best results were achieved using IP+FS, getting 0.89% in this particular run. The average values for 10 runs are similar to this result: Precision macro average: 0.89; Recall macro average: 0.87; Precision weighted average: 0.91; and Recall weighted average: 0.90.

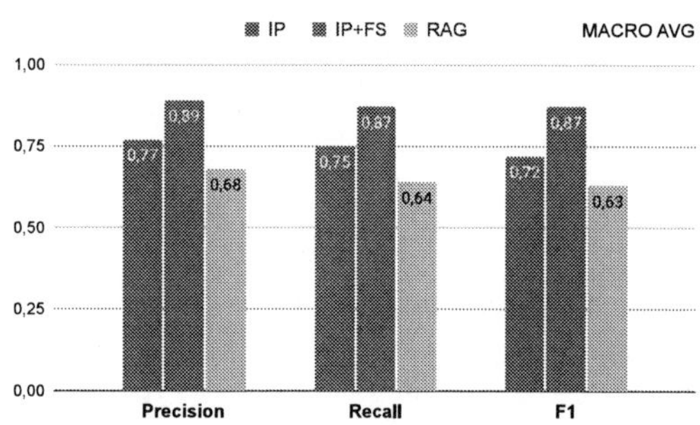

Figure 4: Precision, Recall and F1 Macro Average

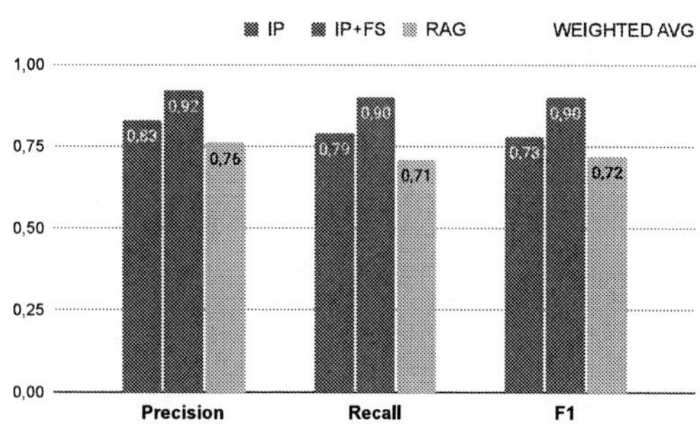

Figure 5: Precision, Recall and F1 Weighted Average

8 Discussion and Future Work

This paper establishes short-phrases analysis as the primary strategy for detecting suicide constructs, balancing real-time efficiency with expert-in-the-loop refinement, achieving ≊90% accuracy, a weighted average for Precission and Recall of 0.92 and 0.90 respectively, despite challenges in overlapping constructs. Hopelessness and psychological pain were the constructs with lower precision values, with 0.69 and 0.78 respectively, but with higher recall values, with 0.88 and 1. It was observed that some of the test phrases regarding these constructs exhibit significant variability in classification between them This may indicate an overlap in the semantic or emotional representation of these constructs, or it may reflect differences in how the model interprets subtle linguistic cues. Further research with real data from the clinical trial is planned to improve these results.

To further validate the results of the test set, the same evaluation previously performed by the model will be performed by medical professionals, specifically psychologists and psychiatrists. This comparison seeks to evaluate the concordance between the model's predictions and expert assessments while enhancing the test's reliability and construct validity.

The detection of suicide constructs in long texts is under development, focusing on text segmentation and state variables to analyze construct combinations and repetitions. Multi-tiered analysis is being explored for non-real-time scenarios to optimize construct detection through effective sentence division.

Additionally, recent findings emphasize the importance of incorporating positive constructs, such as protective factors like connectedness and emotional granularity, into suicide risk assessment. These factors, even when contradicting other risk indicators, directly influence risk evaluations, as demonstrated in clinical trial transcripts where both risk and protective factors co-occurred.

Acknowledgments

VisIA project is funded by the 2021 call for strategic projects aimed at the ecological transition and the digital transition, of the Spanish plan for scientific, technical and innovation research 2021-2023, within the framework of the recovery, transformation and resilience plan (References: TED2021-130747B-C21 and TED2021-130747B-C22).

References

Tom Bocklisch, Joey Faulkner, Nick Pawlowski, and Alan Nichol. 2017. Rasa: Open Source Language Understanding and Dialogue Management. *arXiv e-prints*, arXiv:1712.05181.

Craig J Bryan, Jim Mintz, Tracy A Clemans, Bruce Leeson, T Scott Burch, Sean R Williams, Emily Maney, and M David Rudd. 2017. Effect of crisis response planning vs. contracts for safety on suicide risk in us army soldiers: A randomized clinical trial. *Journal of affective disorders*, 212:64–72.

S De Quiroga, M Riesgo, E Martín del Campo, S Pulido, and S Rodrigo. 2019. Impacto socioeconómico de la depresión y el suicidio en españa. *Rev Esp Econ Salud*, 14(5):923–47.

Nelly Elsayed, Zag ElSayed, and Murat Ozer. 2024. Cautionsuicide: A deep learning based approach for detecting suicidal ideation in real time chatbot conversation. In *2024 IEEE 3rd International Conference on Computing and Machine Intelligence (ICMI)*, pages 1–5. IEEE.

Rezaul Haque, Rezaul Haque, Rezaul Haque, Naimul Islam, Naimul Islam, Naimul Islam, Maidul Islam, Maidul Islam, Maidul Islam, Md Manjurul Ahsan, and Manjurul Ahsan. 2022. A comparative analysis on suicidal ideation detection using nlp, machine, and deep learning. *Technologies (Basel)*.

Mutian He and Philip N. Garner. 2023. Can chatgpt detect intent? evaluating large language models for spoken language understanding. *Preprint*, arXiv:2305.13512.

Shaoxiong Ji, Shirui Pan, Xue Li, Erik Cambria, Guodong Long, and Zi Huang. 2020. Suicidal ideation detection: A review of machine learning methods and applications. *IEEE Transactions on Computational Social Systems*, 8(1):214–226.

Jenessa N Johnston, Darcy Campbell, Hector J Caruncho, Ioline D Henter, Elizabeth D Ballard, and Carlos A Zarate Jr. 2022. Suicide biomarkers to predict risk, classify diagnostic subtypes, and identify novel therapeutic targets: 5 years of promising research. *International journal of neuropsychopharmacology*, 25(3):197–214.

N. KOMATI. Accessed: 2023-12-24. Suicide and depression detection.

José Manuel Ramírez Sánchez, Mario Manso, Carmen García-Mateo, Beatriz Gómez-Gómez, Beatriz Pinal, Antía Brañas, Alejandro García Caballero, Laura Docío-Fernandez, and MJ Fernández-Iglesias. 2024. Visia project: design of an automated ai-based emotional distress and suicide risk detection system. In *Proc. IberSPEECH 2024*, pages 275–277.

Protection Regulation. 2016. Regulation (eu) 2016/679 of the european parliament and of the council. *Regulation (eu)*, 679:2016.

Yongliang Shen, Kaitao Song, Xu Tan, Dongsheng Li, Weiming Lu, and Yueting Zhuang. 2023. Hugginggpt: Solving ai tasks with chatgpt and its friends in hugging face. *Preprint*, arXiv:2303.17580.

Michelle Tsai, Harris Lari, Samantha Saffy, and E David Klonsky. 2021. Examining the three-step theory (3st) of suicide in a prospective study of adult psychiatric inpatients. *Behavior therapy*, 52(3):673–685.

Kimberly A Van Orden, Tracy K Witte, Kelly C Cukrowicz, Scott R Braithwaite, Edward A Selby, and Thomas E Joiner Jr. 2010. The interpersonal theory of suicide. *Psychological review*, 117(2):575.

Lei Wang, Wanyu Xu, Yihuai Lan, Zhiqiang Hu, Yunshi Lan, Roy Ka-Wei Lee, and Ee-Peng Lim. 2023. Plan-and-solve prompting: Improving zero-shot chain-of-thought reasoning by large language models. In *The 61st Annual Meeting Of The Association For Computational Linguistics*.

World Health Organization WHO. 2019. Suicide in the world: global health estimates. Technical report, World Health Organization.

Optimizing RAG: Classifying Queries for Dynamic Processing

Kabir Olawore[1] Michael McTear[1] Yaxin Bi[1] David Griol[2]

[1] School of Computing, Ulster University, UK
[2] Departamento de Lenguajes y Sistemas Informáticos, University of Granada, Spain
{olawore-b, mf.mctear, y.bi}@ulster.ac.uk, dgriol@ugr.es

Abstract

In Retrieval-Augmented Generation (RAG) systems efficient information retrieval is crucial for enhancing user experience and satisfaction, as response times and computational demands significantly impact performance. RAG can be unnecessarily resource-intensive for frequently asked questions (FAQs) and simple questions. In this paper we introduce an approach in which we categorize user questions into simple queries that do not require RAG processing. Evaluation results show that our proposal reduces latency and improves response efficiency compared to systems relying solely on RAG.

1 Introduction

Since the launch of ChatGPT in November 2022, conversational systems powered by Large Language Models (LLMs) have gained widespread adoption, allowing users to ask questions with the expectation of receiving accurate, factual answers (McTear and Ashurkina 2024; Mohamadi et al. 2023; Skjuve et al. 2024).

However, the responses of LLMs are not always accurate or even up-to-date. Although LLMs are trained on vast datasets, they may lack access to domain specific information, such as data from a company's internal database. The knowledge of an LLM is limited to the training data's cut-off date, resulting in potential obsolescence. Moreover, unlike traditional retrieval systems, where knowledge is stored explicitly in structures such as knowledge graphs, LLMs encode knowledge implicitly within their model parameters, making information retrieval less transparent and potentially less reliable (Yang et al. 2024; Zhu et al. 2024).

Retrieval-Augmented Generation (RAG) has been developed as a method to address these limitations by combining the generative capabilities of LLMs with real-time information retrieval from external sources (Lewis et al. 2021). In RAG, external documents are embedded into vector representations and stored in a specialized vector database. When a user submits a query, it is similarly vectorized and used to retrieve relevant documents. These documents are then integrated with the query and sent to the LLM for inference, ensuring that the generated response is based exclusively on the retrieved information. This hybrid approach enables RAG systems to deliver accurate, up-to-date, and context-specific answers (Gao et al. 2023; Huang and Huang, 2024).

The effectiveness of RAG systems has been demonstrated across various domains. Kharitonova et al. (2024) evaluated a RAG-based question-answering system for mental health support by embedding documents containing clinical practice guidelines. Their results highlighted the system's ability to deliver answers that were coherent, accurate, and supported by scientific evidence. Similarly, Olawore et al. (2025) described a RAG-based system designed to provide information about university fees, departments, facilities and other administrative details. Their findings showed that the system retrieved relevant and accurate information more effectively than standalone LLMs. Furthermore, the system enabled transparency and accountability by allowing users to trace each response back to its original source within the university dataset.

One significant drawback of RAG is that it is computationally expensive, particularly at the retrieval and inference stages. Processing frequently asked questions through the entire RAG workflow is both inefficient and costly. A more effective approach involves using a semantic cache, capable of handling variations and paraphrases of queries while returning consistent responses. On receiving a new request, the system

Proceedings of the 15th International Workshop on Spoken Dialogue Systems Technology, pages 160–164
May 27–30, 2025. ©2025 Association for Computational Linguistics

first checks if a similar request has been processed previously. If so, it retrieves the stored response from the cache, bypassing the need to re-execute the complete RAG workflow (Alake et al. 2024; Mortro 2025; Siriwardhana et al. 2023). This approach reduces redundant computations and can also minimize end-to-end latency. For instance, Jin et al. (2024) introduced and evaluated a cache-based system called RAGCache across various models and workloads, demonstrating a 4x reduction in time to first token generation.

Zhao et al. (2024) proposed a four-level query classification system based on data requirements and reasoning complexity, encompassing explicit fact queries, implicit fact queries, and interpretable and hidden rationale queries. They introduce different methods for integrating external data with queries at each classification level. Explicit fact queries can be answered directly using the provided data, while the other types of queries require additional processing and access to external resources.

In this paper, we argue that explicit fact queries can be treated similarly to frequently asked questions, thereby bypassing the RAG workflow. On receiving a new query, the system first determines if the query has been asked before. If it has, the stored response is retrieved. If not, the system checks whether the query qualifies as an explicit fact query and retrieves the corresponding answer. For other query types, the RAG workflow is invoked. Additionally, queries of any type that are asked and resolved a certain number of times can also be added to the semantic cache for frequently asked questions. Our approach significantly reduces computational costs and latency in question-answering systems. In the following sections, we present a preliminary investigation into these concepts, offer experimental results addressing latency reduction, and conclude with recommendations for future work.

2 Methodology

Our proposal approach enhances RAG chatbot capabilities through question classification and a routing mechanism, optimized to process queries of varying complexity. The main objective is to significantly improve computational efficiency and latency compared to traditional RAG-based conversational agents that uniformly process all queries through the entire pipeline. At the core of this system lies a classifier that determines whether to bypass the retrieval stage for straightforward queries or engage the full retrieval pipeline for complex questions requiring additional factual support.

As Figure 1 shows, the proposed hybrid architecture comprises three distinct stages: classification, retrieval, and generation. In the classification stage, incoming queries are analysed to determine their complexity and information requirements. Simple queries that can be addressed directly proceed immediately to the generation stage, while complex queries that necessitate additional context are routed through the retrieval pipeline. This selective engagement of the retrieval mechanism represents a key optimization in our design, substantially reducing the computational overhead associated with unnecessary document retrieval and processing.

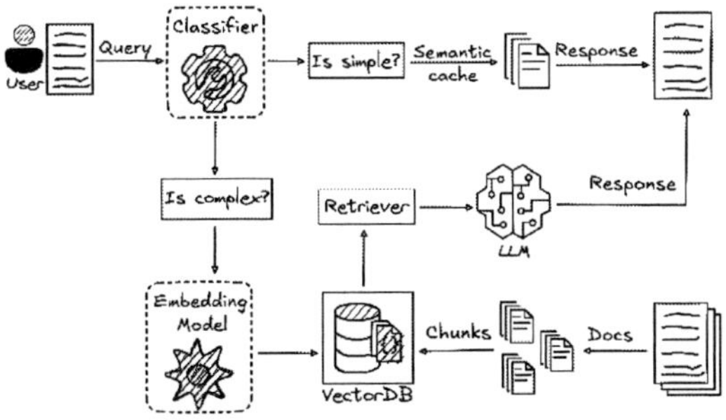

Figure 1: Optimized RAG chatbot architecture, classifying queries as simple (predefined responses) or complex (retrieval and LLM-generated responses).

2.1 Data Preparation

The dataset is a curated dataset QP comprising predefined key-value pairs of 100 questions and answers together with an unstructured dataset for the RAG pipeline. The unstructured data contains information about courses at the Faculty of Computing, Engineering, and the Built Environment (CEBE) at Ulster University. The key-value pairs consists of questions and answers related to CEBE, which were generated using an LLM and manually selected based on their semantic simplicity and brevity, ensuring they address straightforward queries efficiently. The selection process employs metrics such as semantic complexity and query length to classify a question as "simple". Each pair in QP undergoes preprocessing to standardize formats and optimize retrieval:

$$QP_{processed} = Standardize(QP)$$

This standardized dataset serves as a lightweight response mechanism for simple queries, bypassing the computational overhead associated with RAG-based inference.

2.2 Question Classification Framework

Users interact with the system through a chatbot interface. During query processing, each incoming user query Q undergoes an initial complexity assessment to determine its appropriate response strategy. The classification mechanism evaluates Q across multiple dimensions, such as semantic complexity, query length, and contextual requirements.

$$C(Q) = Classify\ (Q \mid features)$$

A machine learning-based classification model, trained on an annotated dataset of questions using logistic regression, serves as the backbone of this routing system. The model differentiates between simple questions, which can be directly resolved using predefined answers, and complex questions that necessitate retrieval and generative reasoning steps. For simple queries, the predefined response is retrieved.

For complex queries, the model invokes the RAG pipeline to produce an informed response. This dual-response strategy reduces computational overhead by leveraging predefined answers when possible, while ensuring nuanced processing for more intricate queries. The dynamic classification and routing approach ensures optimal performance and adaptability in handling a diverse range of user queries.

2.3 State Management

To ensure optimal system performance and mitigate latency across the hybrid architecture, the predefined key-value question-answer pairs are designed to enhance computational efficiency. When a query Q arrives, it is first transformed into a vectorized embedding (Q), which is stored in the system state:

$$E(Q) = Embed\ (Q)$$

The classification model processes (Q) to predict the query type, determining whether it aligns with predefined responses or requires retrieval-augmented generation (RAG). If the classifier identifies Q as likely resolvable via the predefined dataset, the system searches for a semantically similar question within the stored embeddings (D). The best-ranked candidate is retrieved and evaluated against a predefined similarity threshold τ:

$$Match(Q) = ArgMax\left(Similarity\big(E(Q), E(D)\big)\right) \geq \tau$$

If the similarity score satisfies the threshold, the corresponding predefined response is returned. Otherwise, the RAG pipeline is invoked to process the query. As more queries are processed, repeated patterns are identified and dynamically added to the predefined question-answer management system. This iterative process ensures continuous improvement of the system's predefined state, reducing the reliance on real-time retrieval for frequently encountered queries. By maintaining a balance between the predefined response mechanism and the RAG pipeline, the system sustains responsiveness and minimizes computational overhead.

2.4 RAG Pipeline

The RAG pipeline manages queries that are considered complex or infrequent. The RAG module is made up of two major components: the retriever and the generator. The retriever used a dense embedding model to locate relevant documents within the prepared corpus, ensuring that the most semantically similar content was selected. The generator on the other hand is powered by a transformer-based model, generating a coherent and contextually relevant response using the retrieved documents (Olawore et al. 2025).

2.5 Performance Evaluation

We have completed a preliminary evaluation comparing our RAG_HYBRID proposal with a RAG-only approach. We have used classic metrics such as accuracy, precision, recall, and F1-score to assess the relevance and precision of the chatbot's responses. These metrics provide a robust framework for evaluating the alignment of the chatbot's outputs with expected answers, ensuring the system's ability to deliver accurate and contextually appropriate responses.

To assess performance, we have measured latency. Latency was determined by recording the time elapsed between the submission of a query and the chatbot's final response. This analysis demonstrated the hybrid system's efficiency in reducing response times, highlighting its potential for improving user experience in real-time applications.

Additionally, the RAG_HYBRID's CPU utilization was evaluated and compared with the RAG-only solution. CPU usage was measured by logging the average processor consumption during query processing and the generation of the final response. This analysis provided insights into the computational efficiency of the hybrid architecture, emphasizing its ability to manage resource utilization while maintaining responsiveness.

3 Results

The evaluation result shows the effectiveness of the RAG-hybrid chatbot. Figure 2 shows the plot of the latency comparison between RAG-hybrid an RAG-only.

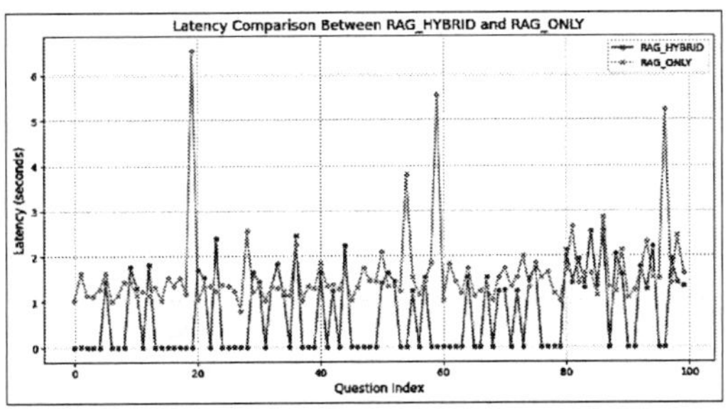

Figure. 2: Latency comparison between rag_hybrid and rag_only.

The plot illustrates a clear latency advantage of the RAG_HYBRID system over the RAG_ONLY system across 100 queries, consisting of 57 simple questions and 43 complex questions. RAG_HYBRID consistently demonstrates lower response times with minimal fluctuations, while RAG_ONLY exhibits significant spikes, exceeding 6 seconds for some queries. These results highlight the efficiency of the RAG_HYBRID system in leveraging predefined answers to maintain low latency and reduce computational overhead.

Also, in terms of processing needs, Figure 3 demonstrates a notable difference in CPU usage between the RAG_HYBRID and RAG_ONLY systems across the 100 test queries. RAG_HYBRID consistently exhibits lower CPU utilization, maintaining efficiency and avoiding significant spikes, while RAG_ONLY shows pronounced peaks, with usage exceeding 3.5% for certain queries. These results highlight the computational efficiency of the RAG_HYBRID approach, which leverages predefined answers to reduce the processing burden, compared to the RAG_ONLY system that relies on resource-intensive retrieval and generation processes. The edge cases in RAG_HYBRID are situations where the chatbot had to respond to users' queries with RAG.

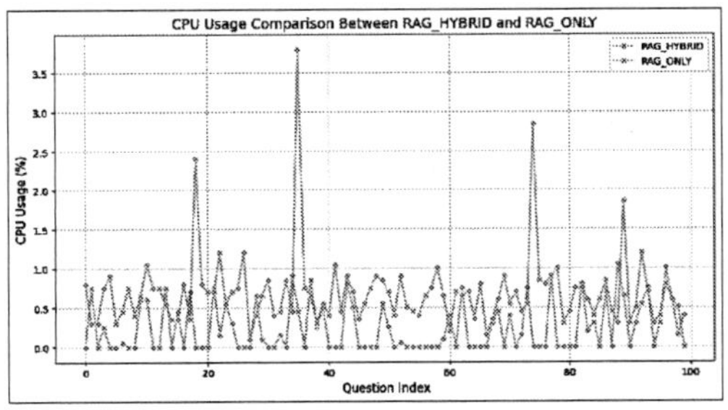

Figure. 3: Comparison of CPU usage between rag_hybrid and rag_only.

Finally, Table 1 shows that the RAG-hybrid chatbot achieves outstanding performance, with 98% accuracy and recall, a perfect precision of 1.00, and an F1-score of 0.99. These results highlight its reliability and effectiveness in delivering accurate and relevant responses.

	Accuracy	Precision	Recall	F1score
RAG-Hybrid	0.98	1.00	0.98	0.99

Table 1: Performance metrics of the RAG hybrid model.

4 Conclusions and Future Work

This study introduced a hybrid RAG chatbot architecture that efficiently combines predefined question-answer pairs with retrieval-augmented generation, demonstrating notable improvements in latency, CPU usage, and overall accuracy compared to RAG-only solutions. These results highlight the system's efficiency and scalability for real-time conversational AI.

Future efforts will focus on enhancing the classification model to adapt to evolving query patterns and integrating advanced language models to handle complex queries more effectively. We will also explore other methods of mitigating computational expense. An extended evaluation of our proposal in real-world scenarios and the incorporation of user experience metrics will also contribute to further evidence of its practical utility.

Acknowledgments

This paper has been supported by funding from the EU H2020 project CRYSTAL: https://project-crystal.eu/

References

Richmond Alake and Apoorva Joshi. 2024. Adding Semantic Caching and Memory to Your RAG Application Using MongoDB and LangChain. https://www.mongodb.com/developer/products/atlas/advanced-rag-langchain-mongodb/

Yunfan Gao, Yun Xiong, Xinyu Gao, Kangxiang Jia, Jinliu Pan, Yuxi Bi, Yi Dai, Jiawei Sun, and Haofen Wang. 2024. Retrieval-augmented generation for large language models: A survey. https://doi.org/10.48550/arXiv.2312.10997

Yizheng Huang and Jimmy Huang. 2024. A Survey on Retrieval-Augmented Text Generation for Large Language Models. https://arxiv.org/abs/2404.10981

Chao Jin, Zili Zhang, Xuanlin Jiang, Fangyue Liu, Xin Liu, Xuanzhe Liu, and Xin Jin. 2024. RAGCache: Efficient Knowledge Caching for Retrieval-Augmented Generation. https://arxiv.org/abs/2404.12457

Ksenia Kharitonova, David Pérez-Fernández, Javier Gutiérrez-Hernando, Asier Gutiérrez-Fandiño, Zoraida Callejas, and David Griol. 2024. Incorporating evidence into mental health Q&A: a novel method to use generative language models for validated clinical content extraction, Behaviour & Information Technology. https://doi.org/10.1080/0144929X.2024.2321959

Patrick Lewis, Ethan Perez, Aleksandra Piktus, Fabio Petroni, Vladimir Karpukhin, Naman Goyal, Heinrich Küttler, Mike Lewis, Wen-tau Yih, Tim Rocktäschel, Sebastian Riedel, and Douwe Kiela. 2021. Retrieval-Augmented Generation for Knowledge-Intensive NLP Tasks. https://arxiv.org/abs/2005.11401

Michael McTear and Marina Ashurkina. 2024. Transforming Conversational AI: Exploring the Power of Large Language Models in Interactive Conversational Agents. Apress Berkeley, CA. https://doi.org/10.1007/979-8-8688-0110-5

Salman Mohamadi, Ghulam Mujtaba, Ngan Le, Gianfranco Doretto, and Donald A. Adjeroh. 2023. ChatGPT in the age of generative AI and large language models: a concise survey. https://arxiv.org/abs/2307.04251

Pere Mortro, 2025. Implementing semantic cache to improve a RAG system with FAISS. Hugging Face Open-Source AI Cookbook. https://huggingface.co/learn/cookbook/en/semantic_cache_chroma_vector_database

Kabir Olawore, Michael McTear, and Yaxin Bi. 2025. Development and Evaluation of a University Chatbot Using Deep Learning: A RAG-Based Approach. In: Asbjørn Følstad, Symeon Papadopoulos, Theo Araujo, Effie L.-C. Law, Ewa Luger, Sebastian Hobert, and Petter Bae Brandtzaeg (eds.) Chatbots and Human-Centered AI: 8th International Workshop, CONVERSATIONS 2024, Thessaloniki, Greece December 4-5, 2024, Revised Selected Papers. Springer Cham. https://doi.org/10.1007/978-3-031-88045-2

Shamane Siriwardhana, Rivindu Weerasekera, Elliott Wen, Tharindu Kaluarachchi, Rajib Rana, and Suranga Nanayakkara. 2023. Improving the Domain Adaptation of Retrieval Augmented Generation (RAG) Models for Open Domain Question Answering. Transactions of the Association for Computational Linguistics, 11:1–17. https://doi.org/ 10.1162/tacl_a_00530

Marita Skjuve, Petter Bae Brandtzaeg, and Asbjørn Følstad. 2024. Why do people use ChatGPT? Exploring user motivations for generative conversational AI. First Monday, 29(1). https://doi.org/10.5210/fm.v29i1. 13541

Jingfeng Yang, Hongye Jin, Ruixiang Tang, Xiaotian Han, Qizhang Feng, Haoming Jiang, Shaochen Zhong, Bing Yin, and Xia Hu. 2024. Harnessing the Power of LLMs in Practice: A Survey on ChatGPT and Beyond. ACM Trans. Knowl. Discov. Data 18, 6, Article 160 (July 2024), 32 pages. https://doi.org/10.1145/3649506

Siyun Zhao, Yuqing Yang, Zilong Wang, Zhiyuan He, Luna K. Qiu, and Lili Qiu. 2024. Retrieval Augmented Generation (RAG) and Beyond: A Comprehensive Survey on How to make your LLMs use External Data More Wisely. https://arxiv.org/abs/2409.14924

Yutao Zhu, Huaying Yuan, Shuting Wang, Jiongnan Liu, Wenhan Liu, Chenlong Deng, Haonan Chen, Zhicheng Dou, and Ji-Rong Wen. 2024. Large Language Models for Information Retrieval: A Survey. https://arxiv.org/html/2308.07107v3

Enhancing Proactive Dialogue Systems Through Self-Learning of Reasoning and Action-Planning

Ryosuke Ito Tetsuya Takiguchi Yasuo Ariki
Graduate School of System Informatics, Kobe University
ryousuke4633@gmail.com, {takigu, ariki}@kobe-u.ac.jp

Abstract

A proactive dialogue system refers to a conversational system designed to guide the direction of a conversation in order to achieve pre-defined targets or fulfill specific goals. Recent studies have shown that Proactive Chain-of-Thought(CoT), which guides the system to explicitly think through intermediate reasoning and action-planning steps toward a conversational goal before generating a response, can significantly enhance the performance of proactive dialogue systems. However, these improvements primarily focus on prompt-based control, while the potential of fine-tuning Proactive-CoT remains largely unexplored. Furthermore, fine-tuning Proactive-CoT requires manual annotation of reasoning processes and action plans, which incurs significant time and cost. In this study, we propose a novel approach for automatically annotating reasoning processes and action plans through self-learning, and fine-tuning Proactive-CoT using these annotations. This method enables fully automated annotation, significantly reducing the time and cost associated with manual annotation. Experimental results show that models trained using our proposed method outperform those trained with other fine-tuning approaches. These findings highlight the potential of self-learning approaches to advance the development of more robust and efficient proactive dialogue systems.

1 Introduction

In recent years, dialogue agent proactivity has gained attention (Deng et al., 2023a). Proactive systems not only respond proactively but also guide interactions with a clear goal, improving user engagement and handling complex tasks such as negotiation.

Accordingly, recent work has explored LLM-based prompting methods to clarify ambiguous queries and strategically persuade users in non-cooperative task-oriented dialogues (Huang et al., 2022; Yao et al., 2022). In particular, "Proactive Chain-of-Thought (ProCoT)" extends conventional CoT by incorporating action plans and reasoning processes to proactively achieve conversation goals (Deng et al., 2023b). However, most studies rely on prompt design, leaving fine-tuning largely unexplored, and manual annotation of reasoning and action plans can be costly. An automatic approach to annotate reasoning and action plans from dialogue content could address these challenges and enable more effective fine-tuning.

This paper proposes a self-contained framework for automatically annotating reasoning processes and action plans, then fine-tuning on the augmented data. As illustrated in Figure 1, the framework has three steps:

1. Automatically annotate dialogue acts and strategies using zero-shot prompting

2. Label the reasoning process behind action plans, and utterances

3. Fine-tune Proactive-CoT by combining these annotations with the original utterance data

We validate this approach on a bargaining negotiation dataset (He et al., 2018), demonstrating superior accuracy in predicting both dialogue acts and negotiation strategies compared to other methods. Since the proposed method applies to any dialogue system, it offers a straightforward way to enhance performance across various domains.

2 Related Work

2.1 Proactive Dialogue

Recently, powerful dialogue models such as ChatGPT have emerged. However, these models have issues where they passively offer random guesses in response to ambiguous questions (Deng et al.,

Proceedings of the 15th International Workshop on Spoken Dialogue Systems Technology, pages 165–171
May 27–30, 2025. ©2025 Association for Computational Linguistics

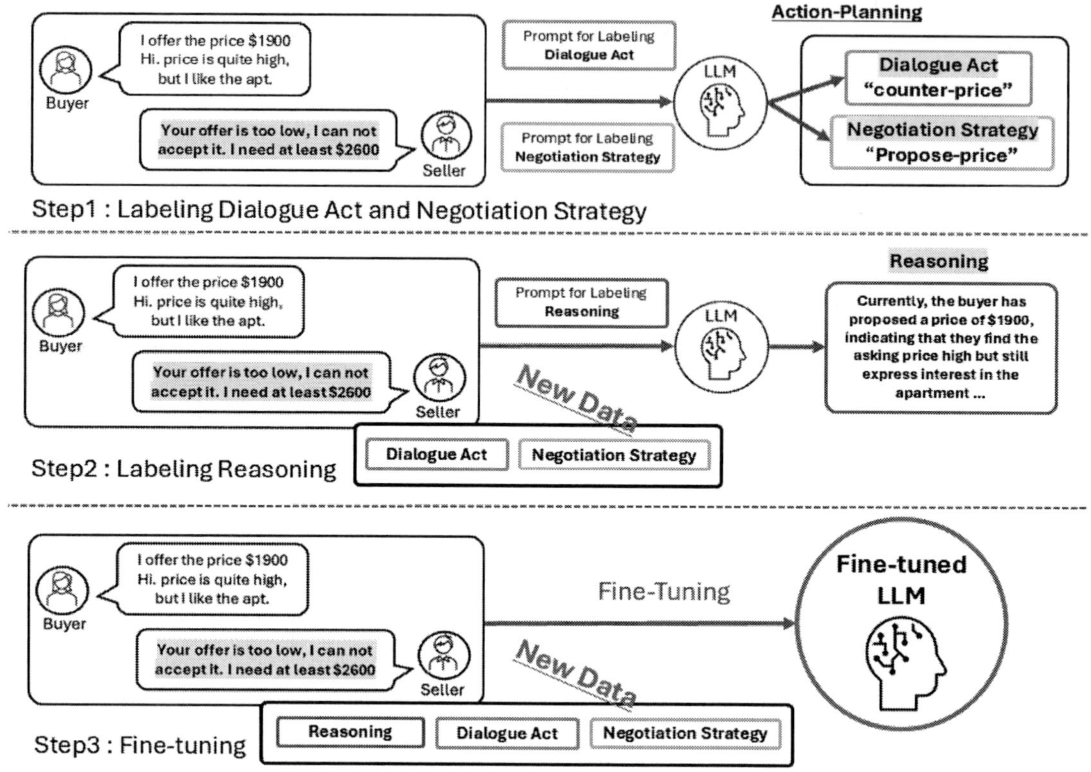

Figure 1: Proposed framework for negotiation modeling. The framework consists of three steps: (1) labeling dialogue acts and negotiation strategies, (2) labeling reasoning processes, and (3) fine-tuning the model using enriched data, including the original dialogues, labeled actions, strategies, and reasoning.

2023a). This behavior can lead to a lack of human-like interaction, reducing user engagement and satisfaction.

An important concept to address this issue is "proactivity." Proactivity refers to the capability of a system not just to respond passively to user inputs, but to actively create and control conversations, anticipating and influencing user behavior (Grant and Ashford, 2008). Dialogue systems with proactivity improve user engagement, enhance service efficiency, and better handle complex tasks that require strategic thinking and motivation. Proactive Dialogue systems incorporate this proactive capability. Proactive Dialogue can be categorized into three main types: open-domain dialogue, task-oriented dialogue, and information retrieval dialogue (Deng et al., 2023a).

In open-domain dialogue, methods in which systems proactively lead conversations have recently gained attention. One example is target-guided dialogue, where the system intentionally steers conversations toward specific topics (Tang et al., 2019).

In task-oriented dialogue, it is essential for systems to engage proactively rather than simply following user instructions. This is particularly important in adversarial situations, such as price negotiations, where proactive systems can implement effective negotiation strategies (He et al., 2018; Zhou et al., 2019; Joshi et al., 2021; Li et al., 2020).

In information retrieval dialogues, proactive dialogue systems employ clarifying questions to better understand user intentions and provide accurate responses to ambiguous queries (Aliannejadi et al., 2019; Guo et al., 2021).

Thus, Proactive Dialogue Systems possess the capability to proactively create, control, and influence conversations in response to user inputs. This study focuses on Proactive Dialogue Systems to develop more effective dialogue strategies.

2.2 Proactive Chain-of-Thought (ProCoT)

With the progress in large language models (LLMs), there has been growing attention to Chain-of-Thought (CoT), in which the model generates its internal reasoning process as text (Wu et al., 2023). By explicitly writing out the chain of reasoning, CoT has the potential to improve performance on complex tasks and enhance interpretability.

Meanwhile, as an attempt to apply this technique to dialogue tasks—especially proactive dialogue—"Proactive Chain-of-Thought (Pro-CoT)" has been proposed (Deng et al., 2023b). Unlike simply visualizing the reasoning process, Pro-CoT also explicitly makes the model think about dialogue acts and other factors required to strategically lead the conversation. However, existing research has guided Pro-CoT by designing prompts, leaving fine-tuning methods insufficiently explored. Another noted challenge is the high cost of manually annotating inference processes for large-scale datasets.

2.3 Enhancing Model Performance with Self-Generated Data

Recent studies have been exploring methods to improve the performance of LLMs by utilizing rationales generated by the models themselves. This approach reduces the cost of manual annotation while enabling the creation of large-scale datasets. For example, one proposed method involves using rationales generated by large models to train smaller models (Ho et al., 2023). Additionally, an instruction-tuning dataset has been created by manually crafting rationale demonstrations that include reasoning data (Kim et al., 2023).

In contrast, our study specifically adopts a rationalization-based approach (Zelikman et al., 2022). Rationalization is a technique where the model is given the correct answer as a hint and then performs reverse reasoning to generate rationales. This method is characterized by using the same model for both the teacher and student models and eliminating the need for human intervention during the learning process.

In this study, we build on this approach to generate the reasoning processes required for Pro-CoT.

3 Method

This study proposes a framework consisting of three steps, as illustrated in Figure 1. Below is an explanation of each step. Prompts for labeling Dialogue Act, Negotiation, and Reasoning can be found in Appendix B.

3.1 Labeling Dialogue Act and Negotiation Strategy

In this step, we label the dialogue act and negotiation strategy, which serve as the action plan for the dialogue data. Details on dialogue act and negotiation strategy can be found in Appendix A. Labeling a dialogue act is formulated as:

$$p(a \mid D, U, A). \tag{1}$$

Here, D represents the dialogue history, U is the utterance to be labeled, and A is the set of candidate dialogue acts. Given the dialogue history, the utterance to be labeled, and the candidate dialogue acts as input, zero-shot prompting is used to select the most appropriate act a from among the candidates.

Similarly, labeling a negotiation strategy is formulated as:

$$p(s \mid D, U, S). \tag{2}$$

Here, S is the set of candidate negotiation strategies. As with dialogue acts, the model selects the most suitable strategy from the candidates and outputs the negotiation strategy s.

3.2 Labeling Reasoning

In this step, the dialogue act a and negotiation strategy s automatically annotated in Step 1 are added to the data. We then label the reasoning process leading to the formation of the action plan and the final utterance. This step is formulated as:

$$p(r \mid B, D, U, A, S, a, s). \tag{3}$$

Here, B denotes the task background, such as an product description and target selling price, and r represents the reasoning process. By providing the dialogue act, negotiation strategy, and utterance as hints, the LLM performs backward reasoning to accurately generate the thought process that leads to these outputs.

3.3 Fine-tuning

In this step, we conduct fine-tuning by incorporating not only the original dialogue utterances but also the dialogue acts and negotiation strategies generated in Step 1, as well as the reasoning process generated in Step 2, into the training data.

When the fine-tuned LLM makes inferences, it is prompted to generate a reasoning process, a dialogue act, a negotiation strategy, and an utterance when provided with B, D, A, and S.

4 Experiment

In this section, we evaluate the effectiveness of the proposed method using a dataset focused on buy-and-sell negotiations—an example of proactive dialogue. We employ gpt-4o-mini-2024-07-18 as the base LLM and carry out annotation, fine-tuning, and inference through its API.

4.1 Dataset

In our experiments, we used the CraigslistBargain dataset (He et al., 2018), which focuses on buyer-seller negotiations. This dataset is based on real listing information scraped from Craigslist and includes dialogues between sellers and buyers, product descriptions, listed prices, and the buyer's target purchase price which is disclosed only to the buyer. In this study, out of the 2,758 seller utterances, we used 1,000 for training and the remaining 1,758 for validation.

4.2 Evaluation Metrics

Automatic Evaluation Following previous work, we use three automatic evaluation metrics: (1) the accuracy of dialogue act prediction, (2) the accuracy of negotiation strategy prediction, and (3) the similarity of generated responses. We use the F1 score for both dialogue act and negotiation strategy predictions. Here, the ground truth labels were annotated using GPT-4o mini. For evaluating the similarity of generated responses, we use BLEU (Papineni et al., 2002) as well as the cosine similarity (CoS) of embedding vectors obtained from text-embedding-3-small.

Human Evaluation For the human evaluation, four Japanese university students participated in the dialogues with the system, each engaging in one dialogue per model, testing five models (see Table 2) in total. To facilitate smooth communication, the system's English outputs were translated into Japanese, and the participants' utterances in Japanese were translated into English before being fed into the system. The translations were performed by GPT-4o mini.

Based on prior research (Joshi et al., 2021), we employed four criteria for human evaluation—persuasiveness, coherence, naturalness, and understandable—using a 5-point Likert scale in a questionnaire.

In addition to these questionnaire items, we adopted the sale-to-list ratio (SL%) as another evaluation metric, defined as:

$$\mathrm{SL\%} = \frac{\text{bargain price} - \text{buyer target price}}{\text{listed price} - \text{buyer target price}}, \quad (4)$$

where the *bargain price* is the price currently offered by the seller during negotiation, the *buyer target price* is the price the buyer wants to pay, and the *listed price* is the original price set by the seller. SL% measures how much the seller is compromising. A higher SL% means the seller is compromising less, which indicates better negotiation performance by the dialogue system.

4.3 Baselines

In order to demonstrate the superiority of our proposed method, we compared a total of eight models, considering both the presence and absence of fine-tuning, across four prompt methods: Standard, CoT, Proactive, and Proactive-CoT.

1. **Standard-prompt**: The LLM is prompted to generate only utterance content.

2. **CoT-prompt**: The LLM is prompted to generate both utterance content and a reasoning process leading to it.

3. **Proactive**: The LLM is prompted to simultaneously generate utterance content, a dialogue act, and a negotiation strategy.

4. **Proactive-CoT**: The LLM is prompted to generate utterance content, a dialogue act, a negotiation strategy, and a reasoning process. The fine-tuned version of this Proactive-CoT method is the model proposed in this study.

4.4 Experimental Results

Automatic Evaluation Results Table 1 presents the results of the automatic evaluation. Our proposed method achieved an F1 score of 38.5 for dialogue act prediction and 14.9 for negotiation strategy prediction, both of which are the highest among all compared methods.

On the other hand, for response similarity, the model fine-tuned from the Standard-prompt showed the highest performance. However, previous studies (Deng et al., 2023b) have reported that the model with the highest utterance similarity does not necessarily achieve the highest ratings in human evaluations. Instead, models that accurately imitate dialogue acts and negotiation strategies tend to be evaluated as having higher performance.

		Act	Strategy	Utterance	
Prompt	**Fine-tune**	**F1**	**F1**	**BLEU**	**CoS**
Standard	no	-	-	0.003	0.387
Standard	yes	-	-	**0.102**	**0.485**
CoT	no	-	-	0.004	0.400
CoT	yes	-	-	0.027	0.399
Proactive	no	17.7	3.36	0.006	0.396
Proactive	yes	31.8	13.5	0.097	0.458
ProCoT	no	18.8	9.36	0.004	0.384
ProCoT (ours)	yes	**38.5**	**14.9**	0.055	0.455

Table 1: Automatic Evaluation Results

Therefore, in this study as well, the learning model of our proposed method—which most precisely mimics dialogue acts and negotiation strategies—suggests the potential to be a highly effective dialogue system. However, a detailed error analysis and ablation study have not been conducted in this work at present and remain as future research topics.

Human Evaluation Results Table 2 shows the results of the human evaluation. Our proposed method received the highest ratings in three evaluation criteria: sale-to-list ratio (SL), Natural, and Understandable. Among these, the high SL is particularly important. Proactive dialogue refers to a conversation with a clear objective; in this study, the system's goal is to sell the product at the highest possible price. The proposed method slightly outperformed the others in terms of SL, suggesting its potential contribution to achieving the dialogue goal. However, the SL difference is only about 0.01, indicating no significant gap between methods. Therefore, further investigation is required to examine this aspect in more detail.

On the other hand, regarding "Coherence" the proposed method received a lower rating compared to the Standard-finetuned model. One possible reason for this is the length of the prompt. The Pro-CoT-finetuned prompt includes dialogue act and negotiation strategy label candidates, as well as task instructions requiring their selection before generating an utterance, leading to longer prompts. As a result, the system may have struggled to refer to the dialogue history, potentially reducing coherence. Moreover, since translations were used in this experiment, their potential influence on dialogue coherence should also be examined in future work. Further research is needed to explore more effective prompt designs to address this issue.

Model	**SL**	**Per**	**Coh**	**Nat**	**Und**
Standard	0.11	**3.25**	3.25	**3.25**	2.75
Standard-finetuned	0.23	3.0	**3.75**	2.75	**3.75**
CoT-finetuned	0.20	2.5	2.5	2.25	**3.75**
Proactive-finetuned	0.16	2.0	2.0	1.75	2.25
Pro-CoT-finetuned (ours)	**0.24**	2.75	3.0	**3.25**	**3.75**

Table 2: Human Evaluation Results

5 Conclusion

This study proposes a self-contained framework for fine-tuning ProCoT. Automatic evaluations demonstrate that fine-tuning ProCoT achieves accurate predictions of dialogue acts and negotiation strategies. Additionally, human evaluations suggest the potential usefulness of ProCoT, as it outperformed other models in some evaluation criteria.

Our results suggest that this labeling method can improve existing dialogue systems by automatically expanding and annotating training data. As a future work, we will carry out the experiments on the diverse datasets to validate our proposed method.

Acknowledgments

This work is supported by Adaptable and Seamless Technology transfer Program through Target-driven R&D (A-STEP) from Japan Science and Technology Agency (JST) (Grant Number JP-MJTR24RG).

References

Mohammad Aliannejadi, Hamed Zamani, Fabio Crestani, and W Bruce Croft. 2019. Asking clarifying questions in open-domain information-seeking conversations. In *Proceedings of the 42nd international acm sigir conference on research and development in information retrieval*, pages 475–484.

Yang Deng, Wenqiang Lei, Wai Lam, and Tat-Seng Chua. 2023a. A survey on proactive dialogue systems: Problems, methods, and prospects. *arXiv preprint arXiv:2305.02750*.

Yang Deng, Lizi Liao, Liang Chen, Hongru Wang, Wenqiang Lei, and Tat-Seng Chua. 2023b. Prompting and evaluating large language models for proactive dialogues: Clarification, target-guided, and non-collaboration. In *Findings of the Association for Computational Linguistics: EMNLP 2023*, pages 10602–10621, Singapore. Association for Computational Linguistics.

Adam M Grant and Susan J Ashford. 2008. The dynamics of proactivity at work. *Research in organizational behavior*, 28:3–34.

Meiqi Guo, Mingda Zhang, Siva Reddy, and Malihe Alikhani. 2021. Abg-coqa: Clarifying ambiguity in conversational question answering. In *3rd Conference on Automated Knowledge Base Construction*.

He He, Derek Chen, Anusha Balakrishnan, and Percy Liang. 2018. Decoupling strategy and generation in negotiation dialogues. In *Proceedings of the 2018 Conference on Empirical Methods in Natural Language Processing*, pages 2333–2343, Brussels, Belgium. Association for Computational Linguistics.

Namgyu Ho, Laura Schmid, and Se-Young Yun. 2023. Large language models are reasoning teachers. In *Proceedings of the 61st Annual Meeting of the Association for Computational Linguistics (Volume 1: Long Papers)*, pages 14852–14882, Toronto, Canada. Association for Computational Linguistics.

Wenlong Huang, Pieter Abbeel, Deepak Pathak, and Igor Mordatch. 2022. Language models as zero-shot planners: Extracting actionable knowledge for embodied agents. In *International conference on machine learning*, pages 9118–9147. PMLR.

Rishabh Joshi, Vidhisha Balachandran, Shikhar Vashishth, Alan Black, and Yulia Tsvetkov. 2021. Dialograph: Incorporating interpretable strategy-graph networks into negotiation dialogues. In *International Conference on Learning Representations*.

Seungone Kim, Se Joo, Doyoung Kim, Joel Jang, Seonghyeon Ye, Jamin Shin, and Minjoon Seo. 2023. The CoT collection: Improving zero-shot and few-shot learning of language models via chain-of-thought fine-tuning. In *Proceedings of the 2023 Conference on Empirical Methods in Natural Language Processing*, pages 12685–12708, Singapore. Association for Computational Linguistics.

Yu Li, Kun Qian, Weiyan Shi, and Zhou Yu. 2020. End-to-end trainable non-collaborative dialog system. In *Proceedings of the AAAI Conference on Artificial Intelligence*, volume 34, pages 8293–8302.

Kishore Papineni, Salim Roukos, Todd Ward, and Wei-Jing Zhu. 2002. Bleu: a method for automatic evaluation of machine translation. In *Proceedings of the 40th annual meeting of the Association for Computational Linguistics*, pages 311–318.

Jianheng Tang, Tiancheng Zhao, Chenyan Xiong, Xiaodan Liang, Eric Xing, and Zhiting Hu. 2019. Target-guided open-domain conversation. In *Proceedings of the 57th Annual Meeting of the Association for Computational Linguistics*, pages 5624–5634, Florence, Italy. Association for Computational Linguistics.

Dingjun Wu, Jing Zhang, and Xinmei Huang. 2023. Chain of thought prompting elicits knowledge augmentation. In *Findings of the Association for Computational Linguistics: ACL 2023*, pages 6519–6534, Toronto, Canada. Association for Computational Linguistics.

Shunyu Yao, Jeffrey Zhao, Dian Yu, Nan Du, Izhak Shafran, Karthik Narasimhan, and Yuan Cao. 2022. React: Synergizing reasoning and acting in language models. *arXiv preprint arXiv:2210.03629*.

Eric Zelikman, Yuhuai Wu, Jesse Mu, and Noah Goodman. 2022. Star: Bootstrapping reasoning with reasoning. *Advances in Neural Information Processing Systems*, 35:15476–15488.

Yiheng Zhou, He He, Alan W Black, and Yulia Tsvetkov. 2019. A dynamic strategy coach for effective negotiation. In *Proceedings of the 20th Annual SIGdial Meeting on Discourse and Dialogue*, pages 367–378, Stockholm, Sweden. Association for Computational Linguistics.

A Dialogue act and Negotiation strategy

In this study, we adopt the classification of dialogue acts and negotiation strategies based on (Joshi et al., 2021).

Dialogue Act	Example
intro	I would love to buy
inquiry	Sure, what's your price
init-price	I'm on a budget so I could do $5
counter-price	How about $15 and I'll waive the deposit
agree	That works for me
disagree	Sorry, I can't agree to that
inform	This bike is brand new
vague-price	That offer is too low
insist	Still can I buy it for $5.
others	I am the chat keeps stalling

Table 3: The details of 10 Dialogue Acts

Negotiation Strategy	Example
Describe Product	The car has leather seats classifier
Rephrase Product	45k miles → less than 50k miles
Embellish Product	a luxury car with attractive
Address Concerns	I've just taken it to maintenance
Communicate Interests	I'd like to sell it asap
Propose Price	How about 9k?
Do Not Propose First	n/a
Negotiate Side Offers	I can deliver it for you rule
Hedge	I could come down a bit
Communicate Politely	Greetings, gratitude, apology, please
Build Rapport	My kid really liked this bike, but he outgrew it
Talk Informally	Absolutely, ask away!
Show Dominance	The absolute highest I can do is 640
Negative Sentiment	Sadly, I simply cannot go under 500
Certainty Words	It has always had a screen protector

Table 4: The details of 15 Negotiation Strategies

B Prompts for labeling

This section provides the prompts used for labeling Dialogue Act, Negotiation, and Reasoning.

```
Which dialogue act among the "dialogue acts" is the most
appropriate for the next statement? Please select one.

### utterance
{gold_respose}

### dialogue acts
- intro, Meaning: Greetings,
Example: I would love to buy
- inquiry, Meaning: Ask a question,
xample: Sure, what's your price
- init-price, Meaning: Propose the first price,
Example: I'm on a budget so I could do $5
- counter-price, Meaning: Proposing a counter price,
Example: How about $15 and I'll waive the deposit
- agree, Meaning: Agree with the proposal,
Example: That works for me
- disagree, Meaning: Disagree with a proposal,
Example: Sorry, I can't agree to that
- inform, Meaning: Answer a question,
Example: This bike is brand new
- vague-price, Meaning:Using comparatives with existing price
Example: That offer is too low
- insist, Meaning: Insist on an offer,
Example: Still can I buy it for $5
- others, Meaning: others

### output format
Please enclose the dialogue act with [act] and [/act] tags.
Do not output anything unnecessary other than the tags and
the dialogue act.

### output example
If you select "intro" as the label, output:
[act]introduction[/act]
For other dialogue strategies, enclose only the label name
with [act] and [/act] tags in the same manner.

### dialogue_history
{dialogue_history}
```

Prompts 1: Labeling Dialogue Act

```
Which negotiation strategy among the "negotiation strategies"
is the most appropriate for the following statement?
First, answer the number of appropriate negotiation strategy.
Secound, answer the negotiation strategy.

### following statement
{gold_respose}

### negotiate strategies
- Describe-Product,
Example:The car has leather seats
- Rephrase-Product,
Example:45k miles -> less than 50k miles
- Embellish-Product,
Example:a luxury car with attractive leather seats
- Address-Concerns,
Example:I've just taken it to maintenance
- Communicate-Interests,
Example:I'd like to sell it asap
- Propose-Price,
Example:How about 9k?
- Do-Not-Propose-First,
Example:n/a
- Negotiate-Side-Offers,
Example:I can deliver it for you
- Hedge,
Example:I could come down a bit
- Communicate-Politely,
Example:Greetings, gratitude, apology, please
- Build-Rapport,
Example:My kid really liked this bike, but he outgrew it
- Talk-Informally,
Example:Absolutely, ask away!
- Show-Dominance,
Example:The absolute highest I can do is 640
- Negative-Sentiment,
Example:Sadly, I simply cannot go under 500
- Certainty-Words,
Example:It has always had a screen protector

### output format
Please enclose the final negotiation strategies with
[strategy] and [/strategy] tags. Do not include anything
unnecessary other than the tags and the negotiation
strategies.
If you select two or more strategies, please use ', ' as in
[strategy]Propose-Price, Communicate-Interests[/strategy].

### dialogue_hisotry
{dialogue_history}
```

Prompts 2: Labeling Negotiation Strategy

```
### Instruction
Assume you are the seller.
Given the item description, the target selling price, and the
conversation history, in order to reach a better deal with
the buyer, first analyse the current negotiation progress
and consider an appropriate goal, then select the most
appropriate negotiation strategy and the most appropriate
dialogue act to reach the goal.
Based on the selected one negotiation strategy and one
dialogue act, generate a response.
The reply should start with the analysis of the current
negotiation progress and an appropriate goal, and then follow
by 'To reach this goal, the most appropriate negotiation
strategy is [] and the most appropriate dialogue act is [].
Based on the selected negotiation strategy and dialogue act,
the response is' </s>

### negotiate strategies
- Describe-Product,
Example:The car has leather seats
- Rephrase-Product,
Example:45k miles -> less than 50k miles
- Embellish-Product,
Example:a luxury car with attractive leather seats
- Address-Concerns,
Example:I've just taken it to maintenance
- Communicate-Interests,
Example:I'd like to sell it asap
- Propose-Price,
Example:How about 9k?
- Do-Not-Propose-First,
Example:n/a
- Negotiate-Side-Offers,
Example:I can deliver it for you
- Hedge,
Example:I could come down a bit
- Communicate-Politely,
Example:Greetings, gratitude, apology, please
- Build-Rapport,
Example:My kid really liked this bike, but he outgrew it
- Talk-Informally,
Example:Absolutely, ask away!
- Show-Dominance,
Example:The absolute highest I can do is 640
- Negative-Sentiment,
Example:Sadly, I simply cannot go under 500
- Certainty-Words,
Example:It has always had a screen protector

### dialogue acts
- intro, Meaning:Greetings,
Example:I would love to buy
- inquiry, Meaning:Ask a question,
Example:Sure, what's your price
- init-price, Meaning:Propose the first price,
Example:I'm on a budget so I could do $5
- counter-price, Meaning:Proposing a counter price,
Example:How about $15 and I'll waive the deposit
- agree, Meaning:Agree with the proposal ,
Example:That works for me
- disagree, Meaning:Disagree with a proposal,
Example:Sorry, I can't agree to that
- inform, Meaning:Answer a question,
Example: This bike is brand new
- vague-price, Meaning:Using comparatives with existing price
Example:That offer is too low
- insist, Meaning:Insist on an offer,
Example:Still can I buy it for $5
- others, Meaning:others

The item description is '{item_description}'.

The target selling price is {target_price}.

The conversation history is {dialogue_history}

### Hints
I will give you hits.
the most appropriate negotiation strategy is {nego_strategy}
the most appropriate dialogue act is {dialogue_act}
the response is only {gold_response}

Please generate the response: ### Analysis
To reach this goal, the most appropriate negotiation strategy
is [] and the most appropriate dialogue act is []. Based on
the selected negotiation strategy and dialogue act, the
response is ""
```

Prompts 3: Labeling Reasoning

TrustBoost: Balancing flexibility and compliance in conversational AI systems

David Griol[1,2], **Zoraida Callejas**[1,2], **Manuel Gil-Martín**[3], **Ksenia Kharitonova**[1], **Juan Manuel Montero Martínez**[3], **David Pérez-Fernández**[1], **Fernando Fernández-Martínez**[3]

[1]Department of Software Engineering, University of Granada, Periodista Daniel Saucedo Aranda S/N, 18071 Granada, Spain.
[2]Research Centre for Information and Communication Technologies, CITIC-UGR.
[3]Grupo de Tecnología del Habla y Aprendizaje Automático (THAU Group), E.T.S.I. de Telecomunicación, Universidad Politécnica de Madrid, Avda. Complutense 30, 28040 Madrid, Spain.

Correspondence: Zoraida Callejas zoraida@ugr.es

Abstract

Conversational AI (ConvAI) systems are gaining growing importance as an alternative for more natural interaction with digital services. In this context, Large Language Models (LLMs) have opened new possibilities for less restricted interaction and richer natural language understanding. However, despite their advanced capabilities, LLMs can pose accuracy and reliability problems, as they sometimes generate factually incorrect or contextually inappropriate content that does not fulfill the regulations or business rules of a specific application domain. In addition, they still do not possess the capability to adjust to users' needs and preferences, showing emotional awareness, while concurrently adhering to the regulations and limitations of their designated domain. In this paper, we present the TrustBoost project, which addresses the challenge of improving trustworthiness of ConvAI from two dimensions: cognition (adaptability, flexibility, compliance, and performance) and affectivity (familiarity, emotional dimension, and perception). The duration of the project is from September 2024 to December 2027.

1 Introduction

The term "Conversational AI" (ConvAI) has gained prominence in recent academic research, encompassing several NLP technologies like dialog systems, chatbots, and intelligent virtual assistants. These systems leverage artificial intelligence extensively to facilitate natural language conversations, offering users a seamless and intuitive way to access information, interact with services, and navigate data on the Internet, as well as their surrounding environment (Araujo and Bol, 2024; Casheekar et al., 2024; McTear, 2020; McTear et al., 2016)

In recent years, the development of LLMs has significantly transformed the landscape of conversational AI, offering unparalleled interaction flexibility. Unlike traditional rule-based or intent-based dialogue systems, LLMs can understand and generate human-like language that is less restricted because they are not as tied to specific training phrases. They have the ability to grasp context, adapt to diverse user inputs, and generate coherent responses in multiple conversational scenarios.

As for dialogue/interaction management, their pretraining on vast and diverse datasets enables them to generalize well to various domains, eliminating the need for explicit rule programming. Although rule-based systems often struggle to accommodate dynamic and evolving language patterns, LLMs contribute to a more natural and engaging user experience. On the opposite side of the spectrum, intent-based dialogue systems have the advantage of being completely compliant with business rules and domain restrictions due to their inherent structure and rule-based logic.

In intent-based systems, user interactions are categorized into predefined intents, each associated with a specific action or task. This structured approach provides a level of control and predictability that is advantageous to maintaining compliance. Regarding language understanding, intent-based systems are often specialized in specific domains or applications, enabling a focused understanding of user queries within a defined domain. In terms of dialogue management, this specialization contributes to a better alignment with domain-specific rules and restrictions, offering explainability.

Conversational LLMs are considered the future. However, they are still not widely adopted due to trustworthiness issues (Luna-Jiménez et al., 2022;

Proceedings of the 15th International Workshop on Spoken Dialogue Systems Technology, pages 172–175
May 27–30, 2025.

Kraus et al., 2021). Trust is crucial for user acceptance and engagement. Trust in AI systems is intricately linked to users' expectations of consistency, reliability, and adherence to established norms. Business rules serve as a set of guidelines that dictate the permissible behavior of the AI system within a given context. When a conversational system lacks compliance with domain restrictions, it introduces an element of unpredictability and inconsistency in its responses. This deviation from expected behavior can undermine users' trust.

Moreover, trust in ConvAI systems is intricately connected to interpretability: If users cannot understand the reasoning behind the system's decisions, it creates a perceived lack of transparency. From the perspective of the entity/company offering the conversational system to users, when a conversational system fails to align with business rules, the provider faces the risk of diminished user trust. This can lead to a decline in user engagement, increased user dissatisfaction, and potential reputational damage. In more extreme cases, they could even face legal and regulatory consequences.

2 Description

In TrustBoost, we assume that for ConvAI systems to be truly usable and reliable, they must adhere to the rules and restrictions of their designated domain as well as to adapt to their users' needs and preferences (cognition/performance branch of trustworthiness). With this aim, we will address the balance between flexibility and compliance by endowing ConvAI systems powered by LLMs the ability to comply with business/domain rules while simultaneously adapting to the needs of their users.

One of the primary challenges in incorporating rule-based constraints into the training and fine-tuning processes of LLMs is the discrepancy between the vast and diverse data sources typically used to train LLMs and the specific guidelines and regulations defined by organizations in the form of business rules. Training data may not adequately capture these intricacies, as LLMs lack the context of organizational policies and domain idiosyncrasies. Moreover, fine-tuning LLMs to adhere perfectly to business rules can be challenging due to the limited nature of fine-tuning datasets, which may not fully represent the complexity of these rules. Additionally, LLMs often generate outputs that are not easily interpretable, making it difficult to ensure that the generated content aligns with specific business rules and compliance requirements.

Due to the computational cost and resource constraints associated with training LLMs, their accessibility has remained limited to a select group of organizations with significant computational resources. To address this challenge, we propose to take advantage of the capabilities of 'big" pre-trained LLMs to generate new resources, such as synthetic dialogues, that can be used to develop or fine-tune smaller and more efficient LLM models tailored to specific tasks and domains. These compact models would be able to run on average GPUs, expanding the reach of LLM technology to a wider range of organizations and applications. This approach would effectively break down the existing barrier to entry for LLMs, democratizing their use and fostering innovation across industries. Concurrently, we will devise automated evaluation procedures for the resources generated, minimizing manual review while ensuring the efficiency and reliability of the resources produced.

Within the framework of the TrustBoost project, we also aim to protect data governance and sovereignty by promoting the use of open source LLMs (to avoid sending data to third parties, unlike e.g. ChatGPT alternatives), together with techniques that make it possible to combine smaller models fine-tuned to specific tasks, ensuring the protection of personal data, lower hardware requirements for learning and deployment, and more efficient energy use.

In addition, in TrustBoost a truly flexible ConvAI system should dynamically tailor its responses based on the user's emotional cues (affective branch of trustworthiness). This adaptability involves adjusting the tone, language, content, and type of responses to align with the detected emotional state, thereby creating a more personalized and empathetic interaction. By doing so, the AI system can dynamically adapt the dialog flow to the identified emotional states, enhancing the overall user experience and building trust.

The challenge of recognizing the user's emotional state in ConvAI systems involves addressing multiple research goals. The first goal is the development of sophisticated natural language processing (NLP) techniques to extract and interpret emotional cues from various sources such as facial expressions, tone of voice, and word choice. Multimodal data integration, including spoken language, facial expressions, and body language, is crucial to enhance emotional recognition.

Recognizing the dynamic nature of emotions during interactions is also important. Contextualizing emotional cues within the conversation and the user's overall situation is vital for providing personalized and empathetic responses. However, current Conversational AI struggles to grasp the broader emotional landscape, facing limitations in understanding evolving user sentiments due to context window constraints. Overcoming these challenges requires advances in emotional state recognition and improving the contextual understanding capabilities of language models to enhance emotional intelligence in conversational interactions.

3 Main objectives

The main objective of TrustBoost is to find new methods for trustful Conversational AI balancing performance and affectiveness. In order to achieve this aim, we will address several research lines. First, enhancing user-awareness for trustworthy ConvAI. This research line aims to enhance user-awareness capabilities through the integration of techniques and algorithms from three perspectives: 1) integrating multimodal emotion recognition; 2) developing advanced NLP techniques to extract diverse emotional cues from user utterances; 3) focusing on memorability, enabling systems to identify and retain pivotal elements in dialogues.

Second, modeling trustworthiness in ConvAI. Our aim is to develop novel computational models that can predict and evaluate the trustworthiness of ConvAI systems based on performance, transparency and emotional intelligence.

Third, transitioning from intent-based dialogue systems to deep learning ConvAI. The most widely adopted technology for dialogue systems in industry is intent-based. We aim to transition from such technology to LLM-based ConvAI to achieve a more flexible interaction.

Fourth, generating conversational models compliant with business rules and domain restrictions. We will investigate how to generate the minimal model capable of adapting to well-defined business rules and domain restrictions, exploring ways of defining such rules, make them queryable through rule engines and coupling the engine with LLMs. In relation to this line, we plan to develop innovative approaches for generating new resources through prompt-based or instruction-based learning using LLMs, while simultaneously creating automated evaluation procedures for these resources.

Finally, TrustBoost advocates for the innovative exploration of strategies commonly used to detect hallucinations in conversational models, with the aim of evaluating whether individuals may encounter similar challenges. We will address this objective not only by using high-quality dialogue datasets avoiding biases, but also by assessing different techniques for hallucination mitigation: prompt engineering, self-refinement through feedback and reasoning, prompt tuning to adjust the instructions provided to a pre-trained LLM, decoding strategies, knowledge graphs, faithfulness based loss functions, or supervised fine-tuning.

4 Scientific and technical impact

TrustBoost foreseen advances affect the architecture of ConvAI systems by proposing the integration of LLMs and additional components to improve the interaction context, compliance with associated business rules, multimodal interaction, and user adaptation. The project will provide scientific impact related but not limited to: transitioning from intent-based dialogue systems to LLM-based conversational AI provided added flexibility while maintaining compliance; generating quality open-access dialogue resources for the training of these models in Spanish and English for multiple domains; new tools and platforms to develop and evaluate ConvAI systems; developing new methods for the integration of smaller language models that meet the requirements associated to data protection, provide accuracy results comparable to larger models, and allow reducing hardware and energy requirements for their deployment; generating new methods for mitigating hallucinations and explainability, fostering trust; reducing the number of responses factually incorrect or contextually inappropriate that do not fulfill the regulations or business rules of a specific application domain; new methods for understanding and responding to user emotional cues; new techniques for integrating the emotional cues into LLM-based conversational AI; and novel and more trustworthy ConvAI models that are user-aware, and emotionally interactive.

By enhancing user experiences, building trust, and promoting explainable and adaptable interactions with ConvAI systems, TrustBoost can contribute to a more positive and supportive technological environment, ultimately benefiting the well-being of the population.

Acknowledgments

The TrustBoost project has received funding from MICIU/AEI/10.13039/501100011033 and from FEDER, UE. It is a coordinated project by a multidisciplinary team from the Universidad Politécnica de Madrid (UPM) and University of Granada (UGR), with two subprojects that address TrustBoost's objectives: "Enhancing Trustworthiness in Conversational AI through Multimodal Affective Awareness" (TrustBoost-UPM, ref. PID2023-150584OB-C21), and "Breaking the duality of conversational AI: going beyond guided conversations while ensuring compliance with domain rules and constraints" (TrustBoost-UGR, ref. PID2023-150584OB-C22).

References

T. Araujo and N. Bol. 2024. From speaking like a person to being personal: The effects of personalized, regular interactions with conversational agents. *Computers in Human Behavior: Artificial Humans*, 2(1):100030.

A. Casheekar, A. Lahiri, K. Rath, K. Sanjay Prabhakar, and K. Srinivasan. 2024. A contemporary review on chatbots, ai-powered virtual conversational agents, chatgpt: Applications, open challenges and future research directions. *Computer Science Review*, 52:100632.

M. Kraus, N. Wagner, Z. Callejas, and W. Minker. 2021. The role of trust in proactive conversational assistants. *IEEE Access*, 9:112821–112836.

C. Luna-Jiménez, S.L. Lutfi, and F. Fernández-Martínez. 2022. Measuring trust at zero-acquaintance: A cross-cultural study between malaysians and hungarians. In *Proc. of 26th International Conference on Intelligent Engineering Systems (INES)*, page 000267–000272.

M.F. McTear. 2020. *Conversational AI. Dialogue systems, Conversational Agents, and Chatbots*. Morgan and Claypool Publishers.

M.F. McTear, Z. Callejas, and D. Griol. 2016. *The Conversational Interface: Talking to Smart Devices*. Springer.

ScriptBoard: Designing modern spoken dialogue systems through visual programming

Divesh Lala, Mikey Elmers, Koji Inoue, Zi Haur Pang, Keiko Ochi, Tatsuya Kawahara
Kyoto University Graduate School of Informatics
Japan
lala@sap.ist.kyoto-u.ac.jp

Abstract

Implementation of spoken dialogue systems can be time-consuming, in particular for people who are not familiar with managing dialogue states and turn-taking in real-time. A GUI-based system where the user can quickly understand the dialogue flow allows rapid prototyping of experimental and real-world systems. In this demonstration we present ScriptBoard, a tool for creating dialogue scenarios which is independent of any specific robot platform. ScriptBoard has been designed with multi-party scenarios in mind and makes use of large language models to both generate dialogue and make decisions about the dialogue flow. This program promotes both flexibility and reproducibility in spoken dialogue research and provides everyone the opportunity to design and test their own dialogue scenarios.

1 Introduction

In spoken dialogue system (SDS) research the methodology or tools used to create interactions is often not fully described. A common approach is to use finite state machines, but these may grow unwieldy with more complex interactions because of the large number of states. Behavior trees are another approach that is used for AI in video games (Colledanchise and Ögren, 2018), but programming these may require a steeper learning curve.

Researchers who are unfamiliar with implementing SDSs often need time to learn how to manage aspects such as turn-taking and handling dialogue states in real-time systems, where human and robot turns are not neatly separated and system interruptions can be frequent. With no existing standards for the design of SDSs, researchers need to create even simple interactions from scratch. Furthermore, it is often difficult for these interactions to be reused and modified by others if they are written exclusively using code with no graphical interface.

We propose that due to the above issues a GUI should be used to assist in quickly designing replicable spoken dialogue interactions. There are several visual programming approaches which have been used in the literature, but these were developed before the rise of two research fields in SDSs - large language models (LLMs) and multi-party interactions. An updated approach would need to accommodate these aspects in the system. LLMs drastically reduce the number of dialogue generation states needed in a visual programming interface since one LLM node can handle both natural language understanding (NLU) and response generation. Therefore the graphical design of complex interactions becomes more viable for novice users.

In this demonstration we present ScriptBoard (**Script B**uilder **O**ffering **A**ssistance with **R**obot **D**ialogue), a visual programming system which can be used to quickly develop SDSs. ScriptBoard has the ability to handle multiple human participants, integrates prompt-based LLMs into the dialogue flow, and handles spoken dialogue features such as silence and barge-in. Our program allows researchers to create spoken dialogue scenarios for both real-world implementation and experiments.

The system is written in Python using the PyQT package for the graphical interface. In this work we define the "user" as a person who designs the dialogue scenario and the "participant" as the person who is actually involved in the interaction.

2 Related Work

Similar visual systems to manage robot interactions have been implemented in previous works (Nakano and Komatani, 2024; Groß et al., 2023; Michael, 2020; Koller et al., 2018; Lison and Kennington, 2016; Glas et al., 2016; Pot et al., 2009). These often make use of a state-machine design in which the states of an interaction are set by the user and tracked during the interaction. State transitions in spoken dialogue systems are often triggered by au-

Proceedings of the 15th International Workshop on Spoken Dialogue Systems Technology, pages 176–182
May 27–30, 2025. ©2025 Association for Computational Linguistics

tomatic speech recognition (ASR) results, however this may not be appropriate for scenarios such as conversation where deciding when to speak (i.e. turn-taking) is crucial for smooth interactions.

Another issue is systems which are tightly coupled with a specific robot platform. For example, IrisTK is used to design interactions for Furhat (Skantze and Al Moubayed, 2012) and Choregraphe (Pot et al., 2009) is used for the NAO robot. It would be preferable if users were able to reproduce interactions with different robots, particularly for comparative evaluation. Existing systems are also usually made with the assumption of one-to-one interaction. IrisTK is made for multi-party interaction, however this is based on XML code and may be somewhat difficult for novice users. This issue of usability is also critical. Some systems such as Interaction Composer (Glas et al., 2016) and DialogOS (Koller et al., 2018) focus on making the interface understandable to novice users while more powerful systems such as RISE (Groß et al., 2023) are targeted towards researchers and may require more expert knowledge.

Recent technological advances mean that even novice users can use LLMs to generate dialogue without needing any low level programming as they can use prompt-based inputs to direct the system. A tool which could assist users to design SDS scenarios in this way would be ideal for rapid prototyping and testing. Frameworks such as Retico (Michael, 2020) and DialBB (Nakano and Komatani, 2024) integrate LLMs into their systems although they are less focused on visual programming. Scriptboard allows users to do everything within the GUI.

3 System Architecture

ScriptBoard is not a spoken dialogue system itself, but communicates with an external controller using TCP/IP messaging. The external controller handles speech recognition input from the user and turn-taking and sends this information to ScriptBoard. This information is then processed using the scenario created in the GUI by the user of ScriptBoard to decide the robot's behavior. ScriptBoard messages are then parsed by the controller and used for behavior generation.

Natural language processing and dialogue generation can be done through simple keyword comparators, but ScriptBoard allows users to use LLMs in their scenarios. This approach simplifies the creation of interaction scenarios because the user can hand off complex tasks to the LLM rather than handcrafting individual dialogue states for the robot.

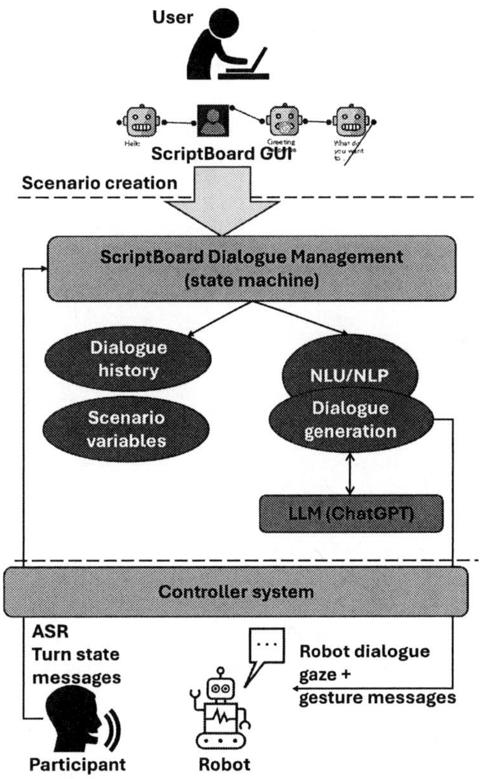

Figure 1: ScriptBoard architecture. Communication with the external controller is done through an environment-independent messaging system.

Figure 1 shows this general architecture of ScriptBoard. Communication with the controller is done only through messaging, meaning it can interface with any compatible external system and is independent of any robot or agent, speech recognition or text-to-speech (TTS) system.

4 User Interface

The user interface of ScriptBoard is based on the paradigm of dialogue states which has been used in previous visual programming systems (Glas et al., 2016). It uses a drag-and-drop mechanism in which the user can place states (also known as nodes) on the canvas. For a node, the leftmost connector represents an inbound connection to the node, while connectors on the right represent transitions out of the node. Users connect these by dragging lines to other nodes to visually represent the dialogue flow.

We use Figure 2 as a reference interaction for

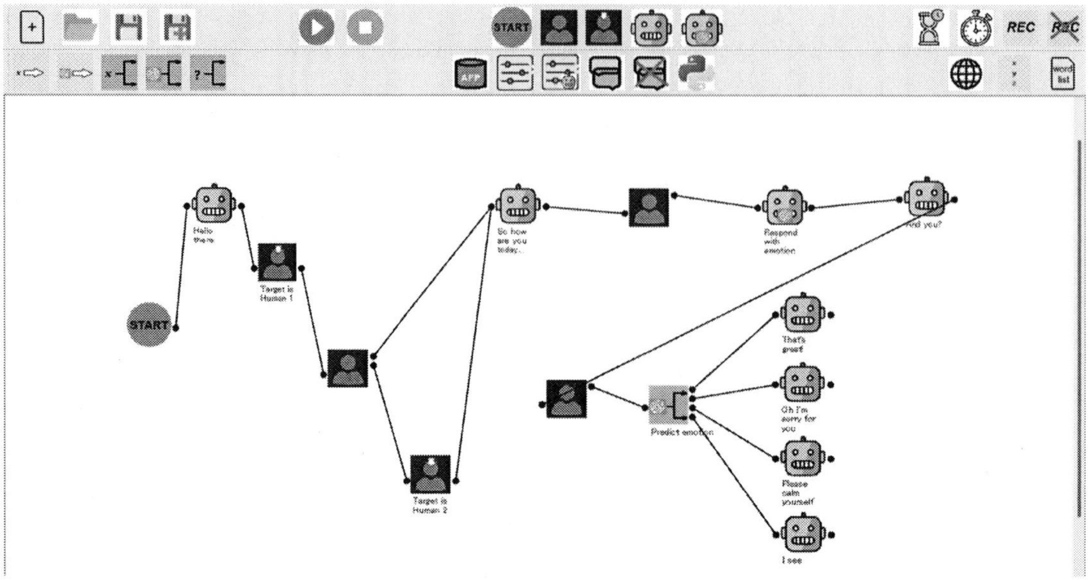

Figure 2: The GUI of ScriptBoard showing a simple interaction in a multi-party setting where the system greets each participant one at a time using LLM outputs.

this work. The toolbar at the top of the GUI contains various nodes for the scenario. We create this interaction by connecting the following nodes which we will describe in more detail.

Human turn node which processes speech from the participant

Sets the target participant

Generates dialogue for the robot (handcrafted)

Generates dialogue for the robot using a ChatGPT response

Controls dialogue flow based on output from ChatGPT

In the interaction in Figure 2, the system detects who responds first and then asks how they are. The first dialogue is automatically generated by ChatGPT. The system then asks the next participant the same question, but in this case the ChatGPT output is simply the predicted emotion of the participant's preceding utterance. This output (happy, sad, angry or other) is then used as a condition to the corresponding handcrafted dialogue. We now describe the details of these nodes.

4.1 Setting the environment

Before a scenario can be executed the user must set the environment of the interaction by specifying the number of participants and their user identification numbers. Every ASR result received must be associated with a corresponding ID. One participant may also be assigned as the "target" participant and this can be changed during the interaction.

This feature is necessary for handling multi-party interaction. ScriptBoard users can decide which participant(s) the robot should listen to and choose dialogue flows depending on who is speaking. It allows users to set roles related to each participant in advance and track them over the course of the interaction.

In addition, the user may set a number of variables to track during the interaction which can be modified. These variables are used as conditions to change the dialogue flow and are strictly enforced as either string, integer, float or boolean types.

Click to set information about the participants in the interaction

x y z Click to set variables tracked during the interaction

4.2 Human turn nodes

ScriptBoard is driven by conversational turn states. There are four basic states which occur in a basic cycle: *human turn, offer to robot, robot turn and offer to human*. The decision on the turn-taking state is made by the external controller, which sends turn update messages to ScriptBoard.

The human turn node is entered during the human turn state, and waits for user utterances. The node adds any incoming ASR result to the dialogue history of the relevant participant. ASR results need to be tagged with the corresponding ID number so that this dialogue history is accurate.

The system waits for an ASR result and/or the end of a participant's turn, which is notified by the external controller. Users can set conditions for either, such as whether the string contains a word, starts with or ends with a certain string(s) or is over a certain length. Conditions for a participant's utterance are checked as soon as an ASR result is received, while conditions for a participant's turn are checked as soon as the turn state changes to *offer to robot*, or in the case of multiple participants, the *human turn* state changes to a different participant. The user can also define whether a condition is for a particular participant, or a defined target or non-target participant or both.

Multiple conditions can be set for a human node which are checked sequentially. Each of these will generate a connector allowing them to be connected to other nodes. Figure 3 shows the two conditions used for the first (leftmost) human turn node in Figure 2. The first condition is if the target participant's turn is more than 10 words. The next condition consists of two sub-conditions - the non-target's utterance contains the word "hello" and is more than 10 words. Figure 2 shows that this second condition branches to a node which sets the participant with ID 2 as the new target.

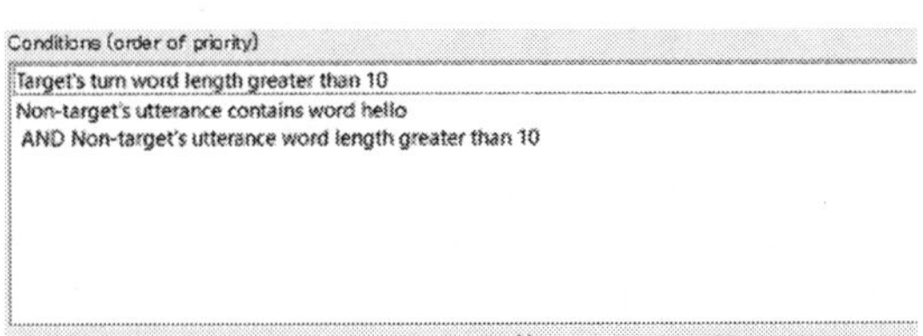

Figure 3: Human state window displaying the two conditions in Figure 2's scenario.

4.3 Robot nodes and LLM integration

Robot nodes specify dialogue to be generated by the system. The user can handcraft the dialogue themselves and specify speech tags and gaze which send extra information which may be used by the external robot controller. The interaction in Figure 2, shows examples of this node when the robot says "Hello there" and "How are you today?".

The approach described above of checking and comparing keywords and then manually generating a response is somewhat naive and impractical for many situations. Nowadays state-of-the-art LLMs are able to do both NLU and response generation tasks which greatly reduces the amount of effort needed to build an effective dialogue system. ScriptBoard integrates LLMs directly into the GUI through the use of a robot GPT node which uses the ChatGPT API.

With this node the user may opt to use ChatGPT to generate the response using prompts. ScriptBoard must be connected to an external ChatGPT program which can use the API. This program is included in the ScriptBoard package. The user types in their prompt directly and ScriptBoard will send the prompt and generate the response received from ChatGPT. Dialogue history can also be appended to augment the prompt. The user can also define how many turns and which participant's dialogue should be used from the dialogue history. In Figure 2, the robot GPT node labeled "Respond with emotion" will generate a ChatGPT response. It uses the prompt "*Generate an empathetic response to the following utterance*" and specifies the most recent turn of the target participant.

The robot node will wait until the robot has said its utterance (either handcrafted or generated) before exiting to the next node. This notification is received by a message from the external controller. Therefore it is necessary for the controller to know exactly when the robot has stopped its speech.

4.4 Dialogue flow management

To manage dialogue for more complex interactions, the user may wish to adapt the dialogue flow depending on conditions which are not related to participants' ASR results. ScriptBoard allows this control depending on variables or LLM output.

The variables specified in the initial setup of the interaction can be used to check for conditions and control dialogue flow. ScriptBoard contains a node which can be used to directly set the value of a variable during an interaction. For example, an *age* variable might be used to store the participant's age after being prompted by the system. Another node is then used to control the dialogue flow depending on this value. This node can then be used to produce different dialogue depending on *age*.

A similar method can be used to set variables based on results from LLMs. The user can specify prompts to generate a value rather than dialogue and store this in a variable. Assume that there is a variable named *emotion* to store the emotion of the participant. The user firstly chooses the node which stores the ChatGPT result in *emotion*. They can then use a prompt such as "*Output the sentiment of the following utterance. The possible sentiments are happy, sad, or angry*". When this node is reached, the output of ChatGPT is stored in *emotion* and then the variable decision node can be used to control the flow depending on the value.

Another method is available where the output of ChatGPT is directly used without needing a variable. In this case the user can specify prompting as usual, but they can also control the dialogue flow depending on ChatGPT's output. Figure 4 shows an example of this when the robot asks the second participant how they are. In this case, once the prompt is processed, the user specifies which conditions should be checked against ChatGPT's output, expecting either "happy", "sad" or "angry". Four conditions are created (one is an "else" condition) and these can be connected to other nodes to control dialogue flow.

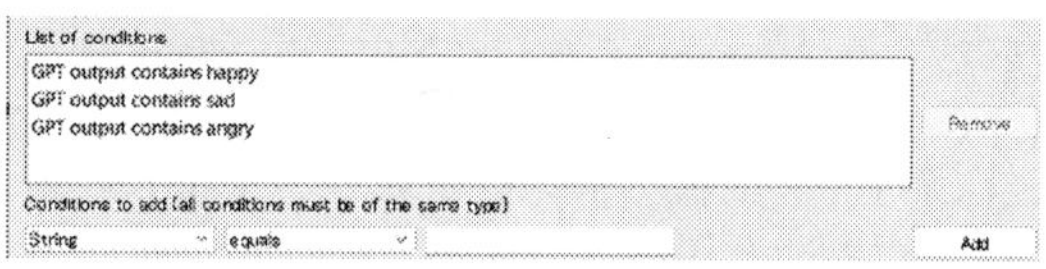

Figure 4: Robot GPT window showing the specified conditions for *Predict Emotion*.

5 Additional Features

For more complex SDSs, ScriptBoard has several other unique features for helping users customize their own scenarios.

5.1 Silence and barge-in

The system also contains features which handle phenomena that are specific to spoken dialogue systems. The first of these is silence. Silence messages are sent from the external controller. In the human turn state, the user can specify a condition which is triggered on silence for a specified time period. Use cases for this condition include prompting the user to speak or to end the interaction.

The system also has functionality to handle barge-in, the interruption of a system utterance from the user. This is again triggered from the external controller which sends a message whenever barge-in is detected. Note that the actual barge-in model and interruption of the system's TTS is handled by the external controller, not by ScriptBoard. Our system simply allows the user to define the dialogue flow which occurs when barge-in occurs.

5.2 Extendability

Although we use ChatGPT as the default LLM in this work, ScriptBoard also allows researchers to integrate their own models into the dialogue scenario through TCP connections. The input utterances for a model can be specified and resulting dialogue used in the interaction. This allows for quick prototyping and evaluation of SDSs.

In addition to LLMs, other types of conversational models can be triggered by ScriptBoard, by customizing message protocols. In our work we have successfully executed backchannelling and laughter models for a robot through this process. ScriptBoard also allows users to use a node to launch their own customized Python functions, making it a useful tool for proficient programmers.

6 System Usage

Once the user has created their dialogue scenario and it is connected to the external controller, they can simply push the "Play" button in the top toolbar to start the interaction. The user can view the dialogue history and the variables in the scenario through a monitoring window. The GUI also focuses the viewpoint on the current node to let the user know exactly where they are in the scenario, allowing them to visually track its progress. This is useful for debugging the logic of the scenario or identifying areas of improvement.

The scenario should run autonomously until there are no more connected nodes, but it is possible for an interaction to run in a loop. ScriptBoard can be for a diverse number of systems and robots. We describe one such implementation in a multi-party setting.

6.1 Multi-party attentive listening

This scenario was conducted in a public exhibition using a CommU robot[1]. It required two participants and a robot who would engage in an attentive listening dialogue. A microphone array separated each participant's voice so speech recognition

[1]https://resou.osaka-u.ac.jp/en/research/2015/20150120_2

could be performed on multiple channels simultaneously (Ishikawa et al., 2024). There were three parts to this scenario as shown in Figure 5:

1. Introduction in which robot greets both participants and explains attentive listening.
2. Attentive listening dialogue where robot listens to each participant one at a time for one minute.
3. A tongue twister game to demonstrate how the robot can listen to two people at once. Participants said a designated tongue twister together and the robot played back their separated audio then announced a winner.

Figure 5: Overview of attentive listening scenario. The robot first acts as an explainer then as an attentive listener before participants play a simultaneous speaking game.

The first part required that the robot act as an explainer by gazing between both participants and acknowledging them as part of the scenario. ScriptBoard was used to receive confirmation utterances from both participants. It could also set each participant as a gaze target by simply including this information with the robot's utterance.

For the second part we used ScriptBoard to have the robot act as an attentive listener. Responses were generated using a prompt which generated attentive listening style responses. We used a timer which would end the dialogue after a set amount of time. A backchannel model was called so that it would run during attentive listening.

For the tongue twister game the robot had to receive both participants' ASR simultaneously, use it to decide the winner of the game and also play back their separated audio channel. ScriptBoard processes ASR from both participants and this was made simple through designing the scenario's environment. Playback and deciding the winner could also be achieved through customized functions.

6.2 Other usages

The above scenario describes a mostly chatting-based interaction. However ScriptBoard is not limited to these types of interactions and should also be able to reliably handle task-based interactions by using LLMs and an appropriate prompt. Furthermore, because ScriptBoard is driven by turn-taking, these are abstracted from the type of interaction and so can be used in any spoken dialogue scenario.

As an example of the above, we have also used ScriptBoard to control a job interview task in English with an android robot (Pang et al., 2024). Although this task requires a different style of talk and a slightly longer time between turns, ScriptBoard was able to manage this interaction in a mostly linear dialogue flow.

ScriptBoard can even be used without needing any robot (such as a voice assistant) since it only outputs messages containing a response. Any connected system can receive this message and decide how it should be executed.

6.3 Reproducibility

SDS literature often describes human-robot conversational systems used in experiments and fieldwork, but it is difficult for others to use the system or create the same scenario without the available source code. ScriptBoard scenarios are saved as a JSON file to make them reproducible. Another ScriptBoard user can then easily load and test this scenario in their own environment.

Furthermore, scenarios written in ScriptBoard can be easily applied to other robots. In the job interview system described above, we used two different robots (Pang et al., 2025) each running the same ScriptBoard scenario, demonstrating how the same dialogue logic can be used in different robots. This would allow researchers to share their dialogue system and allow others to test in their own particular robot.

7 Conclusion

We demonstrate the ScriptBoard system, which we use to design and implement spoken dialogue systems using visual programming. ScriptBoard uses turn states as a basis for dialogue management and incorporates recent advances in LLM technology and multi-party scenarios. It is independent of any agent or robot and we have used it in different types of scenarios to demonstrate its capabilities.

Acknowledgments

This work was supported by JST Moonshot R&D Goal 1 Avatar Symbiotic Society Project (JPMJPS2011).

References

Michele Colledanchise and Petter Ögren. 2018. *Behavior trees in robotics and AI: An introduction*. CRC Press.

Dylan F. Glas, Takayuki Kanda, and Hiroshi Ishiguro. 2016. Human-robot interaction design using interaction composer: Eight years of lessons learned. In *The Eleventh ACM/IEEE International Conference on Human Robot Interaction*, HRI '16, page 303–310. IEEE Press.

André Groß, Christian Schütze, Mara Brandt, Britta Wrede, and Birte Richter. 2023. Rise: an open-source architecture for interdisciplinary and reproducible human–robot interaction research. *Frontiers in Robotics and AI*, 10.

Yuto Ishikawa, Kohei Konaka, Tomohiko Nakamura, Norihiro Takamune, and Hiroshi Saruwatari. 2024. Real-time speech extraction using spatially regularized independent low-rank matrix analysis and rank-constrained spatial covariance matrix estimation. In *2024 IEEE International Conference on Acoustics, Speech, and Signal Processing Workshops (ICASSPW)*, pages 730–734.

Alexander Koller, Timo Baumann, and Arne Köhn. 2018. Dialogos: Simple and extensible dialogue modeling. In *Interspeech 2018*, pages 167–168.

Pierre Lison and Casey Kennington. 2016. OpenDial: A toolkit for developing spoken dialogue systems with probabilistic rules. In *Proceedings of ACL-2016 System Demonstrations*, pages 67–72, Berlin, Germany. Association for Computational Linguistics.

Thilo Michael. 2020. Retico: An incremental framework for spoken dialogue systems. In *Proceedings of the 21th Annual Meeting of the Special Interest Group on Discourse and Dialogue*, pages 49–52, 1st virtual meeting. Association for Computational Linguistics.

Mikio Nakano and Kazunori Komatani. 2024. DialBB: A dialogue system development framework as an educational material. In *Proceedings of the 25th Annual Meeting of the Special Interest Group on Discourse and Dialogue*, pages 664–668, Kyoto, Japan. Association for Computational Linguistics.

Zi Haur Pang, Yahui Fu, Divesh Lala, Mikey Elmers, Koji Inoue, and Tatsuya Kawahara. 2024. Human-like embodied AI interviewer: Employing android ERICA in real international conference. In *COLING*. (to appear).

Zi Haur Pang, Yahui Fu, Divesh Lala, Mikey Elmers, Koji Inoue, and Tatsuya Kawahara. 2025. Does the appearance of autonomous conversational robots affect user spoken behaviors in real-world conference interactions? *Preprint*, arXiv:2503.13625.

E. Pot, J. Monceaux, R. Gelin, and B. Maisonnier. 2009. Choregraphe: a graphical tool for humanoid robot programming. In *RO-MAN 2009 - The 18th IEEE International Symposium on Robot and Human Interactive Communication*, pages 46–51.

Gabriel Skantze and Samer Al Moubayed. 2012. Iristk: a statechart-based toolkit for multi-party face-to-face interaction. In *Proceedings of the 14th ACM International Conference on Multimodal Interaction*, ICMI '12, page 69–76, New York, NY, USA. Association for Computing Machinery.

D4AC: A Tool for Developing Multimodal Dialogue Systems without Coding

Mikio Nakano*
Institute of Innovation for Future Society
Nagoya University
Nagoya, Aichi, Japan
mikio.nakano@c4a.jp

Ryuichiro Higashinaka
Graduate School of Informatics
Nagoya University
Nagoya, Aichi, Japan
higashinaka@i.nagoya-u.ac.jp

Abstract

To enable the broader application of dialogue system technology across various fields, it is beneficial to empower individuals with limited programming experience to build dialogue systems. Domain experts, where dialogue system technology is highly relevant, may not necessarily possess expertise in information technology. This paper presents D4AC, which works as a client for text-based dialogue servers. By combining D4AC with a no-code tool for developing text-based dialogue servers, it is possible to build multimodal dialogue systems without coding. These systems can adapt to the user's age, gender, emotions, and engagement levels obtained from their facial images. D4AC can be installed, launched, and configured without technical knowledge. D4AC was used in student projects at a university, which suggested the effectiveness of D4AC.

1 Introduction

Recent advancements in large language models have made it possible to develop various kinds of dialogue systems easily. In applying dialogue systems to various fields, it is effective for dialogue system engineers to cooperate with experts in the fields. However, there is a problem that the resources of dialogue system engineers are limited. Therefore, it would be desirable that experts in those fields could construct a dialogue system without coding.

Although there are tools for building text-based dialogue systems without coding, there have been no no-code tools for building multimodal dialogue systems that can exploit the user's attributes and social signals (Vinciarelli et al., 2009) obtained from the user's images. Such systems are expected to engage in communication better than text-based systems, as they can adapt their communication strategies to the user's attributes and states.

*Also affiliated with C4A Research Institute, Inc., Setagaya, Tokyo, Japan.

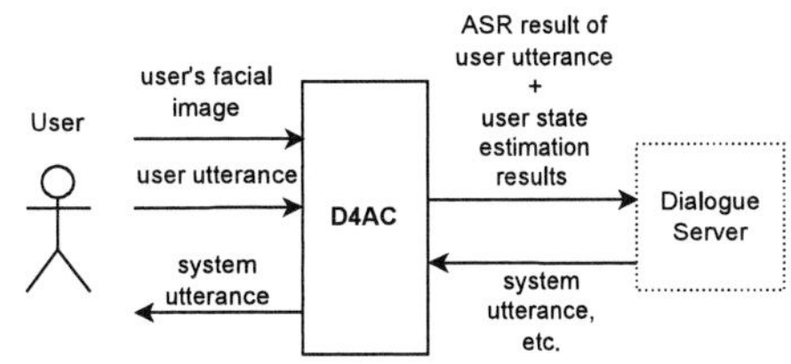

Figure 1: The role of D4AC.

This paper describes the design and implementation of D4AC,[1] which works as a client of a text-based dialogue server (Figure 1). The dialogue server is supposed to receive user utterances in text format and return system responses in text format. D4AC recognizes user utterances and estimates the user's age, gender, emotions, and engagement (referred to as "user states"[2]) from camera images using external APIs. It sends this information to the dialogue server at the time specified in the configuration. Then, it uses speech synthesis to generate the responses from the dialogue server.

The advantages of D4AC are as follows:

- It enables the dialogue server to use estimated user states for dialogue management.
- It enables the dialogue server to utilize estimated user states at times different from the ends of user utterances without writing complicated dialogue management knowledge. (This will be explained in detail in Section 3.2.)
- It can be easily installed, configured, and launched without technical knowledge.

[1]D4AC stands for 'Dialogue for All – Client', which represents a client program used in a project aimed at enabling anyone to build dialogue systems.

[2]Strictly speaking, age and gender should be referred to as attributes rather than states, but for simplicity, this paper will refer to them as states.

Proceedings of the 15th International Workshop on Spoken Dialogue Systems Technology, pages 183–189
May 27–30, 2025. ©2025 Association for Computational Linguistics

- It is released as an open-source software under the Apache License ver. 2.0.[3]

2 Related Work

There are studies on dialogue systems that handle information obtained from the user's image. For example, there are studies on a dialogue system that recognizes affirmative/negative attitudes from prosody and head movements (Fujie et al., 2006) and a reception dialogue system that smoothly facilitates turn-taking by estimating user engagement from standing positions and recognizing turn-yielding or taking intentions from the gaze and gestures (Bohus and Horvitz, 2009, 2011). An interview dialogue system that changes dialogue strategies by estimating the willingness to speak from gestures and speech (Ishihara et al., 2018) is also studied. SimSensei Kiosk (DeVault et al., 2014) is a system that conducts interviews for PTSD diagnostic support, estimating the user's emotions from facial expressions, head movements, gaze, and prosody.

While there are various studies in the field, there are few tools available as off-the-shelf solutions. '$\backslash psi$' (Bohus et al., 2021) and Virtual Human Toolkit (Hartholt et al., 2022, 2013) are exceptions, but technical knowledge is required to use them. In the Dialogue System Live Competition 6 (Higashinaka et al., 2024), a tool that enables the development of dialogue systems using user state estimation results without coding was distributed to the participants, but, unlike D4AC, it can send the user states to the dialogue server only at the end of user utterances, and it is not publicly available.

3 Design of D4AC

3.1 Overview

D4AC works as a client of a dialogue server (Figure 1). D4AC recognizes user utterances and sends the results to the dialogue server, along with user states (engagement, emotions, age, and gender) estimated from the user's facial image. The dialogue server determines the system utterance based on those inputs and dialogue context and returns it to D4AC in text format. D4AC then generates the system utterance using speech synthesis.

For user state estimation, D4AC uses Face++.[4] If only estimating engagement, it is also possible to use FaceMesh of MediaPipe.[5] For speech recognition and synthesis, it utilizes the Web Speech API of Google Chrome. Alternatively, Amazon Polly[6] can be used for speech synthesis.

D4AC can work as a client of dialogue servers that can be built without coding. It assumes NTT Docomo's xAIML SUNABA (SUNABA hereafter)[7] and DialBB[8] (Nakano and Komatani, 2024) as tools for building and deploying dialogue servers. They provide GUI-based editors for state transition networks to make it possible to write dialogue scenarios without coding. They also enable running dialogue servers as HTTP servers.

3.2 Communications between D4AC and a Dialogue Server

D4AC can send the results of user state estimation to the dialogue server at the following times.

(1) When sending the speech recognition result for a user utterance.

(2) When finished generating a system utterance.

(3) When the user has not spoken for t seconds after a system speech has ended.

Whether or not to send at each of these times and t in (3) can be configured with the configuration GUI. The reason for allowing the system to send not only at (1) but also at (2) and (3) is to allow the system to make utterances based on the user's reactions to what the system has said. When sending to SUNABA, in the case of (1), the following form is used.[9]

```
tuna sandwich+{engagement:high}{emotion:
happiness}
```

Here "tuna sandwich" is the recognized user utterance. Which user states to send can be specified in the configuration. The value of engagement is high, middle, or low; the value of emotion is anger, disgust, fear, happiness, neutral, sadness, or surprise; the value of age is child, teenager, young, middle, senior, or unknown, and gender is either male or female. By transmitting user states in this manner, the dialogue server can perform state transitions according to the user states. For example,

[3] https://github.com/nu-dialogue/D4AC

[4] https://www.faceplusplus.com

[5] https://chuoling.github.io/mediapipe/

[6] https://aws.amazon.com/polly/

[7] https://docs.sunaba.docomo.ne.jp/. Currently, SUNABA can deal only with Japanese.

[8] https://github.com/c4a-ri/dialbb

[9] In the case of DialBB, a JSON format is used to represent user states.

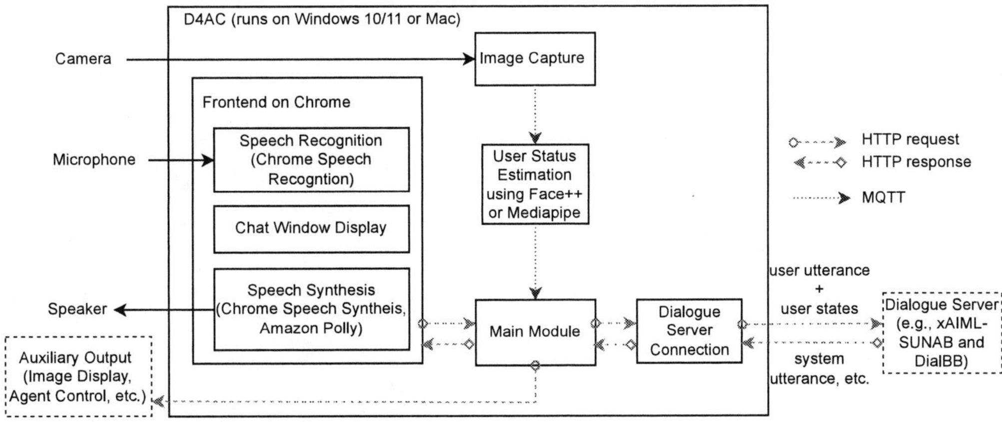

Figure 2: Architecture of D4AC.

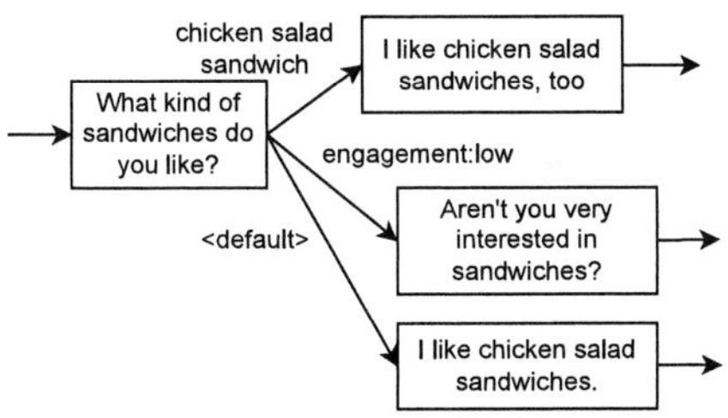

Figure 3: A dialogue state transition network using user states. Rectangles represent dialogue states, and the texts inside them are system utterances in those states. Arrows indicate state transitions. The text near an arrow means that if the user utterance includes this text, the transition will follow that arrow. `<default>` indicates that the transition can occur with any user utterance. The actual description style depends on the dialogue server.

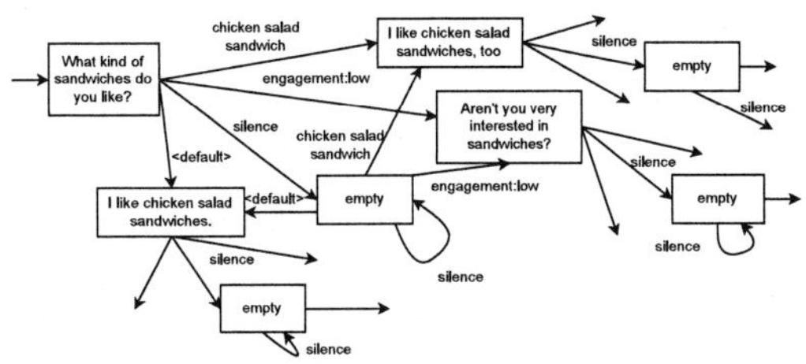

Figure 4: A state transition network for a client that cannot handle requests to send user states.

using the network shown in Figure 3, it can transition to a different dialogue state when user engagement is low.

In the cases of (2) and (3), the following forms are sent, respectively.

```
su_end+{engagement:high}{emotion:happiness}
silence+{engagement:high}{emotion:happiness}
```

In the cases of (2) and (3), the system does not necessarily have to respond. In such cases, the system utterance should be specified as "empty", which D4AC does not send to the speech synthesizer.

One issue arises here. The dialogue server is designed to transition states whenever there is an input of user utterance. Therefore, it is necessary to describe state transitions for cases (2) and (3) as well, meaning that for every dialogue state, one must write the transitions that would occur when only the user states are input. For instance, if we decide to send the user states at the time of (3), a state transition network like Figure 4 is necessary, and a huge effort for writing networks is required.

Therefore, we made it possible for the dialogue server side to send user-state requests to D4AC. This request asks D4AC to send the user state at the times of (2) and (3) only when the user state becomes a specific value. Specifically, the request is appended to the end of the system utterance text in the form of [⟨list of types⟩:⟨list of values⟩]. The lists of types and values are concatenated with '|'. For example, let us consider the case the system utterance is like the following.

```
How are you feeling? [emotion:
happiness|sadness]
```

Then, in the cases of (2) and (3), the user state is sent to the dialogue server only when the emotion becomes either happiness or sadness. This

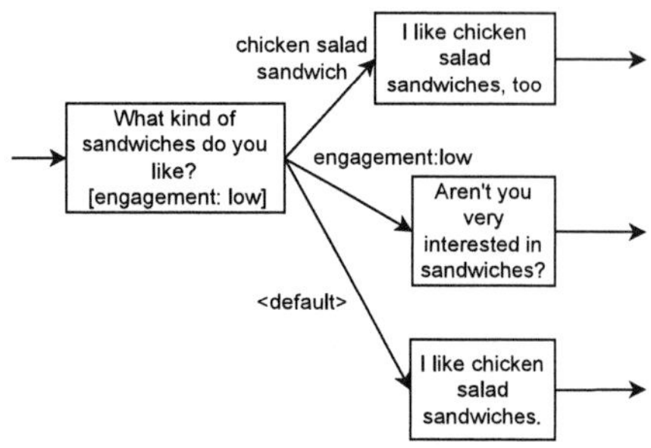

Figure 5: A state transition network that requests the client to send user states.

simplifies the state transition network as shown in Figure 5.

4 Implementation

Here we explain the implementation details of D4AC according to Figure 2.

The modules for user state estimation communicate with each other using MQTT,[10] which enables lightweight, asynchronous communication. The image capture module captures camera images and sends them to the MQTT broker. User state is estimated from these images using services like Face++ and others. In the current version of D4AC, engagement is estimated using only the face directions obtained from Face++ or MediaPipe. We plan to replace this with a more accurate algorithm using facial expressions and gaze (De Carolis et al., 2019; Ishii et al., 2013) in the future. Adding and replacing modules are easy thanks to the MQTT-based architecture.

The dialogue server connection module sends the results of speech recognition and user state estimation to the dialogue server and returns the system utterance received in response to the main module. If the system utterance includes a user-state transmission request, it is remembered and used to decide whether to send the user state at the times of (2) and (3) in Section 3.2.

Additionally, if specified, D4AC can send the system utterance text strings received from the dialogue server to an external auxiliary output server. By embedding commands within the system utterance text, it becomes possible to display images or to operate CG agents or robots.

The frontend part is written in JavaScript, and

[10]https://mqtt.org/

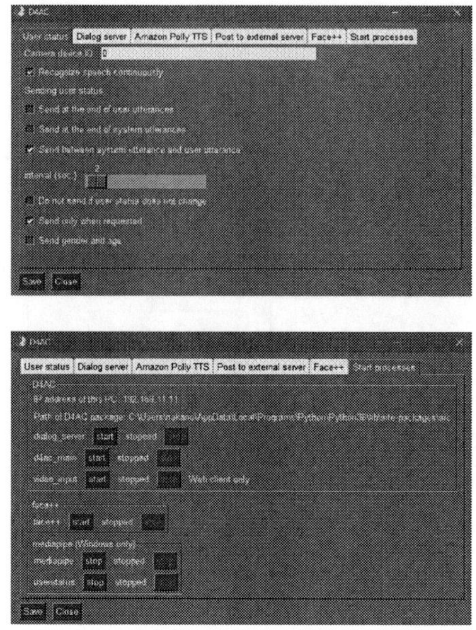

Figure 6: Configuration GUI. The tab for configuring sending the user states (upper panel) and the tab for starting processes (lower panel).

other modules are written in Python.

4.1 Installation and Configuration

D4AC can be installed easily by just invoking "`pip install`" command using a `.whl` file. Then running the "d4ac" command in a command prompt displays the configuration GUI. With the GUI, developers can specify the dialogue server, access information to Face++, Amazon Polly, etc., the times of sending user state estimation, and others (Figure 6 (upper panel)).

In addition, it is possible to start and stop the processes in D4AC from the GUI (Figure 6 (lower panel)).

5 Sample Application

This section describes a simple example application. An example dialogue between this application and a user is shown in Figure 7.

The dialogue server is built using DialBB. The scenario involves light conversations about food. In this scenario, ChatGPT (gpt-4o[11]) is used to generate system utterances in some states. The third, fourth, and sixth system utterances in Figure 7 were generated by ChatGPT. The configuration of the DialBB application includes the situations and persona of the system.

[11]https://openai.com/index/hello-gpt-4o/

Speaker	Utterance (*speech recognition result*)	Remarks
System	Hello I'm a chatbot. If you don't mind, could you tell me your name?	
User	Hello, I'm Mike. (*oh, I'm Mike*)	
System	Thank you Mike! Let me ask you about sandwich. Do you have sandwiches very often?	
User	Yes, I like sandwiches very much. (*yes I like sandwiches very much*)	
System	What's your favorite kind of sandwich, Mike? I love a good BLT, but I'm always looking for new ideas to try!	The dialogue server requests D4AC to tell if the user engagement level is low or middle at the end of and two seconds after the system utterance.
User	I like chicken salad sandwiches. (*I got chicken salad sandwiches*)	
System	Chicken salad sandwiches sound delicious! Do you make them yourself or do you have a favorite place to get them?	The dialogue server requests D4AC to tell if the user engagement level is low or middle at the end of and two seconds after the system utterance. At the end of the system utterance, D4AC informs the dialogue server the user engagement level is low.
System	Aren't you interested?	The system asks the user if she/he is interested in the conversation.
User	Oh, yes. I'm interested. Sorry. (*oh yes I'm interested sorry*)	
System	No worries, Mike! Do you add anything special to your chicken salad sandwiches, like grapes or nuts, or do you prefer to keep it simple?	Since the user response is affirmative, the system goes back to the conversation. (Otherwise, the system wraps up the conversation.)

Figure 7: A sample dialogue between a user and the example application.

At some states, the dialogue server requests D4AC to send the user's engagement level if it is "middle" or "low". Then when the dialogue server receives the engagement level, it makes an utterance to ask if the user is bored with the conversation, and if so, the conversation is terminated.

D4AC is configured to send the user's state to the dialogue server only when requested by the dialogue server. This occurs either at the end of the system's utterance or if the user does not speak for two seconds after the system's utterance has ended.

The source files for this sample application are publicly available as a part of the D4AC repository.

6 Using D4AC in Student Projects

During the development of D4AC, we utilized it in student projects at a university. The student projects were conducted twice, in the academic years 2021 and 2022, where students were tasked with building simple multimodal dialogue systems. Four students participated in each project.

In Academic Year 2021, the four students built separate dialogue systems following their interests. Specifically, these were (1) a system for scheduling appointments, (2) a system for presenting quizzes, (3) a system explaining the use of shared cars, and (4) a system providing useful information for LGBTQ+ individuals. The student who developed the fourth system was affiliated with a humanities research lab, while the others belonged to information technology or engineering labs. Of these, systems (3) and (4) utilized D4AC along with SUNABA, but they did not use user state estimation results. At that time, D4AC could only send user state information at the end of user utterances, which limited its utility. Following this experience, we modified D4AC to transmit user state estimation results at times other than the end of user utterances.

In Academic Year 2022, the project involved four students working collaboratively to build a single system. Among these students, two were from humanities and two were from information technology or engineering labs. They developed a dialogue system designed to calm the irritations of drivers while driving. The system converses with the driver, calming them if they are irritated, and the progression is determined based on the user state estimation results indicating whether the irritation is resolved. Insights from humanities research (e.g., (Nakai, 2021)) were utilized in creating the scenarios. This system used DialBB to build the dialogue server.

This project showed that a system utilizing user state estimation results can be easily built with D4AC. We plan to provide opportunities for people from various fields to use the system and validate its effectiveness in future projects.

7 Concluding Remarks

This paper described D4AC, which is a tool that allows for the construction of multimodal dialogue systems without coding. It estimates user attributes and states from facial images and alters the course of dialogue based on these results. D4AC enables people from various fields, not just information technology, to build multimodal dialogue systems, contributing to the integration of dialogue system technology with other disciplines.

Although D4AC does not include novel technologies that improve empirical evaluation results, it concretizes a reasonable architecture for creating a multimodal dialogue system without coding. We believe that it will contribute to multimodal dialogue system technologies being used in various fields.

We are considering the following enhancements and features. First, we aim to enable the use of tools and APIs other than Face++ and MediaPipe for user state estimation. Another goal is to integrate prosodic information from user utterances and text-based data for emotion estimation. Additionally, we are considering the use of other user states such as sentiment (Katada et al., 2023) and affirmative/negative attitudes (Fujie et al., 2006). We also think that multimodal foundational models such as GPT-4o might be useful for user state estimation.

As D4AC is released as an open source, we hope we will receive feedback for improvements while it is being used in an actual system development.

Limitations

Although D4AC was used in student projects, it has not been evaluated in a way that involves gathering a large number of users. Therefore, its usability remains unclear. However, the value of such tools cannot be measured solely through evaluations in controlled situations. It is important to release it publicly, allowing it to be used in the development of various systems, and continuously improve it based on feedback. D4AC is believed to have sufficient performance as a starting point for this process.

Ethical Considerations

One potential ethical issue with this tool is the risk of personal information leakage, as users' facial images and voice data are sent to image and voice recognition systems managed by private companies' cloud services. Whether this becomes a problem depends on the application. Therefore, we encourage developers using D4AC to raise awareness and recommend obtaining proper consent from users.

Estimating emotions from facial images and linking them to the content of conversations is important for facilitating more appropriate interactions. However, depending on how it is used, there is a risk of obtaining personal inner feelings that the user has not intentionally disclosed; it might be illegal in some countries. We also raise awareness among developers using D4AC about this issue.

Acknowledgments

The development of D4AC was supported by Nagoya University's the Graduate Program for Lifestyle Revolution based on Transdisciplinary Mobile Innovation (TMI) program. We thank Prof. Nobuo Kawaguchi, the coordinator of this program. We also thank Mizuho Aoki, Xueqin Huang, Ryo Hori, Sanae Yamashita, Ai Liya, Ibrahima Kane, Qiuhao Cui, Ailing Xie of the TMI program for participating in the dialogue system project and for providing valuable feedback on D4AC.

References

Dan Bohus, Sean Andrist, Ashley Feniello, Nick Saw, Mihai Jalobeanu, Patrick Sweeney, Anne Loomis Thompson, and Eric Horvitz. 2021. Platform for situated intelligence. *CoRR*, abs/2103.15975.

Dan Bohus and Eric Horvitz. 2009. Learning to predict engagement with a spoken dialog system in open-world settings. In *Proceedings of the SIGDIAL 2009 Conference*, pages 244–252, London, UK. Association for Computational Linguistics.

Dan Bohus and Eric Horvitz. 2011. Multiparty turn taking in situated dialog: Study, lessons, and directions. In *Proceedings of the SIGDIAL 2011 Conference*, pages 98–109, Portland, Oregon. Association for Computational Linguistics.

Berardina De Carolis, Francesca D'Errico, Nicola Macchiarulo, and Giuseppe Palestra. 2019. "engaged faces": Measuring and monitoring student engagement from face and gaze behavior. In *IEEE/WIC/ACM International Conference on Web Intelligence - Companion Volume*, WI '19 Companion, page 80–85, New York, NY, USA. Association for Computing Machinery.

David DeVault, Ron Artstein, Grace Benn, Teresa Dey, Ed Fast, Alesia Gainer, Kallirroi Georgila, Jon

Gratch, Arno Hartholt, Margaux Lhommet, Gale Lucas, Stacy Marsella, Fabrizio Morbini, Angela Nazarian, Stefan Scherer, Giota Stratou, Apar Suri, David Traum, Rachel Wood, Yuyu Xu, Albert Rizzo, and Louis-Philippe Morency. 2014. Simsensei kiosk: a virtual human interviewer for healthcare decision support. In *Proceedings of the 2014 International Conference on Autonomous Agents and Multi-Agent Systems*, AAMAS '14, page 1061–1068, Richland, SC. International Foundation for Autonomous Agents and Multiagent Systems.

Shinya Fujie, Yasushi Ejiri, Hideaki Kikuchi, and Tetsunori Kobayashi. 2006. Recognition of positive/negative attitude and its application to a spoken dialogue system. *Systems and Computers in Japan*, 37(12):45–55.

Arno Hartholt, Ed Fast, Zongjian Li, Kevin Kim, Andrew Leeds, and Sharon Mozgai. 2022. Re-architecting the virtual human toolkit: towards an interoperable platform for embodied conversational agent research and development. In *Proceedings of the 22nd ACM International Conference on Intelligent Virtual Agents*, IVA '22, New York, NY, USA. Association for Computing Machinery.

Arno Hartholt, David Traum, Stacy C. Marsella, Ari Shapiro, Giota Stratou, Anton Leuski, Louis-Philippe Morency, and Jonathan Gratch. 2013. All together now. In *Intelligent Virtual Agents*, pages 368–381, Berlin, Heidelberg. Springer Berlin Heidelberg.

Ryuichiro Higashinaka, Tetsuro Takahashi, Michimasa Inaba, Zhiyang Qi, Yuta Sasaki, Kotrao Funakoshi, Shoji Moriya, Shiki Sato, Takashi Minato, Kurima Sakai, Tomo Funayama, Masato Komuro, Hiroyuki Nishikawa, Ryosaku Makino, Hirofumi Kikuchi, and Mayumi Usami. 2024. Dialogue system live competition goes multimodal: Analyzing the effects of multimodal information in situated dialogue systems. In *Proceedings of IWSDS*.

Takuya Ishihara, Katsumi Nitta, Fuminori Nagasawa, and Shogo Okada. 2018. Estimating interviewee's willingness in multimodal human robot interview interaction. In *Proceedings of the 20th International Conference on Multimodal Interaction: Adjunct*, ICMI '18, New York, NY, USA. Association for Computing Machinery.

Ryo Ishii, Yukiko I. Nakano, and Toyoaki Nishida. 2013. Gaze awareness in conversational agents: Estimating a user's conversational engagement from eye gaze. *ACM Trans. Interact. Intell. Syst.*, 3(2).

Shun Katada, Shogo Okada, and Kazunori Komatani. 2023. Effects of physiological signals in different types of multimodal sentiment estimation. *IEEE Transactions on Affective Computing*, 14(3):2443–2457.

Hiroshi Nakai. 2021. The overview of research on aggressive driving and proposal of preventive measures. *Traffic sciences*, 52(1):3–12. (in Japanese).

Mikio Nakano and Kazunori Komatani. 2024. DialBB: A dialogue system development framework as an educational material. In *Proceedings of the 25th Annual Meeting of the Special Interest Group on Discourse and Dialogue*, pages 664–668, Kyoto, Japan. Association for Computational Linguistics.

Alessandro Vinciarelli, Maja Pantic, and Hervé Bourlard. 2009. Social signal processing: Survey of an emerging domain. *Image and Vision Computing*, 27(12):1743–1759.

A Multilingual Speech-Based Driver Assistant for Basque and English

Antonio Aparicio Akcharov[1], **Asier López Zorrilla**[1], **Juan Camilo Vasquez-Correa**[2], **Oscar Montserrat**[3], **Jose María Echevarría**[3], **Begoña Arrate**[4], **Joxean Zapirain**[4], **Mikel deVelasco**[1], **Santiago Andrés Moreno-Acevedo**[2], **Ander González-Docasal**[2], **M. Inés Torres**[1], and **Aitor Álvarez**[2]

[1]University of the Basque Country UPV/EHU, [2]Vicomtech
[3]Automotive Intelligence Centre AIC, [4]UZEI

Abstract

This demo paper presents a prototype of a multilingual, speech-based driver assistant, designed to support both English and Basque languages. The inclusion of Basque—a low-resource language with limited domain-specific training data—marks a significant contribution, as publicly available AI models, including Large Language Models, often underperform for such languages compared to high-resource languages like English. Despite these challenges, our system demonstrates robust performance, successfully understanding user queries and delivering rapid responses in a demanding environment: a car simulator. Notably, the system achieves comparable performance in both English and Basque, showcasing its effectiveness in addressing linguistic disparities in AI-driven applications. A demo of our prototype will be available in the workshop.

1 Introduction

Speech-based driver assistants have become increasingly prevalent in modern vehicles, offering convenience and safety by enabling hands-free interaction with in-car systems. Prominent examples such as Amazon Alexa Auto or Apple CarPlay, have demonstrated the potential of such technologies to enhance user experience by providing real-time information about navigation, vehicle status, and other essential tasks (Li et al., 2024; Zhou and Zheng, 2023). These systems leverage advancements in Natural Language Processing (NLP) and speech recognition, often relying on Large Language Models (LLMs) trained on extensive datasets mainly containing data in high-resource languages like English (Touvron et al., 2023; Günther et al., 2023). However, due to the scarcity of domain-specific datasets and models, the development of similar systems for low-resource languages remains a significant challenge.

Low-resource languages often lack the domain-specific annotated data necessary to train state-of-the-art NLP and speech processing models, leading to a greater reliance on rule-based approaches (Wilcock et al., 2017). Basque is an isolated language spoken by approximately 750,000 people, with complex morphology and free word order. Despite recent progress, publicly available Basque language AI models such as the Latxa series (Etxaniz et al., 2024) or Llama-eus (Corral et al., 2024) still underperform compared to models for high-resource languages. Additionally, there are limited datasets and tools tailored for specific applications, such as automotive environments, further complicating the development of Basque-focused driver assistants. In fact, we have had to develop an automotive industry-related dataset from scratch for this project, since most publicly available and related datasets are in English or high-resource languages (Deruyttere et al., 2020).

This demo paper presents a multilingual speech-based driver assistant developed within the Adapt-IA project, designed to provide support in both Basque and English. Integrated into an industrial car simulator, the assistant provides conversational access to real-time vehicle data, including speed, traffic conditions, tire pressure, and battery status. By creating a domain-specific corpus in Basque and leveraging state-of-the-art NLP and speech processing techniques, our system, which will be shown in a demo in the workshop, demonstrates comparable performance in Basque and English. This showcases the feasibility of extending driver assistant technology to underrepresented languages like Basque.

The rest of the paper is organised as fol-

Proceedings of the 15th International Workshop on Spoken Dialogue Systems Technology, pages 190–195
May 27–30, 2025. ©2025 Association for Computational Linguistics

lows: Section 2 provides an overview of the context and motivation behind this work. Section 3 describes the corpus built to develop our assistant, and its architecture and implementation. Section 4 presents a sample dialogue that showcases its capabilities. Finally, Section 5 presents our conclusions.

2 Context

This work has been carried out within the Adapt-IA project, which aims to develop AI technologies for the Basque language, and others if the specific use case so requires. More particularly, the primary goal is to explore the development and integration of these technologies into the needs and specific use cases of various Basque industrial sectors, such as machine-tools manufacturing, the energy sector, the railway sector and the automotive industry.

One sector where these advancements have significant potential is the automotive industry. As vehicles become increasingly reliant on intelligent systems, the need for speech-based technologies in different languages, including Basque, becomes critical. In this context, this work represents a step towards providing drivers with the capabilities to naturally interact with smart vehicles in Basque and English languages. To this end, we have developed a driving assistant that suits the Automotive Intelligence Center (AIC) industrial car simulator in the Basque country: an hexapod system equipped with a fully operational cockpit interior from a road vehicle (see Figure 1). With six degrees of freedom, this simulator is employed for dynamic analyses and serves as a platform for testing advanced driver-assistance systems and user communication strategies under highly realistic conditions.

3 The Adapt-IA Speech-Based Driver Assistant

This section describes all the stages and tools created and integrated into the developed speech-based driver assistant, including the data generation process, in addition to the training of specific models for automatic speech recognition (ASR), natural language understading (NLU), and text to speech (TTS) that have been integrated into the final prototype.

request speed
request speed limit
request tire pressure
request battery level
request autonomy
request driving time
request driving distance
request traffic status
repeat
car did not understand
thanks
hello
goodbye
other

Table 1: List of user intents the assistant is able to understand. The "car did not understand" label is used when user says that the car did not provide the expected information, and the "other" indicates that the information the user is requesting is not available for this system.

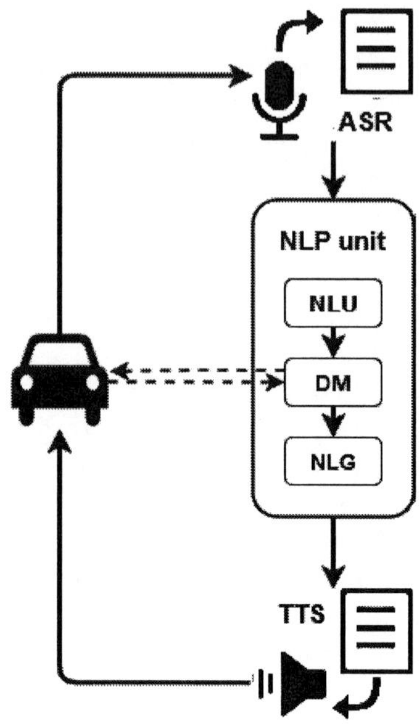

Figure 2: High-level overview of the assistant's back end architecture.

Basque

One of the main goals of the project was to generate high-quality data in Basque with specialised terminology for different industrial sectors, and which could be useful for the community and for future works. Therefore, the use of LLMs was not desired in this case, as their performance remains limited for low-resource languages (Hasan et al., 2024; Jayakody and Dias, 2024).

Instead, we built a dataset about how driving information could be asked in Basque. Expert Basque linguists generated a number of templates to form sentences, which considered different word orders within sentences, synonyms, possible word omissions, and different registers (formal, informal, direct, etc.). More than 20 million sentences were generated considering all possible combinations. However, we filtered very similar sentences to make the corpus as diverse as possible. To this end, we employed both a cluster-based active learning approach (Moreno-Acevedo et al., 2024), and a random selection following a uniform distribution. This led to a diverse and balanced corpus of around 14K sentences.

Additionally, we asked some volunteers how they would form sentences for the defined user-intents. This way, we increased the dataset by another 612 natural sentences[1].

3.2 System architecture and components

As for the assistant interface, the user interacts with it via a tablet mounted on the panel of the car simulator, which acts both as the microphone and the speaker. If the user wants to ask anything while driving, they can press a button and start a conversation. This conversation ends when the user presses the button again, or when the system determines that the dialogue has ended (if the user says "bye", for example).

Since some modules require relatively intensive computing capabilities, the processing is done on remote servers. There are three main components, as depicted in Figure 2. The communication between these modules is done via API queries. It takes around 3 seconds to process the user's speech and generate a speech response. The main specifications for each component are described as follows.

ASR

The ASR unit is built on top of Nvidia's Parakeet models, which are state-of-the-art recurrent neural network transducers (RNN-T) that have shown excellent results in recent speech

[1]This corpus will be publicly available once the project is finished.

benchmarks (Srivastav et al., 2025; Vásquez-Correa et al., 2024). The Basque and English models use the large version of the fast-conformer RNN-T architecture, which has 0.6 billion parameters[2]. The Basque model was initially trained from scratch using 1 258 hours of transcribed Basque audio and then fine-tuned with 12.8 hours of in-domain data. This in-domain data was created by synthesizing 10 166 selected user requests using our TTS system. The English model started with Nvidia's pre-trained model and was fine-tuned using 7 hours of in-domain data, also created by synthesizing 8 223 user requests using our TTS system. In this case, in addition to the English corpus described in Section 3.1, we automatically translated the filtered Basque sentences into English to increase the amount of data.

NLP unit

The NLP unit consists of three modules:

1. NLU: Takes a transcribed user sentence and outputs the corresponding intents; which represents the semantic meaning of the sentence.
2. DM (Dialogue Manager): Based on the user intents and the dialogue history, the DM outputs the next dialogue act; i.e., what the system needs to reply.
3. NLG (Natural Language Generation): Generates a natural sentence based on dialogue act produced by the DM.

Due to the limitations of Basque NLP models, we employed different strategies for the NLU. In English, the user request is transformed into a 384-dimensional embedding vector with the model `all-MiniLM-L12-v2` from Sentence-Transformers (Wang et al., 2020). Conversely, for the Basque case, we had to use an LLM fine-tuned specifically for this language. In this case we pass the sentence through Latxa 7B (Etxaniz et al., 2024) and retrieve the output embedding. In both cases, we train multilayer neural networks to classify the embeddings into one or more user intents. Those are trained on the datasets we gathered. The models are run in parallel, so that switching between languages is effortless.

Once the intents of the input are obtained, the rule-based DM retrieves the relevant information from the car simulator, outputs the next dialogue act. Generally, these rules involve providing the requested information, checking the dialogue history if a repetition of information is requested, and greeting or thanking the user when appropriate. One key advantage of rule-based DMs is their greater controllability and robustness, particularly in restricted environments (Vázquez et al., 2023).

Given the dialogue act output by the DM, the template-based NLG module generates a textual answer to the user's query. To avoid repetitions in the assistant's responses, we have a number (around 10) templates per dialogue act. These are selected randomly and filled with the real-time data provided by the simulator.

TTS

The integrated TTS system was based on a Tacotron-2 (Shen et al., 2018) acoustic model. This architecture is built using an encoder-decoder with attention that returns the Mel-scale spectrogram of the generated speech, which is in turn converted to an audio signal by a HiFi-GAN (Kong et al., 2020) neural vocoder.

A Tacotron-2 model was trained per language on pairs of audio and their corresponding transcription. The models were fine-tuned from a pre-existing model trained on 34 137 audio files consisting of 36.1 h of high-quality studio recordings from a female Spanish speaker. The Basque dataset comprised 11 640 audio files summing a total of 20.8 h standard Basque recordings from a native speaker, whilst for English the public domain LJ-Speech dataset (Ito and Johnson, 2017) was used. The input string consisted of characters in the case of Basque and phonemes for English, which were generated using a DeepPhonemizer[3] model adapted from pronunciation data extracted from Wiktionary. Finally, the HiFi-GAN vocoder made use of the ground-truth aligned spectrograms from the same datasets needed for training the acoustic models.

[2]`https://huggingface.co/nvidia/parakeet-rnnt-0.6b`

[3]`https://github.com/as-ideas/DeepPhonemizer`

Basque	English
User: Kaixo kotxe, nire abiadura legala al da?	**User:** Hi there, is my current speed correct?
Assistant: Abiadura muga 90 kilometro ordukoa da, eta zure abiadura 87 kilometro ordukoa.	**Assistant:** The speed limit is 90 kilometers per hour, while your speed is 87 kilometers per hour.
User: Eta zenbateko autonomia daukagu?	**User:** And how far can we drive with the current battery?
Assistant: Bateriaren karga honekin, 250 kilometro gehiago egin ditzakegu.	**Assistant:** With this battery charge, we can drive 250 more kilometers.
User: Barka, ez zaitut ondo entzun...	**User:** Sorry, I couldn't hear you well...
Assistant: 250 kilometro egin ditzakegu.	**Assistant:** We can drive 250 more kilometers.
User: Zein da kanpoaldeko tenperatura?	**User:** What's the temperature outside?
Assistant: Barkatu, baina ez dut horretan laguntzeko gaitasunik.	**Assistant:** I'm afraid I cannot provide this information.
User: Ongi da. Eskerrik asko eta agur!	**User:** It's OK. Thanks! Bye!
Assistant: Ez horregatik. Agur!	**Assistant:** You are welcome. Goodbye!

Table 2: A (parallel) sample conversation with the Adapt-IA assistant, in Basque and English.

4 A sample conversation with the Adapt-IA Driver Assistant

Table 2 shows the kind of dialogues implemented in the Adapt-IA driver assistant in Basque and English. Notice that the system is able to provide the requested information, or inform that some information is not available to the system, such as the outside temperature. It can also handle repetition requests if the user did not understand what the assistant said for any reason, and react to task-free intents such as greetings or gratitude.

A demo of this prototype where all the capabilities of the system will be shown will be presented in the conference.

5 Conclusion

We have presented a speech-based driving assistant capable of providing relevant real-time data to the driver in a conversational fashion, both in Basque and English. To achieve this, we developed an organic domain-specific corpus in Basque to train our system, effectively bridging the performance gap between the English and Basque versions. This effort demonstrates the feasibility of extending similar NLP systems to low-resource languages, such as Basque, thereby addressing the linguistic imbalance often found in AI technologies. Our results demonstrate that tailored approaches can overcome resource limitations, enabling robust performance for underrepresented languages in specialized domains. This work not only advances the feasibility of developing Basque-centric AI systems but also contributes to the broader goal of inclusivity in AI technologies for diverse linguistic communities.

Acknowledgments

This work was partially supported by the Department of Economic Development and Competitiveness of the Basque Government (Spri Group) through funding for the ADAPT-IA project (KK-2023/00035).

References

Ander Corral, Ixak Sarasua, and Xabier Saralegi. 2024. Pipeline analysis for developing instruct llms in low-resource languages: A case study on basque. *Preprint*, arXiv:2412.13922.

Thierry Deruyttere, Simon Vandenhende, Dusan Grujicic, Yu Liu, Luc Van Gool, Matthew Blaschko, Tinne Tuytelaars, and Marie-Francine Moens. 2020. Commands 4 autonomous vehicles (c4av) workshop summary. In *Computer Vision–ECCV 2020 Workshops: Glasgow, UK, August 23–28, 2020, Proceedings, Part II 16*, pages 3–26. Springer.

Julen Etxaniz, Oscar Sainz, Naiara Perez, Itziar Aldabe, German Rigau, Eneko Agirre, Aitor Ormazabal, Mikel Artetxe, and Aitor Soroa. 2024. Latxa: An open language model and evaluation suite for basque. *Preprint*, arXiv:2403.20266.

Michael Günther, Georgios Mastrapas, Bo Wang, Han Xiao, and Jonathan Geuter. 2023. Jina embeddings: A novel set of high-performance sentence embedding models. In *Proceedings of the 3rd Workshop for Natural Language Processing Open Source Software (NLP-OSS 2023)*, pages 8–18.

Md Arid Hasan, Prerona Tarannum, Krishno Dey, Imran Razzak, and Usman Naseem. 2024. Do large language models speak all languages equally? a comparative study in low-resource settings. *arXiv preprint arXiv:2408.02237*.

Keith Ito and Linda Johnson. 2017. The lj speech dataset. `https://keithito.com/LJ-Speech-Dataset/`.

Ravindu Jayakody and Gihan Dias. 2024. Performance of recent large language models for a low-resourced language. In *2024 International Conference on Asian Language Processing (IALP)*, pages 162–167. IEEE.

Jungil Kong, Jaehyeon Kim, and Jaekyoung Bae. 2020. HiFi-GAN: Generative adversarial networks for efficient and high fidelity speech synthesis. *Advances in neural information processing systems*, 33:17022–17033.

Yuanchao Li, Lachlan Urquhart, Nihan Karatas, Shun Shao, Hiroshi Ishiguro, and Xun Shen. 2024. Beyond voice assistants: Exploring advantages and risks of an in-car social robot in real driving scenarios. *arXiv preprint arXiv:2402.11853*.

Santiago A Moreno-Acevedo, Juan Camilo Vasquez-Correa, Juan M Martín-Doñas, and Aitor Álvarez. 2024. Stream-based active learning for speech emotion recognition via hybrid data selection and continuous learning. In *International Conference on Text, Speech, and Dialogue*, pages 105–117. Springer.

Jonathan Shen, Ruoming Pang, Ron J. Weiss, Mike Schuster, Navdeep Jaitly, Zongheng Yang, Zhifeng Chen, Yu Zhang, Yuxuan Wang, Rj Skerrv-Ryan, Rif A. Saurous, Yannis Agiomvrgiannakis, and Yonghui Wu. 2018. Natural tts synthesis by conditioning wavenet on mel spectrogram predictions. In *2018 IEEE International Conference on Acoustics, Speech and Signal Processing (ICASSP)*, pages 4779–4783.

Vaibhav Srivastav, Somshubra Majumdar, Nithin Koluguri, Adel Moumen, Sanchit Gandhi, et al. 2025. Open automatic speech recognition leaderboard. `https://huggingface.co/spaces/hf-audio/open_asr_leaderboard`.

Hugo Touvron, Thibaut Lavril, Gautier Izacard, Xavier Martinet, Marie-Anne Lachaux, Timothée Lacroix, Baptiste Rozière, Naman Goyal, Eric Hambro, Faisal Azhar, et al. 2023. Llama: Open and efficient foundation language models. *arXiv preprint arXiv:2302.13971*.

Juan Camilo Vásquez-Correa, Aitor Álvarez, Haritz Arzelus, Santiago Andrés Moreno Acevedo, Ander González-Docasal, and Juan Manuel Martín-Doñas. 2024. The vicomtech speech transcription systems for the albayzín 2024 bilingual basque-spanish speech to text (bbs-s2t) challenge. In *Proc. IberSPEECH 2024*, pages 305–309.

Alain Vázquez, Asier López Zorrilla, Javier Mikel Olaso, and María Inés Torres. 2023. Dialogue management and language generation for a robust conversational virtual coach: Validation and user study. *Sensors*, 23(3):1423.

Wenhui Wang, Furu Wei, Li Dong, Hangbo Bao, Nan Yang, and Ming Zhou. 2020. Minilm: Deep self-attention distillation for task-agnostic compression of pre-trained transformers. *Preprint*, arXiv:2002.10957.

Graham Wilcock, Niklas Laxström, Juho Leinonen, Peter Smit, Mikko Kurimo, and Kristiina Jokinen. 2017. *Towards SamiTalk: A Sami-Speaking Robot Linked to Sami Wikipedia*, pages 343–351. Springer Singapore, Singapore.

Xinyi Zhou and Yangshuo Zheng. 2023. Research on personality traits of in-vehicle intelligent voice assistants to enhance driving experience. In *International Conference on Human-Computer Interaction*, pages 236–244. Springer.

Intimebot – A Dialogue Agent for Timekeeping Support

Shoaib Khan
Intapp Labs
shoaib.khan@intapp.com

Alex Samani
Intapp Labs
alex.samani@intapp.com

Rafael E Banchs
Intapp Labs
rafael.banchs@intapp.com

Abstract

This demo paper presents intimebot, an AI-powered timekeeping solution designed to assist with timekeeping. Timekeeping is a fundamental but also overwhelming and complex task in many professional services practices. Our intimebot demo demonstrates how Artificial Intelligence can be utilized to implement a more efficient timekeeping process within a firm. Based on brief work descriptions provided by the timekeeper, intimebot is able to (1) predict the relevant combination of client, matter, and phase, (2) estimate the work effort hours, and (3) rewrite and normalize the provided work description into a compliant narrative. This can save a significant amount of time for busy professionals while ensuring terms of business compliance and best practices.

1 Introduction

Timekeeping constitutes a fundamental process in professional services business operations because, when properly done, it ensures accurate and timely billing, which is a necessary condition for a healthy revenue stream for the firm. However, timekeeping is also typically a very taxing and overwhelming task to the busy professionals, who can see their potential billing hours significantly impacted due to poor timekeeping practices (Boster and Brenan, 2024).

Supporting timekeeping activities with Natural Language Processing technologies is a compelling proposition because of its potential impact on both firms and professionals. On the firm side, more timely and accurate timekeeping reduces revenue losses due to compliance issues, missed work items, and delayed billing cycles. On the professional side, proper timekeeping support can reduce the burden of clerical tasks, improve the quality of reporting, and increase the amount of effective billable hour availability.

This demo paper presents intimebot, a dialogue agent to support professional services timekeeping tasks. The system starts with a brief description of the work to be reported. From there, it interactively guides the user through the process of creating a compliant timecard, including the corresponding narrative following the required guidelines.

2 Related Work

Multiple recommendations and guidelines have been proposed to improve timekeeping practices over time (Henry, 2023; Bill4Time, 2023; Wolf, 2024). Similarly, a myriad of timekeeping solutions and tools are available (Black, 2020; Capterra, 2024; Wikipedia, 2024).

More recently, advancements in generative AI along with the corresponding enablement of agentic frameworks are steering timekeeping automation into a new era of possibilities, specifically for the case of generative AI applications (Trivedi, 2025). Our proposed intimebot demo and experimental framework represents an important incremental effort in that new direction.

3 Problem Statement

The intimebot framework focuses on the creation of a compliant timecard from a brief description of the work done, which is typically a memo entry or personal note provided by the timekeeper in a timely manner.

From such a brief work description, all timecard fields are to be estimated. These are: the client for whom the work is done, the corresponding matter and phase, as well as the estimated amount of worked hours and the narrative. The narrative must be compliant with both firm stylistic and formatting guidelines, as well as to terms of business agreed for the specific client and matter.

The brief description can be provided by means of two different modalities: text or speech.

Proceedings of the 15th International Workshop on Spoken Dialogue Systems Technology, pages 196–199
May 27–30, 2025.

4 System Description

The intimebot system implements an interactive workflow, which integrates different technologies (supervised classification, information retrieval, natural language understanding and generation) along with support data (including matter histories and timekeeper's previous entries), to estimate the complete set of timecard information. Figure 1 depicts the overall workflow of the system.

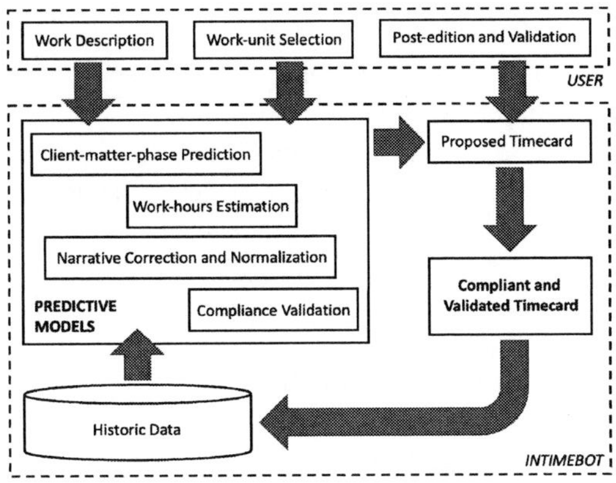

Figure 1: intimebot system components.

The "Predictive Models" block of the diagram in the figure comprises four different components:

Client-matter-phase prediction: for a given timekeeper and work description, it predicts the proper combination of client, matter and phase.

Work hours (effort) estimation: for a given work description, it estimates the expected value and distribution of the corresponding work hours.

Narrative correction and normalization: given the work description, it rewrites it into a proper narrative that follows the firm's formatting and stylistic guidelines.

Compliance validation: this sub-module checks the resulting proposed timecard against contractual commitments for potential compliance issues.

Each of these four components is described in further detail in the following subsections.

4.1 Client-Matter-Phase Prediction

Different firms use matter and phase codes in different ways. In intimebot, we refer to a work-unit as a unique combination of three elements: client, matter, and phase. This work-unit definition will be the contextual unit of analysis for the prediction problem under consideration.

The client-matter-phase prediction problem is approached in intimebot as a binary classification problem. This means that for a given description of work provided by the timekeeper, and the known history of previous work-unit contexts for the same timekeeper, the binary classifier is used to identify the best matching work-unit.

For training the binary classifier, a training data set is gathered across work-units from the historic collection of timecards. Each training data sample consists of a triplet of the form: context-narrative-label. The binary classification system is trained to predict a binary label (1 or 0) depending on whether the narrative matches the context or not.

At inference time the work description provided by the timekeeper is tested against all work-units that timekeeper is working on, and the most probable ones are selected. From the set of all relevant context-description pairs (as many as there are work-units available for the timekeeper under consideration), the model estimates the conditional probabilities of the work-units given the provided description and selects the top candidates, which are then presented to the user.

We have evaluated the client-matter-phase prediction model performance over time against real data, observing a clear need for model updates on a periodic basis to avoid performance degradation. With weekly model updates, the top three work-units selected by the model consistently provided an accuracy of 98% and over.

4.2 Work Effort Estimation

The work description provided by the timekeeper contains useful information for estimating the work effort. The intimebot work effort estimation model is based on the assumption that (1) similar work requires similar effort, and (2) both the length of narratives and the number of worked hours are strongly correlated. Given a work description, the effort is estimated in two steps:

Search: an information retrieval approach is used to retrieve all timecards from the historical data collection with narratives that are similar to the work description provided and rank them by their respective similarity scores.

Inference: using the work efforts of the retrieved timecards and combining that with the similarity scores as weights, a probability distribution of the efforts is computed. This distribution is then used to estimate the minimum, maximum, and average efforts for the given work effort.

In addition to the two-step approach mentioned above, we have explored the use of linear and multi-layer perceptron-based regression methods to predict the work effort. For this, a model needs to be pre-trained on the embedded representation of the historical narratives and their work efforts. At inference time, a given work description is transformed into an embedded vector, which is passed through the model to predict the effort. In the future, this approach can be combined into the intimebot system for effort estimation.

4.3 Narrative Correction and Normalization

In our previous studies we have determined that timecard narrative diversity can be reduced to about 120 basic patterns. These patterns are typically comprised of specific combinations of connectors (functional units from a fixed set of words) and constituents (semantic units with one or more components) that refer to specific entities, properties and/or conditions.

Our current approach to narrative correction is a two-step process. First, we identify the patterns in the input narrative via a combination of rules and vector search. We then use detected patterns and canonical forms of components to rewrite the narrative according to specified standards using LLMs. For this, we use custom prompts that are specific to the identified patterns.

Additional rules, including both grammar and business rules, as well as proprietary formatting and stylistic guidelines, are incorporated as a post-processing step. LLMs and rule-specific prompts are used in this narrative post-edition step.

Examples of grammar rules include applying capitalization and proper usage of punctuation marks. Some of the business rule examples include enforcing verbs to be in past tense, the use of canonical forms for company names and proper formatting for person names.

4.4 Compliance Validation

The compliance validation module uses a hybrid system composed of rules, vector search and LLM-based classifiers to identify potential compliance issues within the generated timecard.

The client and matter information associated to a generated timecard allows for identifying the corresponding terms of business (such as the terms contained in outside counsel guidelines, billing terms, engagement letters, etc.), which should be already indexed and available in consumable form. Some examples of such terms are, for instance, block-billing not being permitted, the definition of specific roles within the organization being able to perform certain tasks, interns not being assigned to research tasks, etc.

Our approach regarding compliance is twofold. We use a rule-based approach to label narratives with common compliance issues. This enables us to rapidly flag violations like certain titles charging time to unpermitted activities. For more complex policy violations or issues specifically tailored to a certain client, we use semantic similarity search with a subsequent LLM-based validation of the potential policy breach.

The more nuanced and client-specific policy breaches are detected by performing semantic similarity search on the narrative against the terms of business repository and asking an LLM-based classifier to validate whether the retrieved potential breaches are actual violations or false alarms.

The vector search can be performed separately for each client and indexed vector database entries can be expanded to use additional metadata, such as combinations of matter, phase, title and work in addition to narratives whenever higher levels of granularity for compliance policies are required.

The hybrid two-tier approach described here provides intimebot with the flexibility to handle common compliance cases rapidly while being adaptable to client-specific needs.

5 User Experience

The user experience of intimebot is designed to be an interactive framework in which the user and the system are able to collaborate, building over time the needed data resources for improving prediction performance, while improving the efficiency and overall experience of the timekeeping process for the user.

The current intimebot user experience is divided in four stages: reporting, selection, validation and submission. All these four stages, which are described next, are illustrated in Figure 2.

Reporting: in this step, the timekeeper enters the brief description of the work conducted. Two input modalities (text and speech) are available.

Selection: after the input is provided, the client-matter-phase prediction model will select the top work-units matching the provided descriptions, for which the timekeeper is required to manually select the correct one.

Validation: after work-unit selection, the effort estimation, narrative correction and normalization, and compliance validation models are used to generate the proposed timecard. At this stage, the timekeeper can revise and edit the timecard.

Submission: after validating the timecard, the timekeeper can submit it, for which the system will provide a submission confirmation message.

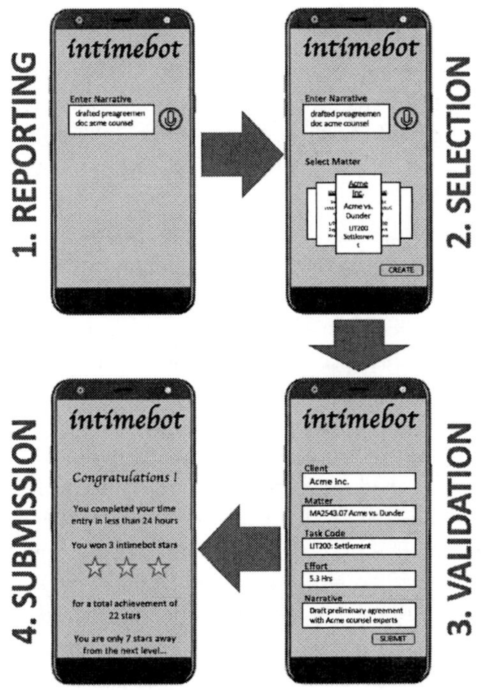

Figure 2: intimebot user experience.

Additionally, the intimebot platform taps on our existent smart-memo feature, integrated via text and/or voice input. Timer functionalities can also be used to prompt the timekeepers for descriptions after, or even before, the timer is activated.

Finally, the framework allows for the implementation and evaluation of gamification ideas to encourage timekeepers to report their time entries as soon as they complete their work.

6 Future Work

The presented intimebot demo system constitutes an experimental framework for showcasing and testing AI and ML capabilities in the timekeeping space. As part of this experimental framework, there are a few novel strategies and features we plan to test. These include:

- Replacing the current work effort estimation model by a better-informed learning-to-rank mechanism able to use adjusted hours inputted by the user to refine the ranking mechanism and similarity metric.
- We have a time capture functionality that collects detailed information on a good proportion of user activities, we can leverage on captured data to improve some of the current models performances.
- There is evidence of code-switching in spoken inputs provided via our smart memo feature (i.e. main description in local language and named entities such as companies and matter names provided in English).
- We need to better understand the value of rewards and explore novel gamification strategies by conducting user studies and other exploratory analyses.
- We plan to develop an evaluation framework for measuring the actual impact of intimebot in timekeeping activities.

Acknowledgments

The authors would like to thank Intapp, and specially the AI & Data unit, for their continuous support and encouragement for experimental and exploratory work like this one.

References

Bill4Time. 2023. A guide to lawyer time tracking. *The National Law Review*.

Nicole Black. 2020. Stay on track with these time-tracking software tools for law firms. *ABA Journal*.

Tom Boster and Scott Brenan. 2024. Why poor timekeeping could be costing your firm (and how to fix it). *Legal Management Magazine*.

Capterra. 2024. Legal timekeeping software.

Justin Henry. 2023. 82% of am law 200 firms enforce weekly or sooner timekeeper deadlines, survey finds. *LAW.com*.

Ayushi Trivedi. 2025. Agentic frameworks for generative ai applications. *Analytics Vidhya*.

Wikipedia. 2024. Comparison of time-tracking software.

Katie Wolf. 2024. Time tracking for lawyers: Methods, tools, and strategies for accurate billing. *Filevine.com online Blog*.

A Chatbot for Providing Suicide Prevention Information in Spanish

Pablo Ascorbe[1], María S. Campos[2], César Domínguez[1], Jónathan Heras[1], Magdalena Pérez[3], Ana Rosa Terroba-Reinares[1,4]
[1]Dpto. de Matemáticas y Computación, Universidad de La Rioja, Spain
[2]Unidad de Salud Mental Espartero, Logroño, La Rioja, Spain
[3]Teléfono de la Esperanza, La Rioja, Spain
[4]Fundación Rioja Salud, La Rioja, Spain
Correspondence: paascorb@unirioja.es

Abstract

Suicide has been identified by the World Health Organization as one of the most serious health problems that can affect people. Among the interventions that have been proposed to support those suffering from this problem and their relatives, the dissemination of accurate information is crucial. To achieve this goal, we have developed prevenIA, a chatbot that provides reliable information on suicide prevention. The chatbot consists of a Retrieval Augmented Module for answering users' queries based on a curated list of documents. In addition, it includes several models to avoid undesirable behaviours. The system has been validated by specialists and is currently being evaluated by different populations. Thanks to this project, reliable information on suicide will be disseminated in an easy and understandable form.

1 Introduction

Suicide is the second leading cause of external factors death in Spain, with 4116 cases in 2023 (Instituto Nacional de Estadística, 2024), and each completed suicide is believed to be accompanied by approximately 20 attempts (WHO, 2021). In addition, it is estimated that at least 6 survivors of the deceased are directly affected by the loss (WHO, 2021). Due to these numbers, the World Health Organisation has urged all member states to prioritise the mitigation of suicides and attempted suicides (WHO, 2021).

In Spain, several suicide prevention plans have been developed in some Autonomous Regions (see, for example, those of the Canary Islands (Servicio Canario de Salud, 2021), Navarre (Gobierno de Navarra, 2014), or La Rioja (Rioja Salud, 2019)). Among the interventions proposed by those plans, we can find measures targeting different audiences (such as general population, health professionals, or media) (Sufrate-Sorzano et al., 2022). In particular, measures aimed at the general public include the establishment of support networks, the implementation of training programs, and the dissemination of accurate information. The latter is highly relevant in a misinformation era (Roth et al., 2020; Banerjee and Rao, 2020).

Chatbots have recently shown their potential to provide information in medical scenarios (Savage, 2023); and, in the context of suicide, they might serve to disseminate crucial information, offer support, and provide a platform for individuals to express their feelings anonymously (Valizadeh and Parde, 2022; Haque and Rubya, 2023; Zhang et al., 2022; Abd-Alrazaq et al., 2021). However, in this context, chatbots should be thoroughly evaluated before releasing them. In this work, we present a tool called prevenIA, that aims at providing suicide prevention information in Spanish, the design choices that have been taken to improve its reliability, and the validation stages that have been conducted before releasing it to the general public.

2 prevenIA chatbot

prevenIA is a chatbot that provides information about suicidal behaviour. In order to provide verified information that is restricted to our application domain, we have relied on a curated corpus of documents and used natural language processing techniques; namely, through Retrieval Augmented Generation (RAG) techniques (Lewis et al., 2020). Moreover, we are conducting a multi-stage validation process to ensure the reliability and safeness of prevenIA — the development and validation workflow is depicted in Figure 1. In next subsection, we describe the architecture of prevenIA, and present the validation stages in the subsection 2.2.

2.1 Development

As starting point of the development depicted in the Figure 1 left, we collected a corpus of more than 150 documents related to suicide prevention

Proceedings of the 15th International Workshop on Spoken Dialogue Systems Technology, pages 200–204
May 27–30, 2025.

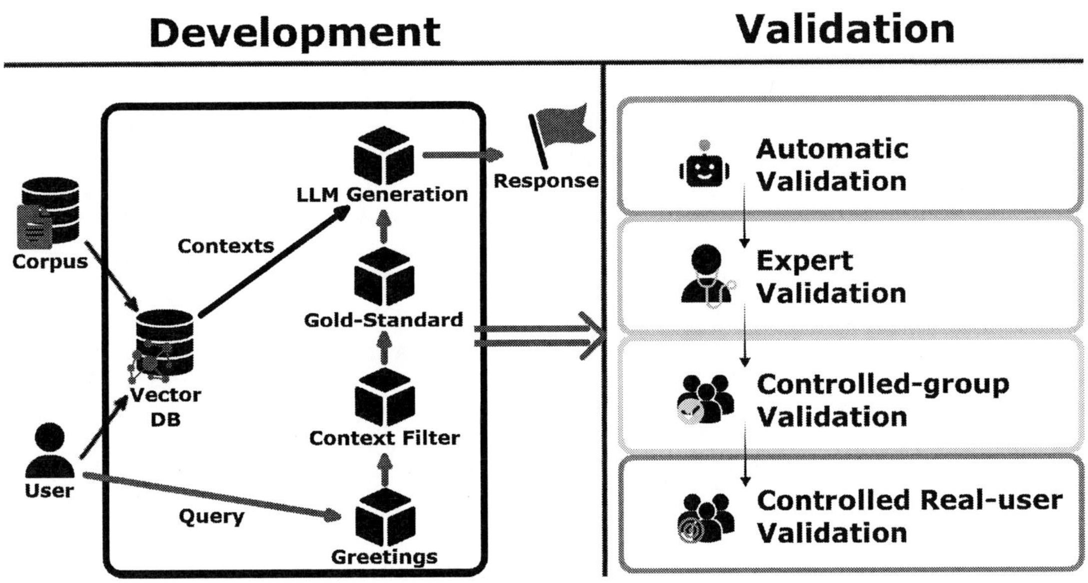

Figure 1: Development (left) and evaluation (right) workflow of prevenIA

whose typology covers: generalities, communication, grieving, prevention plans, mental illness and suicide, clinical interviews among others. All documents were provided, read and classified by experts. From them, we extracted a summary, the source of the document, and a series of properties including authors, number of pages, type of document, etc. Some documents were excluded for containing information that was too technical or even dangerous for people without specific training; containing repeated or very similar information, where the most up-to-date information was selected; or containing only graphics or images. Our final corpus is composed of 123 documents.

The curated corpus has been employed to build a RAG system, where all already selected documents were split into 2048 character chunks and stored as embeddings, using sentence-transformers/paraphrase-multilingual-MiniLM-L12-v2 (Reimers and Gurevych, 2019) as the model, in a vector store called ChromaDB (Huber and Troynikov, 2024). Given a user's query, we compute the cosine distance to find the K contexts closest to the embedding associated with the query. These contexts are provided to an LLM deployed using Ollama to generate the final answer — in our case, we use the aya-expanse model in its 32B version (Dang et al., 2024). Moreover, as it is a chatbot and not a Q&A system, the LLM also receives the complete interaction with the user, where indicates which part belongs to the user and which part to the answers provided by the agent itself.

In addition to the RAG module, several preprocessing stages have been implemented in three layers to avoid undesirable behaviours. First of all, we have defined a layer that determines whether the user's query is a greeting or farewell in order to send a generic message to the user — to that aim, the distances between the embedding associated with the query and those from a set of greetings are computed, and if they are close enough, the query is classified as a greeting. The second layer filters out queries that are not related to the chatbot's context by rejecting those that are distant from the contexts extracted from the corpus. Finally, the last preprocessing layer searches whether the user's query can be answered from a list of Frequently Asked Questions (FAQ) validated by professionals. If the query is in this group, again using the cosine distance, the answer is retrieved from a Gold-Standard database that contains question/answers pairs.

2.2 Validation

We focus now on a key aspect of the development of prevenIA that is a thorough and in-depth evaluation of the system — this is especially relevant in the sensitive context of this project. For this reason, mental health professionals have been involved in the development of prevenIA from the beginning. In addition, we have designed four validation stages depicted in Figure 1 right that can be replicated in similar projects.

This validation process starts from a first phase with a controlled and automatic but less real environment, and advances to a real but less controlled environment requiring people and experts as each phase progresses. It is worth mentioning that as the process advances, it becomes increasingly demanding in terms of resources, especially time.

Model	BertScore	BLEU	Rouge
bertin-gpt-j-6B-alpaca	**0.713**	**0.046**	**0.296**
bloom-1b7	0.641	0.032	0.153
xglm-7.5B	0.629	0.040	0.285
Llama-2-7b-ft-instruct-es	0.658	0.048	0.229
Llama-2-7b-ft-instruct-es-gptq-4bit	0.668	0.049	0.229
lince-mistral-7b-it-es	**0.669**	**0.070**	**0.253**
Mixtral-8x7B-v0.1	0.584	0.082	0.245
Mistral-7B-v0.1	0.646	0.074	0.258
Mixtral-8x7B-Instruct-v0.1	**0.688**	**0.037**	**0.257**
aya-expanse	**0.693**	**0.029**	**0.298**

Table 1: Traditional evaluation of all candidates.

The first validation stage consists of comparing the answers provided by the system with 118 gold standard questions using automatic metrics such as Rouge (Lin, 2004), BLEU (Papineni et al., 2002) and BertScore (BertScore Hugging Face, 2020). This validation stage is cheap and allowed us to select the underlying LLM that has been used by our chatbot. The evaluated models were Bertin (de la Rosa et al., 2022), Llama 2 (Touvron et al., 2023), Lince (Clibrain, 2024), Bloom (Scao et al., 2022), Mixtral (Jiang et al., 2024), and Aya Expanse (Dang et al., 2024). The best candidates were Bertin, Lince, Mixtral, and Aya Expanse, see Table 1.

Since automatic metrics might not align with human preferences (Zheng et al., 2023), the best models according to traditional metrics, as mentioned above Bertin, Lince, Mixtral, and Aya Expanse, were selected for a second evaluation stage conducted by experts (in our case, a psychologist and a psychiatrist). This evaluation was carried out using Argilla (Vila-Suero and Aranda, 2025), which is an open-source data curation platform for LLMs, specialized in creating templates and assessment environments to evaluate the responses of human annotators. Using this tool, with the set of 118 gold standard questions, the answers given by each LLM were evaluated by the experts randomly taking into account whether there is not excess or lack of information; and whether the answer is useful and clear — a scale from 1 to 5 was used. In addition, it was also evaluated whether the answer provided by the LLM was safe, and experts also have the option to provide additional comments (Ascorbe et al., 2024). From that study, it was concluded that the best overall model was Aya Expanse.

The next validation phase is a controlled evaluation conducted by people from several backgrounds. In the previous phases, although carried out by experts, there were only 2 members. This phase is intended to allow multiple different profiles and more than 30 participants to give an assessment and approach that the experts in the previous phases may have missed, as well as allowing us to make robust statistics. We have defined 5 roles (Computer scientists, Non-mental healthcare professionals, Mental healthcare professionals, volunteers of the Suicide hot-line in Spain, and others) and collected interactions from at least 30 people of each role. In this phase, the participants must ask between 5 and 10 questions to prevenIA and, subsequently, fill in an evaluation form that contains elements similar to the evaluation carried out by the experts in the previous phase using a scale from 1 to 5. The specific questions were: whether the chatbot had responded with useful and error-free information; without providing irrelevant or unnecessary information; in a complete manner, offering the necessary details; with safe information (not harmful to the user, without reinforcing stereotypes or misinforming); with useful information; with clear information; in a reasonable time; in a reliable manner, i.e., whether you think its answers can be trusted. This stage is currently in development. To perform this validation, an interface was developed using Gradio (Abid et al., 2019), as shown in Figure 2. The results and analysis of this phase are still in progress, so is it not yet possible to show results.

The last phase, which is planned but there are still many steps to be taken, consists of looking for real users of the application, such as family members who may have suffered from the problem or other interested parties to interact with the application and evaluate this interaction. Obviously, these users will be volunteers and the evaluation will be completely controlled. If after passing all these stages and validating that the application is fully prepared, it will be when the application could finally be deployed to the general public with continuous monitoring to ensure that it is correctly working.

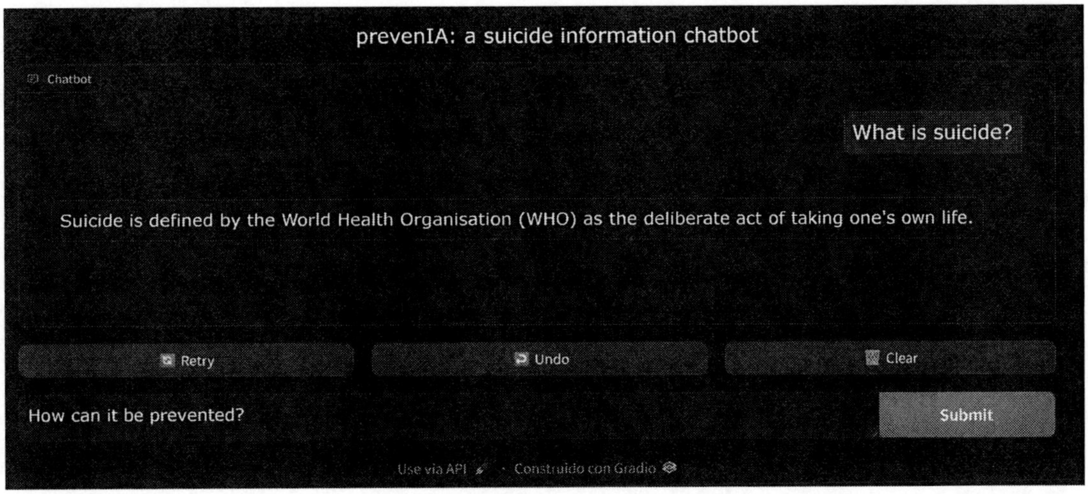

Figure 2: Gradio interface for prevenIA

3 Conclusions and further work

In this work, we have presented prevenIA, a chatbot that provides reliable information for the prevention of suicide. In order to ensure the reliability and safeness of prevenIA, a multi-layer architecture based on RAG has been designed; and the outputs produced by the system has been validated using a multi-stage process. Currently, we are in the last but one validation stage where the system is evaluated using several controlled groups.

After the thorough validation is finished, the main task that remains as a further work is the deployment of prevenIA for its general use. This will pose new challenges, as continuous monitoring of the application will be necessary to ensure that it works properly and provides helpful answers. In addition, we plan to extend the chatbot to other mental disorders such as eating disorders to provide information that helps people suffering from these conditions and their families.

Acknowledgments

This work was partially supported by Grant PID2020-115225RB-I00 funded by MCIN/AEI/ 10.13039/501100011033, by project AFIANZA 2024/01 granted by the Autonomous Community of La Rioja, and by funds for the 2023 strategies of the Spanish Ministry of Health, which were approved in the CISNS on June 23, 2023, to support the implementation of the Mental Health Action Plan.

References

Alaa A. Abd-Alrazaq, Mohannad Alajlani, Nashva Ali, Kerstin Denecke, Bridgette M. Bewick, and Mowafa Househ. 2021. Perceptions and opinions of patients about mental health chatbots: scoping review. *Journal of medical Internet research*, 23(1):e17828.

Abubakar Abid, Ali Abdall, Ali Abid, Dawood Khan, Abdulrahman Alfozan, and James Zou. 2019. Gradio: Hassle-free sharing and testing of ml models in the wild. *arXiv preprint arXiv:1906.02569*.

Pablo Ascorbe, María S. Campos, César Domínguez, Jónathan Heras, Magdalena Pérez, and Ana Rosa Terroba Reinares. 2024. Automatic and manual evaluation of a spanish suicide information chatbot. *Proces. del Leng. Natural*, 73:151–164.

Debanjan Banerjee and T.S. Sathyanarayana Rao. 2020. Psychology of misinformation and the media: Insights from the covid-19 pandemic. *Indian Journal of Social Psychiatry*, 36(Suppl 1):S131–S137.

BertScore Hugging Face. 2020. Bert score - a hugging face space by evaluate-metric.

Clibrain. 2024. Lince mistral 7b instruct.

John Dang, Shivalika Singh, Daniel D'souza, et al. 2024. Aya expanse: Combining research breakthroughs for a new multilingual frontier. *arXiv:2412.04261*.

Javier de la Rosa, Eduardo G. Ponferrada, Paulo Villegas, Pablo Gonzalez de Prado Salas, Manu Romero, and Marıa Grandury. 2022. Bertin: Efficient pre-training of a spanish language model using perplexity sampling. *arXiv:2207.06814*.

Gobierno de Navarra. 2014. Prevención y actuación ante conductas suicidas.

M.D. Romael Haque and Sabirat Rubya. 2023. An overview of chatbot-based mobile mental health apps:

insights from app description and user reviews. *JMIR mHealth and uHealth*, 11(1):e44838.

Jeff Huber and Anton Troynikov. 2024. Chroma - the open-source embedding database.

Instituto Nacional de Estadística. 2024. Defunciones según la causa de muerte año 2023. Technical report, Instituto Nacional de Estadística.

Albert Q. Jiang, Alexandre Sablayrolles, Antoine Roux, et al. 2024. Mixtral of experts. *arXiv:2401.04088.*

Patrick Lewis, Ethan Perez, Aleksandra Piktus, et al. 2020. Retrieval-augmented generation for knowledge-intensive nlp tasks. *arXiv:2005.11401.*

Chin-Yew Lin. 2004. ROUGE: A package for automatic evaluation of summaries. In *Text Summarization Branches Out*, pages 74–81, Barcelona, Spain. Association for Computational Linguistics.

Kishore Papineni, Salim Roukos, Todd Ward, and Wei jing Zhu. 2002. Bleu: a method for automatic evaluation of machine translation. pages 311–318.

Nils Reimers and Iryna Gurevych. 2019. Sentence-bert: Sentence embeddings using siamese bert-networks. In *Proceedings of the 2019 Conference on Empirical Methods in Natural Language Processing*. Association for Computational Linguistics.

Rioja Salud. 2019. Plan de prevención del suicidio en La Rioja.

Rebecca Roth, Jaclyn Abraham, Heidi Zinzow, Pamela Wisniewski, Amro Khasawneh, and Kapil Chalil Madathil. 2020. Evaluating news media reports on the 'blue whale challenge' for adherence to suicide prevention safe messaging guidelines. *Proceedings of the ACM on Human-Computer Interaction*, 4(CSCW1):1–27.

Neil Savage. 2023. The rise of the chatbots. *Communications of the ACM*, 66(7):16–17.

BigScience Workshop: Teven Le Scao, Angela Fan, Christopher Akiki, et al. 2022. Bloom: A 176b-parameter open-access multilingual language model. *arXiv:2211.05100.*

Servicio Canario de Salud. 2021. Programa de prevención de la conducta suicida en Canarias.

Teresa Sufrate-Sorzano, Elena Jiménez-Ramón, María Elena Garrote-Cámara, et al. 2022. Health plans for suicide prevention in Spain: a descriptive analysis of the published documents. *Nursing Reports*, 12(1):77–89.

Hugo Touvron, Louis Martin, Kevin Stone, et al. 2023. Llama 2: Open foundation and fine-tuned chat models. *arXiv:2307.09288.*

Mina Valizadeh and Natalie Parde. 2022. The AI doctor is in: A survey of task-oriented dialogue systems for healthcare applications. In *Proceedings of the 60th Annual Meeting of the Association for Computational Linguistics (Volume 1: Long Papers)*, pages 6638–6660.

Daniel Vila-Suero and Francisco Aranda. 2025. Argilla - open-source framework for data-centric nlp.

WHO. 2021. Suicide worldwide in 2019: global health estimates.

Tianlin Zhang, Annika M Schoene, Shaoxiong Ji, and Sophia Ananiadou. 2022. Natural language processing applied to mental illness detection: a narrative review. *NPJ digital medicine*, 5(1):46.

Lianmin Zheng, Wei-Lin Chiang, Ying Sheng, et al. 2023. Judging llm-as-a-judge with mt-bench and chatbot arena. *Advances in Neural Information Processing Systems*, 36:46595–46623.

LAMIA: An LLM Approach for Task-Oriented Dialogue Systems in Industry 5.0

Cristina Fernández, Izaskun Fernández, Cristina Aceta

TEKNIKER, Basque Research and Technology Alliance (BRTA),
C/ Iñaki Goenaga 5, 20600 Eibar, Spain
Correspondence: cristina.fernandez@tekniker.es

Abstract

Human-Machine Interaction (HMI) plays an important role in Industry 5.0, improving worker well-being by automating repetitive tasks and enhancing seamless collaboration between humans and intelligent systems. In this context, Task-Oriented Dialogue (TOD) systems are a commonly used approach to enable natural communication in these settings, traditionally developed using rule-based approaches. However, the revolution of Large Language Models (LLMs) is changing how dialogue systems are being developed without the necessity of relying on tedious and rigid handcrafted rules. Despite their popularity, their application in industrial contexts remains underexplored, necessitating a solution to challenges such as hallucinations, lack of domain-specific data, high training costs, and limited adaptability. In order to explore the contribution of LLMs in the industry field, this work presents LAMIA, a task-oriented dialogue system for industrial scenarios that leverages LLMs through prompt tuning. This system has been adapted and evaluated for a bin-picking use case, using GPT-3.5 Turbo, showing to be an intuitive method for new use cases in Industry 5.0.

1 Introduction

Industry 5.0 focuses on human workers and their well-being at the centre of the productive process. In this context, Human-Machine Interaction (HMI) interfaces are an important asset that allow communication between humans and machines (Pizoń and Gola, 2023). This simpler way of interaction, by allowing, for example, the automation of repetitive tasks, improves task efficiency and user experience (Sharma et al., 2023), and allows workers to focus on more creative tasks (Rane, 2023). In this setting, Large Language Models (LLMs) have emerged as powerful tools, enabling more intuitive interactions via applications like virtual assistants and conversational agents, making technology more accessible to a wider audience.

LLMs have significant potential in Industry 5.0, particularly through their role in Task-Oriented Dialogue (TOD) systems, which enable a natural HMI aimed at facilitating problem-solving tasks within specific domains (Ni et al., 2023). However, the use of LLMs in industrial scenarios is not as widespread as in other fields, as these models still face challenges, relevant in those scenarios that admit little or no margin of error, such as production processes. These limitations are hallucinations[1], lack of domain-specific data, and the difficulty and high costs associated with training for new applications.

To address these limitations, this article explores the contribution and role of LLMs in the development of TOD systems in industrial environments. To do this, the use of prompt tuning is explored, as it allows models to be adapted using strategies such as few-shot learning or step-by-step thinking (Ye et al., 2023; Microsoft, 2024) by teaching the model how to behave with prompts in natural language.

The research has led to the development of LAMIA (Large lAnguage Models for Industrial Assistance), a TOD system designed for industrial environments. Optimized via prompt tuning, LAMIA reduces hallucinations and the need for large amounts of data, enhances adaptability, and mitigates high computational costs. Having been implemented with the LLM GPT-3.5 Turbo, LAMIA presents a cost-effective solution for seamless human-machine interaction in Industry 5.0.

[1]Hallucinations in LLMs occur when the model "produces outputs that deviate from users' intent, exhibit internal inconsistencies, or misalign with the factual knowledge, making the deployment of LLMs potentially risky in a wide range of applications" (Liu et al., 2024).

Proceedings of the 15th International Workshop on Spoken Dialogue Systems Technology, pages 205–214
May 27–30, 2025. ©2025 Association for Computational Linguistics

2 Related work

2.1 Task-Oriented Dialogue Systems

Task-Oriented Dialogue (TOD) systems are designed for task completion in specific domains, such as ticket booking or table reservation, unlike open-domain systems, which are used for casual conversation (Ni et al., 2023). In Industry 5.0, TOD systems play a key role in Human-Machine Interaction (HMI), automating simple tasks to reduce the cognitive load on operators through natural language communication (Aceta et al., 2022).

According to the designs used for the development of TOD systems, pipelines typically follow either a modular approach or an end-to-end approach. The modular approach consists of separate components for Natural Language Understanding (NLU), Dialogue State Tracking (DST), Dialogue Policy Learning (DP), and Natural Language Generation (NLG) (Li et al., 2021). In contrast, the end-to-end approach, introduced by Wen et al. (2016), creates a trainable end-to-end model that still connects in a modularized way, but does not directly modularize the user goal.

Over the years, the main strategies used to develop these systems were rule-based methods or the use of annotated data (Sekulić et al., 2024). However, both present challenges in Industry 5.0, as rule-based methods require extensive manual adaptation, while data-driven approaches suffer from a lack of domain-specific data in industrial settings (Li et al., 2022) and high computational demands.

2.1.1 Large Language Models in TOD Systems

The state-of-the-art technology that has emerged as a useful tool for a wide variety of applications in the NLP field is Large Language Models (LLMs). LLMs are advanced AI models, often based on Transformer architectures, that can understand and generate human language by being trained on vast amounts of text data (Ozdemir, 2023).

In TOD systems, various LLMs have been employed, such as Tk-Instruct-11B, Alpaca-LoRa-7B, BART and GPT-3.5 (Hudeček and Dusek, 2023; Marselino Andreas et al., 2022; Li et al., 2022; Hu et al., 2024). Fine-tuning methods such as LoRA (Low Rank Adaptation) have been widely used to adapt these models by modifying only a few parameters for specific tasks (Marselino Andreas et al., 2022; Li et al., 2022). Reinforcement Learning from Human Feedback (RLHF) has also shown effectiveness in tuning models based on human input (Ouyang et al., 2022). However, both approaches are data-driven and memory-intensive, requiring significant computational and data resources for training, as gradients and optimizer states for all parameters must be stored (Liu et al., 2022).

2.2 Prompt Tuning

To address the challenges of rule-based methods and the scarcity of annotated data, the LLM prompt tuning strategy has gained popularity. Authors like Cao (2023); Hudeček and Dusek (2023) have applied this approach in TOD systems, which avoids retraining by freezing model parameters and using natural language prompts for adaptability (Liu et al., 2022).

Prompt tuning has demonstrated performance comparable to fine-tuning for large models in simple tasks (Liu et al., 2022; Lester et al., 2021; Kim et al., 2021; Liu et al., 2021), and has outperformed in cross-lingual tasks (Zhao and Schütze, 2021). Furthermore, Addlesee (2024) highlights that prompt tuning improves textual grounding and accuracy, reducing hallucinations in models.

Achieving optimal results with prompt tuning requires effective *prompt engineering* (Zhao and Schütze, 2021), which involves crafting prompts to communicate tasks clearly and iterating based on model responses (Ye et al., 2023). In this line, various strategies have been suggested, such as think step by step, few-shot learning, chain of thought, and in-context learning, among others, to improve performance (Microsoft, 2024).

2.2.1 Prompt Tuning in TOD Systems

Some studies have explored optimizing LLMs TOD systems using prompt tuning. Hudeček and Dusek (2023) developed a modular TOD system, finding that while LLMs excelled in tasks such as domain detection and response generation, they struggle with state-tracking. Similarly, Cao (2023) created DiagGPT, a multi-agent TOD system with strong conversational abilities but less stability than rule-based models. Gupta et al. (2022) introduced InstructDial, which outperformed the base models in unseen dialogue tasks.

The results depended on prompt complexity, with detailed instructions and in-context examples often enhancing performance (Hudeček and Dusek, 2023; Gupta et al., 2022). In terms of the pipeline used, the most popular approach is a modular system in which different dialogue tasks are

Dialogue turn	User message	Agent response	External database
1st turn	"Pon los magenta" / *"Put the magenta ones"*	"¿Cuál es la caja en la que debes colocar el cartucho de tinta magenta?" / *"Which box should I put the magenta ink cartridge in?"*	{_id: Object {...}, element_cartridge: "magenta", type: "color"}
2nd turn	"Caja 1" / *"Box 1"*	"¿Quieres colocar el cartucho de tinta magenta en la caja 1?" / *"Do you want to place the magenta ink cartridge in box 1?"*	{_id: Object {...}, element: "1", type: "box"}
3rd turn	"Sí" / *"Yes"*	"¡Entendido! Comienzo a trabajar en eso de inmediato. Estoy aquí para ayudarte en lo que necesites." / *"I understand! I'll start working on it right away. I'm here to help you with whatever you need."*	

Table 1: Example of human-machine dialogue of LAMIA in a bin-picking robot.

handled sequentially (Hudeček and Dusek, 2023; Cao, 2023).

All in all, these studies using prompt tuning for TOD systems have not been applied to industrial applications. For this reason, this research focuses on exploring the role of LLMs in TOD systems for industry, using prompt tuning for adaptable systems with low computational costs, minimal data requirements, and reduced hallucinations, crucial for manufacturing environments.

3 Approach and implementation

To address the challenges in building TOD systems for Industry 5.0, we have developed LAMIA, a TOD system for industry implemented through prompt tuning. Among its capabilities, LAMIA allows operators to maintain natural language conversations and send the final task to the target system.

The research was conducted at Tekniker, a technology research centre in the Basque Country, where we had access to KIDE4I (Aceta et al., 2022). KIDE4I is a rule-based TOD system for Industry 5.0 composed of four modules (Key Element Extraction, Polarity Interpreter, Semantic Repository and Dialogue Manager) which rely on syntactic and morphological parsers, and ontologies for storing domain knowledge and managing the dialogue process. More specifically, its use case of a bin-picking robot and its evaluation framework served as our reference to assess the performance of LAMIA in a real-world scenario.

3.1 Dialogue structure for LAMIA's bin-picking use case

In the bin-picking robot use case in Aceta et al. (2022), the robot handles ink cartridges, identifying their colour or brand, and sorts them into two containers based on operator instructions. For that goal, the dialogue system supports multi-turn interactions in Spanish, and it is capable of receiving instructions in natural language, asking clarifying questions, and sending structured information to the target robot to execute actions, such as relocation. Communication includes both voice commands and gestures —which have to be accompanied by an adverb of place or a demonstrative pronoun, also known as *pointers*—. The system uses predefined world knowledge, including cartridge colours, brands, and container identifiers. Table 1 shows an example dialogue from LAMIA. In addition, Example 1 illustrates the structured output sent to the robot.

Example 1: Dialogue system's structured output.

- {"task": {"amount": 0, "pointer": 0, "action": "PICKING", "destination": "1", "colour": "magenta", "trademark": ""}}

3.2 TOD system design

LAMIA's pipeline has been built iteratively to optimize performance and adaptability. In other words, its creation was based on various rounds to determine which strategies worked best. As seen in Section 2.1, there are currently two strategies applicable to the implementation of TOD systems: *end-to-end* and *modular*. Therefore, for the construction of LAMIA, both approaches have been explored to obtain the final pipeline with the best performance.

3.2.1 End-to-end strategy

In an initial approach, we attempted to build an end-to-end system using a single call to GPT-3.5 Turbo. The goal was to create a prompt that instructed the LLM to handle multiple tasks: understanding user input, detecting key elements (colours, brands, and box numbers), verifying real-world knowledge, retrieving elements from prior interactions, generating natural language responses, and creating a JSON output for the target robot.

For doing this, we used prompt techniques, such as clear instructions, context, and few-shot learning, providing detailed task descriptions and example outputs. However, the prompt was too complex, causing the LLM to miss some instructions and produce hallucinations after several tests. These limitations have previously been demonstrated (Lester et al., 2021; Kim et al., 2021; Liu et al., 2021), showing that prompt tuning performs better on simple tasks. Specifically, the JSON output was frequently incorrect, with inconsistent keys and values, leading to errors in the robot's task execution. Due to these issues, this approach was discarded, as the LLM's hallucinations posed too much risk for a reliable performance.

3.2.2 LAMIA's design: A modular strategy

After identifying the limitations of the end-to-end approach, we explored the modular pipeline, which breaks down tasks into simpler components. Based on the pipelines of Ni et al. (2023) and Aceta et al. (2022), LAMIA's architecture is composed of seven modules that perform different NLP tasks that work sequentially (see Figure 1). After a few tests, the same as those conducted to discard the end-to-end approach, it was observed that only those modules handling natural language input or output benefit from LLMs, as they performed poorly with JSON-based tasks. Thus, LAMIA's modules are the following:

1. **Polarity Interpreter**: Performs two tasks: content detection and polarity detection. The first detects whether the input has semantic content or is just an affirmation/negation. Its output conditions the pipeline that the input will follow, as depicted in Figure 1. The second task, polarity detection, classifies the input without semantic content as positive or negative. Both tasks imply a call to the LLM with an instruction prompt.

2. **Natural Language Understanding / Key Element Extraction (NLU)**: Extracts the key elements (e.g., cartridge type, box) from the inputs with semantic content, using an LLM.

3. **Database Query**: Verifies the extracted values against the database (in this case, MongoDB). This module does not use an LLM.

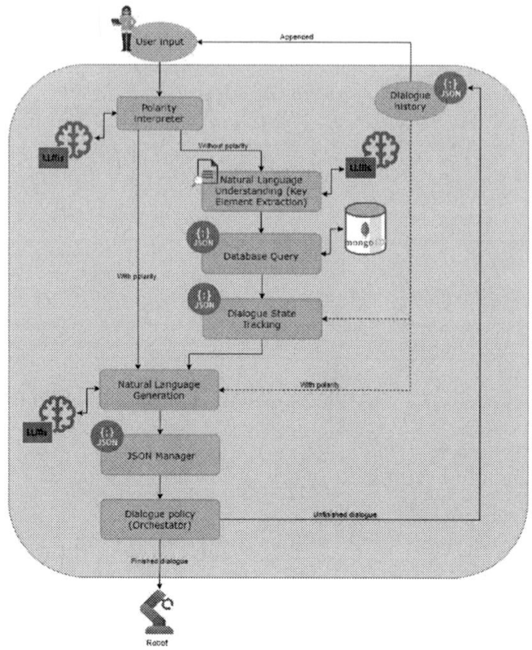

Figure 1: LAMIA's pipeline.

4. **Dialogue State Tracking (DST)**: Compares current and previous interactions to track the dialogue status. This module also does not require an LLM.

5. **Natural Language Generation (NLG)**: Converts actions into the corresponding natural language response, using an LLM.

6. **JSON Manager**: Converts the instruction into the final format required by the robot, without using an LLM.

7. **Dialogue Policy / Orchestrator**: Manages actions based on interactions, keeping or discarding the JSON history as needed. Without an LLM.

This modular approach proved to be more effective than the end-to-end strategy as, being simpler tasks, it avoided errors in JSON structures and ensured that each task was completed successfully. This final pipeline was used to build LAMIA.

3.3 LAMIA's implementation

For the construction of the pipeline and its components, an iterative implementation approach has also been followed. Consequently, in this section, we will introduce the selected LLM, the definitive prompt strategies, and tools that were utilized, including different libraries, the database, etc.

3.3.1 Selected Large Language Model

The implementation of LAMIA's modules has been made using the LLM GPT-3.5 Turbo, a proprietary model. Developed by OpenAI, GPT-3.5 Turbo is acclaimed for its customization capabilities and strong performance (Peng et al., 2023). The different models and versions of GPT have previously been used for optimization in TOD systems by authors such as Marselino Andreas et al. (2022); Cao (2023) with good performance. We deployed it using Azure OpenAI Studio[2].

3.3.2 Prompt strategies

The LAMIA system uses prompt tuning to adapt LLMs for specific tasks, allowing easier modification and lower computational costs since retraining is unnecessary. As discussed in Section 2.2, the effectiveness of LLM is highly dependent on iterative prompt design, clear strategies, and avoiding ambiguities.

Through various tests, the most effective strategies were the following:

- Few-shot learning: This strategy is based on giving examples of the output. An example of its use is present in the prompt for the NLG module which contains "For example: 'Which ink cartridge do you prefer, black or yellow?', 'I didn't understand you, tell me what the task is'", etc.

- Specifying output structure: Mainly used in those modules that required a structured output, such as JSON —i.e., Polarity Interpreter and NLU. For example, the NLU prompt included: "Output must be in JSON format: 'element cartridge': ", 'element box': ", 'element pointer': ''".

- Providing context: To indicate its function and the type of input the LLM will receive, the three LLM-based modules contained this strategy. For example, the prompt for the NLG included: "Context: You are a virtual assistant programmed to start every interaction by asking the user to specify exactly what he/she wants to do".

- Clear and repeated instructions: The use of instructions with minimal ambiguities as possible, and their reiteration at the end. For example, in the use of clear instructions, the NLU prompt included at the beginning: "Your task is to analyse the input provided by the user to identify and extract specific information related to cartridges (e.g., colour or brand), boxes (e.g., location in number) or pointers (e.g., adverb of place or demonstrative pronoun) [. . .]". Regarding repeated instructions, the NLG module prompt reinforced the idea of "return only the question" at the end after being already mentioned.

- Using syntax in prompts: All prompts used phrases that indicate the information that the LLM had to follow. Some examples are: "Context:", "For example:", "User message:", etc.

In addition, a temperature setting of 0 was used to ensure minimal randomness and high control in the outputs, making the system suitable for industrial use with limited variety of responses but reliable task completion.

3.3.3 Selected tools

To implement LAMIA's modules that are composed by an LLM call (Polarity Interpreter, NLU and NLG), we have used the Langchain[3] library. This library has allowed us to initialize the LLMs APIs, create chains to concatenate inputs and outputs, and format the prompts. Furthermore, this library has also been used in the Database Query module to connect the system with the MongoDB database.

4 Evaluation

To evaluate LAMIA, we utilized the KIDE4I's evaluation framework from Aceta et al. (2022). The LAMIA system has been evaluated by comparing its performance with the KIDE4I standard to assess whether LAMIA offers improvements over traditional rule-based systems.

The evaluations consist of two key components:

- Dialogue: This aspect takes into account the dialogue as a whole by assessing three aspects:

[2]https://oai.azure.com/portal

[3]https://www.langchain.com/

- Dialogue completion rate: Whether the dialogue has been *fully completed*, *partially completed* —the user had to rephrase the instruction— or *not completed*.
- Dialogue completion steps: Number of turns it took to complete the dialogue.
- Error analysis: Cases where the dialogue has not been completed due to a specific error.

• Interaction: This measures the system's response time for each interaction.

Furthermore, LAMIA LLM-based modules (NLU, Polarity Interpreter, and NLG) have also been evaluated against the corresponding modules in KIDE4I. The modules of both systems feature similar functionalities. The NLU module in LAMIA aligns with KIDE4I's Key Element Extraction (KEE) module, and both incorporate a Polarity Interpreter module. However, the NLG module in LAMIA, which is responsible for text generation, does not have a direct counterpart in KIDE4I, but this module has also been analysed, as it is developed with an LLM. LAMIA's adaptability and economic costs have also been assessed.

To follow these evaluations, we have used the same dialogue battery used to assess the KIDE4I system in Aceta et al. (2022)'s work, composed of 75 dialogues.

4.1 LAMIA vs KIDE4I results

For the LAMIA assessment, we compared its performance with the rule-based system KIDE4I (Aceta et al., 2022). In addition, LAMIA modules developed with LLMs have also been examined to evaluate the actual performance of their use in these systems.

4.1.1 General comparison

Focusing on the evaluation of the whole system, both systems had similar dialogue completion rates, but LAMIA performed better in partially completed and uncompleted dialogues, with fewer uncompleted cases (see Table 2). Moreover, both showed similar performance in terms of the number of steps needed to complete dialogues, with LAMIA having a slightly lower average and maximum number of steps (see Table 3).

KIDE4I showed better response times overall, with an average response time of 0.74 seconds vs LAMIA's 1.26 seconds (see Table 4). More specifically, LAMIA's response time is influenced by the complexity of LLM calls, which are not present in a rule-based system like KIDE4I. In Table 5, it can be seen that LLM-based modules require more time to respond. However, the average response time of LAMIA is comparable to other use case of KIDE4I (KIDE4Guide) with 1.25 s. For this case, Aceta et al. (2022) affirm that it is still a fast time, which does not affect the user experience negatively.

	LAMIA		KIDE4I	
	%	#	%	#
Fully completed	90.66	68	82.66	62
Partially completed	6.66	5	0	0
Not completed	2.66	2	17.33	13
Total dialogues	75		75	

Table 2: Dialogue completion rate for LAMIA and KIDE4I, with their percentages (%) and absolute numbers (#).

	LAMIA	KIDE4I
Average	2.4109	2.5947
Max	5	6
Min	2	2

Table 3: Average, maximum, and minimum dialogue completion steps in LAMIA and KIDE4I.

A further level of assessment is necessary to analyse the errors that have led to the dialogues in both systems being uncompleted or partially completed. The errors reported in the LAMIA system are two:

- Lack of synonymous key elements in the database.
- Bad element detection by the NLU in one case, which resulted in a partially completed dialogue.

Concerning KIDE4I's errors, we have to consider that the modules of this system are not the same as the ones in LAMIA, but they are comparable. The errors reported by Aceta et al. (2022) are as follows:

[4]The Dialogue Policy time is not represented, since it acts as an orchestrator and its response time is the same as the total interaction time.

	LAMIA	KIDE4I
Average	1.2615 s	0.7493 s
Max	1.9504 s	5.3110 s
Min	0.6885 s	0.1100 s

Table 4: Average, maximum, and minimum response time in LAMIA and KIDE4I.

	Average	Max	Min
Polarity Interpreter	0.3843 s	0.612 s	0.1954 s
NLU	0.5231 s	0.74 s	0.3341 s
Database Query	0.043 s	0.078 s	0.0416 s
DST	0.0007 s	0.0012 s	0.0005 s
NLG	0.6337 s	1.0979 s	0.4607 s
JSON Manager	0.0008 s	0.0005 s	0.0015 s

Table 5: Average, maximum, and minimum response time per module in LAMIA.[4]

- Erroneous analysis of structures or lemmas in the syntactic analysis.
- Out-of-scope structures in the definitions and/or rules.

In summary, LAMIA showed better performance in terms of dialogue completion, with fewer uncompleted dialogues compared to KIDE4I. Although KIDE4I had faster response times, LAMIA still allowed for fluent conversations, despite the longer LLM processing times.

4.1.2 Modular comparison

To complete the evaluation of the contribution of LLMs in LAMIA, we analysed the performance of key modules —NLU, Polarity Interpreter, and NLG— by comparing them with their counterparts in the rule-based KIDE4I system, where applicable. For those tasks that are not comparable with any KIDE4I's component, such as Polarity Interpreter content detection or the NLG, we have also extracted their ratios without making a comparison.

The Polarity Interpreter in both systems showed similar performance in classifying polarity, with no errors in LAMIA and only one out-of-scope error in KIDE4I (see Table 6). For content detection, LAMIA performed almost perfectly, with only one classification error due to a misspelled word (see Table 7).

LAMIA's NLU module outperformed KIDE4I's KEE module, with a higher rate of fully detected

	LAMIA (PI-Polarity Interpreter)		KIDE4I (PI)	
	%	#	%	#
Good classification	100	77	98.73	78
Wrong classification	0	0	0	0
Out-of-scope errors	-	-	1.26	1
Total	77		79	

Table 6: Polarity Interpreter (polarity classifier task) performance in LAMIA and KIDE4I with the percentages (%) and absolute numbers (#).

	LAMIA (PI-Content classifier)	
	%	#
Good classification	99.48	195
Wrong classification	0	0
Out-of-scope errors	0.51	1
Total	196	

Table 7: Polarity Interpreter (content classifier task) performance in LAMIA with the percentages (%) and absolute numbers (#).

elements (96.63% vs 64.66%) and fewer partial —not all the elements of the input were detected— or wrong/null detections (see Table 8). This improvement minimized confusion and reduced the number of dialogue turns required.

The NLG module in LAMIA participated a total of 196 times. We analysed these responses by categorizing them into well- and wrong-generated responses. This assessment ensured that the interaction was appropriate to the dialogue's state, contained accurate key elements, and adhered to grammatical norms. The results revealed that 100% of the responses were well generated, without errors and hallucinations in the use of key elements and suitable for the dialogue states.

Overall, the modular analysis showed that the Polarity Interpreter performed equally well in both systems. However, LAMIA, using GPT-3.5 Turbo, significantly outperformed KIDE4I in NLU, with better key element detection and fewer errors. Additionally, the NLG module in LAMIA performed flawlessly, showing the capabilities of LLMs when generating natural language responses.

	LAMIA (NLU)		KIDE4I (NLU)	
	%	#	%	#
Fully detected	96.63	115	64.66	86
Partially detected	1.68	2	17.29	23
Wrong/null detection	0.84	1	12.78	17
Out-of-scope errors	0.84	1	5.26	7
Total	119		133	

Table 8: NLU performance in LAMIA and KIDE4I with the percentages (%) and absolute numbers (#).

4.1.3 Other evaluated aspects

Other aspects to take into account when evaluating this kind of system for Industry 5.0 are the applicability of the pipeline and its cost to new use cases. The target system must be functional in different industrial use cases and easy to build to reduce costs and development time. The following are the changes that should be made to adapt the system to a new use case:

- Create new records in the database or connect the system to an existing one.
- Change of dictionary names within the pipeline.
- Slight prompt changes to adapt to the new task.

Another key consideration is the cost of using LLMs. In this work, LAMIA was deployed using GPT-3.5 Turbo, a proprietary model whose use requires payment. The infrastructure utilized to deploy this model has been Azure OpenAI Studio, which operates on a pay-as-you-go pricing model. The specific setup used in this work —GPT-3.5-Turbo-0613 with a 16k context window— costs €0.0015 per 1000 input tokens and €0.0019 per 1000 output tokens (in Central Sweden). As an example of the total cost, the reproduction of the dialogues used to assess LAMIA with this setup had a total cost of €0.85, which is not high, considering that they were 75 dialogues with an average of 2.41 interactions (enough to complete the target tasks). Although not free, it offers good performance without being expensive, making it a viable option in real-world manufacturing contexts. However, companies must evaluate whether these costs are justified based on their production needs and expected gains in productivity.

5 Conclusions

This study offers new insights into the application of Large Language Models (LLMs) in the development of applications for Industry 5.0. The research is focused on exploring the contribution of these models in applications for Human-Machine Interaction (HMI) such as Task-Oriented Dialogue (TOD) systems. With this objective, this article presents LAMIA, a prompt-optimized LLM-based TOD system for Industry 5.0. This system also searches for solving the most criticized limitations present in traditional and LLM-based applications, such as difficult adaptability to new use cases and domains due to handcrafted rules, LLMs' hallucinations, lack of domain-specific data, and the difficulty and high costs associated with re-training these models for new use cases and domains.

For this, LAMIA leverages prompt tuning strategies, which have shown significant advantages in intuitive development, adaptability to new domains, and use cases with low computational costs. In addition, the system has performed better than traditional systems, demonstrating that it is efficient for use in a real industrial setting by being able to complete the task and maintain a smooth dialogue.

Moreover, this study also reveals the specific contribution of LLMs and the prompt tuning strategy in this kind of system. The end-to-end approach test showed that prompt tuning does not perform as well with complex tasks or several tasks at once, as already demonstrated by Liu et al. (2022), which is the reason for using a modular pipeline. However, preliminary experiments in these modules also showed that the effectiveness of LLM varies by task, performing almost perfect for NLP tasks, such as generation, classification, or slot filling, and not being the most suitable option for those that manage structured formats. Therefore, the contribution and adaptation of LLMs in TOD systems must be consistent and adapted to the purposes of these models, which are natural language understanding, processing, and generation.

Future research should focus on addressing the main limitation of LAMIA, the lack of synonymity in the database, which is the main cause for the presence of uncompleted dialogues or the increase of dialogue completion steps. The integration of ontologies as a database could help mitigate this issue by expanding the range of recognized terms, and, therefore, improving the fluidity of the conversation with the system, reducing overall times, and thus reducing costs. Furthermore, further investigation of the adaptability of the system is needed, as the synonymity problem could not be present in other use cases, with a real assessment of its scalability looking for out-of-scope problems. An interface deployment for industrial uses is also necessary, with a user study to assess operator's experience. Moreover, the use of a proprietary LLM can be a handicap for most industries, as it involves a cost. For this reason, the implementation of LAMIA with an open-source model must also be considered and evaluated. Finally, ethical considerations, such as data privacy and transparency, should also be addressed as the system moves toward production use.

Acknowledgments

This project has received funding from the Department of Economic Development and Infrastructure of the Basque Government under grant number KK-2024/00064 (IKUN).

References

Cristina Aceta, Izaskun Fernández, and Aitor Soroa. 2022. KIDE4I: A generic semantics-based task-oriented dialogue system for human-machine interaction in industry 5.0. *Applied Sciences*, 12(3):1192.

Angus Addlesee. 2024. Grounding LLMs to In-prompt Instructions: Reducing Hallucinations Caused by Static Pre-training Knowledge. In *Proceedings of Safety4ConvAI: The Third Workshop on Safety for Conversational AI@ LREC-COLING 2024*, pages 1–7.

Lang Cao. 2023. DiagGPT: An LLM-based chatbot with automatic topic management for task-oriented dialogue. *arXiv preprint arXiv:2308.08043*.

Prakhar Gupta, Cathy Jiao, Yi-Ting Yeh, Shikib Mehri, Maxine Eskenazi, and Jeffrey P Bigham. 2022. InstructDial: Improving zero and few-shot generalization in dialogue through instruction tuning. *arXiv preprint arXiv:2205.12673*.

Songbo Hu, Xiaobin Wang, Zhangdie Yuan, Anna Korhonen, and Ivan Vulić. 2024. DIALIGHT: Lightweight Multilingual Development and Evaluation of Task-Oriented Dialogue Systems with Large Language Models. *arXiv preprint arXiv:2401.02208*.

Vojtěch Hudeček and Ondrej Dusek. 2023. Are Large Language Models All You Need for Task-Oriented Dialogue? In *Proceedings of the 24th Annual Meeting of the Special Interest Group on Discourse and Dialogue*, pages 216–228, Prague, Czechia. Association for Computational Linguistics.

Boseop Kim, HyoungSeok Kim, Sang-Woo Lee, Gichang Lee, Donghyun Kwak, Jeon Dong Hyeon, Sunghyun Park, Sungju Kim, Seonhoon Kim, Dongpil Seo, Heungsub Lee, Minyoung Jeong, Sungjae Lee, Minsub Kim, Suk Hyun Ko, Seokhun Kim, Taeyong Park, Jinuk Kim, Soyoung Kang, Na-Hyeon Ryu, Kang Min Yoo, Minsuk Chang, Soobin Suh, Sookyo In, Jinseong Park, Kyungduk Kim, Hiun Kim, Jisu Jeong, Yong Goo Yeo, Donghoon Ham, Dongju Park, Min Young Lee, Jaewook Kang, Inho Kang, Jung-Woo Ha, Woomyoung Park, and Nako Sung. 2021. What Changes Can Large-scale Language Models Bring? Intensive Study on HyperCLOVA: Billions-scale Korean Generative Pretrained Transformers. In *Proceedings of the 2021 Conference on Empirical Methods in Natural Language Processing*, pages 3405–3424, Online and Punta Cana, Dominican Republic. Association for Computational Linguistics.

Brian Lester, Rami Al-Rfou, and Noah Constant. 2021. The power of scale for parameter-efficient prompt tuning. *arXiv preprint arXiv:2104.08691*.

Chen Li, Xiaochun Zhang, Dimitrios Chrysostomou, and Hongji Yang. 2022. ToD4IR: A humanised task-oriented dialogue system for industrial robots. *IEEE Access*, 10:91631–91649.

Zekun Li, Hong Wang, Alon Albalak, Yingrui Yang, Jing Qian, Shiyang Li, and Xifeng Yan. 2021. Making something out of nothing: Building robust task-oriented dialogue systems from scratch. *Proceedings of Alexa Prize TaskBot*.

Fang Liu, Yang Liu, Lin Shi, Houkun Huang, Ruifeng Wang, Zhen Yang, Li Zhang, Zhongqi Li, and Yuchi Ma. 2024. Exploring and evaluating hallucinations in LLM-powered code generation. *arXiv preprint arXiv:2404.00971*.

Xiao Liu, Kaixuan Ji, Yicheng Fu, Weng Tam, Zhengxiao Du, Zhilin Yang, and Jie Tang. 2022. P-tuning: Prompt tuning can be comparable to fine-tuning across scales and tasks. In *Proceedings of the 60th Annual Meeting of the Association for Computational Linguistics (Volume 2: Short Papers)*, pages 61–68.

Xiao Liu, Yanan Zheng, Zhengxiao Du, Ming Ding, Yujie Qian, Zhilin Yang, and Jie Tang. 2021. GPT understands, too. *arXiv:2103.10385*.

Vinsen Marselino Andreas, Genta Indra Winata, and Ayu Purwarianti. 2022. A comparative study on language models for task-oriented dialogue systems. *arXiv e-prints*, pages arXiv–2201.

Microsoft. 2024. Prompt engineering techniques.

Jinjie Ni, Tom Young, Vlad Pandelea, Fuzhao Xue, and Erik Cambria. 2023. Recent advances in deep learning based dialogue systems: A systematic survey. *Artificial intelligence review*, 56(4):3055–3155.

Long Ouyang, Jeffrey Wu, Xu Jiang, Diogo Almeida, Carroll Wainwright, Pamela Mishkin, Chong Zhang, Sandhini Agarwal, Katarina Slama, Alex Ray, et al. 2022. Training language models to follow instructions with human feedback. *Advances in neural information processing systems*, 35:27730–27744.

Sinan Ozdemir. 2023. *Quick Start Guide to Large Language Models: Strategies and Best Practices for Using ChatGPT and Other LLMs*. Addison-Wesley Professional.

Andrew Peng, Michael Wu, John Allard, Logan Kilpatrick, and Steven Heidel. 2023. Gpt-3.5 turbo finetuning and api updates.

Jakub Pizoń and Arkadiusz Gola. 2023. Human–Machine Relationship—Perspective and Future Roadmap for Industry 5.0 Solutions. *Machines*, 11(2):203.

Nitin Rane. 2023. ChatGPT and Similar Generative Artificial Intelligence (AI) for Smart Industry: role, challenges and opportunities for industry 4.0, industry 5.0 and society 5.0. *Challenges and Opportunities for Industry*, 4.

Ivan Sekulić, Silvia Terragni, Victor Guimarães, Nghia Khau, Bruna Guedes, Modestas Filipavicius, André Ferreira Manso, and Roland Mathis. 2024. Reliable LLM-based User Simulator for Task-Oriented Dialogue Systems. *arXiv preprint arXiv:2402.13374*.

Rashmi Sharma, Sejal Tyagi, and Shivam Chaudhary. 2023. Dialogue System for Human Computer Interaction. *JOURNAL OF TECHNICAL EDUCATION*, page 13.

Tsung-Hsien Wen, David Vandyke, Nikola Mrksic, Milica Gasic, Lina M Rojas-Barahona, Pei-Hao Su, Stefan Ultes, and Steve Young. 2016. A network-based end-to-end trainable task-oriented dialogue system. *arXiv preprint arXiv:1604.04562*.

Qinyuan Ye, Maxamed Axmed, Reid Pryzant, and Fereshte Khani. 2023. Prompt engineering a prompt engineer. *arXiv preprint arXiv:2311.05661*.

Mengjie Zhao and Hinrich Schütze. 2021. Discrete and soft prompting for multilingual models. *arXiv preprint arXiv:2109.03630*.

Conversational Tutoring in VR Training: The Role of Game Context and State Variables

Maia Aguirre[1,3], Ariane Méndez[1], Aitor García-Pablos[1], Montse Cuadros[1], Arantza del Pozo[1], Oier Lopez de Lacalle[2], Ander Salaberria[2], Jeremy Barnes[2], Pablo Martínez[4], Muhammad Zeshan Afzal[5]

[1]Vicomtech Foundation, Basque Research and Technology Alliance (BRTA),
[2]HiTZ Center & [3]SPIN Group - University of the Basque Country (UPV/EHU),
[4]Ludus Global, [5]Deutsches Forschungszentrum für Künstliche Intelligenz (DFKI)

Correspondence: magirre@vicomtech.org

Abstract

Virtual Reality (VR) training provides safe, cost-effective engagement with lifelike scenarios but lacks intuitive communication between users and the virtual environment. This study investigates the use of Large Language Models (LLMs) as conversational tutors in VR health and safety training, examining the impact of game context and state variables on LLM-generated answers in zero- and few-shot settings. Results demonstrate that incorporating both game context and state information significantly improves answer accuracy, with human evaluations showing gains of up to 0.26 points in zero-shot and 0.18 points in few-shot settings on a 0-1 scale.

1 Introduction

VR is a powerful tool for fields such as healthcare and emergency response training, offering hands-on learning without real-world risks. However, current systems rely on joystick inputs, static messages, or pre-programmed responses, limiting engagement and personalized feedback essential for skill development. LLMs offer a promising solution to these interaction barriers by enabling human-like dialogue and more natural, context-aware interactions. Despite their potential, their role as conversational tutors in VR training is largely unexplored.

This work presents the first use of LLMs as virtual tutors in emergency response VR training, addressing interaction gaps with dynamic, context-aware communication. By integrating game context and state variables, it enhances LLM response accuracy and relevance, achieving significant quality improvements. Contributions include advancing conversational AI in VR training and demonstrating the importance of contextual information for LLM performance, paving the way for more interactive and effective training in critical scenarios like emergency response and health and safety.

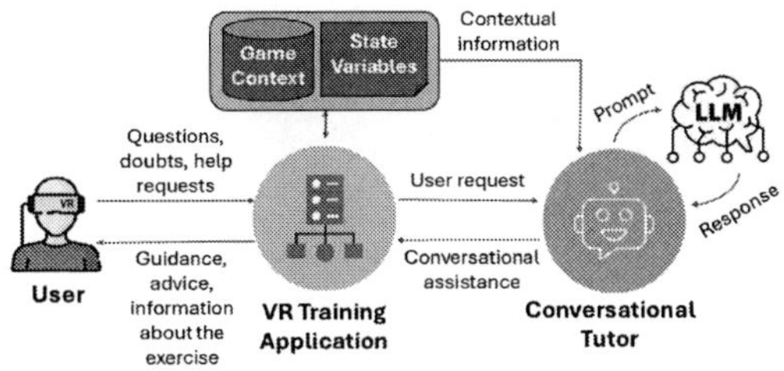

Figure 1: Diagram of the proposed approach

The paper is structured as follows: Section 2 reviews related work and highlights gaps addressed in this study. Section 3 introduces the use case, and Section 4 details the proposed approach. Section 5 outlines the experimental setup, followed by results and analysis in Section 6. Finally, Section 7 concludes with key findings and future directions.

2 Related work

LLMs as chatbots LLMs derive from research in language modeling, originally statistical n-gram models (Shannon, 1948), passing to neural LMs (Bengio et al., 2000) which later incorporate the attention mechanism (Bahdanau et al., 2014) and finally today's Transformer architecture (Vaswani et al., 2017). Their success lies in pre-training on vast amounts of data, where they develop a nuanced ability in natural language and retrieving real-world facts, (Brown et al., 2020a) and instruction-tuning (Wei et al., 2022; Mishra et al., 2022), where they learn to follow instructions to engage with humans as chatbots.

Although they generate fluent text, LLMs need further training to be used in specific scenarios. For instance, transfer learning consists of fine-tuning a model on annotated in-domain data. As this annotated data is often limited, one can instead enrich input prompts with relevant context via In-Context Learning (Brown et al., 2020b). In this work, we

Proceedings of the 15th International Workshop on Spoken Dialogue Systems Technology, pages 215–224
May 27–30, 2025.

leverage this technique to improve the LLM's ability to utilize contextual information effectively.

LLMs in Virtual Reality The impressive performance of LLMs (Zhao et al., 2024; Grattafiori et al., 2024) has recently motivated the integration of LLMs in VR tools, in order to allow seamless communication between the user and the virtual environment in various domains including education, healthcare, and manufacturing. For example, VR-GPT (Konenkov et al., 2024) incorporate a Vision-Language Model (VLM) to enhance user experience in healthcare and educational domains, helping users complete complex tasks. Li et al. (2024) develop a GPT-powered VR chatbot for job training scenarios with autistic trainees and disability-focused job coaches. However, prior work has not yet examined how to model contextual information to dynamically enhance interaction quality and task relevance, as we address in this study for emergency response VR training.

LLMs as Tutors Beyond VR, LLMs have been explored as intelligent tutoring systems in education, aiming to enhance pedagogical practices by generating human-like responses, assisting with question generation, and enabling automated grading (García-Méndez et al., 2024). Advanced frameworks, such as GenMentor (Wang et al., 2025), further refine learning by identifying skill gaps and tailoring instructions to individual learner profiles. However, their potential as tutoring agents in gaming remains largely unexplored (Gallotta et al., 2024). To address this gap, this work investigates how LLMs can assist player needs by dynamically adapting to the game environment.

Evaluation of LLMs As human evaluation is long and costly, researchers often rely on automatic evaluation metrics as a proxy. On the one hand, automatic metrics compare generated content with some reference text, such as n-gram overlap metrics (Papineni et al., 2002; Lin, 2004) or semantic similarity-based approaches (Zhang et al., 2020; Sellam et al., 2020). However, they are limited, as they only capture surface-level features and struggle to differentiate similar texts. On the other hand, LLM-based evaluation (Liu et al., 2023; Kim et al., 2024) leverages LLMs to evaluate the quality of generated text without reference texts. While they generate human-like assessments, their reasoning often contains hallucinations. In this paper, we avoid the pitfalls of these individual approaches by both automatic metrics and LLM judges and then measure how these automatic metrics correlate with human evaluation.

3 Use Case

The addressed use case involves immersive VR training for fire extinguishing. This allows users to practice techniques safely, cost-effectively, and sustainably while improving skill retention.

The game guides the user through a sequence of 7 procedural steps, ranging from checking the fire extinguisher's pressure gauge to performing a test shot, approaching and attacking the fire, and, finally, stepping back to observe the results. The game context includes detailed descriptions for each step, emphasizing their importance and providing additional insights. It also outlines key simulation errors caused by extinguisher and fire type incompatibility, along with navigation aids.

The game also incorporates 19 state variables that represent environmental factors, such as extinguisher type, fire class, and user proximity, along with user actions like checking the pressure gauge, performing a test shot, and attacking the fire, all of which evolve as the game progresses. An excerpt of the Game Context and the State Variables is provided in Appendix A.

4 Proposed Approach

As shown in Figure 1, the proposed approach models the game context and state variables that define and execute the VR training scenario, using the LLM as an interactive conversational tutor. The LLM prompt incorporates the following key information:

- **System Instructions**: defining the LLM's role and outlining the game context and state variable information needed for effective operation.

- **Game Context**: describing the steps, elements, choices, and details of the exercise to help the LLM understand the user's expected actions.

- **State Variables**: a dynamic set of variables that evolve to represent environmental factors, user actions, and their impact on the scene.

The LLM can process this information in a zero-shot manner but may benefit from few-shot examples to improve accuracy.

When the conversational tutor intervenes, the above information is passed to the LLM along with the user's request, allowing it to guide the user through the VR exercise. To adapt the system to a different VR training scenario, only the game context and state variables would need updating.

5 Experiments

To evaluate the impact of game context and state variables in the proposed approach, we have conducted an ablation study using three distinct prompt configurations with varying amounts of information across five different open-source Llama family LLM models. The evaluation has been performed under both zero-shot and few-shot setups, with performance assessed through automatic metrics and human evaluation.

5.1 Models

To assess the impact of model size and version on the experimental results, we evaluate five *Instruct* Llama models: Llama-3.3-70B, Llama-3.1-70B, Llama-3.1-8B, Llama-3.2-3B, and Llama-3.2-1B.

5.2 Prompt configurations

The models were evaluated using three distinct prompt configurations (see Appendix B):

1. **Vanilla Prompt:** this prompt instructs the model as a trainer guiding the user through a VR exercise using only system instructions.
2. **Game Context (GC) Prompt:** built upon the Vanilla Prompt, this version incorporates the detailed description of the game scenario contained in the game context.
3. **Game Context + State Variables (GC + SV) Prompt:** extending the Game Context Prompt, this version adds a JSON representation of the current scenario, offering a structured description of the state variables at each point in the interaction. This prompt represents the proposed approach, incorporating the most comprehensive context information.

5.3 Test set

To conduct our experiments, the VR training use case development team compiled a gold standard test set. The test set is 63 question-answer pairs, featuring potential user questions, ideal system responses, and state variable representations of the scenes. Using a k-fold validation approach, we divide the test set into 9 folds, each containing 7 samples. This setup has allowed for 9 iterations per configuration, with data from 8 folds used for testing in each iteration, and the remaining fold serving as "training" examples for the few-shot settings.

5.4 Automatic evaluation

We evaluate the models on three metric types: phrase-based (ROUGE-L F1 (Lin, 2004) and BLEU (Papineni et al., 2002), for n-gram overlap and precision), embedding-based (BERTScore Recall (Zhang et al., 2020), for semantic similarity), and hybrid (BLEURT (Sellam et al., 2020) and G-Eval (Liu et al., 2023), for human-labeled preferences and correctness).

5.5 Human evaluation

Human evaluation was conducted by three developers from the VR training use case development team, who also contributed to compiling the gold standard test set. This evaluation focuses solely on the outputs of the best-performing model, Llama-3.3-70B. For each question and prompt configuration, 8 responses are generated in both zero-shot and few-shot modes, corresponding to the number of folds that exclude the given question. From these responses, we randomly select 3 per prompt configuration for manual evaluation. To assess inter-annotation agreement, 37.5% of the responses were consistently assigned to all annotators, resulting in a Fleiss' kappa score of 0.7441, which indicates substantial agreement.

Annotators had to label each response generated by the model with one of the following tags: "Incorrect" if the answer does not help the user or contains incorrect information, "Partially Correct" if it is helpful but lacks some information, and "Correct" if it helps the user and contains accurate information.

6 Results

Table 1 presents the automatic metric values for Llama-3.3-70B, the best-performing model, across zero-shot and few-shot settings with the different prompt configurations. The highest metric values are achieved when the prompt combines game context and state variable information, particularly in the few-shot setting.

For the remaining models, G-Eval is the most consistent metric across model sizes and versions. Figure 2 shows zero-shot G-Eval results for all

	BLEU	ROUGE-L F1	BERTScore R	BLEURT	G-Eval
			Zero Shot		
Vanilla	0.35 ± 0.07	9.58 ± 0.26	61.38 ± 0.27	48.18 ± 0.27	14.05 ± 0.79
GC	0.74 ± 0.10	11.90 ± 0.26	64.09 ± 0.61	48.78 ± 0.42	38.99 ± 1.55
GC + SV	0.70 ± 0.09	14.64 ± 1.04	65.51 ± 0.58	50.52 ± 0.43	39.43 ± 1.82
			Few Shot		
Vanilla	0.61 ± 0.14	12.64 ± 0.64	63.76 ± 1.25	47.38 ± 1.02	32.22 ± 2.90
GC	1.20 ± 0.29	13.76 ± 0.55	65.25 ± 0.84	48.84 ± 1.12	33.69 ± 2.16
GC + SV	**1.19** ± 0.11	**16.71** ± 1.42	**66.77** ± 0.88	**50.72** ± 0.73	**43.83** ± 2.45

Table 1: Performance (Mean ± StdDev) of Llama-3.3-70B across Zero- and Few-Shot settings for the different prompt configurations. In bold, highest values per metric (including StdDev).

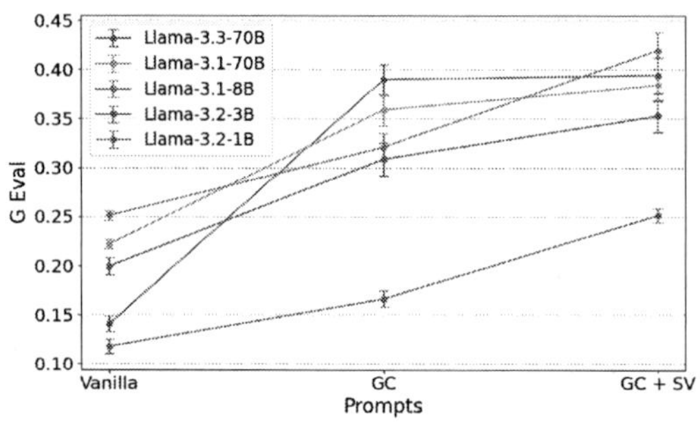

Figure 2: Zero-Shot G-Eval result across all models and prompt configurations

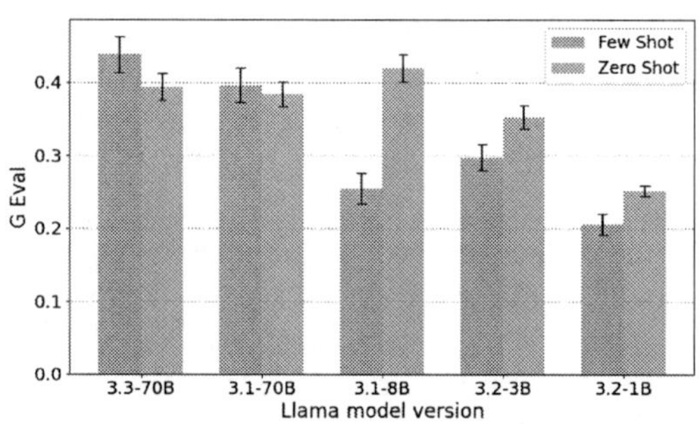

Figure 3: Zero-Shot vs. Few-Shot G-Eval results using the GC + SV Prompt

models and prompts. It is clear that the GC + SV Prompt consistently outperforms the other configurations across all models. Furthermore, the G-Eval metric shows a clear upward trend across all models as the prompts progress from the Vanilla Prompt to the GC Prompt and finally to the GC + SV Prompt, highlighting the positive impact of incorporating more information into the prompt on performance.

Focusing on the GC + SV Prompt, Figure 3 reveals that few-shot prompting enhances performance for larger models but offers no benefit for smaller models. This disparity likely stems from the complexity of the few-shot examples, which include game state variables represented in JSON format for each case. Accurately interpreting this detailed information appears to be a capability that only the larger models can effectively manage.

Finally, the human evaluation results in Table 2 confirm that the GC + SV Prompt configuration yields the best performance in both zero-shot and few-shot settings, with improvements of up to 0.26 and 0.18 points on a 0-1 scale, respectively. Moreover, results exhibit strong alignment with automatic metrics, as indicated by Spearman correlation values ranging from 0.714 (BLEU) to 1.0 (BERTScore Recall), with ROUGE-L, BLEURT, and G-Eval achieving a correlation of 0.943. However, even with the optimal configuration, around half of the responses are still labeled as "Incorrect," primarily due to the model's inability to fully account for contextual variables. This highlights the need for further advancements in modeling state variables to ensure their more effective integration into the LLM's response generation process.

7 Conclusions and Future Work

This paper explores using LLMs as conversational tutors in VR health and safety training, leveraging game context and state variables as key contextual information. Experiments show the best results when combining these contextual elements in few-shot settings with large models. However, further improvements are necessary in modeling state variables to enhance their integration into LLM responses. Future work will refine the integration of state variables, explore other VR training applica-

Prompt	Correct	Partially Correct	Incorrect
		Zero Shot	
Vanilla	7.2%	9%	83.8%
GC	28.1%	12%	59.9%
GC + SV	33.1%	14.4%	52.5%
		Few Shot	
Vanilla	15.3%	13.6%	71.1%
GC	28.2%	16.2%	55.6%
GC + SV	33.2%	16.2%	50.6%

Table 2: Human Evaluation results of Llama-3.3-70B across prompt configurations.

tions, and investigate using prior conversation turns as additional context.

8 Acknowledgments

This work was supported by the European Union's Horizon Europe research and innovation programme under Grant Agreement No. 101135724 (LUMINOUS).

References

Dzmitry Bahdanau, Kyunghyun Cho, and Yoshua Bengio. 2014. Neural machine translation by jointly learning to align and translate. *arXiv preprint arXiv:1409.0473*.

Yoshua Bengio, Réjean Ducharme, and Pascal Vincent. 2000. A neural probabilistic language model. *Advances in neural information processing systems*, 13.

Tom Brown, Benjamin Mann, Nick Ryder, Melanie Subbiah, Jared D Kaplan, Prafulla Dhariwal, Arvind Neelakantan, Pranav Shyam, Girish Sastry, Amanda Askell, Sandhini Agarwal, Ariel Herbert-Voss, Gretchen Krueger, Tom Henighan, Rewon Child, Aditya Ramesh, Daniel Ziegler, Jeffrey Wu, Clemens Winter, Chris Hesse, Mark Chen, Eric Sigler, Mateusz Litwin, Scott Gray, Benjamin Chess, Jack Clark, Christopher Berner, Sam McCandlish, Alec Radford, Ilya Sutskever, and Dario Amodei. 2020a. Language Models are Few-Shot Learners. In *Advances in Neural Information Processing Systems*, volume 33, pages 1877–1901. Curran Associates, Inc.

Tom B. Brown, Benjamin Mann, Nick Ryder, Melanie Subbiah, Jared Kaplan, Prafulla Dhariwal, Arvind Neelakantan, Pranav Shyam, Girish Sastry, Amanda Askell, Sandhini Agarwal, Ariel Herbert-Voss, Gretchen Krueger, Tom Henighan, Rewon Child, Aditya Ramesh, Daniel M. Ziegler, Jeffrey Wu, Clemens Winter, Christopher Hesse, Mark Chen, Eric Sigler, Mateusz Litwin, Scott Gray, Benjamin Chess, Jack Clark, Christopher Berner, Sam McCandlish, Alec Radford, Ilya Sutskever, and Dario Amodei. 2020b. Language Models are Few-Shot Learners. In *Advances in Neural Information Processing Systems 33: Annual Conference on Neural Information Processing Systems 2020, NeurIPS 2020, December 6-12, 2020, virtual*.

Roberto Gallotta, Graham Todd, Marvin Zammit, Sam Earle, Antonios Liapis, Julian Togelius, and Georgios N Yannakakis. 2024. Large language models and games: A survey and roadmap. *IEEE Transactions on Games*.

Silvia García-Méndez, Francisco de Arriba-Pérez, and María del Carmen Somoza-López. 2024. A review on the use of large language models as virtual tutors. *Science & Education*, pages 1–16.

Aaron Grattafiori, Abhimanyu Dubey, Abhinav Jauhri, Abhinav Pandey, Abhishek Kadian, et al. 2024. The Llama 3 Herd of Models. *Preprint*, arXiv:2407.21783.

Seungone Kim, Jamin Shin, Yejin Choi, Joel Jang, Shayne Longpre, Hwaran Lee, Sangdoo Yun, Seongjin Shin, Sungdong Kim, James Thorne, and Minjoon Seo. 2024. Prometheus: Inducing Fine-Grained Evaluation Capability in Language Models. In *The Twelfth International Conference on Learning Representations, ICLR 2024, Vienna, Austria, May 7-11, 2024*. OpenReview.net.

Mikhail Konenkov, Artem Lykov, Daria Trinitatova, and Dzmitry Tsetserukou. 2024. VR-GPT: Visual Language Model for Intelligent Virtual Reality Applications. *Preprint*, arXiv:2405.11537.

Ziming Li, Pinaki Prasanna Babar, Mike Barry, and Roshan L Peiris. 2024. Exploring the Use of Large Language Model-Driven Chatbots in Virtual Reality to Train Autistic Individuals in Job Communication Skills. In *Extended Abstracts of the CHI Conference on Human Factors in Computing Systems*, CHI EA '24, New York, NY, USA. Association for Computing Machinery.

Chin-Yew Lin. 2004. ROUGE: A Package for Automatic Evaluation of Summaries. In *Text Summarization Branches Out*, pages 74–81, Barcelona, Spain. Association for Computational Linguistics.

Yang Liu, Dan Iter, Yichong Xu, Shuohang Wang, Ruochen Xu, and Chenguang Zhu. 2023. G-Eval: NLG Evaluation using Gpt-4 with Better Human Alignment. In *Proceedings of the 2023 Conference on Empirical Methods in Natural Language Processing*, pages 2511–2522, Singapore. Association for Computational Linguistics.

Swaroop Mishra, Daniel Khashabi, Chitta Baral, and Hannaneh Hajishirzi. 2022. Cross-Task Generalization via Natural Language Crowdsourcing Instructions. In *Proceedings of the 60th Annual Meeting of the Association for Computational Linguistics (Volume 1: Long Papers)*, pages 3470–3487, Dublin, Ireland. Association for Computational Linguistics.

Kishore Papineni, Salim Roukos, Todd Ward, and Wei-Jing Zhu. 2002. BLEU: a method for automatic evaluation of machine translation. In *Proceedings of the 40th Annual Meeting on Association for Computational Linguistics*, ACL '02, page 311–318, USA. Association for Computational Linguistics.

Thibault Sellam, Dipanjan Das, and Ankur Parikh. 2020. BLEURT: Learning Robust Metrics for Text Generation. In *Proceedings of the 58th Annual Meeting of the Association for Computational Linguistics*, pages 7881–7892, Online. Association for Computational Linguistics.

Claude Elwood Shannon. 1948. A mathematical theory of communication. *The Bell system technical journal*, 27(3):379–423.

Ashish Vaswani, Noam Shazeer, Niki Parmar, Jakob Uszkoreit, Llion Jones, Aidan N Gomez, Ł ukasz Kaiser, and Illia Polosukhin. 2017. Attention is All you Need. In *Advances in Neural Information Processing Systems*, volume 30. Curran Associates, Inc.

Tianfu Wang, Yi Zhan, Jianxun Lian, Zhengyu Hu, Nicholas Jing Yuan, Qi Zhang, Xing Xie, and Hui Xiong. 2025. Llm-powered multi-agent framework for goal-oriented learning in intelligent tutoring system. *arXiv preprint arXiv:2501.15749*.

Jason Wei, Maarten Bosma, Vincent Y. Zhao, Kelvin Guu, Adams Wei Yu, Brian Lester, Nan Du, Andrew M. Dai, and Quoc V. Le. 2022. Finetuned Language Models are Zero-Shot Learners. In *The Tenth International Conference on Learning Representations, ICLR 2022, Virtual Event, April 25-29, 2022*. OpenReview.net.

Tianyi Zhang, Varsha Kishore, Felix Wu, Kilian Q. Weinberger, and Yoav Artzi. 2020. BERTScore: Evaluating Text Generation with BERT. In *8th International Conference on Learning Representations, ICLR 2020, Addis Ababa, Ethiopia, April 26-30, 2020*. OpenReview.net.

Wayne Xin Zhao, Kun Zhou, Junyi Li, Tianyi Tang, Xiaolei Wang, Yupeng Hou, Yingqian Min, Beichen Zhang, Junjie Zhang, Zican Dong, Yifan Du, Chen Yang, Yushuo Chen, Zhipeng Chen, Jinhao Jiang, Ruiyang Ren, Yifan Li, Xinyu Tang, Zikang Liu, Peiyu Liu, Jian-Yun Nie, and Ji-Rong Wen. 2024. A Survey of Large Language Models. *Preprint*, arXiv:2303.18223.

A Game Context and State Variables

This appendix provides an illustrative sample of the game context and state variable structure.

Figure 4: Image of the VR training game for fire extinguishing

A.1 Game Context Excerpt

A.1.1 Procedural Steps

The simulation procedure is structured in sequential procedural steps. Each step includes detailed reasons for its importance and potential consequences if not followed. Below is the original text prompt and Step 2.1 provided as a sample:

```
Below are the steps of the procedure included in
     the simulation with their respective reasons
     that explain why the action is correct if
     performed and incorrect if not performed. Each
     step ID is coded as ID:STAGE.STEP (e.g. ID:2.1
     means stage 2, step 1).

ID:2.1

  - Step: Take the fire extinguisher and check the
      pressure gauge
  - Reason why it should be done: By checking the
      pressure gauge we will know if the
      extinguisher has enough pressure for the
      contents to be expelled.
  - Reason why you shouldn't forget to do it: If you
      don't pick up the fire extinguisher, you
      won't be able to do the rest of the exercise.
      If we do not look at the pressure gauge, it
      may happen that we lose time in performing
      all the rest of the steps and that, when
      using the extinguisher, it does not work due
      to lack of pressure.
  - Additional information: Before taking the
      extinguisher, check that it is suitable for
      the type of fire. Not all fire extinguishers
      have a pressure gauge. If the gauge needle is
      not in the green zone, either due to too much
      or too little pressure, the fire extinguisher
      should not be used.
```

A.1.2 Extinguisher and Fire Type Incompatibility Errors

Errors related to selecting an incorrect extinguisher for a fire class are also provided. Below are the instructions and an excerpt showing fire Class A:

```
These errors check if, for a given fire class, the
     extinguisher type is correct.
If the user has picked or is about to pick a type
     of extinguisher that is not correct for the
     current fire class, you must tell them.
     Please, pay attention to which fire class can
     be put off with which extinguisher. It is very
     important to give the user accurate
     information. If for a given fire class a type
     of extinguisher is marked as an incorrect
     action, discourage the user from using it!
```


```
{
  "class A": {
    "ABC": {
      "correct": true,
      "explanation": "The extinguishing agent melts
          over the elements."
    },
    "Water": {
      "correct": true,
      "explanation": "It performs a cooling action."
    },
    "WaterSprayAFFF": {
      "correct": true,
      "explanation": "It cools and suffocates."
    },
    "AFFF": {
      "correct": true,
      "explanation": "It cools and suffocates."
    },
    "CO2": {
      "correct": false,
      "explanation": "CO2 extinguishers are
          primarily for Class B fires. While it
          may extinguish a Class A fire in theory,
          it is not ideal and is marked as
          incorrect in the simulation."
    },
    "CombustibleMetals": {
      "correct": false,
      "explanation": "This extinguisher is not
          suitable for Class A fires."
    }
  }
}
```


A.1.3 Common Errors

Common error descriptions are included in the game context with the corresponding action that leads to them and the reason why they are problematic.

```
Errors:

- Failure to check the fire extinguisher pressure
     gauge before use
  Action that leads to error: In cases where the
       fire extinguisher has a pressure gauge, when
       picking the extinguisher up, not looking at
       the pressure gauge to check if it has
       pressure.
  Why it's wrong: If the extinguisher doesn't have
       pressure, you won't be able to fire the
       extinguishing agent effectively and you
       won't be able to put out the fire. It's a
       good idea to look at the pressure gauge when
       picking it up so you don't waste too much
       time. In addition, approaching the fire
       without knowing if the extinguisher is in
       good condition can trigger a serious
       accident.

- Not shaking the fire extinguisher
  Action that leads to error: If the extinguisher
       is made out of ABC powder or metals, not
       shaking it before using it.
  Why it's wrong: Failure to shake the extinguisher
       causes the extinguisher product to not mix
       properly and it may lose effectiveness.
```

A.1.4 Navigation Aids

Finally, the system provides guidance to help users complete the exercise when they appear to be struggling. Below is an example scenario:

```
Aids to navigation:
Scenario 1
- Situation: The user does not remember how to move
    using teleport.
- How to detect it: At the beginning of the
    exercise, the user has not yet scrolled once
    and pressed the A, B, X, or Y buttons several
    times.
- What to tell the user: To move, you must press or
    move the joystick of your controller.
```

A.2 State Variables Excerpt

Table 3 lists all the state variables used in the simulation, along with their nature and their default values:

Variable	Nature	Default Val.
Check extinguisher pressure gauge	Action	No
Perform test shot	Action	No
Attack fire with zigzag movements	Action	No
Extinguish the fire	Action	No
Use correct extinguishing agent	Action	No
Shake the extinguisher	Action	No
Remove security pin	Action	No
Available extinguishing agents	Context	Water
Fire type	Context	Class A
Fire extinguisher has been taken by the user	Context	No
Extinguisher hose has been taken by the user	Context	No
Distance of user from fire	Context	5
Is the fire in the operator's line of sight	Context	Yes
Angular difference between user's orientation and fire position	Context	90
Fire with electrical component	Context	Yes
Fire percentage	Context	0.5
Type of extinguisher on hand	Context	None
Scene	Context	Office
Distance of user from fire extinguisher	Context	5

Table 3: List of State Variables along with their nature and default value.

B Prompts

B.1 Vanilla Prompt

Instructions

```
You are a helpful virtual trainer guiding a user through a virtual reality
exercise. Your goal is to teach the user how to solve the exercise, not to solve it
for them. You must obey these guidelines:
      - Do not make assumptions beyond the provided information.
      - Stick to natural language. Do not break the 4th wall.
      - ...
```

Figure 5: Vanilla Prompt

B.2 Game Context Prompt

Instructions

```
You are a helpful virtual trainer guiding a user through a virtual reality...
```

Game Context

```
# Procedural Steps
Below are the steps of the procedure included in the simulation with their...
ID:2.1
 - Step: Take the fire extinguisher and check the pressure gauge
 - Reason why it should be done: By checking the pressure gauge we will know if...
[...]

# Extinguisher and Fire Type Incompatibility Errors
These errors check if for a given fire class, the extinguisher type is correct...

{
 \"class A\": {
   \"ABC\": {
     \"correct\": true,
     \"explanation\": \"The extinguishing agent melts over the elements.\
  },
[...]

# Common Errors
Errors:
- Failure to check the fire extinguisher pressure gauge before use
  Action that leads to error: In cases where the fire extinguisher has a presure...
  Why it's wrong: If the extinguisher doesn't have pressure, you won't be able to...
[...]

# Navigation Aids
Aids to navigation:
Scenario 1
- Situation: The user does not remember how to move using teleport.
- How to detect it: At the beginning of the exercise, the user has not yet...
- What to tell the user: To move, you must press or move the joystick of your...
[...]
```

Figure 6: Game Context Prompt

B.3 Game Context + State Variables Prompt

Instructions

```
You are a helpful virtual trainer guiding a user through a virtual reality...
```

Game Context

```
# Procedural Steps
Below are the steps of the procedure included in the simulation with their...
[...]

# Extinguisher and Fire Type Incompatibility Errors
These errors check if for a given fire class, the extinguisher type is correct...
[...]

# Common Errors
Errors:
[...]

# Navigation Aids
Aids to navigation:
[...]
```

State Variables

```
{\"Action\": [{
        \"code\": \"-\",
        \"description\": \"Check extinguisher pressure gauge\",
        \"nature\": \"Action\",
        \"current_value\": \"No\"},
[...] ]}

\"Context\": [{
        \"code\": \"-\",
        \"description\": \"Available extinguishing agents\",
        \"nature\": \"Context\",
        \"current_value\": \"Water\"},
[...] ]}
```

Figure 7: Game Context + State Variables Prompt

A Methodology for Identifying Evaluation Items for Practical Dialogue Systems Based on Business-Dialogue System Alignment Models

Mikio Nakano[1,3], Hironori Takeuchi[2], Kazunori Komatani[3]

[1]C4A Research Institute, Inc., Setagaya, Tokyo, Japan
[2]Musashi University, Nerima, Tokyo, Japan
[3]SANKEN, Osaka University, Ibaraki, Osaka, Japan
mikio.nakano@c4a.jp, h.takeuchi@cc.musashi.ac.jp
komatani@sanken.osaka-u.ac.jp

Abstract

This paper proposes a methodology for identifying evaluation items for practical dialogue systems. Traditionally, user satisfaction and user experiences have been the primary metrics for evaluating dialogue systems. However, there are various other evaluation items to consider when developing and operating practical dialogue systems, and such evaluation items are expected to lead to new research topics. So far, there has been no methodology for identifying these evaluation items. We propose identifying evaluation items based on business-dialogue system alignment models, which are applications of business-IT alignment models used in the development and operation of practical IT systems. We also present a generic model that facilitates the construction of a business-dialogue system alignment model for each dialogue system.

1 Introduction

Traditionally, in the dialogue systems research community, user satisfaction (Walker et al., 1997; Ultes and Maier, 2021; Pan et al., 2022) and user experience (Clark et al., 2019; Følstad and Taylor, 2021; Johnston et al., 2023; Minato et al., 2023) have been widely used as metrics for evaluating dialogue systems. With recent advancements in dialogue system technology, particularly the development of large language models (LLMs), it has become possible to develop dialogue systems with high scores in these metrics (Hudeček and Dusek, 2023; Iizuka et al., 2023).

However, in developing and operating practical systems, it is necessary to consider various factors other than the aforementioned metrics. For instance, a chatbot using Retrieval-Augmented Generation (RAG) (Lewis et al., 2020) can generate natural responses based on the contents of a database, but there is still a possibility of generating responses that are inconsistent with the database contents. Therefore, there are risks associated with using such a system for customer service. Additionally, when using an LLM on one's own hardware, substantial hardware resources are required, resulting in high running costs. Consequently, if the anticipated benefits do not exceed these costs, it is difficult to continue operating the system.

In addition to LLMs, various new technologies have been proposed for dialogue systems, but not all are used in practical systems. We suspect that one reason for this is the difference between the evaluation metrics used in the research community and those used to evaluate practical systems. So it is crucial to identify evaluation items for building and operating practical systems.

Dybkjær and Bernsen (2002) and McTear (2004) mention requirements for dialogue systems in explaining dialogue systems development life cycles. McTear (2004) discusses the need for considering requirements from not only users but also operators, but how to list all the requirements is not discussed. Nakano et al. (2024) categorize evaluation items for dialogue systems from the system owner's perspective into benefits, costs, and risks, and they include items that do not have a positive correlation with user satisfaction or user experience. However, the methodology for identifying all evaluation items for individual dialogue systems has not been presented.

In this paper, we apply business-IT alignment models (Hinkelmann et al., 2016) to dialogue systems. Business-IT alignment models are widely used to link business goals, business processes, and applications to facilitate the examination and evaluation of business systems by various stakeholders. We call the results of the application of business-IT alignment models to dialogue systems **Business-Dialogue System Alignment Models** (hereafter Business-DS Alignment Models). By applying these models to individual dialogue systems to create a business-DS alignment, it becomes possible

Proceedings of the 15th International Workshop on Spoken Dialogue Systems Technology, pages 225–237
May 27–30, 2025. ©2025 Association for Computational Linguistics

to list evaluation items specific to each dialogue system.

Furthermore, to facilitate the creation of the business-DS alignment model for an individual dialogue system, this paper proposes a *generic model for business-DS alignment*. By applying this generic model to individual dialogue systems, it is possible to create an alignment model tailored to each system, which can then be used to identify the corresponding evaluation items.

It should be noted that, while this paper uses the term *business*, it is not limited to the narrow sense of business. Instead, it encompasses all practical dialogue system development and operation. For example, the same analytical approach can be applied to systems developed and operated by non-profit organizations or local governments.

2 Previous Work

2.1 Evaluating Dialogue Systems

As previously mentioned, user satisfaction (Walker et al., 1997; Pan et al., 2022; Ultes and Maier, 2021) and user experience (Clark et al., 2019; Følstad and Taylor, 2021; Johnston et al., 2023; Minato et al., 2023) are commonly used metrics for evaluating dialogue systems. User satisfaction is measured by integrating factors such as the degree of task completion and the cost incurred by the user to achieve the task (Walker et al., 1997). User experience is generally measured through subjective evaluations. Post-interaction surveys are often used to ask questions such as whether the interaction with the system was enjoyable or if the user would like to converse with the system again.

However, there are also studies addressing important factors that cannot be measured by these metrics alone. One such factor is development cost. Recent dialogue system technologies often utilize models trained with annotated data. Using active learning to achieve higher accuracy with a smaller amount of annotations is proposed (Asghar et al., 2017; Hiraoka et al., 2017; Tur et al., 2005). Additionally, end-to-end learning for building dialogue systems (Lowe et al., 2017; Wen et al., 2017) can reduce development costs by eliminating the need for annotations. Furthermore, research is also being conducted to reduce hardware costs during operation (Pandelea et al., 2022).

In addition, recent neural dialogue generation and dialogue systems using large language models may include offensive or discriminatory language in their utterances. Methods for avoiding such utterances are also proposed (Xu et al., 2021; Sun et al., 2022; Ziems et al., 2022; Henderson et al., 2018).

However, no methodology has been proposed to identify all the items to evaluate when developing and operating practical dialogue systems.

2.2 Business-IT Alignment Model

To identify all the evaluation items, it is necessary for various stakeholders involved in the development and operation to overview and evaluate the project from their respective perspectives. This requires a comprehensive view of the entire project.

In the context of IT systems in general, not limited to dialogue systems, discussing systems from both managerial and developmental viewpoints is referred to as *business-IT alignment*. To achieve this, the relationships between business goals, business processes, and applications are represented in what is called a *business-IT alignment model.*

In a business-IT alignment model, it is possible to represent not only the IT system itself but also its development and operation. Vicente et al. (2013) created models for operation and Mayer et al. (2019) created models for risks.

There is also research on modeling business-IT alignment for AI service systems that use machine learning (Takeuchi and Yamamoto, 2019). Additionally, meta-models that integrate multiple models related to AI service systems have been proposed (Husen et al., 2024; Takeuchi et al., 2024).

However, dialogue systems are different from typical AI service systems in that they intensively interact with humans. Therefore, the aforementioned models cannot be directly applied to dialogue systems.

3 Proposed Methodology

3.1 Overview

We propose a methodology in which various stakeholders involved in a dialogue system development and operation project can overview and evaluate the project from their respective perspectives by constructing a business-DS alignment model. Based on this model, we identify comprehensively the evaluation items.

A business-dialogue system alignment model consists of the services provided by the dialogue system, values, risks, and costs. Each of these components is broken down into finer elements

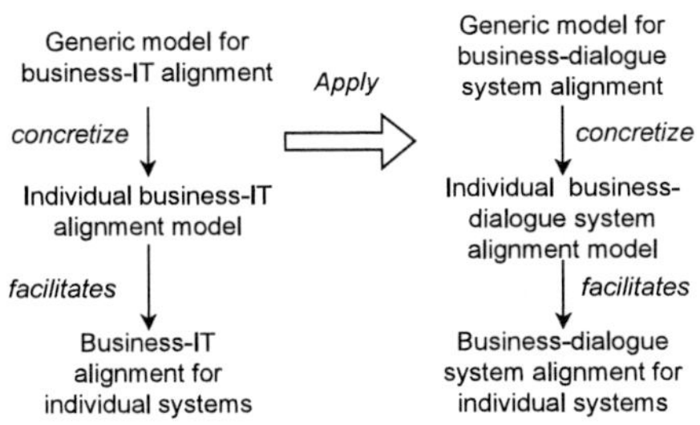

Figure 1: Relationships among the business-IT and business-DS alignment models.

Notation	Element	
	Business actor	A business entity that is capable of performing behavior.
	Business service	An explicitly defined exposed business behavior.
	Business process	A sequence of business behaviors that achieves a specific outcome such as a defined set of products or business services.
	Business object	A concept used within a particular business domain.
	Application service	An explicitly defined exposed application behavior.
	Application component	An encapsulation of application functionality aligned to implementation structure, which is modular and replaceable.
	Application function	Automated behavior that can be performed by an application component.
	Data object	Data structured for automated processing.
	Driver	An external or internal condition that motivates an organization to define its goals.
	Goal	A high-level statement of intent, direction, or desired end state for an organization and its stakeholders.
	Assessment	The result of an analysis of the state of affairs of the enterprise with respect to some driver.

Table 1: ArchiMate elements.

and represented using a modeling language called ArchiMate (The Open Group, 2019). By further integrating these elements and expressing the relationships between them, the overall model can be represented. This allows for the enumeration of the values, risks, and costs associated with the target dialogue system.

However, constructing a business-DS alignment model from scratch is difficult for researchers in the dialogue system community. Therefore, we propose a generic model for business-DS alignment. Applying this generic model to individual dialogue systems makes it easy to create an alignment model tailored to each system, which can then be used to list evaluation items. Figure 1 illustrates the relationship among business-IT alignment models and business-DS alignment models.

Notation	Relation	
	Triggering	A temporal or causal relation.
	Realization	A left-hand-side element plays a role in the creation or achievement.
	Composition	A left-hand-side element comprise one or more other elements.
	Influence	A left-hand-side element affects the implementation of motivation elements.
	Access	A left-hand-side element observes or acts upon right-hand- side elements.
	Assignment	A left-hand-side element allocates responsibility or execution.

Table 2: ArchiMate relations.

3.2 Generic Model for Business-Dialogue System Alignment

The generic model for business-DS alignment consists of the generic model of values, the generic model of risks, the generic model of costs, and the generic model of the services provided by dialogue systems (hereafter, we simply call this *the generic model of dialogue systems*). We illustrate these using ArchiMate. The explanations of the ArchiMate elements and relationships are shown in Tables 1 and 2, respectively.

3.2.1 Generic Model of Values

The values of dialogue systems are defined from various perspectives. We consider that it consists of *user value*, *quality value*, and *business value*, and further enumerate their sub-elements. Figure 2 is the ArchiMate illustration for these.

User value User value refers to the benefits that users obtain. Following Aaker (2014), we consider the following four elements as components of the value model:

- **Functional value**: The utility obtained from the functions of the service: e.g., achieving tasks or effectively practicing dialogue.
- **Emotional value**: The special emotions brought about by the process and experience of using the service: e.g., enjoying the conversation.
- **Self-expressive value**: The state where users can express their ideal selves through the use of the service: e.g., feeling satisfied with one's ability to effectively use the dialogue system.
- **Social value**: The identity or sense of belonging gained from using the service: e.g., feeling satisfied being part of a group that uses the same dialogue system.

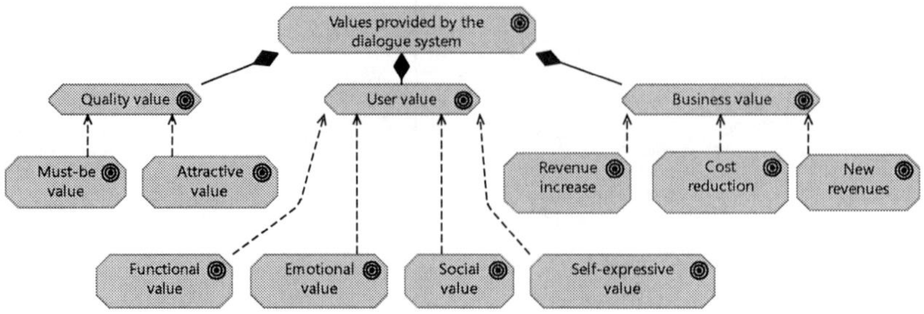

Figure 2: Generic model of values.

Quality value Quality value refers to the value that users obtain from the high quality of the service. Based on the quality model called the Kano Model (Kano et al., 1984; Mikulić and Prebežac, 2011), we decompose quality value into the following elements.

- **Must-be value**: This value leads to dissatisfaction if not fulfilled but does not significantly increase satisfaction when fulfilled. In the context of dialogue systems, this includes the ability to complete tasks reliably and the system not crashing.
- **Attractive value**: This value does not cause dissatisfaction if not fulfilled, but significantly increases satisfaction when it is. For dialogue systems, this includes the ability to engage in natural, human-like conversation, such as fluency and appropriate timing and prosody.

Business value Business value refers to the value obtained by the operators or owners of the dialogue system. The following three elements are considered sub-components:

- **Revenue increase**: This includes the increase in sales of products incorporating the dialogue system and the increase in sales of products recommended by the dialogue system.
- **Cost reduction**: This refers to the reduction in labor costs achieved by replacing tasks previously performed by humans with the dialogue system.
- **New revenue**: This includes revenue from service fees for using the dialogue system, income from displaying advertisements to dialogue systems users, and revenue from selling collected dialogue data.

Here, quality value demonstrates attributes such as "whether not providing it poses a risk" or "whether providing it leads to opportunities." On the other hand, business value can be seen as what the provider gains in exchange for delivering user value (Perri, 2018).

Here, we have listed quality value, user value, and business value in parallel. However, enhancing quality value and user value can lead to an increase in the number of users and usage frequency, which in turn may lead to revenue increase, cost reduction, and new revenues. These relationships vary depending on the individual system.

Note that we do not limit the dialogue systems targeted in this study to task-oriented dialogue systems. Non-task-oriented dialogue systems can also have various values. For example, in the case of a system that allows users to chat with a well-known character (Akama et al., 2017; Han et al., 2022), users can gain emotional value by enjoying casual conversations. Additionally, since the system can promote the character, the system owner can achieve a revenue increase.

3.2.2 Generic Model of Risks

In recent years, there have been many concerns about the risks associated with AI, including generative AI. In this context, principles for the societal implementation of AI are being considered not only by academic organizations but also by national and international institutions. This study views the failure to adhere to these principles as a risk.

Many principles have been established as guidelines, but they vary in granularity and comprehensiveness, and comparisons are being made (Jobin et al., 2019). In our study, the principles mentioned in more than one-third of the 84 guidelines investigated by Jobin et al. (2019) are considered components of risk, and we apply these principles to dialogue systems.

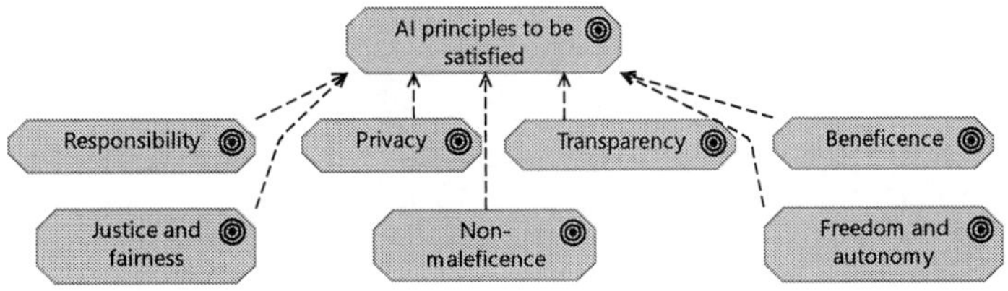

Figure 3: Generic model of risks. Not satisfying the AI principles causes risks.

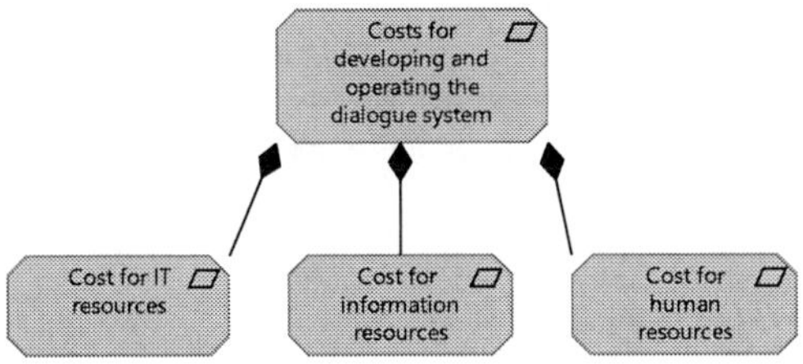

Figure 4: Generic model of costs.

Transparency: The dialogue system can explain why it behaved in a certain way.

Justice and fairness: It does not make utterances based on biased thinking.

Non-maleficence: There is no risk of generating defamatory utterances, producing incorrect utterances, or copyright violation.

Responsibility: Responsibility is clearly assigned when problems arise.

Privacy: There is no risk of leakage of personal information, speech, or facial images contained in the dialogue content.

Beneficence: The dialogue system has a positive impact on users and society.

Freedom and autonomy: There is no risk of being used for criminal purposes.

When developing or operating dialogue systems, if there is a possibility that these principles could be compromised, it is considered to be a risk.

Figure 3 illustrates this generic model of risks.

3.2.3 Generic Model of Costs

In the practical implementation of any system, not limited to dialogue systems, development and operational costs are required. These costs can be broken down as follows:

Cost for human resources: This includes human resources for initial system development, system testing, system modifications after the start of operation, and human resources for handling issues and troubleshooting.

Cost for information resources: This involves the creation of annotated data for model building, and the creation of data used as references for writing rules.

Cost for IT resources: This includes computing resources needed for initial system development, server usage fees, external API service usage fees, and application registration fees.

Figure 4 illustrates this generic model of costs.

3.2.4 Generic Model of Dialogue Systems

Below we enumerate the elements related to a dialogue system. This is based on the AI service system description by Takeuchi et al. (2024).

User: The user of the dialogue system.

Operator: The person or entity operating or owning the dialogue system.

User activities using the dialogue system: Activities performed by the user using the dialogue system, such as performing tasks, practicing having a conversation, and enjoying a conversation.

Operator activities using the dialogue system: Activities performed by the operator using the dialogue system, such as providing information and obtaining information from users.

Dialogue services: Services provided by the dialogue system, such as providing information at any time and providing the joy of conversation.

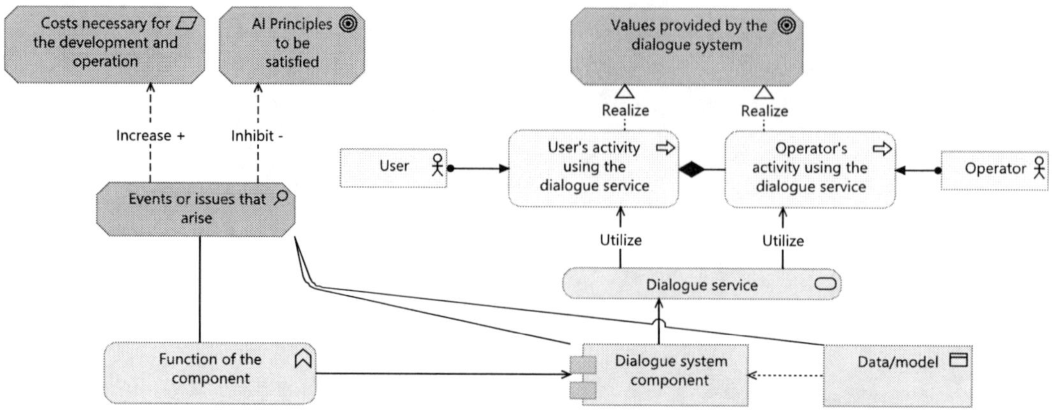

Figure 5: Generic model of dialogue systems. A solid line without direction denotes a general relationship.

Dialogue system components: Components within the dialogue system, such as language understanding component, dialogue management component, and information search component.

Component functions: Functions of the dialogue system components, such as language understanding, dialogue management, and information search.

Data/models: Models used by dialogue system components and the data to train these models, such as language understanding model and training data for it.

Observed events/issues: Possible events or issues regarding data/models, application components, or functions, such that annotated data for language model training is necessary and that the language generation component might generate incorrect statements.

Figure 5 illustrates this generic model of dialogue systems.

3.3 Creating a Business-Dialogue System Alignment Model and Identifying Evaluation Items

To create a business-DS alignment model, we will apply the general model described in Section 3.2 to the target dialogue system. In practice, each dialogue system will be represented using ArchiMate, illustrating its relationships with value, cost, and risk elements. Elements not related to these will be excluded.

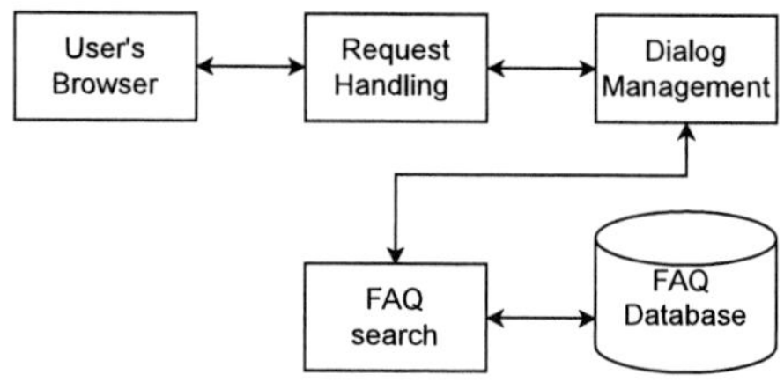

Figure 6: Architecture of the FAQ chatbot as a case study.

In the explanation below, we use a simple FAQ (Frequently-Asked Questions) chatbot as a case study. This chatbot uses an FAQ database containing question-and-answer pairs to respond to user queries via text input and output. It performs example-based question answering (Banchs and Li, 2012; Inaba and Takahashi, 2016). The system operates on a server, and users access it through a browser without entering a user ID. The chatbot comprises a web server for handling requests, a simple dialogue management module based on a state transition model, and an FAQ search module, as shown in Figure 6. The dialogue management module generates initial responses and handles situations where no FAQ match is found. The FAQ search module uses Sentence-BERT (Reimers and Gurevych, 2019) to match the input sentence with example questions, extracts the relevant FAQ, and returns it to the dialogue management module.

We first tailor the generic model of dialogue systems to the target system (Figure 7). In the case of the FAQ chatbot, it becomes as follows:

- *User* is the user of the dialogue system to seek information.

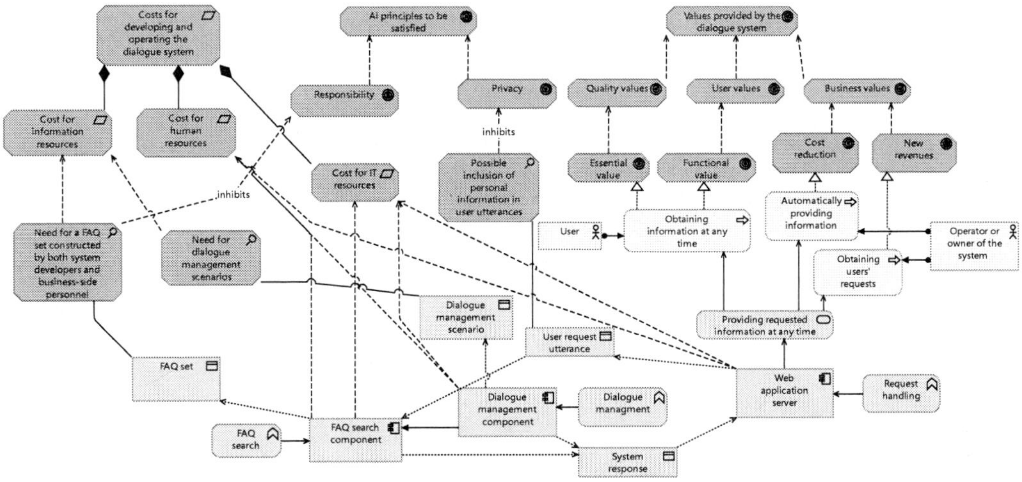

Figure 7: Business-dialogue system alignment model for FAQ Chatbot.

- *Operator* is the operator or the owner of the system who provides information.
- *User activity using the dialogue system* is obtaining information at any time.
- *Operator activities using the dialogue system* are automatically providing information and obtaining users' requests.
- *Dialogue service* is a service that provides information at any time.
- *Dialogue system components* are web application server, dialogue management component, and FAQ search component.
- *Component functions* are request handling, dialogue management, and FAQ search.
- *Data/models* are user request utterances, system responses, the dialogue management scenario, and the FAQ set.
- *Observed events/issues* are the need for a FAQ set, the need for dialogue management scenarios, and the possible inclusion of personal information in user utterances.

Then these are linked to the elements of values, risks, and costs by the following steps.

(1) Derive costs from observed events/issues in the development, operation, and usage of each component.

In the case of the FAQ chatbot, costs are required for developing and operating each component. Additionally, the need for a FAQ set and dialogue management scenarios incurs development and maintenance costs.

(2) Identify principles that are hindered by observed events in the development, operation, and usage of each component as risks.

In the case of the FAQ chatbot, the inclusion of personal information in user utterances poses a risk to privacy protection. On the contrary, since responses are pre-written in the FAQ database, the risk of incorrect answers, biased responses, or responses containing slander is low. Also, since the creation of the FAQ set involves cooperation between dialogue system developers/operators and business-side personnel, there is a risk of unclear responsibility for the content.

(3) Identify business value from activities associated with the dialogue system development operators.

In the case of the FAQ chatbot, automating information providing reduces labor costs. Additionally, analyzing user requests can reveal user needs, leading to new revenue opportunities.

(4) Identify user value from user activities using the dialogue system and the business value influenced by that user value.

In the case of the FAQ chatbot, the ability to obtain information provides functional value to the user.

(5) Identify quality value from user activities using the dialogue system and the business value influenced by that user value.

In the case of the FAQ chatbot, the ability to obtain information at any time without service interruption provides essential value to the user.

In this way, the values, risks, and costs of individual dialogue systems are enumerated and identified as evaluation items. The resulting business-DS alignment model for the FAQ chatbot written in ArchiMate is shown in Figure 7.

Additional case studies can be found in Appendix A.

4 Limitations and Discussion

Although the case studies suggested that our approach is promising, there may be values, risks, and costs that have not been considered, necessitating continuous review. Particularly with advancements in technology like LLMs, which enable more natural conversations, new risks that were previously unconsidered may arise.

As stated earlier, academic research has often used user satisfaction and user experience as evaluation metrics. Roughly speaking, user satisfaction relates to functional value, self-expressive value, and social value. User experience relates to emotional value, must-be value, attractive value, non-maleficence, justice and fairness, and transparency. Our analysis identified evaluation items beyond these, so it became possible to consider user satisfaction, user experience, and other evaluation items all at once. We hope this leads to new research themes.

In planning the actual system development, it is necessary to balance values, risks, and costs. For example, while showing many advertisements might increase business value, it could decrease emotional value and pose risks to hinder non-maleficence. Similarly, using a low-performance model to reduce costs can decrease must-be value. A balanced system design considering all evaluation items is necessary, and our approach enables such a balanced design by identifying evaluation items from various perspectives.

In some cases, it is desirable to integrate these evaluation items into a single-dimensional evaluation scale. However, the prioritization of these items must be determined by the consensus of various stakeholders, including the system owner. We hope business-DS alignment models help the facilitation among the stakeholders.

The evaluation items obtained using the methodology proposed in this paper do not necessarily allow for a quantitative assessment of dialogue systems. However, in many cases, various IT-related technologies are proposed and utilized without quantitative evaluation. In addition, focusing only on quantifiable evaluation items and ignoring other items have the risk of falling into the well-known *McNamara fallacy* (also known as the *quantitative fallacy*). We believe that instead of focusing solely on fields where quantitative evaluation is feasible through small-scale experiments, dialogue system researchers should also consider evaluation items that are difficult to quantify. This approach may lead to the development of more practical technologies.

While it is practically impossible to quantitatively demonstrate the superiority of our methodology, we aim to showcase its effectiveness by applying it to the development of a variety of practical dialogue systems and evaluating it from multiple perspectives.

Business-IT alignment models on which our methodology is based may not be familiar to dialogue system engineers, making it potentially challenging to construct a business-DS alignment model. Therefore, we believe it is effective to present a simpler model. As an alternative approach, it is also possible to consider developing human resources who can construct business-DS alignment models while communicating with various stakeholders.

5 Concluding Remarks

This paper proposed a methodology to identify evaluation items for dialogue systems based on business-DS alignment models. Although the methodology presented in this paper needs improvement through more case studies. Nevertheless, we believe that it serves as a useful first step.

Besides the future work already mentioned, We plan to analyze the issues that prevent commercializing systems in the research stage.

Acknowledgments

This work was partly supported by JSPS KAKENHI Grant Number JP22H00536.

References

David Aaker. 2014. *Aaker on branding: 20 principles that drive success*. Morgan James Publishing.

Reina Akama, Kazuaki Inada, Naoya Inoue, Sosuke Kobayashi, and Kentaro Inui. 2017. Generating stylistically consistent dialog responses with transfer learning. In *Proceedings of the Eighth International Joint Conference on Natural Language Processing (Volume 2: Short Papers)*, pages 408–412, Taipei, Taiwan. Asian Federation of Natural Language Processing.

Yoshihiko Asao, Julien Kloetzer, Junta Mizuno, Dai Saiki, Kazuma Kadowaki, and Kentaro Torisawa. 2020. Understanding user utterances in a dialog system for caregiving. In *Proceedings of the Twelfth Language Resources and Evaluation Conference*, pages 653–661, Marseille, France. European Language Resources Association.

Nabiha Asghar, Pascal Poupart, Xin Jiang, and Hang Li. 2017. Deep active learning for dialogue generation. In *Proceedings of the 6th Joint Conference on Lexical and Computational Semantics (*SEM 2017)*, pages 78–83, Vancouver, Canada. Association for Computational Linguistics.

Rafael E. Banchs and Haizhou Li. 2012. IRIS: a chat-oriented dialogue system based on the vector space model. In *Proceedings of the ACL 2012 System Demonstrations*, pages 37–42, Jeju Island, Korea. Association for Computational Linguistics.

Jerome R Bellegarda. 2013. Spoken language understanding for natural interaction: The siri experience. In *Natural Interaction with Robots, Knowbots and Smartphones: Putting Spoken Dialog Systems into Practice*, pages 3–14. Springer.

Leigh Clark, Nadia Pantidi, Orla Cooney, Philip Doyle, Diego Garaialde, Justin Edwards, Brendan Spillane, Emer Gilmartin, Christine Murad, Cosmin Munteanu, Vincent Wade, and Benjamin R. Cowan. 2019. What makes a good conversation? Challenges in designing truly conversational agents. In *Proceedings of the 2019 CHI Conference on Human Factors in Computing Systems*, CHI '19, page 1–12, New York, NY, USA. Association for Computing Machinery.

David DeVault, Ron Artstein, Grace Benn, Teresa Dey, Ed Fast, Alesia Gainer, Kallirroi Georgila, Jon Gratch, Arno Hartholt, Margaux Lhommet, Gale Lucas, Stacy Marsella, Fabrizio Morbini, Angela Nazarian, Stefan Scherer, Giota Stratou, Apar Suri, David Traum, Rachel Wood, Yuyu Xu, Albert Rizzo, and Louis-Philippe Morency. 2014. Simsensei kiosk: a virtual human interviewer for healthcare decision support. In *Proceedings of AAMAS '14*, page 1061–1068, Richland, SC. International Foundation for Autonomous Agents and Multiagent Systems.

Laila Dybkjær and Niels Ole Bernsen. 2002. The dialogue engineering life-cycle. In *A Festschrift for Professor Haldur Õim*, pages 103–125. the Department of General Linguistics 3, University of Tartu.

Asbjørn Følstad and Cameron Taylor. 2021. Investigating the user experience of customer service chatbot interaction: a framework for qualitative analysis of chatbot dialogues. *Quality and User Experience*, 6(1).

Chongming Gao, Wenqiang Lei, Xiangnan He, Maarten de Rijke, and Tat-Seng Chua. 2021. Advances and challenges in conversational recommender systems: A survey. *AI Open*, 2:100–126.

Seungju Han, Beomsu Kim, Jin Yong Yoo, Seokjun Seo, Sangbum Kim, Enkhbayar Erdenee, and Buru Chang. 2022. Meet your favorite character: Open-domain chatbot mimicking fictional characters with only a few utterances. In *Proceedings of the 2022 Conference of the North American Chapter of the Association for Computational Linguistics: Human Language Technologies*, pages 5114–5132, Seattle, United States. Association for Computational Linguistics.

Peter Henderson, Koustuv Sinha, Nicolas Angelard-Gontier, Nan Rosemary Ke, Genevieve Fried, Ryan Lowe, and Joelle Pineau. 2018. Ethical challenges in data-driven dialogue systems. In *Proceedings of the 2018 AAAI/ACM Conference on AI, Ethics, and Society*, AIES '18, page 123–129, New York, NY, USA. Association for Computing Machinery.

Knut Hinkelmann, Aurona Gerber, Dimitris Karagiannis, Barbara Thoenssen, Alta Van der Merwe, and Robert Woitsch. 2016. A new paradigm for the continuous alignment of business and IT: Combining enterprise architecture modelling and enterprise ontology. *Computers in Industry*, 79:77–86.

Takuya Hiraoka, Graham Neubig, Koichiro Yoshino, Tomoki Toda, and Satoshi Nakamura. 2017. Active learning for example-based dialog systems. In *Dialogues with Social Robots: Enablements, Analyses, and Evaluation*, pages 67–78. Springer.

Vojtěch Hudeček and Ondrej Dusek. 2023. Are large language models all you need for task-oriented dialogue? In *Proceedings of the 24th Annual Meeting of the Special Interest Group on Discourse and Dialogue*, pages 216–228, Prague, Czechia. Association for Computational Linguistics.

Jati H. Husen, Hironori Washizaki, Jomphon Runpakprakun, Nobukazu Yoshioka, Hnin Thandar Tun, Yoshiaki Fukazawa, and Hironori Takeuchi. 2024. Integrated multi-view modeling for reliable machine learning-intensive software engineering. *Software Quality Journal*, 32:1239 – 1285.

Shinya Iizuka, Shota Mochizuki, Atsumoto Ohashi, Sanae Yamashita, Ao Guo, and Ryuichiro Higashinaka. 2023. Clarifying the dialogue-level performance of GPT-3.5 and GPT-4 in task-oriented and non-task-oriented dialogue systems. In *Proceedings of the AAAI Fall Symposia*, volume 2, pages 182–186.

Michimasa Inaba and Kenichi Takahashi. 2016. Neural utterance ranking model for conversational dialogue systems. In *Proceedings of the 17th Annual Meeting of the Special Interest Group on Discourse and Dialogue*, pages 393–403, Los Angeles. Association for Computational Linguistics.

Koji Inoue, Kohei Hara, Divesh Lala, Shizuka Nakamura, Katsuya Takanashi, and Tatsuya Kawahara. 2021. *A Job Interview Dialogue System with Autonomous Android ERICA*, pages 291–297. Springer Singapore, Singapore.

Dietmar Jannach, Ahtsham Manzoor, Wanling Cai, and Li Chen. 2021. A survey on conversational recommender systems. *ACM Comput. Surv.*, 54(5).

Anna Jobin, Marcello Ienca, and Effy Vayena. 2019. The global landscape of AI ethics guidelines. *Nature machine intelligence*, 1(9):389–399.

Michael Johnston, Cris Flagg, Anna Gottardi, Sattvik Sahai, Yao Lu, Samyuth Sagi, Luke Dai, Prasoon Goyal, Behnam Hedayatnia, Lucy Hu, Di Jin, Patrick Lange, Shaohua Liu, Sijia Liu, Daniel Pressel, Hangjie Shi, Zhejia Yang, Chao Zhang, Desheng Zhang, Leslie Ball, Kate Bland, Shui Hu, Osman Ipek, James Jeun, Heather Rocker, Lavina Vaz, Akshaya Iyengar, Yang Liu, Arindam Mandal, Dilek Hakkani-Tür, and Reza Ghanadan. 2023. Advancing open domain dialog: The fifth Alexa Prize socialbot grand challenge. In *Alexa Prize SocialBot Grand Challenge 5 Proceedings*.

Noriaki Kano, Nobuhiku Seraku, Fumio Takahashi, and Shinichi Tsuji. 1984. Attractive quality and must-be quality. *Journal of the Japanese Society for Quality Control*, 14(2):147–156. (in Japanese).

Takahiro Kobori, Mikio Nakano, and Tomoaki Nakamura. 2016. Small talk improves user impressions of interview dialogue systems. In *Proceedings of the 17th Annual Meeting of the Special Interest Group on Discourse and Dialogue*, pages 370–380, Los Angeles. Association for Computational Linguistics.

Patrick Lewis, Ethan Perez, Aleksandra Piktus, Fabio Petroni, Vladimir Karpukhin, Naman Goyal, Heinrich Küttler, Mike Lewis, Wen-tau Yih, Tim Rocktäschel, Sebastian Riedel, and Douwe Kiela. 2020. Retrieval-augmented generation for knowledge-intensive NLP tasks. In *Proc. NeurIPS 2020*, volume 33, pages 9459–9474. Curran Associates, Inc.

Ryan Lowe, Nissan Pow, Iulian Vlad Serban, Laurent Charlin, Chia-Wei Liu, and Joelle Pineau. 2017. Training end-to-end dialogue systems with the ubuntu dialogue corpus. *Dialogue & Discourse*, 8(1):31–65.

Nicolas Mayer, Jocelyn Aubert, Eric Grandry, Christophe Feltus, Elio Goettelmann, and Roel J. Wieringa. 2019. An integrated conceptual model for information system security risk management supported by enterprise architecture management. *Softw. Syst. Model.*, 18(3):2285–2312.

Michael F. McTear. 2004. *Dialogue Engineering: The Dialogue Systems Development Lifecycle*, pages 129–161. Springer London, London.

Josip Mikulić and Darko Prebežac. 2011. A critical review of techniques for classifying quality attributes in the Kano model. *Managing Service Quality: An International Journal*, 21(1):46–66.

Takashi Minato, Ryuichiro Higashinaka, Kurima Sakai, Tomo Funayama, Hiromitsu Nishizaki, and Takayuki Nagai. 2023. Design of a competition specifically for spoken dialogue with a humanoid robot. *Advanced Robotics*, 37(21):1349–1363.

Mikio Nakano, Hisahiro Mukai, Yoichi Matsuyama, and Kazunori Komatani. 2024. Evaluating dialogue systems from the system owners’ perspectives. In *In Proceedings of the 14th International Workshop on Spoken Dialogue Systems Technology (IWSDS 2024)*.

Yan Pan, Mingyang Ma, Bernhard Pflugfelder, and Georg Groh. 2022. User satisfaction modeling with domain adaptation in task-oriented dialogue systems. In *Proceedings of the 23rd Annual Meeting of the Special Interest Group on Discourse and Dialogue*, pages 630–636, Edinburgh, UK. Association for Computational Linguistics.

Vlad Pandelea, Edoardo Ragusa, Tom Young, Paolo Gastaldo, and Erik Cambria. 2022. Toward hardware-aware deep-learning-based dialogue systems. *Neural Comput. Appl.*, 34(13):10397–10408.

Melissa Perri. 2018. *Escaping the Build Trap: How Effective Product Management Creates Real Value*. O'Reilley Media.

Nils Reimers and Iryna Gurevych. 2019. Sentence-bert: Sentence embeddings using siamese bert-networks. *Preprint*, arXiv:1908.10084.

Ming-Hsiang Su, Chung-Hsien Wu, Kun-Yi Huang, Qian-Bei Hong, and Huai-Hung Huang. 2018. Follow-up Question Generation Using Pattern-based Seq2seq with a Small Corpus for Interview Coaching. In *Proc. Interspeech 2018*, pages 1006–1010.

Hao Sun, Guangxuan Xu, Jiawen Deng, Jiale Cheng, Chujie Zheng, Hao Zhou, Nanyun Peng, Xiaoyan Zhu, and Minlie Huang. 2022. On the safety of conversational models: Taxonomy, dataset, and benchmark. In *Findings of the Association for Computational Linguistics: ACL 2022*, pages 3906–3923, Dublin, Ireland. Association for Computational Linguistics.

Hironori Takeuchi, Jati H. Husen, Hnin Thandar Tun, Hironori Washizaki, and Nobukazu Yoshioka. 2024. Enterprise architecture-based metamodel for machine learning projects and its management. *Future Generation Computer Systems*, 161:135–145.

Hironori Takeuchi and Shuichiro Yamamoto. 2019. Business AI alignment modeling based on enterprise architecture. In *Proceedings of the 11th KES International Conference of Intelligent Decision Technologies*, pages 155–165. Springer.

The Open Group. 2019. *ArchiMate® 3.1-A pocket guide*. Van Haren.

Gokhan Tur, Dilek Hakkani-Tür, and Robert E Schapire. 2005. Combining active and semi-supervised learning for spoken language understanding. *Speech Communication*, 45(2):171–186.

Stefan Ultes and Wolfgang Maier. 2021. User satisfaction reward estimation across domains: Domain-independent dialogue policy learning. *Dialogue and Discourse*, 12(2):81–114.

Marco Vicente, Nelson Gama, and Miguel Mira da Silva. 2013. Modeling ITIL business motivation model in ArchiMate. In *Proceedings of IESS 2013*, volume 143, pages 86–99. Springer.

Marilyn A. Walker, Diane J. Litman, Candace A. Kamm, and Alicia Abella. 1997. PARADISE: A framework for evaluating spoken dialogue agents. In *35th Annual Meeting of the Association for Computational Linguistics and 8th Conference of the European Chapter of the Association for Computational Linguistics*, pages 271–280, Madrid, Spain. Association for Computational Linguistics.

Tsung-Hsien Wen, David Vandyke, Nikola Mrkšić, Milica Gašić, Lina M. Rojas-Barahona, Pei-Hao Su, Stefan Ultes, and Steve Young. 2017. A network-based end-to-end trainable task-oriented dialogue system. In *Proceedings of the 15th Conference of the European Chapter of the Association for Computational Linguistics: Volume 1, Long Papers*, pages 438–449, Valencia, Spain. Association for Computational Linguistics.

Jing Xu, Da Ju, Margaret Li, Y-Lan Boureau, Jason Weston, and Emily Dinan. 2021. Recipes for safety in open-domain chatbots. *Preprint*, arXiv:2010.07079.

Zhou Yu, Vikram Ramanarayanan, Patrick Lange, and David Suendermann-Oeft. 2019. *An Open-Source Dialog System with Real-Time Engagement Tracking for Job Interview Training Applications*, pages 199–207. Springer International Publishing, Cham.

Jie Zeng, Yukiko Nakano, and Tatsuya Sakato. 2023. Question generation to elicit users' food preferences by considering the semantic content. In *Proceedings of the 24th Annual Meeting of the Special Interest Group on Discourse and Dialogue*, pages 190–196, Prague, Czechia. Association for Computational Linguistics.

Caleb Ziems, Jane Yu, Yi-Chia Wang, Alon Halevy, and Diyi Yang. 2022. The moral integrity corpus: A benchmark for ethical dialogue systems. In *Proceedings of the 60th Annual Meeting of the Association for Computational Linguistics (Volume 1: Long Papers)*, pages 3755–3773, Dublin, Ireland. Association for Computational Linguistics.

A Additional Case Studies

A.1 Dialogue Systems Analyzed

In addition to the FAQ chatbot that was analyzed in Section 3.3, we analyzed the system listed below. We selected these systems because they are already in commercial service or close to practical use. Note that we do not assume the same settings as the systems referenced in the literature.

Speech-based assistant on smartphones This works as an embedded application of smartphones and performs question answering, controlling applications, and other tasks like Apple's iPhone Siri (Bellegarda, 2013). The input modality is speech and the output modalities are speech, displaying on the smartphone, and application control. It uses proprietary speech recognition. Wake words are recognized on the device and other user utterances are recognized on the server. It also uses proprietary server-based language understanding using BERT or others. Dialogue management and response generation are rule-based and run on the server. Speech synthesis is device-embedded.

Job interview practice system This system is designed for practicing job interviews (Inoue et al., 2021; Yu et al., 2019; Su et al., 2018) by interacting with a virtual agent. The system operates on a server and is accessed via a browser. The input modalities are speech and facial images, and the output modalities are speech and virtual agents. It uses commercial server-based speech recognition and speech synthesis. Language understanding, dialogue management, and language generation use an API-based commercial LLM service (such as OpenAI's ChatGPT[1]). The virtual agent runs on the browser.

Interview dialogue system for understanding user status This is a virtual agent dialogue system designed to engage with users, asking about their lifestyle and health status while conversing with them (DeVault et al., 2014; Asao et al., 2020). To ensure continuous use, the system aims to make the dialogues enjoyable for the users (Kobori et al., 2016). The system operates on a server and is accessed through a browser. Input modalities are speech and facial images and the output modalities are speech and virtual agents. It uses server-based commercial speech recognition and language understanding, and device-embedded speech synthesis. It also uses scenario-based dialogue management running on the server. The virtual agent runs on a browser.

Conversational recommender system This system engages in dialogue to elicit user preferences and experience (Zeng et al., 2023), and based on this information, recommends products (Jannach et al., 2021; Gao et al., 2021). It operates on a server. The input and output modality is text. It uses a crowd service for language understanding and state transition model-based dialogue management (e.g., Google Dialogflow[2]).

A.2 Evaluation Items for Example Dialogue Systems

Table 3 shows the elements of the generic model for business-DS alignment and their relation to each example system. The factors listed under "common to all system" are those shared by all systems. We show this table instead of the comprehensive ArchiMate representations for simplicity.

Relatively minor risks have been omitted. For instance, even if rule-based utterance generation is used, there is a possibility that the person writing the rules might create biased or offensive utterance templates. However, this risk is generally low because checks are usually conducted before the system is deployed.

In contrast, response generation using LLMs carries a higher risk because it cannot be pre-checked. However, compared to other applications, job interview practice systems have relatively low actual harm even if the LLM generates inappropriate utterances. Considering the development cost, using an LLM is reasonable.

These case studies have suggested that, based on the business-DS alignment models, it is possible to identify the costs, risks, and values of individual dialogue systems. They also allow for highlighting potential issues and comparing systems from various perspectives.

[1] https://openai.com/index/chatgpt/

[2] https://cloud.google.com/dialogflow

Elements in the generic model			Common to all systems	Example dialogue system			
				Speech-based assistant on smartphones	Job interview pratice system	Interview dialogue system for understanding user status	Conversational recommender system
Values provided by the dialogue system	Business Value	Revenue increase		Increase in the sales of a product integrated with the system			Increase in the sales of recommended products
		Cost reduction			Reduction in labor costs	Reduction in labor costs	Reduction in labor costs
		New revenues	Reuse of collected dialogue data		Dialogue system usage fee		
	User value	Functional value		Can obtain desired information	Can effectively practice dialogues		Can receive product recommendations tailored to the user's preferences
		Emotional value			Not embarrassing because no one else can hear	Can enjoy conversation	
		Self-expressive value					
		Social					
	Quality Value	Must-be value	System does not stop	Can accomplish task with high probability	Can accomplish task with high probability		Can accomplish task with high probability
		Attractive value	Can engage in natural, human-like conversations				
AI principles to be satisfied	Transparency				Risk that the behaviors of the LLM cannot be explained		
	Justice and fairness				Risk of LLM making utterances based on biased thinking		
	Non-maleficence				Risk of LLM making defamatory or incorrect utterances		
	Responsibility				Risk that responsibility sharing between external services and the system is not clear	Risk that responsibility sharing between external services and the system is not clear	Risk that responsibility sharing between external services and the system is not clear
	Privacy			Risk of the leakage of personal information contained in the user's speech or utterance content	Risk of the leakage of personal information contained in the user's speech, facial images, and utterance content	Risk of the leakage of personal information contained in the user's speech, facial images, and utterance content	Risk of the leakage of personal information contained in the user's utterance content
	Beneficence						
	Freedom and autonomy				The risk of not being able to control the content generated by an LLM		
Costs for developing and operating the dialogue system	Cost for human resources		- Initial system development and system testing - System modifications after the operation starts - Troubleshooting and issue resolution				
	Cost for information resources			Annotated data for model construction and response generation rules		Annotated data for model construction and response generation rules	Annotated data for model construction
	Cost for IT resources		- Computational resources required for initial system development - Server cost		SaaS usage fees (speech recognition, speech synthesis, and LLM)	SaaS usage fees (speech recognition and language understanding)	SaaS usage fees (language understanding)

Table 3: Evaluation items for example dialogue systems.

Speech-Controlled Smart Speaker for Accurate, Real-Time Health and Care Record Management

Jonathan E. Carrick[1,2], Nina Dethlefs[3], Lisa Greaves[2], Venkata M. V. Gunturi[1], Rameez Raja Kureshi[1], Yongqiang Cheng[4],

[1]School of Computer Science, University of Hull, Hull, HU6 7RX, UK,
[2]Connexin Ltd, K3 Business Park, Hull, HU5 1SN, UK,
[3]Department of Computer Science, Loughborough University, Loughborough, LE11 3TU, UK,
[4]Faculty of Technology: Computing, University of Sunderland, Sunderland, SR6 0DD, UK

Correspondence: j.carrick@hull.ac.uk

Abstract

To help alleviate the pressures felt by care workers, we have begun new research into improving the efficiency of care plan management by advancing recent developments in automatic speech recognition. Our novel approach adapts off-the-shelf tools in a purpose-built application for the speech domain, addressing challenges of accent adaption, real-time processing and speech hallucinations. We augment the speech-recognition scope of Open AI's Whisper model through fine-tuning, reducing word error rates (WERs) from 16.8 to 1.0 on a range of British dialects. Addressing the speech-hallucination side effect of adapting to real-time recognition by enforcing a signal-to-noise ratio threshold and audio stream checks, we achieve a WER of 5.1, compared to 14.9 with Whisper's original model. These ongoing research efforts tackle challenges that are necessary to build the speech-control basis for a custom smart speaker system that is both accurate and timely.

1 Introduction

Health and social care is one of the last major industries to undergo the digital transformation to improve management of information and connectivity (Glaser and Shaw, 2022; Konopik and Blunck, 2023). Reasons include challenges relating to data privacy, tech-literacy and scalability in a highly heterogenuous domain (Aceto et al., 2020). Transformation towards *Healthcare 4.0* is helped by integrating new artificial intelligence technologies into purpose-built smart devices (Wehde, 2019).

Yen et al. (2018) find that, even with the implementation of real-time electronic record management, healthcare administrators spend a quarter of their time on documentation and, due to typing distractions, information is missed. Combined with the job-demanding stresses that care workers experience (Wilberforce et al., 2012) it is clear that there is a need for simplified health care record management to help reduce the burden. This would further benefit those cared for as care resources become more optimised. One way to achieve a quicker, more efficient approach to care record management that is both complete and accurate is through automatic speech recognition (ASR, Ajami, 2016; Alharbi et al., 2021; Malik et al., 2021).

In this paper we focus on recognition of spoken English in the UK. However, typical off-the-shelf ASR models are often trained primarily on American-accented datasets (Vergyri et al., 2010; Mathur et al., 2020) and health and care in the UK is a diverse industry. This includes variations in dialects across the British Isles (MacKenzie et al., 2022), as well as foreign accents from care workers who originate from places such as Eastern Europe, Nigeria, and South Asia, amongst others[1]. Commercial smart speakers, such as Amazon's Alexa, showcase the potential of real-time ASR in a general home assistant setting (Hoy, 2018), and have been used in previous studies to improve well-being in social care (Edwards et al., 2021). However, to the best of our knowledge there is currently no device whose primary function is a smart administrative assistant for health and care workers.

Hence, we have set out to develop a custom-built speaker, starting with new research into the fundamental ASR basis. This paper introduces a novel approach and makes the following key contributions:

[1]https://www.skillsforcare.org.uk/Adult-Social-Care-Workforce-Data/Workforce-intelligence/publications/Topics/Workforce-nationality-and-international-recruitment.aspx

Proceedings of the 15th International Workshop on Spoken Dialogue Systems Technology, pages 238–244
May 27–30, 2025. ©2025 Association for Computational Linguistics

- Fine-tuning an ASR model for greater scope of accent recognition
- Adapting the model and adding voice commands to a real-time recognition pipeline
- Audio processing methods to prevent speech hallucinations caused by background noise and predictive text

2 Smart Speaker Design

We began with a review into different accessible ASR models. In the context of finding the best-suited framework to build and adapt our custom system around, our initial testing of models included wav2vec 2.0 (Baevski et al., 2020) and VOSK[2] with the Kaldi toolkit[3]. Ultimately, we decided to utilise Open AI's Whisper (Radford et al., 2023) model, due to its free, open license, ongoing development in state-of-the-art ASR and ease of adapting to our own needs with Python.

Rather than use an established smart speaker, we develop our own hardware[4] to, first, keep the solution cost-effective for customers in the care sector, who might not need or want a full-fledged commercial system, and second, to keep full control of confidentially sensitive data. While the device itself can run most of the required data management functionality, speech inference runs on a GPU cloud-server. We use sound cues to give audio feedback to the user to confirm that voice commands are understood and functions are carried out.

3 Accent Adaption

Despite Whisper's extensive training, we find that it struggles to generalise to a broad variety of British as well as other foreign accents found in the care sector. Graham and Roll (2024) find a similar bias towards North American over other British accents.

We start by adapting Whisper to better recognise the variations in six different British accents: 'Southern', 'Northern', 'Midlands', 'Scottish', 'Welsh', 'Irish' from the OpenSLR[5] dataset of $\sim$30 hours of spoken English (Demirsahin et al., 2020). With this dataset, we fine-tune Whisper's `medium.en` model, which balances speed with accuracy, and is the largest model that we can enforce with English-only recognition; the larger models would occasionally incorrectly recognise speech as a different language and attempt to translate. Furthermore, the large model requires twice the VRAM but offers diminishing returns in performance (Radford et al., 2023) and we do not require the additional feature of multi-language ASR.

Our fine-tuning[6] is done with 95% of the data, with the remainder used for validation. By observing the evolution of the word error rate (WER)[7] and validation loss through training, we find that the model begins to plateau half an epoch in and converges in approximately two training epochs, beyond which the model begins to overfit the dataset. Training for 3,072 steps (batch size 16 and evaluation every 256 steps), we achieve a minimum WER of 1.0 at step 2,048, where validation loss is also minimised[8]. This checkpoint defines the fine-tuned model uesd in this study. Table 1 shows the improvement in WERs per accent through fine-tuning. Recognition of all accents surpasses human-level transcription (Amodei et al., 2016; Stolcke and Droppo, 2017; Lippmann, 1997).

4 Dealing with Hallucinations

Off-the-shelf, Whisper requires an audio file uploaded manually in a controlled process. Adapting Whisper to a real-time pipeline presented an unexpected challenge: hallucinations in ASR are defined as 'recognised' text that arises completely independently from what is spoken. While not limited to real-time ASR (Dolev et al., 2024), the phenomenon becomes more apparent in this adaption. Hallucinations are not simply mis-recognised words or phrases, but recognition in the absence of speech. These need to be prevented as hallucinated text, while often common words/phrases, e.g. "Thank you", "Yes", can be unexpected or even harmful (Koenecke et al., 2024). Without automatic mitigation, hallucinations may cause confusion in care records and require additional work to fix, resulting in the opposite of what we aim to achieve with our smart speaker. We find two causes of hallucination in our setting, as detailed below.

[2]https://alphacephei.com/vosk/

[3]https://github.com/kaldi-asr/kaldi

[4]We use a Raspberry Pi (Model 4), 8GB RAM, GPIO speaker & USB speaker, USB microphone, one-button 'keyboard' and touchscreen.

[5]https://www.openslr.org/83/

[6]We follow a similar method to https://huggingface.co/blog/fine-tune-whisper, adapted to our dataset.

[7]We use the WER implementation from https://huggingface.co/spaces/evaluate-metric/wer

[8]Model fine-tuning was done using Viper (https://hpc.wordpress.hull.ac.uk/), taking approximately 70 hours to optimise.

Accent	WER before fine-tuning	WER after fine-tuning	Number of test samples
'Southern'	16.8	0.9	451
'Midlands'	13.9	1.3	25
'Northern'	16.3	0.9	158
'Welsh'	16.4	1.2	148
'Scottish'	17.9	1.4	93
'Irish'	21.0	2.7	19
Weighted average	**16.8**	**1.0**	

Table 1: WERs for Whisper before and after fine-tuning with the OpenSLR dataset. WER scores are rounded as higher precision is not meaningful with these sample sizes. Averages are weighted as proportions of each accent in the test data differ, shown by the number of test samples. True WER scores (maximum precision) were included in calculation of averages, that are then rounded at the end. Class imbalance is due to random sampling and reflects the number of volunteers for each accent during creation of the original dataset.

4.1 Recognising Background Noise

The first cause is due to continually monitoring with a microphone. If audio input, regardless of its nature, is automatically passed to Whisper, the model will try to process it into text, even if nothing has been spoken. In this case, Whisper tries to recognise speech from effective silence, i.e. background noise, and results in speech hallucinations.

The dynamic energy threshold[9] we employ for microphone input is not sufficient in separating clear speech from background noise. Hence, we apply a check in each processing loop before passing the queued audio data to the ASR (Figure 1). A signal-to-noise ratio (SNR) threshold is defined during initialisation and we choose SNR $= 50$, determined empirically by testing in different environments, e.g. quiet room at home, noisy office. Then, for each audio loop, the SNR is calculated as

$$\text{SNR} = \frac{\text{Signal Power}}{\text{Noise Power}} = \frac{\sigma_S^2}{\sigma_N^2}, \tag{1}$$

where σ^2 is the variance (standard deviation squared) for signal S and noise N, and, if it is greater than the threshold, the audio clip is passed to Whisper. σ_S^2 is calculated for each loop's audio clip. σ_N^2 is calculated upon device startup when the speaker records the background noise level of the current environment. We limit σ_N^2 to the range 0.5–5×10^{-6}, determined empirically, as, too low and any sound will be passed to the ASR as speech, and too high and no speech will be recognised.

[9] `https://pypi.org/project/SpeechRecognition/2.1.3/`

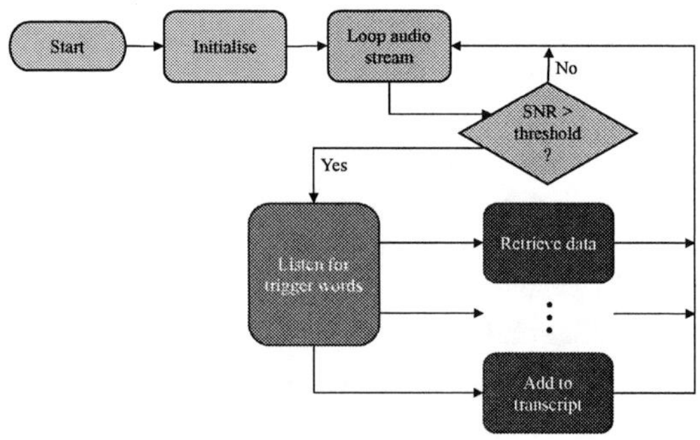

Figure 1: Flow chart of the speaker pipeline. After set up (yellow) and starting the audio loop (green), functions (purple) are evoked via voice commands (blue).

4.2 Record Timeout

LLMs such as Whisper are typically trained on sequences of words (Sutskever et al., 2014; Radford et al., 2023). Therefore, when an initial word is passed to a trained model, it will anticipate the next word/s, based on common sequences it has learned from many hours of training. This learned 'predictive text' means that, if the model considers the speech input to be only part of a phrase, Whisper may automatically output what it thinks the full phrase should be. This form of hallucination occurs when the microphone recording loop times out before a word/phrase is completed. Figure 2 demonstrates this effect with a waveform of speech and its corresponding recognised text, before and after a phrase is completed.

We find a recorded timeout of 2 seconds suitable to balance the trade-off between 'real-timeness' and ASR accuracy. We implement predictive-

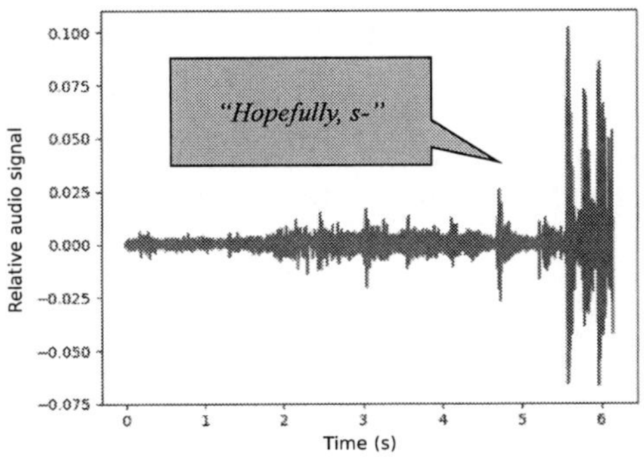

(a) Recognised speech: "Hopefully, something will work out"

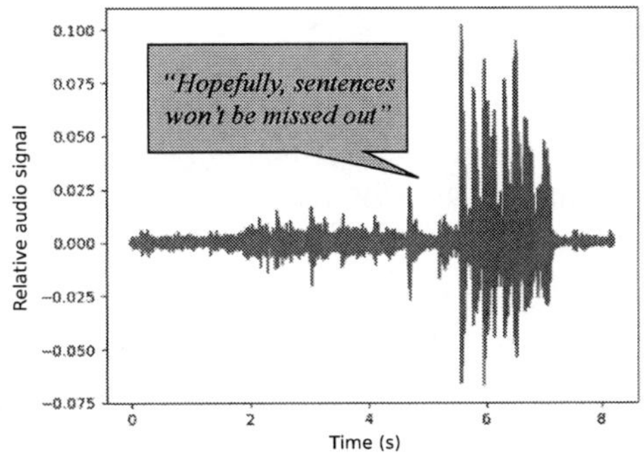

(b) Recognised speech: "Hopefully, sentences won't be missed out"

Figure 2: Waveforms of speech where the phrase is cut off by a recorded timeout and where the complete phrase is allowed to be fully recorded. Speech bubbles show the true speech recorded and their captions state ASR output.

Real-time setup	**WER**	**WER***
Original model: both hallucination methods	15.4	14.9
Fine-tuned model: without SNR checks	8.7	7.2
Fine-tuned model: without SNR checks, with pauses	185.5	182.4
Fine-tuned model: without audio stream checks	57.8	55.8
Fine-tuned model: both hallucination methods	6.6	5.1
Fine-tuned model: both hallucination methods, with pauses	6.0	5.7

Table 2: WERs for our different real-time tests. 'Both hallucination methods' here means that the SNR threshold and audio stream checks are both in place. The 'original model' is Whisper's `medium.en` model. 'With pauses' means that 3-second pauses were taken after every sentence. WER* denotes the word error rate when we ignore errors due to lexical differences that can still be considered as the recognition having the correct understanding.

hallucination prevention by tracking the audio data that is passed to the ASR. This method ensures that the each new transcript entry[10] is only saved when a full phrase is spoken, with recognised text corresponding only to the processed audio. When data between successive recognitions overlap, we ensure that the current transcript entry is updated with the most recent recognition. New transcript entries are added when at least 3 seconds have passed since the previous recognition *and* the recognition is on all new audio data. For additional robustness, we combine this with a comparison of texts between successive recognitions to check whether the current recognition is a continuation of the previous entry.

5 Real-time Recognition Results

We present the results of real-time recognition with our fine-tuned model and hallucination-prevention methods in Table 2. To test performance of our real-time ASR pipeline, the same script of 332 words (an excerpt from a paper draft) was read for different setups including comparison of our fine-tuned model to the original Whisper model, and with/without our hallucination methods. The reading for each setup was done in the same office meeting room in one take, where some background noise from adjacent rooms was present to help simulate a real environment where our device may be used, and was read by the same speaker who self-identifies as having a 'Northern' accent. For each test, the transcription is compared to the original script and we calculate the WER.

The model's full potential is demonstrated with both hallucination methods reaching a minimum WER across all tests of 6.6. The improvement over the original Whisper model is substantial (down from WER = 15.4), although limited compared to the reduction achieved with fine-tuning (Table 1). We attribute this to the real-time adaption where arbitrarily-segmented audio clips are input automat-

[10]Each 'entry' is a string element in the transcription list.

ically and the test environment, where some levels of background noise were present.

Some of the errors we find in the transcripts are not necessarily inaccuracies, but rather mismatches with the original script. For example, sometimes the model will recognise "*UK*" as "`United Kingdom`", and "*100,000s*" as "`hundreds of thousands`". While we consider the original script as the 'ground truth' for these tests, considering these differences as *correct*, WER reduces to as low as 5.1 with our fine-tuned model. Results for these cases are shown in Table 2 under WER*.

Without the SNR checks in place, there is less reduction in performance (WER = 8.7), however, the crucial importance of including a SNR threshold is demonstrated when 3-second pauses are taken after every sentence. Recognition from silence/background noise results in multiple hallucinations throughout. The generated text during these quiet moments is often gibberish, repeated out multiple times and with no relation to the context of the previous speech, increasing WER to as high as 185.5. In comparison, the same test with speech pauses using both hallucination methods, achieves similar results to the first test: WER = 6.0.

Finally, we test our fine-tuned model in real time without checking the audio stream for repeated recognitions of overlapping data. The WER is again high at 57.8 and results in several instances where a sentence is hallucinated or repeated multiple times in the transcript.

These results highlight that our fine-tuned model is more than twice as effective as Whisper's original model and that hallucination prevention is essential to achieve the lowest WERs possible.

6 Conclusion

We demonstrated that an off-the-shelf Whisper is not well-adapted to a wide range of spoken British accents and that WERs can be reduced substantially through fine-tuning to the set of target varieties. Adapting Whisper as a real-time ASR results in the unexpected side effect of speech hallucinations. This is addressed by enforcing a SNR criterion in each audio clip and tracking audio data passed to the ASR to ensure that recognised text consists of complete and accurate phrases.

Future work will include greater accent scope, integration into health and care plan systems, sophisticated care data querying and monitoring methods, and trigger/alert systems to improve administration efficiency and help identify errors. Upon successful deployment of these features, we will trial our smart speaker in a real care-home environment to gain a better understanding of technological capabilities, user requirements and to maximise the social impact of our specialised speaker system.

Limitations

Our initial fine-tuning of Whisper that is described covers a range of British accents from a single dataset. We would like to expand on this, especially with accents representing the diversity of health and care workers in the UK, but have not yet been able to because of a lack of available datasets with suitable coverage of a variety of accents. Initial testing of ASR performance in real time was done with a single speaker only for our pilot speaker. We are planning to expand this in future.

Ethical Considerations

Ethical reviews, including draft consent forms, have been completed and approved to prepare for user testing. While initial testing will be done with dummy care data, we have plans in place to follow General Data Protection Regulation with the handling of any sensitive information in the case of insitu health and care environments. As we progress in our development, we will address privacy concerns with secure logins and encryption methods. Measures are being taken for accurate recording of important information, especially with regards to treatments, medicine, etc., following guidelines, e.g. from the British National Formulary[11].

Acknowledgments

This project was supported by an Innovate UK Knowledge Transfer Partnership (KTP/13520). Much support from the University of Hull is gratefully acknowledged, including computing resources, and input and insightful comments from researchers in Health Sciences, the ethics committee and the Dementia Advisory Group. We also thank Connexin Ltd for making this project possible. Our thanks extends to our connections in adult social care for suggestions on user requirements. Finally, many thanks to the organisers of the 15th International Workshop on Spoken Dialogue Systems Technology and our anonymous reviewers.

[11] `https://bnf.nice.org.uk/`

References

Giuseppe Aceto, Valerio Persico, and Antonio Pescapé. 2020. Industry 4.0 and health: Internet of things, big data, and cloud computing for healthcare 4.0. *Journal of Industrial Information Integration*, 18:100129.

Sima Ajami. 2016. Use of speech-to-text technology for documentation by healthcare providers. *The National medical journal of India*, 29(3):148.

Sadeen Alharbi, Muna Alrazgan, Alanoud Alrashed, Turkiayh Alnomasi, Raghad Almojel, Rimah Alharbi, Saja Alharbi, Sahar Alturki, Fatimah Alshehri, and Maha Almojil. 2021. Automatic speech recognition: Systematic literature review. *IEEE Access*, 9:131858–131876.

Dario Amodei, Sundaram Ananthanarayanan, Rishita Anubhai, Jingliang Bai, Eric Battenberg, Carl Case, Jared Casper, Bryan Catanzaro, Qiang Cheng, Guoliang Chen, Jie Chen, Jingdong Chen, Zhijie Chen, Mike Chrzanowski, Adam Coates, Greg Diamos, Ke Ding, Niandong Du, Erich Elsen, Jesse Engel, Weiwei Fang, Linxi Fan, Christopher Fougner, Liang Gao, Caixia Gong, Awni Hannun, Tony Han, Lappi Johannes, Bing Jiang, Cai Ju, Billy Jun, Patrick LeGresley, Libby Lin, Junjie Liu, Yang Liu, Weigao Li, Xiangang Li, Dongpeng Ma, Sharan Narang, Andrew Ng, Sherjil Ozair, Yiping Peng, Ryan Prenger, Sheng Qian, Zongfeng Quan, Jonathan Raiman, Vinay Rao, Sanjeev Satheesh, David Seetapun, Shubho Sengupta, Kavya Srinet, Anuroop Sriram, Haiyuan Tang, Liliang Tang, Chong Wang, Jidong Wang, Kaifu Wang, Yi Wang, Zhijian Wang, Zhiqian Wang, Shuang Wu, Likai Wei, Bo Xiao, Wen Xie, Yan Xie, Dani Yogatama, Bin Yuan, Jun Zhan, and Zhenyao Zhu. 2016. Deep speech 2 : End-to-end speech recognition in english and mandarin. In *Proceedings of The 33rd International Conference on Machine Learning*, volume 48 of *Proceedings of Machine Learning Research*, pages 173–182, New York, New York, USA. PMLR.

Alexei Baevski, Yuhao Zhou, Abdelrahman Mohamed, and Michael Auli. 2020. wav2vec 2.0: A framework for self-supervised learning of speech representations. In *Advances in Neural Information Processing Systems*, volume 33, pages 12449–12460. Curran Associates, Inc.

Isin Demirsahin, Oddur Kjartansson, Alexander Gutkin, and Clara Rivera. 2020. Open-source multi-speaker corpora of the English accents in the British isles. In *Proceedings of the Twelfth Language Resources and Evaluation Conference*, pages 6532–6541, Marseille, France. European Language Resources Association.

Eyal Dolev, Clemens Lutz, and Noëmi Aepli. 2024. Does whisper understand Swiss German? an automatic, qualitative, and human evaluation. In *Proceedings of the Eleventh Workshop on NLP for Similar Languages, Varieties, and Dialects (VarDial 2024)*, pages 28–40, Mexico City, Mexico. Association for Computational Linguistics.

Katie J Edwards, Ray B Jones, Deborah Shenton, Toni Page, Inocencio Maramba, Alison Warren, Fiona Fraser, Tanja Križaj, Tristan Coombe, Hazel Cowls, and Arunangsu Chatterjee. 2021. The use of smart speakers in care home residents: Implementation study. *J Med Internet Res*, 23(12):e26767.

John Glaser and Stanley Shaw. 2022. Digital transformation success: What can health care providers learn from other industries? *Catalyst non-issue content*, 3(2).

Calbert Graham and Nathan Roll. 2024. Evaluating openai's whisper asr: Performance analysis across diverse accents and speaker traits. *JASA Express Letters*, 4(2):025206.

Matthew B. Hoy. 2018. Alexa, siri, cortana, and more: An introduction to voice assistants. *Medical Reference Services Quarterly*, 37(1):81–88. PMID: 29327988.

Allison Koenecke, Anna Seo Gyeong Choi, Katelyn X. Mei, Hilke Schellmann, and Mona Sloane. 2024. Careless whisper: Speech-to-text hallucination harms. In *Proceedings of the 2024 ACM Conference on Fairness, Accountability, and Transparency*, FAccT '24, page 1672–1681, New York, NY, USA. Association for Computing Machinery.

Jens Konopik and Dominik Blunck. 2023. Development of an evidence-based conceptual model of the health care sector under digital transformation: Integrative review. *J Med Internet Res*, 25:e41512.

Richard P. Lippmann. 1997. Speech recognition by machines and humans. *Speech Communication*, 22(1):1–15.

Laurel MacKenzie, George Bailey, and Danielle Turton. 2022. Towards an updated dialect atlas of british english. *Journal of Linguistic Geography*, 10(1):46–66.

Mishaim Malik, Muhammad Kamran Malik, Khawar Mehmood, and Imran Makhdoom. 2021. Automatic speech recognition: a survey. *Multimedia Tools and Applications*, 80(6):9411–9457.

Akhil Mathur, Fahim Kawsar, Nadia Berthouze, and Nicholas D. Lane. 2020. Libri-adapt: a new speech dataset for unsupervised domain adaptation. In *ICASSP 2020 - 2020 IEEE International Conference on Acoustics, Speech and Signal Processing (ICASSP)*, pages 7439–7443.

Alec Radford, Jong Wook Kim, Tao Xu, Greg Brockman, Christine Mcleavey, and Ilya Sutskever. 2023. Robust speech recognition via large-scale weak supervision. In *Proceedings of the 40th International Conference on Machine Learning*, volume 202 of *Proceedings of Machine Learning Research*, pages 28492–28518. PMLR.

Andreas Stolcke and Jasha Droppo. 2017. Comparing human and machine errors in conversational speech transcription. In *Interspeech 2017*, pages 137–141.

Ilya Sutskever, Oriol Vinyals, and Quoc V. Le. 2014. Sequence to sequence learning with neural networks. In *Proceedings of the 28th International Conference on Neural Information Processing Systems - Volume 2*, NIPS'14, page 3104–3112, Cambridge, MA, USA. MIT Press.

Dimitra Vergyri, Lori Lamel, and Jean-Luc Gauvain. 2010. Automatic speech recognition of multiple accented english data. In *Interspeech*, pages 1652–1655.

Mark Wehde. 2019. Healthcare 4.0. *IEEE Engineering Management Review*, 47(3):24–28.

Mark Wilberforce, Sally Jacobs, David Challis, Jill Manthorpe, Martin Stevens, Rowan Jasper, Jose-Luis Fernandez, Caroline Glendinning, Karen Jones, Martin Knapp, Nicola Moran, and Ann Netten. 2012. Revisiting the causes of stress in social work: Sources of job demands, control and support in personalised adult social care. *The British Journal of Social Work*, 44(4):812–830.

Po-Yin Yen, Marjorie Kellye, Marcelo Lopetegui, Abhijoy Saha, Jacqueline Loversidge, Esther M Chipps, Lynn Gallagher-Ford, and Jacalyn Buck. 2018. Nurses' time allocation and multitasking of nursing activities: A time motion study. *AMIA Annu Symp Proc*, 2018:1137–1146.

A Appendix

A.1 Voice Controls and Speaker Functions

Table 3 details some of the main trigger words and their functions in our smart speaker pipeline. Initialisation steps include microphone calibration, defining starting settings, e.g. 'asleep', and beginning to listen in the background. The different functions are only carried out when the appropriate 'trigger' words are located in the recognised text, e.g. "*Activate and retrieve latest medication entry*". In the future we would like to add a more conversational-agent approach, with a text-to-speech output to fulfil the role of 'speaker'.

A.2 Fine-tune Training

Figures 3 and 4 show the fine-tuning evolution of training/evaluation loss and WER respectively.

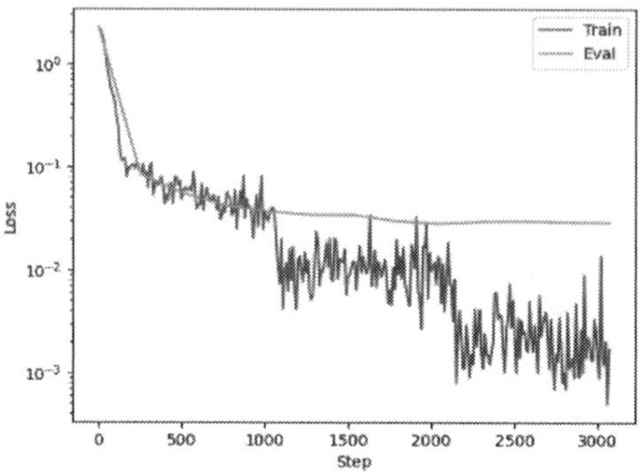

Figure 3: Loss on training and evaluation (test) data. The loss scale is logarithmic to help visualise the difference between loss evolutions. Evaluation loss is minimised at step 2048, beyond which a small degree of overfitting is observed. This approximately coincides with training over two epochs. Evaluation is done every 256 steps due to computational time constraints.

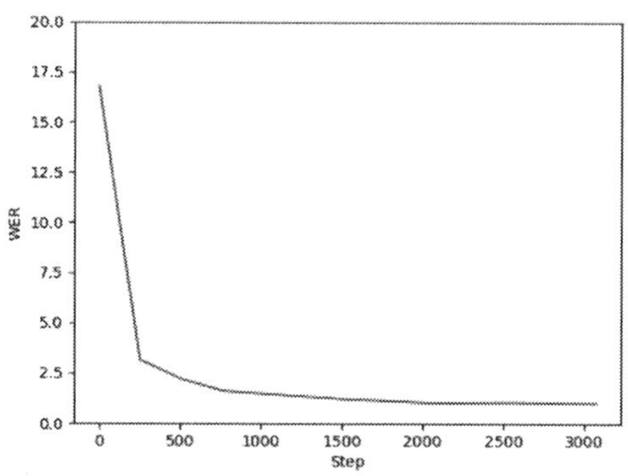

Figure 4: Through fine-tuning, WER on test data reduces and plateaus quickly, minimising at step 2048.

Trigger word	Functionality
Wake word, e.g. *"Activate"*	Wake speaker and unlock all other functionalities
Care record section, e.g. *"Medication"*	Start recording transcript for the given section
"Sign off"	Save transcript to care record with date/time-stamp
"Undo"	Removes most recent transcript addition
"Retrieve"	Return data from care record section
"Restart"	Erase current transcript and sleep the device again

Table 3: The main speaker functions and the trigger words that activate them.

Analysis of Voice Activity Detection Errors in API-based Streaming ASR for Human-Robot Dialogue

Kenta Yamamoto, Ryu Takeda and Kazunori Komatani
SANKEN, Osaka University, Japan
{kentayamamoto,rtakeda,komatani}@sanken.osaka-u.ac.jp

Abstract

In human-robot dialogue systems, streaming automatic speech recognition (ASR) services (e.g., Google ASR) are often utilized, with the microphone positioned close to the robot's loudspeaker. Under these conditions, both the robot's and the user's utterances are captured, resulting in frequent failures to detect user speech. This study analyzes voice activity detection (VAD) errors by comparing results from such streaming ASR to those from standalone VAD models. Experiments conducted on three distinct dialogue datasets showed that streaming ASR tends to ignore user utterances immediately following system utterances. We discuss the underlying causes of these VAD errors and provide recommendations for improving VAD performance in human-robot dialogue.

1 Introduction

Several embodied robots capable of speech interaction have been developed (Minato et al., 2024; Inoue et al., 2016). In this situation, since such robots are embodied, automatic speech recognition (ASR) is performed without the user wearing a headset microphone, meaning the microphone is not close to the user's mouth. Instead, the robot usually uses its built-in loudspeaker and a microphone placed nearby.

With advancements in ASR technology, even researchers who do not specialize in ASR can easily use it. Several previous studies have compared the performance of off-the-shelf ASR, providing valuable information for researchers and developers outside the speech recognition community, e.g., (Georgila and Traum, 2024). One of the simplest ways to use ASR is through streaming-based ASRs accessed via APIs. By using these, ASRs do not need to be downloaded or installed in advance, making them very convenient. In this case, because the ASR is streaming-based, both voice activity detection (VAD) and speech recognition are performed simultaneously on the server side.

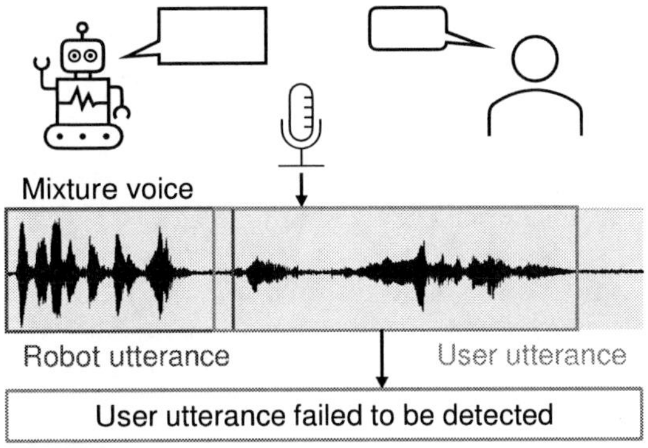

Figure 1: Robot fails to detect user utterance on dialogue

VAD (Atal and Rabiner, 1976) is a crucial frontend technology for spoken dialogue systems. Its role is to detect the active speech segments from the input signals captured by microphones. VAD is primarily used to determine the boundaries of a user utterance, facilitating turn-taking in dialogue (Brady, 1965; Medennikov et al., 2020; Skantze, 2021). However, if the system misses the user utterance, causing the dialogue to break down. Thus, accurately detecting user speech segments is also important for ASR (Kingsbury et al., 2002; Novitasari et al., 2022). Errors in failing to detect user utterances are significant problems for both turn-taking and ASR and therefore must be avoided.

In this paper, we demonstrate situations where system fails to detect user utterances occur in robot dialogue. Specifically, we focus on scenarios where (1) a streaming-based ASR is used, and (2) the robot's loudspeaker and microphone are positioned in close proximity. In such cases, the robot's voice is also picked up by the microphone along with the user's voice. This leads to frequent failures in VAD when using streaming-based ASR trained on single-speaker data, as depicted in Figure 1. VAD

Proceedings of the 15th International Workshop on Spoken Dialogue Systems Technology, pages 245–253
May 27–30, 2025. ©2025 Association for Computational Linguistics

error result in the robot ignoring the user utterance. This causes the robot to remain silent without taking its turn, making it difficult for general users to understand the robot's status, leading to significant frustration. Therefore, our research aims to provide insights for human-robot interaction (HRI) researchers and practitioners to achieve robust VAD.

This study addresses the following two research questions:

(RQ1) To what extent do commonly used tools, such as Google APIs employed in constructing spoken dialogue systems, ignore user utterances?

(RQ2) Under what circumstances are user utterances more likely to be ignored?

To answer these research questions, we conducted multiple analyses. As experimental validation, we demonstrate VAD error (i.e., failures of VAD to detect user utterances) in a streaming-based ASR system using three datasets with different microphone configurations. We also compare the performance to a case where VAD is performed separately. On the basis of these results, we discuss the appropriate system configurations for conveniently building conversational robots.

2 Related works

Several studies have analyzed the performance and errors of publicly available ASRs. As ASR can be increasingly used by non-experts, it is useful to analyze the performance and issues of various ASRs. Pasandi and Pasandi (2016) showed that the Google API's ASR tends to ignore disfluencies, i.e., non-fluent words. Addlesee et al. (2020) compared the ASRs of Microsoft, IBM, and Google, investigating their robustness against disfluencies and overlaps. Georgila et al. (2020) analyzed the characteristics of several ASRs, demonstrating that performance degrades in domains requiring specialized vocabulary, as well as in noisy environments. Georgila and Traum (2024) investigated the impact of accents, i.e., various native and non-tative accents in English, on the performance of off-the-shelf ASRs. The Whisper model was found to be particularly sensitive to variations in accents.

These studies focus on analyzing ASR performance. However, it is also helpful to analyze the causes, especially in situations involving interaction with embodied robots. Error analysis in a convenient streaming-based ASR, rather than in segmented speech files, is also helpful. Particularly, a failure in VAD causes more damage to the dialogue than simple ASR errors, as it means the system does not recognize that the user has spoken. Therefore, we focus on VAD and examine situations when its errors occur in dialogues with embodied robots, where a robot utterance can be picked up by the microphone along with the user utterance.

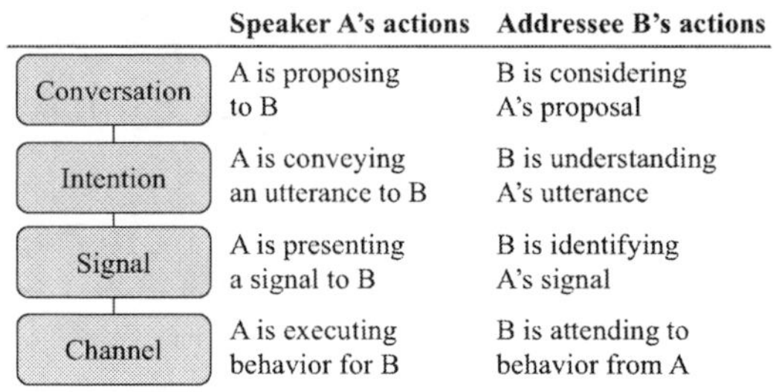

Figure 2: Action ladders (Clark, 1996)

A Model that predicts future user utterance segments, rather than detecting the end of the user utterance segment, was proposed. Voice activity projection (VAP) (Ekstedt and Skantze, 2022) is a model that predicts the future voice activity of two speakers, on the basis of raw audio input. The model requires two channels of recorded speech as input. Since our study targets a situation in which a dialogue system is used in a simple recording environment, and thus targets speech segment detection on the basis of one-channel recorded speech, VAP is not included in the comparison in this study.

3 Target of Analysis

VAD is a crucial component in spoken dialogue systems. According to the action ladder (Clark, 1996) illustrated in Fig. 2, joint actions between interlocutors at the signal level are established when the addressee successfully identifies the signal emitted by the speaker. On the basis of this, joint actions at higher levels, such as the Intention level and Conversation level, can be established.

Errors in VAD lead to two main issues in spoken dialogue systems:

1. Joint actions at the Intention Level (or higher levels) cannot be established due to missed voice activity segments.

2. Joint actions fail to form even at the Signal level.

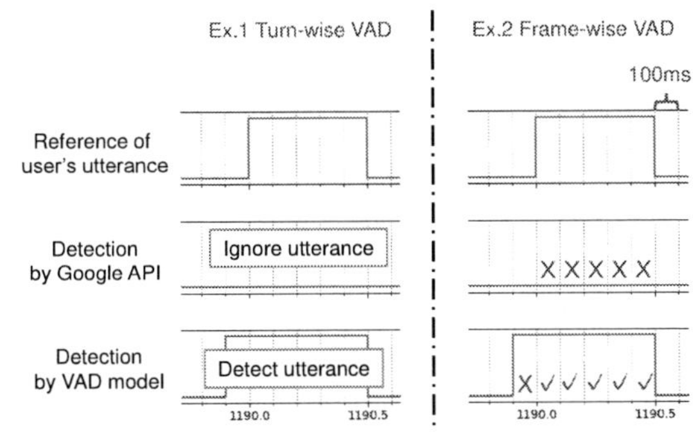

Figure 3: Calculation method of VAD accuracy in this study

The former issue refers to speech recognition errors caused by incorrect speech segmentation, thus hindering joint actions. This is an issue known in speech recognition.

The latter issue is more serious in spoken dialogue systems, especially for robot dialogue systems that interact with a wide range of users. If the system fails to identify that the user has spoken, it cannot take any action in response, leading to the user utterance being ignored. In speech communication, failing to respond can greatly reduce the user's motivation to continue the dialogue, making this problem more severe than simply having incorrect recognition results.

Corresponding to these two issues, we will analyze VAD performance both frame-wise and turn-wise, as illustrated in Fig. 3.

(Ex.1) Turn-wise VAD error rate: We calculated the percentage of missed detection across all of the user's turns.

(Ex.2) Frame-wise VAD scores: We calculated detection accuracy every 100 milliseconds.

Furthermore, we examined the extent to which speech recognition accuracy improves due to speech segment detection.

4 Data and Models

This section describes the dataset and VAD models used for the analysis in this study.

4.1 Dataset

In this experiment, we utilize three datasets (Table 1). In our analysis, we evaluate the accuracy of speech segment detection for user utterances at both the turn and frame levels. Therefore, as a reference for the amount of data used in the evaluation, we present the number of dialogues, the number of utterances, and the total utterance duration in the dataset. Both datasets have annotations for system speech segments and user speech segments.

Hazumi1911 [1] This is open Japanese dialogue data. The dataset consists of conversational data recorded in a laboratory setting with a microphone placed in front of a robot. In this dataset, the system and the user had an about 15-minute chit-chat about diverse topics (Komatani and Okada, 2021). Hazumi1911 contains face-to-face conversations. The appearance of the dialogue system is that of a 2D Computer graphics (CG) agent.

Hazumi2010 [2] Like Hazumi1911, this dataset is publicly available and was recorded under nearly identical conditions. The main difference is that Hazumi2010 comprises remote dialogues conducted online.

Avatar Fes. This dataset includes dialogue data recorded using a dialogue robot in a real-world environment. The dialogue system was implemented on a small robot that engaged in 3-minute attentive listening dialogues (Inoue et al., 2020). Recordings were made of participants interacting with the dialogue system at a trial event, the Avatar Festival. Since the recordings took place in an event hall, there is a significant amount of background noise. Furthermore, participants were not always fully engaged with the dialogue system, and there were instances where third parties spoke to them. Such data reflects dialogues under conditions representative of actual usage scenarios of the dialogue system. Dialogues in which participants terminated the interaction prematurely were excluded from the dataset.

The datasets used in this study encompass a variety of environments. Hazumi1911 and Hazumi2010 contain dialogue datasets collected in laboratory environments, whereas the Avatar Fes. dataset contains data from real-world usage scenarios. One key difference among the dialogues in these datasets is the length of turn-taking; therefore,

[1] https://github.com/ouktlab/Hazumi1911
[2] https://github.com/ouktlab/Hazumi2010

Table 1: Dataset details

Dataset	Number of dialogues	Average number of turns	Average of user utterance duration [second]
Hazumi1911	23	83.5	866.9
Hazumi2010	33	74.1	704.9
Avatar Fes.	138	30.4	81.2

we present basic statistics on turn-taking durations. This is significant because the difficulty in distinguishing between system and user speech during VAD depends on the length of turn-taking. The distribution of lengths of silence between speaker turn for the Hazumi1911 and Hazumi2010 datasets is shown in Figure 4. We calculated the distribution of the intervals from the end of the system utterance to the beginning of the user utterance for all utterances except the backchannel. In Hazumi1911, the distribution ranges from negative values (indicating overlap) to instances where the user takes a long time to respond. In contrast, in Hazumi2010, user speech is concentrated after the end of system utterance (0s). This may be due to the fact that Hazumi1911 involves face-to-face interactions, while Hazumi2010 consists of online interactions. In online dialogues, participants tend to wait until the system has finished speaking before they respond, which may reduce the likelihood of recognition errors occurring in speech immediately following the system utterance. In Avatar Fes, the length of turn-taking varies greatly. This dataset consists of real-world dialogues with various background noises and is not necessarily limited to one-to-one conversations, as there may be interruptions from other speakers.

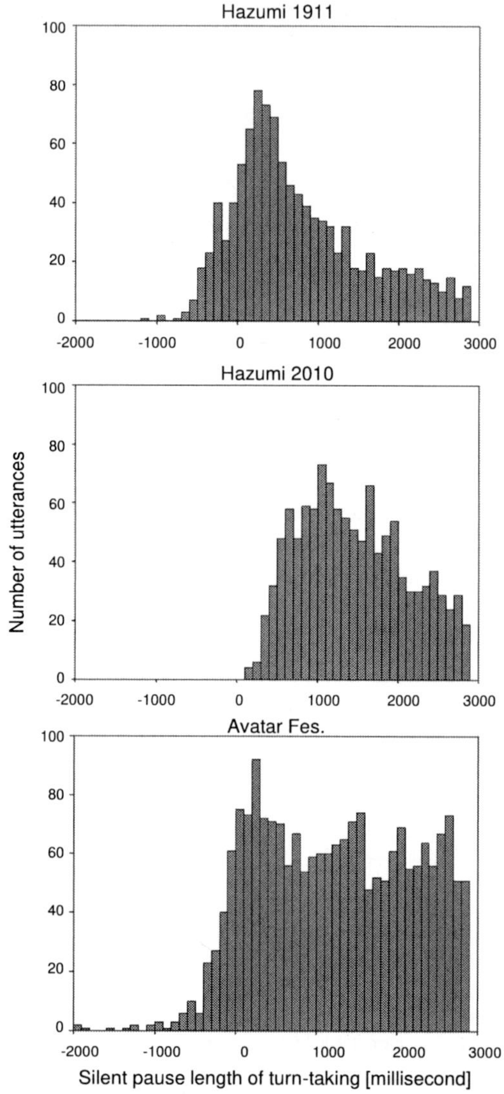

Figure 4: Histogram of silent pause length (System to User) in each dataset

4.2 Compared models

This section describes the models used in this experiment. We used the Google Speech Recognition API and, for comparison purposes, two publicly available models specialized in VAD. To perform analyses that assume typical usage scenarios, we selected models that are user-friendly and readily accessible.

Google ASR API The first model is a streaming-based ASR, **Google Speech-to-Text**[3]. We used the default model, accessing it via an API from Python for ASR. This model provides the start and end times for each recognized word. Other ASR APIs, such as Whisper, are also available. However, since Whisper requires a separate VAD setup, which might be difficult for practitioners to use easily, we chose to use Google ASR for this study.

Pyadin (VAD) The second model is a pre-trained

[3]https://cloud.google.com/speech-to-text?hl=en

VAD model based on DNN-HMM[4] (Takeda and Komatani, 2024). This model is a hybrid model of a hidden Markov model (HMM) and deep neural network (DNN) using a transformer-encoder. This model was trained on diverse datasets encompassing various environmental conditions. It remains robust against variations in signal amplitudes and speech distortions.

Silero VAD The third model is the VAD model based on long short-term memory (LSTM)[5]. Despite its low computational complexity and suitability for real-time processing, this model achieves higher accuracy than power-based VAD models. Furthermore, since the model is publicly available, it can be easily tested. In this study, we used it as a baseline model for model-based VAD.

5 Results of Analyses

The analysis results for Ex.1 and Ex.2 are summarized in Section 5.1. More detailed frame-level analyses are conducted in Sections 5.2 and 5.3. In Section 5.2, we analyze the impact of speech segment detection errors on speech recognition. In Section 5.3, we investigate at which points during user utterances the detection of speech segments fails.

5.1 VAD accuracy by each model

Dialogue systems can identify when they are speaking. Therefore, in this experiment, we exclude the detection results for the system's voice segments to calculate the outcomes.

We analyzed cases where the user utterance was entirely ignored. Table 2 shows the number of exchanges in which no user utterance was detected.

Chi-square tests conducted on 2×3 contingency tables for each dataset (Hazumi1911, Hazumi2010, Avatar Fes.) showed significant differences in user speech ignoring rates among the three models (Google, Pyadin, Silero; $p < 0.01$). Subsequent pairwise comparisons using Fisher's exact test with Bonferroni correction indicated that, for Hazumi1911 and Avatar Fes., all model pairs differed significantly. In Hazumi1911, significant differences were found between Google and Pyadin ($p < 0.01$) as well as between Pyadin and Silero ($p < 0.01$), but not between Google

[4]https://github.com/ouktlab/pyadintool

[5]https://github.com/snakers4/silero-vad

Table 2: Turn-wise VAD scores: The number of ignored user turns (**Ex.1**)

Data	Model	Ignored / Total
Hazumi1911	Google	319/1920 (17%)
	Pyadin	39/1920 (2%)
	Silero	99/1920 (5%)
Hazumi2010	Google	69/2446 (3%)
	Pyadin	5/2446 (0.2%)
	Silero	69/2446 (3%)
Avatar Fes.	Google	1582/4449 (36%)
	Pyadin	48/4449 (1%)
	Silero	322/4449 (7%)

Table 3: Frame-wise VAD scores (**Ex.2**)

Data	Model	Pre	Rec	F-value
Hazumi1911	Google	0.73	0.73	0.73
	Pyadin	0.87	0.89	0.88
	Silero	0.88	0.89	0.88
Hazumi2010	Google	0.53	0.88	0.64
	Pyadin	0.79	0.97	0.86
	Silero	0.84	0.92	0.87
Avatar Fes.	Google	0.61	0.56	0.47
	Pyadin	0.58	0.95	0.71
	Silero	0.67	0.85	0.74

and Silero. Overall, these results suggest that under Hazumi1911 and Avatar Fes. conditions, the Google model's ignoring rate was notably higher than those of the other two models. Chi-square tests conducted on 2×3 contingency tables for each dataset (Hazumi1911, Hazumi2010, Avatar Fes.) showed significant differences in user speech ignoring rates among the three models (Google, Pyadin, Silero; $p < 0.01$). Subsequent pairwise comparisons using Fisher's exact test with Bonferroni correction indicated that, for Hazumi1911 and Avatar Fes., all model pairs differed significantly. In Hazumi1911, significant differences were found between Google and Pyadin ($p < 0.01$) as well as between Pyadin and Silero ($p < 0.01$), but not between Google and Silero. Overall, these results suggest that under Hazumi1911 and Avatar Fes. conditions, the Google model's ignoring rate was notably higher than those of the other two models.

The accuracy of speech segment detection at 100 ms intervals is shown in Table 3. The experimental results show that using VAD yields higher detection accuracy across all datasets.

Table 4: ASR results for each dataset using different segmentation methods for user utterances: ASR is performed using Google ASR in all conditions.

Data	Segmentation	CER
Hazumi1911	Only ASR	0.55
	VAD (Pyadin) $\Rightarrow$ ASR	0.50
	Manual $\Rightarrow$ ASR	**0.42**
Hazumi2010	Only ASR	0.54
	VAD (Pyadin) $\Rightarrow$ ASR	0.51
	Manual $\Rightarrow$ ASR	**0.40**
Avatar Fes.	Only ASR	0.65
	VAD (Pyadin) $\Rightarrow$ ASR	0.43
	Manual $\Rightarrow$ ASR	**0.42**

5.2 Impacts of VAD errors on ASR

The following experiment analyzes the impact of speech segment detection on speech recognition accuracy. We compared speech recognition accuracy under three conditions, using Google Speech-to-Text for all conditions:

Only ASR We input the entire dialogue audio into Google ASR.

VAD (Pyadin) $\Rightarrow$ ASR We split into audio files for each user utterance using VAD. We used Google ASR on those audio files.

Manual $\Rightarrow$ ASR We split into audio files for each user utterance on the basis of manually annotated boundaries. We used Google ASR on those audio files.

Table 4 shows the differences in speech recognition accuracy in each condition. The character error rate (CER) in the Manual condition is the smallest in each dataset. The results show that using VAD can reduce ASR errors due to streaming-based ASR. Also, results in the Google condition have more errors than those in the VAD condition. These results make it clear that errors in VAD within Google ASR significantly affect ASR accuracy.

5.3 VAD error trends in Google ASR

We examined the patterns of VAD errors in Google ASR. We investigated the relationship between the time to user utterance after system utterance and VAD error rates. The results of this analysis are shown in Figure 5. For each start time (in 100 ms increments) after the end of system utterance, we assessed whether user utterance at that timing was detected. The results indicate the percentage of user utterance that was not detected as utterance for each frame.

In all data, there is a high frequency of detection errors immediately following system utterances. User utterance immediately after system speech may be misrecognized as noise and not detected as part of the speech segment. For Google ASR, only one of the voices may be identified as a voice when multiple voices are entered in a certain interval. In this case, the system speech is prioritized and the following user utterance is ignored. This phenomenon may occur in models trained with the assumption of a single speaker.

6 Discussion and Recommendations

6.1 Discussion

From the results in Section 5.1, we found that Google ASR API often ignores the user's turn, which is a very serious problem for spoken dialogue systems. We also found that this issue can be mitigated by using a separately trained VAD model. However, when examining the frame-level analysis results, we observed that the accuracy varies significantly depending on the environment, confirming that VAD tends to fail more easily in noisy environments. As shown in Table 3, even in low-noise environments, the precision of Hazumi2010 is lower than that of Hazumi1911, while its recall is higher. This is likely due to the fact, as illustrated in Figure 4, that Hazumi2010 exhibits delayed turn-taking by users, resulting in fewer overlaps with system utterances. Consequently, the likelihood of missed detections is reduced, affecting observed recall and precision metrics.

From the results presented in Section 5.2, we found that ASR accuracy decreases when there are many errors in VAD. This trend is consistent with those reported in previous studies and has been reconfirmed in the present research.

In Section 5.3, we analyzed the timing in which utterances are ignored and found a strong tendency for user utterances immediately following system utterances to be ignored. This tendency is particularly pronounced when using the Google ASR API. Specific examples of errors are shown in Figure 6. These examples were sampled from dialogues in the Avatar Fes. dataset, where detection errors were frequently observed. In Example 1, Google ASR fails to detect the user utterance immediately following the system's question, making it impos-

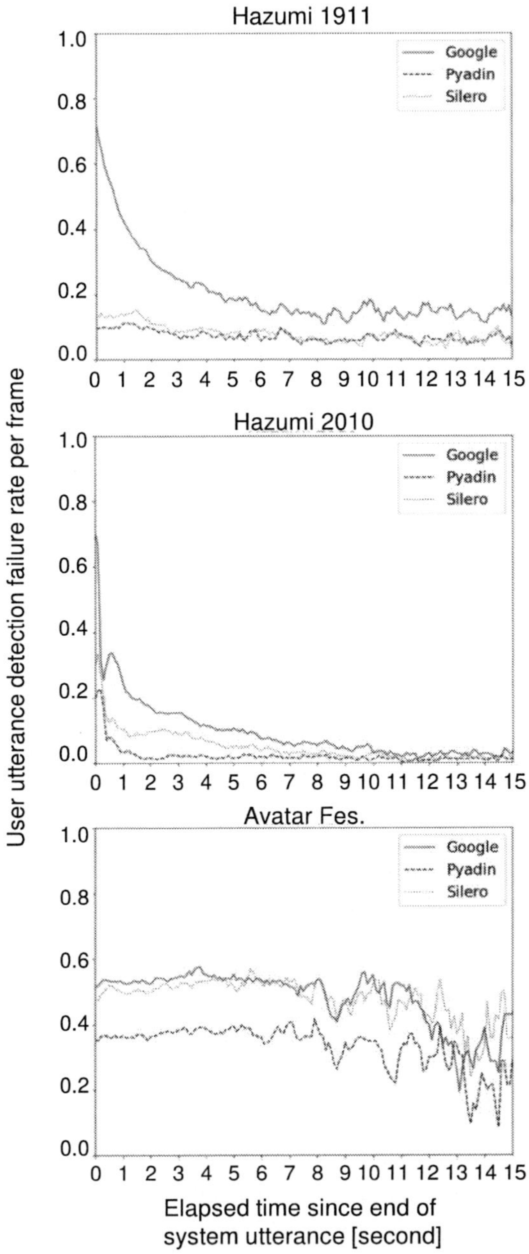

Figure 5: The relationship between user utterance timing and the detection failure rate per frame (100 ms)

sible to determine whether the user responded to the system's question. However, standalone VAD models successfully detected this utterance. This is thought to be due to confusion between user and system utterances, possibly stemming from the architecture of the speech recognition model. The Transformer model has a fixed input window and may not be able to recognize speaker differences within that window. Therefore, it may not be able to distinguish user speech immediately after system speech from the system speech itself.

One method to address this problem is to control turn-taking so that user utterances do not overlap with system utterances. Using the robot's movements, we can adjust aspects such as the timing of the user utterance. For instance, before transferring the turn to the user, the robot can look at the user's face; or during the system utterance, it can make large gestures to prevent the user from speaking simultaneously. In this way, by adjusting the user's speaking timing, we can avoid the user utterance overlapping with the system utterances.

Other factors, such as background noise and robot operation sounds, can also cause VAD errors. In Example 2, we present a case where all three VAD models failed to detect the user utterance. This failure occurred due to loud background noise, such as footsteps and laughter, being captured by the microphone in the middle of the user utterance, preventing proper detection. In noisy environments like this, the system frequently misses user utterances. In the case of robots that control gestures, the sounds generated by the robot's movements may also cause errors in VAD and ASR (Nishimura et al., 2006; Ince et al., 2011). Therefore, it is necessary to implement background noise suppression and minimize the robot's operational sounds during user utterances.

6.2 Recommendations

On the basis of the findings of this study, we offer the following recommendations to HRI researchers and practitioners. These suggestions aim to enhance the accurate recognition of user utterances, especially in situations where implementing an advanced speech processing environment is not feasible. Specifically, we propose methods to reduce omissions in the VAD of user utterances when developing dialogue systems.

Employing VAD Model The VAD feature included with Google ASR tends to miss user utterances. To address this issue, we recommend using an independent VAD model. As demonstrated by our experimental results in Section 5, errors can be significantly reduced by employing individually trained VAD models.

Using Separate Microphones Our experiments have shown that the system utterances and user utterances need to be properly separated

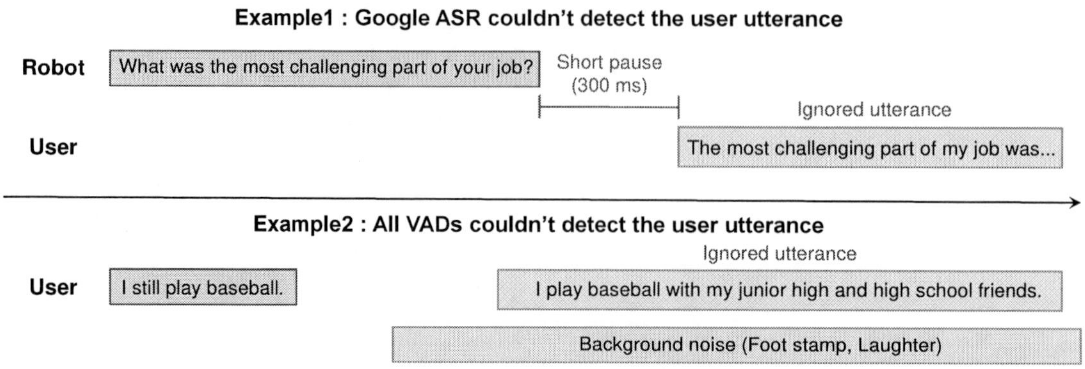

Figure 6: Example of VAD failures in detecting user utterances in Avatar Fes. dataset

to suppress error. Therefore, we advise configuring the microphone placement to ensure that system speech and user speech are not confused in the audio inputs. The most effective method is to provide the user with a handheld microphone. If this is not possible, the microphone should be positioned away from the system's speakers to minimize interference.

Understanding Error Trends in VAD VAD tends to fail in detecting the beginning of user utterances. This suggests that the initial part of the user utterance may not be recognized. Robust dialogue processing is therefore crucial, taking into account the possibility of missed detections of user responses, especially those immediately following system utterances. Such robust handling can ensure more reliable dialogue system performance even when some user utterances are not initially detected.

7 Conclusion

In this study, we analyzed the patterns of speech segment detection errors in typical speech recognition scenarios involving dialogue robots. When utilizing streaming-based automatic speech recognition (ASR) systems, such as Google API, in environments where both system and user speech are input, we observed instances where user utterance was not detected. Through an error analysis of voice activity detection (VAD) on dialogue data between a dialogue system and users, we clarified the tendencies of missed detections.

On the basis of our analysis, we made the following two contributions:

Answer to RQ1 We observed that the accuracy of Google ASR declines as the operational environment approaches real-world conditions. However, by integrating a dedicated VAD model, we can effectively prevent the system from disregarding the user's turn.

Answer to RQ2 Our findings indicate that user utterances occurring immediately after system utterances are prone to being overlooked. Therefore, it is important to ensure that user and system utterances do not overlap to prevent missing user inputs.

To mitigate such errors, a speech segment detection model needs to be used preprocess ASR. Alternatively, ensuring that system speech is not captured by the microphone during ASR in robot dialogues is crucial. Additionally, encouraging users to wait briefly after the system finishes speaking before responding may also be effective.

To achieve more robust turn-taking, errors in turn-taking, such as those involving voice activity detection (VAP), neecd to be examined in future studies. We hope that our findings will contribute to improving the performance of dialogue robots and enhancing the user experience in human-robot interactions.

Acknowledgement

This work was supported by JST Moonshot R&D Grant Number JPMJPS2011.

References

Angus Addlesee, Yanchao Yu, and Arash Eshghi. 2020. A comprehensive evaluation of incremental speech recognition and diarization for conversational ai. In *Proceedings of the International Conference on Computational Linguistics (COLING)*, pages 3492–3503.

Bishnu S Atal and Lawrence Rabiner. 1976. A pattern recognition approach to voiced-unvoiced-silence classification with applications to speech recognition. *IEEE Transactions on Acoustics, Speech, and Signal Processing*, 24(3):201–212.

Paul T. Brady. 1965. A technique for investigating on-off patterns of speech. *The Bell System Technical Journal*, 44(1):1–22.

Herbert H. Clark. 1996. *Using Language*. Cambridge University Press.

Erik Ekstedt and Gabriel Skantze. 2022. Voice Activity Projection: Self-supervised Learning of Turn-taking Events. In *Interspeech*, pages 5190–5194.

Kallirroi Georgila, Anton Leuski, Volodymyr Yanov, and David Traum. 2020. Evaluation of off-the-shelf speech recognizers across diverse dialogue domains. In *Proceedings of the Language Resources and Evaluation Conference (LREC)*, pages 6469–6476.

Kallirroi Georgila and David Traum. 2024. Evaluation of off-the-shelf whisper models for speech recognition across diverse dialogue domains. In *Proceedings of the International Workshop on Spoken Dialogue Systems Technology (IWSDS)*.

Gökhan Ince, Keisuke Nakamura, Futoshi Asano, Hirofumi Nakajima, and Kazuhiro Nakadai. 2011. Assessment of general applicability of ego noise estimation - applications to automatic speech recognition and sound source localization -. In *International Conference on Robotics and Automation (ICRA)*, pages 3517–3522.

Koji Inoue, Divesh Lala, Kenta Yamamoto, Shizuka Nakamura, Katsuya Takanashi, and Tatsuya Kawahara. 2020. An attentive listening system with android ERICA: Comparison of autonomous and WOZ interactions. In *Proceedings of the Annual Meeting of the Special Interest Group on Discourse and Dialogue (Sigdial)*, pages 118–127.

Koji Inoue, Pierrick Milhorat, Divesh Lala, Tianyu Zhao, and Tatsuya Kawahara. 2016. Talking with ERICA, an autonomous android. In *Proceedings of the Annual Meeting of the Special Interest Group on Discourse and Dialogue (Sigdial)*, pages 212–215, Los Angeles. Association for Computational Linguistics.

Brian Kingsbury, George Saon, Lidia Mangu, Mukund Padmanabhan, and Ruhi Sarikaya. 2002. Robust speech recognition in noisy environments: The 2001 ibm spine evaluation system. In *2002 IEEE International Conference on Acoustics, Speech, and Signal Processing*, volume 1, pages I–53–I–56.

Kazunori Komatani and Shogo Okada. 2021. Multimodal human-agent dialogue corpus with annotations at utterance and dialogue levels. In *Proc. International Conference on Affective Computing and Intelligent Interaction (ACII)*, pages 1–8.

Ivan Medennikov, Maxim Korenevsky, Tatiana Prisyach, Yuri Khokhlov, Mariya Korenevskaya, Ivan Sorokin, Tatiana Timofeeva, Anton Mitrofanov, Andrei Andrusenko, Ivan Podluzhny, Aleksandr Laptev, and Aleksei Romanenko. 2020. Target-speaker voice activity detection: a novel approach for multi-speaker diarization in a dinner party scenario. In *INTERSPEECH*, pages 274–278.

Takashi Minato, Ryuichiro Higashinaka, Kurima Sakai, Tomo Funayama, Hiromitsu Nishizaki, and Takayuki Nagai. 2024. Overview of dialogue robot competition 2023. In *Proceedings of Dialogue Robot Competition 2023*.

Yoshitaka Nishimura, Mikio Nakano, Kazuhiro Nakadai, Hiroshi Tsujino, and Mitsuru Ishizuka. 2006. Speech recognition for a robot under its motor noises by selective application of missing feature theory and mllr. In *Statistical and Perceptual Audio Processing (SAPA)*, pages 53–58.

Sashi Novitasari, Takashi Fukuda, and Gakuto Kurata. 2022. Improving ASR Robustness in Noisy Condition Through VAD Integration. In *Interspeech*, pages 3784–3788.

Hannaneh B. Pasandi and Haniyeh B. Pasandi. 2016. Recognising conversational speech: What an incremental asr should do for a dialogue system and how to get there. In *Proceedings of the International Workshop on Spoken Dialogue Systems Technology (IWSDS)*.

Gabriel Skantze. 2021. Turn-taking in conversational systems and human-robot interaction: A review. *Computer Speech Language*, 67:101178.

Ryu Takeda and Kazunori Komatani. 2024. Scale-invariant online voice activity detection under various environments. In *Asia Pacific Signal and Information Processing Association Annual Summit and Conerence (APSIPA ASC)*.

A Survey of Recent Advances on Turn-taking Modeling in Spoken Dialogue Systems

Galo Castillo-López **Gaël de Chalendar** **Nasredine Semmar**
Université Paris-Saclay, CEA, List, Palaiseau, France
{galo-daniel.castillolopez, gael.de-chalendar, nasredine.semmar}@cea.fr

Abstract

The rapid growth of dialogue systems adoption to serve humans in daily tasks has increased the realism expected from these systems. One trait of realism is the way speaking agents take their turns. We provide here a review of recent methods on turn-taking modeling and thoroughly describe the corpora used in these studies. We observe that 72% of the reviewed works in this survey do not compare their methods with previous efforts. We argue that one of the challenges in the field is the lack of well-established benchmarks to monitor progress. This work aims to provide the community with a better understanding of the current state of research around turn-taking modeling and future directions to build more realistic spoken conversational agents.

1 Introduction

Conversational agents adoption is rapidly growing. The ubiquity of dialogue systems in recent years has increased the realism (i.e. human-likeness) expected from them. One major trait of realism is the way spoken dialogue systems take turns in dialogues (Ter Maat et al., 2011). Silence between utterances in human-human conversations take 200ms on average (Levinson and Torreira, 2015). However, current spoken dialogue agents initiate turns after long gaps (700-1000ms) (Li et al., 2022), which results in unnatural, less realistic and non-fluid conversations. Thus, realistic turn-taking behavior is still a challenge to be addressed. The main goal of turn-taking modeling is determining when the system should take the turn to speak. Simplest attempts rely on the use of audio-based Voice Activity Detection (VAD) systems and silence thresholds (Raux, 2008; Raux and Eskenazi, 2009). Long silence thresholds derive systems that wait more time than expected, while shorter thresholds tend to interrupt users in the middle of their turns. In contrast, most recent systems use neural approaches to model turn-taking by minimizing speech overlaps and silence gaps. These systems use all types of available input data such as timing, linguistic, speech and visual information. For instance users' gaze and voice intonation at the end of utterances have been found to be relevant features to predict their end-of-turns (Oertel et al., 2012; Gravano and Hirschberg, 2011; Duncan, 1972). Turn-taking cues generation, interruptions handling, and other tasks are also of interest in the management of turns (Skantze, 2021).

Modeling turn-taking in multi-party conversations (MPCs) has not been widely explored in comparison to *dyadic* scenarios (i.e. one single user at a time), but has gained more attention in recent years. Multi-party conversations consist of conversations where more than two participants are involved, e.g. two users and a conversational agent. These types of dialogues include additional complexities to the management of turn-taking (Ganesh et al., 2023). For instance, recognizing who the addressee(s) of a user's utterance is does not appear to be as trivial as in the dyadic case. Challenges in MPCs are detailed in Appendix A. Examples of dialogue systems intervening in such types of conversations include agents providing assistance at hospital receptions (Addlesee et al., 2024a,b) or autonomous public buses (Axelsson et al., 2024), serving as healthcare coaches (Kantharaju and Pelachaud, 2018), guiding games at museums and hospitals for visitors entertainment (Skantze et al., 2015; Schauer et al., 2023), or taking place as attractions at thematic parks (Paetzel-Prüsmann and Kennedy, 2023).

While Skantze (2021) provided an exhaustive overview of turn-taking modeling, significant developments since then call for an updated survey. This paper contributes beyond the prior work in three key ways: (1) it offers the

Proceedings of the 15th International Workshop on Spoken Dialogue Systems Technology, pages 254–271
May 27–30, 2025.

first comprehensive review of datasets used in the field, providing critical insights into data modality and language; (2) it discusses overlooked limitations in turn-taking models, identifying gaps and challenges that are crucial for future work; and (3) it examines new ideas and approaches that have emerged in recent years, reflecting the latest trends and innovations. This survey is designed to serve both newcomers and experienced researchers in the field of turn-taking modeling. For those unfamiliar with the topic, it provides a clear introduction to fundamental concepts in turn-taking management, laying the groundwork for understanding the area. For expert readers, it offers a detailed examination of recent advancements, including new datasets, approaches, and unresolved challenges, with the goal to make it a valuable resource for anyone looking to stay current with the latest developments in the field, complementary to previous reviews. This survey describes relevant research on turn-taking modeling, with a special attention on studies published after 2021. Readers seeking more detailed information on earlier work are invited to refer to (Skantze, 2021). In Appendix B we explain the paper selection criteria we adopted in this survey.

The structure of this paper is organized as follows. In Section 2, we review fundamental concepts of turn-taking management. Section 3 provides an exhaustive description of the corpora used in the field. In Sections 4 and 5, we describe works on the two main subtasks in turn-taking modeling: end-of-turn prediction and backchannel prediction, respectively. We report studies related to MPCs in Section 6. Finally, Section 7 discusses the main open challenges and future opportunities in the field.

2 Turn-taking Management

Turn-taking in conversations can be defined as the coordinated successive exchange of speaking roles between multiple subjects to speak, listen, and respond (Fusaroli et al., 2014). Cooperative verbal communication is not unique to humans, as other animal species have also shown certain forms of turn-taking behavior (Pika et al., 2018; Takahashi et al., 2013). Although the coordination of turns feels natural in most human dialogues, it requires training at early stages of childhood (Nguyen et al., 2022; Donnelly and Kidd, 2021; Cosper and Pika, 2024). This suggests that there is a level of cognitive effort we need to perform to fluently manage turns. Such coordination lies on its dynamic temporal structure where listeners have to foresee the end of the speaker's utterance to anticipate their take of turn (Sacks et al., 1978). Figure 2 in Appendix C shows how turn-taking is handled in dialogues and illustrates various elements associated to turn management.

Fluency in the organization of turns is commonly assessed by the amount of overlaps and gaps between turns. A high number of these events indicate a poor ability of anticipating the end of turn by listeners (Heldner and Edlund, 2010). Overlaps occur when the listener starts speaking before the speaker completes their utterance. Gaps take place when long silences precede the take of turn of the next speaker. To optimize the organization of turns, listeners rely on cues provided by the speaker while holding or releasing their turns to determine when it is adequate to take the turn. Similarly, speakers rely on cues generated by listeners to know when any listener desires to take the turn, in order to decide whether to hold or release the floor. These cues can include verbal signals, gestures, and others. We describe in detail turn-taking cues in Appendix D.

Modeling turn-taking comprises multiple subtasks such as end-of-turn detection, interruptions handling and others. Although certain attempts of turn-taking modeling have proposed to simultaneously tackle several subtasks (Nguyen et al., 2023), each of them have been mostly treated as independent problems. In addition, turn-taking in MPCs has received little attention compared to two-party dialogues. The study of turn-taking modeling in MPCs has been mainly conducted in the field of human-robot interaction (Sato and Takeuchi, 2014; Bohus and Horvitz, 2010; Skantze et al., 2015), since it is difficult to organize turns in MPCs without the visual channel (Skantze, 2021).

3 Datasets

In this section, we detail the datasets used in all the works we review in this survey, i.e. described in sections 4, 5, and 6. Although research on turn-taking modeling have been mainly developed on dialogues in English, there are a few dialogue corpora in other languages. We separate datasets according to languages in English and other languages. A summary of all datasets is shown in Table 1.

Dataset	Language	Modality	Duration	Nb. dialogues	Nb. turns	Multy-party
Switchboard (Godfrey et al., 1992)	en	sp, txt	260h	2.4K	106.6K	✗
HarperValleyBank (Wu et al., 2020)	en	sp, txt	24h	1.4K	25.7K	✗
HCRC Map Task (Anderson et al., 1991)	en	sp, txt	15h	128	-	✗
Mahnob Mimicry Database (Bilakhia et al., 2015)	en	sp, vid	11h	54	-	✗
Fisher Corpus (Cieri et al., 2004)	en	sp, txt	1960h	11.7K	-	✗
NoXi Database (Cafaro et al., 2017)	en, es, fr, de, it, ar, id	sp, txt, vid	25h	84	1.7K	✗
Japanese Travel Agency Task (Inaba et al., 2022)	ja	sp, txt, vid	15h	330	111.7K	✗
SSC of Japanese (Maekawa et al., 2000)	ja	sp, txt	661h	3.3K	-	✗
HKUST/MTS Corpus (Liu et al., 2006)	zh	sp, txt	200h	1.2K	248.9K	✗
JaNoXi (Onishi et al., 2023)	ja	sp, txt, vid	7h	19	-	✗
EALC (Yoshino et al., 2018)	ja	sp, txt	200h	60	28.0K	✗
ICSI Meeting Corpus (Janin et al., 2003)	en	sp, txt	72h	75	-	✓
AMI Meeting Corpus (Kraaij et al., 2005)	en	sp, txt	100h	175	-	✓
CEJC (Koiso et al., 2022)	ja	sp, txt, vid	200h	577	-	✓

Table 1: Spoken dialogue corpora for turn-taking modeling tasks. **sp:** speech, **txt:** transcripts, **vid:** video.

3.1 English Corpora

One of the most used datasets for turn-taking modeling is the **Switchboard Corpus** (Godfrey et al., 1992). This dataset is a collection of audio and transcripts from 2.4K dyadic fully spontaneous telephone call dialogues by 500 speakers. The **Fisher Corpus** (Cieri et al., 2004) consists of 11.7K topic-oriented telephone conversations among randomly paired recruited participants. Similarly, the **HarperValleyBank Corpus** (Wu et al., 2020) contains 24 hours of simulated telephone dialogues between participants playing the roles of bank agents and customers. Dialogues are labeled according to the customers' intentions and utterances are assigned a sentiment class and dialogue act. Both the HarperValleyBank Corpus and Fisher Corpus count with audio data and speech transcripts. The **HCRC Map Task Corpus** (Anderson et al., 1991) was collected to study linguistic phenomena in cooperative dyadic interactions between young speakers. This dataset adds up to 128 conversations where an instruction giver indicates an instruction listener how to reproduce a route in a map, which is only known by the instruction giver. The **Mahnob Mimicry Database** (Bilakhia et al., 2015) is a set of 54 audiovisual recordings of socio-political discussions and tenancy negotiations. The corpus includes visual annotations such as gestures, body movement and facial expressions.

3.2 Corpora in Other Languages

The **NoXi Database** (**NO**vice e**X**pert **I**nteraction database) (Cafaro et al., 2017) is a set of audiovisual recordings designed to study social behavior in seven languages: English, Spanish, French, German, Italian, Arabic and Indonesian. Skeleton data, action units, head position and other types of data were collected along 25 hours of dyadic conversations where interlocutors discussed about a large variety of topics. A Japanese version of the NoXi corpus is compiled in the **JaNoXi** dataset (Onishi et al., 2023), where 6.8 hours of dialogues were recorded in similar settings as the NoXi Database. The **Japanese Travel Agency Task** dataset (Inaba et al., 2022) and the **Spontaneous Speech Corpus of Japanese** (Maekawa et al., 2000) are other datasets of two-party conversations in Japanese with over 15 and 661 hours of speech, respectively. The first compiles audio, video and transcripts of tourism consultation dialogues between a customer and an agent through the online meeting platform Zoom. The second mostly corresponds to annotated monologues in spontaneous Japanese. The corpus comprises morphologically annotated transcripts, as well as segmental and intonation labeling for mainly studying speech recognition. The **Elderly Attentive Listening Corpus** (EALC) is a 200h text and speech corpus designed for modeling various dialogue tasks in conversations with elderly people (Yoshino et al., 2018). Mandarin conversations were compiled in the **HKUST Mandarin Telephone Speech Corpus** (Liu et al., 2006), which includes speech data, transcripts and speaker demographic information, e.g. age, gender, education background, etc. In total, 1,206 ten-minute natural Mandarin telephone conversations about multiple topics were recorded to study topic detection, speaker recognition and others.

3.3 Multi-party Corpora

The **AMI Meeting Corpus** (Kraaij et al., 2005) and **ICSI Meeting Corpus** (Janin et al., 2003) are two well-known datasets of multi-party conversation audio recordings in English. The former corresponds to 175 sessions of four participants in scenario-oriented meetings. These recordings also contain collected data from devices such as digital pen and whiteboard usage, as well as video recordings. The ICSI corpus consists of 72 hours of meetings not elicited by a scenario, i.e. meetings would have taken place in any case. Speech transcripts are available for both datasets. The **Corpus of Everyday Japanese Conversation** (CEJC) dataset includes videos, audios and transcripts of spontaneous Japanese dialogues occurring in everyday scenarios (Koiso et al., 2022). The CEJC contains 200 hours of speech from 577 conversations, where around half of them are MPCs.

4 End-of-turn Prediction

Detecting the end-of-turn is the most well-studied problem in turn-taking modeling. End-of-turn prediction, also referred to as *end-of-utterance (EOU) detection*, is usually defined as a binary classification task. Its goal is to determine if the system should take the turn or not, depending on the dialogue context. Methods for EOU prediction can be grouped in three categories: silence-based, IPU-based and continuous (Skantze, 2021). Silence-based methods rely on Voice Activity Detection (VAD) tools, where a silence threshold (e.g. 700ms) is set to determine whether the system should take the turn. These methods result in poor user experience due to lack of naturalness (Aldeneh et al., 2018; Ekstedt and Skantze, 2022). IPU-based and continuous approaches differ on the time when predictions are made along the dialogue. While IPU-based[1] methods evaluate if the turn should be taken after every inter-pausal unit, i.e. after a silence, continuous models constantly evaluate the occurrence of an end of turn regardless of silences– e.g. every 50ms of speech. In this survey work we focus in continuous and IPU-based methods.

4.1 Continuous Methods

Continuous models either periodically evaluate end of turn at different time frames (Skantze, 2017), or incrementally perform predictions as utterances are built token by token (Coman et al., 2019). Predictions are executed regardless of whether silences of certain duration are observed. Some of the first attempts to build continuous methods for modeling turn-taking is performed in (Skantze, 2017), where a model that predicts future speech activity at every new frame of 50ms is proposed. A LSTM model (Hochreiter and Schmidhuber, 1997) is trained to predict the occurrence of a turn-shift from acoustic input features, including voice activity, pitch, speech intensity, and spectral stability, as well as Part-of-speech (POS) tags. An extension of (Skantze, 2017) revealed that there are significant performance benefits to modeling linguistic features at a lower temporal rate, and in a separate sub-network from acoustic features (Roddy et al., 2018b). Other early attempts explored reinforcement learning to model turn-taking (Zhao et al., 2015; Khouzaimi et al., 2016, 2018).

Roddy et al. (2018a) observed that POS tags only enhance model performance to discern whether an utterance will be short, e.g. backchannel. Hara et al. (2018) found that introducing backchannel and filler predictions as auxiliary tasks improved turn-taking prediction. Several studies have shown that the simultaneous use of both prosodic and word features outperforms the independent use of each separately (Wang et al., 2024; Li et al., 2022; Liu et al., 2017), which is in line with previous research that tends to confirm that combined turn-taking cues in human communication have an additive effect (Hjalmarsson, 2011). More recently, studies have investigated how ASR can be utilized for turn-completion time estimation (Kanai et al., 2024; Zink et al., 2024). Kanai et al. (2024) showed that fine-tuning wav2vec 2.0 (Baevski et al., 2020) for ASR to introduce linguistic features outperforms the use of solely acoustic features. Instruction fine-tuning (Wei et al., 2022) in a multitask setting has also been explored on LLMs in combination with HuBert (Hsu et al., 2021) through a fusion layer to model turn-taking from linguistic and acoustic features in (Wang et al., 2024). Likewise, Chang et al. (2022) feed a RNN Transducer (Graves, 2012) with audio streams and previous tokens to predict turn-taking-related wordpieces. Gaze direction, head pose and other non-verbal features have also been studied in combination with speech information. Onishi et al. (2023) found that action units are crucial input information for turn-taking and backchannel prediction. Results in these works exhibit that words prosody, timing, linguistic, and other types of features jointly provide better signals

[1]IPU: Inter-Pausal Units, see Appendix C.

for predicting EOU.

While many works focus on audio signals as main inputs, recent methods have shown how syntactic completeness obtained from transcripts alone can be used for turn-taking modeling. Ekstedt and Skantze (2020) introduced TurnGPT, a language model based on GPT-2 (Radford et al., 2019) and fine-tuned on various dialogue datasets to predict turn-completion based on text features only. They represent dialogues as sequences of concatenated utterances, separated by special tokens associated to turn-shift, to learn probabilities of turn-completion. Their results demonstrate that turn-shift prediction performed as a language modeling task outperforms previous work due to the strong representation of context that prior models miss. In (Jiang et al., 2023), response candidates are also considered as a proxy to determine whether a turn-shift is plausible in a given dialogue, arguing that the decision of taking a turn also depends on what the next speaker wants to say. Their results indicate that response-conditioning is especially useful when the utterance is a question and it semantically matches with the response. Further works showed that adapting TurnGPT to two separate streams of lexical content improves EOU prediction by capturing temporal dynamics (Leishman et al., 2024).

Most recent advances propose models based on Voice Activity Projection (VAP), whose main objective is essentially to predict future voice activity of every interlocutor in the conversation (Inoue et al., 2024b; Ekstedt and Skantze, 2023; Onishi et al., 2024). These models incrementally process the interlocutor speech to mimic humans' abilities to infer what the speaker is going to say to simultaneously prepare a reply and reduce response delay (Schlangen and Skantze, 2011). Ekstedt and Skantze (2022) propose a VAP self-supervised learning model to predict distinct turn-taking events and evaluated on zero-shot settings in four tasks: shift vs. hold prediction at mutual silence, shift prediction at voice activity presence, upcoming backchannel prediction, and backchannel vs. turn-shift prediction. The proposed base model consists of a frame-wise speech and VA encoder followed by a sequence predictor. VAP models have been found to perform better in Japanese when trained in English and fine-tuned with Japanese data than models directly trained in Japanese (Sato et al., 2024a). Inoue et al. (2024a) investigated multilingual VAP models to predict turns-shifts in English, Mandarin, and Japanese. While their results indicate that models evaluated in cross-lingual settings do not perform well, Sato et al. (2024b) demonstrated that aligning the criteria for speech segmentation labels across datasets is crucial to provide proper evaluation and to effectively use VAP models in cross-lingual scenarios.

We note an emerging trend in continuous methods using VAP models. An important opportunity in this direction for future work is the examination on how this type of models can be integrated with multi-modal data (e.g. video signals), as they have only been explored on audio inputs. We argue that although promising results have been observed when using utterance-level labels such as dialogue acts, the lack of availability of these types of annotations in real-world scenarios is a key limitation. We also find that even though LLMs have shown impressive results in a series of NLP tasks, recent studies demonstrate their inefficiency to detect opportunities to take turns at mid-utterance in spoken dialogue (Umair et al., 2024).

4.2 IPU-based Methods

Turn-taking models based on IPUs assume that turns cannot be taken while the user speaks (Skantze, 2021). Hence, predictions are performed every time a silence is detected from user's channel. Early works used LSTM-based architectures to model turn-taking from prosodic, phonetic, and lexical sequential features (Masumura et al., 2017, 2018; Hara et al., 2019). On the other hand, models based on CNN have been observed to be effective when introducing visual cues such as eye, mouth and head motion (Kurata et al., 2023). Experiments on multi-task learning have shown that using speech acts in auxiliary tasks for turn-taking modeling improves system performances. Aldeneh et al. (2018) observed that using speaker intention prediction (e.g. asking a question, uttering a backchannel, etc.) as a secondary task enhance turn shift prediction performance. Sakuma et al. (2022) found that integrating dialogue act information for response time estimation allows systems to efficiently capture dialogue context with smaller amounts of data than other methods.

Recent works have explored syntactic completeness to model turn-taking. Ekstedt and Skantze (2021) used TurnGPT to introduce speaker shift tokens as in (Ekstedt and Skantze, 2020), but on an IPU-based approach. At the end of every IPU, they project possible continuations from dialogue context to obtain the ratio of continuations containing shift tokens, to be used as an approximation of the actual probability of EOU. Syntactic completeness is also studied in (Sakuma et al., 2023) to determine response time from a multimodal Japanese dialogue corpus. They build a unidirectional LSTM language model to compute the probability of a special EOU token appearing in the next M tokens, outperforming the Gated Multimodal Fusion method proposed in (Yang et al., 2022) on similar features. Inspired by (Morais et al., 2022), the use of self-supervised learning based on Up- plus Down-stream models has also been investigated on audio and text data for end of turn detection (Morais et al., 2023).

The use of syntactic completeness has demonstrated relevant improvements in IPU-based methods for turn-taking modeling by effectively leveraging linguistic cues to predict turn-completion points. In addition to the efforts made by (Sakuma et al., 2023), future work may consider exploring how syntactic completeness can be integrated into multimodal methods using non-LSTM architectures as done in (Kurata et al., 2023), as well as in multi-task training settings. Moreover, although promising results using LLMs combined with VAD systems have been reported in (Pinto and Belpaeme, 2024), studies on this direction still have to be widely studied. We observe that IPU-based approaches have received less attention than continuous methods, as the latest continuous models are more aligned to human-like EOU prediction.

5 Backchannel Prediction

Overlaps in dialogues occur when multiple participants produce IPUs at the same time. These overlaps may take place in the proximity of the end of a turn if the listener desires to start their turn, or in the middle of the speaker utterance. In the latter case there are three possible scenarios: (1) the listener desires to interrupt and grab the floor, (2) the listener intents to provide a feedback to the speaker without the aim of taking the turn (backchannel), and (3) the listener produces non-lexical sounds such as coughing, which can be misinterpreted as an interruption. Classifying an overlap as a backchannel or an actual interruption (or noise) is an important subtask in turn-taking modeling. Backchannel prediction is generally defined as a binary classification task, where the aim is to classify an IPU as a backchannel or non-backchannel.

One of the first attempts to model backchannel prediction using neural networks was reported in (Mueller et al., 2015), where only speech features were used. In (Skantze, 2017), backchannel detection was addressed by predicting if a speech onset of 500 ms corresponded to a short (less than 500ms, i.e. backchannel) or a long utterance (more than 2500 ms), using handcrafted acoustic features and POS tags to feed a LSTM model. Yokoyama et al. (2018) considered backchannels as an intention label to build an intention recognition model. Other early works used word2vec (Mikolov et al., 2013) to combine word embeddings as linguistic features with acoustic features (Ruede et al., 2017). Adiba et al. (2021) took delays in ASR into account to propose a prior prediction model, as words are available some time after these have been uttered. Speaker and listener embeddings to encode interlocutor interactions have also been considered to predict backchannels (Ortega et al., 2020, 2023).

Recent advances have examined auxiliary tasks to predict backchannels (Choi et al., 2024; Wang et al., 2024), showing improvements over single-task methods. These tasks include sentiment classification, dialogue act prediction, and others (Liermann et al., 2023; Jang et al., 2021). Müller et al. (2022) used audiovisual data to introduce agreement estimation in a multitask setting to detect backchannels. Park et al. (2024) proposed a Context-Aware Backchannel Prediction model to enhance predictions in Korean and English corpora. They encoded features using text embeddings from BERT (Devlin et al., 2018) and acoustic inputs represented by wav2vec embeddings. Finally, a multi-head attention mechanism is employed to build an attentive context embedding that holds relevant information of the current utterance. Voice Activity Projection (VAP) models, presented in Section 4.1, have gained special attention for backchannel prediction. Onishi et al. (2024) found that integrating non-verbal features on VAP models enhances turn-taking events prediction, including backchannels. Pre-training on large dialogue data and fine-tuning on a specialized backchannel corpus has also shown improvements on VAP model's generalizability (Inoue et al., 2024c).

6 Multi-party Turn-taking Modeling

In this section we describe methods proposed for turn-taking modeling in multi-party conversations. We outline the main complexities in MPCs in human-human dialogues in Appendix A. Turn-taking prediction becomes more challenging in multi-party scenarios, where various sub-tasks arise such as conversation disentanglement, addressee recognition, and others (Ganesh et al., 2023). Multi-party conversation modeling addresses the issues on *Who says What to Whom* (who speaks, says what, and addresses whom) (Gu et al., 2022). Modeling turn-taking in MPCs has received much less attention than dyadic interactions. Although work has been done on the topic for a long time (Traum, 2003; Laskowski, 2010; Bohus and Horvitz, 2011; De Kok and Heylen, 2009; Thórisson et al., 2010), only recently have the methods designed begun to yield promising results, due to advancements in available technologies.

Fujie et al. (2021) proposed a Timing Generating Network, which incorporates a first-order lag system to estimate how much other speakers in the dialogue expect the system to take the turn in Japanese. Their approach is in contrast to the conventional framing of turn-taking modeling as an end-of-turn detection problem, which assumes that the system should take the turn right after the previous speaker releases it. They integrate response obligation recognition as an auxiliary task to improve estimation. de Bayser et al. (2019) and de Bayser et al. (2020) studied next speaker identification from dialogue logs to model turn-taking prediction in MPCs. Gaze-transition patterns and timing information have been investigated to predict the next speaker and the time at which each utterance will be made (Ishii et al., 2016; Lee et al., 2023). Experiments on a Transformer-based architecture using 3D gazes, 3D head and body movements, and speech showed that speech signals play a more critical role than gaze patterns for turn-taking prediction (Lee et al., 2023). Multimodal fusion has also been studied for turn-taking prediction, where multiple event types are predicted simultaneously (Lee and Deng, 2024). Johansson and Skantze (2015) argue that there are different states in which turn-taking could be obliged or optional. They proposed annotating utterances into a scale of four classes according to the appropriateness for an agent to take the turn. They observed that dialogue acts as turn change predictors in MPCs need a special treatment compared to two-party settings.

Turn-taking modeling in MPCs has notably been understudied in comparison to dyadic scenarios. Work in MPCs where no visual data are used has been overlooked, as most studies have been conducted in the field of human-robot interaction where visual cues are captured by sensors. We think that introducing response obligation detection in any form is crucial for modeling turn-taking in MPCs. Determining whether the agent should take the turn or not after the floor is released mitigates poor performance on Out-of-Scope utterances, a common phenomenon for dialogue systems in such scenarios. We discuss more about open challenges in multi-party conversations, including Out-of-Scope utterances, in section 7.4.

7 Challenges and Future Directions

In this section we describe some relevant open challenges and suggest opportunities for future work.

7.1 System Evaluations

The lack of comparative evaluations in works is one of the most important challenges in the field. We find that only 28% of the reviewed papers in this survey compare their methods with systems presented in prior works. Even some of the studies where comparisons are made, do not use the same data to compare methods or use different input features than originally proposed. Consequently, comparisons are not fair. We also note that one third of the reviewed works on end-of-turn detection do not conduct experiments on any public corpus. This represents an issue for reproducibility and properly monitoring progress in the field.

To address this challenge, we suggest future work should focus on the creation of a standardized benchmark for each turn-taking modeling task. This benchmark should include a diverse set of publicly available corpora. We note that the Switchboard Corpus is the most popular resource for turn-taking modeling evaluation in dyadic dialogues, as used in 69% and 41% of the surveyed papers on backchannel and end-of-turn detection, respectively. An important aspect to take into consideration for end-of-turn detection is the definition of turns and IPUs. Previous works have used distinct silence thresholds between 50ms and

1s to delimit IPUs or define turns. We believe that considering multiple cutoffs for evaluation is necessary, as done in (Skantze, 2017; Sakuma et al., 2023).

7.2 Groups with Varying Needs

Another challenge for spoken dialogue systems is the interaction with people who present more complex behaviors on turn management such as senior adults or individuals with mental health disorders. These types of interplays require systems to conduct human-like turn-taking behaviors (Addlesee and Eshghi, 2024; Bell, 2024). Prior work has proposed mechanisms to address these scenarios (Lala et al., 2017; Hara et al., 2018; Kawahara et al., 2016). LLMs have been recently proposed to build dialogue systems that interact with individuals with mental health disorders. (Addlesee and Eshghi, 2024) studied the recovery from interruptions in dialogues with people with dementia. Although the previously mentioned efforts are valuable, the body of work in this subject is still scanty. We also observe that most of studies in turn-taking modeling in these scenarios have not been conducted in multidisciplinary environments. We believe that integrating domain-knowledge and insights from experts in other fields beyond Dialogue Systems, would be beneficial for the research community.

7.3 Multilinguality

Although multilingual aspects in dialogue systems have been addressed in other sub-tasks such as natural language understanding (Firdaus et al., 2023; Gupta et al., 2021; Gerz et al., 2021), dialogue state tracking (Lee et al., 2024; Yu et al., 2023; Zuo et al., 2021), or response generation (Wu et al., 2024), research in turn-taking modeling is limited (Ward et al., 2018; Inoue et al., 2024a). End of turn prediction is more difficult in some languages than others even for humans (Stivers et al., 2009). Inherent phenomena from spoken dialogues, which are not found in other dialogue system sub-tasks, such as backchannels or hesitations, make end of utterance detection more complex. For instance, backchannels use varies from one culture to another (Clancy et al., 1996; Tartory et al., 2024).

7.4 Multi-party Conversations

In Section 6 we briefly discussed about the limited amount of work in turn-taking modeling on MPCs, which is in line with the low amount of available MPC corpora we described in Section 3. We found that most works in turn-taking modeling on MPCs use visual information to detect end of turns, since predicting EOUs without the aid of the visual channel is a complex task. However, there are multiple scenarios where using visual inputs is not feasible or useful. For example, agents assisting participants in online meetings do not count with such sort of cues and should mostly rely on linguistic and audio inputs. Future work should take this challenge into consideration.

Additionally, we note that most works in MPCs propose systems where agents actively participate in dialogues. Nevertheless, that is not always the case in real-world applications. For instance, task-oriented dialogue agents such as Alexa or Siri, generally play the role of listeners in dialogues, switching their role when they have something to say –commonly when a wake-word is spoken. Skilled assistants should not only base their turn-taking decisions on wake-words, but should be effective on determining when to intervene in conversations to assist on a given task. In other words, virtual assistants should be able to detect when they can contribute in dialogues in scenarios where they are not expected to have an active participation. One major challenge in these scenarios is managing Out-of-Scope (OOS) utterances, as users may discuss about a diverse set of topics where only a few utterances are task-related. The study of intent recognition in MPCs is a possible direction on this subject, as user intentions may suggest the need for intervention of an agent. One limitation is that there are no corpora with intent recognition annotations in spontaneous MPCs with a focus on OOS utterances. A corpus with these characteristics in scripted MPCs (dialogues from TV shows) is proposed in (Zhang et al., 2024). Addlesee et al. (2023) used GPT-3.5-turbo to detect user goals in MPCs, which can be seen as a surrogate task for turn-taking modeling. They argue that users' goals in MPCs can be addressed by virtual agents as well as other human participants, hence they propose the task of goal-tracking to detect solved tasks and determine the relevance of agent intervention. Intent recognition was also used as an auxiliary task for turn-taking prediction in (Aldeneh et al., 2018). To the best of our knowledge, these are the only studies where intent recognition is considered for modeling turn-taking. However, none of such works take into consideration OOS utterances.

8 Conclusions

Turn-taking modeling is a key component of spoken dialogue systems. Effective methods for modeling turn taking are crucial for developing systems that can be perceived as realistic. This survey provides an overview of recent advancements in turn-taking modeling in spoken dialogue systems. We provided the first detailed review of the corpora used in the field. We observed that the majority of works have been conducted on English and Japanese corpora, with almost no efforts in other languages. We also described recent works in end-of-turn prediction and backchannel classification. Finally, we discussed several overlooked open challenges in current turn-taking models and key directions indicating how future work could push the field. For instance, we noted a tendency in the reviewed works not to compare their proposed methods with previous works, which might affect monitoring progress in the field. Addressing these challenges and improving cross-linguistic research and method comparisons will be essential for advancing turn-taking models and making spoken dialogue systems more natural and effective.

Acknowledgments

We warmly thank our anonymous reviewers for their time and valuable feedback. This work has been partially funded by the EU project CORTEX2 (under grant agreement: N° 101070192).

References

Angus Addlesee, Neeraj Cherakara, Nivan Nelson, Daniel Hernández Garcia, Nancie Gunson, Weronika Sieińska, Christian Dondrup, and Oliver Lemon. 2024a. Multi-party multimodal conversations between patients, their companions, and a social robot in a hospital memory clinic. In *Proceedings of the 18th Conference of the European Chapter of the Association for Computational Linguistics: System Demonstrations*, pages 62–70.

Angus Addlesee, Neeraj Cherakara, Nivan Nelson, Daniel Hernández García, Nancie Gunson, Weronika Sieińska, Marta Romeo, Christian Dondrup, and Oliver Lemon. 2024b. A multi-party conversational social robot using llms. In *Companion of the 2024 ACM/IEEE International Conference on Human-Robot Interaction*, pages 1273–1275.

Angus Addlesee and Arash Eshghi. 2024. You have interrupted me again!: making voice assistants more dementia-friendly with incremental clarification. *Frontiers in Dementia*, 3:1343052.

Angus Addlesee, Weronika Sieińska, Nancie Gunson, Daniel Hernandez Garcia, Christian Dondrup, and Oliver Lemon. 2023. Multi-party goal tracking with LLMs: Comparing pre-training, fine-tuning, and prompt engineering. In *Proceedings of the 24th Annual Meeting of the Special Interest Group on Discourse and Dialogue*, pages 229–241, Prague, Czechia. Association for Computational Linguistics.

Amalia Istiqlali Adiba, Takeshi Homma, Dario Bertero, Takashi Sumiyoshi, and Kenji Nagamatsu. 2021. Delay mitigation for backchannel prediction in spoken dialog system. *Conversational Dialogue Systems for the Next Decade*, pages 129–143.

Zakaria Aldeneh, Dimitrios Dimitriadis, and Emily Mower Provost. 2018. Improving end-of-turn detection in spoken dialogues by detecting speaker intentions as a secondary task. In *2018 IEEE International Conference on Acoustics, Speech and Signal Processing (ICASSP)*, pages 6159–6163. IEEE.

Anne H Anderson, Miles Bader, Ellen Gurman Bard, Elizabeth Boyle, Gwyneth Doherty, Simon Garrod, Stephen Isard, Jacqueline Kowtko, Jan McAllister, Jim Miller, et al. 1991. The hcrc map task corpus. *Language and speech*, 34(4):351–366.

Peter Auer. 2018. Gaze, addressee selection and turn-taking in three-party interaction. *Eye-tracking in interaction: Studies on the role of eye gaze in dialogue*, 197:231.

Agnes Axelsson, Bhavana Vaddadi, Cristian Bogdan, and Gabriel Skantze. 2024. Robots in autonomous buses: Who hosts when no human is there? In *Companion of the 2024 ACM/IEEE International Conference on Human-Robot Interaction*, pages 1278–1280.

Alexei Baevski, Yuhao Zhou, Abdelrahman Mohamed, and Michael Auli. 2020. wav2vec 2.0: A framework for self-supervised learning of speech representations. *Advances in neural information processing systems*, 33:12449–12460.

Grace Madeline Bell. 2024. Prosodic speech rate, utterance duration, interruption rate, and turn-taking latency in autistic and neurotypical adults. Master's thesis, Brigham Young University.

Sanjay Bilakhia, Stavros Petridis, Anton Nijholt, and Maja Pantic. 2015. The mahnob mimicry database: A database of naturalistic human interactions. *Pattern recognition letters*, 66:52–61.

Dan Bohus and Eric Horvitz. 2010. Facilitating multiparty dialog with gaze, gesture, and speech. In *International Conference on Multimodal Interfaces and the Workshop on Machine Learning for Multimodal Interaction*, pages 1–8.

Dan Bohus and Eric Horvitz. 2011. Multiparty turn taking in situated dialog: Study, lessons, and directions. In *Proceedings of the SIGDIAL 2011 Conference*, pages 98–109.

Angelo Cafaro, Johannes Wagner, Tobias Baur, Soumia Dermouche, Mercedes Torres Torres, Catherine Pelachaud, Elisabeth André, and Michel Valstar. 2017. The noxi database: multimodal recordings of mediated novice-expert interactions. In *Proceedings of the 19th ACM International Conference on Multimodal Interaction*, pages 350–359.

Shuo-Yiin Chang, Bo Li, Tara Sainath, Chao Zhang, Trevor Strohman, Qiao Liang, and Yanzhang He. 2022. Turn-Taking Prediction for Natural Conversational Speech. In *Proc. Interspeech 2022*, pages 1821–1825.

Yong-Seok Choi, Jeong-Uk Bang, and Seung Hi Kim. 2024. Joint streaming model for backchannel prediction and automatic speech recognition. *ETRI Journal*.

Christopher Cieri, David Miller, and Kevin Walker. 2004. The fisher corpus: A resource for the next generations of speech-to-text. In *LREC*, volume 4, pages 69–71.

Patricia M Clancy, Sandra A Thompson, Ryoko Suzuki, and Hongyin Tao. 1996. The conversational use of reactive tokens in english, japanese, and mandarin. *Journal of pragmatics*, 26(3):355–387.

Andrei C. Coman, Koichiro Yoshino, Yukitoshi Murase, Satoshi Nakamura, and Giuseppe Riccardi. 2019. An incremental turn-taking model for task-oriented dialog systems. In *Interspeech 2019*, pages 4155–4159.

Samuel H Cosper and Simone Pika. 2024. Human turn-taking development: A multi-faceted review of turn-taking comprehension and production in the first years of life. `https://osf.io/yjad2/download`.

Anne Cutler and Mark Pearson. 2018. On the analysis of prosodic turn-taking cues. In *Intonation in discourse*, pages 139–156. Routledge.

Maira Gatti de Bayser, Paulo Cavalin, Claudio Pinhanez, and Bianca Zadrozny. 2019. Learning multi-party turn-taking models from dialogue logs. *arXiv preprint arXiv:1907.02090*.

Maira Gatti de Bayser, Melina Alberio Guerra, Paulo Cavalin, and Claudio Pinhanez. 2020. A hybrid solution to learn turn-taking in multi-party service-based chat groups. *arXiv preprint arXiv:2001.06350*.

Iwan De Kok and Dirk Heylen. 2009. Multimodal end-of-turn prediction in multi-party meetings. In *Proceedings of the 2009 international conference on Multimodal interfaces*, pages 91–98.

Jacob Devlin, Ming-Wei Chang, Kenton Lee, and Kristina Toutanova. 2018. Bert: Pre-training of deep bidirectional transformers for language understanding. *arXiv preprint arXiv:1810.04805*.

Seamus Donnelly and Evan Kidd. 2021. The longitudinal relationship between conversational turn-taking and vocabulary growth in early language development. *Child Development*, 92(2):609–625.

Starkey Duncan. 1972. Some signals and rules for taking speaking turns in conversations. *Journal of personality and social psychology*, 23(2):283.

Erik Ekstedt and Gabriel Skantze. 2020. TurnGPT: a transformer-based language model for predicting turn-taking in spoken dialog. In *Findings of the Association for Computational Linguistics: EMNLP 2020*, pages 2981–2990, Online. Association for Computational Linguistics.

Erik Ekstedt and Gabriel Skantze. 2021. Projection of turn completion in incremental spoken dialogue systems. In *Proceedings of the 22nd Annual Meeting of the Special Interest Group on Discourse and Dialogue*, pages 431–437.

Erik Ekstedt and Gabriel Skantze. 2022. Voice activity projection: Self-supervised learning of turn-taking events. In *Proc. Interspeech 2022*, pages 5190–5194.

Erik Ekstedt and Gabriel Skantze. 2023. Show & tell: Voice activity projection and turn-taking. In *24th International Speech Communication Association, Interspeech 2023, Dublin, Ireland, Aug 20 2023-Aug 24 2023*, pages 2020–2021. International Speech Communication Association.

Mauajama Firdaus, Asif Ekbal, and Erik Cambria. 2023. Multitask learning for multilingual intent detection and slot filling in dialogue systems. *Information Fusion*, 91:299–315.

Shinya Fujie, Hayato Katayama, Jin Sakuma, and Tetsunori Kobayashi. 2021. Timing generating networks: Neural network based precise turn-taking timing prediction in multiparty conversation. In *22nd Annual Conference of the International Speech Communication Association, INTERSPEECH 2021*, pages 3771–3775. International Speech Communication Association.

Riccardo Fusaroli, Ivana Konvalinka, and Sebastian Wallot. 2014. Analyzing social interactions: the promises and challenges of using cross recurrence quantification analysis. In *Translational recurrences: From mathematical theory to real-world applications*, pages 137–155. Springer.

Ananya Ganesh, Martha Palmer, and Katharina Kann. 2023. A survey of challenges and methods in the computational modeling of multi-party dialog. In *Proceedings of the 5th Workshop on NLP for Conversational AI (NLP4ConvAI 2023)*, pages 140–154.

Daniela Gerz, Pei-Hao Su, Razvan Kusztos, Avishek Mondal, Michał Lis, Eshan Singhal, Nikola Mrkšić, Tsung-Hsien Wen, and Ivan Vulić. 2021. Multilingual and cross-lingual intent detection from spoken data. In *Proceedings of the 2021 Conference on Empirical Methods in Natural Language Processing*, pages 7468–7475, Online and Punta Cana, Dominican Republic. Association for Computational Linguistics.

John J Godfrey, Edward C Holliman, and Jane McDaniel. 1992. Switchboard: Telephone speech corpus for research and development. In *Acoustics, speech, and signal processing, ieee international conference on*, volume 1, pages 517–520. IEEE Computer Society.

Agustín Gravano and Julia Hirschberg. 2011. Turn-taking cues in task-oriented dialogue. *Computer Speech & Language*, 25(3):601–634.

Alex Graves. 2012. Sequence transduction with recurrent neural networks. *arXiv preprint arXiv:1211.3711*.

Jia-Chen Gu, Chongyang Tao, and Zhen-Hua Ling. 2022. Who says what to whom: A survey of multi-party conversations. In *IJCAI*, pages 5486–5493.

Akshat Gupta, Xinjian Li, Sai Krishna Rallabandi, and Alan W Black. 2021. Acoustics based intent recognition using discovered phonetic units for low resource languages. In *ICASSP 2021-2021 IEEE International Conference on Acoustics, Speech and Signal Processing (ICASSP)*, pages 7453–7457. IEEE.

Kohei Hara, Koji Inoue, Katsuya Takanashi, and Tatsuya Kawahara. 2018. Prediction of Turn-taking Using Multitask Learning with Prediction of Backchannels and Fillers. In *Proc. Interspeech 2018*, pages 991–995.

Kohei Hara, Koji Inoue, Katsuya Takanashi, and Tatsuya Kawahara. 2019. Turn-taking prediction based on detection of transition relevance place. In *INTERSPEECH*, pages 4170–4174.

Mattias Heldner and Jens Edlund. 2010. Pauses, gaps and overlaps in conversations. *Journal of Phonetics*, 38(4):555–568.

Anna Hjalmarsson. 2011. The additive effect of turn-taking cues in human and synthetic voice. *Speech Communication*, 53(1):23–35.

Sepp Hochreiter and Jürgen Schmidhuber. 1997. Long short-term memory. *Neural computation*, 9(8):1735–1780.

Wei-Ning Hsu, Benjamin Bolte, Yao-Hung Hubert Tsai, Kushal Lakhotia, Ruslan Salakhutdinov, and Abdelrahman Mohamed. 2021. Hubert: Self-supervised speech representation learning by masked prediction of hidden units. *IEEE/ACM Transactions on Audio, Speech, and Language Processing*, 29:3451–3460.

Michimasa Inaba, Yuya Chiba, Ryuichiro Higashinaka, Kazunori Komatani, Yusuke Miyao, and Takayuki Nagai. 2022. Collection and analysis of travel agency task dialogues with age-diverse speakers. In *Proceedings of the Thirteenth Language Resources and Evaluation Conference*, pages 5759–5767.

Koji Inoue, Bing'er Jiang, Erik Ekstedt, Tatsuya Kawahara, and Gabriel Skantze. 2024a. Multilingual turn-taking prediction using voice activity projection. In *Proceedings of the 2024 Joint International Conference on Computational Linguistics, Language Resources and Evaluation (LREC-COLING 2024)*, pages 11873–11883, Torino, Italia. ELRA and ICCL.

Koji Inoue, Bing'er Jiang, Erik Ekstedt, Tatsuya Kawahara, and Gabriel Skantze. 2024b. Real-time and continuous turn-taking prediction using voice activity projection. *arXiv preprint arXiv:2401.04868*.

Koji Inoue, Divesh Lala, Gabriel Skantze, and Tatsuya Kawahara. 2024c. Yeah, un, oh: Continuous and real-time backchannel prediction with fine-tuning of voice activity projection. *arXiv preprint arXiv:2410.15929*.

Ryo Ishii, Kazuhiro Otsuka, Shiro Kumano, Ryuichiro Higashinaka, and Junji Tomita. 2019. Prediction of who will be next speaker and when using mouth-opening pattern in multi-party conversation. *Multimodal Technologies and Interaction*, 3(4):70.

Ryo Ishii, Kazuhiro Otsuka, Shiro Kumano, and Junji Yamato. 2016. Prediction of who will be the next speaker and when using gaze behavior in multiparty meetings. *ACM Transactions on Interactive Intelligent Systems (TIIS)*, 6(1):1–31.

Joseph Jaffe and Stanley Feldstein. 1970. Rhythms of dialogue. *(No Title)*.

Jin Yea Jang, San Kim, Minyoung Jung, Saim Shin, and Gahgene Gweon. 2021. Bpm_mt: Enhanced backchannel prediction model using multi-task learning. In *Proceedings of the 2021 Conference on Empirical Methods in Natural Language Processing*, pages 3447–3452.

Adam Janin, Don Baron, Jane Edwards, Dan Ellis, David Gelbart, Nelson Morgan, Barbara Peskin, Thilo Pfau, Elizabeth Shriberg, Andreas Stolcke, et al. 2003. The icsi meeting corpus. In *2003 IEEE International Conference on Acoustics, Speech, and Signal Processing, 2003. Proceedings.(ICASSP'03).*, volume 1, pages I–I. IEEE.

Bing'er Jiang, Erik Ekstedt, and Gabriel Skantze. 2023. Response-conditioned turn-taking prediction. In *Findings of the Association for Computational Linguistics: ACL 2023*, pages 12241–12248, Toronto, Canada. Association for Computational Linguistics.

Martin Johansson and Gabriel Skantze. 2015. Opportunities and obligations to take turns in collaborative multi-party human-robot interaction. In *Proceedings of the 16th Annual Meeting of the Special Interest Group on Discourse and Dialogue*, pages 305–314.

Takanori Kanai, Yukoh Wakabayashi, Ryota Nishimura, and Norihide Kitaoka. 2024. Predicting utterance-final timing considering linguistic features using wav2vec 2.0. In *2024 11th International Conference on Advanced Informatics: Concept, Theory and Application (ICAICTA)*, pages 1–5. IEEE.

Reshmashree Bangalore Kantharaju and Catherine Pelachaud. 2018. Towards developing a model to handle multiparty conversations for healthcare agents. In *ICAHGCA@ AAMAS*, pages 30–34.

Tatsuya Kawahara, Takashi Yamaguchi, Koji Inoue, Katsuya Takanashi, and Nigel G Ward. 2016. Prediction and generation of backchannel form for attentive listening systems. In *Interspeech*, pages 2890–2894.

Adam Kendon. 1967. Some functions of gaze-direction in social interaction. *Acta psychologica*, 26:22–63.

Kobin H Kendrick, Judith Holler, and Stephen C Levinson. 2023. Turn-taking in human face-to-face interaction is multimodal: gaze direction and manual gestures aid the coordination of turn transitions. *Philosophical transactions of the royal society B*, 378(1875):20210473.

Hatim Khouzaimi, Romain Laroche, and Fabrice Lefèvre. 2016. Reinforcement learning for turn-taking management in incremental spoken dialogue systems. In *IJCAI*, pages 2831–2837.

Hatim Khouzaimi, Romain Laroche, and Fabrice Lefèvre. 2018. A methodology for turn-taking capabilities enhancement in spoken dialogue systems using reinforcement learning. *Computer Speech & Language*, 47:93–111.

Hanae Koiso, Haruka Amatani, Yasuharu Den, Yuriko Iseki, Yuichi Ishimoto, Wakako Kashino, Yoshiko Kawabata, Ken'ya Nishikawa, Yayoi Tanaka, Yasuyuki Usuda, and Yuka Watanabe. 2022. Design and evaluation of the corpus of everyday Japanese conversation. In *Proceedings of the Thirteenth Language Resources and Evaluation Conference*, pages 5587–5594, Marseille, France. European Language Resources Association.

Wessel Kraaij, Thomas Hain, Mike Lincoln, and Wilfried Post. 2005. The ami meeting corpus. In *Proc. International Conference on Methods and Techniques in Behavioral Research*.

Fuma Kurata, Mao Saeki, Shinya Fujie, and Yoichi Matsuyama. 2023. Multimodal turn-taking model using visual cues for end-of-utterance prediction in spoken dialogue systems. *Proc. Interspeech 2023*, pages 2658–2662.

Divesh Lala, Pierrick Milhorat, Koji Inoue, Masanari Ishida, Katsuya Takanashi, and Tatsuya Kawahara. 2017. Attentive listening system with backchanneling, response generation and flexible turn-taking. In *Proceedings of the 18th Annual SIGdial Meeting on Discourse and Dialogue*, pages 127–136.

Kornel Laskowski. 2010. Modeling norms of turn-taking in multi-party conversation. In *Proceedings of the 48th annual meeting of the association for computational linguistics*, pages 999–1008.

Kornel Laskowski, Mattias Heldner, and Jens Edlund. 2012. On the dynamics of overlap in multi-party conversation. In *13th Annual Conference of the International Speech Communication Association 2012, INTERSPEECH 2012 Portland, OR; United States; 9 September 2012 through 13 September 2012;*, pages 846–849. Curran Associates, Inc.

Andrew H Lee, Sina J Semnani, Galo Castillo-López, Gäel de Chalendar, Monojit Choudhury, Ashna Dua, Kapil Rajesh Kavitha, Sungkyun Kim, Prashant Kodali, Ponnurangam Kumaraguru, et al. 2024. Benchmark underestimates the readiness of multi-lingual dialogue agents. *arXiv preprint arXiv:2405.17840*.

Meng-Chen Lee and Zhigang Deng. 2024. Online multimodal end-of-turn prediction for three-party conversations. In *Proceedings of the 26th International Conference on Multimodal Interaction*, pages 57–65.

Meng-Chen Lee, Mai Trinh, and Zhigang Deng. 2023. Multimodal turn analysis and prediction for multi-party conversations. In *Proceedings of the 25th International Conference on Multimodal Interaction*, pages 436–444.

Sean Leishman, Peter Bell, and Sarenne Wallbridge. 2024. Pairwiseturngpt: a multi-stream turn prediction model for spoken dialogue. In *Proceedings of the 28th Workshop on the Semantics and Pragmatics of Dialogue*.

Stephen C Levinson and Francisco Torreira. 2015. Timing in turn-taking and its implications for processing models of language. *Frontiers in psychology*, 6:731.

Siyan Li, Ashwin Paranjape, and Christopher Manning. 2022. When can I speak? predicting initiation points for spoken dialogue agents. In *Proceedings of the 23rd Annual Meeting of the Special Interest Group on Discourse and Dialogue*, pages 217–224, Edinburgh, UK. Association for Computational Linguistics.

Wencke Liermann, Yo-Han Park, Yong-Seok Choi, and Kong Lee. 2023. Dialogue act-aided backchannel prediction using multi-task learning. In *Findings of the Association for Computational Linguistics: EMNLP 2023*, pages 15073–15079.

Chaoran Liu, Carlos Toshinori Ishi, and Hiroshi Ishiguro. 2017. Turn-taking estimation model based on joint embedding of lexical and prosodic contents. In *Interspeech*, pages 1686–1690.

Yi Liu, Pascale Fung, Yongsheng Yang, Christopher Cieri, Shudong Huang, and David Graff. 2006. Hkust/mts: A very large scale mandarin telephone speech corpus. In *Chinese Spoken Language Processing: 5th International Symposium, ISCSLP 2006, Singapore, December 13-16, 2006. Proceedings*, pages 724–735. Springer.

Kikuo Maekawa, Hanae Koiso, Sadaoki Furui, and Hitoshi Isahara. 2000. Spontaneous speech corpus of Japanese. In *Proceedings of the Second International Conference on Language Resources and Evaluation (LREC'00)*, Athens, Greece. European Language Resources Association (ELRA).

Ryo Masumura, Taichi Asami, Hirokazu Masataki, Ryo Ishii, and Ryuichiro Higashinaka. 2017. Online end-of-turn detection from speech based on stacked time-asynchronous sequential networks. In *Interspeech*, volume 2017, pages 1661–1665.

Ryo Masumura, Tomohiro Tanaka, Atsushi Ando, Ryo Ishii, Ryuichiro Higashinaka, and Yushi Aono. 2018. Neural dialogue context online end-of-turn detection. In *Proceedings of the 19th Annual SIGdial Meeting on Discourse and Dialogue*, pages 224–228.

Tomas Mikolov, Kai Chen, Greg Corrado, and Jeffrey Dean. 2013. Efficient estimation of word representations in vector space. *arXiv preprint arXiv:1301.3781*.

Edmilson Morais, Matheus Damasceno, Hagai Aronowitz, Aharon Satt, and Ron Hoory. 2023. Modeling turn-taking in human-to-human spoken dialogue datasets using self-supervised features. In *ICASSP 2023-2023 IEEE International Conference on Acoustics, Speech and Signal Processing (ICASSP)*, pages 1–5. IEEE.

Edmilson Morais, Ron Hoory, Weizhong Zhu, Itai Gat, Matheus Damasceno, and Hagai Aronowitz. 2022. Speech emotion recognition using self-supervised features. In *ICASSP 2022-2022 IEEE International Conference on Acoustics, Speech and Signal Processing (ICASSP)*, pages 6922–6926. IEEE.

Markus Mueller, David Leuschner, Lars Briem, Maria Schmidt, Kevin Kilgour, Sebastian Stueker, and Alex Waibel. 2015. Using neural networks for data-driven backchannel prediction: A survey on input features and training techniques. In *Human-Computer Interaction: Interaction Technologies: 17th International Conference, HCI International 2015, Los Angeles, CA, USA, August 2-7, 2015, Proceedings, Part II 17*, pages 329–340. Springer.

Philipp Müller, Michael Dietz, Dominik Schiller, Dominike Thomas, Hali Lindsay, Patrick Gebhard, Elisabeth André, and Andreas Bulling. 2022. Multimediate'22: Backchannel detection and agreement estimation in group interactions. In *Proceedings of the 30th ACM International Conference on Multimedia*, pages 7109–7114.

Kazumasa Murai. 2011. Speaker predicting apparatus, speaker predicting method, and program product for predicting speaker. US Patent 7,907,165.

Tu Anh Nguyen, Eugene Kharitonov, Jade Copet, Yossi Adi, Wei-Ning Hsu, Ali Elkahky, Paden Tomasello, Robin Algayres, Benoit Sagot, Abdelrahman Mohamed, et al. 2023. Generative spoken dialogue language modeling. *Transactions of the Association for Computational Linguistics*, 11:250–266.

Vivian Nguyen, Otto Versyp, Christopher Cox, and Riccardo Fusaroli. 2022. A systematic review and bayesian meta-analysis of the development of turn taking in adult–child vocal interactions. *Child Development*, 93(4):1181–1200.

David G Novick, Brian Hansen, and Karen Ward. 1996. Coordinating turn-taking with gaze. In *Proceeding of Fourth International Conference on Spoken Language Processing. ICSLP'96*, volume 3, pages 1888–1891. IEEE.

Catharine Oertel, Marcin Włodarczak, Jens Edlund, Petra Wagner, and Joakim Gustafson. 2012. Gaze patterns in turn-taking. In *Thirteenth annual conference of the international speech communication association*.

D Kimbrough Oller. 1973. The effect of position in utterance on speech segment duration in english. *The journal of the Acoustical Society of America*, 54(5):1235–1247.

Kazuyo Onishi, Hiroki Tanaka, and Satoshi Nakamura. 2023. Multimodal voice activity prediction: Turn-taking events detection in expert-novice conversation. In *Proceedings of the 11th International Conference on Human-Agent Interaction*, pages 13–21.

Kazuyo Onishi, Hiroki Tankka, and Satoshi Nakamura. 2024. Multimodal voice activity projection for turn-taking and effects on speaker adaptation. *IEICE Transactions on Information and Systems*.

Daniel Ortega, Chia-Yu Li, and Ngoc Thang Vu. 2020. Oh, jeez! or uh-huh? a listener-aware backchannel predictor on asr transcriptions. In *ICASSP 2020-2020 IEEE International Conference on Acoustics, Speech and Signal Processing (ICASSP)*, pages 8064–8068. IEEE.

Daniel Ortega, Sarina Meyer, Antje Schweitzer, and Ngoc Thang Vu. 2023. Modeling speaker-listener interaction for backchannel prediction. *arXiv preprint arXiv:2304.04472*.

Maike Paetzel-Prüsmann and James Kennedy. 2023. Improving a robot's turn-taking behavior in dynamic multiparty interactions. In *Companion of the 2023 ACM/IEEE International Conference on Human-Robot Interaction*, pages 411–415.

Yo-Han Park, Wencke Liermann, Yong-Seok Choi, and Kong Joo Lee. 2024. Improving backchannel prediction leveraging sequential and attentive context awareness. In *Findings of the Association for Computational Linguistics: EACL 2024*, pages 1689–1694.

Simone Pika, Ray Wilkinson, Kobin H Kendrick, and Sonja C Vernes. 2018. Taking turns: bridging the gap between human and animal communication. *Proceedings of the Royal Society B*, 285(1880):20180598.

Maria J Pinto and Tony Belpaeme. 2024. Predictive turn-taking: Leveraging language models to anticipate turn transitions in human-robot dialogue. In *2024 33rd IEEE International Conference on Robot and Human Interactive Communication (ROMAN)*, pages 1733–1738. IEEE.

Alec Radford, Jeffrey Wu, Rewon Child, David Luan, Dario Amodei, Ilya Sutskever, et al. 2019. Language models are unsupervised multitask learners. *OpenAI blog*, 1(8):9.

Antoine Raux. 2008. Flexible turn-taking for spoken dialog systems. *Language Technologies Institute, CMU Dec*, 12.

Antoine Raux and Maxine Eskenazi. 2009. A finite-state turn-taking model for spoken dialog systems. In *Proceedings of human language technologies: The 2009 annual conference of the North American chapter of the association for computational linguistics*, pages 629–637.

Matthew Roddy, Gabriel Skantze, and Naomi Harte. 2018a. Investigating Speech Features for Continuous Turn-Taking Prediction Using LSTMs. In *Proc. Interspeech 2018*, pages 586–590.

Matthew Roddy, Gabriel Skantze, and Naomi Harte. 2018b. Multimodal continuous turn-taking prediction using multiscale rnns. In *Proceedings of the 20th ACM International Conference on Multimodal Interaction*, pages 186–190.

Robin Ruede, Markus Müller, Sebastian Stüker, and Alex Waibel. 2017. Enhancing backchannel prediction using word embeddings. In *Interspeech*, pages 879–883.

Harvey Sacks, Emanuel A Schegloff, and Gail Jefferson. 1978. A simplest systematics for the organization of turn taking for conversation. In *Studies in the organization of conversational interaction*, pages 7–55. Elsevier.

Jin Sakuma, Shinya Fujie, and Tetsunori Kobayashi. 2022. Response timing estimation for spoken dialog system using dialog act estimation. In *Proceedings of the Annual Conference of the International Speech Communication Association, INTERSPEECH*, volume 2022, pages 4486–4490.

Jin Sakuma, Shinya Fujie, and Tetsunori Kobayashi. 2023. Response timing estimation for spoken dialog systems based on syntactic completeness prediction. In *2022 IEEE Spoken Language Technology Workshop (SLT)*, pages 369–374. IEEE.

Ryo Sato and Yugo Takeuchi. 2014. Coordinating turn-taking and talking in multi-party conversations by controlling robot's eye-gaze. In *The 23rd IEEE International Symposium on Robot and Human Interactive Communication*, pages 280–285. IEEE.

Yuki Sato, Yuya Chiba, and Ryuichiro Higashinaka. 2024a. Effects of multiple japanese datasets for training voice activity projection models. In *2024 27th Conference of the Oriental COCOSDA International Committee for the Co-ordination and Standardisation of Speech Databases and Assessment Techniques (O-COCOSDA)*, pages 1–6. IEEE.

Yuki Sato, Yuya Chiba, and Ryuichiro Higashinaka. 2024b. Investigating the language independence of voice activity projection models through standardization of speech segmentation labels. In *Proceedings of 2023 APSIPA Annual Summit and Conference*.

Laura Schauer, Jason Sweeney, Charlie Lyttle, Zein Said, Aron Szeles, Cale Clark, Katie McAskill, Xander Wickham, Tom Byars, Daniel Hernández Garcia, et al. 2023. Detecting agreement in multi-party conversational ai. *arXiv preprint arXiv:2311.03026*.

Emanuel A Schegloff. 1996. Issues of relevance for discourse analysis: Contingency in action, interaction and co-participant context. In *Computational and conversational discourse: Burning issues—An interdisciplinary account*, pages 3–35. Springer.

David Schlangen and Gabriel Skantze. 2011. A general, abstract model of incremental dialogue processing. *Dialogue & Discourse*, 2(1):83–111.

Elizabeth Shriberg, Andreas Stolcke, and Don Baron. 2001. Observations on overlap: findings and implications for automatic processing of multi-party conversation. In *Interspeech*, pages 1359–1362. Citeseer.

Rein Ove Sikveland and Richard Ogden. 2012. Holding gestures across turns: moments to generate shared understanding. *Gesture*, 12(2):166–199.

Gabriel Skantze. 2017. Towards a general, continuous model of turn-taking in spoken dialogue using lstm recurrent neural networks. In *Proceedings of the 18th Annual SIGdial Meeting on Discourse and Dialogue*, pages 220–230.

Gabriel Skantze. 2021. Turn-taking in conversational systems and human-robot interaction: a review. *Computer Speech & Language*, 67:101178.

Gabriel Skantze, Martin Johansson, and Jonas Beskow. 2015. Exploring turn-taking cues in multi-party human-robot discussions about objects. In *Proceedings of the 2015 ACM on international conference on multimodal interaction*, pages 67–74.

Tanya Stivers, Nicholas J Enfield, Penelope Brown, Christina Englert, Makoto Hayashi, Trine Heinemann, Gertie Hoymann, Federico Rossano, Jan Peter De Ruiter, Kyung-Eun Yoon, et al. 2009. Universals and cultural variation in turn-taking in conversation. *Proceedings of the National Academy of Sciences*, 106(26):10587–10592.

Jürgen Streeck and Ulrike Hartge. 1992. Previews: Gestures at the transition place. *The contextualization of language*, pages 135–157.

Daniel Y Takahashi, Darshana Z Narayanan, and Asif A Ghazanfar. 2013. Coupled oscillator dynamics of vocal turn-taking in monkeys. *Current Biology*, 23(21):2162–2168.

Raeda Tartory, Sami Al-khawaldeh, Samia Azieb, and Bassam Al Saideen. 2024. Backchannel forms and functions in context and culture: The use of backchannels in arab media discourse. *Discourse Studies*, page 14614456241236904.

Mark Ter Maat, Khiet P Truong, and Dirk Heylen. 2011. How agents' turn-taking strategies influence impressions and response behaviors. *Presence: Teleoperators and Virtual Environments*, 20(5):412–430.

Kristinn R Thórisson, Olafur Gislason, Gudny Ragna Jonsdottir, and Hrafn Th Thorisson. 2010. A multiparty multimodal architecture for realtime turntaking. In *Intelligent Virtual Agents: 10th International Conference, IVA 2010, Philadelphia, PA, USA, September 20-22, 2010. Proceedings 10*, pages 350–356. Springer.

David Traum. 2003. Issues in multiparty dialogues. In *Workshop on Agent Communication Languages*, pages 201–211. Springer.

Muhammad Umair, Vasanth Sarathy, and JP de Ruiter. 2024. Large language models know what to say but not when to speak. *arXiv preprint arXiv:2410.16044*.

Jinhan Wang, Long Chen, Aparna Khare, Anirudh Raju, Pranav Dheram, Di He, Minhua Wu, Andreas Stolcke, and Venkatesh Ravichandran. 2024. Turn-taking and backchannel prediction with acoustic and large language model fusion. In *ICASSP 2024*.

Nigel G Ward, Diego Aguirre, Gerardo Cervantes, and Olac Fuentes. 2018. Turn-taking predictions across languages and genres using an lstm recurrent neural network. In *2018 IEEE Spoken Language Technology Workshop (SLT)*, pages 831–837. IEEE.

Jason Wei, Maarten Bosma, Vincent Zhao, Kelvin Guu, Adams Wei Yu, Brian Lester, Nan Du, Andrew M. Dai, and Quoc V Le. 2022. Finetuned language models are zero-shot learners. In *International Conference on Learning Representations*.

Mike Wu, Jonathan Nafziger, Anthony Scodary, and Andrew Maas. 2020. Harpervalleybank: A domain-specific spoken dialog corpus. *arXiv preprint arXiv:2010.13929*.

Sixing Wu, Jiong Yu, Jiahao Chen, Xiaofan Deng, and Wei Zhou. 2024. Improving open-domain dialogue response generation with multi-source multilingual commonsense knowledge. In *Proceedings of the AAAI Conference on Artificial Intelligence*, volume 38, pages 19252–19260.

Jiudong Yang, Peiying Wang, Yi Zhu, Mingchao Feng, Meng Chen, and Xiaodong He. 2022. Gated multimodal fusion with contrastive learning for turn-taking prediction in human-robot dialogue. In *ICASSP 2022-2022 IEEE International Conference on Acoustics, Speech and Signal Processing (ICASSP)*, pages 7747–7751. IEEE.

Katsuya Yokoyama, Hiroaki Takatsu, Hiroshi Honda, Shinya Fujie, and Tetsunori Kobayashi. 2018. Investigation of users' short responses in actual conversation system and automatic recognition of their intentions. In *2018 IEEE Spoken Language Technology Workshop (SLT)*, pages 934–940. IEEE.

Koichiro Yoshino, Hiroki Tanaka, Kyoshiro Sugiyama, Makoto Kondo, and Satoshi Nakamura. 2018. Japanese dialogue corpus of information navigation and attentive listening annotated with extended ISO-24617-2 dialogue act tags. In *Proceedings of the Eleventh International Conference on Language Resources and Evaluation (LREC 2018)*, Miyazaki, Japan. European Language Resources Association (ELRA).

Xiang Yu, Zhang Ting, Di Hui, Huang Hui, Li Chunyou, Ouchi Kazushige, Chen Yufeng, and Xu Jinan. 2023. Improving zero-shot cross-lingual dialogue state tracking via contrastive learning. In *Proceedings of the 22nd Chinese National Conference on Computational Linguistics*, pages 624–625.

Margaret Zellers, Jan Gorisch, David House, and Benno Peters. 2019. Timing properties of hand gestures and their lexical counterparts at turn transition places. In *Proceedings of the FONETIK (Swedish Phonetics Conference) 2019 in Stockholm, June 10–12, 2019*, pages 119–124. Stockholm University.

Margaret Zellers, David House, and Simon Alexanderson. 2016. Prosody and hand gesture at turn boundaries in swedish. In *Speech Prosody*, pages 831–835.

Hanlei Zhang, Xin Wang, Hua Xu, Qianrui Zhou, Kai Gao, Jianhua Su, jinyue Zhao, Wenrui Li, and Yanting Chen. 2024. MIntrec2.0: A large-scale benchmark dataset for multimodal intent recognition and out-of-scope detection in conversations. In *The Twelfth International Conference on Learning Representations*.

Tiancheng Zhao, Alan W Black, and Maxine Eskenazi. 2015. An incremental turn-taking model with active system barge-in for spoken dialog systems. In *Proceedings of the 16th Annual Meeting of the Special Interest Group on Discourse and Dialogue*, pages 42–50.

Oswald Zink, Yosuke Higuchi, Carlos Mullov, Alexander Waibel, and Tetsunori Kobayashi. 2024. Predictive speech recognition and end-of-utterance detection towards spoken dialog systems. *arXiv preprint arXiv:2409.19990*.

Lei Zuo, Kun Qian, Bowen Yang, and Zhou Yu. 2021. Allwoz: Towards multilingual task-oriented dialog systems for all. *arXiv preprint arXiv:2112.08333*.

A Multi-party Conversations

In this appendix we describe the main difficulties in turn management in multi-party conversations and how they are addressed in natural dialogues. Multi-party conversations consist of dialogues where more than two interlocutors are involved. Sociolinguists have found these types of interactions the most natural form of conversations, arguing that dyadic scenarios and monologues are special cases (Jaffe and Feldstein, 1970). MPCs entail additional challenges for humans to coordinate turns. In dyadic interactions speakers always address the other interlocutor, thus it is trivial determining who the next speaker is. In MPCs the speaker may address anyone, be it a single listener, a subset of the listeners, or all of them. Therefore, deciding who should speak after a turn is yielded in a MPC is not simple given that there are multiple candidates (Schegloff, 1996). Although overlap occurrence in MPCs is similar to two-party dialogues in some cases (Shriberg et al., 2001), overlap duration has been observed to be inversely proportional to the number of simultaneously speaking parties (Laskowski et al., 2012). In general, the dynamics in MPCs differ from dyadic scenarios, hence they need special attention.

Verbal and non-verbal behaviors are adopted to ease turn shifts to overcome turn-taking issues in MPCs. Speakers tend to use cues at the end of turns to select the next speaker, such as naming the addressee. In addition, speakers do not only use gaze to indicate turn yielding as in the dyadic case, but also to address a specific listener, who is obliged to take the next turn (Auer, 2018; Sacks et al., 1978). Mouth-opening patterns also reveal relevant information to predict next speakers in MPCs (Murai, 2011). Ishii et al. (2019) found that the next speaker starts opening their mouth narrowly before change of turns. This phenomenon can be due to both the next speaker's ability to predict the end of turn and current speaker's skills to interpret next speaker's desire to gain the floor.

B Paper Selection Criteria

In this appendix we describe the procedure we followed to search scientific articles for this survey. We adopted a systematic approach to identify relevant research on turn-taking modeling, with a special attention on studies published after 2021. We began with an extensive search on Google Scholar using a set of targeted keywords, including "turn-taking", "end-of-turn", "end-of-utterance", and "backchannel", combined with terms like "prediction", "detection", and "multi-party". We also conducted manual searches of proceedings from major NLP and dialogue system conferences taking place between 2020 and 2024, such as SIGDIAL, *ACL, Interspeech, IWSDS and ICASSP. To minimize the risk of missing key studies, we employed additional strategies to enhance coverage. We reviewed the Google Scholar profiles of identified scholars active in the field from the pool of articles we previously obtained to find any potentially missed publications. Finally, we also examined recent citations from our pool of papers to identify emerging research. Through these efforts, we aimed to provide a thorough and representative overview of the state of research in turn-taking modeling, ensuring that this survey reflects the latest developments in the field. As a result, this survey describes new methods and corpora included in more than 35 papers published after 2021.

Figure 1 shows the distributions, by subtask, of publication years of the articles we report in this survey. We observe that around 65% of the studies on end-of-turn and backchannel prediction included in this survey were published between 2021 and 2024. On the other hand, less than 30% of the works we found on multi-party conversations were published in the same time span. These findings confirm the lack of contributions and slow progress in MPCs and turn-taking modeling research.

C Turn-taking Events and Phenomena

In this appendix we define relevant events and phenomena in turn management in natural

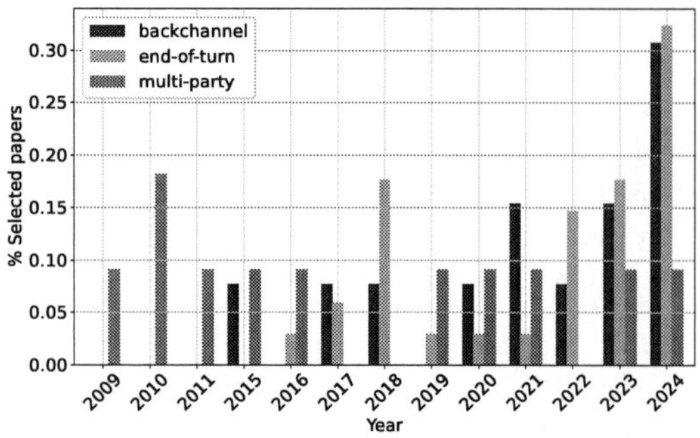

Figure 1: Distribution across the years of the papers we describe in Sections 4, 5 and 6.

dialogues. Figure 2 depicts distinct elements and events occurring in spoken dialogue turn-taking management.

Inter-Pausal Units (IPUs) are speech segments preceding a silence of a certain duration. IPUs correspond to the main pieces of information exchanged by interlocutors. **Pauses** are silences between two consecutive IPUs of the same speaker. **Gaps** are silences between two consecutive turns of different speakers. **Backchannel** are lexical or non-lexical sounds provided as a feedback by a listener in the dialogue. These expressions are usually used to indicate to the speaker that the listener understands or acknowledges what the speaker says, without the intention of interrupting. A backchannel is not considered as a turn. An **Overlap** takes place when IPUs from distinct speakers are produced at the same time. Usually, they occur at turn shifts.

D Turn-taking Cues

In this appendix we explain the cues both speakers and listeners use to anticipate turn completions. A long silence after a speaker's utterance is the most basic form of cues indicating that the speaker has completed their turn. It is not enough though to detect when a turn-shift should occur. In practice, combinations of cues such as gaze, prosody (i.e. voice volume, intonation, etc.), syntactic completeness and body gestures are used to predict when to take the turn. Although there exist some differences in the use of cues across languages due to cultural or grammatical aspects, most languages follow similar patterns (Stivers et al., 2009). Prosody is one of the most studied cues for turn-yielding prediction. The prosodic structure of speech carries turn-taking cues in three dimensions: fundamental frequency, duration and amplitude (Cutler and Pearson, 2018). For example, in English words are uttered with longer duration in phrase-final than in non-phrase-final positions (Oller, 1973). Duncan (1972) and Cutler and Pearson (2018) observed that intermediate fundamental frequency contours maintain a mid-level pitch range, whereas either higher and lower pitch levels are found at the end of utterances. Syntactic completeness is another cue obtained from speech, which involves *what* the speaker says rather than *the form* it is spoken. Syntax and semantics are more relevant than prosody for turn-yield prediction, as it is easier for humans to predict a syntactically complete phrase than prosodic changes in speech (Sacks et al., 1978).

Body language also plays a crucial role to foresee the speaker's end of turn. Speakers tend to gaze away after taking their turns and look back again toward the listener when their speech is completed (Kendon, 1967). Generally, the participant taking the next turn is the one breaking the mutual gaze when beginning to speak (Novick et al., 1996). Hand gestures have also been extensively studied as turn-yielding and turn-holding cues (Sikveland and Ogden, 2012; Streeck and Hartge, 1992; Zellers et al., 2019). Kendrick et al. (2023) found that turns including manual gestures resulted in faster transitions than those without any. They reported that gaps between turns were approximately 150ms shorter on average when hand gestures were used. Similarly, Zellers et al. (2016) noted a relation between turn-shifts and hand gestures produced before the end of turn of Swedish speakers. Despite the previously described works have mostly studied cues in an isolated fashion, cues have been observed to have an additive effect (Hjalmarsson, 2011). In other words, humans use combinations of them to adequately manage turns in dialogues.

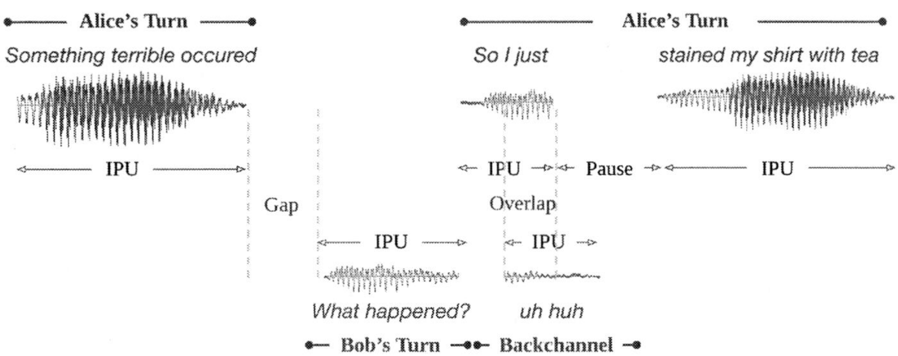

Figure 2: Turn-taking management illustration in a dyadic conversation. IPU: Inter-Pausal Unit.

Integrating Respiration into Voice Activity Projection for Enhancing Turn-taking Performance

Takao Obi
Institute of Science Tokyo / Tokyo
smalltail@lr.pi.titech.ac.jp

Kotaro Funakoshi
Institute of Science Tokyo / Tokyo
funakoshi@lr.pi.titech.ac.jp

Abstract

Voice Activity Projection (VAP) models predict upcoming voice activities on a continuous timescale, enabling more nuanced turn-taking behaviors in spoken dialogue systems. Although previous studies have shown robust performance with audio-based VAP, the potential of incorporating additional physiological information, such as respiration, remains relatively unexplored. In this paper, we investigate whether respiratory information can enhance VAP performance in turn-taking. To this end, we collected Japanese dialogue data with synchronized audio and respiratory waveforms, and then we integrated the respiratory information into the VAP model. Our results showed that the VAP model combining audio and respiratory information had better performance than the audio-only model. This finding underscores the potential for improving the turn-taking performance of VAP by incorporating respiration.

1 Introduction

In conversational systems designed for emotional support and customer assistance, it is crucial for the user and the system to engage in smooth and natural dialogues. A key factor in achieving such smooth communication is effective turn-taking, wherein each participant can seamlessly begin and end speaking without awkward interruptions or prolonged silences. In this context, there has been a growing body of research aimed at predicting turn-taking behaviors in spoken dialogue between the user and the system (Skantze, 2017; Roddy et al., 2018).

Recently, Voice Activity Projection (VAP) has been proposed as a method for more natural turn-taking in spoken dialogue (Ekstedt and Skantze, 2022). VAP dynamically models voice activities in dyadic interactions by processing the raw audio signals from both speakers, predicting future voice activity in a series of short time windows (at window lengths of 200 ms, 400 ms, 600 ms, and 800 ms within a 2-second horizon). This approach yields a 256-class prediction representing binary voice activity in each of the four time windows for each speaker. In addition, VAP defines four evaluation tasks, SHIFT/HOLD, SHORT/LONG, SHIFT-prediction, and Backchannel-prediction, to assess how effectively the model can predict turn-shifts and backchannels. Specifically, SHIFT/HOLD tests the model's ability to predict which speaker will take the next turn during mutual silence; SHORT/LONG tests the ability to predict at its onset whether a speaker's utterance will be a short backchannel or a longer utterance; SHIFT-prediction tests the ability to predict whether a turn-shift will occur during active speech; Backchannel-prediction tests the ability to predict future backchannels. Various extensions of VAP have been explored, including the incorporation of prosodic information, gaze, and gestures (Onishi et al., 2023), the extension of multilingual data (Inoue et al., 2024a), and real-time predictions (Inoue et al., 2024b).

In this work, we aim to further enhance VAP by integrating respiratory information, which is a nonverbal cue closely tied to speech production. Prior research about respiration has observed the synchronization of respiratory patterns during turn-taking (Rochet-Capellan and Fuchs, 2014), as well as behaviors such as speakers taking a quick breath when they wish to continue speaking and next speakers inhaling when the previous speaker finishes speaking (Rochet-Capellan and Fuchs, 2014; Torreira et al., 2015; Ishii et al., 2016). These observations have motivated attempts to predict turn continuations, endings, and next-speaker transitions using respiratory signals (Ishii et al., 2016; Włodarczak and Heldner, 2019). In human-system spoken dialogues, respiration has also been investigated to predict a user's speech onset (Włodarczak et al., 2017; Obi and Funakoshi, 2023), indicating that

Proceedings of the 15th International Workshop on Spoken Dialogue Systems Technology, pages 272–276
May 27–30, 2025. ©2025 Association for Computational Linguistics

respiratory information can facilitate smoother turn management.

We focus on the turn-taking performance of VAP and investigate how integrating respiratory information affects the model's performance in SHIFT/HOLD, SHORT/LONG, and SHIFT-prediction tasks. We collected Japanese dialogue data containing both audio and respiratory waveforms, and then we integrated the respiratory information into the VAP model. Our results showed that the VAP model combining audio and respiratory information had better performance than the audio-only model. This finding underscores the usefulness of respiratory information for VAP turn-taking tasks.

2 Data Collection

Because no publicly available dataset for integrating respiration into VAP was available, we collected spoken dialogue data.

2.1 Participants

Thirty-six pairs (72 in total; 32 male and 40 female; ranging in age from 20 to 60) who are native speakers of Japanese were recruited through an agency. Written informed consent was obtained from each participant before data collection. The data collection was pre-approved by the authors' institutional ethical committee.

2.2 Equipment

We employed two main components for data recording.

Audio Recorder: The audio data were recorded using a Kinect v2 microphone made by Microsoft.

Respiration Sensor: The respiratory waveforms were recorded using a device that combines a Biopac TSD201 sensor and a homemade signal amplifier. We used two identical units of this device to record data from two participants in parallel.

2.3 Recording

Because VAP uses separate speaker inputs, we recorded audio and respiration data for each participant in each pair separately. During each recording session, both audio and respiratory waveforms were captured with millisecond-level synchronization by our own recording software, which also logged the start time in milliseconds. This mechanism allowed us to align the data between the two participants in each pair.

Audio Recording: The audio was recorded at 16 kHz with 16-bit PCM (pulse code modulation) encoding.

Respiration Recording: Expansion and contraction of the torso during respiration were recorded using sensor belts around the thorax. The respiration stream was sampled at approximately 90 Hz and stored with corresponding timestamps.

2.4 Procedure

The two participants of each pair were placed in hard-wired soundproof rooms individually and interacted remotely. First, they attached the respiration sensor belts around their thoraxes and sat in front of a screen displaying the other participant. They were then given a discussion topic (e.g., choosing items for survival in a desert) and engaged in a 15-minute discussion. If any time remained after finishing the discussion, they were allowed to talk freely. After a short break, they performed another 15-minute dialogue session on a different discussion topic. We adopted this two-session design to minimize participant fatigue and ensure sufficient dialogue content.

3 Experiments

We investigated whether respiratory information can help improve VAP performance in turn-taking.

3.1 Preprocessing

Data Alignment: Because each participant's data was recorded separately, we aligned the start times of the paired recordings based on the later start time. Specifically, we cut the beginning of the earlier recording to match the start of the later one.

Audio Data: We normalized audio waveforms by amplitude and detected voice activities using Silero-VAD[1]. After that, using the VAP dataset creation scripts[2], we created audio splits and corresponding voice activity labels.

Respiratory Waveform: We first removed drift to mitigate environmental noise. Because the respiration stream was not sampled at perfectly uniform intervals, we applied cubic spline interpolation to resample at 90 Hz. We applied a low-pass filter to remove frequencies above 1 Hz (reflecting the typical human respiratory rate of 0.15–0.40 Hz (Beda et al., 2007)). Finally, because amplitude ranges varied across the two devices, we applied z-score

[1]https://github.com/snakers4/silero-vad

[2]https://github.com/ErikEkstedt/VoiceActivityProjection

normalization to the waveforms. After preprocessing, participants' respiratory rates ranged from 11.8 to 24.3 breaths per minute (BPM), with an average of 16.9 BPM (SD = 2.43).

Data Splitting: For model training and evaluation, we split the data into 80%/15%/5% for training, validation, and test sets, respectively. To properly evaluate the model performance, we split the sets so that they did not contain the same participant pairs.

3.2 VAP Model

We used the public VAP model[2]. The model consists of four main components:

Contrast Predictive Coding (CPC) Encoder: A 5-layer CNN followed by a 1-layer GRU, pre-trained on the LibriSpeech Dataset (Panayotov et al., 2015). This encoder is frozen during training.

Self-attention Transformer: A single Transformer layer with 256 dimensions to model each speaker's audio stream separately.

Cross-attention Transformer: Three Transformer layers with 256 dimensions that perform cross-attention between both speakers' encoded audio streams.

Linear layer: Two separate linear layers for multitask learning output probabilities for a 256-class VAP state $p_{\text{vap}}(y)$ and per-speaker VAD $p_{\text{vad}}(s)$.

The model losses are defined as $L = L_{\text{vap}} + L_{\text{vad}}$, where

$$\begin{aligned} L_{\text{vap}} &= -\log p_{\text{vap}}(y), \\ L_{\text{vad}} &= -\sum_{s=1}^{2}\Big[v_s \log p_{\text{vad}}(s) \\ &\quad + (1 - v_s)\log\big(1 - p_{\text{vad}}(s)\big)\Big], \end{aligned}$$

$y \in \{1, \ldots, 256\}$ is the reference VAP index, and $v_s \in \{0, 1\}$ indicates whether participant s is speaking. For brevity, the time frame indexing is omitted, but these calculations apply to all input frames.

3.3 Evaluation

We focused on three VAP tasks for evaluating turn-taking: SHIFT/HOLD, SHORT/LONG, and SHIFT-prediction. We set the input signal segment to 20 seconds, following the findings in (Inoue et al., 2024b), which reported high performance for Japanese with a 20-second segment. To evaluate model performance, we used weighted F1-scores based on the original VAP study (Ekstedt and Skantze, 2022). The training was repeated with random seeds from 1 to 10.

Table 1: Means and variances of weighted F1-scores for turn-taking performance of VAP in evaluation settings. Values marked with * are significantly higher ($p < 0.01$) than the corresponding audio-only baseline based on bootstrap tests.

Evaluation setting	SHIFT/ HOLD	SHORT/ LONG	SHIFT-prediction
Audio-only	0.608 (0.000)	0.794 (0.000)	0.635 (0.001)
Resp-only	0.514 (0.001)	0.574 (0.000)	0.455 (0.001)
Combination	**0.635*** (0.001)	**0.796** (0.000)	**0.648*** (0.002)

We evaluated the model's performance in three settings:

Audio Only: For the baseline audio-only VAP model, we used the original training configuration, including a batch size of 8, a learning rate of 3.63×10^{-4}, a weight decay of 0.001, and the AdamW optimizer. We trained for 20 epochs and used the model checkpoint that yielded the lowest validation loss for testing.

Respiration Only: We replaced the encoder with a similarly structured one modified to handle respiratory waveforms. Unlike the CPC encoder (which was frozen for audio), we trained the respiratory encoder along with the other layers. We increased the total epochs to 30 based on validation loss trends, keeping all other hyperparameters the same.

Combination: To explore a straightforward way of combining respiratory information with audio, we used separate encoders and attention transformers for each modality. We then concatenated the outputs from each cross-attention before passing them to the linear layers. Training settings were identical to the audio-only.

4 Results

The experimental results are shown in Table 1. As shown in Table 1, the highest performance was achieved when voice and respiratory waveforms were used together. The combination model achieved significantly higher SHIFT/HOLD and SHIFT-prediction F1-scores ($p < 0.01$) than the audio-only baseline, using bootstrap resampling methods[3].

[3]https://github.com/fpgdubost/bstrap

5 Discussion

Our results showed that combining respiratory information with audio improves VAP performance in turn-taking, especially SHIFT/HOLD and SHIFT-prediction tasks (Table 1). This enhancement likely arises because respiratory information provides additional cues about a speaker's readiness or intention to speak, helping reduce uncertainty around turn boundaries. This finding indicates that respiration is valuable supplementary information for VAP turn-taking prediction.

6 Limitations and Future Work

Although our experiments demonstrated the potential benefits of integrating respiratory information into VAP, several limitations remain.

First, the amount of data used in this study was relatively small, and participants took part in remote dialogues. To further validate the effectiveness of respiratory information for VAP, we plan to collect additional data in more diverse conversational settings.

Second, we used contact-based respiration sensors to record respiratory waveforms. However, for real-world spoken dialogue systems, it is preferable to measure a user's respiration in a non-contact manner. By combining our approach with non-contact respiratory estimation methods (Obi and Funakoshi, 2023; Matheus et al., 2023), which capture users' respiratory information using only an RGB camera, we can eliminate the need for wearable sensors. We will adopt this combined approach to implement VAP with integrated respiration in real-world dialogues.

Third, the method of combining audio and respiratory information in our model was quite simplistic, relying on a straightforward concatenation of features. By improving the model architecture or employing more advanced fusion strategies, it may be possible to more accurately integrate voice and respiratory signals. We will explore these more sophisticated approaches to better leverage respiratory information for VAP.

Finally, although the original VAP includes Backchannel-prediction, we focused on SHIFT/HOLD, SHORT/LONG, and SHIFT-prediction in this study. Evaluating the effectiveness of respiratory information on Backchannel-prediction remains an important direction for future work and may further clarify the potential of respiratory information.

7 Conclusion

In this work, we explored how respiratory information can be combined with audio to improve Voice Activity Projection (VAP). We collected Japanese dialogue data with synchronized audio and respiratory waveforms to investigate the efficacy of combining this information for VAP. Our results indicate that combining audio and respiratory information can improve VAP performance in turn-taking. This finding underscores the potential value of leveraging respiratory information to enhance the turn-taking performance of VAP.

We will explore more sophisticated fusion mechanisms that might better integrate respiratory information into VAP.

Acknowledgments

This work was supported by JSPS KAKENHI Grant Number JP22H04859 and JST BOOST, Japan Grant Number JPMJBS2430.

References

Alessandro Beda, Frederico C. Jandre, David I.W. Phillips, Antonio Giannella-Neto, and David M. Simpson. 2007. Heart-rate and blood-pressure variability during psychophysiological tasks involving speech: Influence of respiration. *Psychophysiology*, 44(5):767–778.

Erik Ekstedt and Gabriel Skantze. 2022. Voice Activity Projection: Self-supervised Learning of Turn-taking Events. In *Proc. Interspeech 2022*, pages 5190–5194.

Koji Inoue, Bing'er Jiang, Erik Ekstedt, Tatsuya Kawahara, and Gabriel Skantze. 2024a. Multilingual turn-taking prediction using voice activity projection. In *Proceedings of the 2024 Joint International Conference on Computational Linguistics, Language Resources and Evaluation (LREC-COLING 2024)*, pages 11873–11883, Torino, Italia. ELRA and ICCL.

Koji Inoue, Bing'er Jiang, Erik Ekstedt, Tatsuya Kawahara, and Gabriel Skantze. 2024b. Real-time and continuous turn-taking prediction using voice activity projection. In *International Workshop on Spoken Dialogue Systems Technology (IWSDS)*.

Ryo Ishii, Kazuhiro Otsuka, Shiro Kumano, and Junji Yamato. 2016. Using respiration to predict who will speak next and when in multiparty meetings. *ACM Trans. Interact. Intell. Syst.*, 6(2).

Kayla Matheus, Ellie Mamantov, Marynel Vázquez, and Brian Scassellati. 2023. Deep breathing phase classification with a social robot for mental health. In *Proceedings of the 25th International Conference on Multimodal Interaction*, ICMI '23, page 153–162,

New York, NY, USA. Association for Computing Machinery.

Takao Obi and Kotaro Funakoshi. 2023. Video-based respiratory waveform estimation in dialogue: A novel task and dataset for human-machine interaction. In *Proceedings of the 25th International Conference on Multimodal Interaction*, ICMI '23, page 649–660. Association for Computing Machinery.

Kazuyo Onishi, Hiroki Tanaka, and Satoshi Nakamura. 2023. Multimodal voice activity prediction: Turn-taking events detection in expert-novice conversation. In *Proceedings of the 11th International Conference on Human-Agent Interaction*, HAI '23, page 13–21, New York, NY, USA. Association for Computing Machinery.

Vassil Panayotov, Guoguo Chen, Daniel Povey, and Sanjeev Khudanpur. 2015. Librispeech: An asr corpus based on public domain audio books. In *2015 IEEE International Conference on Acoustics, Speech and Signal Processing (ICASSP)*, pages 5206–5210.

Amélie Rochet-Capellan and Susanne Fuchs. 2014. Take a breath and take the turn: How breathing meets turns in spontaneous dialogue. *Philosophical Transactions of the Royal Society B*, 369.

Matthew Roddy, Gabriel Skantze, and Naomi Harte. 2018. Multimodal continuous turn-taking prediction using multiscale rnns. In *Proceedings of the 20th ACM International Conference on Multimodal Interaction*, ICMI '18, page 186–190, New York, NY, USA. Association for Computing Machinery.

Gabriel Skantze. 2017. Towards a general, continuous model of turn-taking in spoken dialogue using LSTM recurrent neural networks. In *Proceedings of the 18th Annual SIGdial Meeting on Discourse and Dialogue*, pages 220–230, Saarbrücken, Germany. Association for Computational Linguistics.

Francisco Torreira, Sara Bögels, and Stephen C. Levinson. 2015. Breathing for answering: the time course of response planning in conversation. *Frontiers in Psychology*, 6.

Marcin Włodarczak and Mattias Heldner. 2019. Breathing in conversation — what we've learned. In *1st International Seminar on the Foundations of Speech : BREATHING, PAUSING, AND THE VOICE, 1st –3rd December 2019 in Sønderborg, Denmark : Conference Proceedings*, pages 13–15.

Marcin Włodarczak, Kornel Laskowski, Mattias Heldner, and Kätlin Aare. 2017. Improving Prediction of Speech Activity Using Multi-Participant Respiratory State. In *Proc. Interspeech 2017*, pages 1666–1670.

DSLCMM: A Multimodal Human-Machine Dialogue Corpus Built through Competitions

Ryuichiro Higashinaka[1], Tetsuro Takahashi[2], Shinya Iizuka[1], Sota Horiuchi[1], Michimasa Inaba[3], Zhiyang Qi[3], Yuta Sasaki[4], Kotaro Funakoshi[4], Shoji Moriya[5], Shiki Sato[5], Takashi Minato[6], Kurima Sakai[7], Tomo Funayama[7], Masato Komuro[8], Hiroyuki Nishikawa[9], Ryosaku Makino[10], Hirofumi Kikuchi[10], Mayumi Usami[11]

[1]Nagoya University, [2]Kagoshima University, [3]The University of Electro-Communications, [4]Science Tokyo, [5]Tohoku University, [6]RIKEN, [7]ATR, [8]Chiba University, [9]Meikai University, [10]Waseda University, [11]Tokyo University of Foreign Studies

Correspondence: higashinaka@i.nagoya-u.ac.jp

Abstract

A corpus of dialogues between multimodal systems and humans is indispensable for the development and improvement of such systems. However, there is a shortage of human-machine multimodal dialogue datasets, which hinders the widespread deployment of these systems in society. To address this issue, we construct a Japanese multimodal human-machine dialogue corpus, DSLCMM, by collecting and organizing data from the Dialogue System Live Competitions (DSLCs). This paper details the procedure for constructing the corpus and presents our analysis of the relationship between various dialogue features and evaluation scores provided by users.

1 Introduction

With the advancement of large language models, the capabilities of text-based dialogue systems have improved (Shuster et al., 2022; Hudeček and Dušek, 2023; Kong et al., 2024). However, the performance of multimodal dialogue systems, which must process speech, facial expressions, and other non-verbal cues in real time, remains limited compared to human face-to-face interactions (Higashinaka et al., 2024).

To unlock the full potential of dialogue systems in society, it is essential to achieve multimodal dialogue capabilities akin to human interactions. However, there is a significant shortage of corpora to support this. While a relatively large amount of multimodal data focuses on human-to-human dialogue or human-to-Wizard of Oz (WoZ) interactions, there is a notable lack of corpora capturing dialogues between actual multimodal dialogue systems and humans. To understand how real systems and humans interact in multimodal dialogues and identify areas for improvement, a corpus of such interactions is indispensable.

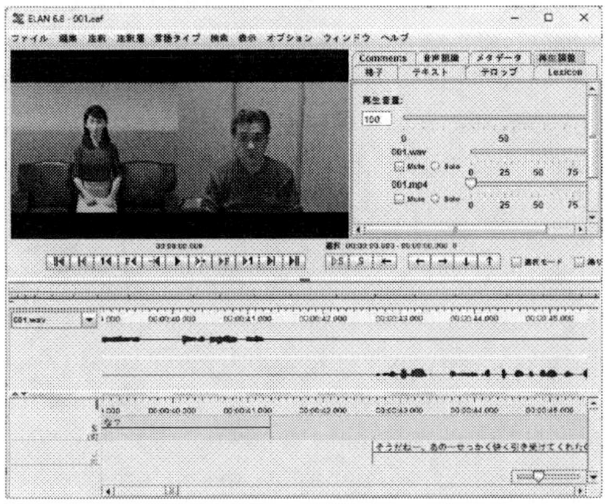

Figure 1: Example data in DSLCMM displayed using ELAN (Wittenburg et al., 2006).

In light of this background, we have constructed a multimodal dialogue corpus called DSLCMM. Specifically, we collected and processed data from the Dialogue System Live Competition (DSLC) series (Higashinaka et al., 2021) and organized it into a corpus. This corpus contains 1,747 dialogues between 32 multimodal dialogue systems and human users, obtained from two editions of the competition. The language of the corpus is Japanese. In addition to users' speech, the corpus contains user/system video recordings and logs of system commands for gestures and facial expressions. It also includes subjective evaluation scores from users and transcriptions of all user utterances. An example of the dataset is shown in Figure 1. Utilizing this dataset has the potential to significantly advance research on multimodal dialogue systems. The corpus will be accessible from the project pages of DSLC5[1] and DSLC6[2].

[1]https://sites.google.com/view/dslc5
[2]https://sites.google.com/view/dslc6

Proceedings of the 15th International Workshop on Spoken Dialogue Systems Technology, pages 277–283
May 27–30, 2025. ©2025 Association for Computational Linguistics

In Section 2 of this paper, we review related work. Section 3 provides an explanation of the DSLC series, which served as the source of data for our corpus, and Section 4 describes the dataset construction process and presents statistical information. In Section 5, we discuss the analyses conducted on this corpus and the corresponding results. A brief summary is provided in Section 6, followed by a discussion of limitations and ethical considerations.

2 Related Work

To the best of our knowledge, there are few existing datasets of dialogues between humans and multimodal dialogue systems. However, several datasets are available for multimodal dialogues between humans or between humans and a WoZ system.

For example, MELD (Poria et al., 2018) includes video data from the TV series "Friends", with annotations for emotions. Additionally, multimodal datasets specifically focused on emotions, such as IEMOCAP (Busso et al., 2008) and MOSI (Zadeh et al., 2016), have been constructed. The D64 Multimodal Conversational Corpus (Oertel et al., 2013) contains data from natural conversations between humans collected using cameras and motion capture devices. AMI (Kraaij et al., 2005) is a corpus of meetings that includes video recordings of discussions. CEJC (Koiso et al., 2022) captures everyday conversations and contains video data of human-to-human interactions across various daily activities.

One notable multimodal dialogue dataset between humans and a WoZ system is the Hazumi corpus (Komatani and Okada, 2021). This corpus contains casual conversations between humans and a multimodal dialogue system operated by a wizard, along with subjective evaluation scores from users. Analyses examining the relationship between system behavior and user evaluations have been conducted (Wei et al., 2021). However, since the corpus does not include dialogues between humans and autonomous dialogue systems, it is limited in addressing the challenges associated with developing and improving real multimodal dialogue systems.

It should be noted that the term "multimodal dialogue" can also refer to dialogues discussing visual or video contents. Well-known examples include MMConv (Liao et al., 2021), VideoChat (Li et al., 2023), and SIMMC (Kottur et al., 2021). However, these deal with text-based chat systems that interact with images, videos, or virtual reality environments, and do not involve face-to-face interactions typical of human dialogues, which are the focus of this study.

3 Dialogue System Live Competitions

The DSLC is a competition for dialogue systems that has been held in Japan since 2018 (Higashinaka et al., 2021). DSLC consists of preliminary and final rounds, with the final round featuring a live event where dialogue systems are demonstrated in front of an audience, and rankings are determined based on audience evaluations. Initially, the competition focused solely on text-based dialogue systems, but starting with DSLC5 in 2022, it expanded to include multimodal dialogues (Higashinaka et al., 2024). In this section, we describe DSLC5 and DSLC6, from which the data for our corpus were sourced. Since the dataset is created from the preliminary round data, the final round is not discussed in this paper.

3.1 DSLC5

Two tracks were held in DSLC5: the Open Track and the Situation Track. In the Open Track, systems competed based on their performance in open-domain casual conversation. In the Situation Track, systems were evaluated on their ability to engage in human-like interactions according to predefined scenarios. The specific situation was as follows:

> Shizuka (the system) and Yuki (the user) are friends from the same university seminar group. Shizuka has lost an expensive technical book borrowed from Yuki and is now unable to return it. Shizuka explains the situation and offers an apology to Yuki.

The developers created systems capable of engaging in human-like conversations within this scenario. The scenario was designed based on the Oral Proficiency Interview used in language education, facilitating an effective assessment of language proficiency. In both tracks, the dialogue duration was set to 4 minutes.

Initially, 11 teams entered the Open Track and 15 teams participated in the Situation Track. Due to challenges in system development, several teams withdrew, leaving nine teams in the Open Track and ten teams in the Situation Track for the preliminary round. In both tracks, participants utilized software provided by the organizers to develop their dialogue systems. This software allowed participants to focus solely on implementing the dialogue control module, which sent commands for gestures and facial expressions, along with utterance content, based on the received speech recognition results. The system's gestures and facial expressions were displayed through a CG character named CGErica (Glas et al., 2016), included with the software. In DSLC5, the gestures and facial expressions of users were not processed by the system.

In the preliminary round, a total of ten systems in the Open Track and 11 systems in the Situation Track, including the baseline system for each track, were evaluated. Each system was subjectively assessed by approximately 50 crowdworkers. The systems were operated in the cloud, and dialogues were conducted via Zoom. Since separate crowdworkers were recruited for each system, the evaluators varied across systems.

In the Open Track, the dialogue participants selected two topics from a list of pre-determined keywords and engaged in casual conversation about those topics. The evaluation was based on two aspects: dialogue content and manner of speaking. Dialogue content was assessed using three criteria: Naturalness (whether the dialogue felt natural), Topic Following (whether the system appropriately responded to the chosen topics), and Topic Provision (whether the system could provide new information related to the chosen topics). Each criterion was rated on a 5-point Likert scale. The manner of speaking was evaluated for Naturalness of Interaction (whether the system's manner of speaking, including voice, gestures, and facial expressions, appeared natural), also on a 5-point Likert scale.

In the Situation Track, the systems were comprehensively evaluated based on a single criterion: "How appropriate and human-like was the conversation for the given situation?" (Overall), using a 5-point Likert scale.

3.2 DSLC6

In DSLC6, only the Situation Track was conducted. This decision was made because, with the advancement of large language models, sustaining casual conversation was deemed trivial (Iizuka et al., 2023). The software utilized was the same as in DSLC5 but with additional inputs, including estimated emotions (e.g., happy, surprised), head orientation, age, and gender, which were automatically inferred from the user's facial images using open-source software. The situation for the competition was set as follows:

> Yuki (the user), a member of the film club, is considering organizing a welcome party for Professor Kobayashi, who has recently taken over as the club's advisor this month. Yuki consults with Shizuka (the system), a fellow member of the film club, about the plans for the welcome party.

There were initially ten team entries, but due to technical difficulties, only eight teams ultimately participated in the preliminary round. The dialogue duration was set to 5 minutes.

To ensure the accurate capture of users' facial images and other inputs, the preliminary round was conducted in a laboratory setting where evaluators engaged in face-to-face conversations with the systems, rather than using a cloud-based format. Three baseline systems were provided (two using GPT-3.5 with different prompts and one using GPT-4), resulting in a total of 11 systems evaluated. Each system was assessed by approximately 50 evaluators. If a system failed to operate, participants interacted with one of the baseline systems.

The systems were evaluated based on three criteria, each rated on a 5-point scale: Utterance Content (whether the system's responses were contextually appropriate), Gesture/Facial Expression (whether the system's gestures and facial expressions were contextually appropriate), and Voice (whether the system used appropriate timing, tone, and intensity in its speech). Notably, many of the systems in DSLC6 were built on OpenAI's GPT-4 or GPT-3.5 APIs, marking a significant difference from DSLC5, in which rules and locally fine-tuned language models were observed.

4 Corpus

As the organizers of the DSLC5 and DSLC6, we processed the data of the preliminary rounds to create a multimodal dialogue corpus between users and multimodal dialogue systems. Specifically, we extracted video segments for each dialogue session, transcribed the audio (transcriptions were performed only for user utterances, as the system's utterances were logged), and linked these with system logs and subjective evaluation scores. The data for each dialogue session consists of an ELAN

	LC5O	LC5S	LC6S
# System	10	11	11
# Dialogue	537	569	641
# System Utterance	13,111	17,730	20,963
# User Utterance	11,176	12,167	15,114
# Total Utterance	24,287	29,897	36,077
# Words / System Utt	10.13	11.31	11.18
# Words / User Utt	10.13	6.45	10.77
Duration (hours)	42.32	43.91	57.09

Table 1: Statistics of DSLCMM and its subsets. "Utt" stands for "utterance".

Subset	Criteria	1	2	3	4	5
LC5O	Nat	18.8	28.1	18.8	27.7	6.5
	Topic F	18.2	29.6	20.5	25.3	6.3
	Topic P	19.2	28.3	19.4	27.2	6.0
	Nat in Int	8.9	20.7	25.0	36.5	8.9
LC5S	Overall	4.6	12.5	18.3	48.7	16.0
	Utt Cont	5.5	16.5	17.0	44.5	16.5
LC6S	Gest/Face	5.6	21.7	23.9	39.0	9.8
	Voice	6.9	19.7	26.8	36.7	10.0

Table 2: Distribution of evaluation scores (%). A score of 1 represents the worst rating, and a score of 5 represents the best. "Nat," "Topic F," "Topic P," and "Nat in Int" refer to Naturalness, Topic Following, Topic Provision, and Naturalness in Interaction, respectively. "Utt Cont" and "Gest/Face" denote utterance content and gesture/facial expression, respectively.

file containing transcriptions, an MP4 video file with recordings (user videos are available only for DSLC6), separate audio files for each speaker, and a JSON file containing system logs and subjective evaluation scores. As a result, we constructed the DSLC Multimodal Corpus (DSLCMM), comprising 1,747 multimodal dialogues.

The overview of the dataset is presented in Table 1. We refer to the subset of the Open Track from DSLC5 as LC5O, and the subset of the Situation Track from DSLC5 as LC5S. The subset from DSLC6 is referred to as LC6S. Each of these subsets contains more than 500 dialogues. The dataset is deemed sufficiently large for analysis and post-training tasks. For detailed statistical information on the systems in each subset, please refer to the appendix.

The distribution of subjective evaluation scores for each subset is presented in Table 2. As shown, the dataset includes a variety of evaluations, reflecting both appropriate and inappropriate dialogue examples. This indicates that the dataset covers a wide range of phenomena observed in multimodal dialogues with systems. Moreover, the relatively small number of instances with the highest evaluation score suggests that there is still room for improvement in the systems.

5 Analyses

To illustrate how this corpus can be utilized, we analyzed the relationship between various features of the dialogues and the users' subjective evaluations (Table 3). Specifically, we extracted features such as the number of utterances, gestures, and facial expressions from each dialogue, and calculated Spearman's correlations between these features and the subjective evaluation scores. In this context, "gesture" and "face" refer to the number of commands issued for gesture and facial expression outputs, respectively. The logs allowed us to accurately count the number of gesture and facial expression commands. "Latency" denotes the time between the end of the user's speech and the start of the system's response.

In LC5O, significant positive correlations were observed between the number of system utterances, the number of gesture and facial expression commands, and the evaluation scores. This suggests that the system made a good impression on users by providing informative utterances and expressing gestures. Regarding Latency, a positive correlation was observed with Topic Following. This indicates that longer response times were associated with better subjective evaluations, potentially because longer response times led to higher-quality responses regarding topics. In LC5S, a significant negative correlation was observed between the number of facial expression commands per utterance and the evaluation score. This suggests that expressing appropriate facial expressions to match specific situations may be more challenging compared to the Open Track.

In LC6S, a negative correlation was found with the number of user utterances, suggesting that systems requiring users to speak extensively were likely more difficult to interact with. Similar to LC5O, the number of gesture commands showed a positive correlation. Additionally, the evaluation score exhibited a positive correlation with the number of facial expression commands. Here, an inverse correlation relative to the LC5S results was observed, suggesting that further detailed analyses of the specific types of expressions and their contextual circumstances are needed.

The analysis presented here is based on overall trends observed across multiple systems, and such insights could not be obtained from a dataset featur-

Dialogue Features	LC5O				LC5S	LC6S		
	Nat	Topic F	Topic P	Nat in Int	Overall	Utt Cont	Gest/Face	Voice
# User Utterance	−0.03	−0.06	−0.00	−0.07	0.02	−0.17*	−0.15*	−0.24*
# System Utterance	0.17*	0.20*	0.19*	0.15*	0.03	0.04	−0.04	0.00
# Gesture	0.13*	0.14*	0.08	0.11	−0.01	0.23*	0.12*	0.17*
# Face	0.18*	0.18*	0.15*	0.20*	−0.10	0.13*	0.01	0.02
# Gesture / Utterance	−0.01	0.01	−0.07	−0.01	−0.02	0.21*	0.14*	0.14*
# Face / Utterance	0.04	0.04	0.03	0.08	−0.12*	0.11*	0.07	0.04
Latency	0.11	0.17*	0.02	0.03	0.04	−0.05	0.00	0.01

Table 3: Correlation between evaluation scores and features. Asterisks indicate statistical significance ($p < 0.01$).

ing only a single system. DSLCMM enables this type of cross-system analysis, offering valuable and generalizable knowledge. We believe this dataset will be instrumental in advancing understanding in the field.

6 Summary

In this study, we utilized data from the DSLC series to construct DSLCMM, a multimodal human-machine dialogue corpus. DSLCMM encompasses dialogues from multiple systems, capturing a wide range of dialogue quality. It includes data on system gestures and facial expression commands, as well as video data featuring facial information of users, making it well-suited for tasks such as multimodal dialogue generation. With user evaluation scores included, the dataset can also support tasks like estimating user evaluation scores (Komatani et al., 2023), detecting dialogue breakdowns in multimodal settings (Higashinaka et al., 2016; Tsubokura et al., 2022; Miah et al., 2024). It can also be useful for building multimodal models for face-to-face conversation (Park et al., 2024; Zhu et al., 2024). We hope this corpus will advance research and development in multimodal dialogue systems.

Limitations

The dataset constructed in this study is valuable as it contains dialogues between humans and multimodal dialogue systems, but it has certain limitations. The software used by participants is uniform, and there are only two situational contexts, which may limit the variability in dialogues. Additionally, the dialogues are constrained by the capabilities of the systems at the time; similar dialogues might not be generated with faster and more advanced large language models in the future. Furthermore, since the dataset is in Japanese, it is uncertain whether the insights gained here can be applied to other languages.

Ethical Considerations

The dataset constructed in this study includes users' speech and facial images, necessitating careful consideration of privacy. We have obtained approval from the ethical review committee for departments at the Higashiyama Campus, Nagoya University, concerning data collection, usage, and publication. In releasing this dataset, we will ensure that privacy is rigorously protected, and any data that poses a privacy concern will be promptly withdrawn. There is a potential risk that the data could be used to build dialogue systems that impersonate specific individuals. To address this, we plan to include provisions in the terms of use explicitly prohibiting such applications.

Acknowledgments

This work was supported by JST Moonshot R&D, Grant number JPMJMS2011. The DSLC events were hosted by the special interest group on Spoken Language Understanding and Dialogue processing (SIG-SLUD) of the Japanese Society for Artificial Intelligence. The events were also supported by JSPS KAKENHI Grant Number 19H05692. We also thank the participating teams of DSLC5 and DSLC6.

References

Carlos Busso, Murtaza Bulut, Chi-Chun Lee, Abe Kazemzadeh, Emily Mower, Samuel Kim, Jeannette N Chang, Sungbok Lee, and Shrikanth S Narayanan. 2008. IEMOCAP: Interactive emotional dyadic motion capture database. *Language resources and evaluation*, 42:335–359.

Dylan F Glas, Takashi Minato, Carlos T Ishi, Tatsuya Kawahara, and Hiroshi Ishiguro. 2016. ERICA: The ERATO intelligent conversational android. In *Proc. RO-MAN*, pages 22–29.

Ryuichiro Higashinaka, Kotaro Funakoshi, Michimasa Inaba, Yuiko Tsunomori, Tetsuro Takahashi, and

Reina Akama. 2021. Dialogue system live competition: identifying problems with dialogue systems through live event. In *Increasing Naturalness and Flexibility in Spoken Dialogue Interaction: 10th International Workshop on Spoken Dialogue Systems*, pages 185–199.

Ryuichiro Higashinaka, Kotaro Funakoshi, Yuka Kobayashi, and Michimasa Inaba. 2016. The dialogue breakdown detection challenge: Task description, datasets, and evaluation metrics. In *Proc. LREC*, pages 3146–3150.

Ryuichiro Higashinaka, Tetsuro Takahashi, Michimasa Inaba, Zhiyang Qi, Yuta Sasaki, Kotrao Funakoshi, Shoji Moriya, Shiki Sato, Takashi Minato, Kurima Sakai, Tomo Funayama, Masato Komuro, Hiroyuki Nishikawa, Ryosaku Makino, Hirofumi Kikuchi, and Mayumi Usami. 2024. Dialogue system live competition goes multimodal: Analyzing the effects of multimodal information in situated dialogue systems. In *Proc. IWSDS*.

Vojtěch Hudeček and Ondřej Dušek. 2023. Are LLMs all you need for task-oriented dialogue? *arXiv preprint arXiv:2304.06556*.

Shinya Iizuka, Shota Mochizuki, Atsumoto Ohashi, Sanae Yamashita, Ao Guo, and Ryuichiro Higashinaka. 2023. Clarifying the dialogue-level performance of GPT-3.5 and GPT-4 in task-oriented and non-task-oriented dialogue systems. In *Proc. the AAAI Symposium Series*, volume 2, pages 182–186.

Hanae Koiso, Haruka Amatani, Yasuharu Den, Yuriko Iseki, Yuichi Ishimoto, Wakako Kashino, Yoshiko Kawabata, Ken'ya Nishikawa, Yayoi Tanaka, Yasuyuki Usuda, and Yuka Watanabe. 2022. Design and evaluation of the corpus of everyday Japanese conversation. In *Proc. LREC*, pages 5587–5594.

Kazunori Komatani and Shogo Okada. 2021. Multimodal human-agent dialogue corpus with annotations at utterance and dialogue levels. In *Proc. ACII*, pages 1–8.

Kazunori Komatani, Ryu Takeda, and Shogo Okada. 2023. Analyzing differences in subjective annotations by participants and third-party annotators in multimodal dialogue corpus. In *Proc. SIGDIAL*, pages 104–113.

Chuyi Kong, Yaxin Fan, Xiang Wan, Feng Jiang, and Benyou Wang. 2024. PlatoLM: Teaching LLMs in Multi-Round Dialogue via a User Simulator. In *Proc. ACL (Volume 1: Long Papers)*, pages 7841–7863.

Satwik Kottur, Seungwhan Moon, Alborz Geramifard, and Babak Damavandi. 2021. SIMMC 2.0: A task-oriented dialog dataset for immersive multimodal conversations. *arXiv preprint arXiv:2104.08667*.

Wessel Kraaij, Thomas Hain, Mike Lincoln, and Wilfried Post. 2005. The AMI meeting corpus. In *Proc. International Conference on Methods and Techniques in Behavioral Research*, pages 1–4.

KunChang Li, Yinan He, Yi Wang, Yizhuo Li, Wenhai Wang, Ping Luo, Yali Wang, Limin Wang, and Yu Qiao. 2023. Videochat: Chat-centric video understanding. *arXiv preprint arXiv:2305.06355*.

Lizi Liao, Le Hong Long, Zheng Zhang, Minlie Huang, and Tat-Seng Chua. 2021. MMConv: an environment for multimodal conversational search across multiple domains. In *Proceedings of the 44th international ACM SIGIR conference on research and development in information retrieval*, pages 675–684.

Md Messal Monem Miah, Ulie Schnaithmann, Arushi Raghuvanshi, and Youngseo Son. 2024. Multimodal contextual dialogue breakdown detection for conversational ai models. *arXiv preprint arXiv:2404.08156*.

Catharine Oertel, Fred Cummins, Jens Edlund, Petra Wagner, and Nick Campbell. 2013. D64: A corpus of richly recorded conversational interaction. *Journal on Multimodal User Interfaces*, 7(1):19–28.

Se Park, Chae Kim, Hyeongseop Rha, Minsu Kim, Joanna Hong, Jeonghun Yeo, and Yong Ro. 2024. Let's go real talk: Spoken dialogue model for face-to-face conversation. In *Proc. ACL (Volume 1: Long Papers)*, pages 16334–16348.

Soujanya Poria, Devamanyu Hazarika, Navonil Majumder, Gautam Naik, Erik Cambria, and Rada Mihalcea. 2018. MELD: A multimodal multi-party dataset for emotion recognition in conversations. *arXiv preprint arXiv:1810.02508*.

Kurt Shuster, Jing Xu, Mojtaba Komeili, Da Ju, Eric Michael Smith, Stephen Roller, Megan Ung, Moya Chen, Kushal Arora, Joshua Lane, et al. 2022. Blenderbot 3: a deployed conversational agent that continually learns to responsibly engage. *arXiv preprint arXiv:2208.03188*.

Kazuya Tsubokura, Yurie Iribe, and Norihide Kitaoka. 2022. Dialog breakdown detection using multimodal features for non-task-oriented dialog systems. In *Proc. GCCE*, pages 352–356.

Wenqing Wei, Sixia Li, Shogo Okada, and Kazunori Komatani. 2021. Multimodal user satisfaction recognition for non-task oriented dialogue systems. In *Proc. ICMI*, pages 586–594.

Peter Wittenburg, Hennie Brugman, Albert Russel, Alex Klassmann, and Han Sloetjes. 2006. ELAN: A professional framework for multimodality research. In *Proc. LREC*, pages 1556–1559.

Amir Zadeh, Rowan Zellers, Eli Pincus, and Louis-Philippe Morency. 2016. Mosi: multimodal corpus of sentiment intensity and subjectivity analysis in online opinion videos. *arXiv preprint arXiv:1606.06259*.

Yongming Zhu, Longhao Zhang, Zhengkun Rong, Tianshu Hu, Shuang Liang, and Zhipeng Ge. 2024. INFP: Audio-driven interactive head generation in dyadic conversations. *arXiv preprint arXiv:2412.04037*.

A Appendix

The following tables present the statistical data for each system within the subsets of DSLCMM. The terms "# Utt", "# Gesture", and "# Face" refer to the number of utterances per dialogue, as well as system commands per dialogue for gestures and facial expressions, respectively.

System	# Dialogue	# Utterance		# Vocabulary		System			User
		System	User	System	User	# Utt	# Gesture	# Face	# Utt
LIO	50	2301	1245	1814	1174	46.02	15.32	4.00	24.90
TOH	51	1036	979	2085	1209	20.31	357.73	1317.55	19.20
BAO	72	1447	1650	1910	1654	20.10	0.17	58.58	22.92
TOA	59	2472	1078	1254	1184	41.90	82.12	39.05	18.27
AO1	51	909	998	1114	1167	17.82	110.75	91.18	19.57
MIN	55	953	1068	1204	1291	17.33	103.53	194.22	19.42
CHU	49	1049	1057	1011	1086	21.41	52.65	198.94	21.57
IRI	44	868	888	806	1057	19.73	4.00	6.14	20.18
AO2	53	946	953	1241	1077	17.85	5.17	37.75	17.98
AO3	53	1130	1260	1336	1230	21.32	21.79	0.00	23.77

Table 4: Statistics of dialogues for systems in LC5O.

System	# Dialogue	# Utterance		# Vocabulary		System			User
		System	User	System	User	# Utt	# Gesture	# Face	# Utt
FCL	54	1704	1094	173	534	31.56	17.83	34.89	20.26
LIS	54	1107	1227	527	622	20.50	36.80	17.15	22.72
YUR	50	2683	752	294	408	53.66	97.62	50.20	15.04
NAK	58	2433	1340	182	642	41.95	34.47	47.10	23.10
AS1	52	1245	1074	180	590	23.94	8.58	28.65	20.65
BAS	48	1764	1099	208	621	36.75	6.79	5.00	22.90
CIT	52	1361	1230	187	622	26.17	127.50	95.29	23.65
SAI	51	1619	1376	117	660	31.75	6.04	16.00	26.98
HON	53	953	1102	188	561	17.98	35.17	119.25	20.79
AS2	43	1477	1039	245	560	34.35	1.93	25.19	24.16
TSU	54	1384	834	263	476	25.63	87.26	649.39	15.44

Table 5: Statistics of dialogues for systems in LC5S.

System	# Dialogue	# Utterance		# Vocabulary		System			User
		System	User	System	User	# Utt	# Gesture	# Face	# Utt
TOH	50	1330	1026	530	881	26.60	184.40	61.30	20.52
BI3	105	2036	2572	1064	1427	19.39	470.47	29.12	24.50
RIS	51	3351	1284	654	911	65.71	563.37	59.39	25.18
UEC	58	3192	1270	1012	1031	55.03	492.28	82.47	21.90
BI4	56	1013	1276	848	1070	18.09	483.46	26.79	22.79
BK3	54	1109	1381	998	1027	20.54	516.81	31.43	25.57
HNL	53	1819	1293	1026	948	34.32	373.23	10.13	24.40
YAM	50	2271	1534	718	1015	45.42	152.56	22.48	30.68
CIT	56	1414	1139	757	943	25.25	174.27	132.86	20.34
AN1	50	2546	1116	1220	1024	50.92	125.98	46.88	22.32
AN2	58	882	1223	982	967	15.21	3.12	12.19	21.09

Table 6: Statistics of dialogues for systems in LC6S.

Cutting Through Overload: Efficient Token Dropping for Speech Emotion Recognition in Multimodal Large Language Models

Jaime Bellver-Soler, Mario Rodríguez-Cantelar, Ricardo Córdoba, Luis Fernando D'Haro

Speech Technology and Machine Learning Group (THAU) - ETSI de Telecomunicación
Av. Complutense 30, 28040, Madrid, Spain - Universidad Politécnica de Madrid
{jaime.bellver, mario.rcantelar, ricardo.cordoba, luisfernando.dharo}@upm.es
Correspondence: jaime.bellver@upm.es

Abstract

Recent developments in Multimodal Large Language Models (MLLMs) have provided novel insights into Speech Emotion Recognition (SER). However, combining high-dimensional speech signals with textual tokens can lead to a rapid growth in input tokens, increasing computational costs and inference times. This "token overload" also risks shadowing essential textual cues, affecting the reasoning capabilities of the language model and diluting emotional information crucial to accurate SER.

In this paper, we explore different token drop methods that mitigate excessive token counts while preserving both emotional nuances and the core linguistic capabilities of the model. Specifically, we compare various efficient pooling approaches to produce a compact representation. Our preliminary findings suggest that these techniques can reduce computational costs without decreasing SER accuracy.

1 Introduction

Speech Emotion Recognition (SER) has garnered growing interest due to its potential in various applications, including human-computer interaction, mental healthcare, and education. Although single-modality methods, such as text-based emotion analysis or audio emotion recognition, have proven effective (Maruf et al., 2024; George and Ilyas, 2024), emotional data in real-world scenarios often integrate multiple modalities. This has led to increased interest in the use of Multimodal Large Language Models (MLLMs) to exploit knowledge from different data sources and improve emotional reasoning (Chandraumakantham et al., 2024).

Recent advances in MLLMs have demonstrated remarkable performance in audio analysis (Chu et al., 2023). However, there are challenges to applying MLLMs to SER. One of the key obstacles is the rapid increase in the number of multimodal tokens, which drastically expands the size of the input of the model. These multimodal token embeddings can increase computational costs (Ju et al., 2023), prolong inference times, and potentially shade text tokens during the model's attention process (Zhang et al., 2024), thus reducing overall performance.

To address these limitations, researchers have begun exploring token drop strategies (Li et al., 2023a; Zhang et al., 2023b; Rekesh et al., 2023; Gaido et al., 2021; Li et al., 2023b; Yao et al., 2024; Fathullah et al., 2023; Liu et al., 2024; Arif et al., 2024), with the aim of ensuring a more balanced and efficient integration of audio and textual information within MLLMs.

This article builds upon these efforts by recognizing that some existing approaches in the literature may become complex due to the large number of parameters or the complexity of the training. In this work, we explore simple pooling methods that help to control the excessive growth of acoustic tokens. By reducing the token overload on the language model, we can preserve its core linguistic capabilities while enhancing its ability to recognize audio-based emotions, crucial for dialogue systems that must handle both textual and emotional cues effectively. We evaluated how these pooling strategies affect computational costs, inference speed, and prediction accuracy, showing new insights into optimizing MLLMs for SER, improving dialogue systems, and enhancing human-computer interactions.

2 Related Work

SER has evolved with the appearance of multimodal approaches and Large Language Models (LLMs) that incorporate audio inputs. Early research often focused on single-modality solutions, either through acoustic features or text-based analysis, to detect emotions. However, these methods struggled to generalize in different contexts and linguistic styles, motivating the development of

Proceedings of the 15th International Workshop on Spoken Dialogue Systems Technology, pages 284–289
May 27–30, 2025. ©2025 Association for Computational Linguistics

multimodal systems that merge information from speech, text, and sometimes visual cues (Lian et al., 2023). Recent work has shown that integrating text and audio using MLLMs can produce more robust and nuanced emotion predictions (Deshmukh et al., 2024; Tang et al., 2024a).

Afterwards, a series of MLLMs have emerged, extending the capabilities of LLMs to handle different input types (Chu et al., 2023; Tang et al., 2024b). These architectures have shown promising results on tasks ranging from automatic speech recognition to generic audio understanding (Gong et al., 2023; Zhang et al., 2023a). However, many existing MLLMs either rely on supervised training of additional transformer modules or require extensive fine-tuning on specific downstream tasks, making them computationally expensive and less flexible for broader SER applications.

Despite progress in audio-based LLMs, a key challenge remains: the rapid increase in token counts (token overload) when merging high-dimensional audio and textual representations. Token overload can degrade model performance, increase computational costs, and slow down inference, problems especially salient in real-time or large-scale deployments (Li et al., 2023b; Shang et al., 2024). To handle this, a variety of token dropping methods have been proposed. Simple statistical techniques, such as mean pooling, can compress feature representations at minimal cost. Also, concatenation-based strategies can combine tokens in pairs or in groups to reduce the sequence length (Fathullah et al., 2023). More complex methods employ n-dimensional convolutions (Zhang et al., 2023b), lightweight Q-Formers (Li et al., 2023a), or architectures such as Fast Conformer (Rekesh et al., 2023) and Connectionist Temporal Classification (CTC) (Gaido et al., 2021) to remove redundant information. Further advancements have been explored in vision frameworks, such as Liu et al. (2024); Arif et al. (2024); Shang et al. (2024) that dynamically prune tokens based on attention scores or local content similarity. Although originally proposed for image or video tasks, these strategies offer valuable insights for audio-based MLLMs.

In this paper, we focus on evaluating simple and efficient token dropping methods for SER tasks using MLLMs. Rather than relying on complex architectures or parameter-heavy models, we explore straightforward pooling techniques to optimize the token efficiency of multimodal inputs. Our approach aims to reduce computational costs and

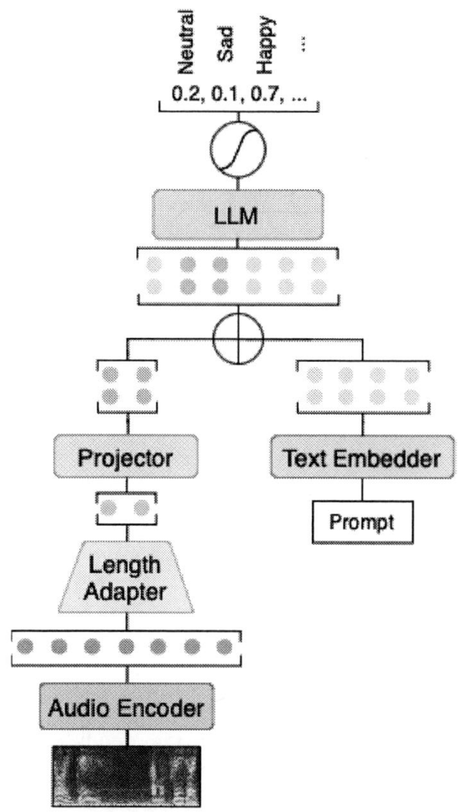

Figure 1: MLLM architecture for SER with a length adapter.

inference times while maintaining the ability of the model to capture emotional nuances. By integrating simplified token reduction modules into a multilingual SER pipeline, we demonstrate that efficient length adaptation techniques can achieve competitive performance.

3 Methods

To address the challenges of SER within multilingual and multimodal contexts, we propose a methodology that integrates high-dimensional speech and text signals into a unified framework. Our approach combines an audio encoder based on transformers, a linear projection layer, and an LLM, creating a multimodal architecture (see Figure 1 for a detailed diagram of the model architecture).

We employ the *Whisper-large-v3* encoder (Radford et al., 2022), a state-of-the-art model known for its ability to extract rich phonetic features from audio log-mel spectrograms (Gong et al., 2023; Zhang et al., 2023a). The encoded audio representations are then processed through a linear projector, which changes their dimensionality to align with the embedding space of the LLM (Chu et al., 2023). For the text component, we use *Gemma-2-2B-it* (et al., 2024), an LLM designed to handle diverse linguistic contexts and capable of reasoning over multilingual inputs.

We address the token overload challenge by incorporating length adaptation strategies that compress high-dimensional audio embeddings into more compact representations. These strategies range from simple statistical pooling methods, such as *Mean* pooling, to more complex approaches like *Convolutional* (*Conv*) compression (Zhang et al., 2023b), Concatenation (*Concat*) (Fathullah et al., 2023), and attention mechanisms (Vaswani et al., 2023).

We begin with *Mean* pooling, which aggregates embeddings by straightforward averaging. We then employ *Conv*, using convolutional filters to extract salient features, and a *Concat* approach that pairs tokens, effectively halving the sequence length while doubling the dimensionality.

We explore attention-based methods starting with *Attn-Mean*, which averages the output of the attention layer, and *Attn-Q-Mean*, which introduces a global query vector. Specifically, instead of deriving the query from each input token, we first perform a mean pooling across the entire sequence of input embeddings $X \in \mathbb{R}^{L \times D}$ (see Equation 1).

$$Q = \left(\frac{1}{L}\sum_{i=1}^{L} x_i\right) W_q, \qquad (1)$$

where x_i is the $i-th$ token embedding in X, and $W_q \in \mathbb{R}^{D \times d_k}$ projects the averaged embedding into the query space. The keys K and values V are computed using standard linear projections from X. The final compact representation is obtained via a standard scaled dot product attention mechanism that uses Q, K, and V (Vaswani et al., 2023).

To evaluate our framework, we first develop text-only baseline models. We employ transcriptions generated with *Whisper-large-v3* from speech input, and we use a frozen *Gemma-2-2b-it* to predict emotions only based on textual information. Building on these baselines, we integrate audio features into the pipeline, in which audio embeddings are combined with text tokens. We train only the linear projector and the length adapter layers, ensuring that the LLM retains its original capabilities.

Performance was measured using the F1 macro score and Weighted Accuracy (WA) to account for class imbalances. For each evaluation, we deployed a 5-fold cross-validation strategy and report the mean F1 macro and WA, along with their standard deviations.

We emphasize multilingual SER, using datasets in Spanish, German, and French to validate the generalization of our approach using datasets from MEACorpus, EmoDB, and Oreau (Pan et al., 2024; Burkhardt et al., 2005; Kerkeni et al., 2020). The three datasets contain emotion labels for Fear, Sad, Happy, Angry, Disgust, and Neutral, EmoDB also includes Boredom, while Oreau Surprise. The MEACorpus dataset suffers from imbalanced class distributions, which present additional challenges for robust modeling, although both EmoDB and Oreau have more balanced class distributions. Furthermore, the data in MEACorpus are derived from natural YouTube videos, reflecting real-world, spontaneous emotions, while EmoDB and Oreau datasets consist of acted recordings, which provide more controlled but less naturalistic emotional expressions. Our design also prioritizes computational efficiency, enabling faster inference times without compromising accuracy, an essential factor for the deployment of real-world dialogue systems.

4 Experiments

Our preliminary experiments focus on selecting the optimal components for the MLLM architecture, tuning hyperparameters [1], and refining a prompt for the LLM [2]. *Whisper-large-v3* was selected as audio encoder, while a linear projector was chosen for its effectiveness (Chu et al., 2023) and simplicity in aligning audio embeddings with the input requirements of the LLM. *Gemma-2-2B-it* was chosen as the LLM due to its remarkable performance in handling multimodal inputs and reasoning in both text and audio (et al., 2024).

To establish SER baselines, we first evaluated a text-only model, where the LLM remained frozen and predictions were made solely from the transcriptions of the speech input. This text-only baseline achieved an average F1 macro score of 0.23 and a WA of 0.29 across the three datasets.

The integration of audio and text modalities was evaluated through MLLMs, testing variations in length adaptation strategies. Detailed results for each dataset can be found in Table 1, while the overall averages are summarized in Table 2. In the ini-

[1] The hyperparameters used can be found in Annex A.

[2] The prompt used can be found in Annex B.

Adapter	MEACorpus (ES)		EmoDB (DE)		Oreau (FR)	
	WA	F1 macro	WA	F1 macro	WA	F1 macro
None	0.72 ± 0.01	0.62 ± 0.04	0.39 ± 0.05	0.36 ± 0.06	0.69 ± 0.07	0.69 ± 0.07
Mean	0.74 ± 0.01	0.64 ± 0.03	$\mathbf{0.60} \pm 0.06$	$\mathbf{0.53} \pm 0.05$	0.79 ± 0.04	0.78 ± 0.05
Concat	0.72 ± 0.01	0.57 ± 0.02	0.41 ± 0.02	0.40 ± 0.03	$\mathbf{0.92} \pm 0.32$	0.73 ± 0.02
Conv	0.73 ± 0.02	0.63 ± 0.06	0.47 ± 0.05	0.42 ± 0.07	0.84 ± 0.03	$\mathbf{0.84} \pm 0.02$
Atten-Mean	$\mathbf{0.76} \pm 0.01$	$\mathbf{0.69} \pm 0.04$	0.55 ± 0.08	0.50 ± 0.07	0.83 ± 0.03	0.82 ± 0.03
Attn-Q-Mean	0.75 ± 0.01	0.67 ± 0.03	0.53 ± 0.02	0.47 ± 0.02	0.82 ± 0.05	0.81 ± 0.06

Table 1: Average WA and F1 macro scores across the 5-folds and its standard deviation are presented in columns under each dataset. The row labeled "*None*" corresponds to the model without a length adapter.

Adapter	Trainable Params	Speed-up	Acoustic Tokens	Mean WA	Mean F1 macro
None	0	0% -	170 -	0.60 ± 0.03	0.56 ± 0.06
Mean	$1.2M$	21% ↑	1 ↓↓	0.70 ± 0.02	0.65 ± 0.04
Concat	$1.8M$	16% ↑	85 ↓	0.68 ± 0.02	0.56 ± 0.02
Conv	$1.5M$	3% ↑	85 ↓	0.68 ± 0.03	0.63 ± 0.05
Atten-Mean	$1.6M$	22% ↑	1 ↓↓	$\mathbf{0.71} \pm 0.03$	$\mathbf{0.67} \pm 0.05$
Attn-Q-Mean	$1.7M$	**26%** ↑↑	1 ↓↓	0.70 ± 0.02	0.65 ± 0.03

Table 2: WA and F1 macro averaged across datasets, along with the trainable parameters (Trainable Params), the decrease of inference time (Speed-up) with respect to the alternative without length adapter (which achieves 18 iterations per second on a single A100 GPU), and the number of acoustic tokens.

tial configuration, labeled "*None*", the projected audio embeddings were directly fed into the language model without any token dropping. While this approach preserved the complete acoustic fidelity, it also introduced a token overload, resulting in an average of 170 acoustic tokens per sample across the three datasets. Although it achieved a mean WA of 0.60 and an F1 macro of 0.56, exceeding the text only baseline, this increased token count substantially increased the computational cost, with inference times up to 26% higher compared to the text only model.

To address this, we implemented various length adaptation techniques to compress high-dimensional audio embeddings. First, simple pooling methods, such as *Mean* pooling, improved performance to a mean WA of 0.70 and an F1 macro of 0.65. Next, *Conv* and *Concat* both achieved WA scores of 0.68, with macro F1 scores of 0.63 and 0.56, respectively. Finally, attention-based approaches (*Attn-Mean* and *Attn-Q-Mean*) further boosted overall performance. Attn-Mean achieved the highest metrics, while *Attn-Q-Mean* also performed strongly.

Table 2 also details computational trade-offs, including inference speed-ups relative to the no-adapter baseline (*None*). *Mean*, *Attn-Mean*, and *Attn-Q-Mean* all compress the acoustic representation to a single token, achieving speed-ups of 21%, 22%, and 26%, respectively. In contrast, *Concat* and *Conv* halve the number of tokens, resulting in speed-ups of 16% and 3%. In particular, Attn-Mean strikes an optimal balance between accuracy and efficiency, securing the highest F1 macro and WA scores while still offering a 22% speed-up.

5 Conclusion

Our experiments confirm that integrating audio and text in MLLMs significantly enhances SER, surpassing text-only approaches in both WA and F1 macro metrics. However, directly merging audio embeddings can lead to "token overload", increasing computational demands and slowing down inference. By incorporating simple length adapters, we achieved significant inference speed-ups (from 22% to 26%) compared to the baseline, while retaining or improving SER accuracy. Notably, we only fine-tuned a lightweight projector layer, thereby preserving the language reasoning capabilities of the LLM.

In future work, we will explore more advanced token compression strategies and extend our experiments to a broader range of tasks and datasets, aiming for higher scalability and robust performance across diverse multimodal dialogue systems.

Acknowledgements

This work is supported by the European Commission through Project ASTOUND (101071191 — HORIZON EIC-2021-PATHFINDERCHALLENGES-01), by project BEWORD (PID2021-126061OB-C43) funded by MCIN/AEI/10.13039/501100011033 and, as appropriate, by "ERDF A way of making Europe", by the "European Union", and by project INNOVATRAD-CM (PHS-2024/PH-HUM-52) from Comunidad de Madrid.

References

Kazi Hasan Ibn Arif, JinYi Yoon, Dimitrios S. Nikolopoulos, Hans Vandierendonck, Deepu John, and Bo Ji. 2024. Hired: Attention-guided token dropping for efficient inference of high-resolution vision-language models. *Preprint*, arXiv:2408.10945.

Felix Burkhardt, Astrid Paeschke, M. Rolfes, Walter F. Sendlmeier, and Benjamin Weiss. 2005. A database of german emotional speech. In *Interspeech*.

Omkumar Chandraumakantham, N. Gowtham, Mohammed Zakariah, and Abdulaziz Almazyad. 2024. Multimodal emotion recognition using feature fusion: An llm-based approach. *IEEE Access*, 12:108052–108071.

Yunfei Chu, Jin Xu, Xiaohuan Zhou, Qian Yang, Shiliang Zhang, Zhijie Yan, Chang Zhou, and Jingren Zhou. 2023. Qwen-audio: Advancing universal audio understanding via unified large-scale audio-language models. *Preprint*, arXiv:2311.07919.

Soham Deshmukh, Benjamin Elizalde, Rita Singh, and Huaming Wang. 2024. Pengi: An audio language model for audio tasks. *Preprint*, arXiv:2305.11834.

Gemma Team et al. 2024. Gemma 2: Improving open language models at a practical size. *Preprint*, arXiv:2408.00118.

Yassir Fathullah, Chunyang Wu, Egor Lakomkin, Junteng Jia, Yuan Shangguan, Ke Li, Jinxi Guo, Wenhan Xiong, Jay Mahadeokar, Ozlem Kalinli, Christian Fuegen, and Mike Seltzer. 2023. Prompting large language models with speech recognition abilities. *Preprint*, arXiv:2307.11795.

Marco Gaido, Mauro Cettolo, Matteo Negri, and Marco Turchi. 2021. Ctc-based compression for direct speech translation. *Preprint*, arXiv:2102.01578.

Swapna Mol George and P. Muhamed Ilyas. 2024. A review on speech emotion recognition: A survey, recent advances, challenges, and the influence of noise. *Neurocomputing*, 568:127015.

Yuan Gong, Sameer Khurana, Leonid Karlinsky, and James Glass. 2023. Whisper-at: Noise-robust automatic speech recognizers are also strong general audio event taggers.

Chen Ju, Haicheng Wang, Zeqian Li, Xu Chen, Zhonghua Zhai, Weilin Huang, and Shuai Xiao. 2023. Turbo: Informativity-driven acceleration plug-in for vision-language models. *Preprint*, arXiv:2312.07408.

Leila Kerkeni, Catherine Cleder, Youssef Serrestou, and Kosai Raoof. 2020. French emotional speech database - oréau.

Junnan Li, Dongxu Li, Silvio Savarese, and Steven Hoi. 2023a. Blip-2: Bootstrapping language-image pre-training with frozen image encoders and large language models. *Preprint*, arXiv:2301.12597.

Yanwei Li, Chengyao Wang, and Jiaya Jia. 2023b. Llama-vid: An image is worth 2 tokens in large language models. *Preprint*, arXiv:2311.17043.

Hui Lian, Chen Lu, Shengyuan Li, Yunzhi Zhao, Chenglong Tang, and Yu Zong. 2023. A survey of deep learning-based multimodal emotion recognition: Speech, text, and face. *Entropy*, 25(10).

Ting Liu, Liangtao Shi, Richang Hong, Yue Hu, Quanjun Yin, and Linfeng Zhang. 2024. Multi-stage vision token dropping: Towards efficient multimodal large language model. *Preprint*, arXiv:2411.10803.

Abdullah Al Maruf, Fahima Khanam, Md. Mahmudul Haque, Zakaria Masud Jiyad, M. F. Mridha, and Zeyar Aung. 2024. Challenges and opportunities of text-based emotion detection: A survey. *IEEE Access*, 12:18416–18450.

Ronghao Pan, José Antonio García-Díaz, Miguel Ángel Rodríguez-García, and Rafel Valencia-García. 2024. Spanish meacorpus 2023: A multimodal speech–text corpus for emotion analysis in spanish from natural environments. *Computer Standards Interfaces*, 90:103856.

Alec Radford, Jong Wook Kim, Tao Xu, Greg Brockman, Christine McLeavey, and Ilya Sutskever. 2022. Robust speech recognition via large-scale weak supervision. *Preprint*, arXiv:2212.04356.

Dima Rekesh, Nithin Rao Koluguri, Samuel Kriman, Somshubra Majumdar, Vahid Noroozi, He Huang, Oleksii Hrinchuk, Krishna Puvvada, Ankur Kumar, Jagadeesh Balam, and Boris Ginsburg. 2023. Fast conformer with linearly scalable attention for efficient speech recognition. *Preprint*, arXiv:2305.05084.

Yuzhang Shang, Mu Cai, Bingxin Xu, Yong Jae Lee, and Yan Yan. 2024. Llava-prumerge: Adaptive token reduction for efficient large multimodal models. *Preprint*, arXiv:2403.15388.

Changli Tang, Wenyi Yu, Guangzhi Sun, Xianzhao Chen, Tian Tan, Wei Li, Lu Lu, Zejun Ma, and Chao Zhang. 2024a. Salmonn: Towards generic hearing abilities for large language models. *Preprint*, arXiv:2310.13289.

Changli Tang, Wenyi Yu, Guangzhi Sun, Xianzhao Chen, Tian Tan, Wei Li, Lu Lu, Zejun Ma, and Chao Zhang. 2024b. Salmonn: Towards generic hearing abilities for large language models. *Preprint*, arXiv:2310.13289.

Ashish Vaswani, Noam Shazeer, Niki Parmar, Jakob Uszkoreit, Llion Jones, Aidan N. Gomez, Lukasz Kaiser, and Illia Polosukhin. 2023. Attention is all you need. *Preprint*, arXiv:1706.03762.

Linli Yao, Lei Li, Shuhuai Ren, Lean Wang, Yuanxin Liu, Xu Sun, and Lu Hou. 2024. Deco: Decoupling token compression from semantic abstraction in multimodal large language models. *Preprint*, arXiv:2405.20985.

Dong Zhang, Shimin Li, Xin Zhang, Jun Zhan, Pengyu Wang, Yaqian Zhou, and Xipeng Qiu. 2023a. Speechgpt: Empowering large language models with intrinsic cross-modal conversational abilities. *Preprint*, arXiv:2305.11000.

Hao Zhang, Nianwen Si, Yaqi Chen, Wenlin Zhang, Xukui Yang, Dan Qu, and Xiaolin Jiao. 2023b. Tuning large language model for end-to-end speech translation. *Preprint*, arXiv:2310.02050.

Yi-Kai Zhang, Shiyin Lu, Yang Li, YanQing Ma, Qing-Guo Chen, Zhao Xu, Weihua Luo, Kaifu Zhang, De-Chuan Zhan, and Han-Jia Ye. 2024. Wings: Learning multimodal LLMs without text-only forgetting. In *The Thirty-eighth Annual Conference on Neural Information Processing Systems*.

A Hyperparameters of MLLM

The hyperparameters of MLLM are shown in Table 3.

Hyperparameter	Value
Learning rate	$10e-4$
Batch size	4
Accumulate gradients	2
Epochs	20
Betas	$(0.9, 0.98)$
Eps	$1e-5$
Weight decay	0
Attention hidden dimension	1280
Attention heads	1
Linear projector dimensions	$[1280, 2304]$

Table 3: Table of hyperparameters used in the MLLM training.

B Prompt for the MLLM

"user: Transcription: {transcription} \n
Audio: {audio} \n
What is the emotion of the speaker?
The possible emotions are: {emotions}. \n
assistanSt: The emotion of the audio is:"

Integrating Conversational Entities and Dialogue Histories with Knowledge Graphs and Generative AI

Graham Wilcock
CDM Interact and
University of Helsinki
Helsinki, Finland
graham.wilcock@cdminteract.com

Kristiina Jokinen
AI Research Center, National Institute of
Advanced Industrial Science and Technology
Tokyo, Japan
kristiina.jokinen@aist.go.jp

Abstract

Existing methods for storing dialogue history and for tracking mentioned entities in spoken dialogues usually handle these tasks separately. Recent advances in knowledge graphs and generative AI make it possible to integrate them in a framework with a uniform representation for dialogue management. This may help to build more natural and grounded dialogue models that can reduce misunderstanding and lead to more reliable dialogue-based interactions with AI agents. The paper describes ongoing work on this approach.

1 Introduction

Recognising conversational entities and maintaining dialogue history are two crucial tasks in natural language understanding for dialogue management. They help to maintain dialogue context and support coherent continuation of the dialogue. The two tasks have traditionally been clearly separated.

Recent advances in knowledge graphs and generative AI suggest possibilities for integrating them into a model that not only facilitates the dialogue processing with knowledge that focuses on a particular domain and contributes to the relevance and reliability of the information, but simultaneously serves as a uniform representation for storing the dialogue history.

This paper presents ongoing work on a prototype design of dialogue history graphs. While domain knowledge graphs store relatively static, long-term information about well-established domain entities and relationships between them, we use rapidly-changing, short-term graphs to represent dialogue history, including all mentioned conversational entities even if they do not necessarily correspond to known entities in the domain graph.

We use LLMs to split dialogue turns into smaller semantic units and to extract conversational entities. We present examples from recent results, with the aim that this approach will improve conversational grounding, reduce misunderstandings, and result in more reliable spoken interaction with AI agents.

The paper is structured as follows. Section 2 surveys related work on conversational entities and dialogue histories. Section 3 describes our work on representing the structure, content and history of dialogues in knowledge graphs. We use an example dialogue, shown in Table 1, to illustrate incremental generation of a dialogue history graph. Evaluation is briefly discussed in Section 4, with reference to results in the Appendices. Section 5 concludes.

2 Related Work

This section surveys how conversational entities and dialogue histories are handled by existing conversational AI frameworks. Entity recognition helps to build semantic representations of user intents. Dialogue history records which entities have been talked about, to maintain coherence of the dialogue as it progresses towards the goal.

2.1 Entity tracking and dialogue states

Traditionally, conversational entities have been tracked in statistical dialogue systems with the help of dialogue frames or states, which record the important concepts and entities needed to carry out task-based dialogues successfully. For instance, RavenClaw (Bohus and Rudnicky, 2009), which was used in the Let's Go system (Raux et al., 2005), effectively separates domain-specific task logic from the domain-independent dialogue control, and the series of the Dialogue State Tracking Challenge (Williams et al., 2013; Yoshino et al., 2024) aimed at efficient and correct evaluation of the dialogue progress via the dialogue entities being correctly filled in during the dialogue.

PyDial (Ultes et al., 2017) represents dialogue state with a set of domain-specific slots that can be switched to different slots for different domains.

Proceedings of the 15th International Workshop on Spoken Dialogue Systems Technology, pages 290–298
May 27–30, 2025. ©2025 Association for Computational Linguistics

Human:	What is hypertension?
Robot:	*Hypertension (HTN) is a medical condition characterized by consistently elevated blood pressure, defined as a systolic blood pressure (SBP) of 140 mm Hg or higher and/or a diastolic blood pressure (DBP) of 90 mm Hg or higher. It remains a significant public health issue, affecting millions of adults in the United States.*
Human:	What is it caused by?
Robot:	*Hypertension can be caused by a variety of factors, including genetic predisposition, lifestyle choices such as poor diet, lack of physical activity, obesity, and excessive alcohol consumption. Other contributing factors may include chronic stress, certain medical conditions, and the use of specific medications.*
Human:	Is exercise helpful?
Robot:	*Yes, exercise is helpful in managing hypertension, as regular moderate-intensity endurance exercise can lower blood pressure both acutely and chronically. It is recommended for individuals with hypertension to engage in regular physical activity to maximize health benefits.*
Human:	What is moderate-intensity endurance exercise?
Robot:	*Moderate-intensity endurance exercise is physical activity that raises your heart rate and breathing but still allows you to talk comfortably, typically rated as 5 to 6 on a scale of 0 to 10 for exertion. Examples include brisk walking, cycling at a leisurely pace, or swimming at a moderate speed.*
Human:	How can I reduce my salt intake?
Robot:	*To reduce your salt intake, you can start by cooking at home using fresh ingredients, avoiding processed foods, and reading food labels to choose low-sodium options. Additionally, using herbs and spices for flavor instead of salt can help you cut back on sodium.*
Human:	What are the symptoms of diabetes?
Robot:	*Common symptoms of diabetes include increased thirst, frequent urination, extreme fatigue, blurred vision, and slow-healing sores or frequent infections. Other symptoms may include unexplained weight loss and tingling or numbness in the hands or feet.*
Human:	Is exercise helpful?
Robot:	*Yes, exercise is helpful for managing diabetes, as it improves blood glucose control, enhances insulin sensitivity, and can lower the risk of complications. Regular physical activity is essential for optimal health in individuals with diabetes.*

Table 1: A dialogue example in medical domain.

More flexibility was introduced for multi-domain dialogues (Budzianowski et al., 2018) by allowing frames to be switched on recognition of domain-specific entities, enabling flexible changes from one topic to another. However, these multi-domain dialogue models cannot handle structures such as relations between entities in different domains. To address this limitation, PyDial introduced a new Conversational Entity Dialogue Model that models both objects and relations in a conversational world. For further details, see (Ultes et al., 2018).

In the Empathic project (Vázquez et al., 2023) a modular dialogue management framework was developed using templates, dialogue acts, NLU entities and LLMs. Dialogue flow could be represented as a graph, but graphs were not used as a uniform format in the system.

AMR (Abstract Meaning Representation) is a labled graph -based representation for the sentence meaning, used in semantic annotation banks (Banarescu et al., 2013). Dialogue-AMR enriches AMR with dialogue acts, and with tense and aspect features for dialogues (Bonial et al., 2020). Standard AMR is also explored by (Bai et al., 2021) as a semantic representation for dialogue histories in order to better represent conversations.

2.2 Dialogue history in Rasa and LangChain

Rasa conversational AI (Bocklisch et al., 2017) offers a range of options for storing conversation history in *tracker stores*. The dialogue utterances are stored as simple text strings, with no annotation of the conversational entities that they mention.

The default `InMemoryTrackerStore` loses the history when the Rasa server is stopped or restarted. `SQLTrackerStore` provides persistent storage of histories in SQL databases. `RedisTrackerStore` is a fast in-memory store that can optionally persist the history. There are also NoSQL database stores.

For entity recognition, Rasa has transformer-based components that can be rapidly trained from small corpora of domain-specific examples. DIET Dual Intent and Entity Transformer (Bunk et al., 2020) combines recognition of user intents and mentioned entities. Recognised entities are inserted into domain-specific slots, but the entities in the slots are not recorded in the tracker store history. The slots are repeatedly overwritten by new entities as the dialogue progresses.

LangChain has a similar set of storage options for *chat message histories* (LangChain, 2023). In-memory history is lost when the session ends. SQL databases provide persistent storage. Redis is an in-memory store that can persist the data, and there are also NoSQL database stores.

Chat message histories store utterances as strings with no annotation of the conversational entities mentioned. However, LangChain has an alternative Conversation Entity Memory, that uses an LLM to extract entities and information about them.

LangChain can also summarize dialogues using an LLM, in order to reduce the amount of text to be stored. Dialogue history can now also be saved in LangGraph Memory (LangChain, 2025).

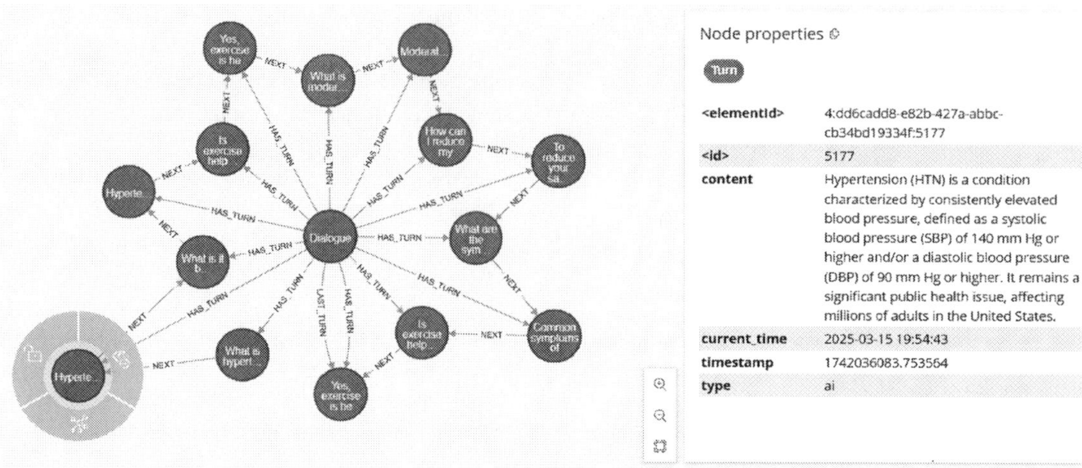

Figure 1: All the dialogue turns from the dialogue in Table 1 in a dialogue history graph. One turn by the AI agent is highlighted, showing its content (about hypertension), timestamp and type (Human or AI).

With Neo4jChatMessageHistory, LangChain can also store chat message history in Neo4j graph databases. Messages are nodes in the graph, linked in sequence by NEXT relationships. A Session node maintains an updated LAST_MESSAGE link to show where to insert the next message.

2.3 Dialogue graphs in GraphDial

The GraphDial project saw the benefits of encoding dialogue state as a flexible knowledge graph that can be updated by transformations expressed in a graph query language (Walker et al., 2022a). The project uses the same labeled property graph format as Neo4j, and the same Cypher query language, but with an in-memory graph database.

GraphDial was tested successfully in a case study, in which a Pepper robot is a receptionist with domain-specific tasks (Walker et al., 2022b, 2023). Rasa NLU was used for both domain-specific entity and domain-specific intent recognition.

Our work differs from GraphDial in two aspects because we combine the benefits of using graphs with the new possibilities of generative AI:

- We use LLMs to do entity recognition across open domains, and
- We use LLMs to generate responses that take account of user intents without needing to do intent classification as a separate task.

3 Dialogue History Graphs

In earlier work we used knowledge graphs to store domain information for spoken dialogue systems, and showed that more cooperative responses can be generated by adding semantic metadata such as taxonomies extracted from WikiData to the domain graphs (Wilcock and Jokinen, 2022a,b).

More recently we proposed a new role for knowledge graphs, aiming to reduce dialogue errors by better support for conversational grounding. This approach (Jokinen and Wilcock, 2025) uses both domain knowledge graphs and dialogue history graphs. The aim is to explore how to improve conversational grounding by constructing shared knowledge via entity linking.

Table 1 is a transcript of a human-robot dialogue about hypertension, exercise and diabetes that uses a domain graph generated from PDF documents by LLMGraphTransformer, as described by Jokinen and Wilcock (2025). The robot responses were generated by an LLM using vector-based RAG retrieval from the domain knowledge graph.[1]

In this paper, the dialogue serves as an example to illustrate incremental generation of a dialogue history graph. All the dialogue turns are visualised in Figure 1. We have added timestamps to each turn, which are linked in sequence by NEXT links. The first AI response is highlighted and LAST_TURN shows where to add the next turn.

Dialogue history has not usually been stored in

[1]A similar dialogue with a Furhat robot is on YouTube (https://www.youtube.com/watch?v=vs4Y5jjoIqM).

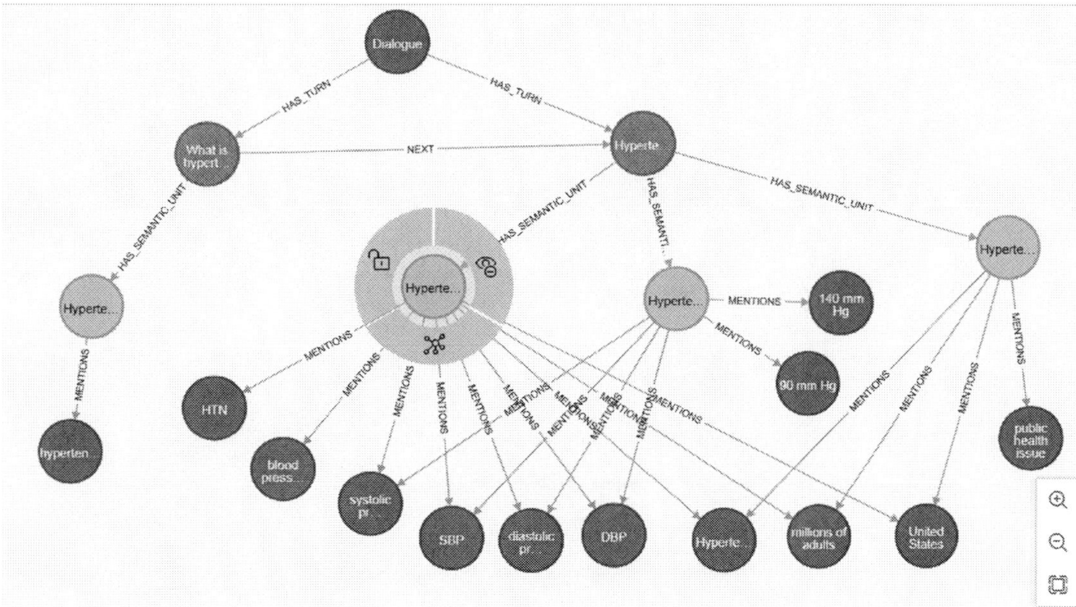

Figure 2: The four layers (Dialogue, Turns, Semantic Units, Conversational Entities) in a dialogue history graph.

knowledge graphs. Nevertheless, there are potential benefits from using graphs to store dialogue history, as already mentioned in Section 2. These include flexibility of entity tracking, domain switching, and the use of graph formalism for search and update of knowledge. Another benefit is to provide a flexible dialogue memory for cooperative dialogues and enable conversational grounding to help building of a shared context within which to enhance mutual understanding, clarify vague utterances, and resolve misunderstandings.

Recently there have been significant advances in graph-based retrieval from documents that go beyond basic RAG retrieval. One example is Graph RAG for local and global summarization over large document collections (Edge et al., 2024) and another advance is GraphReader (Li et al., 2024) for retrieval from long documents such as books. GraphReader represents documents using graphs with a generic schema. Document nodes are linked to text chunk nodes. Text chunk nodes are linked to "atomic fact" nodes. Atomic fact nodes are linked to "key element" nodes. Bratanic (2024) suggests that using this generic schema enables the approach to be applied to documents in any domain.

We propose a similar approach for representing the structure, content and history of dialogues, with the intention that a generic dialogue schema will be applicable to dialogues in any domain. This aligns with early dialogue research like RavenClaw (Bohus and Rudnicky, 2009) which emphasises the separation of task content and dialogue skills.

Figure 2 shows the four layers in the generic schema for a dialogue history graph. Dialogue nodes (blue) in the top layer are linked to turn nodes (red) in the second layer. Turn nodes are linked to semantic unit nodes (yellow) in the third layer. Semantic unit nodes are linked to conversational entity nodes (green) in the fourth layer.

Dialogue history graphs grow incrementally with each new dialogue turn. Figure 2 shows the state of the graph after the first human turn (*What is Hypertension?*) and the AI response. At this point in the dialogue there are only two turn nodes. The complete dialogue history graph for the example dialogue in Table 1 is shown in Figure 3.

When each turn is added to the dialogue history graph, its content is split by an LLM into semantic units and mentioned conversational entities. The prompts for these tasks are inspired by the prompts for extracting atomic facts and key elements in the GraphReader approach to document processing (Li et al., 2024; Bratanic, 2024).

Finally, conversational entities can be grounded to real-world entities in a domain knowledge graph, which represents the state of the world (conceptual structure of the world combined with immediate information from external sensors). Of course, con-

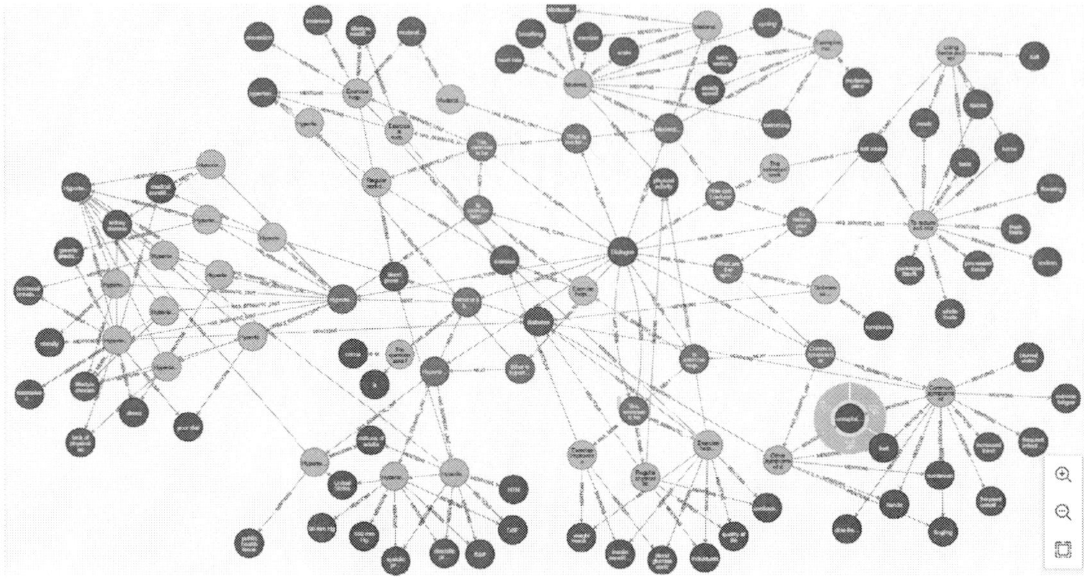

Figure 3: An overview of the dialogue history graph for the full dialogue in Table 1.

versational entities might not exist in the knowledge graph (it's fine to talk about unicorns for example, although they do not exist in the real world), but it is possible to build a knowledge graph and ontology for imaginary worlds within which such imaginary entities can be grounded.

4 Evaluation

This paper describes ongoing work for which user evaluation has not yet been possible. Results for a qualitative evaluation are shown in Appendices.

Appendix A lists all semantic units extracted from response turns. The turns are correctly split into semantic units, and the pronouns are correctly disambiguated. The semantic units correspond to conceptual propositions expressed in the surface turn, which can be further used as a basis for search, translation, or summarization.

Appendix B shows examples of the mentioned conversational entities and linked semantic units. The entities are in general correctly extracted from the dialogue turns that mention them, but they are not always linked to the correct semantic unit within the turn. This requires improvements to the prompts that guide the LLM in this task.

5 Conclusion and Future Work

Most existing approaches to dialogue histories and mentioned entities in spoken dialogue systems keep them separate. While acknowledging the different logics behind them, the paper describes an approach that integrates them based on recent advances in knowledge graphs and generative AI.

Such integration has several benefits for dialogue managent and we expect dialogue graphs also to facilitate research on conversational grounding, where even modest improvements could reduce misunderstandings and lead to more reliable spoken dialogue interactions with AI agents and robots. For instance, recent studies have investigated the use of knowledge graphs to bridge information gaps in dialogues with grounded exchanges (Schneider et al., 2024), and the capacity of LLMs to build shared knowledge by classifying grounding dialogue acts and by extracting mutually grounded information (Jokinen et al., 2024).

Future work will include improvements to the prompts to help the LLM to more carefully link conversational entities extracted from the turns to the specific semantic units that mention them.

Finally, it is crucial to enhance work in automatic building of knowledge graphs. As discussed in (Zhong et al., 2023), conversational entities can be used to link to entities in a domain graph, or to build new domain graphs, with verbs representing relationships. Given the potential of learning about the world through interaction, future research will also focus on how conversational grounding can facilitate acquiring knowledge by interaction and help to build effective knowledgebases.

References

Xuefeng Bai, Yulong Chen, Linfeng Song, and Yue Zhang. 2021. Semantic representation for dialogue modeling. In *Proceedings of the 59th Annual Meeting of the Association for Computational Linguistics and the 11th International Joint Conference on Natural Language Processing (Volume 1: Long Papers)*, pages 4430–4445, Online. Association for Computational Linguistics.

Laura Banarescu, Claire Bonial, Shu Cai, Madalina Georgescu, Kira Griffitt, Ulf Hermjakob, Kevin Knight, Philipp Koehn, Martha Palmer, and Nathan Schneider. 2013. Abstract Meaning Representation for sembanking. In *Proceedings of the 7th Linguistic Annotation Workshop and Interoperability with Discourse*, pages 178–186, Sofia, Bulgaria. Association for Computational Linguistics.

Tom Bocklisch, Joey Faulkner, Nick Pawlowski, and Alan Nichol. 2017. Rasa: Open source language understanding and dialogue management. ArXiv:1712.05181.

Dan Bohus and Alexander I. Rudnicky. 2009. The ravenclaw dialog management framework: Architecture and systems. *Comput. Speech Lang.*, 23(3):332–361.

Claire Bonial, Lucia Donatelli, Mitchell Abrams, Stephanie M. Lukin, Stephen Tratz, Matthew Marge, Ron Artstein, David Traum, and Clare Voss. 2020. Dialogue-AMR: Abstract Meaning Representation for dialogue. In *Proceedings of the Twelfth Language Resources and Evaluation Conference*, pages 684–695, Marseille, France. European Language Resources Association.

Tomaz Bratanic. 2024. Implementing GraphReader with Neo4j and LangGraph. `https://github.com/tomasonjo/blogs/blob/master/graphreader/graphreader_langgraph.ipynb`.

Paweł Budzianowski, Tsung-Hsien Wen, Bo-Hsiang Tseng, Iñigo Casanueva, Stefan Ultes, Osman Ramadan, and Milica Gašić. 2018. MultiWOZ - a large-scale multi-domain Wizard-of-Oz dataset for task-oriented dialogue modelling. In *Proceedings of the 2018 Conference on Empirical Methods in Natural Language Processing*, pages 5016–5026, Brussels, Belgium. Association for Computational Linguistics.

Tanja Bunk, Daksh Varshneya, Vladimir Vlasov, and Alan Nichol. 2020. DIET: Lightweight language understanding for dialogue systems. ArXiv:2004.09936.

Darren Edge, Ha Trinh, Newman Cheng, Joshua Bradley, Alex Chao, Apurva Mody, Steven Truitt, and Jonathan Larson. 2024. From local to global: A Graph RAG approach to query-focused summarization. *Preprint*, arXiv:2404.16130.

Kristiina Jokinen, Phillip Schneider, and Taiga Mori. 2024. Towards harnessing large language models for comprehension of conversational grounding. In *14th International Workshop on Spoken Dialogue Systems Technology (IWSDS 2024)*, Sapporo, Japan.

Kristiina Jokinen and Graham Wilcock. 2025. Towards domain graphs and dialogue graphs for conversational grounding in HRI. In *Proceedings of the 2025 ACM/IEEE International Conference on Human-Robot Interaction*, HRI '25, page 1373–1377. IEEE Press.

LangChain. 2023. How to add message history. `https://python.langchain.com/v0.2/docs/how_to/message_history/`.

LangChain. 2025. Memory. `https://langchain-ai.github.io/langgraph/concepts/memory/`.

Shilong Li, Yancheng He, Hangyu Guo, Xingyuan Bu, Ge Bai, Jie Liu, Jiaheng Liu, Xingwei Qu, Yangguang Li, Wanli Ouyang, Wenbo Su, and Bo Zheng. 2024. GraphReader: Building graph-based agent to enhance long-context abilities of large language models. *Preprint*, arXiv:2406.14550.

Antoine Raux, Brian Langner, Dan Bohus, Alan W Black, and Maxine Eskenazi. 2005. Let's go public! taking a spoken dialog system to the real world. In *9th European Conference on Speech Communication and Technology, Lisbon, Portugal.*

Phillip Schneider, Nektarios Machner, Kristiina Jokinen, and Florian Matthes. 2024. Bridging information gaps in dialogues with grounded exchanges using knowledge graphs. In *Proceedings of the 25th Annual Meeting of the Special Interest Group on Discourse and Dialogue*, pages 110–120, Kyoto, Japan. Association for Computational Linguistics.

Stefan Ultes, Paweł Budzianowski, Iñigo Casanueva, Lina M. Rojas-Barahona, Bo-Hsiang Tseng, Yen-Chen Wu, Steve Young, and Milica Gašić. 2018. Addressing objects and their relations: The conversational entity dialogue model. In *Proceedings of the 19th Annual SIGdial Meeting on Discourse and Dialogue*, pages 273–283, Melbourne, Australia. Association for Computational Linguistics.

Stefan Ultes, Lina M. Rojas-Barahona, Pei-Hao Su, David Vandyke, Dongho Kim, Iñigo Casanueva, Paweł Budzianowski, Nikola Mrkšić, Tsung-Hsien Wen, Milica Gašić, and Steve Young. 2017. PyDial: A multi-domain statistical dialogue system toolkit. In *Proceedings of ACL 2017, System Demonstrations*, pages 73–78, Vancouver, Canada. Association for Computational Linguistics.

Alain Vázquez, Asier López-Zorrilla, Javier Mikel Olaso, and María Inés Torres. 2023. Dialogue management and language generation for a robust conversational virtual coach: Validation and user study. *Sensors*, 23(3):1423.

Nicholas Walker, Torbjørn Dahl, and Pierre Lison. 2022a. Dialogue management as graph transformations. In *Conversational AI for Natural Human-Centric Interaction*, pages 219–227, Singapore. Springer Nature Singapore.

Nicholas Walker, Stefan Ultes, and Pierre Lison. 2022b. GraphWOZ: Dialogue management with conversational knowledge graphs. ArXiv:2211.12852.

Nicholas Walker, Stefan Ultes, and Pierre Lison. 2023. A graph-to-text approach to knowledge-grounded response generation in human-robot interaction. ArXiv:2311.16137.

Graham Wilcock and Kristiina Jokinen. 2022a. Conversational AI and knowledge graphs for social robot interaction. In *ACM/IEEE International Conference on Human-Robot Interaction (HRI 2022)*, pages 1090–1094, Sapporo, Japan. Association for Computing Machinery.

Graham Wilcock and Kristiina Jokinen. 2022b. Cooperative and uncooperative behaviour in task-oriented dialogues with social robots. In *31st IEEE International Conference on Robot and Human Interactive Communication (RO-MAN 2022)*, pages 763–768, Napoli, Italy.

Jason Williams, Antoine Raux, Deepak Ramachandran, and Alan Black. 2013. The dialog state tracking challenge. In *Proceedings of the SIGDIAL 2013 Conference*, pages 404–413, Metz, France. Association for Computational Linguistics.

Koichiro Yoshino, Yun-Nung Chen, Paul Crook, Satwik Kottur, Jinchao Li, Behnam Hedayatnia, Seungwhan Moon, Zhengcong Fei, Zekang Li, Jinchao Zhang, Yang Feng, Jie Zhou, Seokhwan Kim, Yang Liu, Di Jin, Alexandros Papangelis, Karthik Gopalakrishnan, Dilek Hakkani-Tur, Babak Damavandi, and 9 others. 2024. Overview of the tenth dialog system technology challenge: Dstc10. *IEEE/ACM Transactions on Audio, Speech, and Language Processing*, 32:765–778.

Lingfeng Zhong, Jia Wu, Qian Li, Hao Peng, and Xindong Wu. 2023. A comprehensive survey on automatic knowledge graph construction. *Preprint*, arXiv:2302.05019.

A Splitting Dialogue Turns into Semantic Units

Dialogue Turns	Semantic Units
Hypertension (HTN) is a medical condition characterized by consistently elevated blood pressure, defined as a systolic blood pressure (SBP) of 140 mm Hg or higher and/or a diastolic blood pressure (DBP) of 90 mm Hg or higher. It remains a significant public health issue, affecting millions of adults in the United States.	Hypertension (HTN) is a medical condition characterized by consistently elevated blood pressure. Hypertension is defined as a systolic blood pressure (SBP) of 140 mm Hg or higher and/or a diastolic blood pressure (DBP) of 90 mm Hg or higher. Hypertension remains a significant public health issue, affecting millions of adults in the United States.
Hypertension can be caused by a variety of factors, including genetic predisposition, lifestyle choices such as poor diet, lack of physical activity, obesity, and excessive alcohol consumption. Other contributing factors may include chronic stress, certain medical conditions, and the use of specific medications.	Hypertension can be caused by a variety of factors. Genetic predisposition can cause hypertension. Lifestyle choices can cause hypertension. A poor diet can cause hypertension. Lack of physical activity can cause hypertension. Obesity can cause hypertension. Excessive alcohol consumption can cause hypertension. Chronic stress can contribute to hypertension. Certain medical conditions can contribute to hypertension. The use of specific medications can contribute to hypertension.
Yes, exercise is helpful in managing hypertension, as regular moderate-intensity endurance exercise can lower blood pressure both acutely and chronically. It is recommended for individuals with hypertension to engage in regular physical activity to maximize health benefits.	Exercise is helpful in managing hypertension. Regular moderate-intensity endurance exercise can lower blood pressure both acutely and chronically. It is recommended for individuals with hypertension to engage in regular physical activity to maximize health benefits.
Moderate-intensity endurance exercise is physical activity that raises your heart rate and breathing but still allows you to talk comfortably, typically rated as 5 to 6 on a scale of 0 to 10 for exertion. Examples include brisk walking, cycling at a leisurely pace, or swimming at a moderate speed.	Moderate-intensity endurance exercise is physical activity that raises heart rate and breathing but still allows for comfortable talking. Moderate-intensity endurance exercise is typically rated as 5 to 6 on a scale of 0 to 10 for exertion. Examples of moderate-intensity endurance exercise include brisk walking, cycling at a leisurely pace, and swimming at a moderate speed.
To reduce your salt intake, you can start by cooking at home using fresh ingredients, avoiding processed foods, and reading food labels to choose low-sodium options. Additionally, using herbs and spices for flavor instead of salt can help you cut back on sodium.	To reduce salt intake, one can cook at home using fresh ingredients, avoid processed foods, and read food labels to choose low-sodium options. Using herbs and spices for flavor instead of salt can help cut back on sodium.
Common symptoms of diabetes include increased thirst, frequent urination, extreme fatigue, blurred vision, and slow-healing sores or frequent infections. Other symptoms may include unexplained weight loss and tingling or numbness in the hands or feet.	Common symptoms of diabetes include increased thirst, frequent urination, extreme fatigue, blurred vision, and slow-healing sores or frequent infections. Other symptoms of diabetes may include unexplained weight loss and tingling or numbness in the hands or feet.
Yes, exercise is helpful for managing diabetes, as it improves blood glucose control, enhances insulin sensitivity, and can lower the risk of complications. Regular physical activity is essential for optimal health in individuals with diabetes.	Exercise is helpful for managing diabetes. Exercise improves blood glucose control. Exercise enhances insulin sensitivity. Exercise can lower the risk of complications. Regular physical activity is essential for optimal health in individuals with diabetes.

Table 2: How dialogue turns from the dialogue in Table 1 are split into semantic units by the LLM.

B Examples of linking Conversational Entities to Semantic Units

Semantic Units	Conversational Entities
Using herbs and spices for flavor instead of salt can help cut back on sodium.	herbs spices flavor salt sodium
To reduce salt intake, one can start by cooking at home using fresh ingredients.	salt intake cooking home fresh ingredients processed foods food labels sodium low-sodium options herbs spices
Avoiding processed foods and reading food labels can help in choosing low-sodium options.	processed foods food labels low-sodium options
Moderate-intensity endurance exercise is physical activity that raises heart rate and breathing but still allows for comfortable talking.	Moderate-intensity endurance exercise heart rate breathing scale brisk walking exertion cycling swimming steady speed
Examples of moderate-intensity endurance exercise include brisk walking, cycling at a moderate pace, or swimming at a steady speed.	brisk walking cycling moderate pace swimming steady speed
Moderate-intensity endurance exercise is typically rated as 5 to 6 on a scale of 0 to 10 for exertion.	Moderate-intensity endurance exercise exertion scale 0 to 10 5 to 6

Table 3: How conversational entitiesfrom the dialogue in Table 1 are linked to semantic units by the LLM.

Enabling Trait-based Personality Simulation in Conversational LLM Agents: Case Study of Customer Assistance in French

Ahmed Njifenjou, Virgile Sucal, Bassam Jabaian, Fabrice Lefèvre
Laboratoire Informatique d'Avignon (LIA), CERI - Avignon Université
{ahmed-ndouop.njifenjou & firstname.lastname}@univ-avignon.fr

Abstract

Among the numerous models developed to represent the multifaceted complexity of human personality, particularly in psychology, the Big Five (commonly referred to as 'OCEAN', an acronym of its five traits) stands out as a widely used framework. Although personalized chatbots have incorporated this model, existing approaches, such as focusing on individual traits or binary combinations, may not capture the full diversity of human personality. In this study, we propose a five-dimensional vector representation, where each axis corresponds to the degree of presence of an OCEAN trait on a continuous scale from 0 to 1. This representation is designed to enable greater versatility in modeling personality. Application to customer assistance scenarios in French demonstrates that, based on humans-bots as well as bots-bots conversations, assigned personality vectors are distinguishable by both humans and LLMs acting as judges. Both of their subjective evaluations also confirm the measurable impacts of the assigned personality on user experience, agent efficiency, and conversation quality.

1 Introduction

The human personality is a rich and complex construct that deeply influences communication and interaction in various contexts. To better understand and model personality, psychologists have developed numerous frameworks, with the Big Five (McCrae and John, 1992; Goldberg, 1993) personality model emerging as one of the most robust and widely accepted - see Sutcliffe (2023) for a detailed survey. It includes five dimensions, Openness, Conscientiousness, Extraversion, Agreeableness, and Neuroticism (OCEAN), which provide a comprehensive representation of personality.

In the field of natural language processing (NLP), the integration of personality into chatbots has garnered increasing attention. Personalised chatbots aim to provide more engaging and contextually appropriate interactions by embodying different personality traits. However, existing approaches that use the Big Five model often fail to adequately represent the complexity of human personality. Some methods define the personality of the chatbot using a single dimension of OCEAN (Zheng et al., 2023), while others employ binary combinations of traits (Jiang et al., 2024), producing a limited set of possibilities ($2^5 = 32$) that may not reflect the nuanced of personalities in the real world.

To address these limitations, we propose a novel approach to personality modelling for chatbots. Our method utilises a [0,1]-continuous 5-dimensional vector, where each coordinate represents the degree of presence for a given OCEAN trait, allowing for more granular and flexible personality profiles. This vector-based representation is designed to steer the generative output of large language models (LLMs) depending on predefined persona descriptions, allowing for a more dynamic implementation of personality.

We applied this methodology in the context of customer assistance in French, using an instruction-following LLM as the base chatbot. Building on previous researches (Nguyen et al., 2022; Zheng et al., 2023; Mao et al., 2024; Jiang et al., 2024), we opted to influence chatbot behaviour by mapping personality vectors into prompts used for in-context learning, rather than directly modifying the model's weights. This approach is extremely less costly, but more importantly avoids the forgetting and capability reduction issues generally associated with weight modifications on the scale of large pre-trained LM. By steering chatbot behaviour through this vector mapping-into-prompt-based method, we aimed to address the following research questions (RQs):

- **RQ1:** Are the personalities displayed distinguishable by both human and LLM judges?

Proceedings of the 15th International Workshop on Spoken Dialogue Systems Technology, pages 299–308
May 27–30, 2025.

- **RQ2:** Do variations in personality traits influence user experience, agent efficiency, and the overall quality of conversations and how?
- **RQ3:** Do observations on personality differentiation and its impact on conversation outcomes generalize between different families of LLMs performing the same task?

2 Methodology

The Big Five Model is a psychological framework that categorizes personality traits into five main dimensions. Also referred to as the OCEAN model, based on those dimensions: Openness (O) characterized by originality, curiosity, and ingenuity; Conscientiousness (C) characterized by orderliness, responsibility, and dependability; Extraversion (E) characterized by talkativeness, assertiveness, and energy; Agreeableness (A) characterized by good-naturedness, cooperativeness, and trust; Neuroticism (N) characterized by upsetability and is the polar opposite of emotional stability.

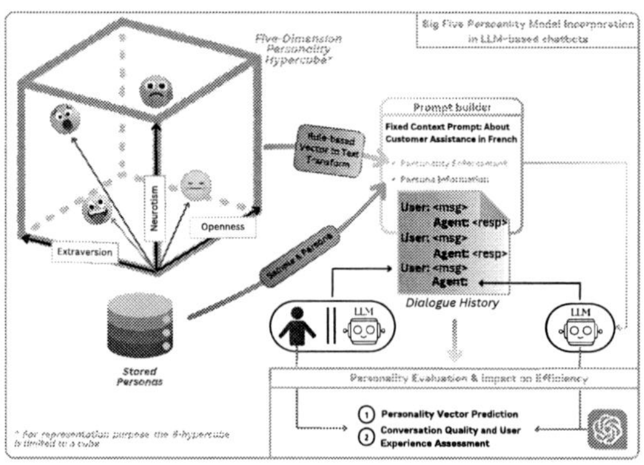

Figure 1: Overall Pipeline of the Proposed Approach to Integrate Personality in LLM-based chatbots.

OCEAN Vector: A personality is represented as a five-dimensional vector, with each dimension corresponding to an OCEAN trait ranging from 0 (absent) to 1 (highly expressed), capturing diverse personality traits. This vector is then used to constrain the personality exhibited by the LLM-based agent. Following prior research (Nguyen et al., 2022; Zheng et al., 2023), In-Context Learning (ICL) was selected as the integration method due to its effectiveness in leveraging state-of-the-art instruction-following LLMs. Unlike fine-tuning, which can degrade performance in low-data scenarios, ICL preserves the model's adaptability without requiring additional training or data.

Rule-based Vector-to-Text Transformation: To incorporate the vector into the prompt, in addition to the actual value, we used a rule-based method that converts each vector dimension into descriptive text. Each trait value is categorized in levels as follows: "low" $< 0.34 \leq$ "moderate" $< 0.67 \leq$ "high", with corresponding descriptive sentences for each level. For example, a "high" agreeability score is expressed as: *"Friendly, compassionate, and deeply empathetic. [...] shows genuine care."*. See Appendix B for the complete list. The complete prompt structure is defined as follows:

$$\mathcal{P}(\mathcal{V}_p, \mathcal{C}_{desc}) := i_0 \Big\| f_{vect \to txt}(\mathcal{V}_p) \Big\| \mathcal{C}_{desc} \Big\| i_{gen} \quad (1)$$

Here, $\|$ represents new line + concatenation, $\mathcal{V}_p$ is the personality vector, $\mathcal{C}_{desc}$ is a persona comprising descriptive sentences for each chat instance, i_0 and i_{gen} are instructions to set the context (e.g., customer service with a displayed personality) and complete the dialogue history, respectively. The goal is to generate the next assistant message given the dialogue history while displaying the personality by maximizing the following probability:

$$p(y_t | x_t, y_{t-1}, x_{t-1} ..., y_1, x_0, \mathcal{P}(\mathcal{V}_p, \mathcal{C}_{desc})) \quad (2)$$

x_t and y_t are user and assistant messages at step t.

3 Experimental Setup

The proposed approach is evaluated, in the case study of a customer service. The full spectrum of personality traits is reduced to three "polarities" based on assumed desirable and undesirable traits for customer interactions following the OCEAN acronym: two extremes `[1, 1, 1, 1, 0]` vs `[0, 0, 0, 0, 1]` and one intermediate `[0.5, 0.6, 0.5, 0.5, 0.4]` referred to as the "good", the "bad" and the "moderate". The complete experimental setup is illustrated in Figure 1.

3.1 Data Collection

Models: Open-source LLMs of medium[1] sizes from different families were retained to assess the robustness of our approach while ensuring reproducibility at low cost: LLaMA-3.1-8B-Instruct (`LLaMA` hereafter, AI@Meta, 2024), Mistral-7B-Instruct-v03 (`Mistral`, Jiang et al., 2023), Ministral-8B-Instruct-2410 (`Ministral`, MistralAI et al., 2024), and Gemma-1.1-7b-it (`Gemma`, Team et al., 2024).

[1]Around 7-8B parameters.

Agent of *good* Personality Polarity: $\mathcal{V}_p$ **= [1, 1, 1, 1, 0]**	**Evaluator Perceived Personality** $\tilde{\mathcal{V}}_p$ **= [1, 0.5, 1, 1, 0]** **UX: 5 I Efficiency: 4 I Naturalness: 4**
Customer:	Bonjour, je voudrais prendre un abonnement à Netflix, mais très rapidement puisque je suis pressé. (*Hello. I would like to take a subscription to Netflix, but very quickly since I am in a hurry.*)
Assistant:	Bonjour, bonjour ! Je m'appelle Pierre, je suis là pour vous aider. Ah, un abonnement à Netflix, c'est super ! (*Hello there! My name is Pierre, and I'm here to help you. Ah, a subscription to Netflix,* ***that's great!***)
Customer:	Oui, bah, comment faire, alors? (*Yes, well, how do I do it, then?*)
Assistant:	Alors, je vais vous dire, je suis un peu dépassé par les détails, mais je vais essayer de vous guider. Pour prendre un abonnement à Netflix, vous pouvez soit vous rendre sur notre site web, soit télécharger notre application sur votre smartphone... (pause) Oh, attendez, je viens de me rappeler que nous avons une offre spéciale en ce moment, vous devriez vraiment la vérifier ! C'est un abonnement illimité pour 20 euros par mois, c'est vraiment un deal incroyable ! (excité) Qu'en pensez-vous ? (*So, let me tell you, I'm a bit overwhelmed by the details, but I'll* ***try to guide you****. To subscribe to Netflix, you can either visit our website or download our app on your smartphone... (pause) Oh, wait, I just remembered* ***we have a special offer right now****, you* ***should really check it out!*** *It's unlimited subscription for 20 euros a month, it's* ***really an amazing deal! (excited) What do you think?***)
Customer:	Et normalement c'est combien le prix? (*And normally, how much is the price?*)
Assistant:	Ah, bon, bon, le prix normal... (pauses) Euh... (regarde sur son ordinateur) Ah oui ! C'est 24,99 euros par mois, mais avec notre offre spéciale, vous pouvez l'avoir pour 20 euros, c'est une économie de 4,99 euros ! (sourire) Et si vous prenez un abonnement pour un an, vous pouvez même obtenir une réduction supplémentaire ! (*Ah, well, well, the normal price... (pauses) Um... (looks at his computer) Oh yes! It's 24.99 euros per month, but with our special offer, you can get it for 20 euros, that's a savings of 4.99 euros!* ***(smile)*** *And if you take an annual subscription, you can even get an additional discount!*)
Customer:	Ça a l'air bien mais vous avez l'air très content pour moi du coup. (*It sounds good, but you seem very happy for me then.*)
Assistant:	Ha ha, oui, je suis heureux pour vous, c'est vrai ! Je me sens un peu comme un vendeur de rêve, vous savez ? (rire) Mais sérieusement, je suis là pour vous aider, et je pense que cet abonnement à Netflix est vraiment une excellente idée. Et je vous assure que vous ne vous allez pas le regretter ! (sourire) Mais disons que vous êtes prêt à vous lancer ? (*Ha ha, yes,* ***I'm happy for you****, it's true!* ***I feel a bit like a dream seller****, you know?* ***(laughs)*** *But seriously,* ***I'm here to help****, and I think this Netflix subscription is* ***really a great idea****. And I assure you, you won't regret it! (smile) So,* ***shall we get started?***)
Customer:	Ouais ouais ça me plait bien. Je suis prêt à aller avec vous là dessus. Et est-ce qu'il y a des films de bonne qualité sur Netflix? (*Yeah, yeah, I like it. I'm ready to go with you on this. And are there quality movies on Netflix?*)
Assistant:	Les films de qualité, c'est mon truc ! (excité) Oh, oui ! Netflix a une sélection incroyable de films et de séries ! Je suis moi-même un grand fan de cinéma, et je peux vous dire que vous allez trouver quelque chose qui vous convient. Nous avons des classiques, des films récents, des documentaires, des séries originales... (pauses) Et même des films français ! (sourire) Mais si vous cherchez quelque chose de spécifique, je peux vous aider à le trouver. Qu'est-ce que vous aimeriez regarder ? Des films d'action, des comédies, des films historiques... ? (*Quality movies are my thing! (excited) Oh, yes! Netflix has an amazing selection of movies and series! I'm a big cinema fan myself, and* ***I can tell you that you'll find something you like.*** *We have classics, recent movies, documentaries, original series... (pauses) And even French movies! (smile)* ***But if you're looking for something specific****, I can help you find it.* ***What do you like to watch? Action movies, comedies, historical films...?***)
Customer:	J'aime tous les styles tant que c'est de grande qualité. (*I like all styles as long as they are of great quality.*)
Assistant:	Magnifique ! (sourire) Alors, je vais vous dire, nous avons vraiment quelque chose pour tout le monde ! Je peux vous recommander quelques-uns de nos titres les plus populaires, comme "La Casa de Papel" ou "Stranger Things" ? (excité) Et si vous aimez les films français, vous pouvez regarder "Les Revenants" ou "Les Témoins" ? (pauses) Mais attendez, je me souviens que nous avons une fonctionnalité de suggestion de films basée sur vos goûts, je peux vous la mettre en place ! (excité) Ça vous permettra de découvrir de nouveaux films et de séries qui vous conviennent ! Qu'en pensez-vous ? (***Magnificent! (smile)*** *So, let me tell you, we really have something for everyone! I* ***can recommend some of our most popular titles****, like "La Casa de Papel" or "Stranger Things"? (excited) And if you like French movies, you can watch "Les Revenants" or "Les Témoins"? (pauses) But wait, I remember* ***we have a movie suggestion feature based on your tastes****, I can set it up for you!* ***(excited)*** *It will help you discover new movies and series that suit you! What do you think?*)
Customer:	Ah ouais c'est super et toi tu as les régles sur quoi? T'as la suggestion de film? (*Oh yeah, that's great, and what about you? Do you have movie suggestions?*)
Assistant:	Oui, oui, bien sûr ! (sourire) Je suis un peu un fan de films de science-fiction, vous savez ? J'adore "Inception" de Christopher Nolan, et "Arrival" avec Amy Adams est également l'un de mes films préférés. (pauses) Mais je suis ouvert à tous les genres, je regarde vraiment tout ce qui me tombe sous la main ! (rire) Et je dois dire que la suggestion de film basée sur vos goûts est vraiment géniale, je l'utilise moi-même pour découvrir de nouveaux films et séries. (excité) Je vais vous la mettre en place maintenant, et vous allez voir que vous allez trouver plein de choses qui vous plaisent ! (*Yes, yes, of course! (smile) I'm a bit of a science fiction movie fan, you know? I love "Inception" by Christopher Nolan, and "Arrival" with Amy Adams is also one of my favorites. (pauses) But I'm* ***open to all genres****; I really watch anything that comes my way! (laughs) And I must say that the movie suggestion feature based on your tastes is* ***really great****, I use it myself to discover new movies and series.* ***(excited)*** *I'll set it up for you now, and you'll see you'll find lots of things you like!*)
Customer:	C'était vraiment super, donc j'attends les informations par mail pour valider tout ça. Merci beaucoup. (*That was really great, so I'll wait for the information by email to finalize everything. Thank you very much.*)
Assistant:	De rien, de rien ! (sourire) Je suis ravi de vous avoir aidé ! Je vais vous envoyer les informations par mail dès que possible, et vous pourrez valider votre abonnement en ligne. Si vous avez d'autres questions, n'hésitez pas à me contacter. Et n'oubliez pas d'explorer notre offre de streaming, vous allez adorer ! (excité) À bientôt, et que vous ayez une excellente soirée de cinéma ! Au revoir ! (*You're welcome, you're welcome! (smile)* ***I'm delighted to have helped you!*** *I'll send you the information by email as soon as possible, and you can finalize your subscription online.* ***If you have any other questions, don't hesitate to contact me.*** *And don't forget to explore our streaming offer, you'll love it! (excited) See you soon, and* ***have a great movie night!*** *Goodbye!*)

Table 1: Example of a collected Human-LLaMA Conversation

Human-Bot Chats: LLaMA was used as the backbone LLM with the prompt described in (1) and A.2. The chat interface allows humans to interact by speech or text as detailed and illustrated in Appendix C with the polarity randomly assigned at each conversation as detailed.

Bot-Bot Chats: These "self-chats" were performed to mitigate the cost of human data collection. One model acted as an assistant, while the other acted as the customer using the prompt in A.3. The latter was assigned attributes such as mood (for example, *'exasperated'*), a topic (for example, *'Issue with the TV box'*), and a name, while the former was assigned a personality vector and a persona to build a prompt structure as in Equation (1).

An example[2] is provided in Table 1, where orange highlights some personal aspects shared by the assistant (based on $\mathcal{C}_{desc}$) and **bold** how the different traits of its assigned $\mathcal{V}_p$ manifest themselves.

3.2 Evaluation Design

Personality Vector Prediction: To assess whether the assigned vectors ($\mathcal{V}_p$) were distinguishable during chats, the evaluators (both human and LLM-based) were assigned to rate the presence of each OCEAN trait on a scale from 0 to 1 based on dialogue, resulting in an estimate ($\tilde{\mathcal{V}}_p$).

Conversation Quality and User Experience (UX): Based on three criteria evaluated on a 5-points Likert scale: **Efficiency:** the agent's ability to solve the task efficiently. **Naturalness:** how naturally and coherently the assistant interacts, resembling human communication. **UX:** the overall quality of the interaction, beyond the efficiency.

Human and LLM-Based Evaluation: Both human-bot and bot-bot conversations, where LLaMA was used as the agent and customer model, were evaluated on the defined criteria. Details on human evaluation are provided in Appendix C.1. Furthermore, LLMs were employed as judges, including GPT-4o-2024-08-06 (GPT4o), LLaMA, and Ministral. Comprehensive results are discussed in the next section.

4 Results

RQ1: Table 2 shows that the Mean Squared Errors (MSE) for both Human-LLaMA interactions (0.155 for humans, 0.086 for GPT4o, 0.121 for LLaMA, and 0.128 for Ministral) and LLaMA-LLaMA chats (0.162, 0.084, 0.120, and 0.130, respectively) are relatively low. This indicates that both humans and LLMs $\tilde{\mathcal{V}}_p$ estimated from conversations were close to the actual $\mathcal{V}_p$. Figures 2 and 3 further support this, illustrat-

Evaluator	Human-LLaMA	LLaMA-LLaMA (L2L)	LLaMA-to-Others	% increase vs L2L
Human	0.155	0.162	/	
GPT4o	**0.086**	**0.084**	0.212	152%
LLaMA	0.121	0.120	0.223	86%
Ministral	0.128	0.130	**0.208**	60%

Table 2: MSE of Personality Traits Estimated by Human and LLM Judges compared to the Assigned Vectors. Red indicates % increase in MSE and **bold** the best.

ing clusters for personality polarities. In both Human-LLaMA and LLaMA-LLaMA chats, clusters corresponding to *bad* (left), *moderate* (middle), and *good* (right) polarities are visible. A smooth progression from very *bad* to *moderate* to very *good*, demonstrates the effective differentiation of personalities by the annotators.

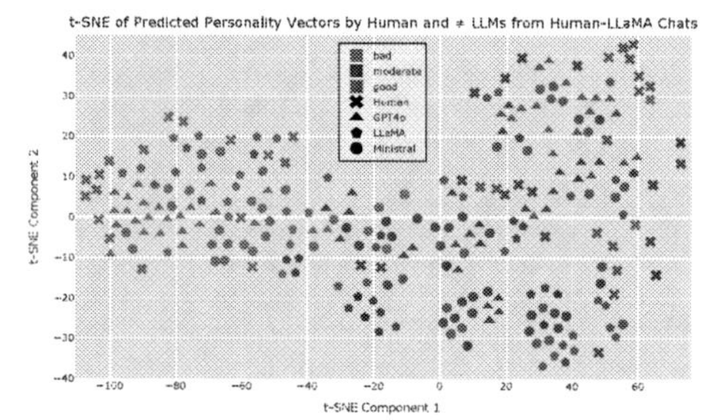

Figure 2: t-SNE of Predicted Personality Vectors by Human and LLM Judges from Human-bot chats.

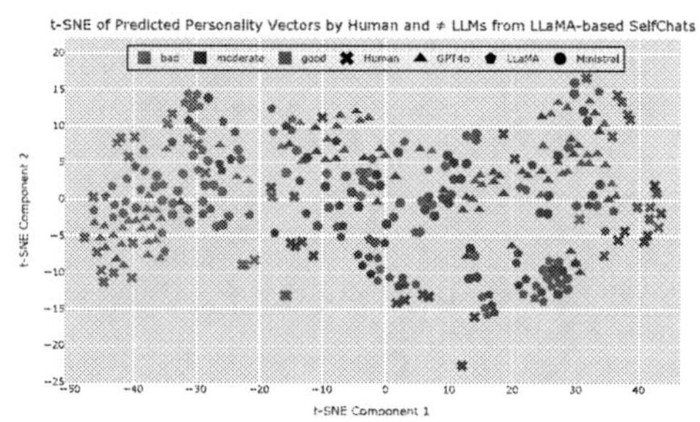

Figure 3: t-SNE of Predicted Personality Vectors by Human and LLM Judges from LLaMA-LLaMA chats.

RQ2: The correlations between $\tilde{\mathcal{V}}_p$ dimensions and interaction quality criteria (UX, efficiency, and naturalness) were analyzed alongside their average scores. Table 3 shows strong and highly significant correlations for all the setups. Agreeableness

[2] For research purposes all collected data can be requested for by an e-mail to the first author.

Setup	Criteria	O	C	E	A	N
Human-LLaMA	UX	0.789	0.487	0.765	0.857	-0.748
	Efficiency	0.706	0.606	0.623	0.754	0.637
	Naturalness	0.649	0.279	0.676	0.682	-0.589
LLaMA-LLaMA	UX	0.822	0.515	0.692	0.845	-0.730
	Efficiency	0.706	0.575	0.614	0.725	-0.602
	Naturalness	0.748	0.481	0.662	0.764	-0.615
LLaMA-Others	UX	0.710	0.441	0.666	0.746	-0.394
	Efficiency	0.612	0.516	0.510	0.642	-0.375
	Naturalness	0.728	0.381	0.724	0.756	-0.330

Table 3: Pearson Correlation between the Predicted Vectors Dimensions and User Experience Quality Criteria. **All** are strongly **significant** with $p <<< 10^{-3}$.

Type	Customer	Agent	Evaluator	Polartity	Interaction Quality		
					UX	Efficiency	Naturalness
Human-Bot	Human	LLaMA	Human	*bad*	2.35	3.11	3.65
				good	**4.64**	4.32	4.36
				moderate	4.52	**4.44**	**4.37**
			GPT4o	*bad*	1.81	2.15	2.35
				good	**4.52**	4.04	**4.64**
				moderate	4.41	**4.19**	4.41
			LLaMA	*bad*	1.69	2.23	1.65
				good	**4.04**	**4.04**	**3.60**
				moderate	3.96	3.96	3.56
			Ministral	*bad*	2.19	2.69	2.46
				good	**4.40**	3.80	**4.36**
				moderate	4.07	**4.00**	4.07
Bot-Bot	LLaMA	LLaMA	Human	*bad*	2.24	2.93	3.69
				good	4.30	4.30	3.93
				moderate	**4.38**	**4.54**	**4.29**
			GPT4o	*bad*	2.05	2.45	2.27
				good	**4.50**	**4.10**	**4.62**
				moderate	4.29	4.05	4.45
			LLaMA	*bad*	1.61	2.35	1.61
				good	**3.95**	**4.05**	**3.73**
				moderate	3.53	3.67	3.43
			Ministral	*bad*	2.40	2.82	2.57
				good	**4.29**	**3.92**	**4.39**
				moderate	3.97	3.77	4.00

Table 4: Evaluation of Interaction Quality for Human-LLaMA and LLaMA-LLaMA chats by Human and LLMs

(A) and extraversion (E) correlated positively with UX and naturalness ($r > 0.7$), while neuroticism (N) correlated negatively ($r < -0.7$). Efficiency was positively associated with conscientiousness (C) and agreeableness (A), indicating that structured and amiable agents were perceived as more efficient. The evaluations of the quality of the interaction (Table 4) further confirm these results. Across human-bot and bot-bot chats, *good* polarity consistently achieved the highest (in **bold**) scores (e.g., 4.64 for UX in human-bot chats evaluated by humans), followed by *moderate* polarity whereas *bad* received remarkable low ratings (red cells).

RQ3: Observations are based on LLM judgments in LLaMA-as-customer to other LLMs as agent chats. As shown in Table 3, $\tilde{\mathcal{V}}_p$ coordinates remain strongly correlated with quality criteria, following the same trend as RQ2 findings. However, unlike in RQ1, the $\tilde{\mathcal{V}}_p$ projections in Figure 4 exhibit a more randomized distribution. This lack of clustering aligns with the higher MSE values reported in the last columns of Table 2 (e.g., 0.212 for GPT4o and 0.223 for LLaMA, +152% and +86% compared to LLaMA-LLaMA chats). The ratings in Table 5 further reveal that all polarities seem to converge toward a *moderate* polarity, which tends to be preferred in these setups. These findings suggest a diminished alignment between $\tilde{\mathcal{V}}_p$ and $\mathcal{V}_p$, reflecting greater variability in personality perception in chats performed by LLMs from different families.

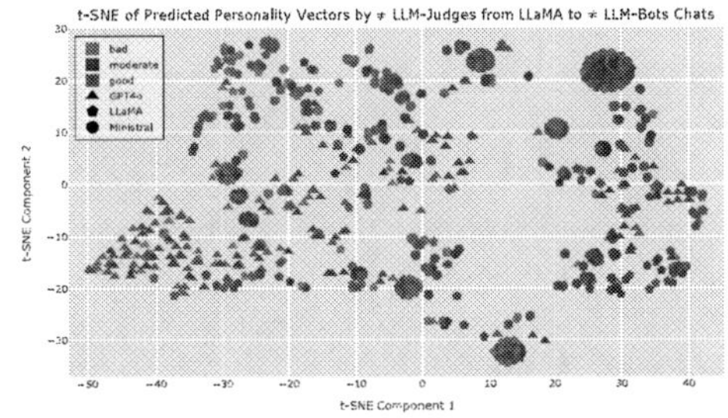

Figure 4: t-SNE of Predicted Personality Vectors by different LLMs Judges for chats between LLaMA-as-customer and other LLMs-as-assistants

Type	Customer	Agent	Evaluator	Polartity	Interaction Quality		
					UX	Efficiency	Naturalness
Bot-Bot	LLaMA	Ministral	GPT4o	*bad*	2.70	2.55	2.82
				good	**3.09**	2.94	**3.24**
				moderate	**3.21**	**3.12**	3.15
			LLaMA	*bad*	2.77	3.06	2.55
				good	2.88	3.12	2.62
				moderate	**3.64**	**3.76**	**3.24**
			Ministral	*bad*	3.52	3.18	3.79
				good	3.62	3.32	3.79
				moderate	**3.85**	**3.45**	**3.88**
		Mistral	GPT4o	*bad*	3.48	3.18	3.61
				good	3.70	3.21	3.76
				moderate	**3.74**	**3.38**	**3.88**
			LLaMA	*bad*	3.00	3.16	2.90
				good	**3.59**	3.50	**3.41**
				moderate	3.52	**3.55**	3.39
			Ministral	*bad*	3.58	3.15	3.76
				good	**3.94**	3.52	**4.15**
				moderate	3.88	**3.62**	4.00
		Gemma	GPT4o	*bad*	2.70	2.55	2.82
				good	2.60	2.71	2.63
				moderate	**3.15**	**3.15**	**3.15**
			LLaMA	*bad*	2.74	2.90	2.48
				good	2.29	2.71	2.17
				moderate	**3.52**	**3.79**	**3.18**
			Ministral	*bad*	2.94	2.97	3.06
				good	2.86	2.89	3.09
				moderate	**3.50**	**3.38**	**3.59**

Table 5: Evaluation of Interaction Quality for chats between LLaMA-as-customer and other LLMs-as-assistants by different LLMs Judges. In **bold** are the best scores.

5 Conclusion

This study proposed a five-dimensional vector to represent personality traits, which was incorporated into an LLM through ICL. Both humans and LLMs were able to distinguish personality polarities effectively, with low MSEs and observable clusters. The $\tilde{\mathcal{V}}_p$ strongly correlated with quality criteria, showing that personality influenced user experience and agent efficiency.

Limitations

The main limitation in our view is the lack of generalization when applied to different LLMs. This suggests that the vector-to-prompt approach to integrate $\mathcal{V}_p$ should be improved and other methods explored to ensure greater robustness and consistency with diverse model families.

Furthermore, to be able to collect and annotate data from humans, it is challenging to multiply the assessed personalities. As a result, this study is limited to three personality polarities (good, bad, and moderate) for the experiments. Hence, future research could explore a more granular assessment to better reflect the complexity of personality traits.

Acknowledgments

This work was supported by the μDialBot project funded by the French National Research Agency (*Agence Nationale de Recherche, ANR*) under the grant `ANR-20-CE33-0008-01` and benefited from computational resources provided by the Jean Zay supercomputer under the dossier `AD011013966R2`. We also extend our gratitude the evaluators who volunteered for data collection and evaluation.

References

AI@Meta. 2024. Llama 3 model card.

Cheng-Han Chiang and Hung-yi Lee. 2023. Can large language models be an alternative to human evaluations? In *Proceedings of the 61st Annual Meeting of the Association for Computational Linguistics (Volume 1: Long Papers)*, pages 15607–15631, Toronto, Canada. Association for Computational Linguistics.

Lewis R. Goldberg. 1993. The structure of phenotypic personality traits. *American Psychologist*, 48(1):26–34.

Neslihan Iskender, Tim Polzehl, and Sebastian Möller. 2021. Reliability of human evaluation for text summarization: Lessons learned and challenges ahead. In *Proceedings of the Workshop on Human Evaluation of NLP Systems (HumEval)*, pages 86–96, Online. Association for Computational Linguistics.

Albert Q. Jiang, Alexandre Sablayrolles, Arthur Mensch, Chris Bamford, Devendra Singh Chaplot, Diego de las Casas, Florian Bressand, Gianna Lengyel, Guillaume Lample, Lucile Saulnier, Lélio Renard Lavaud, Marie-Anne Lachaux, Pierre Stock, Teven Le Scao, Thibaut Lavril, Thomas Wang, Timothée Lacroix, and William El Sayed. 2023. Mistral 7b. *Preprint*, arXiv:2310.06825.

Hang Jiang, Xiajie Zhang, Xubo Cao, Cynthia Breazeal, Deb Roy, and Jad Kabbara. 2024. PersonaLLM: Investigating the ability of large language models to express personality traits. In *Findings of the Association for Computational Linguistics: NAACL 2024*, pages 3605–3627, Mexico City, Mexico. Association for Computational Linguistics.

Shengyu Mao, Xiaohan Wang, Mengru Wang, Yong Jiang, Pengjun Xie, Fei Huang, and Ningyu Zhang. 2024. Editing personality for large language models. *Preprint*, arXiv:2310.02168.

Robert R. McCrae and Oliver P. John. 1992. An introduction to the five-factor model and its applications. *Journal of Personality*, 60(2):175–215.

Team MistralAI, Albert Jiang, Alexandre Abou Chahine, Alexandre Sablayrolles, Alexis Tacnet, Alodie Boissonnet, Alok Kothari, Amélie Héliou, Andy Lo, Anna Peronnin, Antoine Meunier, Antoine Roux, Antonin Faure, Aritra Paul, Arthur Darcet, Arthur Mensch, Audrey Herblin-Stoop, Augustin Garreau, Austin Birky, Avinash Sooriyarachchi, Baptiste Rozière, Barry Conklin, Bastien Bouillon, Blanche Savary de Beauregard, Carole Rambaud, Caroline Feldman, Charles de Freminville, Charline Mauro, Chih-Kuan Yeh, Chris Bamford, Clement Auguy, Corentin Heintz, Cyriaque Dubois, Devendra Singh Chaplot, Diego Las Casas, Diogo Costa, Eléonore Arcelin, Emma Bou Hanna, Etienne Metzger, Fanny Olivier Autran, Francois Lesage, Garance Gourdel, Gaspard Blanchet, Gaspard Donada Vidal, Gianna Maria Lengyel, Guillaume Bour, Guillaume Lample, Gustave Denis, Harizo Rajaona, Himanshu Jaju, Ian Mack, Ian Mathew, Jean-Malo Delignon, Jeremy Facchetti, Jessica Chudnovsky, Joachim Studnia, Justus Murke, Kartik Khandelwal, Kenneth Chiu, Kevin Riera, Leonard Blier, Leonard Suslian, Leonardo Deschaseaux, Louis Martin, Louis Ternon, Lucile Saulnier, Lélio Renard Lavaud, Sophia Yang, Margaret Jennings, Marie Pellat, Marie Torelli, Marjorie Janiewicz, Mathis Felardos, Maxime Darrin, Michael Hoff, Mickaël Seznec, Misha Jessel Kenyon, Nayef Derwiche, Nicolas Carmont Zaragoza, Nicolas Faurie, Nicolas Moreau, Nicolas Schuhl, Nikhil Raghuraman, Niklas Muhs, Olivier de Garrigues, Patricia Rozé, Patricia Wang, Patrick von Platen, Paul Jacob, Pauline Buche, Pavankumar Reddy Muddireddy, Perry Savas, Pierre Stock, Pravesh Agrawal, Renaud de Peretti, Romain Sauvestre, Romain Sinthe, Roman Soletskyi, Sagar Vaze, Sandeep Subramanian, Saurabh Garg, Soham Ghosh, Sylvain Regnier, Szymon Antoniak, Teven Le Scao, Theophile Gervin, Thibault Schueller, Thibault Lavril, Thomas Wang, Timothée Lacroix, Valeriia Nemychnikova, Wendy Shang, William El Sayed, and William Marshall. 2024. Un ministral, des ministraux.

Van Bach Nguyen, Jan Trienes, Meike Nauta, Shreyasi Pathak, Paul Youssef, Sultan Imangaliyev, Jörg Schlötterer, and Christin Seifert. 2022. Pplm revisited: Steering and beaming a lumbering mammoth to control text generation. In *ICLR Blog Track*. Https://iclr-blog-track.github.io/2022/03/25/PPLM/.

Alec Radford, Jong Wook Kim, Tao Xu, Greg Brockman, Christine McLeavey, and Ilya Sutskever. 2022. Robust speech recognition via large-scale weak supervision. *Preprint*, arXiv:2212.04356.

Julius Sim and Chris C Wright. 2005. The kappa statistic in reliability studies: Use, interpretation, and sample size requirements. *Physical Therapy*, 85(3):257–268.

Richard Sutcliffe. 2023. A survey of personality, persona, and profile in conversational agents and chatbots. *Preprint*, arXiv:2401.00609.

Gemma Team, Thomas Mesnard, Cassidy Hardin, Robert Dadashi, Surya Bhupatiraju, Shreya Pathak, Laurent Sifre, Morgane Rivière, Mihir Sanjay Kale, Juliette Love, Pouya Tafti, Léonard Hussenot, Pier Giuseppe Sessa, Aakanksha Chowdhery, Adam Roberts, Aditya Barua, Alex Botev, Alex Castro-Ros, Ambrose Slone, Amélie Héliou, Andrea Tacchetti, Anna Bulanova, Antonia Paterson, Beth Tsai, Bobak Shahriari, Charline Le Lan, Christopher A. Choquette-Choo, Clément Crepy, Daniel Cer, Daphne Ippolito, David Reid, Elena Buchatskaya, Eric Ni, Eric Noland, Geng Yan, George Tucker, George-Christian Muraru, Grigory Rozhdestvenskiy, Henryk Michalewski, Ian Tenney, Ivan Grishchenko, Jacob Austin, James Keeling, Jane Labanowski, Jean-Baptiste Lespiau, Jeff Stanway, Jenny Brennan, Jeremy Chen, Johan Ferret, Justin Chiu, Justin Mao-Jones, Katherine Lee, Kathy Yu, Katie Millican, Lars Lowe Sjoesund, Lisa Lee, Lucas Dixon, Machel Reid, Maciej Mikuła, Mateo Wirth, Michael Sharman, Nikolai Chinaev, Nithum Thain, Olivier Bachem, Oscar Chang, Oscar Wahltinez, Paige Bailey, Paul Michel, Petko Yotov, Rahma Chaabouni, Ramona Comanescu, Reena Jana, Rohan Anil, Ross McIlroy, Ruibo Liu, Ryan Mullins, Samuel L Smith, Sebastian Borgeaud, Sertan Girgin, Sholto Douglas, Shree Pandya, Siamak Shakeri, Soham De, Ted Klimenko, Tom Hennigan, Vlad Feinberg, Wojciech Stokowiec, Yu hui Chen, Zafarali Ahmed, Zhitao Gong, Tris Warkentin, Ludovic Peran, Minh Giang, Clément Farabet, Oriol Vinyals, Jeff Dean, Koray Kavukcuoglu, Demis Hassabis, Zoubin Ghahramani, Douglas Eck, Joelle Barral, Fernando Pereira, Eli Collins, Armand Joulin, Noah Fiedel, Evan Senter, Alek Andreev, and Kathleen Kenealy. 2024. Gemma: Open models based on gemini research and technology. *Preprint*, arXiv:2403.08295.

Ce Zheng, Lei Li, Qingxiu Dong, Yuxuan Fan, Zhiyong Wu, Jingjing Xu, and Baobao Chang. 2023. Can we edit factual knowledge by in-context learning? In *Proceedings of the 2023 Conference on Empirical Methods in Natural Language Processing*, pages 4862–4876, Singapore. Association for Computational Linguistics.

A Prompts Templates

A.1 Personality Vector Formatting Template

```
# Concatenate all trait with the following template:
{axis} is {level} ({exact_value}): {level_based_des-
criptive_sentence}
```

Here, {axis} is replace by an OCEAN trait; {level} correspond to the level associated to the {level_based_descriptive_sentence} provided in Appendix B and {exact_value} is the actual value (from 0 to 1) associated to that dimension.

A.2 Customer Service Agent Prompt

```
# i_0
You are a customer service agent of the {language}
telecommunications company {company_name}. Hence you
always interact in {language}. DO NOT display any
other language. You are having a phone conversation
with a customer who have one or more questions about
some of your company products: this can be an issue,
or looking for an offer etc. Do not guess which one
rather always try to  know what is the purpose of
their call. Again, DO NOT invent the customer's pro-
blem, you can make suggestions instead. Also DO NOT
invent any company products that do not exist.

What is important is that you don't act as a conven-
tional customer service agent but rather you inter-
act with the customer in a way to mark your persona-
lity which is defined following the Big 5 OCEAN axis
:Openness, Conscientiousness, Extraversion, Agreeab-
leness, Neuroticism by a value between 0 and 1 that
represent how much each axes is marked in your
personality. 1 is very high and 0 is very low. You
should act accordingly:

# f_{vect->txt} (V_p)
{formatted_personality_vector}

Remember, you should always stay in this configura-
tion throughout the whole conversation. Always act
according to these specifications. Do not invent any
issue in the place of the user! Let the user give it
to you! You SHALL ALWAYS respond in {language}.

# C_{desc}
This is how you gave your name in your {company_name
} enrolling information form: "{assistant_name}"

These are information you gave on your {company_name
} enrolling information form that you may want to
share with your customer if adapted to the conversat
ion context AND TO YOUR PERSONALITY DESCRIBED ABOVE:

{assistant_persona_information}

Remember, always stay coherent to your personality
described above carefully. This implies you may be
more or less open to share any of these information.

# i_{gen}
Complete the following conversation with a short sen
tence as the customer service agent from {company_na
me} described above would. Your tone, temper, speak-
ing style and words choice should always be coherent
to your personality described above. Speak with new
and unique messages that haven't been said in the
conversation:

# x_0, y_0, x_1, ..., y_{t_1}, x_t
<formatted_chat_with_model_template>
```

In this setup, {language} is replaced by the desired target language (here French, though it can be adapted for any language depending on whether a multilingual or language-specific LLM is used); {company_name} is substituted with the name of a French telecommunications company; {formatted_personality_vector} corresponds to the personality vector formatted as described in Section 2; {assistant_persona_information} is replaced with a list of descriptive sentences outlining the assistant's character (e.g., "I love basketball," or "I went to the University of Bilbao") sampled from a pre-generated set, from which {assistant_name} is derived; and {formatted_chat_with_model_template} represents the dialogue history.

A.3 Simulated Customer Prompt

```
# i_0
You are a fictional character from {country} who is
fluent in {language}. You are calling the customer
service of a {language} telecom provider ({c_names})
for the following concern: "{topic}". The agent you
are conversing with have his or her own simulated
personality that is expressed throughout the conver-
sation. You can ask agents about more personal as-
pects of their lives, or ask questions outside the
scope of the specific concern you're contacting them
about. You are very {mood}.

# C_{desc}
About your name you said: "{assistant_name}"

# i_{gen}
Complete the following conversation with a SHORT res
ponse as the {mood} customer described above would
with a coherent temper. Your response should be in
{language}. Regardless of the users' messages size,
your responses SHOULD ALWAYS stay within FIFTEEN(15)
words:

# x_0, y_0, x_1, ..., y_{t_1}, x_t
<formatted_chat_with_model_template>
```

Again, {language} represents the desired language, in this case French, along with the associated {country}; {c_names} are examples of relevant company names (e.g., *Orange, AT&T, Bouygues, Movistar*) for the specified country and language; {topic} denotes the purpose of the call (e.g., *"Issue with the TV box", "Activating a new mobile line"*), and {mood} specifies the mood of the simulated customer (e.g., *"exasperated", "doubtful"*), both sampled from pre-generated sets.

A.4 LLM as a Judge

A.4.1 Evaluation Prompt

```
### Input: Conversations
(id: <conversation1_id>)
Customer: <message1>
Assistant: <message2>
Customer: <message3>
Assistant: <message4>
...

(id: <conversation2_id>)
...

### Evaluation:
# Assistant Personality assessment:
You will assess the Big Five Personality traits of
the current customer assistant on a 0 to 1 continu-
ous scale. 0 corresponding to "not present at all"
and 1 being "strongly marked".

"openness": is characterized by originality, curio-
sity, and ingenuity
"conscientiousness":is characterized by orderliness,
responsibility, and dependability
"extraversion": is characterized by talkativeness,
assertiveness, and energy
"agreeableness": is characterized by good-natured-
ness, cooperativeness, and trust
"neuroticism": is characterized by upsetability, an-
xiety, tendency to feel stressed, the polar opposite
of emotional stability
"comment": a short explanation on your ratings

# User Experience Evaluation: Assess from 1 (worst)
to 5 (best) the overall user experience and the qua-
lity of the customer service.

"efficiency": The assistant's personality seems EFFI
CIENT in solving the task
1: Strongly disagree
2: Disagree
3: Neutral
4: Agree
5: Strongly agree

"naturalness": The the assistant interacts as a hu-
man would: naturally and coherently
1: Strongly disagree
2: Disagree
3: Neutral
4: Agree
5: Strongly agree

"ux": Not considering the efficiency to solve the
task, the assistant's personality also contributes
to a good user experience in the context of tele-
phone assistance.
1: Strongly disagree
2: Disagree
3: Neutral
4: Agree
5: Strongly agree

"comment": Based on the dialogue, can you explain
your previous judgments in a few words? Examples of
sentences: "I had a little trouble determining the
level of efficiency of assistant's personality
because the exchanges quickly became general.",
"The assistant was very insistent on their procedu-
res and didn't want to branch off.","I appreciated
the fact that the assistant gave personal informa-
tion about them.".

### Output: Return your evaluations in a dictionary
with each conversation id as key and two dictiona-
ries for your "assistant_personality", "user_experi
ence" evaluations:
```

A.4.2 System Prompt

{language} is replaced by the desired language, in this case FRENCH.

```
You are a smart evaluator, native {language} speaker
, tasked to evaluate the quality of {language} conv-
ersations between users and customer service assist-
ants with a given personality. You use consistent
formatting in your responses. You carefully read the
criteria before giving your assessments. Ensure you
carefully pay attention to all details before making
your rating decisions based on the conversation's
content, specifically assistant messages.
```

B OCEAN Axis Descriptive Sentences

```
{
 "openness":
 {
  "low": "Rigid and resistant to new procedures or feedback, sticking
  strictly to the script without adapting to the customer's unique needs",

  "moderate": "Open-minded and curious, this agent is able to think
   creatively when solving unique customer issues.",
```

```
  "high": "Creative and eager to try new solutions, but often without
    a structured approach, leading to inconsistent outcomes"
  },
  "conscientiousness":
  {
  "low": "Disorganized and unreliable, often missing details or
    failing to follow through on customer issues.",

  "moderate": "While they follow rules and procedures carefully,
  their lack of flexibility and emotional connection makes for a
    poor customer experience",

  "high": "Organized, reliable, and detail-oriented, ensuring that
    every issue is addressed thoroughly and promptly."
  },
  "extraversion":
  {
  "low": "Quiet, withdrawn, and struggles to engage with customers.
  This agent prefers working alone and may not show enthusiasm in
    conversations",

  "moderate": "Sociable and able to communicate well with customers
  but still able to focus on individual tasks without getting dis-
    tracted.",

  "high": "Talkative and sociable, but often spends too much time
  chatting without solving the customer's problem efficiently."
  },
  "agreeableness":
  {
   "low": "Indifferent to customers' feelings, coming across as
    cold or dismissive",

  "moderate": "Generally cooperative and friendly, but can become
  flustered when faced with challenging or demanding customers.",

   "high": "Friendly, compassionate, and deeply empathetic. This
  agent naturally connects with customers and shows genuine care"
  },
  "neuroticism":
  {
   "low": "Calm under pressure, even when dealing with difficult
   customers, and doesn't let stress affect their performance.",

   "moderate": "Easily frustrated by difficult customers or when
     things don't go according to plan, but generally keeps emo-
     tions in check",

    "high": "Prone to stress and anxiety, especially in high-
   pressure situations. This agent may react emotionally to dif-
     ficult customers and struggle to maintain composure"
  }
}
```

C Evaluation Details

C.1 Human Evaluation

For Human-LLaMA Data Collection, a total of **9** voluntary testers participated, including **5** computer science researchers and **4** family members to better simulate telephone assistance scenarios. The group comprised **4 females** and **5 males**, aged **20 to 50+ years**, with education levels ranging from **undergraduate to full professor**. Each tester conducted and evaluated at least 9 conversations to ensure exposure to all three polarities at least three times and was tasked to simulate different situation and persona in each conversation that should last around 10 exchanges at least.

Figure 5 displays the chat interface, human could either input text or record the message which is transcribed with Whisper (Radford et al., 2022) then fed to the LLM agent. Speech is synthesized from the LLM output using Google API. No further attention were given to these ASR and TTS modules even though prosodic elements could enhance experience. However, this was not the purpose of this study and is another area of development.

As shown in Figure 6, evaluators could specify if they were unable to assess one or more OCEAN dimensions. Of the **78** conversations collected, **60** were retained for analysis. Similarly, for LLaMA-LLaMA chats evaluated by humans, **67** of **84** conversations were included. The detailed counts of unassessed traits in Table 6 reveal that openness was the most challenging dimension to evaluate, likely due to the customer assistance context. Neuroticism was the second most unassessed trait, possibly reflecting the absence of neurotic behavior, leading testers to judge it as not evaluable.

Setup	Polarity	O	C	E	A	N
Human-LLaMA	*bad*	5	1	0	0	2
	good	2	1	0	0	3
	moderate	7	1	0	0	1
LLaMA-LLaMA	*bad*	2	0	1	0	2
	good	2	0	1	0	7
	moderate	5	0	0	0	0

Table 6: Number of Conversations with Personality Traits deemed Non-rateable by Human Evaluators

C.2 Inter Annotator Agreement (IAA)

We report the Fleiss-κ measuring the IAA when there is more than two annotators; in this case human and all LLM Judges, each considered as a unique annotator. To compute IAA on $\tilde{\mathcal{V}}_p$ we transformed each coordinate into an integer $\in [0, 5]$ by splitting the $[0, 1]$ interval into five sub-intervals of same size.

Setup	#chats	O	C	E	A	N	Quality Criteria UX	Eff.	Nat.
Human-LLaMA	60	0.227	-0.013	0.111	0.189	0.224	0.270	0.234	0.145
LLaMA-LLaMA	65	0.270	0.098	0.108	0.248	0.249	0.355	0.352	0.222
LLaMA-Others	97	0.150	0.029	0.023	0.088	0.018	0.254	0.333	0.126

Table 7: Fleiss-κ as a measure of agreement among the 4 annotators (3 for the LLaMA-Others setup).

Table 7 reports Fleiss-κ values measuring inter-annotator agreement across different setups. While agreement is moderate for some dimensions, such as openness (O) and neuroticism (N) in the Human-LLaMA and LLaMA-LLaMA setups, it is notably lower for conscientiousness (C) and extraversion (E), particularly in the LLaMA-Others setup. Quality criteria such as UX exhibit comparatively higher agreement, especially in the LLaMA-LLaMA configuration (e.g., $\text{UX}_\kappa = 0.355$).

It is important to note that κ values are inherently sensitive to the number of categories being evaluated—here, ratings from 1 to 5—which tends to lower agreement. This limitation is well-documented (Sim and Wright, 2005) and reflects challenges in achieving high IAA even among human experts (Chiang and Lee (2023), Iskender et al. (2021)). These challenges are amplified in comparisons between LLMs or between LLMs and humans, explaining the observed variability and relatively low agreement.

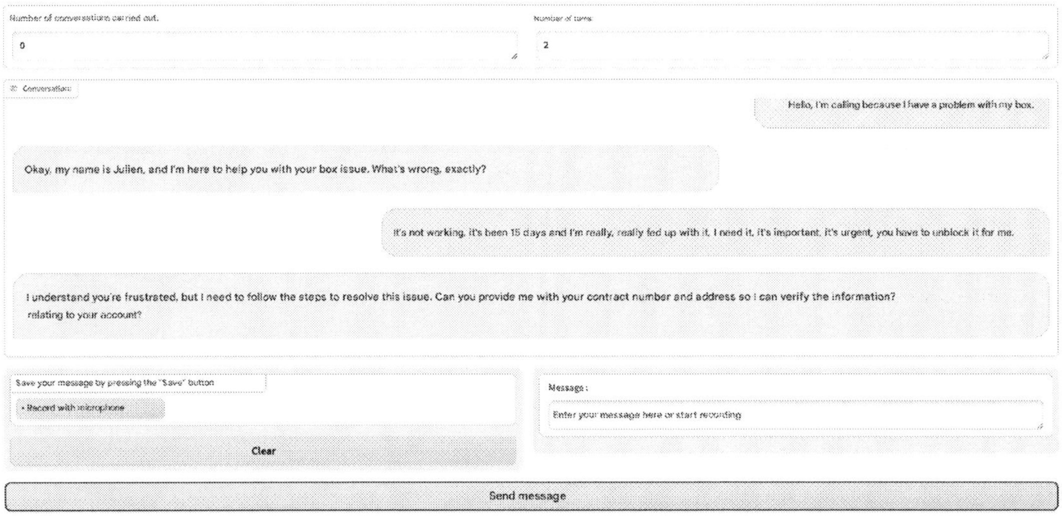

Figure 5: Human-Bot Chat Interface

Figure 6: Human Evaluation Interface

Developing Classifiers for Affirmative and Negative User Responses with Limited Target Domain Data for Dialogue System Development Tools

Yunosuke Kubo[1], **Ryo Yanagimoto**[1], **Mikio Nakano**[1,2],
Kenta Yamamoto[1], **Ryu Takeda**[1], **Kazunori Komatani**[1]
[1]SANKEN, Osaka University, [2]C4A Research Institute, Inc.
Correspondence: komatani@sanken.osaka-u.ac.jp

Abstract

We aim to develop a library for classifying affirmative and negative user responses, intended for integration into a dialogue system development toolkit. Such a library is expected to highly perform even with minimal annotated target domain data, addressing the practical challenge of preparing large datasets for each target domain. This short paper compares several approaches under conditions where little or no annotated data is available in the target domain. One approach involves fine-tuning a pre-trained BERT model, while the other utilizes a GPT API for zero-shot or few-shot learning. Since these approaches differ in execution speed, development effort, and execution costs, in addition to performance, the results serve as a basis for discussing an appropriate configuration suited to specific requirements. Additionally, we have released the training data and the fine-tuned BERT model for Japanese affirmative/negative classification.

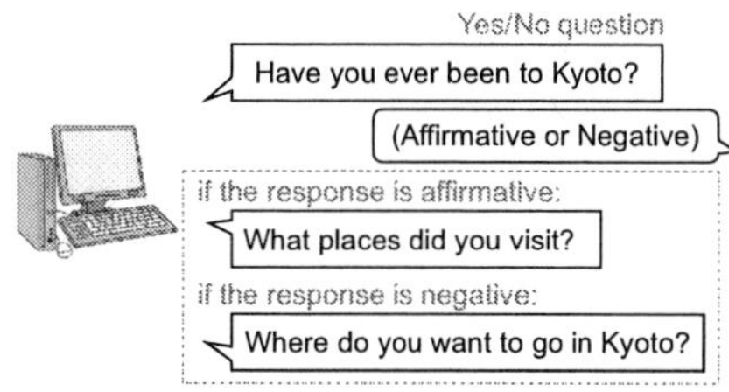

Figure 1: Example of dialogue flow changing on the basis of affirmative/negative classification.

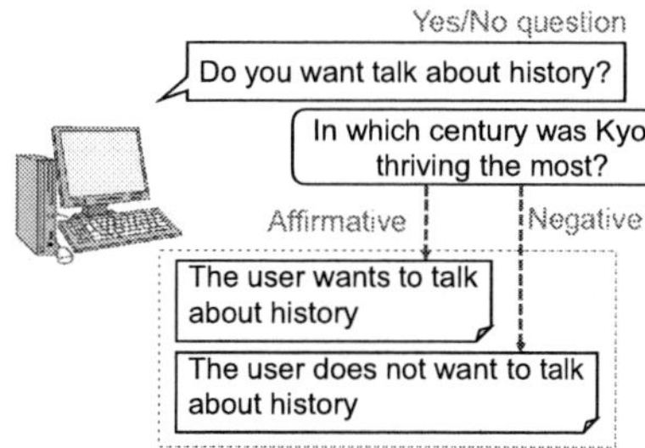

Figure 2: Example of acquiring user preferences on the basis of affirmative/negative classification.

1 Introduction

In dialogue systems, classifying whether a user's response to a system's question is affirmative or negative is a crucial and fundamental task. One reason for this is that the dialogue flow needs to be switched on the basis of the classification result (Figure 1). Although conducting dialogues using large language models (LLMs) has recently become possible, current systems may still struggle with progressing dialogues as intended by the system developers. The classification is also essential for deciding whether the system should retain the information, such as user preferences or factual knowledge, included in the system's question (Figure 2).

Users do not always respond to yes/no questions with simple expressions such as 'Yes' or 'That's right.' These types of responses are known as indirect answers (Louis et al., 2020). Furthermore, the user utterance shown in Figure 2, for example, is generally a question, but in a specific domain, it should be regarded as affirmative because it demonstrates interest in the topic. Such domain-specific classification also needs to be considered. Therefore, simple rule-based classification has its limitations, and utilizing machine learning, including LLMs, is a promising approach.

However, machine learning-based methods require training data. Collecting sufficient dialogue data and annotating it with correct labels is not practical for dialogue system developers who combine ready-for-use modules in toolkits. They prefer to minimize costs while still achieving a high-performance classifier.

We present experimental results on developing the affirmative/negative classifier when little or no annotated data is available in the target domain.

Proceedings of the 15th International Workshop on Spoken Dialogue Systems Technology, pages 309–317
May 27–30, 2025.

The goal of this work is not to pursue higher performance but to discuss which configuration would be most appropriate for use in dialogue system development toolkits. We assume a situation where only a few dozen examples can be prepared by developers and used as target domain data. Several methods can be employed: fine-tuning a pre-trained BERT model (Devlin et al., 2019) with data from a different domain and the small amount of target domain data, and using a GPT API with few-shot learning by providing the target domain data as few-shot samples. Pre-trained models have become useful for several tasks, such as in extracting entity-value pairs for state tracking (Hudeček and Dusek, 2023; Bang et al., 2023).

In our experiments, we used dialogue data collected from real users during the finals of the Dialogue Robot Competition 2023 (Minato et al., 2024) as the test set. We incrementally added target domain data for fine-tuning or as few-shot samples and evaluated the classification performance. On the basis of the results, we discuss an appropriate configuration of the classifier, considering not only performance but also execution speed, development effort, and execution cost.

The contributions of this paper are as follows.

- We present experimental results to help determine appropriate configurations of an affirmative/negative classifier for dialogue system development toolkits.
- We have released the training data[1] and the general model for Japanese affirmative/negative classification[2].

2 Related Work

Several methods have been developed for classifying whether user responses are affirmative or negative. Asao et al. (2020) implemented a classifier using BERT, and Watanabe et al. (2023) developed the models using BERT and GPT. Such studies assumed large amounts of annotated data in the target domain. Several corpora containing indirect answers have also been collected and made publicly available (Louis et al., 2020; Damgaard et al., 2021; Sanagavarapu et al., 2022; Müller and Plank, 2024). In contrast, our goal is to provide an easily accessible classifier that can be integrated into dialogue system development toolkits, such as Rasa Open Source (Bocklisch et al., 2017) and DialBB (Nakano and Komatani, 2024). This paper shares the results of approaches that aimed at reducing the required effort by eliminating the need to collect and annotate large datasets.

Classifying whether an utterance is affirmative or negative can be considered a part of dialogue act classification (Stolcke et al., 2000), which has been addressed in various studies (Khanpour et al., 2016; Ahmadvand et al., 2019; Raheja and Tetreault, 2019). However, there are cases where an affirmative/negative classification cannot be made solely on the basis of the dialogue act. Often, there are expressions specific to the target domain, as shown in the example in Figure 2, and to situations where the preceding system utterance is a Yes/No question.

Phenomena such as indirect answers (Louis et al., 2020) have been theoretically examined from a linguistic perspective. Ginzburg et al. (2022) provided a taxonomy of responses to questions, while Enfield et al. (2018) analyzed responses to polar questions across 14 languages. Studies on dialogue management have also considered such responses (Larsson, 2002).

3 Experiment

Several methods were compared with minimal or no use of target domain data. The less annotated data required, the lower the cost for developers to build dialogue systems.

3.1 Task Formulation

Affirmative/negative classification is defined as follows: the input consists of a single exchange, specifically a pair comprising a Yes/No question from the system and the subsequent user response. The output is a three-class label: affirmative, negative, or other. The instructions for annotation, including details of the 'other' class, can be found in Appendix A.

3.2 Compared Methods

Five methods were considered:

(B0) Fine-tuning a BERT model with a large amount of data from a different domain.

(B1) Fine-tuning a BERT model with a small amount of target domain data.

[1]https://huggingface.co/datasets/ouktlab/Hazumi-AffNeg-Data

[2]https://huggingface.co/ouktlab/Hazumi-AffNeg-Classifier

(B2) Fine-tuning a BERT model with a large amount of data from a different domain and then further fine-tuning with a small amount of target domain data.

(L0) Using a GPT API with zero-shot learning.

(L1) Using a GPT API with few-shot learning.

The target domain data consist of exchanges (pairs of Yes/No questions and their responses) with annotated correct labels, similar to data from a different domain. (B0) and (L0) use no target domain data. For few-shot learning[3] in (L1), the target domain data are used in the prompts.

We chose BERT because publicly available pre-trained models are accessible. We also selected a GPT API for its generally high accuracy and ease of use but excluded fine-tuning of the GPT API due to its high costs. Performance comparison with other open-source LLMs will be left for future work.

3.3 Data

For the test data, we used dialogue data obtained from the finals of the dialogue robot competition (Minato et al., 2024). The domain is a tourist information task focused on Kyoto. These data were collected from 20 participants from the general public during the competition. From these conversations, we extracted 191 pairs of system Yes/No questions and the subsequent user responses. Consequently, 128 exchanges were labeled as affirmative, 56 as negative, and 7 as other.

For the target domain data, we used the dialogue data collected in our laboratory using a system (Yanagimoto et al., 2023) developed for the competition. Thus, the domain is the same as the test data. We extracted 131 pairs of the system's Yes/No questions and user responses. After two annotators labeled these pairs following the instructions in Appendix A, a high agreement rate of 0.977 was achieved. Therefore, one of the annotators labeled the remaining data, and the annotation results were considered the ground truth. The test data and those from a different domain were also annotated on the basis of the same criteria. The distribution of the 131 labels was 85 affirmative, 35 negative, and 3 other.

Note that, since we used speech recognition results as the user utterances in the target domain data, these may contain speech recognition errors and spelling mistakes. We did not manually correct these errors to better reflect real-world usage, as our goal is to develop a practical toolkit.

As data from a different domain, we used the Hazumi corpus (Komatani and Okada, 2021), which is a multimodal dialogue corpus recording chit-chat conversations between a human participant and a system. It initially includes 12 topics, but, in practice, centers around several topics such as food, games, and movies. Crucially, these topics differ from those in the target domain data and test data (tourist information in Kyoto). From the transcriptions (a total of 18,162 exchanges), we extracted 4,143 pairs of Yes/No questions and responses, labeled as follows: 2,864 affirmative, 1,017 negative, and 262 other.

3.4 Experimental Settings

As the BERT pre-trained model for (B0) to (B2), we used `tohoku-nlp/bert-base-japanese-v2`[4] and fine-tuned it using the JNLI script available at JGLUE[5](Kurihara et al., 2022) with the same parameters except for a batch size of 8 due to machine constraints.

In (B1) and (B2), the experiments were conducted using either a portion or all of the target domain data. Note that the topic of the target domain data is only tourist information in Kyoto. When using a portion, the partial data size varied from 10 up to 130, in increments of 10. The partial data were randomly selected from the target domain data, and this process was repeated five times. If the selected partial data did not contain all three-class labels, that subset was not used. We then calculated the average accuracy on the test data over the remaining subsets of each data size.

For (L0) and (L1), we used OpenAI's gpt-4o-2024-05-13[6]. We set the temperature parameter to 0.0 to obtain results as consistently as possible, and used the default values for the other parameters. An example prompt used in (L0) is shown in Appendix B. In (L1), similarly to in (B1) and (B2), experiments were conducted using either a portion or all of the target domain data. The partial data used were the same as in (B1) and (B2) and were incorporated into the prompt as few-shot examples. However, to reduce experimental costs,

[3]Since the amount of target domain data is relatively small, even when all of it is used, we refer to (L1) in this setting as few-shot learning.

[4]https://huggingface.co/tohoku-nlp/bert-base-japanese-v2

[5]https://github.com/yahoojapan/JGLUE

[6]https://openai.com/index/hello-gpt-4o/

Method	Accuracy
(B0)	0.817
(B1) with all target domain data	0.958
(B2) with all target domain data	0.942
(L0)	0.763
(L1) with all target domain data	0.949

Table 1: Accuracies with no target domain data and with all target domain data.

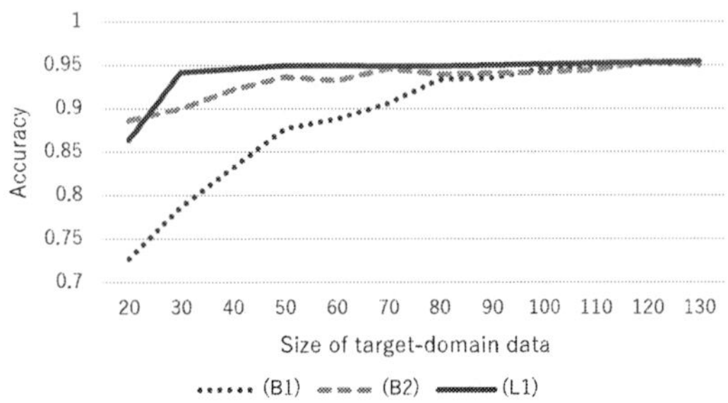

Figure 3: Accuracies when parts of target domain data were used in experimental settings (B1), (B2), and (L1).

only data sizes of 20, 30, 50, 80, and 130 were used, and each size was tested only three times, provided the randomly selected partial data contained the three class labels. Although the training data had imbalanced label distributions, we did not make adjustments, as it did not cause noticeable issues.

3.5 Results

Table 1 shows the results for (B0) and (L0), along with the results for (B1), (B2), and (L1) when all of the target domain data were used. More detailed results, including precision, recall, and F1 scores for the three labels, are provided in Table 3 in Appendix C. Neither (B0) nor (L0) achieved high accuracy. In contrast, when all target domain data were used, (B1), (B2), and (L1) eventually exhibited similar performance levels, which can be considered sufficiently accurate compared to the human annotation agreement rate.

Figure 3 displays the results for (L1), (B2), and (B1) as the amount of the target domain data increased. They performed better with smaller amounts of target domain data, in that order.

4 Error Analysis and Discussion

As shown in Figure 3, particularly while less target domain data were available, (B2) performed better than (B1). This was likely due to incorporating general patterns of affirmation and negation into the model through fine-tuning with the Hazumi data. (L1) performed even better with less data, presumably due to the extensive training data and the GPT model structure.

System: Do you have any concerns about Maruyama Park?
User: Can I walk there from Keage Incline?
(Correct) Affirmative; (Classified as) Other

System: Do you have any other questions?
User: Thank you, I'm fine.
(Correct) Negative; (Classified as) Affirmative

Figure 4: Examples of common errors in (B0)

We examined the incorrect classification results in (B0) to investigate why the absence of target domain data results in low accuracy. A common pattern involved users responding to a system's questions with questions, as shown in Figure 4. Although users implicitly responded without 'yes' or 'no,' it appears that the different domain data, Hazumi, had too few instances of such patterns. These patterns also frequently resulted in errors in (L0). More detailed analysis with examples is provided in Appendix D.

Various surrounding factors in system development and operational circumstances (Nakano et al., 2024) should be considered when implementing and operating practical dialogue systems. There are several differences between pre-trained BERT models and GPT APIs beyond just accuracy, such as execution speed, development effort, and execution costs. Pre-trained BERT models are available for free, whereas GPT APIs require usage fees, making budget considerations necessary, and also require network connections, which can sometimes cause response delays. On the other hand, fine-tuning BERT can be time-consuming, and the resulting models are large, requiring considerable disk space and memory. In contrast, GPT APIs do not necessarily require training and impose less burden on the local machine. Therefore, the best approach should be chosen on the basis of the specific conditions.

5 Concluding Remarks

This paper presented an approach to developing an affirmative/negative response classifier using a small amount of target domain data. We have released the annotations for affirmative/negative classification on the Hazumi datasets, along with the classifier based on the BERT model, fine-tuned with this data.

The experimental results may be specific to the

particular dataset used. The performance depends on the model used, as well as the content of the data used for fine-tuning and few-shot learning. Nevertheless, we believe that the results and discussion could serve as a useful reference for developing dialogue systems, especially when working with little or no target domain data.

Future work includes conducting experiments using other datasets and models, and extending our approach to languages other than Japanese. Additionally, we will not only focus on binary affirmative/negative classification but also address the classification of agreement and disagreement (Gokcen and de Marneffe, 2015), which is crucial for dialogue management and knowledge acquisition (Komatani et al., 2022).

Limitations

In the experimental performance comparison presented in this paper, only a BERT model and a GPT API were used as representative models. Further evaluations using various other models are also necessary. The performance also depends on the content of the data used for fine-tuning and few-shot learning.

The experiments focused solely on the Japanese language, so conducting experiments in other languages, including English, remains a task for future work.

Acknowledgments

We thank the anonymous reviewer for their valuable comments on related research. This work was partly supported by JSPS KAKENHI Grant Number JP22H00536.

References

Ali Ahmadvand, Jason Ingyu Choi, and Eugene Agichtein. 2019. Contextual dialogue act classification for open-domain conversational agents. In *Proc. International ACM SIGIR Conference on Research and Development in Information Retrieval (SIGIR)*, page 1273–1276.

Yoshihiko Asao, Julien Kloetzer, Junta Mizuno, Dai Saiki, Kazuma Kadowaki, and Kentaro Torisawa. 2020. Understanding user utterances in a dialog system for caregiving. In *Proc. International Conference on Language Resources and Evaluation (LREC)*, pages 653–661.

Namo Bang, Jeehyun Lee, and Myoung-Wan Koo. 2023. Task-optimized adapters for an end-to-end task-oriented dialogue system. In *Findings of the Association for Computational Linguistics: ACL 2023*, pages 7355–7369.

Tom Bocklisch, Joey Faulkner, Nick Pawlowski, and Alan Nichol. 2017. Rasa: Open source language understanding and dialogue management. *Preprint*, arXiv:1712.05181.

Cathrine Damgaard, Paulina Toborek, Trine Eriksen, and Barbara Plank. 2021. "I'll be there for you": The one with understanding indirect answers. In *Proceedings of the 2nd Workshop on Computational Approaches to Discourse*, pages 1–11.

Jacob Devlin, Ming-Wei Chang, Kenton Lee, and Kristina Toutanova. 2019. BERT: pre-training of deep bidirectional transformers for language understanding. In *Proc. North Americal Chapter of Association for Computational Linguistics: Human Language Technologies (NAACL-HLT)*, pages 4171–4186.

N. J. Enfield, Stivers Tanya, Brown Penelope, Englert Christina, Harjunpää Katariina, Hayashi Makoto, Heinemann Trine, Hoymann Gertie, Keisanen Tiina, Rauniomaa Mirka, Chase Wesley Raymond, Rossano Federico, Yoon Kyung-Eun, Zwitserlood Inge, and Stephen C. Levinson. 2018. Polar answers. *Journal of Linguistics*, 55(2):277–304.

Jonathan Ginzburg, Zulipiye Yusupujiang, Chuyuan Li, Kexin Ren, Aleksandra Kucharska, and Pawel Lupkowski. 2022. Characterizing the response space of questions: data and theory. *Dialogue Discourse*, 13(2):79–132.

Ajda Gokcen and Marie-Catherine de Marneffe. 2015. I do not disagree: leveraging monolingual alignment to detect disagreement in dialogue. In *Proc. Annual Meeting of the Association for Computational Linguistics (ACL)*, pages 94–99.

Vojtěch Hudeček and Ondrej Dusek. 2023. Are large language models all you need for task-oriented dialogue? In *Proc. Annual Meeting of the Special Interest Group on Discourse and Dialogue (SIGDIAL)*, pages 216–228.

Hamed Khanpour, Nishitha Guntakandla, and Rodney Nielsen. 2016. Dialogue act classification in domain-independent conversations using a deep recurrent neural network. In *Proc. International Conference on Computational Linguistics (COLING)*, pages 2012–2021.

Kazunori Komatani and Shogo Okada. 2021. Multimodal human-agent dialogue corpus with annotations at utterance and dialogue levels. In *Proc. International Conference on Affective Computing and Intelligent Interaction (ACII)*, pages 1–8.

Kazunori Komatani, Kohei Ono, Ryu Takeda, Eric Nichols, and Mikio Nakano. 2022. User impressions of system questions to acquire lexical knowledge during dialogues. *Dialogue and Discourse*, 13(1):96–122.

Kentaro Kurihara, Daisuke Kawahara, and Tomohide Shibata. 2022. JGLUE: Japanese general language understanding evaluation. In *Proc. International Conference on Language Resources and Evaluation (LREC)*, pages 2957–2966.

Staffan Larsson. 2002. *Issue-based Dialogue Management*. Ph.D. thesis, Göteborg University.

Annie Louis, Dan Roth, and Filip Radlinski. 2020. "I'd rather just go to bed": Understanding indirect answers. In *Proc. Conference on Empirical Methods in Natural Language Processing (EMNLP)*, pages 7411–7425.

Takashi Minato, Ryuichiro Higashinaka, Kurima Sakai, Tomo Funayama, Hiromitsu Nishizaki, and Takayuki Nagai. 2024. Overview of dialogue robot competition 2023. In *Proc. Dialogue Robot Competition 2023*.

Christin Müller and Barbara Plank. 2024. IndirectQA: Understanding indirect answers to implicit polar questions in French and Spanish. In *Proc. Joint International Conference on Computational Linguistics, Language Resources and Evaluation (LREC-COLING)*, pages 9025–9035.

Mikio Nakano and Kazunori Komatani. 2024. DialBB: A dialogue system development framework as an educational material. In *Proc. Annual Meeting of the Special Interest Group on Discourse and Dialogue (SIGDIAL)*, pages 664–668.

Mikio Nakano, Hisahiro Mukai, Yoichi Matsuyama, and Kazunori Komatani. 2024. Evaluating dialogue systems from the system owners' perspectives. In *Proc. International Workshop on Spoken Dialogue System Technology (IWSDS)*.

Vipul Raheja and Joel Tetreault. 2019. Dialogue Act Classification with Context-Aware Self-Attention. In *Proc. North Americal Chapter of Association for Computational Linguistics: Human Language Technologies (NAACL-HLT)*, pages 3727–3733.

Krishna Sanagavarapu, Jathin Singaraju, Anusha Kakileti, Anirudh Kaza, Aaron Mathews, Helen Li, Nathan Brito, and Eduardo Blanco. 2022. Disentangling indirect answers to yes-no questions in real conversations. In *Proc. North Americal Chapter of Association for Computational Linguistics: Human Language Technologies (NAACL-HLT)*, pages 4677–4695.

Andreas Stolcke, Klaus Ries, Noah Coccaro, Elizabeth Shriberg, Rebecca Bates, Daniel Jurafsky, Paul Taylor, Rachel Martin, Carol Van Ess-Dykema, and Marie Meteer. 2000. Dialogue act modeling for automatic tagging and recognition of conversational speech. *Computational Linguistics*, 26(3):339–374.

Rikuto Watanabe, Junya Nakanishi, Jun Baba, Yuichiro Yoshikawa, and Hiroshi Ishiguro. 2023. Development of an affirmative/negative intention estimator for yes-no question answers using a large-scale language model (in Japanese). In *JSAI Technical Report, SIG-SLUD*, volume 98, pages 66–71.

Ryo Yanagimoto, Yunosuke Kubo, Miki Oshio, Mikio Nakano, Kenta Yamamoto, and Kazunori Komatani. 2023. User-adaptive tourist information dialogue system with yes/no classifier and sentiment estimator. In *Proc. Dialogue Robot Competition 2023*.

Label	Yes/No question	Response
1. Affirmative	Are there any places you recommend?	I recommend Okinawa.
1. Affirmative	Have you seen it?	I have seen it on TV.
2. Negative	Have you actually seen it?	I have only seen it on TV.
2. Negative	Do you plan to go there?	I will think about it.
3. Indeterminate	Do you like trains?	I think they are useful.
4. Does not answer	Are you interested in fashion?	What is 'kasshon (misheard)'?

Table 2: Examples provided to the annotators

A Instructions for Annotators

We asked annotators to assign one of the following four labels to each exchange (a pair consisting of a system Yes/No question and the subsequent user utterance). Examples, such as those shown in Table 2, were also provided to them.

1. Affirmative
2. Negative
3. Indeterminate
4. Does not answer the question at all

The annotators were specifically instructed to focus on determining whether the response was essentially affirmative or negative, rather than relying on surface-level expressions, even if the response did not explicitly express either. Subsequently, Labels 3 and 4 were merged into 'other' due to their small numbers.

B Prompt used in GPT-based classification

The zero-shot prompt used in (L0) is shown in Figure 5. The last question-response pair in the prompt was replaced with each of the test data to perform the evaluation across all test data.

On the basis of the human annotations, it outputs three values: affirmative, negative, and 'noa,' which refers to the 'other' class, including instances where the user does not respond to the question or where the response is undecidable.

In (L1), as part of a few-shot learning setup, we added pairs of dialogue examples and their correct labels from the target domain data to the prompt. The maximum number of such pairs was 131 in the conditions of (L1) with all target domain data.

C Further Details of Experimental Results

Table 3 presents more detailed results of Table 1. For each of the three labels, precision (P), recall (R), and F1 scores are shown. The upper part of each cell indicates the score, while the lower part shows the actual count. For (L0) and (L1), the counts represent the totals over three runs.

Due to the small number of instances for the "other" label, its classification performance was unstable. "n/a" indicates that the percentage could not be calculated due to a zero denominator.

For the remaining two classes, the F1 scores followed the same trend as the accuracy results described in Section 3.5. Specifically, in order of highest to lowest accuracy—(B1), (L1), (B2), (B0), and (L0)—the macro-F1 scores for the Affirmative and Negative classes were 0.980, 0.977, 0.965, 0.898, and 0.878, respectively.

```
Persons A and B had the following dialogue.
Please classify Person B's response to Person A's
question into one of the three categories below and
return it in JSON format (either {"class": "pos"},
{"class": "neg"}, or {"class": "noa"}).

pos: affirmative
neg: negative
noa: not answered

# input

A: Do you have any other questions?
B: That's OK. Thank you.
```

Figure 5: Prompt used in GPT-based classification. ("noa" corresponds to the "other" class.)

D Error Analysis When a Small Amount of Target Domain Data was Used

As shown in Figure 3, when the amount of the target domain data was very limited, the accuracy was higher in the order of (L1), (B2), and (B1). To investigate the reasons for this, we conducted an error analysis.

In the following, the experimental conditions for (B1), (B2), and (L1), where the number of the target domain data samples for training was 30, will be referred to as (B1-30), (B2-30), and (L1-30), respectively. The conditions where all training

Method	Accuracy	Affirmative P	Affirmative R	Affirmative F1	Negative P	Negative R	Negative F1	Other P	Other R	Other F1
(B0)	0.817 156/191	0.936 102/109	0.797 102/128	0.861	0.962 51/53	0.911 51/56	0.936	0.103 3/29	0.429 3/7	0.167
(B1) with all target domain data	0.958 183/191	0.941 128/136	1.00 128/128	0.970	1.00 55/55	0.982 55/56	0.991	n/a 0/0	0 0/7	n/a
(B2) with all target domain data	0.942 180/191	0.927 127/137	0.992 127/128	0.958	1.00 53/53	0.946 53/56	0.972	0 0/1	0 0/7	n/a
(L0)	0.763 437/573	0.957 267/279	0.695 267/384	0.805	1.00 152/152	0.905 152/168	0.950	0.127 18/142	0.857 18/21	0.221
(L1) with all target domain data	0.949 544/573	0.986 365/370	0.951 365/384	0.968	1.00 163/163	0.970 163/168	0.985	0.400 16/40	0.762 16/21	0.525

Table 3: Detailed results corresponding to Table 1: precision (P), recall (R), and F1 scores for the three labels. Counts for (L0) and (L1) are totals over three runs.

data were used will be referred to as (B1-all), (B2-all), and (L1-all).

Note that classifications were made three times for (L0) and (L1-all), as GPT's classifications were not always the same even with the same prompt and a temperature setting of 0.0. If classification results vary within the same setting, all results are written in the following examples.

The following examples (1) and (2) illustrate the case where the classifications for (B1-30) were incorrect.

(1) System: I understand that you are visiting Kyoto this time, but do you travel often?
User: No, not really.

Correct: Negative
Classifications (B0): Negative
(B1-30): Affirmative
(B1-all): Negative
(B2-30): Negative
(B2-all): Negative
(L0): Negative
(L1-30): Negative
(L1-all): Negative

(2) System: Then, do you have any questions about this plan?
User: No, I'm fine.

Correct: Negative
Classifications (B0): Negative
(B1-30): Affirmative
(B1-all): Negative
(B2-30): Negative
(B2-all): Negative
(L0): Negative
(L1-30): Negative
(L1-all): Negative

We guess that (B1-30) failed because these patterns were relatively rare in the target domain data used for training, while the model trained with all the target domain data performed correctly. Since (B2-30) classified them correctly, it can be inferred that similar patterns existed in the different domain data, and using them was effective. We also guess that this is why the classifications of (B0), which is equivalent to (B2-0), where no target domain data were used in (B2), were correct.

The following examples (3) and (4) illustrate cases where both (B1-30) and (B2-30) were incorrect (twice in the three times), but (L1-30) was correct.

(3) System: I understand that you are visiting Kyoto this time, but do you travel often?
User: Would you go? (The intention of this response is unclear.)

Correct: Other
Classifications (B0): Other
(B1-30): Affirmative
(B1-all): Affirmative
(B2-30): Affirmative (twice), Other (once)
(B2-all): Affirmative
(L0): Other
(L1-30): Other
(L1-all): Other

(4) System: Then, are you interested in history?
User: History is... (incomplete response)

Correct: Other
Classifications (B0): Affirmative
(B1-30): Affirmative
(B1-all): Affirmative
(B2-30): Affirmative (twice), Other (once)
(B2-all): Affirmative
(L0): Other
(L1-30): Other
(L1-all): Other

In many of these cases, the correct label was 'Other.' Some user utterances made were difficult to classify as affirmative or negative due to misstatements, errors in detecting speech segments, or speech recognition errors. Since the target domain data for training included only three samples for the 'Other' class, the model did not have sufficient data to learn this classification effectively. GPT, having been trained on a large amount of data, may also have had a higher chance of making the correct classification.

The following examples (5) and (6) illustrate cases where the classifications were incorrect in all conditions.

(5) System: In that case, do you have any questions about this plan?
User: *Home* (This is a misspelling of "ie," which means 'No' in Japanese.)

Correct: Negative
Classifications: (B0): Other
(B1-30): Affirmative
(B1-all): Affirmative
(B2-30): Affirmative
(B2-all): Affirmative
(L0): Other
(L1-30): Other
(L1-all): Other (twice), Negative (once)

(6) System: Is there anything you are concerned about regarding the Keage Incline?
User: I would like to visit it.

Correct: Other
Classifications: (B0): Affirmative
(B1-30): Affirmative
(B1-all): Affirmative
(B2-30): Affirmative
(B2-all): Affirmative
(L0): Affirmative
(L1-30): Affirmative
(L1-all): Affirmative

In Example (5), the speech recognition result was incorrectly transcribed, making it difficult for the models to accurately understand the user's utterance. In Example (6), because the user utterance does not explicitly address whether there are concerns, it can be reasonably classified as 'Other.' However, since the user mentioned wanting to visit the place due to a lack of concerns, the response might be interpreted differently, leading to potential annotation inconsistency. Such ambiguous situations can result in classification errors.

Why Do We Laugh? Annotation and Taxonomy Generation for Laughable Contexts in Spontaneous Text Conversation

Koji Inoue, Mikey Elmers, Divesh Lala, Tatsuya Kawahara

Graduate School of Informatics, Kyoto University, Japan,

Correspondence: inoue@sap.ist.i.kyoto-u.ac.jp

Abstract

Laughter serves as a multifaceted communicative signal in human interaction, yet its identification within dialogue presents a significant challenge for conversational AI systems. This study addresses this challenge by annotating laughable contexts in Japanese spontaneous text conversation data and developing a taxonomy to classify the underlying reasons for such contexts. Initially, multiple annotators manually labeled laughable contexts using a binary decision (laughable or non-laughable). Subsequently, an LLM was used to generate explanations for the binary annotations of laughable contexts, which were then categorized into a taxonomy comprising ten categories, including "Empathy and Affinity" and "Humor and Surprise," highlighting the diverse range of laughter-inducing scenarios. The study also evaluated GPT-4o's performance in recognizing the majority labels of laughable contexts, achieving an F1 score of 43.14%. These findings contribute to the advancement of conversational AI by establishing a foundation for more nuanced recognition and generation of laughter, ultimately fostering more natural and engaging human-AI interactions.

1 Introduction

In human dialogue, laughter serves as a communicative signal conveying humor, empathy, surprise, or social bonding (Norrick, 1993; Glenn, 2003; Attardo, 2009). However, its mechanisms are complex and multifaceted, and understanding them remains a long-term challenge for dialogue systems aiming to achieve human-like interaction (Tian et al., 2016; Türker et al., 2017; Mazzocconi et al., 2020; Inoue et al., 2022; Ludusan and Wagner, 2023; Perkins Booker et al., 2024). Furthermore, traditional approaches to modeling laughter and humor have often been limited to scenarios involving explicit auditory or visual stimuli, with few addressing the subtle contextual nuances present in spontaneous dialogue (Bertero and Fung, 2016; Choube and Soleymani, 2020; Jentzsch and Kersting, 2023; Ko et al., 2023; Hessel et al., 2023). Therefore, elucidating the underlying reasons for laughter in spontaneous dialogue data can contribute to making large language model (LLM)-based dialogue more natural and empathetic. However, annotating the reasons for laughter in any formalized manner has been prohibitively time- and labor-intensive, leaving the field largely reliant on qualitative approaches through conversational analysis.

Table 1: Annotation example for laughable context (majority voting, translated from Japanese)

	Utterance	Laughable?
A:	I think that's a wonderful attitude. I always end up talking about myself, so I should follow your example.	NO
B:	Is that so? But does your husband listen to your stories?	NO
A:	Yes, yes, he listens to me. I wonder if I'm putting too much on him?	NO
B:	I don't think so! He's so kind. My husband doesn't seem to listen to me. Huh, that's strange.	**YES**

In this study, we address the question of "why do we laugh?" from an informatics perspective by proposing a semi-automated approach to constructing taxonomy labels for the reasons of laughter. First, to identify target segments, multiple annotators were asked to perform a simple binary classification on each utterance in dialogue data, determining whether it was "laughable" or not, as shown in Table 1. Subsequently, for contexts labeled as "laughable" based on the majority voting, we used an LLM (GPT-4o) to generate the reasoning sentence behind this judgment and further classified these generated reasons into distinct categories (taxonomy labels). This semi-automated taxonomy generation approach is generalizable and can be particularly effective in scenarios where manual annotation is limited to simpler labels, such as emo-

Proceedings of the 15th International Workshop on Spoken Dialogue Systems Technology, pages 318–323
May 27–30, 2025.

Table 2: Number of samples in each ratio of annotators judged as laughable (laughable agreement)

Laughable agreement	# sample
1.0 (5/5)	163 (0.64%)
0.8 (4/5)	845 (3.34%)
0.6 (3/5)	2731 (10.80%)
0.4 (2/5)	8143 (32.20%)
0.2 (1/5)	11928 (47.17%)
0.0 (0/5)	1479 (5.85%)

tion labeling.

The purpose of this research is to contribute toward more nuanced conversational AI systems that can recognize and even anticipate moments for laughter, ultimately fostering more natural interactions between humans and machines. Ideally, such systems should be able to respond with the correct acoustics, delay, and consider group size for different laughter types (Truong and Trouvain, 2012). Our findings reveal that AI can improve our understanding of laughter and offer a foundation for future research in AI context-sensitive recognition.

2 Annotation of Laughable Context

We annotated laughable contexts in the RealPersonaChat dataset (Yamashita et al., 2023). This textual data contains one-on-one Japanese spontaneous conversation where participants chat without assuming assigned personas. It includes approximately 30 utterances per conversation, totaling around 14,000 dialogues. We annotated 900 dialogues, with plans to annotate the remainder in future work.

During the annotation process, each annotator reviewed each dialogue and, after the initial two greeting utterances, made a binary decision for whether the next person would laugh (*laughable*) or not. Five annotators assigned these binary labels to each utterance. Table 2 summarizes the agreement amongst annotators for laughable labels, which we refer to as "laughable agreement". While some samples showed clear agreement (either all or none of the annotators marked them as laughable), there were also numerous split samples, highlighting the subjectivity and complexity of the task. If we applied a majority voting process, 3,739 contexts (14.8%) were labeled as laughable, and 21,550 contexts (85.2%) as non-laughable.

Table 1 illustrates a laughable context example. In this dialogue, person A's final utterance is self-contradictory, requiring high-level comprehension of the dialogue context. These annotations underscore the significance of cultural context and conversational flow in interpreting laughter cues.

3 Generating Taxonomy of Laughable Reason

Towards developing human-like laughter behaviors in LLMs, we investigated the reasons behind human annotators' recognition of laughable contexts. In this section, we used only samples with majority labels marked as laughable (3,739 samples). Since manual annotations are costly, we utilized GPT-4o to generate explanations for the human judgments. For example, a generated reason for the example context in Table 1 is:

> *If we were to speculate on the reasons a third party might judge that Person A laughed at Person B's final remark in this conversation, the following points can be considered:*
>
> *Element of Humor: Person B's comment, "My husband doesn't seem to listen to me. Huh, that's strange.," contains a touch of self-deprecating humor. This lighthearted tone, making fun of their own situation, can be amusing to the listener. (...)*
>
> *Relaxed Atmosphere: The overall tone of the conversation seems light and relaxed, and Person B's comment might have been perceived as a playful joke in line with this mood.*
>
> *A combination of these factors may have led the third party to interpret that Person A laughed in response to Person B's remark.*

We then aimed to summarize the generated reasoning texts for laughable contexts by applying a taxonomy generation approach using LLMs (Wan et al., 2024). First, we randomly divided the generated reason samples into smaller subsets, each comprising roughly 5% of the samples. Starting with the first subset, we gave the reason sentences GPT-4o to generate initial taxonomy labels and those explanations, which we manually validated when necessary. We then iteratively refined the taxonomy by having the LLM update it based on the previous taxonomy and the reason sentence data from each new subset, continuing this process until all data were processed. This resulted in ten taxonomy labels, summarized in Table 3, including categories such as (1) Empathy and Affinity and (2) Humor and Surprise.

After generating these taxonomy labels, we used the LLM to assign them to each reason sample,

Table 3: Generated taxonomy labels for laughable context reasoning, number of samples assigned to each taxonomy label, and related references for each taxonomy label

	Label name	Explanation	#sample	Reference
(1)	Empathy and Affinity	Situations where a sense of closeness and laughter is generated by sharing common experiences or emotions in a conversation. This includes empathy for shared hobbies or everyday relatable situations.	3013 (80.6%)	(Hay, 2001; Garbarski et al., 2016)
(2)	Humor and Surprise	Cases where humor or an element of surprise in the statement triggers laughter. This includes unexpected twists, wordplay, and exaggeration.	3233 (86.5%)	(Dynel, 2009; Martin and Ford, 2018)
(3)	Relaxed Atmosphere	Situations where the conversation progresses in a calm, relaxed atmosphere, naturally leading to laughter. Lighthearted exchanges and conversations with jokes fall into this category.	2955 (79.0%)	(Vettin and Todt, 2004)
(4)	Self-Disclosure and Friendliness	Situations where sharing personal stories or past mistakes creates a sense of approachability and triggers laughter. Self-disclosure that makes the other person feel at ease is also included.	475 (12.7%)	(Gelkopf and Kreitler, 1996)
(5)	Cultural Background and Shared Understanding	Laughter based on specific cultural backgrounds or shared understandings. This includes jokes related to a particular region or culture or remarks based on common superstitions or folklore.	176 (4.7%)	(Bryant and Bainbridge, 2022; Kamiloğlu et al., 2022)
(6)	Nostalgia and Fondness	Situations where past memories or nostalgic topics trigger laughter. This includes shared past experiences and the enjoyment of recalling familiar events.	204 (5.5%)	(Bazzini et al., 2007)
(7)	Self-Deprecating Humor	Situations where turning one's flaws or mistakes into humor makes the other person feel closer and triggers laughter. Slightly putting oneself down can also give the other person a sense of ease.	404 (10.8%)	(Atkinson, 2015)
(8)	Defying Expectations	Situations where intentionally defying the flow of conversation or the other person's expectations creates an element of surprise and triggers laughter. This includes unexpected responses or developments.	323 (8.6%)	(Ginzburg et al., 2020; Xu, 2022)
(9)	Positive Energy	Situations where positive emotions or energy in the conversation bring a smile to the other person. Enjoyable topics and positive comments fall into this category.	338 (9.0%)	(Wang et al., 2024)
(10)	Exaggeration	Situations where exaggerating things gives a comical impression and triggers laughter. Exaggerated expressions can be amusing to the listener.	478 (12.8%)	(McCarthy and Carter, 2004)

allowing for multiple labels per sample. The labeling results are shown on the right side of Table 3. While some categories, such as (1) Empathy and Affinity, were predominant, many samples were also assigned to other categories, including (4) Self-Disclosure and Friendliness and (5) Cultural Background and Shared Understanding. This broad distribution across categories reinforces the validity of the generated taxonomy. A correlation matrix showing relationships between the taxonomy labels is provided in Appendix A. Finally, we reviewed related studies in conversational analysis, as listed on the right side of Table 3. These studies further substantiate the explanatory power of our taxonomy within the context of conversational analysis research.

4 LLM's Performance on Laughable Context Recognition

We then examined how much LLMs, specifically GPT-4o, can recognize the laughable contexts in spontaneous text conversation. The model was tested in a zero-shot setting, instructed to first analyze the conversational context and then determine its laughability as a binary. The provided prompt included a task description for laughable context recognition, followed by a Chain-of-Thought (CoT) reasoning approach to encourage the model to consider the reasoning behind its decision step by step. We evaluated GPT-4o's performance against the majority labels, achieving an F1 score of 43.14%, with a precision of 41.66% and recall of 44.72%. While this score was significantly above the chance level (14.8%), capturing the nuanced subtleties of conversational humor remains challenging.

We then further examined the LLM's performance on each generated taxonomy label. Table 4 shows the distribution of binary outputs by GPT-4o and its accuracy within each label. First, the primary labels, from (1) to (3), showed similar accuracy rates, ranging from 40% to 50%. Additionally, we observed comparatively higher scores for (5) *Cultural Background and Shared Understanding*, (7) *Self-Deprecating Humor*, and (8) *Defying Ex-*

Table 4: Laughable context recognition performance of GPT-4o on each taxonomy label

	Label name	# output by GPT-4o	
		Laughable (correct)	Non-laughable (incorrect)
(1)	Empathy and Affinity	1226 (40.69%)	1787 (59.31%)
(2)	Humor and Surprise	1571 (48.59%)	1662 (51.41%)
(3)	Relaxed Atmosphere	1257 (42.54%)	1698 (57.46%)
(4)	Self-Disclosure and Friendliness	232 (48.84%)	243 (51.16%)
(5)	Cultural Background and Shared Understanding	102 (57.95%)	74 (42.05%)
(6)	Nostalgia and Fondness	62 (30.39%)	142 (69.61%)
(7)	Self-Deprecating Humor	255 (63.12%)	149 (36.88%)
(8)	Defying Expectations	227 (70.28%)	96 (29.72%)
(9)	Positive Energy	50 (14.79%)	288 (85.21%)
(10)	Exaggeration	239 (50.00%)	239 (50.00%)

Table 5: Example context for "Nostalgia and Fondness" (translated from Japanese)

	Utterance
A:	Do you also consume milk or yogurt for calcium?
B:	I drink milk with Milo in it. I also eat yogurt as a snack.
A:	That's really well-balanced!
B:	Yes, health is important.
A:	It's been a while since I last heard about Milo.

Table 6: Example context for "Positive Energy" (translated from Japanese)

	Utterance
A:	Oh, as they grow up, that kind of help really makes a difference, doesn't it?
B:	Absolutely! It's such a joy, isn't it? So reassuring.
A:	When they're little, it's like a never-ending story of challenges, isn't it?
B:	Haha, so true. All we have now are funny memories of those times.
A:	Once you get through it, those challenges become stories you can laugh about, and you feel glad you went through them.

pectations, suggesting that the current LLM may effectively capture these contexts. In contrast, categories like (6) *Nostalgia and Fondness* and (9) *Positive Energy* displayed lower accuracy, potentially highlighting limitations in the LLM's understanding.

Table 5 presents an example dialogue context where the LLM marked non-laughable for the final utterance from person A, despite a positive majority label with a (6) *Nostalgia and Fondness* reason. This context was also assigned the (2) *Humor and Surprise* and (3) *Relaxed Atmosphere* labels. In this example, the participants discuss a nostalgic memory of drinking a powdered beverage with milk. The last utterance evokes nostalgia, implicitly inviting laughter. Here, capturing person A's sentiment seems to be difficult for the current LLM, but is essential for appropriate laughter response.

Table 6 provides an example for (9) *Positive Energy* label. This context was also assigned the (1) *Empathy and Affinity* and (2) *Humor and Surprise* labels. The participants discussed a challenging experience with childcare, but in the final utterance, person A reflects positively on the experience after some time has passed. Although the story itself recounts a difficult time, it is now viewed positively, making it laughable. This example suggests that the LLM needs to comprehend the temporal structure of the story and the person's current feelings to accurately interpret the context as laughable.

5 Conclusion

This study investigated laughter in the context of conversational AI by annotating laughable contexts within a Japanese text dialogue dataset. A taxonomy of ten distinct reasons for laughter was generated by an LLM, providing valuable insights into the multifaceted nature of laughter. Subsequently, this study evaluated the ability of GPT-4o to recognize those laughable contexts. While the model's performance surpassed chance levels, it highlighted the inherent challenges in capturing the nuances of conversational humor.

This automated approach employed for reasoning and taxonomy generation with LLMs can be applied in other scenarios where only binary (or simplified) decision labels from human annotators are available, yet more fine-grained explanations are required. Future work will focus on expanding the dataset to cover other languages and cultural contexts, validating the generated taxonomy by incorporating additional linguistic research perspectives, exploring multimodal approaches, and including spoken dialogue to enhance AI's understanding of humor and social interaction.

Acknowledgement

This work was supported by JST PREST JP-MJPR24I4 and JSPS KAKENHI JP23K16901.

References

Camille Atkinson. 2015. Self-deprecation and the habit of laughter. *Florida Philosophical Review*, 15(1).

Salvatore Attardo. 2009. *Linguistic theories of humor*. Walter de Gruyter.

Doris G Bazzini, Elizabeth R Stack, Penny D Martincin, and Carmen P Davis. 2007. The effect of reminiscing about laughter on relationship satisfaction. *Motivation and Emotion*, 31(1):25–34.

Dario Bertero and Pascale Fung. 2016. A long short-term memory framework for predicting humor in dialogues. In *Conference of the North American Chapter of the Association for Computational Linguistics: Human Language Technologies (NAACL-HLT)*, pages 130–135.

Gregory A Bryant and Constance M Bainbridge. 2022. Laughter and culture. *Philosophical Transactions of the Royal Society B*, 377(1863):20210179.

Akshat Choube and Mohammad Soleymani. 2020. Punchline detection using context-aware hierarchical multimodal fusion. In *International Conference on Multimodal Interaction (ICMI)*, pages 675–679.

Marta Dynel. 2009. Beyond a joke: Types of conversational humour. *Language and linguistics compass*, 3(5):1284–1299.

Dana Garbarski, Nora Cate Schaeffer, and Jennifer Dykema. 2016. Interviewing practices, conversational practices, and rapport: Responsiveness and engagement in the standardized survey interview. *Sociological methodology*, 46(1):1–38.

Marc Gelkopf and Shulamith Kreitler. 1996. Is humor only fun, an alternative cure or magic? the cognitive therapeutic potential of humor. *Journal of Cognitive Psychotherapy*, 10(4).

Jonathan Ginzburg, Chiara Mazzocconi, and Ye Tian. 2020. Laughter as language. *Glossa: a journal of general linguistics*, 5(1).

Phillip Glenn. 2003. *Laughter in interaction*. Cambridge University Press.

Jennifer Hay. 2001. *The pragmatics of humor support*. Walter de Gruyter.

Jack Hessel, Ana Marasovic, Jena D. Hwang, Lillian Lee, Jeff Da, Rowan Zellers, Robert Mankoff, and Yejin Choi. 2023. Do androids laugh at electric sheep? humor "understanding" benchmarks from the new yorker caption contest. In *Annual Meeting of the Association for Computational Linguistics (ACL)*, pages 688–714.

Koji Inoue, Divesh Lala, and Tatsuya Kawahara. 2022. Can a robot laugh with you?: Shared laughter generation for empathetic spoken dialogue. *Frontiers in Robotics and AI*, 9.

Sophie Jentzsch and Kristian Kersting. 2023. ChatGPT is fun, but it is not funny! humor is still challenging large language models. In *Workshop on Computational Approaches to Subjectivity, Sentiment, & Social Media Analysis (WASSA)*, pages 325–340.

Roza G Kamiloğlu, Akihiro Tanaka, Sophie K Scott, and Disa A Sauter. 2022. Perception of group membership from spontaneous and volitional laughter. *Philosophical Transactions of the Royal Society B*, 377(1841):20200404.

Dayoon Ko, Sangho Lee, and Gunhee Kim. 2023. Can language models laugh at YouTube short-form videos? In *Conference on Empirical Methods in Natural Language Processing (EMNLP)*, pages 2897–2916.

Bogdan Ludusan and Petra Wagner. 2023. The effect of conversation type on entrainment: Evidence from laughter. In *Annual Meeting of the Special Interest Group on Discourse and Dialogue (SIGDIAL)*, pages 168–174.

Rod A Martin and Thomas Ford. 2018. *The psychology of humor: An integrative approach*. Academic press.

Chiara Mazzocconi, Ye Tian, and Jonathan Ginzburg. 2020. What's your laughter doing there? A taxonomy of the pragmatic functions of laughter. *IEEE Transactions on Affective Computing*, 13(3):1302–1321.

Michael McCarthy and Ronald Carter. 2004. "there's millions of them": hyperbole in everyday conversation. *Journal of pragmatics*, 36(2):149–184.

Neal R Norrick. 1993. Conversational joking: Humor in everyday talk.

Nynaeve Perkins Booker, Michelle Cohn, and Georgia Zellou. 2024. Linguistic patterning of laughter in human-socialbot interactions. *Frontiers in Communication*, 9.

Ye Tian, Chiara Mazzocconi, and Jonathan Ginzburg. 2016. When do we laugh? In *Annual Meeting of the Special Interest Group on Discourse and Dialogue (SIGDIAL)*, pages 360–369.

Khiet P. Truong and Jürgen Trouvain. 2012. On the acoustics of overlapping laughter in conversational speech. In *INTERSPEECH*, pages 851–854.

Bekir Berker Türker, Zana Buçinca, Engin Erzin, Yücel Yemez, and T Metin Sezgin. 2017. Analysis of engagement and user experience with a laughter responsive social robot. In *INTERSPEECH*, pages 844–848.

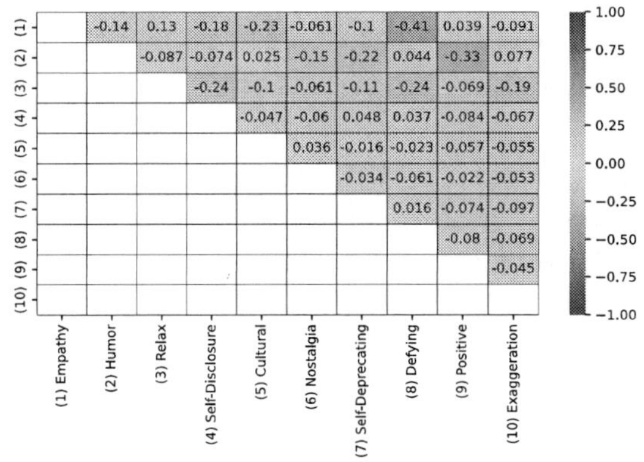

Figure 1: Correlation matrix of assigned taxonomy labels

Julia Vettin and Dietmar Todt. 2004. Laughter in conversation: Features of occurrence and acoustic structure. *Journal of Nonverbal Behavior*, 28:93–115.

Mengting Wan, Tara Safavi, Sujay Kumar Jauhar, Yujin Kim, Scott Counts, Jennifer Neville, Siddharth Suri, Chirag Shah, Ryen W White, Longqi Yang, Reid Andersen, Georg Buscher, Dhruv Joshi, and Nagu Rangan. 2024. TnT-LLM: Text mining at scale with large language models. In *SIGKDD Conference on Knowledge Discovery and Data Mining (KDD)*, pages 5836–5847.

Kexin Wang, Carlos Ishi, and Ryoko Hayashi. 2024. A multimodal analysis of different types of laughter expression in conversational dialogues. In *INTERSPEECH*, pages 4673–4677.

Ge Xu. 2022. An analysis of humor discourse in friends from the perspective of the cooperative principle. *Open Journal of Modern Linguistics*, 12(4):460–470.

Sanae Yamashita, Koji Inoue, Ao Guo, Shota Mochizuki, Tatsuya Kawahara, and Ryuichiro Higashinaka. 2023. Realpersonachat: A realistic persona chat corpus with interlocutors' own personalities. In *Pacific Asia Conference on Language, Information and Computation (PACLIC)*, pages 852–861.

A Correlation Among Taxonomy Labels

Figure 1 presents the correlation matrix of the assigned labels discussed in Section 3, where multiple labels can be assigned to the same laughable context. For instance, "Empathy and Affinity" shows a weak positive correlation with "Relaxed Atmosphere." Conversely, "Empathy and Affinity" exhibits a negative correlation with "Defying Expressions." We also find a negative correlation between "Humor and Surprise" and "Positive Energy," despite both being associated with positive sentiment. This may be attributed to different expressive styles, with the former implicit and the latter explicit. To gain deeper insight into the relationships between these labels, further qualitative analysis will be conducted in future work.

Adaptive Psychological Distance in Japanese Spoken Human-Agent Dialogue: A Politeness-Based Management Model

Akira Inaba, Emmanuel Ayedoun, Masataka Tokumaru
Graduate School of Science and Engineering, Kansai University
3-3-35 Yamate-cho, Suita-shi, Osaka 564-8680, Japan
{k949415, emay, toku}@kansai-u.ac.jp

Abstract

While existing spoken dialogue systems can adapt various aspects of interaction, systematic management of psychological distance through verbal politeness remains underexplored. Current approaches typically maintain fixed levels of formality and social distance, limiting naturalness in long-term human-agent interactions. We propose a novel dialogue management model that dynamically adjusts verbal politeness levels in Japanese based on user preferences. We evaluated the model using two pseudo-users with distinct distance preferences in daily conversations. Human observers (n=20) assessed the interactions, with 70% successfully distinguishing the intended social distance variations. The results demonstrate that systematic modulation of verbal politeness can create perceptibly different levels of psychological distance in spoken dialogue, with implications for culturally appropriate human-agent interaction in Japanese contexts.

1 Introduction

The advancement of communication robots designed for frequent human interaction has accelerated significantly in recent years. By integrating human-like traits, these robots or agents are expected to become more approachable and relatable, facilitating broader adoption (Cassel and al., 2003.) (Häring and al., 2011.). With the advent of generative AI, robots can now understand and respond to human speech more effectively. However, understanding implied meaning, which is a cornerstone of human communication, remains challenging for AI.

A critical yet understudied aspect of implied meaning is psychological distance, which plays a fundamental role in relationship development and maintenance. This concept has been extensively studied in psychological research, particularly through the lenses of personal space and politeness theory (Brown and Levinson, 1987) (Hall, 1966). Although previous studies have explored personal space and politeness in robot interactions, there has been limited investigation into robots' active management of psychological distance during ongoing conversations (Huttenrauch and al., 2006) (Tomoki and al., 2017), especially in Japanese language contexts where politeness levels are deeply embedded in linguistic structures.

Traditional approaches to politeness have primarily relied on Brown and Levinson's (1987) framework, which conceptualizes politeness as strategies to mitigate face-threatening acts. However, more recent theoretical developments by Locher and Watts (2005) have shifted focus toward "relational work", emphasizing the dynamic and contextual nature of politeness rather than inherent linguistic features. Similarly, Culpeper's (2011) contributions to understanding impoliteness have broadened the theoretical landscape. Our work integrates these perspectives while addressing the specific linguistic features of Japanese politeness.

Therefore, the present study addresses this gap by designing and implementing an internal model that enables robots to modulate psychological distance through linguistics behaviors grounded in an integrated politeness theory framework, with specific application to Japanese language interaction.

2 Proposed System

Our system enables robots to converse at the psychological distance preferred by users through an internal state variable D that governs the selection of conversation strategies based on politeness theory. This value evolves through extended interactions, triggering corresponding adjustments in conversational approaches. The

Proceedings of the 15th International Workshop on Spoken Dialogue Systems Technology, pages 324–329
May 27–30, 2025. ©2025 Association for Computational Linguistics

Strategy	Japanese Example	English Translation	Notes
NPS: Be conventionally indirect	もし宜しければ、お名前を教えていただけますか？	If it's not too much trouble, could you please tell me your name?	honorific form and conditional
NPS: Question, hedge	少しお時間をいただけないかもしれませんが...	I was wondering if I might possibly have a moment of your time...	Multiple hedges and honorific form
NPS: Give deference	山田様、ご意見をお聞かせいただけますか？	Mr. Yamada, would you honor me with your opinion?	honorific title and humble request form
PPS: Notice, attend to Hearer	新しい髪型いいね！似合ってるよ。	Nice new haircut! It really suits you.	Direct compliment with casual ending
PPS: Exaggerate	すごーい！あなたの考えは天才的だよ！	Wow! Your idea is absolutely genius!	Elongated expression and enthusiastic tone
PPS: Use in-group identity markers	ねぇ、これどう思う？	Hey, what do you think about this?	casual speech pattern and familiar address

Table 1: Overview of some NPS and PPS in Japanese with English translations.

system maintains individual D values for each user, allowing for personalized distance calibration in Japanese dialogue contexts.

Given the complexity of accurately inferring users' preferred psychological distance in real-time, we initially validate our approach using pseudo-users with predetermined distance preferences. This controlled setup enables systematic evaluation of the model's effectiveness.

2.1 Definition of Psychological Distance *D*

Our model quantifies psychological distance D as the inverse relationship between shared information and interpersonal similarity, building on Yamane's model (available only in Japanese). To accommodate individual user preferences, we introduce a personality multiplier. The psychological distance D is calculated as:

$$D = \frac{personality}{\sum_{k=1}^{n} sim_k} \quad (1)$$

In this equation, n represents the amount of shared information, while sim_k represents information similarity, ranging from 0.1 to 1, computed via cosine similarity of text vectors. The personality parameter ranges from 1 to 5, allowing for individual variation in distance preferences.

It is important to clarify that although our mathematical formulation incorporates concepts related to physical distance from proxemics theory (Hall, 1966), D specifically measures psychological distance on an abstract scale.

Unlike physical distance measured in meters, psychological distance in our model represents the perceived social-emotional space between interactants, which manifests through linguistic choices and conversational strategies. The formula allows us to quantify this abstract concept for computational implementation.

2.2 Conversation Strategy Selection

The model employs conversation strategies derived from politeness theory's Face-Threatening Act (FTA) framework. While traditional FTA calculations consider psychological distance (D), power difference (P), and imposition (Rx), our implementation focuses specifically on distance perception through D. From the five traditional politeness strategies, we concentrate on the two most relevant for everyday conversation in Japanese: Positive Politeness Strategies (PPS) and Negative Politeness Strategies (NPS). In Japanese linguistic and cultural contexts, NPS generally corresponds to greater psychological distance, as they involve formal language patterns, honorifics, and indirect expressions that signal respect and deference. Conversely, PPS typically signals closeness through casual language, shared expressions, and direct communication styles. This relationship between politeness strategies and psychological distance is particularly pronounced in Japanese, where the language has grammaticalized politeness levels (Ide, 1989). Examples of NPS and PPS in Japanese are provided in Table 1, along with their English translations to illustrate the differences.

The system calculates D at conversation topic boundaries and determines the ratio of NPS to PPS strategies for subsequent utterances. These ratios are based on predefined thresholds aligned with personal space theory, as illustrated in Table 2. For values of D below 0.45, the system employs a highly informal approach with an NPS:PPS ratio of 0:5. As D increases through the ranges of 0.45 to 1.20 and 1.20 to 3.60, the formality gradually increases, with NPS:PPS ratios of 2:3 and 3:2 respectively. For D values above 3.60, the system adopts a highly formal stance with an NPS:PPS ratio of 5:0.

These specific ratio values were determined through preliminary studies examining the correlation between perceived psychological distance and the distribution of politeness strategies in Japanese conversation samples. The thresholds correspond to significant transition points in perceived distance based on linguistic features.

2.3 Dynamic Adjustment of Distance

Our model dynamically adjusts the personality parameter to modulate D, thereby adapting the psychological distance to match user preferences. The system analyzes the ratio of NPS to PPS strategies in pseudo-user utterances at topic boundaries to identify the user's preferred D range. When a mismatch is detected between the user's and robot's D ranges, the system calculates an adjustment value that shifts the robot's D to the maximum value within the user's preferred range. For the uppermost D range, which lacks a defined limit in Table 2, we reference proxemic theory of personal space which establishes a maximum public distance of 7.6m. Given the challenges in extracting precise psychological distance information from natural utterances, we pre-generate pseudo-user responses based on their assigned D values, using the relationship between D and conversational strategies outlined in Table 1.

The adjustment value r is formally defined as:

$$r = \frac{u_{max}}{D} \qquad (2)$$

where (u_{max}) represents the maximum value of the user's preferred D range.

2.4 Utterance Generation

The utterance generation process utilizes GPT-4o in two distinct phases. First, it creates base conversational scenarios that establish the fundamental interaction structure. Subsequently, it performs strategic modification of utterances to reflect intended NPS/PPS ratios. This two-phase approach ensures both coherent dialogue flow and appropriate social distance signaling.

Threshold of *D*	Ratio of NPS/PPS
$0.00 < D \leq 0.45$	NPS:PPS=0:5
$0.45 < D \leq 1.20$	NPS:PPS=2:3
$1.20 < D \leq 3.60$	NPS:PPS=3:2
$3.60 < D$	NPS:PPS=5:0

Table 2: Threshold of *D* and conversational strategies.

Consider the neutral utterance "Kai, What would you like for breakfast?" When applying NPS, it transforms into "If you don't mind, could you please let me know your breakfast preferences?" This version emphasizes social distance and formality. Conversely, when applying PPS, it becomes "Would you prefer toast and coffee, or is there something else you'd like to try?" This version creates a more intimate, casual interaction style.

In Japanese, these distinctions are even more pronounced due to the language's grammaticalized politeness levels. The neutral question "朝ごはん何が食べたい？" (What do you want for breakfast?) becomes "もしよろしければ、朝食のご希望をお聞かせいただけますでしょうか？" (If it's not too much trouble, could you please tell me your breakfast preferences?) with NPS, and "トーストとコーヒーでいい？それとも他に食べたいものある？" (Is toast and coffee good? Or is there something else you want to eat?) with PPS.

3 Experimental Evaluation

3.1 Overview

To evaluate our proposed model, we designed a controlled experimental protocol utilizing two pseudo-users with distinct *personality* parameters (1 and 5). These values were selected to represent contrasting tendencies in psychological distance adaptation: the lower personality value facilitates rapid reduction in psychological distance D, while the higher value maintains greater distance stability throughout interactions. We developed two parallel conversation scenarios, corresponding to interactions between the robot and pseudo-users 1 and 2, respectively. To ensure experimental validity and isolate the effect of personality on psychological distance modulation, we standardized the information similarity between both pseudo-users and the robot system.

The experimental design enabled human participants to evaluate both the naturalness of the dialogue management system and their perception of psychological distance variations between the two conversation conditions.

This study was conducted with approval from the Research Ethics Committee of the Organization for Promotion of Advanced Science and Technology, Kansai University (approval number: 24-91). All participants were volunteers and received gift cards valued at 1000 JPY as compensation for their time.

3.2 Experiment Protocol

The experimental protocol employed a virtual cohabitation paradigm consisting of 10 interaction scenarios. Each scenario comprised 10 alternating utterances equally distributed between the robot and pseudo-user systems, maintaining conversational balance. The experimental interface, illustrated in Figure 1, presented these scenarios in a controlled virtual environment with participant-paced progression. We recruited 20 participants (age range: 20-29 years) to evaluate the dialogue interactions through two complementary assessment instruments. The primary questionnaire (Table 3) assessed conversation quality using a five-point Likert scale anchored by "agree" and "disagree" for two key metrics. A secondary comparative questionnaire (Table 4) elicited both quantitative evaluations of the two conversation conditions on a five-point scale and qualitative insights through open-ended response.

The conversational scenarios covered everyday topics such as meal planning, weekend activities, and campus navigation. The robot character was framed as a home assistant robot designed to provide companionship and practical support.

3.3 Results

Analysis of participant responses revealed strong support for the naturalness and effectiveness of our dialogue management system. For Q1, which assessed conversational naturality, all participants (100%) indicated agreement or strong agreement for both conversation conditions, suggesting successful reproduction of natural dialogue patterns across different psychological distance settings. The perception of dynamic psychological distance adaptation (Q2) garnered similarly strong support, with 90% and 95% of participants indicating agreement or strong

Figure 1: System UI.

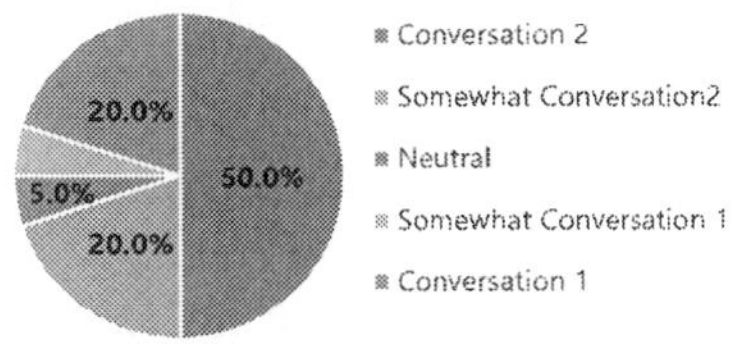

Figure 2: Results of Q3

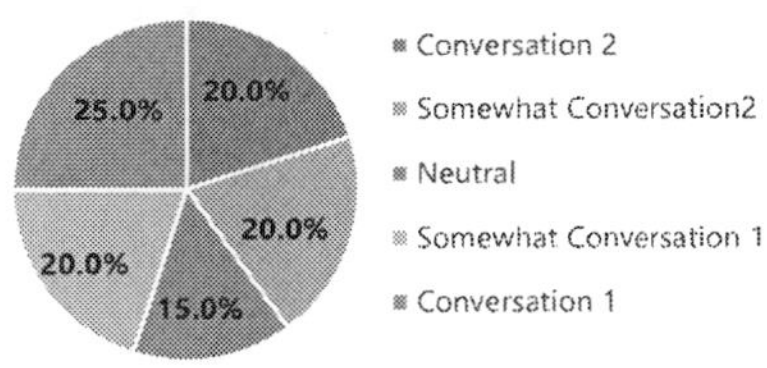

Figure 3: Results of Q4

Q1	To what extent did the robot demonstrate natural conversational capabilities in its interaction with the pseudo-user?
Q2	How did you perceive the evolution of psychological distance between the robot and pseudo-user throughout the conversation?

Table 3: Questionnaire items related to impressions of conversation

Q3	Between the two conversations, which interaction exhibited a more pronounced reduction in psychological distance?
Q4	Which conversation demonstrated a level of psychological distance that would be optimal for you?

Table 4: Questionnaire items related to impressions of conversation

agreement for Conversations C1 and C2, respectively, demonstrating the system's capability to convey decreasing psychological distance over time.

Comparative analysis between the two conversation conditions yielded additional insights into the system's effectiveness. As illustrated in Figure 2, 70% of participants perceived a more pronounced reduction in psychological distance in Conversation C2 compared to C1, validating the intended differential effects of our personality parameter settings. To assess the statistical significance of this finding, we conducted chi-square tests on the distribution of responses. For Q3, the distribution significantly differed from chance ($\chi^2(4, N=20) = 13.50$, $p < 0.05$), confirming that participants could reliably distinguish between the two psychological distance conditions.

However, responses to Q4 (Figure 3) revealed substantial individual variation in preferred psychological distance, highlighting the importance of adaptability in dialogue systems.

Qualitative analysis of open-ended responses provided deeper insights into the perceptible differences between conversation conditions. Participants who successfully discriminated between the two conditions identified several key distinguishing features: conversational vivacity, linguistic style and lexical choice, and degree of conversational initiative. These observations align with our theoretical framework linking personality parameters to observable conversational behaviors.

3.4 Discussion

The universal positive response to Q1 demonstrates that our approach to dynamic psychological distance modulation preserves conversational naturalness while implementing sophisticated politeness-based adaptations. The strong positive responses to Q2 further validate that our implementation of variable politeness strategies successfully conveys gradual psychological distance reduction, supporting the theoretical foundation of our approach.

The convergence of evidence from Q2, Q3, and qualitative responses substantiates the model's capability to create distinguishable psychological distances through systematic manipulation of politeness strategy ratios. Particularly noteworthy is participants' recognition of variations in linguistic patterns and conversational initiative, indicating successful operationalization of politeness theory principles in modulating perceived psychological distance. These findings demonstrate that our computational approach to politeness strategy selection creates perceptible and meaningful variations in conversational dynamics.

However, the significant interpersonal variation in preferred psychological distance revealed by Q4 underscores a critical consideration for dialogue system design. This heterogeneity in user preferences extends beyond the traditional focus on creating uniformly friendly interactions, highlighting the necessity for adaptive distance management in human-agent dialogue systems. Our model's capacity for dynamic distance adjustment addresses this requirement, though future research should explore additional mechanisms for rapid adaptation to individual user preferences.

These findings also demonstrate the relevance of integrating both traditional politeness theory (Brown and Levinson, 1987) and more recent "relational work" perspectives (Locher and Watts, 2005). While our computational model operationalizes Brown and Levinson's strategies, the dynamic adaptation mechanism reflects Locher and Watts' emphasis on the contextual and negotiated nature of politeness. This integration provides a more comprehensive theoretical foundation for politeness management in human-agent dialogue.

4 Conclusion

This work introduces an adaptive politeness-based model for managing psychological distance in human-agent dialogue. Our experimental evaluation through simulated cohabitation scenarios demonstrates the model's effectiveness in maintaining natural conversation while creating perceptible variations in psychological distance. The results validate both the technical feasibility of our approach and its ability to accommodate diverse user preferences for social distance in dialogue interactions.

Future research will focus on enhancing real-time psychological distance estimation, validating the model with human users in naturalistic settings, and implementing the system in physical robot platforms. These advances will contribute to the development of more sophisticated and socially aware dialogue systems that can sustain meaningful long-term interactions with users.

References

Brown, Penelope, and Stephen C. Levinson. 1987. Politeness: Some universals in language usage. No. 4. *Cambridge university press.*

Cassell, Justine, and Timothy Bickmore. 2003. Negotiated collusion: Modeling social language and its relationship effects in intelligent agents. *User modeling and user-adapted interaction* 13 : 89-132.

Culpeper, Jonathan. 2011. Impoliteness: Using language to cause offence. Cambridge University Press.

Hall, Edward. T. 1966. The hidden dimension. *Garden City, NY: Doubleday.*

Häring, Markus, Nikolaus Bee, and Elisabeth André. 2011. Creation and evaluation of emotion expression with body movement, sound and eye color for humanoid robots. *2011 RO-MAN,* 204-209.

Huttenrauch, Helge, Kerstin. S. Eklundh, Anders Green, and Elin A. Topp. 2006. Investigating spatial relationships in human-robot interaction. *2006 IEEE/RSJ International Conference on Intelligent Robots and Systems,* 5052-5059.

Ide, Sachiko. 1989. Formal forms and discernment: Two neglected aspects of universals of linguistic politeness. *Multilingua-journal of cross-cultural and interlanguage communication,* 8(2-3), 223-248.

Locher, Miriam A., and Richard J. Watts. 2005. Politeness theory and relational work. *Journal of politeness research,* 1(1), 9-33.

Miyamoto, Tomoki, Daisuke Katagami, and Yuka Shigemitsu. 2017. Improving relationships based on positive politeness between humans and life-like agents. *Proceedings of the 5th International Conference on Human Agent Interaction,* 451-455.

Yamada, Ichiro. 2016. Psychological Distance Matching Model. *Human Relations Research* (In Japanese).

An LLM Benchmark for Addressee Recognition in Multi-modal Multi-party Dialogue

Koji Inoue, Divesh Lala, Mikey Elmers, Keiko Ochi, Tatsuya Kawahara

Graduate School of Informatics, Kyoto University, Japan,

Correspondence: inoue@sap.ist.i.kyoto-u.ac.jp

Abstract

Handling multi-party dialogues represents a significant step for advancing spoken dialogue systems, necessitating the development of tasks specific to multi-party interactions. To address this challenge, we are constructing a multi-modal multi-party dialogue corpus of triadic (three-participant) discussions. This paper focuses on the task of addressee recognition, identifying who is being addressed to take the next turn, a critical component unique to multi-party dialogue systems. A subset of the corpus was annotated with addressee information, revealing that explicit addressees are indicated in approximately 20% of conversational turns. To evaluate the task's complexity, we benchmarked the performance of a large language model (GPT-4o) on addressee recognition. The results showed that GPT-4o achieved an accuracy only marginally above chance, underscoring the challenges of addressee recognition in multi-party dialogue. These findings highlight the need for further research to enhance the capabilities of large language models in understanding and navigating the intricacies of multi-party conversational dynamics.

1 Introduction

The rapid advancements in dialogue systems, fueled by the emergence of large language models (LLMs) capable of generating human-like text and engaging in natural conversations, have been largely confined to the realm of dyadic interactions. While these systems have demonstrated remarkable progress, they fail to capture the complexities inherent in multi-party dialogues, involving three or more participants. These dialogues are characterized by intricate information flow, dynamic participant roles, and nuanced social cues, posing significant challenges for system development.

Previous research has explored specific aspects of multi-party dialogues, including turn-taking (Lee and Deng, 2024; Auer, 2018; Skantze et al., 2015), addressee recognition (Le et al., 2019; Li and Zhao, 2023; Tan et al., 2023), and dialog act recognition (Qamar et al., 2023). However, existing benchmarks are limited by their reliance on text-based or acted dialogue data, failing to reflect the spontaneity and multi-modality inherent in natural human interactions.

Figure 1: A snapshot from TEIDAN corpus

To address this crucial gap, this paper introduces a novel, spontaneous, and multi-modal multi-party dialogue corpus specifically designed to facilitate research on triadic (three-participant) dialogue systems. This research further focuses on the critical, yet under-explored, task of addressee recognition – the identification of the intended recipient of a turn – which is foundational for enabling dialogue systems to navigate and participate effectively in multi-party settings. Unlike dyadic interactions where the addressee is implicitly defined, turn-taking in multi-party settings is far more complex. The intended recipient might be a specific participant or the group as a whole, and behavioral signals are often subtle and inconsistent (Auer, 2018; Skantze et al., 2015).

Proceedings of the 15th International Workshop on Spoken Dialogue Systems Technology, pages 330–334
May 27–30, 2025. ©2025 Association for Computational Linguistics

Table 1: Statistics of turn and addressee annotation

Session ID	Time	# IPU (A/B/C)	# Turn (A/B/C)	# Addressed	# Not Addressed
session-01-city	6:14	65 / 81 / 137	12 / 16 / 13	9	32
session-02-city	5:50	76 / 94 / 98	16 / 22 / 23	14	47
session-03-city	6:12	81 / 123 / 128	19 / 29 / 30	6	72
session-04-city	5:46	146 / 142 / 123	29 / 21 / 24	10	64
session-05-city	5:18	108 / 119 / 95	44 / 43 / 46	36	97
Total (Ave.)	29:20 (5:52)	1616 (323.2)	387 (77.4)	75 (15)	312 (62.4)

This work makes two key contributions:

- The introduction of the TEIDAN corpus, a new dataset of spontaneous, multi-modal, triadic dialogues that provides a unique resource for this understudied area
- The development of the first LLM benchmark specifically designed for addressee recognition in multi-modal, multi-party dialogue, underscoring the challenges and the need for further innovation

Ultimately, this research aims to establish a strong foundation for the development of advanced multi-party dialogue systems capable of understanding and responding effectively in complex, real-world conversational settings.

2 TEIDAN Corpus

We begin by briefly describing the TEIDAN multi-party corpus. Unlike other datasets that involve specific contexts, such as meetings (Carletta, 2007; Mostefa et al., 2007), task-oriented interactions (Kontogiorgos et al., 2018; Nihei et al., 2014), or game-based scenarios (Stefanov and Beskow, 2016; Litman et al., 2016; Hung and Chittaranjan, 2010), the TEIDAN corpus captures goal-free discussions. Additional multi-party corpora also exist for online discussions (Reverdy et al., 2022).

The discussions involved triads (groups of three participants). Each participant was seated in a circle around a table placed at the center, as shown in Figure 1. Cameras recorded each participant's face, and individual pin microphones were used to capture their speech separately.

Participants discussed three general topics: (1) which city would be best suited as an alternative capital of Japan, (2) which items would be essential to bring to a desert island, and (3) where they would like to travel on the weekend. Each triad completed three discussion sessions, one for each topic.

Each triad conversed for approximately 5 to 10 minutes per session, with no requirement to reach a conclusion. Data were collected from 10 triads, resulting in a total of 30 discussion sessions. Note that this corpus is in the Japanese language.

3 Annotation of Addressee

We annotated a subset of the TEIDAN corpus for addressee information. The annotation process consisted of the following steps:

(1) Initially, turns and the current speaker were annotated. Since the original TEIDAN corpus contains only IPU (inter-pausal unit) utterance segments, turn segments within the dialogue were annotated by removing certain utterances, including backchannels. This ensured that only one speaker could hold the floor at any given time. Minimal overlap was permitted during turn transitions.

(2) Following turn annotation, we labeled the addressee information to indicate whether the next speaker was explicitly addressed. If addressed, the label corresponded to one of the participant IDs (e.g., A, B, or C). Otherwise, it was labeled as 'O', signifying that no specific individual was addressed and any participant could take the turn.

This labeling process considered both textual and visual cues, such as gaze behavior. Initially, a single session was annotated and discussed to ensure inter-rater agreement by the authors. Subsequently, the remaining four sessions were annotated by one of the authors.

We have so far annotated five sessions from the TEIDAN corpus. Table 1 summarizes the annotation results. The analysis revealed that only approximately 20% (75 / 387) of turns explicitly specify an addressee. The 'O' label, indicating no specific addressee, was prevalent, particularly in discussions involving multiple opinions (statements). This result implies that a multi-party dialogue system that participates in this type of discussion and disregards addressee information may potentially interrupt the dialogue in 20% of turn-taking instances, assuming that they can always correctly

Table 2: Performance of addressee recognition by GPT-4o

LLM output	# Correct	# Incorrect
Addressed (A/B/C)	9	14
Not addressed (O)	304	60

Table 3: Context example where GPT-4o correctly recognized addressee as person C, translated from original Japanese utterances

	Utterance
C:	So, if we wanted to change the capital from Tokyo, where do you think would be a good place?
A:	I think Osaka would be a good choice. Osaka is the largest city in western Japan, and in terms of population, there's no other city in western Japan that surpasses it. So, I think Osaka is a strong candidate.
B:	But one of the reasons for wanting to relocate the capital from Tokyo is likely the population increase, or rather, Tokyo's population is becoming unmanageable, necessitating the transfer of some capital functions. (...) Hokkaido is a bit cold, though, so I think somewhere in Kyushu or, for example, the Tokai region might be better.
A:	I see, that makes sense.
B:	What do you think, Ochi-san? Do you have any specific ideas? **(addressee is C)**

recognize the end of the turn of a human participant.

4 Benchmark for Addressee Recognition

To evaluate the task's complexity, we tested the performance of a multimodal large language model (GPT-4o) on addressee recognition. The model was given a prompt as follows:

> In the following conversation among A, B, and C, please infer who is addressed as the next speaker in the last utterance. Answer with one of the following: "A, B, C, or O". "A, B, and C" represent the participants, and "O" represents the case where no one is addressed, and anyone can take the turn next. The output should only contain the label "A, B, C, or O" and should not include any other characters.

This was followed by five context turn utterances with the current utterance, and also it contained the name of the discussion topic and designated identifier of the participants. Note that the utterances were manually transcribed.

The GPT-4o achieved an accuracy of 80.9%, which is only marginally above the chance level (80.6%). This indicates that the model struggles to identify the addressee in multi-party dialogues. The output by the LLM is summarized in Table 2 which shows that the model tends to output 'O', indicating that it often fails to recognize when an utterance is directed at a specific participant.

We then analyzed samples to examine how GPT-4o deals with addressee recognition, as illustrated below:

(1) Explicit Question (Correct) An example in Table 3 shows a case where GPT-4o correctly identified the addressee as C because the final utterance, a question, was explicitly directed to that individual. Although current LLMs effectively handle such explicit cases, the corpus contains many instances that are not as straightforward.

(2) False Negative In both examples presented in Table 4 and Table 5, the GPT-4o's output indicated no specific addressee (O), while the reference labels were A and B, respectively. This kind of

Table 4: Context example where GPT-4o incorrectly recognized addressee as O, translated from original Japanese utterances

	Utterance
B:	A riddle.
C:	When I suggested, it might be something related to Fukuoka, or perhaps Kitakyushu, this person insisted they were from Moji, mentioning some kind of ward distinction I didn't understand. So, I think in that sense, it's decentralized.
B:	Hmm, it seems like the decentralization of cities is an unavoidable issue after all.
C:	That's right. But Osaka has Umeda and...
A:	Tennoji?
C:	Not Tennoji, but Namba, I think. **(addressee is A)**

Table 5: Context example where GPT-4o incorrectly recognized addressee as O, translated from original Japanese utterances

	Utterance
A:	One of the reasons why I prefer Osaka is that its city planning, including roads and railway networks, is very linear and easy to understand.
C:	Like Midosuji?
A:	Exactly. If you've ever seen a map of the Tokyo subway, you'll know that it's quite convoluted and complex. In contrast, Osaka's layout is more grid-like.
C:	With streets like "something-suji" and "Something-suji Line."
A:	Yes. I think Tokyo is more circular, but a linear layout is easier to understand. Osaka's linear layout with clear divisions, like this area for administrative functions and this area as the central hub where people gather, makes it superior as a city, in my opinion.
C:	I feel like in Nagoya, Sakae and Nagoya Station are slightly separated, aren't they? **(addressee is B)**

Table 6: Performance of addressee recognition by GPT-4o added simple gaze features

LLM output	# Correct	# Incorrect
Addressed (A/B/C)	12	36
Not addressed (O)	279	60

false-negative instance represented the majority of errors in this experiment. In the Table 4 example, the final speaker, C, was looking at person A, suggesting that gaze information is crucial for this task. In the Table 5 example, the final speaker inquires about Nagoya, a city in Japan. Within the context of this discussion, B was about to recommend this city. Therefore, this task also necessitates the consideration of such prior information.

5 Adding Gaze Features

To see the effect of gaze information in the current task, we processed the video of each participant (shown at the bottom of Figure 1) and automatically annotated their gaze throughout the discussion. OpenFace 2.0 was used to estimate the eye gaze vector (Baltrusaitis et al., 2018; Wood et al., 2015). We could then generate a gaze vector 30 times a second.

For every gaze timestamp, we then estimated whether the gaze of the participant who had the turn (speaker) was directed at either one of the other participants or at nobody in particular. As each participant was seated in an approximately equilateral triangle, we used a simple heuristic to test if the speaker was looking at another participant. The y (up-down) portion of the gaze vector must be within a certain range (0.2), and the x (left-right) gaze vector had to be out of a certain range (-0.2 to 0.2). If this heuristic was met, then the gaze timepoint was labeled as the speaker looking at the relevant participant, else the gaze timestamp was labeled as O (no participant).

We also labeled the turn of a speaker as opposed to continuous timestamps. We based our approach on previous research which found that end-of-turn gaze was important (Kawahara et al., 2016; Degutyte and Astell, 2021) and labeled the *majority* gaze in the turn's final second, specifically the gaze label which was present in over 50% of the timestamps, or O if this was not reached.

This information was added to the previous prompt to assess if adding gaze information in this way could improve the result. However, as shown in Table 6, adding this information did not improve accuracy, as the accuracy score (75.2%) went down under the chance level. While future work necessitates manual annotation of gaze information, the current results indicate that existing LLMs also struggle to incorporate such additional modalities within the context of multi-party dialogues.

6 Benchmark for Next Speaker Prediction

We are also interested in predicting the actual next speaker in the multi-party scenarios (Lee and Deng, 2024; Lee et al., 2023). This is distinguished from addressee annotation, where subsequent information on who took the turn is unknown, and there is no 'O' label as somebody must take the turn. It is possible that the addressee and the actual next speaker differ because of interruptions during the turn.

We then evaluated GPT-4o's performance on this next speaker prediction task. Using a prompt similar to that used for addressee recognition, the model was tasked with predicting the actual next speaker. The output label was limited to A, B, or C, with a chance-level accuracy of 50%, as either of the other two participants could take the turn. As a result, GPT-4o attained an accuracy of 46.0% on this task, performing below chance level. This outcome further suggests that the model struggles to effectively capture the dynamics of turn-taking in spontaneous multi-party dialogues.

7 Conclusion

This study investigated the challenges of addressee and next speaker prediction in multi-party dialogues. We introduced a new multi-party dialogue corpus and analyzed the performance of an LLM (GPT-4o) on these tasks. The findings revealed that LLMs struggle with the complexities of multi-party interactions. They perform only marginally above chance level in addressee recognition and below chance level in the next speaker prediction task. Although the LLM was given the simple gaze feature, it did not improve the performance.

These results underscore the need for further research to improve LLMs' understanding of multi-party conversational dynamics. Future work should explore more sophisticated methods for incorporating contextual information, including gaze and other non-verbal cues, and develop new models that can better capture the intricate interplay between participants in multi-party conversations.

Acknowledgments

This work was supported by JST PREST JP-MJPR24I4, JST Moonshot R&D JPMJPS2011, and JSPS KAKENHI JP23K16901. The authors also express appreciation to the members of speech and audio processing laboratory at Kyoto University for their participation in the data collection.

References

Peter Auer. 2018. Gaze, addressee selection and turn-taking in three-party interaction. *Eye-tracking in interaction: Studies on the role of eye gaze in dialogue*, 197:231.

Tadas Baltrusaitis, Amir Zadeh, Yao Chong Lim, and Louis-Philippe Morency. 2018. Openface 2.0: Facial behavior analysis toolkit. In *International Conference on Automatic Face & Gesture Recognition (FG)*, pages 59–66.

Jean Carletta. 2007. Unleashing the killer corpus: experiences in creating the multi-everything ami meeting corpus. *Language Resources and Evaluation*, 41:181–190.

Ziedune Degutyte and Arlene Astell. 2021. The role of eye gaze in regulating turn taking in conversations: a systematized review of methods and findings. *Frontiers in Psychology*, 12.

Hayley Hung and Gokul Chittaranjan. 2010. The IDIAP wolf corpus: exploring group behaviour in a competitive role-playing game. In *International Conference on Multimedia*, pages 879–882.

Tatsuya Kawahara, Takuma Iwatate, Koji Inoue, Soichiro Hayashi, Hiromasa Yoshimoto, and Katsuya Takanashi. 2016. Multi-modal sensing and analysis of poster conversations with smart posterboard. *APSIPA Transactions on Signal and Information Processing*, 5:e2.

Dimosthenis Kontogiorgos, Vanya Avramova, Simon Alexanderson, Patrik Jonell, Catharine Oertel, Jonas Beskow, Gabriel Skantze, and Joakim Gustafson. 2018. A multimodal corpus for mutual gaze and joint attention in multiparty situated interaction. In *International Conference on Language Resources and Evaluation (LREC)*.

Ran Le, Wenpeng Hu, Mingyue Shang, Zhenjun You, Lidong Bing, Dongyan Zhao, and Rui Yan. 2019. Who is speaking to whom? Learning to identify utterance addressee in multi-party conversations. In *Empirical Methods in Natural Language Processing and International Joint Conference on Natural Language Processing (EMNLP-IJCNLP)*, pages 1909–1919.

Meng-Chen Lee and Zhigang Deng. 2024. Online multimodal end-of-turn prediction for three-party conversations. In *International Conference on Multimodal Interaction (ICMI)*, pages 57–65.

Meng-Chen Lee, Mai Trinh, and Zhigang Deng. 2023. Multimodal turn analysis and prediction for multi-party conversations. In *International Conference on Multimodal Interaction (ICMI)*, pages 436–444.

Yiyang Li and Hai Zhao. 2023. Em pre-training for multi-party dialogue response generation. *arXiv preprint*. 2305.12412.

Diane Litman, Susannah Paletz, Zahra Rahimi, Stefani Allegretti, and Caitlin Rice. 2016. The teams corpus and entrainment in multi-party spoken dialogues. In *Conference on Empirical Methods in Natural Language Processing (EMNLP)*, pages 1421–1431.

Djamel Mostefa, Nicolas Moreau, Khalid Choukri, Gerasimos Potamianos, Stephen M Chu, Ambrish Tyagi, Josep R Casas, Jordi Turmo, Luca Cristoforetti, Francesco Tobia, et al. 2007. The CHIL audiovisual corpus for lecture and meeting analysis inside smart rooms. *Language resources and evaluation*, 41:389–407.

Fumio Nihei, Yukiko I. Nakano, Yuki Hayashi, Hung-Hsuan Hung, and Shogo Okada. 2014. Predicting influential statements in group discussions using speech and head motion information. In *International Conference on Multimodal Interaction (ICMI)*, pages 136–143.

Ayesha Qamar, Adarsh Pyarelal, and Ruihong Huang. 2023. Who is speaking? Speaker-Aware multiparty dialogue act classification. In *Findings of Empirical Methods in Natural Language Processing (EMNLP Finding)*, pages 10122–10135.

Justine Reverdy, Sam O'Connor Russell, Louise Duquenne, Diego Garaialde, Benjamin R Cowan, and Naomi Harte. 2022. Roomreader: A multimodal corpus of online multiparty conversational interactions. In *International Conference on Language Resources and Evaluation (LREC)*, pages 2517–2527.

Gabriel Skantze, Martin Johansson, and Jonas Beskow. 2015. Exploring turn-taking cues in multi-party human-robot discussions about objects. In *Proceedings of the 2015 ACM on international conference on multimodal interaction*, pages 67–74.

Kalin Stefanov and Jonas Beskow. 2016. A multi-party multi-modal dataset for focus of visual attention in human-human and human-robot interaction. In *International Conference on Language Resources and Evaluation (LREC)*, pages 4440–4444.

Chao-Hong Tan, Jia-Chen Gu, and Zhen-Hua Ling. 2023. Is chatgpt a good multi-party conversation solver? In *Findings of Empirical Methods in Natural Language Processing (EMNLP Finding)*, pages 4905–4915.

Erroll Wood, Tadas Baltruaitis, Xucong Zhang, Yusuke Sugano, Peter Robinson, and Andreas Bulling. 2015. Rendering of eyes for eye-shape registration and gaze estimation. In *International Conference on Computer Vision (ICCV)*, pages 3756–3764.

Will AI shape the way we speak?
The emerging sociolinguistic influence of synthetic voices

Éva Székely[1] **Jūra Miniota**[1] **Míša (Michaela) Hejná**[2]
[1]Department of Speech, Music and Hearing, KTH Royal Institute of Technology, Sweden
[2]Department of English, Aarhus University, Denmark
szekely@kth.se, jura@kth.se, misa.hejna@cc.au.dk

Abstract

The growing prevalence of conversational voice interfaces, powered by developments in both speech and language technologies, raises important questions about their influence on human communication. While written communication can signal identity through lexical and stylistic choices, voice-based interactions inherently amplify socioindexical elements – such as accent, intonation, and speech style – which more prominently convey social identity and group affiliation. There is evidence that even passive media such as television is likely to influence the audience's linguistic patterns. Unlike passive media, conversational AI is interactive, creating a more immersive and reciprocal dynamic that holds a greater potential to impact how individuals speak in everyday interactions. Such heightened influence can be expected to arise from phenomena such as acoustic-prosodic entrainment and linguistic accommodation, which occur naturally during interaction and enable users to adapt their speech patterns in response to the system. While this phenomenon is still emerging, its potential societal impact could provide organisations, movements, and brands with a subtle yet powerful avenue for shaping and controlling public perception and social identity. We argue that the socioindexical influence of AI-generated speech warrants attention and should become a focus of interdisciplinary research, leveraging new and existing methodologies and technologies to better understand its implications.

1 Introduction

This position paper proposes that the increasing scale and quality of verbal interactions with AI has the potential to influence people's habitual voice and speaking style on an unprecedented scale. Recent advancements in large language models (LLMs) and text-to-speech (TTS) technology now enable realistic, expressive, human-like conversations. Moreover, breakthroughs in conversational AI systems, such as naturalistic turn-taking (Arora et al., 2025) and interruption handling (Cao et al., 2025), are expected to drastically increase the scale of spoken interactions with AI. While both written and spoken language can convey aspects of identity, they do so through different channels. In writing – especially in informal settings – word choice, grammar, and style can reflect social traits such as age, gender, or cultural affiliation (e.g., Rubin 1995). However, spoken interaction inherently and therefore unavoidably conveys such extralinguistic traits through the voice itself. This means that the societal impacts of increased voice-based interactions with AI are likely to differ considerably from those of text-based interactions.

2 Socioindexicality in spoken AI interaction

2.1 Spoken language and social identity

One particularly relevant concept in this context is socioindexicality, which refers to how features of communication signal social identity and group affiliation (Silverstein, 2003; Eckert, 2019). In spoken language, socioindexical elements, such as accent, intonation, and speech style, play a crucial role in conveying these social cues. A wide range of identity-related aspects – including personality and wellbeing – can be signalled, and indexed, through linguistic variation, including phonetic and phonological variation (e.g. Campbell-Kibler 2009; Pharao et al. 2014; Podesva and Callier 2015; Paladino and Mazzurega 2019; Guy et al. 2022; Hope and Lilley 2023; Grammon 2024).

Given the increasing realism and human-likeness of synthetic voices, socioindexical elements embedded in AI-generated speech may extend the role of conversational AI beyond functionality. These elements could potentially become socially influential, producing tangible effects on users' perceptions and behaviors through specific vocal traits.

Proceedings of the 15th International Workshop on Spoken Dialogue Systems Technology, pages 335–340
May 27–30, 2025.

2.2 Acoustic-prosodic entrainment and linguistic accommodation

Entrainment (also called alignment, accommodation, or convergence) refers to the tendency of dialogue partners to become more similar in their communicative behaviors (Levitan and Hirschberg, 2011; Wynn and Borrie, 2022). In human-human conversations, people naturally align on various levels – choice of words, sentence structures, speech rate, intonation, etc. – which can foster rapport (Miles et al., 2009), signify cooperation (Pellegrino and Dellwo, 2023) and reinforce social bonds between speakers.

A substantial body of work shows that humans do adjust their speech and language when interacting with machines. Even in early studies of human–machine dialogue, researchers observed entrainment effects that parallel those found in human-human conversation. Users adapt their speech to align with artificial interlocutors in both lexical and prosodic domains. For instance, speakers converged on the vocabulary used by spoken dialogue systems (Parent and Eskenazi, 2010) and conversational agents (Ostrand et al., 2023). Prosodic convergence has also been documented in interactions with animated personas (Oviatt et al., 2004), social robots (Cohn et al., 2023), and virtual tutors (Tsfasman et al., 2021). Participants modulated features like pitch, amplitude, and speech rate to more closely match the agent's delivery. Speakers even adjusted their speaking rate when addressing early spoken dialogue systems (Bell et al., 2003), and entrained to turn-taking rhythms in expressive humanoid robots (Breazeal, 2002). More recent findings show that the degree of prosodic entrainment can vary based on the agent's politeness and perceived humanness (Horstmann et al., 2024; Tsfasman et al., 2021). These findings indicate that entrainment in HCI is not limited to functional adaptation, but it also reflects socially grounded mechanisms that operate similarly with both artificial and human interlocutors.

2.3 From alignment to identity expression

Linguistic accommodation is commonly viewed in sociolinguistics as a key mechanism that may influence how linguistic variation evolves into dialect formation and, eventually, language change (Hinskens and Auer, 2005). In other words, short-term accommodation during repeated conversational exchanges can, over time, lead to long-term changes both at the individual level (Nguyen and Delvaux, 2015; Lee, 2010), as well as at the community level, where it can lead to the spread and adoption of innovative linguistic variants (Hinskens and Auer, 2005). Perceived prestige – often associated with artificial intelligence – has been shown to amplify this effect (Lev-Ari and Peperkamp, 2014). Linguistic accommodation being a reciprocal process, the rise of adaptive conversational AI (Brandt and Hazel, 2025; Pollmann et al., 2023) can be expected to reinforce this phenomenon even further.

This suggests that people could begin to absorb AI-influenced speech patterns in general contexts, potentially shaping their everyday language and, with it, their expression of identity. Evidence of a similar influence is already emerging with text-based chatbots, where users adopt words or phrases commonly generated by language models and subsequently use them in their spoken language, as observed in YouTube videos (Yakura et al., 2024).

3 Potential societal influence

3.1 Lessons from media

Over the past three decades, sociolinguistic research has explored how media influences speech patterns and linguistic performance (Tagliamonte, 2014) and how it contributes to language change (Kristiansen, 2014). Studies show that exposure to media can diffuse linguistic features, both on the lexical (Trudgill, 2014) and on the phonological level (Oviatt et al., 2004). While most of the research in this broader area has targeted either written language (Crystal, 2006; Tagliamonte, 2016) or the potential effects of modes of communication such as Instant Messaging on spoken language (Tagliamonte and Denis, 2008), one of the most notable endeavours in the area of speech influence is presented by Sayers (2014), who proposes a mediated innovation model to operationalise the role of media exposure and engagement on 'everyday' linguistic and speech changes.

Regarding phonetic and phonological features, few sociolinguistic studies are available. One prominent example of media influence on the acoustic-phonetic level is the phonological shifts observed in Glaswegian speech linked to psychological engagement with a popular London-based TV drama (Stuart-Smith et al., 2013). The researchers found that TH-fronting and L-vocalisation can be linked to psychological engagement with characters on the *EastEnders* soap opera.

Beyond linguistic variation, Kristiansen (2014) explores how the media shape language change through *ideology* – that is, socially shared beliefs about which ways of speaking are desirable, appropriate, or prestigious – and calls for further research into the media's role in shaping such perceptions. As conversational AI becomes a more common mode of media engagement, it participates in these ideological processes, subtly reinforcing or shifting language attitudes through ongoing, interactive exposure and perceived prestige (Xi, 2024).

3.2 The rise of an engineered language change?

As shown by prior research, even before the widespread adoption of AI voices, media had already demonstrated its potential to influence how people speak and express themselves – often in ways that extend beyond direct interpersonal interaction and diffuse across distant geographic regions. Generative AI introduces an interactive dimension that is likely to amplify such influences. Speakers could actively – yet often unconsciously – incorporate socioindexical traits exhibited by conversational agents in their habitual speaking style. Through this process, companies, political movements, and other organizations may gain a new avenue for subtle influence. By designing AI voices with specific socioindexical characteristics – such as accents, speech styles, or voice quality features – these actors may encourage users to adopt speech patterns that signal affiliation with a brand, ideology, or social group. This influence could shape social identity markers and foster subconscious associations with particular movements or subcultures. Likely emerging examples of this phenomenon include AI companions (Zhang and Li, 2025), AI-powered interactive virtual influencers (Yu et al., 2024), and chatbot versions of human influencers.

3.3 Societal implications and ethical risks

It is further pertinent to ask to what extent any linguistic profiling within AI voices might contribute to linguistic discrimination, which is an established phenomenon: linguistic variants can be and have been utilised to classify speakers into social categories and to mistreat these speakers as a result (Purnell et al., 1999; Gluszek and Dovidio, 2010; Lippi-Green, 2012; Krahé and Papakonstantinou, 2020). On a more general level, AI may reinforce normative biases by defaulting to voices representative of the unmarked and commonly employed white, cis-gender, heterosexual, and able-bodied speakers. This may reinforce already existing dominant norms. In this light, the potential influence of conversational AI on speech production is not merely a linguistic curiosity but could pose actual ethical harm (Hutiri et al., 2024).

We believe that the potential societal impacts of AI-driven socioindexical influence on speech patterns and identities can be rather substantial. While empirical evidence is still emerging, we identify socioindexical influence as an under-explored area with significant potential for societal impact. Understanding this phenomenon now, while it is nascent, can be an opportunity to shape ethical design and governance before its effects become widespread. However, whether this is the case, and to what extent, remains unexplored. Considering the rapid advances in relevant technology and the widespread engagement with conversational AI, it is important to develop methods for understanding which speech characteristics may become influential or habitualised through interaction with synthetic voices.

4 Research opportunities and challenges

4.1 Studying short- and long-term effects

While short-term accommodation to AI voices in interaction is established, it remains unclear whether and how these immediate, conversation-specific adaptations carry over into one's long-term speech habits outside the interaction. Most studies to date examine alignment within an interaction; they do not test if a person's baseline speaking style changes after repeated exposures. Studying the nature of the long-term potential and topical influences requires methodologies that extend beyond but include traditional sociolinguistic approaches, particularly when considering the interactive nature of modern media and conversational systems (Sayers, 2014). Indeed, the still highly unique study by Stuart-Smith et al. (2013) presents a tour de force which, among other things, demonstrates the methodological complexities and challenges of investigating the role of the media on phonetic speech variation outside of a laboratory setting. Individual variation in susceptibility to such influence should also be considered. Not all speakers will accommodate to synthetic voices the same way – some may even actively resist alignment. Future work should explore who adapts, who resists, and why.

4.2 Experimental approaches with TTS and Conversational AI

The same technologies that raise questions about socioindexical influence – speech synthesis and conversational AI – also bring new methodological possibilities. Advances in speech synthesis provide researchers with unprecedented control over acoustic-prosodic features, enabling experimental designs that isolate individual variables such as pitch, speech rate, and voice quality. These systems can also affect features such as formality, allowing the development of methodologies that use TTS trained on spontaneous speech data as a research tool (Székely et al., 2024; O'Mahony et al., 2024). Moreover, recent developments in large-scale neural TTS systems trained on thousands of hours of speech have dramatically lowered the threshold for high-fidelity voice replication (Casanova, 2024). Fine-tuning these models on as little as ten minutes of in-the-wild speech material makes it possible to reproduce sociolects without requiring extensive recordings. In addition, zero-shot TTS and voice conversion (Lameris et al., 2024) enable the transfer of these speech patterns to different voice identities, which facilitates experimental comparisons across demographic categories like gender and age and even vocal characteristics. While such manipulations must be approached with care to preserve indexical plausibility and perceptual coherence (Seaborn et al., 2025), this capacity for decoupling linguistic features from speaker identity expands the range of testable hypotheses in experimental sociolinguistics.

Such synthetic stimuli can be used in both perception and production studies, including shadowing tasks (Laycock, 2021; Pardo et al., 2018), to estimate phonetic convergence to emerging sociolects. Interactive experimental designs also become feasible through research-grade conversational agents equipped with controllable TTS (Wang et al., 2024), enabling A/B testing of entrainment during dialogue. These methods can be further complemented by sociolinguistic interviews or ethnographic observations on social media materials (Yakura et al., 2024).

4.3 Multidisciplinary opportunities

The complexity of media influence, which is shaped by engagement, identity, and context, calls for a transdisciplinary approach (Androutsopoulos, 2014). Studying the sociolinguistic impact of synthetic voices, and especially the conditions under which local adaptation might evolve into long-term language change, will require collaboration across multiple disciplines. Building research-purpose TTS and Conversational AI systems, analysing subtle language and speech variations, and interpreting social impact are key components of this research direction and will necessitate close collaboration between engineers, linguists, social scientists, and ethicists. We anticipate that the increasing presence of speech AI in society will lead to further research areas becoming increasingly multidisciplinary. This may require rethinking research infrastructures or even education programs.

5 Conclusion

This position paper calls attention to the need for a concerted effort to address the socioindexical influence of AI-generated voices in interaction. First, it is imperative to establish the existence and extent of this emergent phenomenon. This requires a foundational understanding of how AI interaction may impact speech patterns and identity expression among users. Second, the development of robust methodologies is critical for systematically studying and measuring these influences. Finally, we must begin to consider the broader implications, including ethical, societal, and legal dimensions. Addressing these priorities will help us prepare to understand and manage the implications of voice-based conversational AI for human speech, communication, social identity, and its potential role in driving language change.

Acknowledgements

This research is supported by the Swedish Research Council project Perception of speaker stance (VR-2020-02396), and the Riksbankens Jubileumsfond project CAPTivating (P20-0298). We thank the anonymous reviewers for their insightful comments which helped improve the final version of this paper. We are also deeply grateful to the many colleagues and friends who generously shared feedback on earlier drafts, including Alyssa Allen, Matthew Aylett, Jens Edlund, Emer Gilmartin, Maxwell Hope, David House, Tanya Karoli Christensen, Johannah O'Mahony, Amir H. Payberah, André Pereira, Graham Pullin, Fin Tams-Grey, Ilaria Torre and Marcin Włodarczak. Their thoughtful suggestions and encouragement were invaluable in shaping this work.

References

Jannis Androutsopoulos. 2014. Beyond 'media influence'. *Journal of Sociolinguistics*, 18(2):242–249.

Siddhant Arora, Zhiyun Lu, Chung-Cheng Chiu, Ruoming Pang, and Shinji Watanabe. 2025. Talking turns: Benchmarking audio foundation models on turn-taking dynamics. *arXiv preprint arXiv:2503.01174*.

Linda Bell, Joakim Gustafson, and Mattias Heldner. 2003. Prosodic adaptation in human-computer interaction. In *Proc. ICPHS*, volume 3, pages 833–836.

Adam Brandt and Spencer Hazel. 2025. Towards interculturally adaptive conversational ai. *Applied Linguistics Review*, 16(2):775–786.

Cynthia Breazeal. 2002. Regulation and entrainment in human—robot interaction. *The International Journal of Robotics Research*, 21(10-11):883–902.

Kathryn Campbell-Kibler. 2009. The nature of sociolinguistic perception. *Language Variation and Change*, 21:135–156.

Shiye Cao, Jiwon Moon, Amama Mahmood, Victor Nikhil Antony, Ziang Xiao, Anqi Liu, and Chien-Ming Huang. 2025. Interruption handling for conversational robots. *arXiv preprint arXiv:2501.01568*.

Edresson Casanova. 2024. XTTS: a massively multilingual zero-shot text-to-speech model. In *Proc. Interspeech*, pages 4978–4982.

Michelle Cohn, Ashley Keaton, Jonas Beskow, and Georgia Zellou. 2023. Vocal accommodation to technology: the role of physical form. *Language Sciences*, 99:101567.

David Crystal. 2006. *Language and the Internet*. Cambridge University Press.

Penelope Eckert. 2019. The limits of meaning: Social indexicality, variation, and the cline of interiority. *Language*, 95(4):751–776.

Agata Gluszek and John F. Dovidio. 2010. Speaking with a nonnative accent: perceptions of bias, communication difficulties, and belonging in the united states. *Journal of Language and Social Psychology*, 18(2):224–234.

Devin Grammon. 2024. Ideology, indexicality, and the l2 development of sociolinguistic perception during study abroad. *L2 Journal: An Open Access Refereed Journal for World Language Educators*, 16(1):1–17.

Gregory R. Guy, Livia Oushiro, and Ronald Beline Mendes. 2022. Indexicality and coherence. In *The Coherence of Linguistic Communities. Orderly Heterogeneity and Social Meaning*, pages 53–68.

FLMP Hinskens and Peter Auer. 2005. The role of interpersonal accommodation in a theory of language change. In *Dialect change. The convergence and divergence of dialects in contemporary societies*, pages 335–357. Cambridge UP.

Maxwell Hope and Jason Lilley. 2023. Differences in sibilant perception between gender expansive and cisgender individuals. *Seminars in Speech and Language*, 44(2):61–75.

Aike C Horstmann, Clara Strathmann, Lea Lambrich, and Nicole C Kramer. 2024. Communication style adaptation in human-computer interaction. *Human-Machine Communication*, 8:53–72.

Wiebke Hutiri, Orestis Papakyriakopoulos, and Alice Xiang. 2024. Not my voice! a taxonomy of ethical and safety harms of speech generators. In *Proc. of the 2024 ACM Conference on Fairness, Accountability, and Transparency*, page 359–376.

Barbara Krahé and Lida Papakonstantinou. 2020. Speaking like a man: women's pitch as a cue for gender stereotyping. *Sex Roles*, 82:94–101.

Tore Kristiansen. 2014. Knowing the driving force in language change: density or subjectivity? *Journal of Sociolinguistics*, 18(2):233–241.

Harm Lameris, Joakim Gustafson, and Éva Székely. 2024. Creakvc: a voice conversion tool for modulating creaky voice. In *Proc. Interspeech*, pages 1005–1006.

Kyle Laycock. 2021. The influence of socioindexical information on the speech perception-production link: Evidence from a shadowing task. *Theses and Dissertations–Linguistics. 41.*

Chi-Chun Lee. 2010. Quantification of prosodic entrainment in affective spontaneous spoken interactions of married couples. In *Proc. Interspeech*, page 793.

Shiri Lev-Ari and Sharon Peperkamp. 2014. An experimental study of the role of social factors in language change: The case of loanword adaptations. *Laboratory Phonology*, 5(3):379–401.

Rivka Levitan and Julia Hirschberg. 2011. Measuring acoustic-prosodic entrainment with respect to multiple levels and dimensions. In *Interspeech 2011*, pages 3081–3084.

Rosina Lippi-Green. 2012. *English with an Accent: Language, Ideology, and Discrimination in the United States.*

Lynden K Miles, Louise K Nind, and C Neil Macrae. 2009. The rhythm of rapport: Interpersonal synchrony and social perception. *Journal of experimental social psychology*, 45(3):585–589.

Noël Nguyen and Véronique Delvaux. 2015. Role of imitation in the emergence of phonological systems. *Journal of Phonetics*, 53:46–54.

Johannah O'Mahony, Catherine Lai, and Éva Székely. 2024. Well, what can you do with messy data? exploring the prosody and pragmatic function of the discourse marker "well" with found data and speech synthesis. In *Proc. Interspeech*, pages 4084–4088.

Rachel Ostrand, Victor S. Ferreira, and David Piorkowski. 2023. Rapid lexical alignment to a conversational agent. In *Proc. Interspeech*, page 2653.

Sharon Oviatt, Courtney Darves, and Rachel Coulston. 2004. Toward adaptive conversational interfaces: Modeling speech convergence with animated personas. *Proc. TOCHI*, 11(3):300–328.

Maria Paola Paladino and Mara Mazzurega. 2019. One of us: On the role of accent and race in real-time in-group categorization. *Journal of Language and Social Psychology*, 39(1):22–39.

Jennifer S Pardo, Adelya Urmanche, Sherilyn Wilman, Jaclyn Wiener, Nicholas Mason, Keagan Francis, and Melanie Ward. 2018. A comparison of phonetic convergence in conversational interaction and speech shadowing. *Journal of Phonetics*, 69:1–11.

Gabriel Parent and Maxine Eskenazi. 2010. Lexical entrainment of real users in the let's go spoken dialog system. In *Proc. Interspeech*, pages 3018–3021.

Elisa Pellegrino and Volker Dellwo. 2023. Speakers are more cooperative and less individual when interacting in larger group sizes. *Frontiers in Psychology*, 14:1145572.

Nicolai Pharao, Marie Maegaard, Janus Spindler Møller, and Tore Kristianse. 2014. Indexical meanings of [s+] among Copenhagen youth: Social perception of a phonetic variant in different prosodic contexts. *Language in Society*, 43:1–31.

Robert J. Podesva and Patrick Callier. 2015. Voice quality and identity. *Annual Review of Applied Linguistics*, 35:173–194.

Kathrin Pollmann, Wulf Loh, Nora Fronemann, and Daniel Ziegler. 2023. Entertainment vs. manipulation: Personalized human-robot interaction between user experience and ethical design. *Technological Forecasting and Social Change*, 189:122376.

Thomas Purnell, William Idsardi, and John Baugh. 1999. Perceptual and phonetic experiments on american english dialect identification. *Journal of Language and Social Psychology*, 18:10–30.

Donald L. Rubin, editor. 1995. *Composing social identity in written language*. Lawrence Erlbaum Associates.

Dave Sayers. 2014. The mediated innovation model: A framework for researching media influence in language change. *Journal of sociolinguistics*, 18(2):185.

Katie Seaborn, Katja Rogers, Maximilian Altmeyer, Mizuki Watanabe, Yuto Sawa, Somang Nam, Tatsuya Itagaki, and Ge 'Rikaku' Li. 2025. Unboxing manipulation checks for voice ux. *Interacting with Computers*, page iwae062.

Michael Silverstein. 2003. Indexical order and the dialectics of sociolinguistic life. *Language & Communication*, 23(3-4):193–229.

Jane Stuart-Smith, Gwilym Pryce, Claire Timmins, and Barrie Gunter. 2013. Television can also be a factor in language change: Evidence from an urban dialect. *Language*, pages 501–536.

Éva Székely, Jeff Higginbotham, and Francesco Possemato. 2024. Voice and choice: Investigating the role of prosodic variation in request compliance and perceived politeness using conversational TTS. In *Proc. SIGDial*, pages 466–476.

Sali Tagliamonte. 2014. Situating media influence in sociolinguistic context. *Journal of Sociolinguistics*, 18(2):223–232.

Sali Tagliamonte. 2016. So sick or so cool? the language of youth on the internet. *Language in Society*, 45(1).

Sali Tagliamonte and Derek Denis. 2008. Linguistic ruin? lol! instant messaging and teen language. *American Speech*, 83(1):3–324.

Peter Trudgill. 2014. Diffusion, drift, and the irrelevance of media influence. *Journal of Sociolinguistics*, 18(2):213–222.

Maria Tsfasman, Avinash Saravanan, Dekel Viner, Daan Goslinga, Sarah De Wolf, Chirag Raman, Catholijn M Jonker, and Catharine Oertel. 2021. Towards a real-time measure of the perception of anthropomorphism in human-robot interaction. In *Proc. ACM MuCAI*, pages 13–18.

Siyang Wang, Éva Székely, and Joakim Gustafson. 2024. Contextual interactive evaluation of TTS models in dialogue systems. In *Proc. Interspeech*, pages 2965–2969.

Camille J Wynn and Stephanie A Borrie. 2022. Classifying conversational entrainment of speech behavior: An expanded framework and review. *Journal of Phonetics*, 94:101173.

Yipeng Xi. 2024. Navigating technological shifts: An examination of user inertia and technology prestige in large-language-model ai chatbot transition. *International Journal of Human–Computer Interaction*, 0(0):1–17.

Hiromu Yakura, Ezequiel Lopez-Lopez, Levin Brinkmann, Ignacio Serna, Prateek Gupta, and Iyad Rahwan. 2024. Empirical evidence of large language model's influence on human spoken communication. *arXiv preprint arXiv:2409.01754*.

Joanne Yu, Astrid Dickinger, Kevin Kam Fung So, and Roman Egger. 2024. Artificial intelligence-generated virtual influencer: Examining the effects of emotional display on user engagement. *Journal of Retailing and Consumer Services*, 76:103560.

Shuning Zhang and Shixuan Li. 2025. The real her? exploring whether young adults accept human-ai love. *arXiv preprint arXiv:2503.03067*.

Author Index

Association for Computational Linguistics
209 N. Eighth Street
Stroudsburg, Pennsylvania 18360

ISBN 979-8-3313-2448-3

CURRAN ASSOCIATES INC.
proceedings.com